FILE AND DATA BASE TECHNIQUES

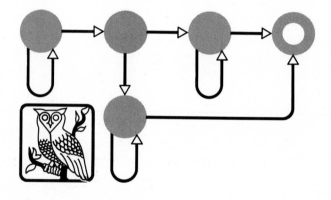

HRW SERIES IN COMPUTER SCIENCE

Seymour V. Pollack, Series Editor

Seymour V. Pollack and Theodor Sterling
    Guide To PL/1 and Structured Programming, Third Edition

Will Gillett and Seymour V. Pollack
    Introduction to Engineered Software

James Bradley
    File And Data Base Techniques

FILE AND DATA BASE TECHNIQUES

James Bradley
The University of Calgary

Holt, Rinehart and Winston
New York   Chicago   San Francisco   Philadelphia
Montreal   Toronto   London   Sydney   Tokyo
Mexico City   Rio de Janeiro   Madrid

ACKNOWLEDGEMENTS

A product of CODASYL is not the property of any individual, company, or organization or of any group of individuals, companies, or organizations.

No warranty, expressed or implied, is made by any contributor or by any CODASYL committee as to the accuracy and functioning of any system developed as a result of this product.

Moreover, no responsibility is assumed by any contributor or by any committee in connection therewith.

This product neither states the opinion of, nor implies concurrence of, the sponsoring institutions.

COBOL is an industry language and is not the property of any company or group of companies, or of any organization or group of organizations.

No warranty, expressed or implied, is made by any contributor or by the CODASYL COBOL Committee as to the accuracy and functioning of the programming system and language. Moreover, no responsibility is assumed by any contributor, or by the committee, in connection therewith.

CBS College Publishing
Holt, Rinehart and Winston
The Dryden Press
Saunders College Publishing

PREFACE

For many reasons, probably all connected with rapid growth, data base management is still a somewhat disorganized subject, and many who have tried to teach it have found more than the usual number of difficulties to overcome. It was largely with the intention of eliminating many of these difficulties that this book was written.

The book is designed primarily for courses in computer science, although as much material as possible was chosen to satisfy the needs of business students and computer professionals. Part 1 of the book is devoted exclusively to conventional file processing techniques, and for two good reasons. First of all, conventional files are used side by side with data bases in most data processing environments, so that a knowledge of conventional file processing is required for the creation and updating of data bases. Secondly, many of the principles of conventional file processing still apply to the underlying storage files of data bases, so that a knowledge of conventional file processing is useful in areas such as data base design and tuning, data base system implementation, and the design of optimum data base retrieval algorithms. The material in Part 1 is designed for a one-semester file processing course which should be a prerequisite for a subsequent course on data base management. Some of the material in Part 1 is quite elementary, particularly in the beginning of Chapter 2 on sequential files. Thus the instructor who wishes to proceed at a fast pace in the file processing course could quite conveniently include Chapter 6 from Part 2 on data base techniques.

Chapter 6 is specially designed to help the student to move easily from files to data bases. In my experience, the transition from conventional files to data bases is never an easy one for most students, for there is a large conceptual gap between the two areas. Chapter 6 bridges that gap. It begins with conventional storage files, and step by step leads the student to conceptual data base structures, the ANSI/SPARC 3 level data base system organization, and the three main approaches to data base management. A brief chapter on data base design principles follows (Chapter 7), for it is helpful for students to become comfortable with the notion of a Fourth Normal Form data base at an early stage. However, the material in subsequent chapters is so designed that most of the more difficult material in Chapter 7 may be skipped over initially. The remaining chapters of Part 2 deal with the three main approaches to data base management, first CODASYL, and then the relational and hierarchical approaches.

Should an instructor desire it, the design of the book lends itself reasonably well to teaching relational data bases first and then CODASYL. However, instructors are strongly urged not to do this, even if they are convinced of the superiority of the relational approach. The latest CODASYL may not be to everyone's liking, but it is well worthy of study, and has the decided advantage of being much closer to the world of conventional file processing than the sophisticated but more abstract relational approach, thus enabling the beginner to more quickly gain a grasp of what data base management is all about. Furthermore, a student who has absorbed the CODASYL approach is in a much stronger position to appreciate the promise of the relational approach.

Few dispute that students learn best by working with files and data bases, rather than by just reading about them, and in both parts of the book every effort is made to balance theory and practice by including a reasonable number of programming examples illustrating the creation and manipulation of both files and data bases. But here we encounter a problem. Only PL/1 and COBOL are equipped with the file processing facilities necessary for a book of this sort. Use of both languages was clearly out of the question, and use of no language at all was clearly inconsistent with the aims of the book. PL/1 was chosen, since this language is more convenient for students and instructors in computer science. I realize that there are many, particularly in commercial data processing, who would have preferred COBOL. For this reason, the simplest possible subset of PL/1 is employed, in order that the programs could be read and understood by non PL/1 programmers. Apart from the file processing *READ/WRITE* commands, which are similar in both PL/1 and COBOL, use was made only of common programming constructs such as arrays, structure variables, *WHILE* and *DO* loops, and logical variables. In only a few instances was use made of a more advanced PL/1 facility, as for example at the end of Chapter 2 on sequential files. In that instance, PL/1 *BASED* variables were used in buffer and variable length record processing, for lack of any alternative.

As was said earlier, there are many problems connected with a course on data base management, and another one is encountered with the use of PL/1 in the material on CODASYL. Although PL/1 may be employed with most commercial CODASYL data base systems, and while CODASYL has a data manipulation language specification for COBOL, a PL/1 equivalent has not yet appeared, and is long overdue. This problem was dealt with by a translation of the CODASYL COBOL syntax to a readable PL/1 syntax consistent with the style of PL/1. Naturally, the official CODASYL semantics were preserved, except in a few minor instances where it would have been unrealistic. This is the course taken by major implementors of CODASYL, such as Cullinane Corporation, Honeywell, and Sperry Rand. Readers should be aware that such a PL/1 translation is easier for a CODASYL implementor, since all data base system access in practice is by means of *CALL* statements. Use of such primitive calls in this book was not considered acceptable, as they would have drastically reduced readability of the material. Instead, a great effort was made to find an easily readable CODASYL PL/1 syntax. Where such CODASYL PL/1 commands are used in programs and program excerpts, there is a cross reference to where the command is described and to the COBOL equivalent, should it be of interest. The CODASYL COBOL data manipulation language commands are given in Appendix 2.

An additional problem with including practical examples of file and data base processing programs is the choice of operating system on which to base it all. The processing of files, and underlying data base storage files, is intimately connected with the input/output facilities of the operating system. Again a difficult choice had to be made, and it was decided to base it all on OS/MVS, the widely used IBM operating system. OS/MVS is also of theoretical importance, and even if it is not available on the campus computer, most students will learn about it in courses on operating systems. However, it is not assumed that the reader is familiar with OS/MVS, or indeed with operating systems of any kind, and necessary operating system concepts are described in Chapter 1. An effort was made to keep operating system involvement to a minimum, and, although readers must normally assume an OS/MVS background operating system, associated details, particularly Job Control Language details, are either omitted or included only for purposes of illustration. Thus the book is also intended for use with courses for which the practical work is based on other operating systems. I have not experienced any difficulty, for example, in using the book in a course in which the MULTICS operating system from Honeywell was used. But no matter what operating system is used in practice, students can not escape having to make use of the relevant manuals.

Another significant problem, somewhat related to the operating system, is the storage medium for files and data bases. In most cases the medium is the disk unit, and in order to meaningfully deal with the storage densities and access times, some practical device is needed for examples. The IBM 3350 was chosen because of its wide use, although there are occasional references to its recently announced successor, the IBM 3380 disk. Even if students use other disks in practice, the material on these disks should be useful for gaining insight into underlying input/output processes and for purposes of comparison.

The existence of three main approaches to data base management is a problem in itself for many instructors, time limitations often resulting in only a cursory treatment of each approach. I believe that it is better to cover two approaches thoroughly than three superficially. To make the task of comparing the approaches as easy as possible, essentially the same data base, namely the FOR-ESTRY data base, is used with all three approaches.[1] This particular data base is sufficiently rich

---

[1] *The idea of including a recursive relationship (involving generations of trees) in this* FORESTRY *data base was developed from material in a Ph.D. thesis entitled* 'Electronic Data Processing of Forestry Tree-breeding Information,' *by B. Ditlevsen, of the Royal Veterinary and Agricultural University in Copenhagen, 1977 (not in English).*

in properties that it brings out most of the positive and negative features of the three approaches, without requiring that the reader become familiar with one or more new data bases for each new approach, as is common with other texts. A further problem is a consistent diagrammatic technique for representing data bases. There is no widely accepted method for doing this, and the proponents of each approach have traditionally been careful to avoid diagrams which could be associated with any of the competing approaches. This problem was easily solved by employing extended Bachman diagrams everywhere. This type of diagram is quite new, but is easy to grasp, and has the advantage of applying well to all three approaches. Extended Bachman diagrams may even be used to illustrate functional and other dependencies, and, with some further extensions, for illustrating retrieval expressions, an area to which diagrammatic techniques have not traditionally been applied. In my experience, all who have ever tried to use this diagrammatic technique have been enthusiastic about its power and applicability.

Terminology is often a problem for the instructor and student in this field, and it has also been a problem for me. The book covers a wide span of accumulated knowledge and techniques. Unfortunately it is common in practice for a term to be used in two different areas with two different meanings, and vice versa. For example, in conventional file processing, an 'external' file commonly means a collection of records on an external storage device such as a disk, the term 'external' being used in the sense of external to the main memory of a computer; however, when dealing with data bases, an external file is an abstract file, and a constitutent of an ANSI/SPARC external data base, which is something entirely different. Nevertheless, I have taken pains to use terminology which is acceptable and as near to common usage as possible, and which is consistent from one part of the book to another. Should I be found to have lapsed, the responsibility is entirely mine, but the reader is asked to consider the difficulty of the task.

There is a final problem for the data base instructor, about which little can be done in a textbook, and that is the problem of student access to suitable data base management systems. I believe that at the present time the CODASYL and relational approaches are the most important from an educational point of view. Yet it is still rare for an institution to have access to both systems, and there are some that have access to neither. Fortunately there is an acceptable solution for lack of access to a CODASYL system. Students should be made to write five procedures, namely STORE, CONNECT, FIND, FIND-MEMBER-N, and MODIFY. These modules should be able to manipulate a specific data base with three files, such as that in Figure 6.8. The manipulation should be along the lines of that accomplished by execution of the corresponding CODASYL commands, but of course with a minimum capability. The modules should interface with application programs by means of three global structure variables, each capable of holding a record from one of the files of the data base. A STATUS variable can also be used for a minimum number of return codes. The structure variables and STATUS thus serve as a User Working Area. Students should then be made to write about five application programs that make use of these modules. Suggested application programs are a loading program, a program to dump the data base, an update program, and two fairly sophisticated retrieval programs. Students are capable of writing these modules and application programs in a period of six to eight weeks of the course. The insight gained compares favourably with that obtained from use of a CODASYL system.

The difficulties are greater when a relational system is not available, and the solution we can propose is not nearly as satisfactory. Students should write procedures JOIN, SELECT, DIVIDE, and PROJECT for manipulation of a data base such as the one in Figure 6.8. STORE and MODIFY procedures should also be constructed. The primitive relational algebra thus constructed can then be used with application programs to manipulate the data base. However, that still leaves the student without practical experience of such powerful relational retrieval languages as SQL, even small scale implementations of which would probably be far too demanding to ask a beginning student to construct. There is in this case no alternative to setting and marking assignments in which students have to construct SQL, DSL ALPHA, and perhaps EOS expressions, an activity which will reveal a great deal to the instructor about the relative difficulty with which expressions in these languages can be formulated and read.

Data-base management is still under rapid development, and it has been a struggle to keep the manuscript abreast of the constant advances. In this respect, the patience and co-operation of the editors and staff of Holt, Rinehart and Winston must be acknowledged, particularly for acquiescing in requests to significantly update not only the copy-edited manuscript, but also the galley proofs. A continually vexing currency problem concerned System R, the comprehensive relational data base system under development at IBM. While the book was being written, there were few published reports on the progress of this project, and most of the limited information in the author's possession seemed to indicate that release of System R was unlikely in the foreseeable future. Consequently, in early 1980, it was finally decided that it would be premature to include a chapter on this system. Then in late 1980 and early 1981, the 'fog' surrounding the progress of System R lifted, significant and encouraging publications from IBM sources appeared, and IBM announced SQL/DS, a system using SQL (the language of System R) that interfaced to DL/1 and DOS/VSE. As a result of these developments, the author became convinced that the System R prototype had now progressed so far, that its omission from the book would be a serious deficiency. Fortunately Brete Harrison, the senior editor, was of a similar opinion, and at a rather late stage it was decided that it would be sufficient to include the specifics of System R in Appendix 3, since most of the relational theory on which the system is based was already covered in the rest of the book. Appendix 3 should therefore be treated by instructors as a continuation of Chapters 13 through 16 on the relational approach. It is thus an important appendix, although readers should be aware that the author has no privileged access to IBM sources, and that, in consequence, the description and diagrams in Appendix 3 are entirely the author's original interpretation of published material on the System R prototype.

While I have tried to reference all the many sources I have drawn upon, there will inevitably be omissions, for which I must accept responsibility. My greatest single source was without doubt the CODASYL DDLC and COBOL Journals of Development, and I offer the CODASYL data base committees the customary acknowledgment for the liberal use I have made of their work. I hope, in addition, that they will understand that the PL/1 data manipulation language translation used in Chapters 9 and 10 was developed only out of necessity, and in a spirit of co-operation rather than competition. The members of these committees will certainly understand, as should all readers, that the effort on my part to produce this translation was modest compared with the effort required to develop the current CODASYL specifications. (I should add that I know first hand of the work that is required to prepare a standards recommendation, having once served on an international standards committee.)

The material on the EOS CODASYL Enhancement and the EOS predicate calculus (Chapter 11 and the last part of Chapter 15) is based largely on my own published research, and deals with the application of Bachman's owner-coupled set concept to non-procedural retrieval languages. While it is not for me to recommend that this material be taught at undergraduate level, I would hope that instructors would study it and decide for themselves. They will probably be surprised, as have many others, that retrieval languages as expressive as those described in this material could possibly be based on the pragmatic owner-coupled set concept. The material is certainly not difficult. Students can easily master it, gaining as a result a deeper understanding of the role of quantifiers and of the nature of the established set theoretic relational languages such as DSL Alpha and SQL. In addition, as the late M. E. Senko has pointed out, the EOS language provides a useful bridge between the CODASYL and relational approaches.

Finally, readers will notice that the last chapter ends with a quotation about the 'road' going ever on and on. And indeed it does. A large number of emerging and advanced data-base topics are either given only preliminary treatment in the book, or are not covered at all. Many of these topics, such as distributed data-bases, are expected to grow in importance in years to come. It is fortunate that these more advanced topics are seldom covered in a first course in data-base management, for space limitations would not have permitted them to be covered adequately in this text. However, the topics that *are* covered in Part 2 are more than sufficient for a first course in the subject, and Part 2 may be regarded as complete in itself. It is expected that the more advanced material will eventually be placed in a planned companion volume.

There remains the pleasure of thanking all of those who directly or indirectly contributed to the book. In particular, but with some sadness, I wish to acknowledge the contribution of the late M. E. Senko at IBM. His encouragement and support during the last six months of his life was generously given, and was decisive in stimulating me to carry on and complete the book. I am also deeply indebted to E. H. Sibley at Sibley Data Systems, first of all for his support during a difficult period, and secondly for reading the manuscript, uncovering errors and suggesting improvements. The following must also be thanked for reading the manuscript and suggesting improvements, namely A. G. Dale at the University of Texas in Austin, S. P. Ghosh at the IBM Thomas J. Watson Research Center, J. Gray at IBM in San Jose, S. G. Navathe at the University of Florida, and S. Pollack at the University of Washington in St. Louis. Thanks are due as well to F. Groenbeck of the Technical University of Denmark for his support, and to A. K. Bradley who did the artwork for almost all the diagrams. Finally the diligence of my students at the University of Calgary in uncovering errors is gratefully appreciated.

J. B.

Calgary, Alberta
August, 1981

TABLE OF CONTENTS

PART 1

FILE TECHNIQUES

"Whirling machines, as the simplest means of obtaining quick motion with inconsiderable changes of place, play a part."

Ernest Mach, in Popular Scientific Lectures, *1898.*

Input/Output Facilities   1

1.1 INTRODUCTION

A *data base* is a collection of cross-referenced files. In theory, it need not have anything to do with computers, for it is possible to construct a data base with pencil, paper, and a stack of filing cabinets. Unfortunately, if such a data base were to contain the amount of data stored in many computer data bases today, its manipulation and maintenance would be a time-consuming affair.

A computer data base is made up of computer files, physically stored on the tapes, disks, and other media that make up the computer's external storage. User programs update and retrieve information from the data base, but only indirectly. As we shall see later, a complex software product known as a *Data-Base Management System* (DBMS) acts as a go-between for user-Application Programs (user APs) and the data base.

While data bases are becoming widespread, there is no sign that the conventional computer file will disappear from the scene. Such conventional computer files reside on external storage units such as disk or tape. A computer file is made up of records, each of which normally describes some entity in the physical world. There are many possible file types and methods of organizing them, and for a given file there are usually several ways of processing it by means of a user-application program.

In the final analysis, because the physical data base is a collection of physical computer files, and because the evolution of data bases and data-base management systems was to a large extent the result of the twin attempts to reduce data redundancy in files and to make application programs less dependent on the organization of files, the study of computer files makes a good foundation for the study of data bases. The fact that a wide variety of file organizations are in common use is a further indication of their fundamental importance. For this reason, Part 1 of this book will be devoted to computer files, with only occasional references to data bases. Data bases are introduced in Part 2.

1.1.1 Data Transfer

In computer installations, data is transferred between the computer's main memory and files on external storage units, under the supervision of a *multiprogramming operating system*. This transfer is carried out as a result of requests for input/output services made by a user-application program to the Operating System (OS). An operating system is the basic software component that manages all the resources of the computer. Thus the operating system is heavily involved in input/output [Habermann, 1976; Tanenbaum, 1976]. Figure 1.1 is a simple illustration of data transfer in which the operating system is involved.

The transfer of data between the data area of an application program and the external storage media is relatively slow because of the electromechanical nature of these media. It is therefore important that the Input/Output (I/O) facilities of the operating system be properly used, and a basic understanding of the essentials of I/O facilities and operating systems is necessary for the evaluation, design, and performance tuning of data-base and file systems.

We shall start in Section 1.2 with a look at the functional properties of some of the special hardware devices necessary for efficient I/O. Then, in Section 1.3, we shall look at the essentials of multiprogramming operating systems, paying particular attention to operating system I/O mechanisms. Finally, in Section 1.4, we shall look in some detail at the storage and timing parameters of the more important external storage devices, namely, tapes and disks. Because of the widespread use of System/370 and equivalent computers [Davis, 1977; Flores, 1973; Rindfleisch, 1978], we shall use hardware devices and operating systems for these machines for purposes of illustration.

1.2 HARDWARE AND I/O

The historical development of computer systems has been accompanied by a marked disparity between the speed of access of the Central Processing Unit (CPU) to main-memory programs and data and the speed of access to external storage units such as disk and tape devices. The speed disparity is of the order of a thousand to one and is caused by the fact that the CPU and main memory operate at electronic speeds (microseconds and less), while the external storage devices operate at electromechanical speeds (milliseconds). With advancing technology, the speed of external storage devices is increasing all the time, but CPU and main-memory speeds are also getting faster, so that the disparity in speeds can be expected to prevail for the foreseeable future.

The problems caused by this mismatch have been solved by the use of special *I/O processors* or *channels*. Input/output activities, which would otherwise have severely delayed the activities of the CPU, are offloaded onto channels. These devices are capable of independently transmitting data to and from external storage while the CPU is engaged in executing some other program in main memory [Madnik, 1974].

1.2.1 Channels

A channel is a small computer, but it has no memory of its own and executes special Channel Programs (CP) that reside in main memory. Thus a channel must have direct access to main memory. A channel starts execution only when turned on by a special component of the operating system. When a channel is executing, the execution is concurrent with that of the CPU; when a channel has carried out its task, it informs the CPU (by interrupting execution) and then stops.

As can be seen from Figure 1.1, a channel is not connected to an external storage device directly but to a *Device Controller* (DC), which is in turn connected to one or more storage devices. It is the device controller that actually carries out the commands executed by the channel. In addition (see Figure 1.1), a channel may also be connected to more than one controller, but at any given instant it is servicing just one external storage unit via one controller. A large machine normally has more than one channel.

Channel Functions   The main function carried out by the channel is the assembly and disassembly of data. Data are transmitted between external storage devices and main memory in user-specified amounts of data known as *data blocks*. A data block might typically be 2000 bytes, but it nevertheless comes off a disk track in bits, is assembled into bytes by the controller, and is further assembled into words (4 bytes) by the channel. The channel continues to place these bytes in a specially designated area of main memory known as a *buffer* area until the transfer of at least 1 data block is complete (see Figure

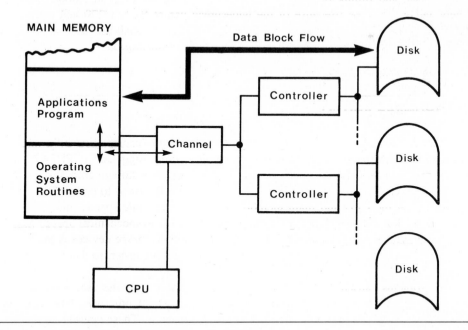

FIGURE 1.1.   *Overview of the input/output process in a mainframe computer.*

1.1). This process is reversed for transmission from memory buffer area to an external storage device. Additional functions of the channel are:

a. Fetching of channel program commands;

b. Transmission of commands to the device controller;

c. Transmission of sensory or status information to the CPU, for example, end of file or end of transmission of a block.

Types of Channels   Three types of channels are used with System/370 computers, namely *selector, byte-multiplexor,* and *block-multiplexor* channels.

Selector channels are normally used with high-speed storage devices such as disk and tape units. However, during channel operation only one storage device can be transmitting data via the channel.

Block-multiplexor channels are used to interleave the transmission of data blocks from different storage devices. As mentioned earlier, the prime function of a channel is the assembly of words from bytes, and vice versa. But the unit of data transmission is the *data block,* and where several blocks have to be transferred from a device, there will be a time period between the transmission of two consecutive data blocks when the channel can switch to the transmission of a block from a different device. Block-multiplexor channels are used with fast storage devices, and in a limited way are thus capable of servicing several storage devices concurrently.

Byte-multiplexor channels are used to service more than one slow external device concurrently. They interleave the transmission of bytes from different slow devices.

1.2.2 Device Controllers

The device controller primarily analyzes and carries out the commands transmitted to it from the channel program [Flores, 1973; IBM, 1976a]. These channel-program commands cause data to be written and read and, with direct access devices such as disks, enable data to be located. A controller has three other important functions.

a. The controller passes sensory or status information via the channel to the CPU, indicating, for example, the end of transmission of a data block.

b. Where necessary (for example, in the case of disks) the controller assembles bits into bytes for transmission to the channel (and vice versa).

c. The controller carries out validity checks (parity checks) on the data being transmitted. If an error is detected, the CPU is informed via the channel as in (a).

We now look at the commands carried out by device controllers in a little more detail. An understanding of these commands will be useful in Chapters 2, 3, and 4.

Controller Commands   We can identify four types of commands that may be carried out by a controller, namely *control commands, search commands, read commands,* and *write commands.*

Control commands cause the read/write mechanism or heads to be positioned so that either a search for a data block or the reading or writing of a data block in the storage medium can begin. For example, in the case of disk units, a *seek* command positions the read/write heads and selects an individual read/write head.

Search commands permit the controller to search one or more tracks of a disk unit in search of a data block with a key that either (a) matches the one in the channel program in main memory, or (b) satisfies other specified search conditions involving a search parameter in the channel program.

Read commands cause all or a specified part of a data block to be transferred to main memory. *Write* commands cause a data block to be transferred from a main-memory buffer area to a specified location on the storage medium. In the case of disk devices, a successful search command and subsequent execution of a *read* or *write* command can be carried out in one rotation of the disk. Thus a controller can search along a disk track until it finds the right data block and then transmit it, all within the period of revolution of the disk.

1.2.3 Direct Memory-Access (DMA) Devices

A channel is an example of a *direct memory-access device*. It can access main memory either to transmit data to and from a buffer area or to fetch channel-program commands and parameters. Thus a channel does not operate completely concurrently with the CPU. Only one processor can access the main memory at a time; thus when a channel is accessing, the CPU is shut out. This only occasionally slows the CPU down, however, because the CPU fetches most of its instructions from a high-speed *look-ahead cache memory,* into which its current instructions have been fed ahead of time.

Another example of a direct memory-access device is a *DMA controller.* These are used primarily with minicomputers and combine the essential channel- and device-controller functions in one device [Eckhouse, 1979].

1.3 MULTIPROGRAMMING AND I/O

The use of channels alone is not enough to solve the problem of the CPU and peripheral storage-device speeds. The channels merely relieve the CPU of the problem of servicing the slow peripheral devices. In many cases, execution of a user-application program would have to wait while a channel filled or emptied a buffer area. The standard solution to this problem is the multiprogramming operating system, which permits several user-application programs to be in the main memory at the same time. When a user program has to wait for a channel, the operating system switches control to another program that does not need to wait [Davis, 1977; Rus, 1979; Tanenbaum, 1976].

There are two main types of multiprogramming operating systems. There is the *memory partition* (or *nonvirtual*) *operating system* exemplified by OS/MVT [Davis, 1977]. This type of system is now outmoded, but it is useful to consider it because it greatly contributes to an understanding of the other type of operating system, namely, *virtual* or *demand-paged operating systems*. Such systems are in wide use at the time of writing. The widely used virtual system OS/MVS (originally called OS/VS2–2) is an upgraded version of OS/MVT [Scherr, 1973].

In this section we shall consider the workings of the two types of operating system in general terms and consider the input/output mechanisms for these systems in some detail.

1.3.1 Memory Partition-Type Operating Systems

The most widely used memory partition operation system was probably OS/MVT (MVT is an acronym for Multiprogramming with a Variable number of Tasks), and systems of this type were common in the early 1970s.

Main memory was basically divided into *partitions* (with OS/MVT, the term *region* was used). Some of the partitions were occupied by components of the operating system and others by user jobs, as shown in Figure 1.2. A user job was typically a user-application program with accompanying routines and data structures. We shall have more to say about these routines and data structures later. The control program for the operating system controlled the resources of the computer and had three major components, the *multiprogramming supervisor*, the *job scheduler*, and *data management services*. The job scheduler read in new jobs and placed them in a suitable partition in main memory. Data management services was responsible for carrying out I/O for the user jobs (and the job scheduler), while the multiprogramming supervisor continually switched execution control among the user jobs, job scheduler, and data management services, thus ensuring the interleaved execution of the various jobs.

Typically, if a user job needed input of data from an external storage device, a request was passed to a component of data management services known as the *I/O supervisor*. The multiprogramming supervisor then gave control to the I/O supervisor, which arranged for a channel to transmit the required data to the user partition. While the channel was transmitting, the multiprogramming supervisor would probably have given execution control to any of the user jobs that were not waiting for I/O data. It is useful to look more closely at the I/O mechanisms of OS/MVT, for they provide a basis for understanding the I/O mechanisms of the virtual operating systems such as OS/MVS, which are somewhat difficult to visualize. But first of all, we need to examine more closely the contents of a typical user partition.

User-Partition Contents   Accompanying each application program in a user partition are a group of routines and data structures provided by the operating system. We list and describe four of these that are necessary for our exposition.

1. *Data-Control Block*. This is a data structure containing all the information necessary for accessing a storage file, for example, the length of a data block or the type of file organization involved. (The information in the Data-Control Block (DCB) comes partly from the file declaration in a PL/1 or COBOL program, partly from a file definition statement (*Dataset Definition* or *DD* statement) or equivalent statement accompanying the program

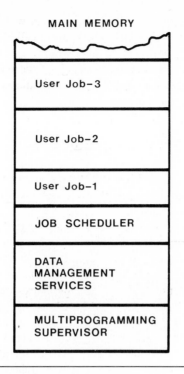

MAIN MEMORY

User Job–3
User Job–2
User Job–1
JOB SCHEDULER
DATA MANAGEMENT SERVICES
MULTIPROGRAMMING SUPERVISOR

FIGURE 1.2. *Division of the main memory into partitions (or regions) under the operating system OS/MVT.*

when it was submitted to the system, and partly from a label in the storage file, when the file is first accessed [Rindfleisch, 1978].)

2. *Access Method.* This is an often large and complex routine that is constructed from standard-access method modules by the data management services system when the file is first opened. It is the Access Method (AM) that analyzes requests for I/O from the user-application program, transmits data records between the applications-program data area and the file buffer, and issues requests to the I/O supervisor for input/output services.[1]

3. *Channel Program.* The channel program is constructed by the access method when the file is first opened and may be executed only by a channel.

4. *Buffers.* A buffer is capable of holding exactly one data block. Both access-method and channel-program modules have access to the buffers. The number of buffers is specified by the user when a file is declared or in a DD statement. We distinguish between *input buffers,* used with an access method that delivers data to the buffer, and *output buffers,* used with an access method that transmits data from the buffer. Note that a data block contains records, and that the number of records in a block is called the *block factor.*

---

[1]*It is not strictly true that the access method is in a user partition in OS/MVT; certain access-method modules reside in a* link-pack area *of main memory and are shared among user jobs.*

I/O Mechanisms   We shall now look in some detail at the mechanism by which I/O is carried out for a typical user-application program in a user partition (see Figure 1.3). We consider a user-application program in one partition, accompanied by a DCB, channel program, and buffer. The I/O supervisor is shown as residing in a separate partition. To keep the presentation as simple as possible, we assume that the user partition contains only one buffer. (More than one buffer is often more efficient, and the subject of double buffering is dealt with in Chapter 2.)

Let us now suppose that the application program issues a READ request for input of a record. There are two possibilities. Either the record is already in the buffer because of an earlier input operation or it is not in the buffer. We take the case of the record in the buffer first.

The READ request from the applications program causes the access method to gain control as a subroutine of the applications program. The access method searches the buffer, finds the record, and delivers it to the applications-program data area. Control is then returned to the applications program. During the whole process, the same user partition has control and the operating system, represented by the I/O supervisor, is not involved.

The operating system is involved when the record is not in the buffer. Specifically, we involve the access method, channel program, buffer, and I/O supervisor. (Other data structures are also involved, but they are ignored here for the sake of simplicity.) Referring to Figure 1.3, the important activities are as follows.

1. The READ statement is executed.

2. Control passes to the access method, which checks the buffer.

3. Using the DCB, the access method formulates and sends a request for I/O services to the I/O supervisor. The I/O request or *request element* is placed in a channel queue; there is a channel queue for the service of each channel. The request element contains the address of the correct channel program, identifiers for the channel and storage device, and other control information.

4. The user partition loses control because it lacks I/O data.

5. The multiprogramming supervisor gives control to another partition.

6. We assumed that the channel for our I/O was busy; when it is ready for a new activity, the CPU is interrupted.

7. The multiprogramming supervisor gives control to the I/O supervisor.

8. If the request is first in line in the channel queue for the channel, it will be dealt with by the I/O supervisor; otherwise, we may have to wait.

9. Assuming that it is our turn, the I/O supervisor passes the address of the channel program to a standard location in main memory containing the *channel address word*.

10. The I/O supervisor turns on the storage device and device controller and starts the channel program.

11. a. Assuming that there are no other idle channels for the I/O supervisor to service, the multiprogramming supervisor gives control to another partition.

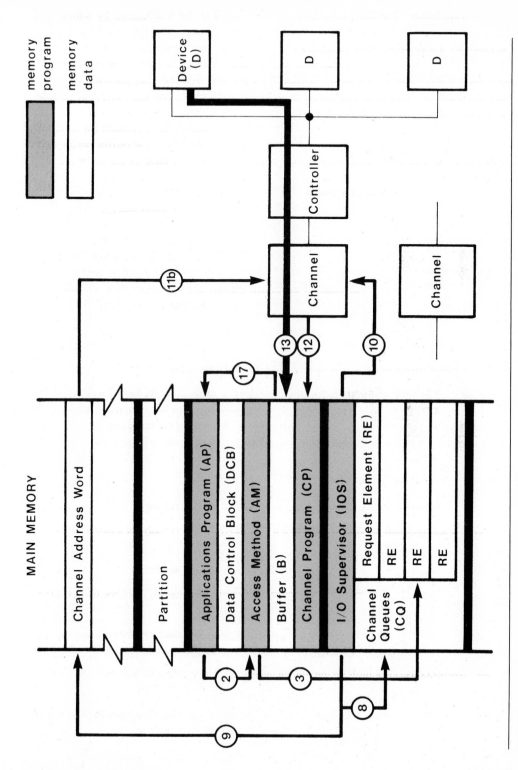

FIGURE 1.3. Sequence of I/O events under OS/MVT.

b.   The channel accesses the channel address word, retrieving the address of the channel program in the user partition.

12. The channel executes the channel program.

13. A block of data is transferred to the buffer in our user partition.

14. When the channel is finished, it interrupts the CPU.

15. The multiprogramming supervisor gives control to the I/O supervisor, which starts the channel's next activity. Servicing idle channels has very high priority.

16. Our user partition is eventually given control by the multiprogramming supervisor.

17. The access method in the user partition resumes execution and delivers the required record from the buffer to the applications-program data area.

18. The access method returns control to the user-application program, which then processes the record.

A similar sequence of events takes place when a user applications program executes a WRITE statement. In the simplest case, the output buffer is not full, and when a WRITE request is received the access method merely transfers the required record from the user-program data area to the buffer. However, if the buffer is filled by the record, then the I/O supervisor is involved and a process is set in motion that is very similar to that for the case of a READ request with the required record not in the buffer. The main difference is that this time the channel program transmits a block from the buffer to the storage device.

Move- and Locate-Mode Processing   The type of processing described above is known as *move-mode processing* because, with both reading and writing of records, movement of records between buffer and program data area is involved. A variation described in more detail in Chapter 2 is known as *locate-mode processing*.

With *locate-mode* processing, in a case such as a READ request being issued by the applications program, instead of the required record being transmitted from the buffer to the program data area, the address of the record in the buffer is delivered to the applications-program data area. The applications program then processes the record on location in the buffer, with a resulting saving in transmission time.

1.3.2 Virtual or Demand-Paged Operating Systems

The most widely used system of this type is probably OS/MVS (MVS is an acronym for Multiple Virtual Storage). OS/MVS is based on OS/MVT (described in the previous subsection), but with some fundamental extensions that require modification of the basic I/O mechanisms described for OS/MVT. The extensions permit the CPU to execute a user job with only a small portion (that is, a few pages, each 4K bytes in length) of the job in main storage at any given time. The remainder of a job being executed resides on a very fast disk in *external page storage*. Furthermore, a user job is not restricted in size to the largest amount of the main memory available, since only a few pages of a job are required in main memory for execution. It is thus possible for a job to be larger than the main

---

memory, the actual limiting size being determined by the addressing system of the computer. With System/370 machines under OS/MVS, a user job plus the space required by the operating system could in theory be as large as 16 megabytes. Each user is said to have a virtual memory at his or her disposal, the virtual memory being 16 megabytes of storage [Scherr, 1973].

To understand clearly the concept of a user's virtual memory, it is necessary to examine the computer's addressing system. System/370 machine instructions permit an instruction to reference or operate on data in an address contained within the instruction. Such addresses can be up to 24 bits long, and can therefore contain values up to about 16 million. It is thus possible to have a System/370 machine-language program up to 16 million bytes long, including data areas. This maximum theoretical program length is a user's virtual memory. Of course, this possibility exists for all users and even for some operating system components, and OS/MVS is an operating system that provides each user with a virtual memory. (As OS/MVS is implemented, a user's virtual memory is reduced by the size of the main components of the operating system.)

We may still imagine that each user job occupies a user partition as with OS/MVT, except that (a) the size of the partition is now limited only by the size of the virtual memory, and (b) the user partition no longer resides in main memory, but is best imagined as residing in the user's virtual memory (see Figure 1.4). In reality, of course, the contents of a user partition reside in external page storage on a fast disk.

System Operation   When a new user job is loaded for execution, as with OS/MVT, it is the job-scheduler component of the operating system that carries out the loading operation. The job scheduler places the job not in main memory, but in its virtual memory; that is, in external page storage. The job is thus placed in external page storage much as it would have been placed in main memory under OS/MVT and is ready for execution. However, at the same time, the job scheduler divides the job up into segments (64K bytes long), and the segments are further divided into pages (4K bytes). Sooner or later, the multiprogramming supervisor gives execution control to the new job; to permit it to execute, a component of the operating system called the *paging supervisor* reads in, or *pages in,* sufficient pages from external page storage for the job to begin execution. If the CPU at some point then executes an instruction that references data in a page not in main memory, the paging supervisor pages the least recently used page in main memory out to the external page storage and pages in the required page. In the meantime, the multiprogramming supervisor will probably have given control to pages of some other job.

We thus see that the main operational difference between a virtual system and a conventional system is that the multiprogramming supervisor switches control between the main-memory pages of different user jobs, while the paging supervisor sees that the user job pages required for execution are in main memory. In order for the paging supervisor to be able to function, the operating system maintains sets of tables with information about segments and pages. There is a table describing locations of pages in external page storage, there is a table describing the status of the slots of main memory (page slots) that can contain pages, and there are tables giving the start addresses of the locations of pages being executed in main memory (page tables). These latter tables are important for our exposition.

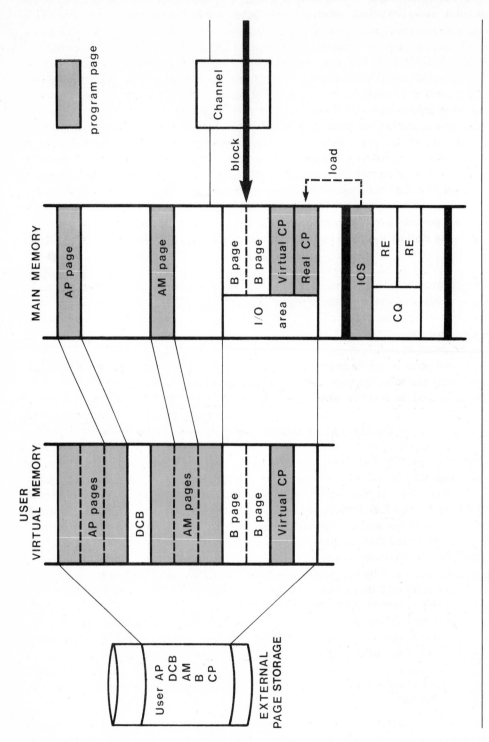

FIGURE 1.4. *The equivalent of an OS/MVT partition in external page storage, virtual memory, and main memory under OS/MVS, showing details of the I/O mechanisms.*

All addresses in user jobs in external page storage are virtual and can range up to 16 megabytes, as we have seen. When a page is paged into real memory for execution, it still contains these virtual addresses. Thus an instruction referring to an address 1000 bytes from the start of page 10 in segment 100 (virtual address approximately 100∗64,000 + 10∗4000 + 1000, or 6,441,000), would actually be referring to main-memory address 301,000, or address 300,000 + 1000, if the page in question had been paged into main-memory location 300,000.

Thus in order for the CPU to execute the segments paged in by the paging supervisor, it must have a method of translating the instruction virtual addresses to real-memory addresses. It uses the page tables, listing locations of pages in main memory for this purpose. However, if software routines had to be used to translate the addresses, this would slow execution unacceptably. To solve this problem, special fast table look-up hardware, called *Dynamic Address Translation* (DAT) hardware, is used by the CPU [Auslander, 1973].

We are now in a position to examine the I/O mechanisms under OS/MVS for external *user files* (as distinct from external *page storage* under the control of the paging supervisor).

I/O Mechanisms The I/O mechanisms for virtual systems such as OS/MVS are much the same as those described in the previous subsection for OS/MVT, allowing for the fact that the equivalent of the OS/MVT partition can now be much larger than the main memory and is undergoing constant paging. There are some additional differences of which we should be aware as well.

The first point is that there is an even greater opportunity for sharing access methods between different jobs. Suppose two different jobs need the same access method. It is necessary to load the access method only once into external page storage, and let external page-storage tables for each job refer to the same external page-storage location. Thus it is possible to avoid the situation where an access method for a job is paged out, to be followed by the paging in of the same access method for another job.

The other point is that when a job is loaded into virtual storage, that is, placed in external page storage, allowance is made for having channel programs in external page storage; when a channel program is constructed by the access method, it will join the rest of the job (including DCB, buffers, and access methods) in external page storage. However, the channel programs will contain addresses (for example, channel programs reference buffer locations), and these addresses are *virtual*. So, when a page containing a channel program is paged into main memory, it must have its *virtual* addresses translated into *real* addresses before it can be executed by a channel. Only the CPU is equipped with DAT hardware for automatic translation, and software translation must be used with channel programs.[1] This is carried out by the I/O supervisor.

We shall now follow the sequence of events following the execution of a READ statement in a user job. As in the case with OS/MVT, for tutorial purposes we shall assume that there is only one buffer available. Referring to Figure 1.4, we can see that the user

---

[1]*While this book was in press IBM announced new machines for OS/MVS with channels equipped with DAT hardware.*

job involved is stored in external page storage, and we imagine it to exist as a partition (limited in size only by the size of virtual memory) in its virtual memory. In addition, some pages from the applications program are being executed in main memory. We consider the case where the record required is not in the input buffer.

1. The READ statement is executed in a main-memory page of the application program.

2. Control goes to the access method, paged in if necessary.

3. Using the DCB, paged in if necessary, the access method formulates and places an I/O request element in the appropriate I/O supervisor channel queue.

4. The multiprogramming supervisor gives control to the pages of another application.

5. The required channel eventually interrupts the CPU, when it has run out of work.

6. The multiprogramming supervisor gives control to the I/O supervisor (not paged in and out). Assuming our I/O request element is at the head of the queue, it is dealt with.

7. The I/O supervisor commands the paging supervisor to suspend paging of the buffer and channel program area of main storage for our job. One reason for doing this is to prevent an entirely different page from being paged into the location that the channel is using as a buffer. The channel is operating concurrently with the CPU and has no DAT hardware. Consequently, the paging supervisor could overwrite and thus wipe out our partly transmitted data block with a page of some other application.

8. The I/O supervisor now processes our channel program in main memory and produces a copy of it with real addresses, which it places in the I/O area, where paging has been suspended.

9. The I/O supervisor places the address of the real-address channel program in the channel address word (see I/O sequence for OS/MVT) and starts the channel.

10. a. The multiprogramming supervisor switches control to the pages of some other application.

    b. The channel fetches the contents of the channel address word and starts executing the (real-address) channel program copy.

11. The channel delivers a block of data to the input buffer.

12. The channel is out of work, so it interrupts the CPU; the multiprogramming supervisor then gives control to the I/O supervisor again.

13. The I/O supervisor informs the paging supervisor that it may resume paging of the I/O area for our job.

14. The I/O supervisor arranges for the channel to start some new activity (going through Steps 7, 8, and 9 for some other application).

15. The multiprogramming supervisor gives control to the pages of some job, probably not ours; one result may be that our newly filled buffer will be paged out to external page storage.

16. Eventually the multiprogramming supervisor gives control to the pages of our job, and the access method delivers a record from the buffer (paged back in if necessary) to the applications-program data area.

It is thus clear that, apart from the continual paging, the essential difference between I/O in virtual and nonvirtual operating systems is the need for translation of the virtual channel-program addresses into real addresses by a software routine.

User Written Access Methods   It is possible for users to write their own access methods since the access method functions as a subprogram of an applications program. Such application programs need to be written in assembler language, and the programmer must also construct the DCB, channel program, and certain other data structures [IBM, 1970; Kuo, 1974]. This is a major task, and it can pay to construct such special access methods only if there is likelihood of very frequent use of nonstandard file organizations.

As shown in Figure 1.5, a data-base management system runs in most cases as a subprogram of a user-application program. To obtain input from a data base, a user application program first passes a request to the data-base control system. The data-base control system analyzes the request and passes I/O requests to one or more access methods, which deal with them as outlined above for applications programs. There is thus a possibility of constructing special access methods for use with data-base systems, but at the time of writing, as far as the author is aware, there is no data-base system in which such access methods have been incorporated. All such systems use the standard access methods provided with the operating system.

System Diagrams with Virtual Operating Systems   Virtual operating systems are difficult for most people to visualize and are even harder to describe diagrammatically. To simplify diagrams in this book, we shall adopt the convention that user jobs occupy a partition in the main memory which is arbitrarily large and are accompanied by all necessary access methods, buffers, and channel programs. It is to be understood that in practice such a partition would probably occupy noncontiguous space in external page storage and be paged into the main memory for execution. This convention can be applied at once to Figure 1.5.

MULTICS Virtual Files   Before leaving the subject of I/O with virtual operating systems, the MULTICS operating system from Honeywell [Honeywell, 1977; Tanenbaum, 1976] deserves mention. Because of the use of a 36-bit address in machine instructions, the virtual memory of a user is $6*10^{12}$ bytes (9-bit "bytes"), which is approximately $1.5*10^5$ times larger than the IBM System/370 virtual memory. This huge virtual memory allows a user to place storage files in external page storage, that is, in virtual memory, in the same way as user-program data accompanies a program in a program-data area. Thus what is usually regarded as a storage file now may be regarded almost as a part of the program-data area. When a record is required, it is simply obtained from a page, paged in if necessary. Nevertheless, under MULTICS, user programs written in higher languages continue to require the specification of separate storage files. Storage files of this type are sometimes referred to as *virtual files;* in MULTICS, they are called *segments.*

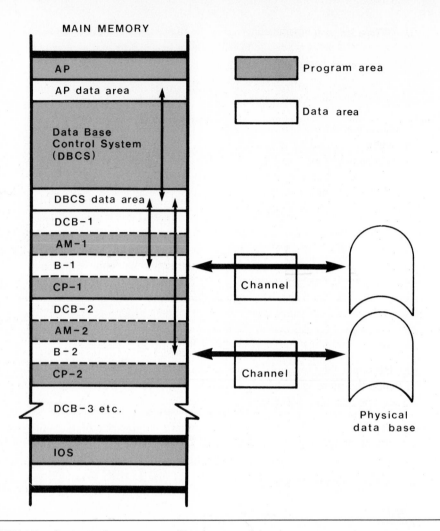

FIGURE 1.5. *Contents of a memory partition for a user job employing a data-base management system.*

1.4 TAPE AND DISK PARAMETERS

We shall now consider the physical parameters that govern data storage and transfer with tape and disk units, the most widely employed storage media.

1.4.1 Tapes

Data Storage Here the relevant parameters are

$d:$ Storage density (nominal) in card-images per foot;

$L:$ Tape length in feet;

$g:$ InterBlock Gap (IBG) in card-images;

$B:$ Block length in card-images.

However, manufacturers usually quote d in bits per inch (bpi) and g in inches, necessitating conversions when it is required to relate them to a file-storage problem.

The main technical factor to be considered is the effect of the interblock gap. Data is transmitted between buffers and tape in blocks, and because the fast-moving tape requires time in between block transmissions in which to stop, space is wasted on the tape. Thus there is a need for an IBG (see Figure 1.6).

FIGURE 1.6.   *Physical tape data format.*

Clearly, the larger the number of blocks on the tape, the larger will be the number of IBGs, and hence the more space will be wasted. Thus the utilization factor for a given tape will always be less than 100 percent. The percent utilization factor will be given by

tape utilization (percent): $\dfrac{100B}{B + g}$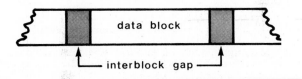

Thus a tape that can nominally store Ld card-images will in practice only be able to hold

$$\dfrac{BLd}{B + g}$$

card-images. We can see from the above that as B becomes large in relation to g, the storage density tends to the nominal. When $B = g$, the utilization is only 50 percent.

As a further illustration, we can look at some typical figures for the relevant parameters. A widely used industry tape is 2400 feet in length and has a storage density of 240 card-images per foot (1600 bits[1] per inch) and an interblock gap of 12 card-images (0.6 inches). This tape can nominally store

2400 * 240   or   576,000 card-images

---

[1] *Note that a byte of data is stored* across *and not* along *a tape. A density of 1600 bits per inch of length therefore implies a density of 1600 bytes per inch of physical tape.*

However, with a block size of 12 card-images, it is only 50 percent utilized, and with a block size of 24 (which is fairly typical), it is 66.6 percent utilized. The effect of block size is illustrated in Figure 1.7.

Data Transmission   We need the following parameters:

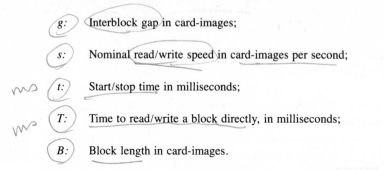

- *g:*   Interblock gap in card-images;

- *s:*   Nominal read/write speed in card-images per second;

- *t:*   Start/stop time in milliseconds;

- *T:*   Time to read/write a block directly, in milliseconds;

- *B:*   Block length in card-images.

The main point is that the effective rate of data transmission is reduced by two factors:

1.   The time required to start and stop the tape.

2.   The time spent by the read/write heads in the interblock gap.

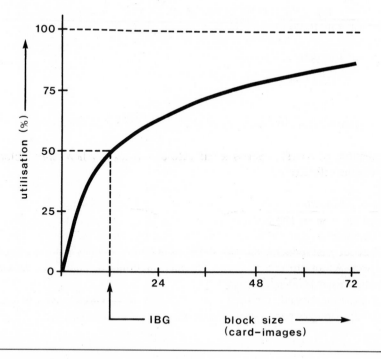

FIGURE 1.7.   *Effect of block size on a 1600-bpi industry tape percentage utilization.*

These two factors are not unrelated. First consider the case where many blocks are being read without the tape stopping. The time wasted due to a typical interblock gap will be g/s seconds. Now consider the case where just one block is read. The time spent by the heads in the gaps before and after reading a block will be $(g/s + t/1000)$ seconds. Here t is the *additional* time in milliseconds required for the tape to start and stop.

We can now deduce an expression for the effective data transmission rate. If the time spent directly reading a block is T, then this time is

$$\frac{100T}{T + t + 1000g/s} \quad \text{percent}$$

of the total time to read a block. However, if n blocks are read without stopping the tape, the corresponding percentage is:

$$\frac{100Tn}{Tn + t + 1000gn/s} \quad \text{percent}$$

which reduces to the first expression when $n = 1$.

Thus the effective data transmission rate must be the above percentage of the nominal transmission rate:

$$\frac{Tns}{Tn + t + 1000gn/s} \quad \text{card-images per second}$$

Because $T = 1000B/s$, we can rewrite the expression for the effective data transmission rate as

$$\frac{1000Bns}{1000Bn + st + 1000gn} \quad \text{card-images per second}$$

This expression, of course, applies to the case of n blocks. Where only 1 block is being transmitted, the effective rate is

$$\frac{1000Bs}{1000B + st + 1000g} \quad \text{card-images per second}$$

Thus we can see that reducing the block size reduces the effective read/write speed, as we would expect. As an illustration, let us consider the effect of block size on the data rate for the widely used 1600-bpi industry tape.

As already mentioned, for such tapes g is close to 12 card-images; in addition, s is about 2000 card-images per second and t is about 1 millisecond. The effective transmission rate is thus given by

$$\frac{2000Bn}{Bn + 2 + 12n} \quad \text{card-images per second}$$

Representative curves are shown in Figure 1.8. It can clearly be seen that a block size of at least 25 card-images is desirable with these tapes.

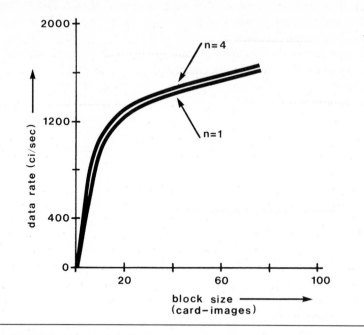

FIGURE 1.8. *Effect of block size on effective data-transmission rate. The number of blocks (n) transmitted at a time has little effect on the rate. Curves are for industry 1600-bpi tapes.*

1.4.2 Disks

Cylinder Concept   In dealing with a disk-pack, it is usual to consider that a set of tracks of the same radius makes up a *cylinder* of tracks. Thus a disk-pack with, for example, 19 recording surfaces will have 19 tracks in a cylinder, and if there are, for instance, 400 tracks on a surface, there will be 400 cylinders in the disk-pack. A cylinder may also be regarded as a set of tracks that may be read without seeks, that is, movement of the read/write arms.

Data Storage   There are two main ways of formatting a disk track. One is the hardware technique of dividing a track into fixed-length, hardware-addressable sectors. Here a sector is the smallest addressable length of track, but it can contain more than one data block. This means that the address of a data block is specified by the cylinder, track, and sector numbers of the sector in which it is contained. If data blocks do not fit evenly into a sector, unused space at the end of each sector may result.

The other method is the software approach of recording a block number for each data block on the track. A block number is stored in a *count subblock* of the stored block or *storage block*. This method is used with System/370, and such a storage block is also called a *count-data block*. A variation, which is also used, is the *count-key data block*. Here the block number is recorded with the data block, along with an identifying key. This key is stored in a *key subblock* of the storage block. Further, the (transmitted) data block is stored as a *data subblock* of the storage block.

Software formats are shown diagrammatically in Figures 1.9a, 1.9b, and 1.9c. These formats permit a block's address to be constructed from cylinder, track, and block number, or from cylinder, track number, and block key, or from a combination of both. Because the software approach is used with System/370, we shall restrict the following analysis to this approach.

a. Track-block capacity estimations   The following parameters are required:

$S:$ Nominal track storage (bytes);

$c:$ Number of bytes required for (1) interblock gap, plus (2) count subblock, plus (3) intersubblock gap;

$B:$ Data subblock in bytes;

$k:$ Number of bytes for the key;

$r:$ c, plus the bytes for the key intersubblock gap.

The nominal track storage is not the total on the track. As we can see from Figure 1.9a, at the beginning of the track some space is reserved for use by the system (for the purposes of track identification and track status).

It is important to understand that only whole numbers of blocks are allowed on a track. (Contrast this with the sector formatting approach, where only whole numbers of blocks are allowed in a sector.) Thus, using Figure 1.9b, we can see that the number n of count-data blocks that can fit on a track is given by

$$n = \text{Trunc}\left(\frac{S}{c+B}\right) \tag{1}$$

With count-key data blocks, using Figure 1.9c, the number n is given by

$$n = \text{Trunc}\left(\frac{S}{r+k+B}\right) \tag{2}$$

Thus if

$$\frac{S}{2} < r + k + B \leq S$$

then there is room for only one count-key data block.

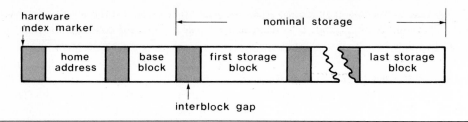

FIGURE 1.9a. *Disk track format: The areas taken up by the home address and base block are not available for storage blocks.*

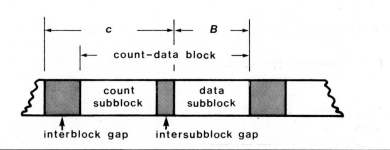

FIGURE 1.9b. *Format of a count-data block. The data subblock is the usual (transmitted) data block.*

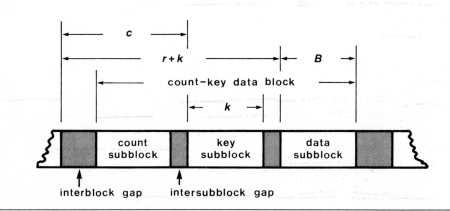

FIGURE 1.9c. *Format of a count-key data block. The key in the key subblock is the key of the last record in the data subblock.*

To take a practical example, consider the parameter values for the widely used IBM 3350 disk unit: $S = 19,254$, $c = 185$, and $r = 267$. Thus for count-data blocks and count-key data blocks, respectively, the number n of blocks per track is given by

$$n = \text{Trunc}\ [19,254/(185 + B)]$$

and

$$n = \text{Trunc}\ [19,254/(267 + (k + B))]$$

From these relationships, it is convenient [IBM, 1976a] to construct a table giving the maximum and minimum allowed values of B and $k + B$ for a given value of n. Such values are shown in Table 1.1.

In the case of count-data blocks, for a given n the maximum value of B is that which, if increased in size by 1 byte, would decrease n to $n - 1$. The minimum value of B is that which, if decreased by 1 byte, would increase n to $n + 1$. We can similarly deduce maximum and minimum values of $k + B$ for the case of count-key data blocks.

b. Track utilization   It is clear that in the software formatting approach, there are two kinds of nominal track space not containing user data. First, we have the block and subblock gaps, together with key and count subblocks. And, second, we have possible unused space at the end of a track. The more of this type of track space there is, the lower the track utilization for user data.

We may define the percentage track utilization as the total length of the data subblocks on a track taken as a percentage of the total nominal track length. That gives

$$100nB/S$$

where n is the total number of blocks on a track, as deduced from relationships such as (1) and (2).

The utilization is generally improved by keeping the block size high. Nevertheless, low utilization can result with large blocks from unused storage at the end of a track. Thus in the case of a 3350 device with count-data format, a data block of 9443 bytes, although large, allows only one block in a 19,254-byte nominal storage, so that the utilization is less than 50 percent. The moral is that the designer needs to take care.

Data Transmission   We can use the following parameters:

s: Nominal read/write speed in bytes per second;

R: Rotation time in milliseconds;

P: Average head positioning or seek time in milliseconds;

B: Data block size in bytes.

TRACK CAPACITY—IBM 3350 DISK				
Count-data blocks		**Count-key data blocks**		**Blocks per track (n)**
Bytes in a data subblock (B)		Bytes in key and data subblocks ($k + B$)		
Min.	Max.	Min.	Max.	
9443	19069	9361	18987	1
6234	9442	6152	9360	2
4629	6233	4547	6151	3
3666	4628	3584	4546	4
3025	3665	2943	3583	5
2566	3024	2484	2942	6
2222	2565	2140	2483	7
1955	2221	1873	2139	8
1741	1954	1659	1872	9
•	•	•	•	•
•	•	•	•	•
•	•	•	•	•

TABLE 1.1

Data transmission in disk units is dominated by the rotation and head-positioning (seek) times. To access a given track, the head must move; to access a given block (either by block number or key), the device controller has to examine the blocks on the track one by one until the required block is found. Only then is it transmitted.

The head positioning delay can be avoided by using a fixed head disk; however, such devices are very expensive and are used mainly for system purposes. It is also worth noting here that when a disk file is created sequentially, it is loaded cylinder by cylinder, the tracks of each cylinder being loaded consecutively. This permits the file to be processed sequentially, cylinder by cylinder, with few seeks being necessary. In such cases, the effect of rotational delay will dominate. Nevertheless, disk units are used primarily for direct access, and we shall consider data transmission for that case. The time to transmit a block of data will be given by

$$\frac{R}{2} + P + \frac{B}{s}$$

INPUT/OUTPUT FACILITIES

This time is, of necessity, an average. The term $R/2$ is thus half the rotation time. The last term is normally fairly small compared to the other two. If we again consider a 3350 device for purposes of illustration, R is 16.7 milliseconds, P is 25 milliseconds and s is about 1.2 million bytes per second. (Compare this last figure with that for the 2400-foot, 1600-bpi industry tape exemplified earlier.) Thus $R/2 + P$ comes to 33.4 milliseconds, while B/s contributes 1.7 milliseconds for a typical 2000-byte block.

The effective transmission rate with direct access will clearly be

$$\frac{B}{R/2 + P + B/s}$$

Using the parameters for the 3350 device and a 2000-byte block length, this is close to 57,000 bytes per second. This should be compared to the nominal 1,200,000 bytes per second and to typical tape data transmission speeds.

Disk access is clearly slow, so that in the design of direct-access files and of procedures for processing them, great attention must be paid to techniques for reducing the number of file accesses required. This is even more true in the case of data bases. Disk specifications for the IBM 3350 and 3380 disks are given in Appendix 1.

EXERCISES

1. Assuming that there is room for only one more record in the output buffer, list the activities that follow a WRITE request under OS/MVS.

2. Records of length 200 bytes are stored in blocks that are 25 card-images in size. An industry 1600-bpi tape is filled with these records.

   a. How many records can the tape hold?

   b. How much space is wasted by interblock gaps?

   c. How long would it take to read the whole tape without stops.

   d. If the tape is read three blocks at a time, how much time is spent in reading it?

3. Complete the entries for $n = 10$ and $n = 50$ in Table 1.1. Why can there not be an entry for $n = 110$?

4. A file with 48,000 records is loaded as an IBM PL/1 CONSECUTIVE file (blocks in count-data format) on a 3350 disk. The records are each 200 bytes long and the number of records in a data block is 16. Using the 3350-track specifications given in Appendix 1, determine each of the following.

   a. The number of tracks required for the file.

   b. The percentage utilization of the nominal track space used by the records.

5. Records of a PL/1 (index sequential) file are stored on a 3350-disk in count-key data format. If the record key is 13 bytes long, a record is 100 bytes long, the number of records in a data block is 30, and the tracks are completely full of records, determine each of the following using the 3350 track and timing specifications given in Appendix 1:

   a. The number of records on a track.

   b. The time to read all the records on a track sequentially.

   c. The time to read all the records on a track by direct access in random order.

6. A PL/1 CONSECUTIVE file (blocks in count-data format) contains eight 200 byte records in each data block. The file fills a complete IBM 3350 disk pack. What would be the minimum increase in the block factor required to permit the file to fit into 7 of the 1600-bpi industry tapes described in this chapter? A 3350-disk unit has 555 cylinders, with 30 tracks per cylinder.

7. The CONSECUTIVE file in the previous question is to be reorganized as a REGIONAL(1) file (count-data format, block factor 1). How many extra cylinders will be required?

8. A PL/1 CONSECUTIVE file (count-data format) contains records of varying lengths in 16,000 blocks with two types of makeup. One type has 49 records of total length 1090 bytes, and the other has 74 records of total length 1140 bytes. The block types alternate in the file, and the first block is the type with 49 records. How many tracks of a 3350 disk are needed for the file? (Note that in the data subblock of a storage block that can vary in length, a 4-byte length indicator is attached to *each* record, with an additional 4-byte length indicator being attached to the data subblock.)

9. For the file in Exercise 8, calculate the amount of unused space at the end of a track.

10. For the file in Exercise 8, if the maximum length of a data block was specified in the accompanying DD statement as being 1800 bytes, what is the least possible length of the first record in the 74-record block?

11. Make up a table like Table 1.1 for an IBM 3380 disk unit (see Appendix 1).

12. Repeat Exercises 4, 5, 7, 8, 9, and 10 for an IBM 3380 disk (see Appendix 1).

REFERENCES

Auslander, M. A., and J. F. Jaffe, 1973, "Influences of Dynamic Address Translation on Operating System Technology," *IBM Sys. J.*, **12**(4):368–81.

Davis, W. S., 1977, *Operating Systems: A Systematic View,* Addison-Wesley, Reading, Mass.

Eckhouse, R. H., and L. R. Morris, 1979, *Minicomputer Systems,* Prentice-Hall, Inc., Englewood Cliffs, N.J.

Flores, I., 1973, *Peripheral Devices*, Prentice-Hall, Inc., Englewood Cliffs, N.J.

Habermann, A. N., 1976, *Introduction to Operating System Design*, SRA Inc.

Honeywell, 1977, *MULTICS Introductory User's Guide*, Order Form AL40.

IBM, 1970, *System Programmer's Guide, Order Form GC28–6550*.

IBM, 1976a, *Introduction to IBM Direct Access Storage Devices and Organization Methods*, Student Text, Order Form GC20–1649.

IBM, 1976b, *Introduction to IBM 3350 Direct Access Storage*, Order Form GA26–1638.

Kuo, S. S., 1974, *Assembler Language for FORTRAN, COBOL and PL/1 Programmers*, Addison-Wesley, Reading, Mass.

Madnik, S. E., and J. J. Donovan, 1974, *Operating Systems*, McGraw-Hill, New York.

Rindfleisch, D. H., 1978, *Utilizing System 360/370 OS and VS Job Control Language and Utility Programs*, Prentice-Hall, Inc., Englewood Cliffs, N.J.

Rus, T., 1979, *Data Structures and Operating Systems*, John Wiley, New York.

Scherr, A. L., 1973, "OS/VS2-2 Concepts and Philosophies," *IBM Sys. J.*, **12**(4):381–400.

Tanenbaum, A. S., 1976, *Structured Computer Organization*, Prentice-Hall, Inc., Englewood Cliffs, N.J.

Sequential Files

2

Sequential files are characterized by the fact that the constituent records are stored in sequence; that is, such a file is tape-like, although it may also reside on a direct access device.

The sequential file is probably the earliest type of computer file, and conceptually it is also the simplest. However, when records with different structures are included in the same file, unavoidable complexity is introduced. Sequential files are in very wide use.

Computer files (and, for that matter, data bases) require a language or sublanguage (that is, a part of a more general-purpose language) for their creation and manipulation. The best known file manipulation sublanguages are embodied in PL/1 and COBOL. The two are quite similar, and we shall employ PL/1 throughout this book. In this chapter, we shall look at the PL/1 sublanguage for manipulating sequential files [IBM, 1976a; Weinberg, 1970].

As mentioned in the previous chapter, when a file is to be used by a program, there has to be a DCB or its equivalent for the access method to use. For programs running under OS/MVT or OS/MVS, the DCB is, to a large extent, constructed from *DCB parameters* included in a special statement known as a *Data Definition* (DD) statement. There is one DD statement for each file being manipulated. The DD statements must be constructed by the user and are placed just after the program being submitted to the system (for an example, see the program CREATE in Section 2.2.1).

The DD statements are a part of OS *Job Control Language* (JCL), which is a field of study in itself. The user wishing to set up files under OS/MVS must have a knowledge of this language. However, the subject is beyond the scope of this text [Rindfleisch, 1978; IBM, 1976b], but JCL is included with examples where it is instructive.

2.1 PL/1 SEQUENTIAL FILE MANIPULATION SUBLANGUAGE

Before examining PL/1 syntax and semantics for sequential file manipulation, we must first clarify the distinction between two types of sequential files, *record* and *stream files*.

2.1.1 Record and Stream Files

Record and stream files may be distinguished by the way in which they are created, that is, by the way in which data is transmitted between user-program data areas and storage devices. Nevertheless, during both record and stream file creation, data is transmitted between buffers and external devices in blocks. It is in the transmission of the data between program *data area* and *buffer* that the difference is to be found. With record transmission, the data in the form of *records* is moved between the program data area and buffer. With stream transmission, the data is transmitted from the program data area to the buffer in the form of a discontinuous stream of *data elements*. In this process, numerical data elements are converted from machine binary and binary coded decimal formats to character format. There are no conversions with record transmission. Thus a record file is not necessarily in character format; a stream file always is.

While stream transmission can be used with sequential files on tape and disk, its main application is to card readers and line printers. We shall therefore restrict our discussion to sequential files employing record transmission. In PL/1, a sequential record-transmission file is known as a CONSECUTIVE file [IBM, 1976a].

2.1.2 CONSECUTIVE File Organization

A CONSECUTIVE file may reside on tape, disk, or even punched cards. There is a first and last record, and the records can only be accessed sequentially one after another. With disks, count-data format is used, and the records are laid out sequentially on consecutive cylinders. In a user AP, such a file will be

1. Declared, thus allocating storage for the DCB, access method, buffers, and so on;

2. Opened, so that the operating system can build the DCB, access method, and channel program;

3. Subjected to

   a. read operations, or

   b. write operations, or

   c. rewrite operations, if residing on a disk, or

   d. any combination of (a), (b) or (c);

4. Closed, freeing the storage space used by the file DCB, and so on;

5. Associated with a DD statement or its equivalent.

File Declaration   The most useful general declaration is

DCL *(ddname)* FILE RECORD ENV (CONSECUTIVE);

The *ddname* refers to the DD statement, which describes the file, and also serves as the file name for the program. (It is possible to include some of the DCB parameters from the DD statement in the parenthesis following the ENV (or ENVIRONMENT) option. It should be noted however, that the DD statement is overridden if there is a conflict.)

OPEN Statement   The following general statement is useful.

$$\text{OPEN FILE } (ddname) \begin{Bmatrix} \text{OUTPUT} \\ \text{INPUT} \\ \text{UPDATE} \\ \text{INPUT BACKWARDS} \end{Bmatrix}$$

It must be understood that the file can be opened for only one purpose at a time. If it is opened for INPUT, we may read records from it into the AP data area. We may not write records on to the end of it; that would require that the file be opened for OUTPUT.[1]

Only a disk file may be opened for UPDATE; as we shall see, this permits updating of a record that has just been read. INPUT BACKWARDS allows us to read records from a tape moving in the reverse direction.

More than one file may be opened by a single open statement:

OPEN FILE (BETA) INPUT, FILE (DELTA) OUTPUT, FILE (GAMMA) UPDATE;

Here the files with ddnames BETA, DELTA, and GAMMA are opened for different purposes. As already mentioned, an OPEN statement causes the operating system to construct the DCB, access method, and channel program. This takes some time, primarily due to the fact that the required operating system routines have to be loaded dynamically for execution. It is therefore more efficient to open as many files as possible with one OPEN statement.

WRITE Statement, File Opened for OUTPUT   The normal WRITE statement syntax is:

WRITE FILE *(ddname)* FROM *(program variable)*;

---

[1]*To extend an existing file,* DISP = (MOD,...) *must be coded in the DD statement.*

affect of WRITE

As a result of the execution of this statement, the contents of the program variable (the record) are placed in the file buffer. If this fills the buffer, then the buffer contents are transmitted to external storage.

Normally the program variable is a PL/1 structure variable, with byte length equal to the record length specified in the DD statement. A string variable is sometimes used instead of a structure variable.

READ Statement, File Opened for INPUT In the remaining file-handling statements, we may assume that we have to deal with a file BETA (ddname) and a program structure variable S, as this simplifies the explanation of syntax and semantics.

In the case of reading, we have two possible statements:

READ FILE (BETA) INTO (S);

and

READ FILE (BETA) IGNORE *(PL/1 numerical expression);*

With the first statement, when first executed, the first record in the file is delivered to S; when next executed, the next record is delivered, and so on. If, however, the second READ statement above is executed at some point, the next *n* records are skipped, where *n* is the value of the numerical expression (with any fractional part truncated).

Updating Statements, File on Disk Opened for UPDATE Here we have three possible statements. We can explain their use by the following program excerpt.

READ FILE (BETA) INTO (S);
    /* First READ statement after file is opened; effect is to deliver record 1 in BETA to user AP
    data area at S */
. . . . ;
READ FILE (BETA) IGNORE (3);
    /* Records 2, 3, and 4 skipped */
. . . . ;
READ FILE (BETA) INTO (S);
    /* Record 5 delivered to S */
S.A. = *expression;*
S.B. = *expression;*
    /* Fields A and B for record 5 updated */
REWRITE FILE (BETA) FROM (S);
    /* Record from S replaces record 5 in external storage */

Thus the use of a disk permits us to alter records as they read sequentially. For this to be possible with a tape, its direction of motion would have to be continually reversed, which is not feasible in practice.

CLOSE Statement   This is simply

CLOSE FILE (BETA);

When this is executed, the memory taken up by the access method, DCB, channel program, and buffers is freed. A file opened for OUTPUT, for example, must be closed again before being opened again for some other purpose.

Effect of CLOSE

2.2 PROCESSING OF CONSECUTIVE FILES

A new file is created by a file-creation program. A file which is frequently used and always kept up-to-date is usually referred to as a master file. During the life of a master file, it will be processed by update programs and information retrieval programs. We now look at some file creation and updating techniques with a CONSECUTIVE (master) file.

2.2.1 File Creation

To create a file, the necessary source data must be available in machine-readable form. The necessary data may come from different sources; a fairly typical situation is depicted in Figure 2.1. Here the file-creation program uses data from both an existing stack of cards (a card file) and a file on disk. The disk file could just be a control file, employed to check the validity of data from the card file.

  As an illustration, we take a simple example of a file creation problem. Again referring to Figure 2.1, let us suppose that a shipping firm is going to create a master file called MASTERF which will contain records, each describing one of its ships.

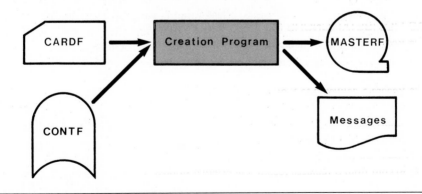

FIGURE 2.1. *System diagram for the creation of a master file* (MASTERF) *using a card file* (CARDF) *and control file* (CONTF).

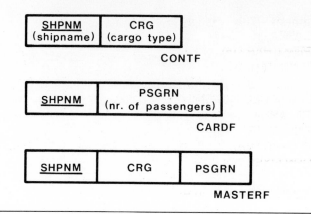

FIGURE 2.2. *Simple field compositions for the files from Figure 2.1. Key fields are underlined.* MASTERF *records are composed of fields from* CARDF *and* CONTF.

The file MASTERF will have the following fields.

1.   SHPNM, the shipname; the values of SHPNM are unique, so that the field may be used as a key or identifier for the file.

2.   CRG, the type of cargo on board a ship.

3.   PSGRN, the number of passengers on board a ship.

MASTERF is to be created by integrating data in two existing files, namely the card file CARDF, and the control file CONTF. As shown in Figure 2.2, SHPNM and CRG are the fields of CONTF, while CARDF has the fields SHPNM and PSGRN.

Elementary File-Creation Program   In the following program, we read in cards from CARDF in sequence, check that the SHPNM value is valid by accessing the control file, at the same time obtaining the value of the CRG field, and then assemble the new MASTERF record and store it in MASTERF. Both CARDF and CONTF are assumed sorted in ascending key or SHPNM sequence.

```
CREATE: PROC OPTIONS (MAIN);

    /*  Program creates a new MASTERF file by integrating the card file CARDF and the
        control file CONTF   */

DCL BEOF BIT (1) INIT ('1'B);              /*  Logical variable: Before End Of File   */
DCL CARDF FILE RECORD ENV (CONSECUTIVE),
    1 CARDF_AREA,                          /*  Holds CARDF records   */
        2 SHPNM CHAR (15),
        2 PSGRN PIC '99999',
        2 FILLER CHAR (60);                /* A CARDF record is a complete card */
```

```
DCL CONTF FILE RECORD ENV (CONSECUTIVE),
      1 CONTF_AREA,                         /*  Holds CONTF records   */
          2 SHPNM CHAR (15),
          2 CRG CHAR (10);

DCL MASTERF FILE RECORD ENV (CONSECUTIVE),
      1 MASTERF_AREA,                       /*  Holds MASTERF records   */
          2 SHPNM CHAR (15),
          2 CRG CHAR (10),
          2 PSGRN FIXED BIN (31);

ON ENDFILE (CARDF) BEOF = '0'B;

/*   Loading begins   */
OPEN FILE (CARDF) INPUT,
     FILE (CONTF) INPUT,
     FILE (MASTERF) OUTPUT;
READ FILE (CARDF) INTO (CARDF_AREA);
DO WHILE (BEOF);
    READ FILE (CONTF) INTO (CONTF_AREA);
    IF CARDF_AREA.SHPNM = CONTF_AREA.SHPNM     /*  Keys match?  */
        THEN DO;     /*  Assemble MASTERF record   */
            MASTERF_AREA.SHPNM   =   CARDF_AREA.SHPNM;
            MASTERF_AREA.CRG     =   CONTF_AREA.CRG;
            MASTERF_AREA.PSGRN   =   CARDF_AREA.PSGRN;
            WRITE FILE (MASTERF) FROM (MASTERF_AREA);
            READ FILE (CARDF) INTO (CARDF_AREA);
        END;
        ELSE DO;  /*  Keys do not match   */
            PUT SKIP LIST ('ERROR: MISMATCHED KEYS');
            PUT SKIP DATA (CARDF_AREA, CONTF_AREA);
            BEOF = '0'B;      /*  Stop execution*/
        END;
END;
END CREATE;
/*
//GO. CONTF DD DSNAME = SHIPCONTROL,DISP = (OLD,KEEP),UNIT = DISK
//GO.MASTERF DD DSNAME = SHIPMAST,DISP = (NEW,CATLG),UNIT = TAPE,
//              DCB = (RECFM = FB,LRECL = 29,BLKSIZE = 2900),
//              VOL = SER = 123
//GO.CARDF DD   *
        Physical cards placed here
/*
```

The JCL tells the operating system that CONTF is an old disk file already described in the system catalogue and that MASTERF is to be a new tape file with fixed-length records of

---

length 29 bytes, which are to be transmitted in blocks of 100 records.[1] The records thus have a *block factor* of 100. The record length specified is the length in bytes of the program structure variable that holds the record.

Creation of Large Files   If the file MASTERF were a very large file, the creation program just given would hardly be acceptable. As it is written, the program merely matches CARDF and CONTF record keys, assembles the corresponding MASTERF record, and places it in the buffer. If a key mismatch occurs, the program ceases execution.

However, if MASTERF is large, there may well be many records in CARDF or CONTF, which would give rise to a mismatch. When a mismatch occurs with the above program, it would be necessary to run it again after the cause of error had been corrected (remembering to alter the MASTERF DD statement, since MASTERF is now an old file catalogued in the system catalogue). If a subsequent mismatch occurred, we might have to do the same again, and so on. Of course, if MASTERF is large, then CARDF would likely be a tape file.

The above program is said to lack *robustness;* that is, it can stand very little misuse, and the files CARDF and CONTF have to be perfectly matched for it to work satisfactorily.

A more robust version of CREATE would be able to tolerate more imperfection in the two files CARDF and CONTF. It could perhaps be designed to detect common types of mismatch and print out sufficient information to correct the errors, but continue processing of the files until all the matched records had been integrated. The corrected mismatches could then later be processed as updates to the created master file MASTERF.

As an illustration of a more robust program for creation of MASTERF, we shall design and write a new version of CREATE that can tolerate the more commonly occurring mismatches.

Suppose that

1. $A_1, A_2, ..., A_i, ...$ is the set of key values from CARDF, sorted in ascending order;

2. $O_1, O_2, ..., O_i, ...$ is the set of key values from CONTF, sorted in ascending order.

We use the above notation to describe the situations the new program can handle.

a. $A_i = O_i$; matching keys, program continues.

b. $A_i = O_i$, $A_{i+1} \neq O_{i+1}$, and $A_{i+1} = O_{i+2}$; missing CARDF record, corresponding O_{i+1} key printed out, program continues.

c. $A_i = O_i$, $A_{i+1} \neq O_{i+1}$, and $A_{i+2} = O_{i+2}$; probable error in CARDF key value, A_{i+1}, O_{i+1} values printed out, program continues.

d. $A_i = O_i$, $A_{i+1} \neq O_{i+1}$, and $A_{i+2} = O_{i+1}$; CARDF record with no corresponding CONTF record, CARDF key printed out, program continues.

---

[1] *With disk files, the specifications of block size* (BLKSIZE) *in a DD statement is the length of the data subblock, not that of the storage block.*

---

e. None of the above four situations; that is, multiple mismatches, program cannot handle, program stops.

We now give the corresponding, more robust version of CREATE. Robust programs are of necessity more complex and somewhat more difficult to read. For this reason, none of the subsequent programs used in this book to illustrate file or data base principles are in any way robust. The following is thus a lone example involving the simplest kind of file organization.

```
CREATE: PROC OPTIONS (MAIN);

    /*  Program creates MASTERF sequential file on tape from card file CARDF and disk
        control file CONTF as shown in Figures 2.1 and 2.2.
        Program can tolerate:

    a.  Missing cards;

    b.  Incorrect card key values;

    c.  Card records with no corresponding CONTF record;

        and after printing out relevant error information, will continue processing    */

DCL (BEOF, NEXTCARD) BIT (1) INIT ('1'B),
    TROUBLE BIT (1) INIT ('0'B);                /*  Logical variables  */
DCL CARDF FILE RECORD ENV (CONSECUTIVE),
    1 CARDF_AREA,                               /*  Holds CARDF record  */
      2 SHPNM CHAR (15),
      2 PSGRN PIC '99999',
      2 FILLER CHAR (60),
    1 CARDF_RES LIKE CARDF_AREA;                /*  Space for 2nd CARDF record */

DCL CONTF FILE RECORD ENV (CONSECUTIVE),
    1 CONTF_AREA,                               /*  Holds CONTF record  */
      2 SHPNM CHAR (15),
      2 CRG CHAR (10),
    1 CONTF_RES LIKE CONTF_AREA;                /*  Space for 2nd CONTF record  */

DCL MASTERF FILE RECORD ENV (CONSECUTIVE),
    1 MASTERF_AREA,                             /*  Holds MASTERF record  */
      2 SHPNM CHAR (15),
      2 CRG CHAR (10),
      2 PSGRN FIXED BIN (31);

ON ENDFILE (CARDF) BEGIN;
    BEOF = '0'B;                                /*  Stop main processing loop  */
    IF TROUBLE                                  /*  If mismatch investigation in
                                                    progress  */
```

```
                THEN CARDF_RES.SHPNM = '   ';
                /*   Permits 2nd mismatch investigation   */
        END;


        ON ENDFILE (CONTF) BEGIN;
            PUT SKIP (2) LIST ('PROCESSING STOPPED; END OF CONTF FILE');
            IF ⌐ TROUBLE                            /*   No mismatch investigation in
                                                         progress   */
                THEN PUT SKIP LIST ('DURING PROCESSING OF CARD WITH KEY:',
                    CARDF_AREA.SHPNM);
                ELSE                                /*   File ends during mismatch
                                                         investigation   */
                    PUT SKIP LIST ('FOLLOWING MISMATCHED KEY OF CARD WITH KEY:',
                        CARDF_AREA.SHPNM);
            STOP;
        END;


        OPEN
            FILE (CARDF) INPUT,
            FILE (CONTF) INPUT,
            FILE (MASTERF) OUTPUT;


            /*   We now start main processing loop   */
        READ FILE (CARDF) INTO (CARDF_AREA);
        J = 1;    /*   J is used to count CARDF records   */
        DO WHILE (BEOF);
        READ FILE (CONTF) INTO (CONTF_AREA);
        IF CONTF_AREA.SHPNM ⌐ = CARDF_AREA.SHPNM
                /*   Then investigate cause of this mismatch   */
        THEN DO;
            TROUBLE = '1'B;                         /*   Mismatch investigation in progress,
                                                         trouble flag set   */


                /*   First investigation: check for missing CONTF record   */

            READ FILE (CARDF) INTO (CARDF_RES);
            J = J + 1;
            IF CARDF_RES.SHPNM = CONTF_AREA.SHPNM
                /*   Missing CONTF record confirmed   */
            THEN DO;
                PUT SKIP (2) LIST ('CONTF RECORD MISSING, WITH KEY:',
                    CARDF_AREA.SHPNM);
                PUT SKIP LIST ('CORRESPONDS TO CARD NUMBER:', J − 1);
                CARDF_AREA = CARDF_RES;
```

```
        END;                                      /*  And program may now proceed
                                                      normally   */

    ELSE
                /*  Missing CONTF record not confirmed   */

                /*  Second investigation:
                    check for a missing CARDF record   */

DO;
    READ FILE (CONTF) INTO (CONTF_RES);
    IF CONTF_RES.SHPNM = CARDF_AREA.SHPNM
        /*  Missing CARDF record confirmed   */
    THEN DO;
        PUT SKIP (2) LIST ('CARDF RECORD MISSING, WITH KEY:',
            CONTF_ AREA.SHPNM);
        PUT SKIP LIST ('FOLLOWS CARD NUMBER:',' ', J − 2);
        CONTF_AREA = CONTF_RES;
        NEXTCARD = '0'B;
        /*  Program can now proceed normally, except that there is no need to read the
            next CARDF record as it is already in CARDF_RES as a result of first
            mismatch investigation   */
    END;
    ELSE
    /*  Missing CARDF record not confirmed   */


    /*  Third investigation:
        check for probable error in key value for CARDF record in CARDF_AREA   */

    IF CONTF_RES.SHPNM = CARDF_RES.SHPNM
        /*  Probable error in CARDF record key value confirmed   */
    THEN DO;
        PUT SKIP (2) LIST ('PROBABLE MISPUNCHED CARD, WITH KEY:',
            CARDF_AREA.SHPNM);
        PUT SKIP LIST ('CARDF RECORD KEY PROBABLY SHOULD BE:',
            CONTF_AREA.SHPNM);
        PUT SKIP LIST ('CARDF RECORD NUMBER IS: ',' ', J − 1);
        CARDF_AREA = CARDF_RES;
        CONTF_AREA = CONTF_RES;
            /*  Program can now proceed normally   */
    END;

    ELSE       /*  First three investigations negative, either multiple key errors or
                   unmatched last card; better stop processing   */
```

```
        IF BEOF THEN DO;                          /*  If not unmatched
                                                       last card    */
                PUT SKIP (2) LIST ('MULTIPLE KEY ERRORS, PROCESSING
                    STOPPED WITH CARDS:', J - 1, J);
                PUT SKIP LIST ('WITH CARD KEYS:', CARDF_AREA.SHPNM,
                    CARDF_RES.SHPNM);
                STOP;   END;
          ELSE DO;
                PUT SKIP (2) LIST ('LAST CARD UNMATCHED');
                STOP;   END;

     END;
     TROUBLE = '0'B;                         /*  End of mismatch investigation   */
END;
ELSE;   /*  No key mismatch detected   */


       /*  Assembly of MASTERF record can now begin   */


MASTERF_AREA.SHPNM     = CARDF_AREA.SHPNM;
MASTERF_AREA.CRG       = CONTF_AREA.CRG;
MASTERF_AREA.PSGRN     = CARDF_AREA.PSGRN;
WRITE FILE (MASTERF) FROM (MASTERF_AREA);

IF NEXTCARD THEN DO;
               /*   Second mismatch investigation was not successful   */
     READ FILE (CARDF) INTO (CARDF_AREA);
     J = J + 1;
     END;
ELSE DO;
     CARDF_AREA = CARDF_RES;
     NEXTCARD = '1'B;  /*  Reset flag for next time around   */
END;
END;                              /*  End of main processing loop   */


PUT SKIP LIST ('CAUTION: CARDF MAY END BEFORE CONTF');
END CREATE;
/*
// JCL AS IN FIRST VERSION
```

To help you understand how this program works, sample input record keys are given in Table 2.1a and b, with the resulting output data in Table 2.1c and d.

Assuming that the program is not stopped by multiple key errors, we have two methods of completing the creation of the master file, MASTERF. One method entails examining the printout and correcting all the errors detected in CARDF and CONTF. The program could then be run again; this time there should be no errors.

Alternatively, we could construct a transaction file TRANS (on cards, tape, or disk) using the errors listed in the printout. The TRANS records would have the same format as

SAMPLE I/O DATA FOR THE ROBUST VERSION OF **CREATE**		
CARDF.SHPNM values	**CONTF.SHPNM values**	**MASTERF.SHPNM values**
ANNA	ANNA	ANNA
BLUEBELL	BLUEFIN	BLUEFIN
BLUEFIN	PENNY	PENNY
PENNY	ST. HELEN	SWEENY
ST. HELENE	SWEENY	TITAN
SWEENY	TAYLOR	
TITAN	TITAN	
TYPHON	TAIFON	
	VALIANT	
(a)	(b)	(c)

Error messages from CREATE

CONTF RECORD MISSING, WITH KEY:	BLUEBELL	
CORRESPONDS TO CARD NUMBER:		2
PROBABLE MISPUNCHED CARD, WITH KEY:	ST. HELENE	
CARDF RECORD KEY PROBABLY SHOULD BE:	ST. HELEN	
CARDF RECORD NUMBER IS:		5
CARDF RECORD MISSING, WITH KEY:	TAYLOR	
FOLLOWS CARD NUMBER:		6
LAST CARD UNMATCHED		

(d)

TABLE 2.1

MASTERF records, so that the records in TRANS are those missing from MASTERF. The TRANS records could be inserted in MASTERF by means of a (standard) update program. Updating principles for sequential files are discussed in the next subsection.

We may conclude that even with the comparatively simple task of creating a CON-SECUTIVE file, an effort should be made to select the optimum strategy, especially when the file is large, and this strategy should be reflected in the file-creation program (see Exercises 6 and 7).

2.2.2 Updating of Sequential Files

Sequential files are usually updated using the batch technique, which originated in the early days of tape installations, before disk units were economically viable.

With the batch technique, updates for a given master file are first batched together and sorted in key order. The master file records are then read in one at a time during execution of the update program, until a record with the same key as the first transaction record is reached. This record is then updated. A new transaction record is read in, the process of finding the next master record is repeated, and so on.

Normally when the master file is on tape, a new tape file for the updated master file is created by the process. This represents the classic method of computer-file processing and is illustrated in Figure 2.3.

If the master file is on disk and if no insertions of new records are involved, it is possible to update the file without writing it out again on some other storage medium. Thus the original or old master is destroyed in the process of updating it, which is a disadvantage as far as maintaining the accuracy, or *integrity,* of the data is concerned.

We can thus see that while it may be faster to update on a disk, it is not as safe as doing it on tape. The choice between the two methods clearly involves two factors, namely, timing and integrity. We look at these two factors in turn.

Timing   To deal with timing, we introduce the concept of *search length* (for update). Search length is defined as the number of master file accesses (that is, block transmissions) required to service a given transaction.

Suppose we have a master file with M blocks, which is being updated from a transaction file with r records. Then the *average search length* (S) when the file is on tape will be

$$S = \frac{2M}{r}$$

since the total number of file accesses to read and write the old and new tape files is $2M$.

When the file is on disk, it will not be necessary to write out more than r blocks, so that the total number of file accesses required will be $(M + r)$. Thus the average search length is given by

$$S = \frac{(M + r)}{r}$$

It will frequently be the case that r is much smaller than M, so that for a disk file we have

$$S = \frac{M}{r}$$

which is half the value required for tape files.

Not only is the average search length significantly smaller for disk files, the time required for a disk access can also be shorter with modern disk units. To see this, consider a typical block size of 25 card-images. From Section 1.4.1, we see that the time to read in one block from a 1600-bpi industry tape will be about 20 milliseconds. From Section 1.4.2, and remembering that a sequential disk file is processed cylinder by cylinder with

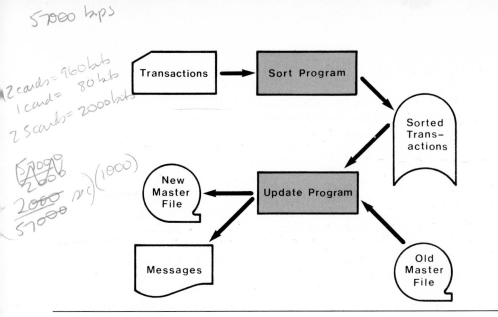

(handwritten annotations in left margin:)
57000 bps

2 cards = 960 bits
1 card = 80 bits
25 cards = 2000 bits

1000
2000
2000 p/g (1000)
57000

FIGURE 2.3. *Classic batch-updating system with sequential files.*

few seeks, the corresponding time for a 3350 disk is about 10 milliseconds. Thus, in this case, the disk file could be processed about four times faster than the tape file.

However, we must be careful here. The above time for retrieving a block from a 3350 disk will be true only if there are no other files on the disk pack being processed concurrently. If there are other concurrent files on the disk, each block retrieval may be associated with a seek operation, and this could put the time for a retrieval up to 35 milliseconds. Of course, we could always increase the block size to take up a complete track. Unfortunately this is usually detrimental to other users, since the multiprogramming supervisor (see Chapter 1) switches control to other users following interrupts caused by I/O completion, and with longer blocks there will be fewer interrupts.

It is thus clear that the relative merits of disk or tape updating with sequential files, insofar as timing is concerned, must be investigated in each individual case, with allowance made for the introduction of faster tape and disk drives in the course of time.

Integrity   As far as integrity is concerned, batch processing with tape files is clearly superior; the classic method is to have three generations of master files, namely, grandfather, father, and son files.

With disk files, an uncalled-for update will result in the loss of useful data, unless other measures have been taken. A common solution is to use a tape file as a backup. The contents of the disk master file are "dumped" onto the tape at regular intervals, weekly or monthly, depending on the activity of the file. At the same time, all transactions carried out since the previous dump are saved. Thus, in the event of an accident, it is possible to regenerate the current master file from the backup tape and saved transactions.

The practice of using a backup tape is widespread for all kinds of disk files as well as sequential files. The method is also used with data-base files. Here again the data-base files are dumped onto tapes at regular intervals, and the transactions carried out since the previous dump are stored in what are called *log files*.

Updating Program Example We now consider a simple example of updating the file MASTERF, the creation of which was described in the previous subsection; its field formats are shown in Figure 2.2. The main purpose of the example is the illustration of the use of the requisite PL/1 file sublanguage.

We assume that the updating is to be carried out on the basis of transaction records in a file TRANS on a disk. The TRANS records have the same format as MASTERF records and are sorted in ascending SHPNM order. We also assume that the MASTERF file is now on a *disk* unit, as this permits us to illustrate the use of the REWRITE statement. The updating consists of altering the nonkey fields of a MASTERF record to match those of a corresponding TRANS record.

```
UPDATE: PROC OPTIONS (MAIN);

DCL BEOF BIT (1) INIT ('1'B);                    /*  Logical variable   */
DCL MASTERF FILE RECORD ENV (CONSECUTIVE),
    1 MASTERF_AREA,                              /*  Holds MASTERF record  */
        2 SHPNM CHAR (15),
        2 CRG CHAR (10),
        2 PSGRN FIXED BIN (31);


DCL TRANS FILE RECORD ENV (CONSECUTIVE),
    1 TRANS_AREA LIKE MASTERF_AREA;              /*  Holds TRANS record   */

OPEN FILE (MASTERF) UPDATE,
    FILE (TRANS) INPUT;
ON ENDFILE (TRANS) BEGIN;
    PUT SKIP LIST ('UPDATE COMPLETED');
    BEOF = '0'B;
END;
ON ENDFILE (MASTERF) MASTERF_AREA.SHPNM = '99999';

/*  Main processing loop begins   */

READ FILE (TRANS) INTO (TRANS_AREA);
MASTERF_AREA.SHPNM = ' ';

DO WHILE (BEOF);

    DO WHILE (MASTERF_AREA.SHPNM < TRANS_AREA.SHPNM);
        /*  Search for matching MASTERF record   */
        READ FILE (MASTERF) INTO (MASTERF_AREA);
    END;
```

```
        IF MASTERF_AREA.SHPNM ¬ = TRANS_AREA.SHPNM THEN
            PUT SKIP LIST ('NO MASTERF RECORD FOUND FOR TRANS RECORD WITH KEY:',
               TRANS_AREA.SHPNM);
                    ELSE DO;
            MASTERF_AREA = TRANS_AREA;
            REWRITE FILE (MASTERF) FROM (MASTERF_AREA);
            END;
READ FILE (TRANS) INTO (TRANS_AREA);
END;
END UPDATE;
/*
//GO.TRANS DD DSN = TRANSACT,DISP = (OLD,KEEP),UNIT = DISK
//GO.MASTERF DD DSN = SHIPMAST,DISP = (OLD,KEEP),UNIT = DISK
```

This program cannot handle every conceivable thing that could go wrong and could be made much more robust.

2.3 BUFFER TECHNIQUES

2.3.1 Double Buffering

Double buffering is a technique widely employed with sequential files. Normally a file-processing program with sequential files running under OS/MVS will have double buffers assigned by default, although the programmer can change this either in the PL/1 file declaration statement or in the DD statement.

The memory map for an application program which is reading in a sequential file A, and—as a result—writing out an updated file B, is shown in Figure 2.4. For A we have an access method, DCB, channel program, and two input buffers, while for B we have an access method, DCB, channel program, and two output buffers. The processing mode is the move mode (see Chapter 1 and next section).

When A is first read, two blocks are fetched filling both buffers; thereafter only one block is fetched from external storage at a time, to fill a buffer whose records have already been processed by the AP. Thus there is often at least one "full" buffer of records waiting to be processed.

When the records of B are written out, a block is transmitted from the buffer to external storage when one output buffer is full. Each time a buffer fills up, the access method requests the I/O supervisor to empty it. Thus there is often at least one empty buffer available.

This means that the AP is not required to wait solely because of a full output buffer or an empty (that is, fully processed) input buffer. If there were only one input and one output buffer, then, as described in Chapter 1, an application program could not run from, for example, the point at which an input buffer was emptied until the point at which the input channel had completed a block transfer and the access method had completed a

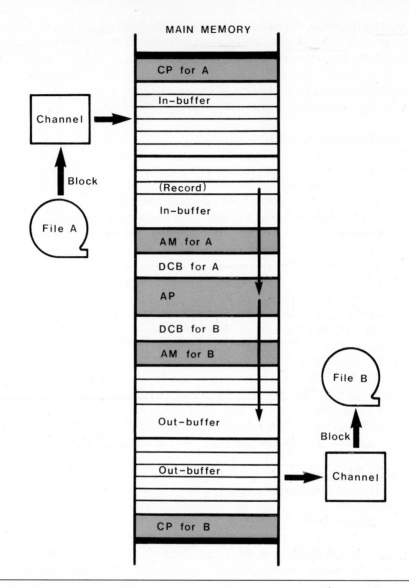

FIGURE 2.4. *Showing an AP partition, where the AP is reading an input file A and writing an output file B. Double buffering is employed for both input and output, reducing the chance of the AP having to wait because of either an empty input buffer or full output buffer.*

record transfer. However, the situation is not clear-cut. With double buffering when, for example, an input buffer empties, an input/output request is passed to the I/O supervisor, and although the AP partition could theoretically run because of the other full buffer, it may not do so because the operating system may give control to some other partition. Thus double buffering reduces the time during which an AP is not eligible to run, thus—in general—speeding up processing.

2.3.2 Locate Mode Processing

It can be clearly seen from Figure 2.4 that conventional sequential file processing in the move mode, as the name implies, involves a lot of moving of records around. Records first come in a block to the input buffer, then a record is moved to an AP data area, then possibly again to another AP data area, then to an output buffer, and finally, as part of a block, to the storage file. Some of this moving around can be avoided, as mentioned in Chapter 1, by employing the locate mode.

In the locate mode, instead of passing the record to the AP data area, the access method passes only the address of the record, thus permitting the AP to process the record in the buffer. We shall now see how this may be carried out in practice using PL/1. Slight modifications of the basic file handling READ and WRITE statements are necessary to permit utilization of the record addresses in the buffer.

We shall illustrate by taking as an example the simple update of the master file MASTERF created on tape in an earlier section. The format of the file is as shown in Figure 2.2. The MASTERF file (on tape) will be updated to produce a new version NEW-MASTER, also on tape. The update consists in changing the cargo (CRG) from 'WHEAT' to 'BARLEY' for all ships carrying wheat.

There are two basic methods of using the locate mode; the processing can take place either in the input buffer or the output buffer. We shall look at each in turn.

Input Buffer Processing The following is a simple program for updating the MAS-TERF records in the input buffer.

```
INBUFF: PROC OPTIONS (MAIN);

/*  Program reads MASTERF tape records, updates cargo (CRG) values from 'WHEAT' to
    'BARLEY', and outputs new NEWMAST tape file. Processing takes place in Input
    Buffer   */

DCL BEOF BIT (1) INIT ('1'B);          /*  Logical variable   */
DCL 1 MASTERF_AREA BASED (LOC),¹       /*  Holds MASTERF, NEWMAST
                                           record   */

2 SHPNM CHAR (15),
2 CRG CHAR (10),
```

_____

¹MASTERF_AREA *is an example of a PL/1* BASED *variable*.

2 PSGRN FIXED BIN (31);

```
/*  Here we have implicitly declared a pointer or address variable LOC as well as the structure
    MASTERF_AREA. When LOC is assigned a value, storage is (dynamically) assigned to
    MASTERF at the address held by LOC   */
DCL (NEWMAST,                               /*  New file created by update
                                                process   */

MASTERF) FILE RECORD ENV (CONSECUTIVE);

ON ENDFILE (MASTERF) BEOF = '0'B;

OPEN FILE (MASTERF) INPUT,
     FILE (NEWMAST) OUTPUT;
     READ FILE (MASTERF) SET (LOC);        /*  Locate mode READ statement   */
/*  Semantics:

    1.   The double input buffers are filled by blocks from MASTERF.

    2.   Address of first record in buffers placed in LOC.

    3.   MASTERF_AREA allocated storage at this address, so that the contents of
         MASTERF_AREA is the first buffer record.

    4.   This first record may now be processed in buffer */

DO WHILE (BEOF);
     IF CRG = 'WHEAT'
         THEN CRG = 'BARLEY';
            /*  Processing of this record completed; record can be moved to output buffer   */
     WRITE FILE (NEWMAST) FROM (MASTERF_AREA);
                                            /*  Normal write statement   */
     READ FILE (MASTERF) SET (LOC);        /*  Locate mode READ statement   */
         /*  Address of next input buffer record placed in LOC, so that MASTERF_AREA is
             allocated a new storage location coincident with this record   */
END;
END INBUFF;
/*
//GO.MASTERF DD DSN = SHIPMAST,UNIT = TAPE,DISP = (OLD,KEEP)
//GO.NEWMAST DD DSN = BARSHIP,UNIT = TAPE,DISP = (NEW,CATLG),
//                DCB = (LRECL = 29,RECFM = FB,BLKSIZE = 2900),
//                VOL = SER = 123
```

The process is also illustrated in Figure 2.5a. The important point is that the location of the program-data area for the receipt of records is variable and is determined by the address of the next record delivered by the access method to the AP.

From the diagram, we can see that we have eliminated movement of records between input buffer and AP. However, records still have to move between input buffer and output buffer. We thus have the possibility illustrated in Figure 2.5b, and discussed below.

locate-mode processing :

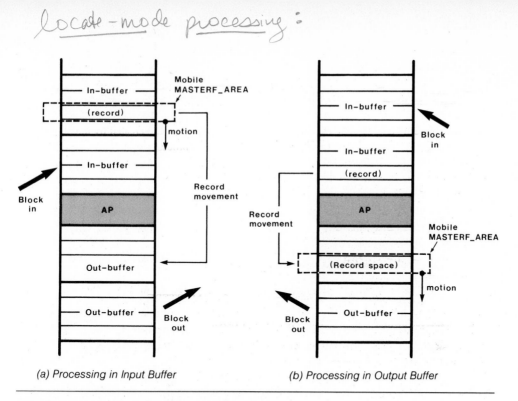

(a) Processing in Input Buffer   (b) Processing in Output Buffer

FIGURE 2.5.   *Partial memory partition maps, showing how a mobile, that is, a pointer allocated, AP data area permits processing in a buffer, thus reducing data movements. This type of processing is called* locate-mode processing.

Output Buffer Processing   Here we eliminate movement of records between AP and the output buffer. However, prior to processing, we must now move them one at a time from input buffer to output buffer, where processing takes place.

We repeat the program INBUFF, but this time we carry out the processing in the output buffer.

OUTBUFF: PROC OPTIONS (MAIN);

/*   Program carries out same updating as previous program INBUFF   */

DCL BEOF BIT (1) INIT ('1'B);   /*   Logical variable   */

DCL 1 MASTERF_AREA BASED (LOC),   /*   Holds MASTERF, NEWMAST record   */

    2 SHPNM CHAR (15),
    2 CRG CHAR (10),
    2 PSGRN FIXED BIN (31);
    /*   As in previous program, MASTERF_AREA has a mobile memory location, depending on the value of the pointer variable LOC   */

```
DCL (NEWMAST,                                    /*  New file created by update
                                                     process   */
    MASTERF) FILE RECORD ENV (CONSECUTIVE);

ON ENDFILE (MASTERF) BEOF = '0'B;
OPEN FILE (MASTERF) INPUT,
    FILE (NEWMAST) OUTPUT;

DO WHILE (BEOF);
    LOCATE (MASTERF_AREA) FILE (NEWMAST);        /*  Locate mode WRITE
                                                     statement   */
```

/*   Semantics:

1.   Address of next free NEWMAST output buffer record *space* placed in LOC.

2.   MASTERF_AREA is allocated storage at this address, so that MASTERF_AREA is ready to receive a record.

3.   If the next free record space was output buffer-2, indicating that output buffer-1 was full, output buffer-1 is transmitted, and vice versa   */

```
    READ FILE (MASTERF) INTO (MASTERF_AREA);
```
/*   Normal READ statement, but remember that MASTERF_AREA is overlaid on an empty output buffer space   */
```
IF BEOF                                          /*  i.e., we are not at the end of the
                                                     file   */

    THEN IF CRG = 'WHEAT'
        THEN CRG = 'BARLEY';
```
/*   Processing has taken place in output buffer, the NEWMAST record is ready for block transmission as soon as remaining part of buffer is filled, and MASTERF_AREA moved to the first record space in the next buffer   */
```
END;
END OUTBUFF;
/*
//JCL AS IN PREVIOUS EXAMPLE
```

This type of processing in the output buffer is more difficult to visualize than processing in the input buffer. The main conceptual difference is that with input buffer processing, the mobile MASTERF_AREA is located coincident with a record to be processed; however, with output buffer processing, the mobile MASTERF_AREA is coincident with an empty record space in the output buffer, in anticipation of receiving the next record.

2.3.3 Variable Length and Format Records

Continuing our discussion of buffer techniques, it is convenient to consider techniques for processing variable length or format records, even though strictly speaking only one of

---

the techniques to be described involves special buffer techniques. We shall first consider how the need for variable length/format records arises and then discuss techniques for dealing with them.

Need for Variable Length/Format Records   The need for variable length/format records commonly arises because of the existence of categories of entities. Records in a file ordinarily describe entities of a given class, such as people, ships, trees, or oilwells. However, if a given class consists of several disjoint categories, it is likely that the records for entities from one category will have to differ significantly from the records for another category. This happens because different categories from the same entity class tend to have different kinds of attributes [Kent, 1979; Smith, 1977].

As a commonly occurring example, consider the entity class "person." Suppose a firm needs to have a record for each person connected with the firm. There are different categories of persons to be dealt with. We have persons who are employees, persons who are customers, persons who are stockholders, persons who are both stockholders and customers, and so on. Each category of person will have distinct attributes; for example, an employee will have a salary, while a stockholder will have a certain number of shares. Thus if the firm constructs a file containing records for all of the persons connected with the firm, the records will, of necessity, have variable length/format.

As a second—and deliberately simplified—example, consider the entity class *ship*. We could have two categories of ships, as shown in Figure 2.6. One category (*P*) consists of passenger and cargo ships, while the other category (*T*) consists of oil tankers. Category *P* records have the distinct fields CRG and PSGRN (cargo and number of passengers), while category *T* records have the distinct field BRL (barrels of oil). However, records for both categories have some fields in common: SHPNM, the key field giving the ship name, CAT, giving the category the ship belongs to, and WT, giving the weight of the ship.

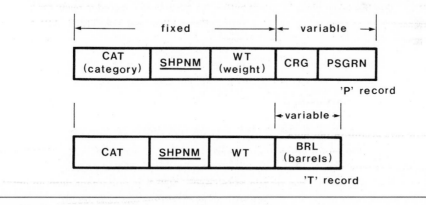

FIGURE 2.6.   *Record formats for two categories of records describing the entity* ship. *Ships are categorized according to whether they can carry passengers (category* P*) or oil (category* T*). Records may be divided into two parts, a fixed part, with format independent of category and a variable part, with format dependent on category.*

We can see that it is normally possible to divide each record in a variable length/format file into two segments, namely, a fixed segment containing those fields that are common to all categories, and a variable segment containing fields that reflect the category involved. We now consider how a file with variable length/format records may be created.

File Creation   It is quite a simple matter to create a file with variable length/format records. It is necessary only to have program structure variables corresponding to the different categories of record. Referring again to Figure 2.6, if we wished to create a file for the entity class *ship,* we could use the structures P_AREA and T_AREA, capable of holding category *P* and category *T* records, respectively. In the creation program we would use the following WRITE statements:

WRITE FILE (MASTER) FROM (P_AREA);
. . . . ;
WRITE FILE (MASTER) FROM (T_AREA);

With these statements, records with different lengths and field formats will be transmitted to the file MASTER.

Of course, the operating system must be informed to expect variable records, so that a suitable access method can be in place. This is done in the DD statement. For example, we could specify that the format is VB, Variable length Blocks, and give the maximum record length that can occur and the maximum block size (that is, buffer size) to be used. To enable the records to be deblocked by the access method on input, on output the access method attaches to each record a 4-byte field containing its length (see Exercise 8).

Thus when the file is later read, the access method will deliver a record (stripped of its length field) to the application program. The problem is: To which AP data-structure variable should the record be delivered? For instance, if we write at random

READ FILE (MASTER) INTO (T_AREA);

when the record being delivered is of category *P,* then we have a small disaster. The problem can be solved in three main ways, and we shall now take them in turn.

Use of Fixed Format Files   The simplest method of reading in variable records is by not writing them out in the first place. This can be a reasonable solution if the entity class involved does not have too many categories. With the records for the entity class *ship,* as shown in Figure 2.6, we have only two categories, so in that case it would be feasible.

The technique consists in setting up a file for the fixed segments from all the records, such as the file SHIP in Figure 2.7. We must also set up a file for each category of variable segment, with the corresponding key field SHPNM attached to each segment. This gives us the files PASSENGER and TANKER, also depicted in Figure 2.7.

To process the records, the application program reads in SHIP records sequentially and, depending on whether the CAT field has the value *P* or *T,* the program reads the next PASSENGER or TANKER record, respectively. We assume here that the files are

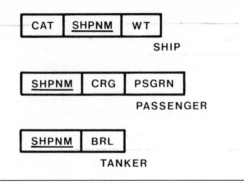

FIGURE 2.7. *We could avoid variable length or format records, by placing the fixed part of each record in one file* **SHIP,** *the variable part for category P in a separate file* **PASSENGER** *with the key field* **SHPNM** *added, and the variable part for the category T in the separate file* **TANKER,** *again with the* **SHPNM** *key field added.*

sequential files, but we could also have them as direct-access files, as described in Chapters 3 and 4.

You will notice that the three files from Figure 2.7 cross-reference each other; that is, from a SHIP record, we can use the CAT and SHPNM fields to come to a corresponding record in PASSENGER or TANKR, and vice versa. A collection of cross-referenced files is a data base, so that these three files thus constitute a primitive data base. This suggests the possibility of a variation of this technique, namely the use of a DBMS to implement storage structures for entity classes with different constituent categories.

Use of Next-Record-Category Field   The method of next-record-category fields involves reading in variable records. However, when the file is originally constructed, a category field is attached to each record that indicates not the category that record belongs to, but the category the subsequent record belongs to. For the file with the two categories of records shown in Figure 2.6, the CAT field could be used for this purpose.

On reading the file, provided we know the category the first record belongs to, we can then read the second record, and so on. This method is very simple to use but clearly cannot be used with direct access files.

Use of Overlay Techniques   An overlay technique can also be used to read variable records. It is widely used, has many variations, and has the advantage of being applicable to both sequential and direct-access files.

In principle, this method consists in having the required record delivered to a memory location that is either in the input buffer or a program-data area and is large enough to take the largest type of record in the file. The address of this memory location is then used to allocate storage, coincident with (or overlaying) this record location, to all program-data structures that match the records of the file.

Since the fixed segment of a variable record is always the first part of the record and since this will contain the field indicating which category the record belongs to, it may be read by the application program and used to select the correct program-data structure to enable the complete record to be processed.

We consider the case of the entity class *ship*, with its two categories *P* and *T*, as shown in Figure 2.6, where we suppose that we have a file MASTER containing records belonging to these categories. The following retrieval program, which sums the total number of barrels of oil and passengers on board ships described by MASTER records, should clarify the principles involved.

```
REPORT: PROC OPTIONS (MAIN);

    /*   Program processes MASTER variable records, and sums the values in the BRL field and
         in the PSGRN field   */

DCL BEOF BIT (1) INIT ('1'B);      /*   Logical variable   */
DCL MASTER FILE RECORD ENV (CONSECUTIVE),
        1 P_AREA BASED (P_ADDR),       /*   For P-type records   */
        2 CAT CHAR (1),      /*   Category   */
        2 SHPNM CHAR (15),
        2 WT FIXED BIN (31),
        2 CRG CHAR (10),
        2 PSGRN FIXED BIN (31),

        1 T_AREA BASED (T_ADDR),       /*   For T-type records   */
        2 CAT CHAR (1),
        2 SHPNM CHAR (15),
        2 WT FIXED BIN (31),
        2 BRL FIXED BIN (31),

        1 TEST CHAR (34) CHAR VARYING;
                    /*   Can hold either a P-type or T-type record   */

ON ENDFILE (MASTER) BEOF = '0'B;
OPEN FILE (MASTER) INPUT;

P_ADDR, T_ADDR = ADDR(TEST);
                    /*   The structures P_AREA and T_AREA are now assigned storage space
                         overlaying TEST as shown in Figure 2.8   */

JTOTAL = 0;      /*   JTOTAL sums barrels of oil   */
KTOTAL = 0;      /*   KTOTAL sums passengers   */
    /*   Processing loop begins   */

READ FILE (MASTER) INTO (TEST);
DO WHILE (BEOF);
```

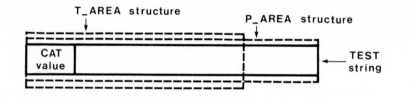

FIGURE 2.8. *The structures* T_AREA *and* P_AREA *are overlaid on the string* TEST. TEST *can hold the largest records in the file, in this case P-type records.*

```
        /*   We first determine what category of record is in TEST following previous READ
              statement   */
IF P_AREA.CAT  =  'P' THEN
            KTOTAL   =   KTOTAL + PSGRN;      /*   Sum passengers   */
         ELSE JTOTAL   =   JTOTAL + BRL;      /*   Sum barrels of oil   */
READ FILE (MASTER) INTO (TEST);
END;


PUT SKIP LIST (KTOTAL, 'PASSENGERS',
                JTOTAL, 'BARRELS');
END;
```

In the above program we have used move mode. With sequential files, a common variation is to employ location mode, permitting processing in the buffer with resulting improvement in performance.

Use of buffer processing is illustrated in Figure 2.9. Here the structures P_AREA and T_AREA are mobile and both overlay the record to be processed in the input buffer. We no longer need the string TEST used in the move mode version. We assume that processing takes place in the input buffer.

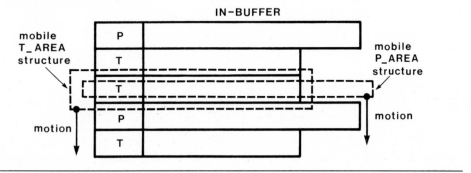

FIGURE 2.9. *This shows the input buffer with* T- *and* P-*type records. The mobile structures* T_AREA *and* P_AREA *are placed coincident with the next record to be read. The type of record can be determined using the* CAT *field from either structure.*

```
REPORT: PROC OPTIONS (MAIN);

        /*   New version of the previous program which employs
             locate-mode input buffer processing   */

DCL BEOF BIT (1) INIT ('1'B);   /*   Logical variable   */
DCL MASTER FILE RECORD ENV (CONSECUTIVE),
        1 P_AREA BASED (PT),    /*   For P-type records   */
            2    /*   And so on, as in previous version   */   ,

        1 T_AREA BASED (PT),    /*   For T-type records   */
            2    /*   And so on, as with previous version   */   ;

ON ENDFILE (MASTER) BEOF  =  '0'B;
OPEN FILE (MASTER) INPUT;
JTOTAL, KTOTAL  =  0;    /*   For oil and passenger totals   */

READ FILE (MASTER) SET (PT);    /*   Locate mode READ statement   */
DO WHILE (BEOF);
        /*   Following the previous READ statement, both T_AREA and P_AREA now overlay the
             correct record in the buffer   */
    IF P_AREA.CAT  =  'P' THEN
            KTOTAL  =  KTOTAL + PSGRN;    /*   Sum passengers   */
    ELSE JTOTAL  =  JTOTAL + BRL;        /*   Sum barrels of oil   */
    READ FILE (MASTER) SET (PT);
END;

PUT SKIP LIST (KTOTAL, 'PASSENGERS',
               JTOTAL, 'BARRELS');
END;
```

EXERCISES

1. Write a new version of the updating program UPDATE from Section 2.2.2 that allows for both changes to existing master records and insertion of new master records.

2. A file with 10,000 fixed-length records, each 500 bytes long, is processed in the input buffer using locate-mode processing. Discuss possible savings in processing time compared with the use of move mode.

3. Write a version of the retrieval program REPORT from Section 2.3.3, which uses the files SHIP, PASSENGER, and TANKER from Figure 2.7.

4. Write the file creation program for the file MASTER used in the program REPORT in

Section 2.3.3. We may assume that *P*-type records are available in an existing file PSOURCE and the *T*-type records in a file TSOURCE.

5. Create a file with the variable records from Figure 2.7 that will be read by means of a next-record-category field in each record, that is, in this case the CAT field.

6. Arrange for CARDF and CONTF files with a good selection of mismatches such as those shown in Table 2.1. Use the robust version of CREATE to generate a list of all mismatches. Then write an update program to complete creation of MASTERF using the data in the mismatch list.

7. Generate a new version of the robust CREATE program, which, in addition to printing mismatches which occur within CARDF and CONTF, prints out a list of unprocessed CARDF keys if CONTF finishes first, and vice versa.

8. Assuming that MASTERF has been created, write a report program which lists each cargo type being carried by ships in MASTERF and, for each type of cargo, the number of ships involved.

9. Assume that there exist two versions of MASTERF, namely MASTERA and MASTERB, both sorted in ascending key order. If there can be records common to both files, write a program that merges the two files into one file.

10. Write a report program to print the records from MASTERA and MASTERB from Exercise 9 that are common to both files.

11. Suppose that in addition to MASTERF, we have another master file CREW, which contains a record for each crew member on board ships in MASTERF. The key field in CREW is PERSON_NUMB and additional fields are AGE, SALARY, NATIONALITY, and SHPNM, where SHPNM is the name of the ship on which a crew member is sailing. If CREW is sorted in ascending SHPNM order, write a program to produce a new file JOIN, where JOIN records describe crew members as in CREW, but also have the fields CRG and PSGNR that give the cargo and number of passengers of the ship of a crew member, respectively. (In effect, this program carries out a join operation; see Chapter 16.)

12. If CREW from the previous question is sorted on the key field PERSON_NUMB, write a report program to print the maximum and minimum salaries earned by sailors of each nationality.

13. MASTERF and CREW taken together form a simple data base, since the records of the two files are related through the field SHPNM. Assuming that CREW is sorted in ascending SHPNM order, write a report program to find the nationalities and ages of sailors on ships carrying grain. (CREW is described in Exercise 11.)

14. Write an update program to add new crew members (taken from an update file TRANS) to the file CREW. The program should check that the SHPNM value in a new CREW record actually exists in MASTERF. It may be assumed that two versions of TRANS are available, one sorted on PERSON_NUMB and the other sorted on SHPNM. TRANS records have the same fields as CREW. (CREW is described in Exercise 11.)

REFERENCES

IBM, 1976a, *OS PL/1 Optimizing Compiler, Language Reference Manual,* Order Form GC 33–0009.

IBM, 1976b, *OS PL/1 Optimizing Compiler, Programmer's Guide,* Order Form FC33–0006.

Kent, W., 1979, "Limitations of Record Based Information Models," *ACM Trans. on Data Base Systems,* **4**(1):107–31.

Rindfleisch, D. H., 1978, *Utilizing System 360/370 OS and VS Job Control Language and Utility Programs,* Prentice-Hall, Inc., Englewood Cliffs, N.J.

Smith, J. M., and D. C. P. Smith, 1977, "Data Base Abstraction Aggregates," *Comm. ACM,* **20**(6):405–13.

Weinberg, G. M., 1970, *PL/1 Programming: A Manual of Style,* McGraw-Hill, New York.

Hash Files 3

Sequential files suffer from the disadvantage that records must always be sequentially accessed; that is, to extract a record with a given key, all the preceding records in the file have to be accessed. In an extreme case, if we had a file with 10,000 blocks and had to update 10 records, on average this would require 1001 accesses per record, or an average search length of 1001.

The solution is to permit a record to be accessed directly on presentation of a key, and this is possible if the file is on a direct-access device such as a disk (or drum).

As we saw in Chapter 1, records on a disk are located at disk addresses. For example, count-data format enables a record to be located by the system at an address made up of cylinder number, track number, and block number. Thus the system must have a record address to locate a record directly, while the user wishes to retrieve a record on the basis of the record key. In the case of the master file for ships used in Chapter 2, the ship name (SHPNM) is the record key, since it may be used to uniquely identify each record.

Thus, for the system to retrieve a record on the basis of a record key, there must be a way for it to obtain the record address using the record key. There are two main ways this may be done. One method involves using an index (see Chapter 4). The other method, which we shall study in this chapter, involves using a hashing routine. Files for which hashing routines are required are called *hash files*.

Hashing consists of employing a standard routine, which permits the record address to be deduced from the record key. When a hash file is first created, the records are placed in the addresses obtained by applying the hashing routine to the record key. Thus, for retrieval purposes, if the record key is known, application of the same routine will generate the record's address and permit it to be retrieved [Horowitz, 1977; Knuth, 1973].

As an example of a simple hashing routine, if we had an idealized disk with record addresses going from 001 to 100 and 90 records with keys from 10 to 900, the hashing routine could consist of dividing the key by 10 to give addresses from 1 to 90, which would fit the device. However, most hashing routines are more involved than this one and require considerable development. The hashing process is depicted in Figure 3.1.

The following are two major disadvantages of hash files.

a. Hash files cannot be read out in record-key sequence, since the records are stored in address sequence.

b. Hash files cannot grow substantially in size without either a redesign of the hashing routine or an increase in address capacity (Section 3.3.4).

Nevertheless, despite major advances in the facilities for direct-access files that employ indexes (index sequential files), there has been a continued increase in the use of hash files in the last decade. Direct access is faster with hash files than with any other kind of file, and we can therefore expect that they will be of continued importance in the future [Fagin, 1979].

3.1 THEORY OF HASH FILES

3.1.1 Record Distributions

Hashing routines give rise to record distributions in the storage device that are almost always nonuniform. A distribution may be depicted diagrammatically as in Figure 3.2. Here 20 records have been assigned to 31 addresses. We see that addresses 0, 5, 9, 12, 18, and 23 have been assigned no records, while addresses 3 and 14 have been assigned 3 records.

Such a diagram, while useful, displays the distribution in far too clumsy a manner. We rarely are directly interested in knowing exactly how many records have been assigned to a given physical address. The information required is more of a statistical nature. For example, with some patience we may deduce from Figure 3.2 that out of the 26 addresses, there are 6 addresses that have been assigned no records, 13 assigned 1 record, 4 assigned 2 records, 2 assigned 3 records, and 1 assigned 4 records.

This statistical information can be used to construct a distribution function for the particular hashing routine, as illustrated in Figure 3.3. The graph charts the number of

FIGURE 3.1.   *The function of a hashing routine is the conversion of a (sparse) set of record keys or identifiers to a (dense) set of physical addresses on a direct-access device.*

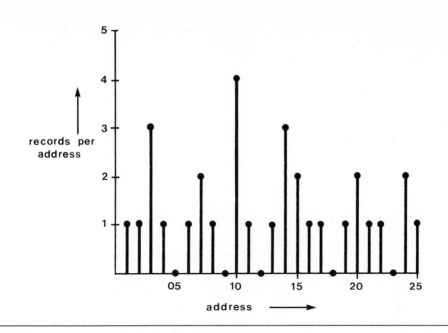

FIGURE 3.2. *Simple representation of the distribution of records assigned to addresses by a hashing routine. Some addresses are assigned one record, some none, and some more than one.*

addresses with x records against x. It is also possible sometimes to construct a mathematical function $D(x)$, which gives the number of addresses with x records. Different distributions may conveniently be compared using their distribution functions. Many of the records assigned to the same address are relegated to an overflow area, and—as we shall see later—the distribution function may be used in addition to estimate the size of this overflow area.

Uniform Distribution   The uniform distribution is the ideal distribution, but, although it may be approached, it almost never achieved in practice. With this distribution there are no overflow records; that is, if an address can hold n records, no more than n are ever assigned. However, fewer than n may well be assigned.

This is illustrated in Figure 3.4a. Here we assign 1000 records to 1000 addresses. If we assume that each address can hold only one record, only one uniform distribution is possible, assigning one record to each address as shown. Had we only 800 records to assign, then the uniform distribution function would entail 200 addresses without records, and 800 with 1 record.

Going back to the case in which we have assigned 1000 records to 1000 addresses, if each address could hold 2 records, then there are many possible uniform distributions; that is, distributions that do not give rise to overflow. In this case, a typical uniform distribution would have some addresses with no records, some with 1 record, and some with 2 records; there would be none with more than 2 records.

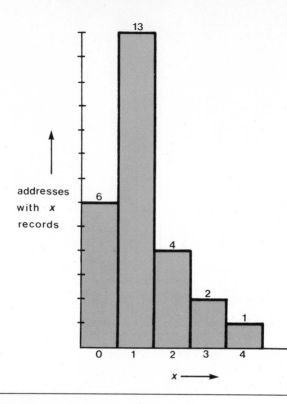

FIGURE 3.3. *Distribution function for the distribution from Figure 3.2. We can see, for example, that 4 addresses have each been assigned 2 records.*

We shall not now examine the merits of what is best: addresses that can hold only one record or addresses that can hold more than one. The question is important, but the answer hinges on complex and conflicting considerations that are best discussed later.

Random or Poisson Distributions   Random distributions come about when the records are assigned *randomly* to addresses or, in other words, when all addresses have the same chance of being assigned a record. We can do a very simple analysis of random assignments by considering the case of 5 records being assigned by a *randomizing* hashing routine to 10 addresses.

We take the records one at a time and carry out the assignment. For each record there is a probability of getting an empty address and a probability of getting a full address. As more records are assigned, the chance of the remaining records getting an empty address diminishes and the chance of getting a full address increases. This is shown in Table 3.1.

It follows that the probability of all 5 records coming to an empty address is

$$0.6*0.7*0.8*0.9*1.0$$

PROBABILITIES OF EACH SUCCESSIVE RECORD BEING ASSIGNED TO AN EMPTY ADDRESS AND A FULL ADDRESS WHEN 5 RECORDS ARE RANDOMLY ASSIGNED TO 10 ADDRESSES		
Record Number	Probability of Empty Address	Probability of Full Address
1	1.0	0.0
2	0.9	0.1
3	0.8	0.2
4	0.7	0.3
5	0.6	0.4

TABLE 3.1

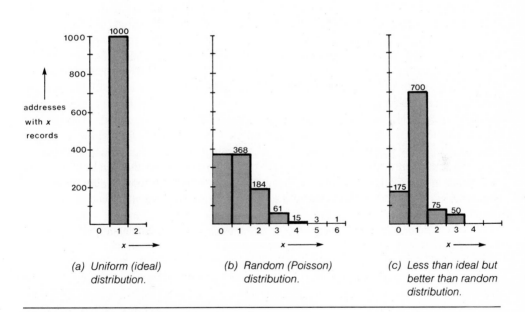

(a) Uniform (ideal) distribution.

(b) Random (Poisson) distribution.

(c) Less than ideal but better than random distribution.

FIGURE 3.4. *Some distribution functions for 1000 records assigned to 1000 addresses by a hashing routine. The aim is always a distribution as close to uniform as possible. However, a distribution may be even worse than random, that is, have fewer than 368 addresses with 1 record assigned. Note that both the numbers of records and addresses add up to 1000.*

or 30%. This means that the chance that not all of the 5 records will get an empty address is 70%. It should be noted that only 5 records are being assigned to 10 addresses—that is, the address space is only 50% full—yet there is a 70% chance of overflow.

In practice, significant overflow with a random distribution is unavoidable. The distribution function resulting from the assignment of 1000 records to 1000 addresses is shown in Figure 3.4b. It is quite clear that there is a very large difference between a random distribution and the ideal uniform distribution. With the random distribution, only 368, or little more than a third of the addresses, have been assigned 1 record. The number of overflow records, assuming one address can hold one record, is

$$184(2 - 1) + 61(3 - 1) + 15(4 - 1) + 3(5 - 1) + 1(6 - 1)$$

or 368 records. Thus about 37% of the records must be assigned to an overflow area.

The random distribution is not, therefore, particularly desirable, and we generally try to do better if at all possible. A distribution that is better than random is shown in Figure 3.4c. Generally if there is uniformity in the distribution of record keys, it is possible to find a hashing routine that preserves a large part of this uniformity. However, if the key distribution is itself approaching random, then a little better than random distribution of records in the address space is the best that can be hoped for.

However, despite the fact that we wish to have better than random distributions, these distributions do have one advantage: There is a large body of mathematical theory available for dealing with them. Although this theory is not very applicable for nonrandom distributions, it is frequently used for lack of any alternative. Its use is also often justified by the assumption that it introduces a safety factor. For example, if we use the Poisson distribution to estimate the number of overflow records, and hence the size of the overflow area (a critical design parameter), we shall get a figure that is larger than necessary if the distribution is better than random, and hence a safety factor is introduced. Of course, if the distribution is worse than random, the estimated overflow area will be too small. It is important to know if the hashing routine is generating a distribution which is better or worse than random.

Random distributions are therefore important, and a more detailed theory is given in the last section of this chapter. One of the important results of this theory is the random or Poisson distribution function $F(x)$. This gives us the number of addresses with x records, given that r records are being assigned to R addresses [Bratbergsengen, 1973; Knuth, 1973]. We have

$$F(x) = R\left(\frac{r}{R}\right)^x \left(\frac{1}{x!}\right) \exp\left(-\frac{r}{R}\right)$$

If we make r/R equal to one and R equal to 1000, then we have the case of 1000 records being assigned to 1000 addresses, and the above reduces to

$$F(x) = \frac{R}{x!}\left[\exp(-1)\right] = \frac{1000}{2.7183}\frac{1}{x!} = \frac{368}{x!}$$

which gives us the distribution shown in Figure 3.4*b*. The formula for $F(x)$ is somewhat awkward to use, while tables for various values of x and r/R are quite convenient (see Table 3.2). However, if an electronic calculator is available, it is probably no more work to use the formula directly.

We can also display the information in the formula for $F(x)$ graphically, as in Figure 3.5. Here we have a distribution for r/R equal to 0.5, 1.0, 2.0, 3.0, 6.0, and 10. It is important to note that values of r/R greater than 1 are of practical significance only when each address is capable of physically storing more than 1 record. For example, if r is 2000 and R is 1000, giving $r/R = 2$, then to store 2000 records in 1000 addresses, each address would have to be capable of holding at least two records. Furthermore, *the curves are quite independent of the number of physical records an address can hold, and merely indicate how many records are assigned to an address.* From the number of records assigned, together with the number an address can hold, the number of overflow records can be deduced.

3.1.2 Hashing Methods

Development   The main point to be grasped is that the generation of a suitable hashing routine for a large file can be a project in itself. As such, many different routines can be tried and the results analyzed before an acceptable routine is chosen.

The usual method of development is systematic trial and error. No other method is available. Thus, with a large file, several different and competing routines are first developed. The results are then analyzed, usually by producing distribution functions for each

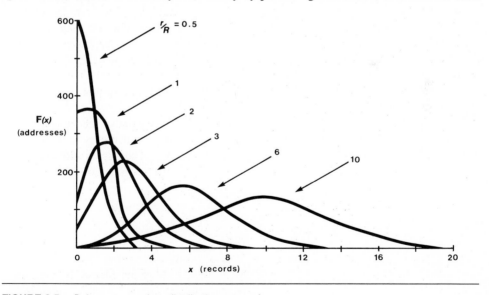

FIGURE 3.5.   *Poisson or random distribution curves for different values of r/R, starting with 0.5. The curves are all calculated on the assumption that there are 1000 addresses available.*

	POISSON DISTRIBUTION FUNCTION					
	Records per Address (r/R)					
	0.5	**1**	**2**	**3**	**6**	**10**
F(0)/R	.607	.368	.135	.050	.002	
F(1)/R	.303	.368	.271	.149	.015	
F(2)/R	.076	.184	.271	.224	.045	.002
F(3)/R	.013	.061	.180	.224	.089	.008
F(4)/R	.002	.015	.090	.168	.134	.019
F(5)/R		.003	.036	.101	.161	.038
F(6)/R		.001	.012	.050	.161	.063
F(7)/R			.003	.022	.138	.090
F(8)/R			.001	.008	.103	.113
F(9)/R				.003	.069	.125
F(10)/R				.001	.041	.125
F(11)/R					.023	.114
F(12)/R					.011	.095
F(13)/R					.005	.073
F(14)/R					.002	.052
F(15)/R					.001	.035
F(16)/R						.022
F(17)/R						.013
F(18)/R						.007
F(19)/R						.004
F(20)/R						.002
F(21)/R						.001

TABLE 3.2   The table is used as follows: Suppose we are assigning 200,000 records to 100,000 addresses. That means r/R is 2. From the table, the number of addresses that are assigned only 1 record (F(1)) is: 0.271*R, or 27,100 addresses.

method. As a result of the analysis, refinements in the initial routines or combinations of them are introduced. If that does not give satisfactory results, the process is repeated. To reduce the amount of processing necessary for analyzing the trial hashing routines with large sets of record keys, typical subsets of the keys or file models may be used.

The conversion of a record key to an address is usually carried out in two stages. First, the alphabetic characters in the record key are converted to numeric, which is usually quite straightforward. For example, alphabetic characters are stored in IBM machines as single bytes using the EBCDIC[1] representation. The numerical values of the bytes for *A*, *B*, *C*, . . . are 193, 194, 195, . . . , so that in the first stage we could convert *A* to 93, *B* to 94, and so on. Many other equally good methods could also be used.

The next stage is the difficult one. At the end of the first stage, we have numeric record keys. We must now use a suitable transformation to fit these keys into a certain number of addresses. We also have to decide how many and what kind of addresses to use; that is, how many records an address can accommodate. However, we shall look into that later; for now we shall restrict ourselves to the key-to-address transformation, assuming the number and type of addresses to be given.

We can now look at some well-known transformation methods that often give acceptable results. These methods, variations, or combinations of the two can be used for the trial hash routines [Lum, 1971, 1973; Maurer, 1975].

Prime Division   The principle behind the technique of *prime division* is simple. Suppose we wish to assign 20 records with 4 digit keys to 20 addresses numbered from 0 through 19. If we divide each key by 20, the remainder must be between 0 and 19; thus this transformation maps keys that range from 0000 through 9999 into addresses ranging from 0 through 19. So far so good; but now let us look at the kind of distribution we can expect in this simple example. Consider now two different series of keys: series-1 and series-2, and the result of a transformation that consists of dividing by 20 and taking the remainder.

The results are shown in Table 3.3. The first series of records is uniform, and dividing by 20 preserves this uniformity. The second series is also uniform, but division by 20 results in a nonuniform distribution, with clusters of records around addresses 0, 5, 10, and 15. The clustering occurs because of common factors in the record keys.

Thus the distribution resulting with series-2 keys when the divisor is 20 is considerably worse than random. We get no addresses with 1 record, none with 2, none with 3, none with 4, and 4 addresses each with 5 records. We recall from Figure 3.4*b* that a random distribution would give about 7 addresses with one record.

The clustering, or skew distribution, can be to a large extent avoided by using a prime number as a divisor, usually a prime number nearest to but greater than the number of addresses that would otherwise have been used. With series-1 and series-2 records in Table 3.3, we have tried 23. This choice results in a uniform series of addresses with both series; that is, a distribution that is superior to a random distribution.

Generally prime division is an excellent method for preserving whatever uniformity there is in the keys and for avoiding clustering (skew distributions); it tends to give

---

[1]*Extended Binary Coded Decimal Interchange Code.*

THE DIVISION METHOD OF KEY-TO-ADDRESS TRANSFORMATION					
Series-1			**Series-2**		
Record key	Division by 20	Division by 23	Record key	Division by 20	Division by 23
3000	00	10	3000	00	10
3001	01	11	3025	05	12
3002	02	12	3050	10	14
3003	03	13	3075	15	16
3004	04	14	3100	00	18
3005	05	15	3125	05	20
3006	06	16	3150	10	22
3007	07	17	3175	15	01
3008	08	18	3200	00	03
3009	09	19	3225	05	05
3010	10	20	3250	10	07
3011	11	21	3275	15	09
3012	12	22	3300	00	11
3013	13	00	3325	05	13
3014	14	01	3350	10	15
3015	15	02	3375	15	17
3016	16	03	3400	00	19
3017	17	04	3425	05	21
3018	18	05	3450	10	00
3019	19	06	3475	15	02

TABLE 3.3 Two series of 20 four-digit keys are assigned to files with 20 and 23 addresses. With series-2, it can be seen that division with the prime number 23 results in a more uniform distribution.

distributions that are better than random. However, for a given set of keys, one prime number may be better than another, so that in the development stage more than one prime should be tested (see Section 3.3.1). While prime division is the best method in general, with some keys other methods may prove superior and should also be attempted.

Truncation, Extraction, and Folding The *truncation, extraction,* and *folding* methods are essentially variations of the division method.

1. *Truncation.* Truncation is the division method using a power of 10 (or of the radix in which the keys are expressed). Suppose 8-digit keys are to be assigned to 3-digit addresses. Then the rightmost 3 digits of the key are used as the address. Thus if we have a key 12345678, the address is 678.

    Truncation gives reasonable results where the keys are uniform. However, where the keys are inclined to cluster, the resulting distribution is usually worse than random. But even with severe clustering, the method may find use for reducing the length of a long key prior to application of the prime-division method.

2. *Extraction.* Extraction is a variation on the truncation method. Instead of taking the rightmost digits of the key to form the address, we extract digits from other locations within the key. Thus with the 8-digit key 12345678 assigned to a 3-digit address, we might extract digits from the middle to form the key 456, for example. The digits selected do not have to be contiguous, so we might have used 357 instead.

    Extraction is probably superior to truncation, in that we may select the digits that demonstrate the greatest variation over the set of keys. It gives good results with uniformly varying keys and poor results where the keys tend to cluster.

3. *Folding.* Folding involves extracting digits—usually half of them—from the key and adding them to the remaining digits. Thus the key is "folded" upon itself. For example, with the key 12345678 we could take 1234 and add it to 5678, giving 6912. One of the methods already described can then be applied to the folded keys if their range is still too large.

    A further variation of the folding technique involves reversing the digits from the right half of the key before addition. This is known as *boundary folding.* Taking the record key 12345678 again, we take the left-most 4 digits 1234, reverse their order—giving 4321—and add this number to 5678, giving 9999.

    Folding has the advantage in some cases of using all the digits in the key, whereas with truncation and extraction, some of them are discarded. The discarded digits may have been able to make a contribution to the uniformity of the addresses; with folding, the variability of the whole key is retained.

Randomizing and Radix Transformation With *randomizing,* we deliberately aim for a random or near random distribution. You may wonder why, when we have so far attempted to obtain a distribution that was better than random and as near uniform as possible.

The answer lies in the fact that with certain key sets, because of nonuniformity and severe clustering, methods such as prime division—which otherwise tend to give reasonably uniform distributions—fail completely and give distributions that are worse than random. In such situations, methods that give random distributions are an improvement.

The most widely used technique for randomizing is *radix transformation.* Decimal numbers have the radix 10. The key 12345678 may thus be written:

$$1*10^7 + 2*10^6 + 3*10^5 + 4*10^4 + 5*10^3 + 6*10^2 + 7*10^1 + 8*10^0$$

The usual procedure is to change the radix 10 to 11, giving the following expression for the transformed key.

$$1*11^7 + 2*11^6 + 3*11^5 + 4*11^4 + 5*11^3 + 6*11^2 + 7*11^1 + 8*11^0$$

On evaluation, this gives 23579476. If the resulting value is too long, truncation may be applied. Thus if the addresses ranged from 000 to 999, the radix-11 transformation for the key 12345678 would give 476 for the address.

There are other methods of randomizing, but radix transformation is usually quite effective. It is worth repeating that a randomizing transformation is best regarded as a transformation of last resort, to be used only when other methods have produced distributions which are worse than random.

3.1.3 Theory of Overflow

When dealing with overflow, we need two additional terms: *load factor* and *address size* or *capacity*. The load factor is the fraction of the available space in the file that is used. Thus, if a file could hold 100,000 records when all its addresses were full but the file only had 70,000 records, then its load factor is 0.7, or 70%.

The address size tells us how many records may be assigned to an address without overflow. In most cases an address will be able to hold a block, so that block factor and address size are the same.

Let us suppose we have a distribution $D(x)$, not necessarily random, for a given file. Then $D(x)$ gives the number of addresses that have been assigned x records. If b is the address size, addresses that have b records assigned have no overflow records, while addresses that have $b + n$ records assigned have n overflow records per address. From the $D(b + 1)$ addresses with one overflow record per address, we get $D(b + 1)$ overflow records; from the $D(b + 2)$ addresses each with 2 overflow records, we get $2D(b + 2)$ overflow records; and from the $D(b + n)$ addresses with n overflow records per address, we get $nD(b + n)$ overflow records.

We can deduce an expression for the total number of overflow records from a distribution $D(x)$ with an address size b:

$$\text{Total overflow records} = \sum_{n=1} nD(b + n)$$

If the total number of addresses in the file is R, the total capacity of the file is Rb. If r is the number of records in the file, the load factor is

$$\frac{r}{Rb}$$

and the fraction of the records that overflow is

$$\frac{1}{r} \sum_{n=1} nD(b + n)$$

In the case of a random distribution, we replace $D(b + n)$ by $F(b + n)$ in the above expressions; recall that $F(x)$ is the random distribution function for r records assigned to R addresses and given by

$$F(x) = R\left(\frac{r}{R}\right)^{x}\left(\frac{1}{x!}\right) \exp\left(-\frac{r}{R}\right)$$

To see just how much overflow we are liable to get in a practical situation, we can construct a table on the basis of the above expressions (or on the basis of the data in Table 3.2). The results are shown in Table 3.4; it should be noted that this data applies to random distributions. Instead of a table, a set of overflow curves could be constructed, as in Figure 3.6.

This table is rich in information and, using the above formulas or more detailed Poisson tables, additional columns may be incorporated for values of r/R other than the 0.5, 1, 2, and 3 shown. When r/R is 2, we are assigning, for instance, 2000 records to 1000 addresses. If we are assigning 1500 records to 1000 addresses, we would use a column for r/R equal to 1.5.

For a given r/R, we see that the load factor (expressed as a percent in the table) declines with increasing address size or capacity. The reason for this is not hard to see. Take r/R equal to 1, which could occur with 1000 records to 1000 addresses. If the address size is 1, then the 1000 addresses can at most hold 1000 records so that the load factor is 100%. Now if we increase the address size to 4, the 1000 addresses have room for 4000 records so that the load factor falls to 25%.

We also note that for a given r/R, the overflow falls with increasing address size. This is also reasonable. Increasing address size means that the likelihood of more than one record being assigned to an address leading to overflow is much reduced.

Looking at the rows instead of the columns for a given address size or capacity, if we reduce the ratio r/R, which of necessity reduces the load factor, we have a reduction in

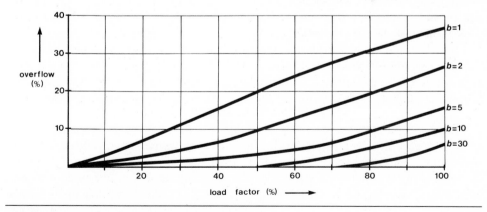

FIGURE 3.6. *Overflow against load factor for various address capacities (b) for randomized files. The curves are an alternative to tables of the type in Table 3.4.*

Address Size (b)	Total Records / Total Addresses (r/R)				
	0.5	1	2	3	
1	50% / 20%	100% / 36%	— / —	— / —	Load Factor Overflow
2	25% / 2%	50% / 10%	100% / 27%	— / —	Load Factor Overflow
3	17% / 0%	33% / 2%	66% / 11%	100% / 22%	Load Factor Overflow
4	12% / 0%	25% / 0.3%	50% / 3.6%	75% / 10%	Load Factor Overflow
5	10% / 0%	20% / 0%	40% / 1%	60% / 4.5%	Load Factor Overflow
6	8% / 0%	16% / 0%	33% / 0%	50% / 2.5%	Load Factor Overflow

PERCENTAGE LOAD FACTOR AND OVERFLOW FOR DIFFERENT ADDRESS SIZES AND RATIO OF TOTAL RECORDS TO TOTAL ADDRESSES (r/R). THE TABLE IS VALID FOR RANDOM DISTRIBUTIONS ONLY.

TABLE 3.4

overflow. Reduced overflow is always a major design aim. Let us look at the row for address size equal to 2. When we assign 2000 records to 1000 addresses, the file is 100% full but we have 27% of the records as overflow records. If, instead, we choose to place only 1000 records in the 1000 addresses, so that the file is only 50% full, we now find that the overflow is down to 10% of the records.

This is one of the most common methods of reducing overflow. We are simply willing to waste space in the physical storage to avoid wasting time searching for overflow records, which will have to be located somewhere other than in their home addresses, that is, the addresses obtained by applying the hashing routine to the keys of these records.

However, another method of reducing the overflow is by *increasing* the address capacity while holding the load factor constant. We can see the effect of this from looking at the diagonals in the table. Consider the case where we assign 1000 records to 2000 addresses ($r/R = 0.5$) and where the address capacity is 1.0. The result is shown in the top left corner of the table; we have a 50% load factor and 20% overflow.

In practice, a 50% load factor is under the acceptable limit, which is usually about 65%. To reduce this 20% overflow without going even further down in load factor, we could cut the number of addresses in half, to 1000, and double the size of an address, to 2. The load factor is thus unchanged. But from the table we see that the overflow is now 10%, a significant reduction. We can go further; from the table, we see that by decreasing the number of addresses to 500 (r/R is now 2) and increasing the address size to 4, we can get the overflow down to 3.5%.

There are thus two practical methods of reducing overflow, *given the hashing routine*.

a. Increasing the capacity of the individual addresses.

b. Increasing the number of addresses in the storage file relative to the number of records.

As we will see, (a) turns out to be the better method. Consider the second method. We have seen that with randomizing routines and with an address capacity of one, a load factor of 100% would give 36% overflow, which is not acceptable. Admittedly, a better than randomizing routine would give less. With randomizing, reducing the load factor to 50% gives 20% overflow. We apparently waste 50% of the space in the file to achieve this.

However, this conclusion is superficial. Far more space is being wasted. For example, with OS/MVS the file could be stored using either count-data or count-key data format, as described in Section 1.4. If the address capacity is 1, then the data subblock will contain either a record or nothing. With count-data format, the percentage of the available space used on an IBM 3350 disk is

$$\frac{100B}{185 + B}$$

With count-key data format, it is

$$\frac{100B}{267 + (K + B)}$$

where K is the length of the record key and B is the capacity of an address in bytes.

In the above case, if the record length is 80 bytes, then the utilization of the space with 100% load factor is about 30% for count-data and about 22% for count-key-data format (assuming the key length to be 15 bytes). However, if we reduce the load factor to 50% to give 20% overflow, the space utilization falls to about 15% and 11% for count-data and count-key-data formats, respectively.

Thus keeping the address capacity low and the load factor low as well results in very poor utilization of the available space on a disk unit. The other method of reducing overflow requires that we increase the address size or capacity (with count-data or count-key-data formats, this in effect means increasing the number of records in the data subblock). This method is to be preferred, although it gives rise to increased transmission time.

To illustrate, let us take the case of an address capacity of 3 and a 100% load factor. From Table 3.4, we see that the overflow is 22%, not too different from that in the previous example (20%) with a 50% load factor. For comparison purposes, we shall again assume that the record length is 80 bytes with a key of 15 bytes. This means space utilizations of 56% and 46% for count-data and count-key-data formats, respectively, using the formulas above. This is a considerable improvement over the previous case.

However, to retrieve a record, all three records in the data subblock have to be retrieved and deblocked. We saw in Section 1.4 that the time to retrieve a block of data is the sum of the seek time, rotation time, and data-transmission time. Since we are interested in only one record in the block (or data subblock), time is wasted in transmitting the unwanted records.

It is useful to examine the quantities involved. With an IBM 3350 disk, the average seek and rotation time is about 34 milliseconds. The data transmission rate is 1198 bytes per millisecond, so that the time to find and transmit a block with 80 bytes is 34.06 milliseconds (on the average) and for a block with 240 bytes (or with three 80-byte records), it is 34.18 milliseconds, which is not a significant increase. The difference between one 800-byte record per address and three 800-byte records would still be only 1.3 milliseconds. Thus the extra time wasted in transmitting the unwanted records is usually acceptable, provided the record lengths and address capacities are not abnormally large.

The conclusion is clear: the best way to reduce overflow is to have a hash routine which gives a distribution as near uniform as possible. The next best way is to keep the address capacity high and the load factor as close to 100% as possible, with allowance being made for growth or fluctuation in the size of the file. The least acceptable method, normally used only where fast access with large records is a critical requirement, is to keep the address capacity close to 1 and employ a low load factor, often in the range of 60 to 70%. Finally, in particular cases, combinations of these methods may be used to advantage.

Search Length   Overflow records can never be entirely avoided, and they are normally placed either in separate files, in reserved portions of the main file, or in unused address spaces. The question then arises as to the efficiency with which records from a hash file may be retrieved when *synonyms* (overflow records) are present.

When a record is to be retrieved, the home address is calculated by means of the hashing routine. If the record in the home address is not the required one, then the required record may be an overflow record, and—as such—a search will have to be made for it, requiring additional accesses or retrievals until it is found.

In this chapter we will use the concept of *search length* (for retrieval), or the number of accesses to retrieve a given record. Records in their home addresses have a search length of unity by definition, while overflow records normally have a search length greater than one.

An average search length for the whole file may be computed by adding the search lengths for each record and dividing by the number of records. The average search length is a very important design parameter. It gives the average number of accesses to retrieve a record; using the average time per access, the average time per retrieval may be obtained.

Generally, average search lengths greater than 2 are unacceptable; we should aim for those less than 1.5. As we shall see later, it is normal practice for the file-loading program to compute the search length. The search length is affected by many factors, including load factor, address capacity, and overflow technique employed. We shall therefore examine next the options available for managing overflow.

3.1.4 Overflow Management Techniques

Progressive Overflow   *Progressive overflow* (sometimes called *open addressing*) is widely used, simple to manage, and involves placing each overflow record in the nearest empty address greater than the home address. Thus if a record to be retrieved is not in its home address, each succeeding address is accessed until the record is found. With this technique, the file is normally loaded in two stages. First, all the home-address records are loaded. Then the remaining synonyms are written out in the remaining free addresses. Were a synonym written out before other records were permitted to occupy their home addresses, then additional overflow would be produced, resulting in an increased average search length.

With the course of time, additions and deletions to the file cause it to deteriorate, resulting in an increase in the average search length. For example, when a record is to be added to the file, it may not be possible to place it in its home address because it is occupied by a synonym from another home address. In such a case the updating routine could either (1) treat the new record as a synonym and place it in the next empty address, or (2) move the record occupying the home address to the nearest empty address instead, thus permitting the new record to be placed in its home address. Either way, the search length increases. Because the majority of the records can be expected to be in their home addresses in the beginning, deletions will tend to remove records from home addresses, again increasing the average search length.

The relationship between average search length and load factor has been determined experimentally by Peterson in a classic series of experiments on progressive overflow files [Peterson, 1957]. The relationship has also been deduced mathematically using the Poisson distribution function [Tainiter, 1963], but the deduction is unusually complex.

Peterson's curves for search length versus load factor after initial loading are shown in Figure 3.7. For a given load factor, the search length decreases with increasing address capacity because the more records an address can hold, the more likely it is that the address following a full address will not be full and the fewer overflow records there are in the

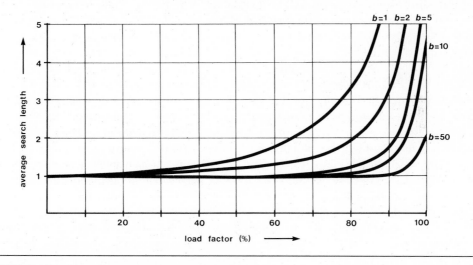

FIGURE 3.7 *Average search length versus load factor for randomized files with different address capacities* (b); *curves are for progressive overflow and are valid after initial loading. (Copyright 1957 by International Business Machines Corporation; reprinted with permission.)*

first place. It is also clear that the average search length will increase with load factor; with the increasing load factor, it becomes less likely that the address following a full address will not be full.

From the curves in Figure 3.7, it can be seen that an average search length less than 2.0 is not difficult to attain. Even with an address capacity of 1, a 60% load factor gives an average search length of 1.8. However, it cannot be stressed enough that these curves describe the situation immediately after initial loading.

As pointed out already, the search length increases as deletions and insertions take place. However, after between about 50% and 150% turnover of records, an equilibrium situation is reached in which an insertion or deletion is just as likely to reduce the average search length as increase it. The file is said to have reached a state of *dynamic equilibrium* [Peterson, 1957].

Thus it is insufficient to measure the average search length just after loading; it should also be periodically monitored, perhaps during updating. Study of Peterson's progressive overflow results reveals that, as a rule of thumb, average search length increases during updating in accordance with the formula

$$S_e = 1 + 3(S_0 - 1)$$

where S_0 and S_e are initial and dynamic-equilibrium search lengths, respectively. The increase is thus substantial. If search lengths are to be kept under 1.5 during the life of the file and if periodic reorganizations are not envisaged then, for example, with address capacity of 10, the load factor should not exceed 80%. These considerations, it must be remembered, are for randomized files; where the hashing routine gives a better than random distribution, less stringent parameters could be used.

In Section 3.3, we shall give examples of loading and updating routines for hash files with progressive overflow using PL/1. We shall continue here with other methods of handling overflow.

Count-Key Progressive Overflow   The *count-key progressive overflow* technique is quite effective, is fairly widely used, and gives a very low average search length—usually near 1. It has also some severe disadvantages, making it suitable only in restricted cases. The technique is very easy to use, as it is built into OS/MVS and PL/1; file organizations permitting it are in PL/1 terminology called REGIONAL (2) files.

With REGIONAL (2) files, each record in storage is the data subblock in a count-key data block, as described in Section 1.4. The block serves as an addressable region, which can contain a record. The address of the region depends on the cylinder and track numbers, together with the block number as contained in the count subblock.

To place a record in the file, a hashing routine first produces an address A from a key K. If the record were in a PL/1 structure S and were to be written in a file BETA, then the WRITE statement would be

WRITE FILE (BETA) FROM (S) KEYFROM (K/ /A);

where both K and A are CHARACTER, or string, variables. We note that the access method requires the record (in S), the address of the addressable region (in A), and the record key (in K, but also redundantly in S).

To store the record (which is treated as a block), the controller under channel-program control uses the count subblock to count the addressable regions or blocks on the track until the desired region is found. If the address is empty, the record is placed in the data subblock and the key is placed in the key subblock. If the address is full, the controller searches further under channel-program control (note this is a continuation of the access, not a new access) until the next empty address or region is encountered. The record and key are deposited in the data and key subblocks, respectively, of this address.

It is thus clear that the overflow is progressive, but not under programmer control. It is under *access-method control*. Let us see what happens when we try to retrieve a record from the file.

In this case we would use a READ statement of the type

READ FILE (BETA) INTO (S) KEY (K/ /A);

This time the record found will be placed in the structure S. The record sought has the key K and, as a result of applying the hashing routine to K, the home address has been calculated and is the value in A.

To access the record, the controller, under channel-program control, counts through the records on the appropriate track until the address given in A matches that of a block as determined by the current count subblock. The key in K is then compared with the key in the key subblock (the channel program sees to this); if the two match, the record is transmitted. If they do not match, the required record is most likely to be an overflow record, and the controller continues to examine the subsequent blocks on the track; however, it now inspects the key subblock and not the count subblock. It is important to note that this inspection of the subsequent blocks is not a new access, but a continuation of the original access. When a block is found that has a key subblock which matches the key K, the block is transmitted. In this way, an overflow record is retrieved in a time equivalent to little more than that for one access. Thus, for such a file, the average search length will be close to unity.

The major drawback with these files is that the records cannot be blocked; that is, the address capacity is always unity. Because load factors must be kept considerably below 100% (otherwise many overflow records would end up in subsequent tracks) to avoid excessive search times, and because the format is count-key data, the utilization of the space on the track can be poor. With an 80% load factor, 80-byte records and a 10-byte key, the track utilization for a 3350 device is

$$\frac{80*80}{(267 + 10 + 80)}, \quad \text{or} \quad 18\%$$

using the disk storage capacity expressions from Section 1.4. Thus the method is only acceptable when the record length is quite large. If, in the calculation above, we used a record length of 600 bytes instead of 80, the space utilization would climb to 55%. Unfortunately we are not always in a position to change record lengths.

There is a variation of REGIONAL(2) file organization, which may be used with PL/1; it is known as REGIONAL(3). However, since the records cannot be blocked and count-key-data format is used, it suffers from the same drawbacks as REGIONAL(2). You are referred to the manuals [IBM, 1976a, 1976b].

Chained Progressive Overflow   With conventional progressive overflow, the chief disadvantage is that the search length is relatively large during retrieval. If the home address of a record is, for instance, 100, and it is in fact located at address 110 as an overflow record, then 11 accesses will have to be made to retrieve it. It is this problem that the count-key progressive technique is designed to overcome.

Another method of overcoming this problem involves chaining the overflow records together and to the home address by means of a pointer system. Unfortunately, especially with deletions and insertions, the task of maintaining the pointer system can be burdensome. For a file *with address capacity equal to unity,* the complexity of the maintenance algorithms and the average search length are both kept low if the following are observed.

1.   When an overflow record is deleted, the overflow chain should be repaired. Thus if P, Q, and R are consecutive records in an overflow chain starting at the home address for the three records, when Q is deleted, the pointer field in P should be updated to point to the address of R.

2.   When a record in its home address is to be deleted, if there is a chain of overflow records for that address, then a record from the chain (usually the first) should be deleted and placed in the vacated home address.

3.   If home address HR has no space for a new record R, and if in HR there is an overflow record B belonging to an overflow chain starting at home address HB, then B should be deleted and R inserted in its home address HR. Then B should be reinserted at the end of the overflow chain for the home address HB.

If these rules are followed, orderly overflow chains will result. Similar rules can be devised for *address capacity greater than unity.* All chains should begin at a home address, and there should be no empty records in the chains to increase search length. The main drawback to chained progressive overflow is quite clear, however: Insertion and deletion can involve many accesses for maintenance of the chaining system.

With this overflow method, it is instructive to derive an expression (and associated curves) for the average search length involved. We undertake the derivation both for address size (b) equal to 1 and greater than 1.

1.   *Average search length for* $b = 1$ Suppose that the hashing routine gives rise to a distribution $D(x)$. There will be $D(1)$ chains with only 1 record, $D(2)$ chains with 2 records, $D(3)$ chains with 3 records, and $D(x)$ chains with x records.

If we take a chain of 3 records, the number of accesses required to access the 3 records independently is

$$1 + 2 + 3$$

The number of accesses needed to access a chain of x records independently is

$$1 + 2 + 3 + \cdots + x, \text{ or } \frac{x(x + 1)}{2} \text{ accesses}$$

There are $D(x)$ chains with x records. Thus the number of accesses to access the records in all chains with x records is

$$\frac{x(x + 1)}{2} D(x)$$

The number of accesses to access all the records in the file must therefore be

$$\sum_{x=1} \frac{x(x + 1)}{2} D(x) \tag{1}$$

The average search length is thus

$$\frac{1}{r} \sum_{x=1} \frac{x(x + 1)}{2} D(x) \tag{2}$$

This expression is valid for any distribution. If the distribution is known, Expression 2 may be used to deduce a curve for average search length versus load factor, as is done in Figure 3.8 for the random distribution $F(x)$. With a random distribution, Expression 2 becomes

$$\frac{1}{r} \sum_{x=1} \frac{x(x + 1)}{2} F(x) \tag{3}$$

With this expression and with the help of a table like Table 3.2, we may deduce the curve for $b = 1$ in Figure 3.8.

To understand how this is done, suppose we wish to know the average search length for load factors equal to 100% and 50%, respectively, with $b = 1$. For the 100% load factor, we could take the case of 1000 records assigned to 1000 addresses; that is, r/R equal to 1, so that the values $F(1)$, $F(2)$, ... may be obtained from the table. For the 50% load factor, we could take 500 records assigned to 1000 addresses, or r/R equal to 0.5, so that the values for $F(x)$ may again be obtained from the table.

Expression 3 may be reduced [Bratbergsengen, 1973] to approximately

$$1 + \frac{r}{2R}$$

This is reasonably close to the values shown in Figure 3.8, which the author obtained numerically.

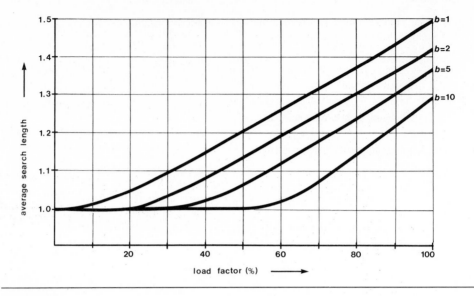

FIGURE 3.8. *Average search length versus load factor for a randomized file with block factor* b *and chained overflow records. The set of curves may be applied to three chained overflow situations:*
1. *Chained progressive overflow; for* b > 1*, the curves are worst case.*
2. *Separate overflow area with same block factor as main file; for* b > 1*, curves are worst case and may be meaningfully extrapolated.*
3. *Separate overflow area with block factor 1, regardless of* b *for main file; curves are exact and may be meaningfully extrapolated.*

It must be remembered that Expression 3 applies just after initial loading. However, if orderly chains are maintained, it is likely that a file in dynamic equilibrium will have very close to the same average search length.

2. *Average search length for* b > 1   For *b* > 1, the average search length will depend on the character of the overflow chains. We can distinguish three distinct cases.

   a. *Best case:* Overflow records from a given home address have addresses exclusively reserved for overflow records from this home address. Thus if we have 13 overflow records with an address size of 5, the overflow records use up 2.3 addresses.

   b. *Worst case:* There is never more than one overflow record from a given home address in any address. Thus if we have 13 overflow records, they will be in 13 different addresses.

   c. *Typical case:* Overflow records from a given home address use a number of addresses somewhere between the worst case and the best case.

Derivation of an expression for the average search length for the typical case is difficult, and we shall be content with a derivation for the worst case, which will be useful in most practical situations.

Suppose we have x overflow records from a single home address. The number of accesses to retrieve all these records independently will be

$$2 + 3 + 4 + \cdots + x + (x + 1)$$

If we agree to call the above expression $S(x)$, we have

$$S(x) = \frac{(x + 1)}{2} ((x + 1) + 1) - 1$$

If b is the size of an address, then there are $D(b + x)$ addresses, each of which has x overflow records. Hence, to independently retrieve all the overflow records from these $D(b + x)$ addresses we need

$$S(x)D(b + x) \quad \text{accesses}$$

To retrieve all the overflow records, we shall need

$$\sum_{x=1} S(x)D(b + x) \quad \text{accesses} \tag{4}$$

The number of overflow records must be altogether

$$\sum_{x=1} xD(b + x)$$

Hence the number of nonoverflow records, that is, records in their home addresses, must be

$$r - \sum_{x=1} xD(b + x) \tag{5}$$

However, any home-address record may be retrieved in a single access. Thus the total number of accesses required to independently retrieve all the records in the file is the sum of Expressions 4 and 5:

$$\sum_{x=1} S(x)D(b + x) + r - \sum_{x=1} xD(b + x) \quad \text{accesses}$$

Hence the average search must be

$$\frac{1}{r} \left[\sum_{x=1} S(x)D(b + x) + r - \sum_{x=1} xD(b + x) \right] \tag{7}$$

This expression applies to any record distribution $D(x)$. The average search length for a random distribution $F(x)$ may be obtained by substituting $F(x)$ for $D(x)$ in Expression 7.

Incidentally, Expression 7 reduces to Expression 2 when $b = 1$, as indeed we should expect.

Using different values of r, R, and b, the curves in Figure 3.8 may be deduced (for $b > 1$) from Expression 7 and possibly also from a table such as Table 3.2.

The fact that the average search length is calculated for the worst possible case implies that when the file reaches dynamic equilibrium, the average search length will not exceed the value for the worst case, provided orderly chains are maintained.

It is clear that chained progressive overflow results in quite a low average search length, and the method can be recommended. Nevertheless, maintenance of the chaining system usually gives rise to substantial overhead if the file is subjected to a great deal of insertion and deletion of records.

Separate Overflow Area   With the separate overflow area technique, an entirely separate area is reserved for overflow records. This separate area can be either a reserved part of the file space, or it can be an entirely different file. If the home-address records and overflow records are in the same file, the same address size will apply to both types of records. On the other hand, if the overflow records are in a different file, we have the possibility of one address size for the overflow records and another for the home-address records.

When the file is loaded initially, overflow records are placed in chains in the overflow area, the records of any chain all having overflowed from a single home address. Normally the records in each chain are loaded contiguously in storage, with space left between chains to allow for additional records as a result of insertions.

Thus, although the chains are separated from each other just after loading, following sufficient deletions and insertions the chains will tend to become interleaved. When the file is in dynamic equilibrium, the chaining situation will not be much different from the case where the overflow technique is chained progressive. In fact, in the worst case (where each record of a chain is in a distinct address), the average search length will be exactly as in the worst case with chained progressive overflow, so that Expressions 2 and 7 and the curves in Figure 3.8 apply. In fact, if the block factor of the separate overflow area is unity, then the curves of Figure 3.8 apply exactly.

You should be aware that when applying either Expressions 2 and 7 or the curves of Figure 3.8 to the worst case of the average search length with the separate overflow technique, r is the total number of records in the file (or files if there are two of them), R is the total number of addresses *available to home-address records,* and the load factor (expressed as a fraction) is r/Rb. The load factor can thus exceed unity (or 100%) and still be meaningful, so that the curves of Figure 3.8 can in this case usefully be extrapolated.

The best case average search length with a separate overflow area occurs just after initial loading. It is instructive to deduce an expression for the average search length for this case, if only for purposes of comparing with the average search length in the worst case.

In the following derivation, we also assume that r records are attempted assigned to R addresses of home-address space and that the distribution function is $D(x)$.

It is clear that in the best case, which is just after initial loading, the overflow records are packed into a contiguous set of addresses. Thus if we have 12 records overflowing from a home address and if the address size is 5, the chain takes up 3 addresses. The number of independent accesses to retrieve all 12 of these records will be

$$2 + 2 + 2 + 2 + 2 + 3 + 3 + 3 + 3 + 3 + 4 + 4 \quad \text{accesses}$$

or

$$5(2 + 3) + 4 + 4 \quad \text{accesses}$$

Similarly, if there are x overflow records from a home address, if b is the address size, c is the integer closest to but less than or equal to x/b, and g is the integer closest to but greater than or equal to x/b, then the total number of accesses $S(x)$ to independently retrieve all the x records is given by

$$S(x) = b \left[\frac{(c + 1)}{2} ((c + 1) + 1) - 1 \right] + (g + 1)(x - bc) \tag{8}$$

We may now proceed precisely as in the previous derivation. We obtain an expression to access the records in all chains with x overflow records, and by summation get Expression 4 for the accesses to retrieve all records. Taking into account the accesses to retrieve the home-address records (Expression 5), we again come to Expression 7 for the average search length. That is,

$$\frac{1}{r} \left[\sum_{x=1} S(x)D(b + x) + r - \sum_{x=1} xD(b + x) \right]$$

except that in this case $S(x)$ is as in Expression 8.

Using Expressions 7 and 8, we obtain the curves in Figure 3.9. They give the search length for a hash file with a separate overflow area just after initial loading. This search length will increase as the file tends to dynamic equilibrium. Note that the load factor r/Rb is computed in this case using an R value equal to the number of addresses available to the home-address records, so that load factors greater than 100% are physically significant and the curves may usefully be extrapolated. The curves may also be interpreted as giving the best-case search lengths for chained progressive overflow.

It is clear that there is not much basis for choosing between the use of chained progressive and separate overflow area techniques. Both give a low average search length, at the expense of considerable deletion and insertion overhead. However, when combined with a large address size, hash files using these overflow techniques are probably the ultimate at present as far as fast retrieval is concerned.

3.2 PL/1 HASH FILES

REGIONAL(1), REGIONAL(2), and REGIONAL(3) are the three file organizations available in PL/1 for constructing hash files, and the sublanguages associated with them are quite

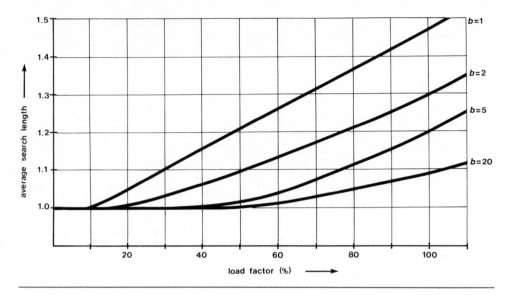

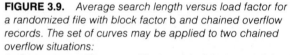

FIGURE 3.9. *Average search length versus load factor for a randomized file with block factor* b *and chained overflow records. The set of curves may be applied to two chained overflow situations:*

1. *Separate overflow area with same block factor as main file; for b > 1, curves are the best case in general, but apply exactly just after initial loading. Curves may be meaningfully extrapolated.*
2. *Chained progressive overflow; for b > 1, curves are the best case, but hardly ever attainable.*

similar. With all three methods, there are directly and relatively addressable *regions* for holding records; a relative address is called a *region number*. With REGIONAL(1), a region corresponds to a block in count-data format, while with REGIONAL(2) and REGIONAL(3), a block or region is in count-key-data format [Rindfleisch, 1978; IBM, 1976a; IBM, 1976b].

The use of count-key-data format with REGIONAL(2) and REGIONAL(3) permits the count-key-progressive overflow technique to be incorporated into the access method. However, as we have seen, this technique tends to result in low track utilization, since a block (or region) is restricted to containing no more than that one record.

With REGIONAL(1) file organization, overflow must be managed by the application program. Since the formatting on a track is count-data, there is no possibility of using count-key progressive overflow. Addressable regions can contain more than one record; that is, the address capacity can be greater than one. Unfortunately, the access method does not block and deblock records automatically and is in fact designed to handle blocks containing only one record. However, it is not difficult to incorporate blocking and deblocking facilities in application programs.

We therefore select REGIONAL(1) organization for more detailed study, as it is both the simplest and most flexible. You are referred to the manuals for the manipulation sublanguages for REGIONAL(2) and REGIONAL(3) file organizations; these sublanguages are very similar to that for REGIONAL(1) files.

3.2.1 REGIONAL(1) and File Organization

Strictly speaking, REGIONAL(1) is designed to permit one record per addressable region, where *a region corresponds to a count-data block*. The count subblock contains the information needed to determine the region number, and the data subblock contains the record. The region number is not the physical address of the count-data block or region, in terms of cylinder and track number and block number. It is the relative address taken from the start of the file in the physical disk, since there could be more than one REGIONAL(1) file on the disk.

Because REGIONAL(1) permits only one record per addressable region, it is necessary to construct composite records using structure arrays in the PL/1 program to increase the address capacity. Each element in the structure array is a record, and the whole array or composite record can be transmitted using the REGIONAL(1) file sublanguage. We shall see later how this works in practice. We look first at the sublanguage, which—we again emphasize—handles one record per region.

File Declaration   A useful file declaration statement is

DCL BETA FILE RECORD ENV (REGIONAL(1));

where, as with the description of the sublanguage for CONSECUTIVE files, we employ BETA as a file (or ddname) name.

OPEN Statement   It is important to distinguish between how a file is organized (for example, REGIONAL(1)) and how it is to be processed. REGIONAL(1) files can be processed in six basic ways. The processing method is specified at open time. The OPEN statement possibilities are given by

OPEN FILE (BETA)
$$
\begin{cases}
\text{SEQUENTIAL OUTPUT KEYED} \\
\text{DIRECT OUTPUT KEYED} \\
\\
\text{SEQUENTIAL INPUT \ \ [KEYED]} \\
\text{SEQUENTIAL UPDATE [KEYED]} \\
\\
\text{DIRECT INPUT KEYED} \\
\text{DIRECT UPDATE KEYED}
\end{cases}
$$

In the following sections, we shall deal with each of these processing modes in turn. To permit the operating system to construct access methods, DCB, and so on as efficiently as possible, as many files as possible should be opened in one OPEN statement. Thus we might have

OPEN FILE (BETA) DIRECT UPDATE KEYED, FILE (DELTA) INPUT;

where DELTA is not a REGIONAL(1) file.

CLOSE Statement   This is simply

CLOSE FILE (BETA);

Creation of REGIONAL(1) Files   The file may be created in either of two ways: when it is open for SEQUENTIAL OUTPUT KEYED and when it is open for DIRECT OUTPUT KEYED. We shall examine the two separately.

1. *Creation with* SEQUENTIAL OUTPUT KEYED   First, the file is opened with

    OPEN FILE (BETA) SEQUENTIAL OUTPUT KEYED;

    Records are assumed to be available sorted in ascending order by region number. To do this, the hashing algorithm will have been applied to the record keys at some earlier stage, followed by a sort by region number.
    Records are written out in ascending region number sequence (an out-of-sequence record will cause the PL/1 KEY on-condition to be raised). We use the WRITE statement

    WRITE FILE (BETA) FROM (S) KEYFROM (REG);

    where S is the variable containing the record to be transmitted. Following KEYFROM, we may use an expression or a variable, such as REG. The region number is obtained from the *rightmost 8 characters* in the *character string value* of REG or equivalent expression. These 8 characters must contain the *unsigned* region number *right justified,* for example bbbbb123 for region 123. The first region number is bbbbbbbO.[1] (If REG or the equivalent expression is FIXED, a useful rule is that the 8 characters used are those that would be output by a PUT EDIT statement that uses format item F(8).)
    We note the following. Presentation of a duplicate region number will cause the PL/1 KEY on-condition to be raised; a duplicate region number signals an overflow record that the program must be prepared to handle. Regions not used in the creation of the file are marked empty by a '11111111'B in the first byte of the region.

2. *Creation with* DIRECT OUTPUT KEYED   First the file is opened with

    OPEN FILE (BETA) DIRECT OUTPUT KEYED;

    As well as creating the access method, DCB, and so on, following OPEN, the file is filled with empty regions; that is, the first byte in each region contains '11111111'B.
    Records may be written out in any sequence using the WRITE statement

---

[1]*The number of regions required is specified in the DD statement, up to a maximum of 16,777,215 regions.*

WRITE FILE (BETA) FROM (S) KEYFROM (REG);

where, as before, **S** has the record and **REG** the region number. However, in this case presentation of a duplicate region number does not cause the **KEY** on-condition to be raised, so that the program must have some other method of determining when a record is an overflow record. A record with a duplicate region number is simply written in the correct region; its original contents are then lost.

Record Retrieval from REGIONAL(1) Files   Records may be retrieved either sequentially by region number or by direct access in any sequence. We take each separately.

1. *Retrieval with* SEQUENTIAL INPUT KEYED   The file is opened with

    OPEN FILE (BETA) SEQUENTIAL INPUT KEYED;

    We use **KEYED** in the open statement only when it is desired to read the region number as well as the record.
    The file may now be read sequentially.

    READ FILE (BETA) INTO (S);

    The first or next record is read in sequence by region number. The region number is not read. If we encounter

    READ FILE (BETA) INTO (S) IGNORE (N);

    then the next record is read after skipping the next **N** records. At this stage, it is well to point out that a region is read or IGNOREd even when empty. The program must be prepared to handle empty regions. If we execute

    READ FILE (BETA) INTO (S) KEYTO (REG);

    then the next record in region number sequence is read and placed in **S** and the region number placed in the variable **REG** (right justified). This **KEYTO** option can only be used if **KEYED** is coded in the **OPEN** statement.

2. *Retrieval with* DIRECT INPUT KEYED   The file is opened with

    OPEN FILE (BETA) DIRECT INPUT KEYED;

    The file may now be read by presenting the region number of the required region:

    READ FILE (BETA) INTO (S) KEY (REG);

    The record in the region which has region number given by the value of the string variable **REG** is transmitted to **S**. The region is read even when empty and the program must be prepared for empty regions.

Updating of REGIONAL(1) Files   The files may be updated either in sequence by region number or by direct access in any sequence. Again we take them separately.

1. *Updating with* SEQUENTIAL UPDATE KEYED   The file is opened with

    OPEN FILE (BETA) SEQUENTIAL UPDATE KEYED;

    When the KEYED option is coded, the region number associated with a record may be read.

    All the READ statements useable with SEQUENTIAL INPUT KEYED may be employed and with the same effect. However, following a statement such as

    READ FILE (BETA) INTO (S);

    in which the next record in region number sequence is read and placed in S, S may be subsequently updated by the applications program, and a rewrite statement executed:

    REWRITE FILE (BETA) FROM (S);

    The record in S is stored in the same region as was accessed in the previous READ statement.

2. *Updating with* DIRECT UPDATE KEYED   We open the file:

    OPEN FILE (BETA) DIRECT UPDATE KEYED;

    We may write and read in any sequence:

    READ FILE (BETA) INTO (S) KEY (REG);

    The contents of the region corresponding to REG are read into S, even when the region is empty. Now, if we execute

    WRITE FILE (BETA) FROM (S) KEYFROM (REG);

    the contents of S are written into the region corresponding to REG, even when the region is full already. To delete a record we may write

    DELETE FILE (BETA) KEY (REG);

    Following this, '11111111'B is written in the first byte of the region corresponding to REG; that is, the region is rendered empty.

The KEY On-Condition   As already mentioned, the KEY on-condition is raised when we present a duplicate or out-of-sequence region number during sequential file creation.

The KEY on-condition is always enabled and cannot be disabled. (If no KEY on-unit has been coded, normal system action is to terminate execution of the program.)

3.3 CREATION AND UPDATING STRATEGIES

3.3.1 Testing of Hashing Routines

As discussed in Section 3.1, the development of a suitable hashing routine for a file can be a development project in itself. In that section, the various methods that can be used were also analyzed. More than one hashing routine will normally be developed and tested until a suitable one has been chosen.

Testing the hashing routine often consists of ascertaining whether the resulting distribution of records is uniform, random, better than random, or worse than random. This can be done by applying a test load program to the record keys, using the hashing routine under test.

A test-load program may load the actual records into regions. If it does so, it will have to be able to take care of overflow. However, the test-load program may not in fact load the records, but simply keep track of the number of records that would otherwise be loaded into a region. Thus each region could effectively contain a one-field record. The numerical value of the field is incremented each time a record is "loaded" into the region.

Following "loading" of the records, the test-load program could determine the number of regions (addresses) with x records and thus determine and print out the distribution of records in the file. The distribution can then be compared with uniform and random distributions. An important test parameter is the ratio of records to regions (r/R); with a promising hashing routine, we could have the distribution printed out for a range of values of r/R.

A Test-Load Program   If the test-load program is not actually going to load the records, only the record keys are needed. However, the records have to be somewhere, and we may assume that they are in a sequential file on tape or disk. To keep the exercise reasonably realistic let us assume that the file describes holes drilled by an oil company. The record key is alphanumeric and identifies a given hole; to keep the record short we can take the attributes to be depth, cost, and location, as displayed in Figure 3.10. Although we need only the record keys, the whole record will have to be read in, so that the program

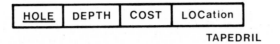

TAPEDRIL

FIGURE 3.10.   *Field format for the file* **TAPEDRIL** *used in the examples. The record describes a drill-hole. Key field is underlined.*

will deal with two files: a CONSECUTIVE file TAPEDRIL (on tape), and a REGIONAL(1) file HASHDRIL. However, as we shall see shortly, use of a REGIONAL(1) file here can often be wasteful. Nevertheless, the following program illustrates use of the PL/1 REGIONAL(1) sublanguage.

```
TEST: PROC OPTIONS (MAIN);
          /*  Program prints distribution resulting from hashing routine HASH for r equal to
              value in TESTPARM   */


DCL TAPEDRIL FILE RECORD ENV(CONSECUTIVE),   /*  Source records  */
      1 TDRIL,      /*  Holds a source record  */
          2 HOLE CHAR (6),      /*  Key field  */
          2 DEPTH FIXED FIN (15),
          2 COST FIXED DEC (8),
          2 LOC CHAR (3);


DCL HASHDRIL FILE RECORD ENV(REGIONAL(1)),   /*  Pseudo hash file  */
      1 HDRIL,                                /*  Holds a HASHDRIL
                                                  record  */

          2 TAG BIT (8) INIT ('00000000'B),  /*  For empty records  */
          2 COUNTER FIXED BIN (15);          /*  Counts records assigned  */


DCL HASH ENTRY;                              /*  Hashing routine, compiled
                                                 separately  */

DCL REG CHAR (8),                           /*  Holds a region number  */
      K BIT (1),                            /*  Used for checking operation
                                                of hashing routine  */

      TESTPARM FIXED BIN (31);              /*  Value of r  */


GET LIST (TESTPARM);
OPEN FILE (HASHDRIL) DIRECT OUTPUT KEYED;   /*  File formatted with empty
                                                records  */

CLOSE FILE (HASHDRIL);


    /*  First step: fill up HASHDRIL  */


OPEN FILE (HASHDRIL) DIRECT UPDATE KEYED,   /*  We now update
                                                HASHDRIL  */

      FILE (TAPEDRIL) INPUT;
DO J = 1 TO TESTPARM;
      READ FILE (TAPEDRIL) INTO (TDRIL);
      CALL HASH (HOLE, REG, K);             /*  HASH accepts record key
                                                and returns region number to
                                                REG, and an OK signal to
                                                K  */
```

```
IF K = '0'B                                    /*   Not OK   */
    THEN DO;
        PUT SKIP LIST (HOLE, REG, 'HASH ERROR');
        STOP;
    END;
    ELSE DO;
        READ FILE (HASHDRIL) INTO (HDRIL) KEY (REG);

        /*   We check to see if a record has been previously assigned to this region */

        IF TAG = '11111111'B     /*   Nothing previously assigned   */
        THEN DO;
            TAG = '00000000'B;   /*   Something has now been assigned   */
            COUNTER = 1;         /*   That is, the first record   */
        END;
        ELSE                     /*   Something previously assigned   */
            COUNTER = COUNTER + 1;

            /*   Additional record assigned to the region whose address is in
                     REG   */
        WRITE FILE (HASHDRIL) FROM (HDRIL) KEYFROM (REG);
    END;
END;  /*   End of DO loop   */
    /*   For each region with TAG '11111111'B no records have been assigned; with TAG
         '00000000'B the value of COUNTER gives the number of records that have been
         assigned   */
CLOSE FILE (HASHDRIL), FILE (TAPEDRIL);

    /*   Second step: analysis of distribution in HASHDRIL   */

BEGIN;                                      /*   Start of BEGIN block   */
DCL BEOF BIT (1) INIT ('1'B);               /*   Logical variable   */
DCL TOTALREC (0:30) FIXED BIN (31) INIT/*   Holds distribution   */
((31)0);

ON ENDFILE (HASHDRIL) BEOF = '0'B;
OPEN FILE (HASHDRIL) SEQUENTIAL            /*   We process sequentially   */
INPUT KEYED;

READ FILE (HASHDRIL) INTO (HDRIL);
DO WHILE (BEOF);
    IF TAG = '00000000'B THEN
        IF COUNTER >= 30 THEN TOTALREC(30) = TOTALREC(30) + 1;
        ELSE TOTALREC(COUNTER) = TOTALREC(COUNTER) + 1;
        ELSE TOTALREC(0) = TOTALREC(0) + 1;
    READ FILE (HASHDRIL) INTO (HDRIL);
```

END;

/ Last step; output distribution function */*

```
PUT SKIP LIST ('RECORDS', TESTPARM);
PUT SKIP (2) LIST ('RECORD DISTRIBUTION');
PUT SKIP (3) LIST ('X', 'TOTALREGIONS');
DO J = 0 TO 30;
     PUT SKIP (J, TOTALREC(J)); END;
END;  /*  End of BEGIN block  */
END TEST;
/*
//GO.SYSIN DD *
TESTPARM value
/*
//GO.TAPEDRIL DD DSN = TAPEDRIL,DISP = (OLD,KEEP)
//GO.HASHDRIL DD DSN = HASHDRIL,DISP = (NEW,CATLG),UNIT = DISK,
//                DCB = (BLKSIZE = 3,RECFM = F,DSORG = DA),
//                SPACE = (3,100000), VOL = SER = 123
```

We notice from the DD statement for HASHDRIL that the records in this test file are only 3 bytes long and that we have assumed 100,000 regions (SPACE parameter). Because of the small record size, the utilization of the disk storage will be very poor. Since the storage format is count-data, with an IBM 3350 disk, the utilization in this case would be

$$\frac{3}{185 + 3} \; 100\%$$

that is, about 1.6%. In addition, when the file is open for direct access, as in the first part of the program, records must be read before they can be updated, which will cost an average of about 70 milliseconds per update.

Thus if we calculate keys for 60,000 records for the 100,000 regions, for example, the file accesses during the updating portion of the program would take about an hour. We should recall that this is a test program that needs to be run for different hashing routines under consideration and for different numbers of records (that is, different r/R ratios). Unless the data in HASHDRIL needs to be retained for further analysis or the number of records involved is very large (more than 100,000), then it could pay to use a faster version of the program TEST where the REGIONAL(1) file is replaced by a very large array of COUNTER elements. This faster version would be limited in speed by the time required to read in the records in TAPEDRIL.

Hash File Models   Another method of testing hashing routines with a minimum of computer processing and disk storage utilization involves using scaled-down models of files instead of the file itself. The hashing routine to be tested can be used only with the file model, but with a relatively simple modification, it can be scaled up to handle the real

---

file. With the scaled down hashing routine, testing would involve determining the record distribution for, as an example, 600 records being assigned to 1000 regions.

An advantage of this method is that the search length can be obtained from the test program for different overflow techniques; because, in the last analysis, it is a low search length that is required, the search length can be used instead of the record distribution resulting from the hashing routine as the comparison basis.

We shall not go into the construction of models in detail, but simply consider the main idea. For example, suppose we have a file where the key consists of 3 letters: IBM, RCA, AEC, and so on. Such a file could conceivably hold about 15,000 records, if all letter combinations were used. Let us suppose that there are, in fact, 10,000.

To construct the model of the file, we could include records with keys whose constituent letters come from the first 10 letters of the alphabet (or any other 10 letters). The model file would then have a maximum of 1000 records. If we select about 660 records for the file, it may now be regarded as a scaled-down version of the original file. Assigning these 660 records to 1000 regions would be roughly equivalent to assigning the original 10,000 records to 15,000 regions. The hashing routine could be scaled down in a similar manner.

The first part of the hashing routine will convert the alphabetic keys to numerals. Here the scaling factor would involve the fact that with the original keys, letters could be assigned values from 0 to 25, while with the model, the values would be from 0 to 9, and so on.

The main drawback with this approach is that sometimes a valid scaling down is very difficult to achieve because of complex key constructions that not infrequently occur in practice. However, with very large files, its use can sometimes result in considerable savings.

3.3.2 Creation of a REGIONAL(1) File with Progressive Overflow

We may now assume that a suitable hashing routine has been developed and that we are in a position to load the file. From the previous program (and Figure 3.10), the records from TAPEDRILL are 6 + 2 + 5 + 3, or 16, bytes long. In practice, such a record would probably be several hundred bytes long.

A critical question now is whether or not to block the records; that is, to have more than one record to an address. REGIONAL(1) does not support blocked records unless the blocking and deblocking facilities are included in the application program. However, as we have seen, there are very great advantages in blocking; these include very high utilization of the disk space and reduced overflow, resulting in shorter average search length. We shall assume that as a result of a careful analysis, a block factor of 50 is chosen (50 records per address) with a loading factor of 90% and progressive overflow. To aid the blocking and deblocking of records, a structural array capable of holding 50 records will be used in the creation program. With only 16-byte records, a block factor of 1, and 90% loading factor, the space utilization is about 7% on a 3350 disk. With a block factor of 50, it is about 73%. With IBM 3350 disks, block sizes greater than 800 bytes should be aimed at.

There are two basic methods of loading a hash file, namely, *direct loading* and *sequential loading*. With direct loading, the records are read in (probably from a tape file), the hashing routine is applied to each record, and the record is placed directly in the appropriate addressable region. If the region already has a record, it is placed in an overflow file as an overflow record. When the home-address records are loaded, the overflow records are read in and placed in the hash file in accordance with the overflow technique being used.

Sequential loading involves reading in the records, applying the hashing routine, and then loading the records, with a new field attached for the region number, into a sequential file. The sequential file is then sorted in ascending region number sequence, and these records are used as the source file for loading the hash file sequentially. As with direct loading, overflow records are placed in a temporary sequential file and loaded separately.

We shall take sequential loading as an example. We assume that the records from TAPEDRIL (Figure 3.10) are in the sequential file TAPEHASH, which has an extra field REG that holds the address obtained by hashing the record key HOLE. We also assume that the TAPEHASH records are sorted in ascending REGION number sequence.

The resulting hash file is DRILHASH; the loading takes place in two stages, as shown in Figure 3.11. As mentioned earlier, a region is assigned many records in this program; that is, the records are blocked by the program and not automatically by the access method. The block structure used is shown in Figure 3.12.

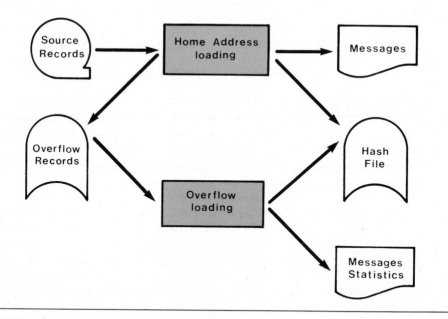

FIGURE 3.11. *Two-stage loading of a hash file with progressive overflow. Actually, four stages are involved. The records in* **TAPEHASH** *are assumed to have had the hashing routine applied at an earlier stage and to have been sorted in ascending region number sequence.*

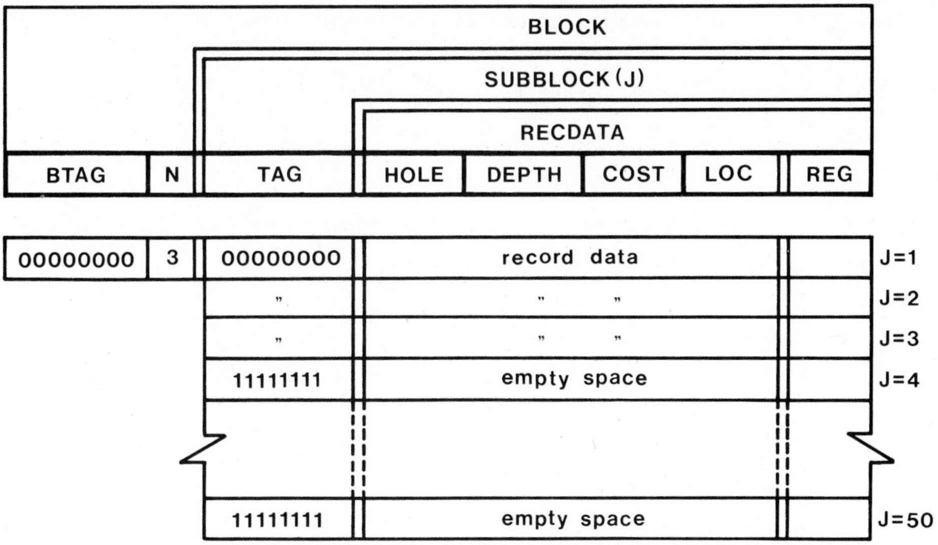

FIGURE 3.12. *Structure of the block used in the creation of a hash file* **DRILHASH** *using the loading program* **LOADHASH.** *The file organization used is PL/1* **REGIONAL(1),** *which does not allow blocked records. Blocked records are desirable on grounds of increased efficiency for retrievals and increased space utilization. Blocking and deblocking of the records in the structure* **BLOCK** *above is carried out by the loading program* **LOADHASH.**

The second field, **N**, of the block keeps track of the number of records in the block. The rest of the block is divided into 50 record spaces. Each record has attached an 8-bit field, which informs about the status of the record (deleted or valid) together with an 8-byte field for the region number. This region number is useful but not strictly necessary; for example, since the block will contain both home address and overflow records, a record's (home) region number can be used to distinguish between the two types.

LOADHASH: PROC OPTIONS (MAIN);

/* 1. This program loads a hash file called DRILHASH, which has records that describe holes drilled in the ground.

 2. The source records to create DRILHASH come from the sequential file TAPEHASH, which has records that:

   a. Have the home-region number already attached;

   b. Are sorted in ascending sequence by region number.

 3. Two-stage sequential loading is used.

a. Home-address records are loaded sequentially in ascending region number sequence, with overflow records temporarily placed in the file OVFLOW.

b. Then these overflow records are loaded using the progressive overflow technique.

4. File statistics are collected in the two stages, and the initial search length is calculated.

5. The structure array BLOCK is used to store many records per region (not provided for by the REGIONAL(1) access method, but most desirable on grounds of space utilization and efficiency). The structure is shown in Figure 3.12.   */

```
DCL     TAPEHASH FILE RECORD ENV (CONSECUTIVE),    /* Source records */
        1   TPAREA,                                 /* Holds a source record */
            2   HOLE CHAR (6),                      /* Record key */
            2   DEPTH FIXED BIN (15),
            2   COST FIXED DEC (8),
            2   LOC CHAR (3),
            2   REG CHAR (8);                        /* Hashed using HOLE value */


DCL     (DRILHASH) FILE RECORD ENV (REGIONAL(1) ),        /*   Hash file   */
        1   BLOCK,                      /*   Holds up to 50 DRILHASH records   */
            2   BTAG BIT (8),                   /*   Can indicate empty block   */
            2   N FIXED BIN (15),               /*   Number of records in block   */
            2   SUBBLOCK (50),          /*   Each element holds a DRILHASH record   */
                3   TAG BIT (8),                    /*   For record deletion   */
                3   RECDATA LIKE TPAREA;


DCL     OVFLOW FILE RECORD ENV (CONSECUTIVE),      /*   For overflow records   */
        1   OFAREA LIKE TPAREA;                     /*   Holds an overflow record   */


                    /*   Statistical variables   */


DCL     (TOTREC,                        /*   Total records in TAPEHASH   */
        TOTBLOCK,                       /*   Total blocks containing records   */
        TOTHA)                          /*   Total home address records   */
        FIXED BIN (31) INIT (0);
DCL     B   FIXED BIN (31);             /*   Total regions available   */
DCL     SL  FIXED BIN (15);             /*   Used for search length calculation   */


                    /*   Other auxiliary variables   */


DCL     (BEOF, LOG) BIT (1);            /*   Logical variables   */
DCL     J FIXED BIN (15);               /*   Loop control variable   */
DCL     KAY PIC '99999999';             /*   Holds region number   */
DCL     (K, M) FIXED DEC (8);           /*   Control variables   */
```

```
                    /*   First stage: loading of home address records    */

OPEN FILE (TAPEHASH) INPUT,
    FILE (OVFLOW) OUTPUT,
    FILE (DRILHASH) SEQUENTIAL OUTPUT KEYED;
ON ENDFILE (TAPEHASH) BEOF = '0'B;

READ FILE (TAPEHASH) INTO (TPAREA);
TOTREC = 1;                           /*   First record read    */
BEOF = '1'B;
DO WHILE (BEOF);                      /*   Main loading loop    */
    KAY = TPAREA.REG;

    /*   Following loop places records in the structure BLOCK    */
    DO J = 1 TO 50 WHILE (KAY = TPAREA.REG & BEOF);
        TAG(J) = '00000000'B;              /*   Valid record    */
        RECDATA(J) = TPAREA;
        READ FILE (TAPEHASH) INTO (TPAREA);
        TOTREC = TOTREC + 1;          /*   Statistics    */
    END;

                    /*   Now complete this block    */
    N = J;                                /*   Number of records in block    */
    BTAG = '00000000'B;                   /*   Block-with-records mark    */
    IF J < 50 THEN DO L = J + 1 TO 50;
        /*   Mark unfilled record spaces    */
        TAG(L) = '11111111'B;
    END;

    /*   Now transmit the block    */
    WRITE FILE (DRILHASH) FROM (BLOCK) KEYFROM (KAY);
    TOTBLOCK = TOTBLOCK + 1;
    TOTHA = TOTHA + J;                     /*   Statistics    */

        /*   If J was 50 there may well be overflow records from this block or region; these are
        now placed in OVFLOW    */
    IF J = 50 THEN DO;
    DO WHILE (KAY = TPAREA.REG & BEOF);
        WRITE FILE (OVFLOW) FROM (TPAREA);
        READ FILE (TAPEHASH) INTO (TPAREA);
        TOTREC = TOTREC + 1;
    END;
    END;
END;                                  /*   End of main loading loop    */
```

```
TOTREC = TOTREC − 1;                    /*   Adjustment for endfile effect   */
CLOSE FILE (DRILHASH), FILE (OVFLOW), FILE (TAPEHASH);
PUT SKIP LIST ('HOME ADDRESSES LOADED');


                    /*   Second stage: loading of overflow records   */


SL = 0;                                 /*   Statistics   */
GET LIST (B);                           /*   Get total regions in file   */
OPEN FILE (DRILHASH) DIRECT UPDATE KEYED,
    FILE (OVFLOW) INPUT;
ON ENDFILE (OVFLOW) BEOF = '0'B;
BEOF = '1'B;


/*   Main overflow loading loop follows   */
READ FILE (OVFLOW) INTO (OFAREA);
DO WHILE (BEOF);
    KAY = OFAREA.REG;
    K = 0;                              /*   Control variable   */


      /*   Following loop fills regions subsequent to region KAY with overflow records from
      region KAY   */
    LOG = '1'B;
    DO WHILE (LOG);
        K = K + 1;                      /*   Get ready for next region   */


      /*   If we go past the end of the hash file, continue progressive overflow with first
      region of file   */
      IF K + KAY > = B
          THEN M = −B;                  /*   Means back to start of file   */
          ELSE M = 0;                   /*   M has no effect   */
      READ FILE (DRILHASH) INTO (BLOCK) KEY (K + KAY + M);
          /*   We are K regions past home address in KAY. KEY expression is FIXED DEC
          (10), with character string value 13 characters long   */
      IF BTAG = '11111111'B
              THEN J = 1;               /*   Empty region   */
              ELSE J = N + 1;           /*   Fill up from position J   */


      IF J < 51 THEN DO;                /*   Safe to place records in region   */
          DO I = J TO 50 WHILE (KAY=OFAREA.REG & BEOF);
              RECDATA(I) = OFAREA;
              TAG(I) = '00000000'B;  /*   Ith record in BLOCK   */
              READ FILE (OVFLOW) INTO (OFAREA);
          END;                          /*   Filling of this region completed   */
```

```
                    /*   However there is still some housekeeping   */
        N = I;                              /*   Number of records in region   */
        SL = SL + (K + 1)(N − J + 1);      /*   Contribution to total accesses   */
        IF J = 1 THEN DO;                  /*   That is, if region was empty at
                                                start   */
            BTAG = '00000000'B;            /*   There are now records in region   */
            IF N < 50 THEN DO L = N + 1 TO 50
                TAG(L) = '11111111'B;      /*   Mark unused space   */
                END;
            TOTBLOCK = TOTBLOCK + 1 /*   Statistics   */
        END;
                            /*   Housekeeping completed   */


        WRITE FILE (DRILHASH) FROM (BLOCK) KEYFROM (K + KAY + M);
            /*   We may need additional regions to accommodate all the records
            overflowing from region KAY   */


        IF N < 50                              /*   No additional regions needed   */
            THEN LOG = '0'B;
            ELSE IF (KAY = OFAREA.REG & BEOF) THEN; /*   Regions
                                                          needed   */
                        ELSE LOG = '0'B;       /*   Not needed   */
        END;
        ELSE;                              /*   No room in block, repeat inner loop   */
    END;                                   /*   End of DO WHILE (LOG) loop   */
END;                                       /*   End of DO WHILE (BEOF) loop   */
PUT SKIP LIST ('OVERFLOW RECORDS LOADED');


        /*   Third stage: statistical results   */


PUT SKIP (4) LIST ('**FILE STATISTICS**');
PUT SKIP (2) LIST ('TOTAL RECORDS IN FILE = ', TOTREC);
PUT SKIP LIST ('TOTAL BLOCKS WITH RECORDS = ', TOTBLOCK);
PUT SKIP LIST ('TOTAL HOME ADDRESS RECORDS = ', TOTHA);
PUT SKIP LIST ('AVERAGE SEARCH LENGTH = ', (TOTHA + SL)/TOTREC);
END;
/*
//GO.SYSIN DD   *
    1000
/*
//GO. TAPEHASH DD DSN = TAPEHASH, DISP = (OLD,KEEP)
//GO.OVFLOW DD DSN = OVFLOW,DISP = (NEW,DELETE),UNIT = DISK,
//                VOL = SER = 345,DCB = (LRECL = 24,RECFM = FB,BLKSIZE = 2400),
//                SPACE = (TRK,n)
```

```
//GO.DRILHASH DD DSN = DRILHASH,DISP = (NEW,CATLG),UNIT = DISK,
//                    VOL = SER = 567,DCB = (BLKSIZE = 1253,RECFM = F,DSORG = DA),
//                    SPACE = (1253,1000)
```

Observe that the above loading program calculates the initial average search length for the file. The method is based on the definition of average search length; that is, that it is the number of accesses required to retrieve every record in random order divided by the total number of records.

The total accesses to retrieve the records in their home addresses will be TOTREC, the total number of home-address records. The number of retrievals to fetch t overflow records k regions away from their home-address region is $t(k + 1)$. Thus, if every time we put overflow records in an overflow block, we compute

$$SL = SL + t(k + 1)$$

at the end of the program, SL will have the number of retrievals needed to fetch all of the overflow records.

Thus TOTHA + SL is the number of accesses to retrieve all records, so that (TOTHA + SL)/TOTREC is the average search length.

Another useful statistic not included in the above program is the maximum search length encountered; it is the maximum value of $k + 1$. It could be obtained by inserting

```
IF MAX < K + 1   THEN MAX = K + 1;
```

in the second processing stage just after the point where K is incremented.

A common pitfall in constructing programs for dealing with hash files that employ progressive overflow is to neglect to allow for the case where the progression in search of blocks with space goes past the last block in the file. When this happens, the search should be permitted to continue from the first block in the file.

Figure 3.13 shows some sample input/output data for the program LOADHASH.

3.3.3 Updating of a REGIONAL(1) Hash File

In general there are two main methods of updating a hash file, and they correspond closely to the two methods of creating hash files. The *single-stage* or *direct* method involves reading in a transaction record, using the hashing routine to determine the region number, and then accessing this and successive regions until the record with the same key as the transaction record is found.

The *two-stage* or *sequential* method first involves processing the transaction records using the hashing routine until they are available with region number attached and sorted in ascending region number. Then both the transaction and hash files are read in sequentially. If a home-address record with the same key as the transaction record is not found, then the transaction record is placed in a temporary overflow file. When all home-address transactions have been processed, the hash file is opened for direct access and the trans-

---

HOLE	—	REG
GA66	—	0
P999	—	0
MA80	—	2
KA90	—	2
G333	—	2
DAV4	—	4
HIB7	—	4
L345	—	4
PEN7	—	4

TAPEHASH

HOLE	—	REG
G333	—	2
L345	—	4
PEN7	—	4

OVFLOW

Region	BTAG	N	TAG	HOLE	—	REG
0	8('0')	2	8('0')	GA66	—	0
			8('0')	P999	—	0
1	8('0')	2	8('0')	L345	—	4
			8('0')	PEN7	—	4
2	8('0')	2	8('0')	MA80	—	2
			8('0')	KA90	—	2
3	8('0')	1	8('0')	G333	—	2
			8('1')			
4	8('0')	2	8('0')	DAV4	—	4
			8('0')	HIB7	—	4

DRILHASH

FIGURE 3.13. *Sample data for the records of the source file* **TAPEHASH,** *the intermediate file* **OVFLOW,** *and output file* **DRILHASH.** *To make the diagram possible, we have assumed that the address size for* **DRILHASH** *is 2 and not 50, as in the creation program* **LOADHASH.** *Overflow records are shaded.*

actions in the overflow file are then processed by the direct method. The two-stage method is illustrated in Figure 3.14.

Unlike file creation programs, file updating programs are run repeatedly, so that it is important to make the correct choice between single- and two-stage updating strategies. If the updating takes place as part of a real-time system, then there is no choice: the direct method is necessary.

When the updating takes place in the batch mode, either method may be used. The trade-off analysis in this case is complex and involves many factors; we shall not go into it in detail here. However, it is clear that if the number of transactions is large and the number of records not in their home addresses not large, then the two-stage method will be the most efficient in many cases. This is so because the sequential reading of the hash file records will rarely cause a block to be read unnecessarily and because the file will be read in cylinders, thus eliminating many seek times.

On the other hand, when the number of transactions is small or when the number of records not in their home addresses is large, then the direct method will clearly be more efficient. The following program illustrates the direct method, chosen for no other reason than that the sequential method was used with the file creation program LOADHASH in Section 3.3.2.

To keep the exercise reasonably realistic, we shall imagine that the transaction

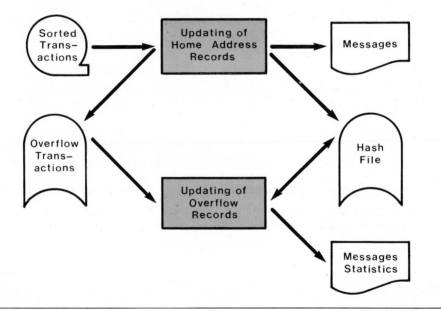

FIGURE 3.14. *The two-stage or sequential method of updating a hash file. It may be employed only in the batch mode. Transaction records are submitted to the hashing routine and sorted on region number at an earlier stage. In the first stage, home-address records are updated with sequential processing. In the second stage, overflow records are updated using direct processing.*

(TRANS) records have the fields HOLE, DEPTH, and COST, and that the file DRILHASH created previously is being updated. The TRANS records describe holes in the process of being drilled, and contain the latest depth and cost data. To include some deletions, we shall assert that holes with depth less than 1000 feet and cost to date greater than $200,000 will be abandoned and therefore deleted from DRILHASH.

UPDATE: PROC OPTIONS (MAIN):

/* 1. This program uses the direct or single stage updating technique to update the hash file DRILHASH (created in the previous subsection) from the transaction file TRANS.

  2. DRILHASH is a REGIONAL(1) file, but has up to 50 records per region or block. The structure of a block is illustrated in Figure 3.12, and corresponds to the structure variable BLOCK used in this program.

  3. The update involves both modification and deletion of records. When a record in a region is deleted, the last record in that region is moved into the deleted record's position, in order to avoid gaps in blocks.   */

```
DCL TRANS FILE RECORD ENV (CONSECUTIVE).
    1 TRAREA,                       /*  Holds a TRANS record   */
      2  HOLE CHAR (6),             /*  Record key   */
      2  DEPTH FIXED BIN (15),      /*  Latest depth data   */
      2  COST FIXED DEC (8);        /*  Latest cost data   */

DCL DRILHASH FILE RECORD ENV (REGIONAL (1)),
    1 BLOCK,                        /*  Holds complete region   */
      1  BTAG BIT (8),
      2  N FIXED BIN (15),          /*  Number of records in region   */
      2  SUBBLOCK (50),
        3 TAG BIT (8),
        3 HOLE CHAR (6),            /*  Record key   */
        3 DEPTH FIXED BIN (15),
        3 COST FIXED DEC (8),
        3 LOC CHAR (3),
        3 REG CHAR (8);            /*  Home address   */

DCL (BEOF, FOUND, OK) BIT (1);      /*  Logical variables   */
DCL KAY PIC '99999999';             /*  Used for region numbers   */
DCL (K, M) 'FIXED DEC (8);          /*  Control variables   */

                        /*   Statistical variables   */
DCL
        (TOTACCESS,                 /*  Total retrievals from HASHDRIL   */
        TOTTRANS                    /*  Total TRANS records read   */
        B)                          /*  Total regions in file   */
```

```
                    FIXED BIN (31);
DCL   (LIMIT,                       /*   Limit length of search   */
       MAX) FIXED BIN (15);         /*   Maximum search length encountered   */
DCL   HASH ENTRY;                   /*   Hashing routine, compiled separately   */


ON ENDFILE (TRANS) BEOF = '0'B;
BEOF = '1'B
OPEN FILE (TRANS) INPUT,
      FILE (DRILHASH) DIRECT UPDATE KEYED;


            /*   We must have size of hash file and maximum length of search   */
                GET LIST (B, LIMIT);
MAX = 0;
TOTACCESS, TOTTRANS = 0;            /*   Statistics   */
READ FILE (TRANS) INTO (TRAREA);


        /*   Main Processing Loop   */


DO WHILE (BEOF);
      TOTTRANS = TOTTRANS + 1;         /*   Statistics   */
      CALL HASH (TRAREA.HOLE, KAY, OK);

      IF OK = '0'B                  /*   Something wrong with hashing   */
      THEN DO;
          PUT SKIP LIST ('POSSIBLE HASHING ERROR', TRAREA.HOLE, KAY);
          TOTTRANS = TOTTRANS − 1;  /*   Dud   */
      END;
      ELSE DO;                       /*   Everything OK   */


                /*   Now retrieve corresponding DRILHASH record   */
      FOUND = '0'B;
      K = −1                        /*   Start of progressive search   */
      DO WHILE ( ¬ FOUND & K + 1 < LIMIT);
          K = K + 1;                /*   We are K regions past home address   */
          IF KAY + K > = B THEN M = −B;   /*   Watch out for end of file   */
                    ELSE M = 0;
          READ FILE (DRILHASH) INTO (BLOCK) KEY (KAY + K + M);
          IF BTAG = '00000000'B THEN      /*   Records in this region   */

                /*   Let us check through them   */
          DO J = 1 TO N WHILE ( ¬ FOUND);
              IF TRAREA.HOLE = BLOCK.HOLE(J) THEN DO;
                  L = J;
                  FOUND = '1'B; END;
      END;                          /*   End of checking thru a block   */
```

```
END;                                    /*   End of progressive search of blocks   */


                        /*   Maybe record was not found   */
    IF ¬ FOUND THEN DO;
        PUT SKIP LIST ('NO RECORD WITH KEY = ', TRAREA.HOLE, 'FOUND');
        TOTTRANS = TOTTRANS − 1;  /*  Cannot use in search length calculation   */
    END;

    ELSE DO;                             /*   Record was found   */
        IF MAX < K THEN MAX = K;        /*   Statistics   */
        TOTACCESS = TOTACCESS + K + 1; /*   Statistics   */


                    /*   Now update found record in BLOCK   */
        IF TRAREA.DEPTH < 1000 & TRAREA.COST > 200000
        THEN
                        /*   Hole abandoned; delete record   */
        IF N = 1 THEN BTAG = '11111111'B;          /*   Region now empty   */
            ELSE DO;                               /*   No gaps allowed in region   */
                SUBBLOCK(L) = SUBBLOCK(N);   /*   Move last record   */
                TAG(N) = '11111111'B;        /*   Delete last record   */
                N = N − 1;                   /*   Update number of records   */
            END;
        ELSE DO;                        /*   Modify record found   */
            BLOCK.DEPTH(L) = TRAREA.DEPTH;
            BLOCK.COST(L)  = TRAREA.COST;
        END;

        WRITE FILE (DRILHASH) FROM (BLOCK) KEYFROM ( KAY + K + M);
    END;                                /*   Of updating found record   */
    END;                                /*   Of all processing for current
                                             transaction   */
    READ FILE (TRANS) INTO (TRAREA);
END;                                    /*   End of DO WHILE (BEOF) loop   */

            /*   We now compute average and max. search lengths   */

PUT SKIP (4) LIST ('**STATISTICS**');
PUT SKIP (2) LIST ('AVERAGE SEARCH LENGTH FOR RETRIEVALS = ',
                TOTACCESS/TOTTRANS,
                'MAX. SEARCH LENGTH = ', MAX);
END;
/*
//GO.SYSIN DD        *
    1000, 20
/*
```

```
//GO.TRANS DD DSN = TRANS,DISP = (OLD,KEEP)
//GO.DRILHASH DD DSN = DRILHASH,DISP = (OLD,KEEP)
```

As with the creation of the hash file, a common error is to neglect to allow for a progressive search that goes past the last region in the file. The search in such cases should continue from the start of the file; that is, at region number zero.

We must also consider the case where the record sought is not in the file; that is, we must limit the search to a reasonable number of accesses. A reasonable rule of thumb is to permit searches up to twice the longest known search length for the file. This maximum or longest known search length can be printed out when the file is created, as mentioned earlier, and, because it will tend to increase as the file ages, also following each update.

In the above program, the quantity limiting the length of search, LIMIT, is read in at the start of the program.

Finally, as illustrated in the file creation and updating programs in this section, the use of blocks with REGIONAL(1) files does involve some extra programming and a little extra time for data transmission. However, this is not excessive and the reward is much increased space utilization and reduced search length.

3.3.4 Growth of Hash Files

Growth of hash files is something of a problem. The obvious way for a hash file to grow is by allowing the number of addressable regions to increase. The trouble with this is that if the increase is significant, a new hashing routine will be required, and the whole process of testing and selection may need to be repeated. The file will, of course, have to be reloaded.

Another obvious method of growth is to start out with a low load factor, and thus allow the growth of the file to bring the load factor up to an acceptable level in the course of time. The disadvantage is clearly the wasted storage space at the start.

A more subtle, and probably the best, method is to permit the address capacity to grow, with the number of addresses remaining constant. Thus all loading and update programs would have to be written to allow for the blocking factor (as in LOADHASH or UPDATE) to be read in as a control parameter (see Exercise 16). Of course, at the point where an increase in the address capacity became necessary, the file would have to be reloaded. A variation [Fagin, 1979] is to allow the capacity of a separate overflow area to increase.

3.4 RANDOM DISTRIBUTION FUNCTION DERIVATION

The random distribution function in tabular form is useful for design of hash files, as we have seen. The following derivation may be skipped without loss of continuity and is included only for the sake of completeness.

We shall suppose that r records are being assigned to R addresses or regions, and that the assignment is random; that is, as a record is assigned, each region has an equal probability of receiving a record.

The probability that region K, a definite region, will be assigned a record following the hashing operation on its key is

$$p = \frac{1}{R}$$

The probability that records $C_1, C_2, \ldots, C_x$, *and only these records,* will be assigned to the region with region number K is

$$\left(\frac{1}{R}\right)^x \left(1 - \frac{1}{R}\right)^{r-x} \tag{1}$$

This expression needs some explanation. Suppose we consider only the assignment of one definite record, such as C_1. We want the probability that *just this record* will be assigned to region K. This probability will be the product of the probability that the record will be assigned,

$$\frac{1}{R}$$

and the probability that the other records will be assigned to the remaining regions,

$$\left(1 - \frac{1}{R}\right)^{r-1}$$

since the probability that one record will not be assigned to the region K is

$$\left(1 - \frac{1}{R}\right)$$

Thus the probability that the record C_1 will be assigned to region K is

$$\frac{1}{R}\left(1 - \frac{1}{R}\right)^{r-1}$$

Similarly, the probability that the x definite records $C_1, C_2, \ldots, C_x$ will be assigned to the region K and that other records will be assigned elsewhere is the product of the probability that the records will be assigned to region K,

$$\left(\frac{1}{R}\right)^x$$

and the probability that the other records will not go to region K,

$$\left(1 - \frac{1}{R}\right)^{r-x}$$

which gives us Expression 1. This is illustrated in Figure 3.15.

However, Expression 1 is the probability that x given records go to K. We need the probability that any x, but no more than x, records will come to the region K. The number of groups of x records we can have in the total r records is the same as the number of ways we can take x records out of r records; that is,

$$\frac{r!}{(r-x)!\,x!} \tag{2}$$

Thus the probability that any x but no more than x records come to a given region (K) is

$$\frac{r!}{(r-x)!x!}\left(\frac{1}{R}\right)^{x}\left(1 - \frac{1}{R}\right)^{r-x} \tag{3}$$

obtained by multiplying Expressions 1 and 2.

Thus we have the probability that any region K will get x, and no more than x, records.

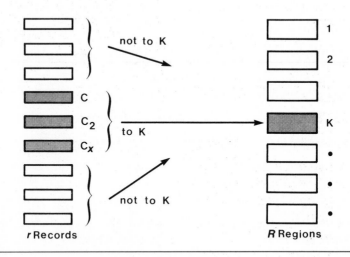

FIGURE 3.15.   *The core of the derivation of the random distribution expression consists in pinpointing the probability that a given (but not any) x records (such as $C_1, \ldots, C_x$) from the r records, and not any other than those x records, will be assigned to a given region K.*

If we multiply by the total number of regions R, we have the number of regions with x records, which is what we are seeking; we shall call the distribution $F(x)$:

$$F(x) = \frac{Rr!}{(r - x)!x!}\left(\frac{1}{R}\right)^x\left(1 - \frac{1}{R}\right)^{r-x}$$

(4)

This expression can be simplified, if we allow that r and R are both large in relation to x, which will be true in practice. Thus Expression 4 becomes

$$F(x) = \frac{Rr^x}{x!}\left(\frac{1}{R}\right)^x\left(1 - \frac{1}{R}\right)^r$$

Expanding using the binomial theorem, the above reduces to

$$F(x) = R\left(\frac{r}{R}\right)^x\left(\frac{1}{x!}\right)\exp\left(-\frac{r}{R}\right)$$

(5)

which is the standard expression for a random or Poisson distribution.

EXERCISES

1. Extend the table in Table 3.2 to include the case where r/R is 4.

2. Prepare a small file of r company records. The record key is the company name, and for the purpose of the exercise it is sufficient for this to be the only field. The company records are to be stored in a hash file with 1000 addresses ($R = 1000$). Write a selection of hashing routines and compare the resulting distributions. Observe the effect of varying r for a given routine.

3. Add the entry for the case where r/R is 4 and b is 5 to Table 3.4.

4. Obtain the curve for $b = 10$ in Figure 3.8.

5. Suppose we have a hash file employing the separate (linked) overflow area technique, but where the address size in the home-address area is h and in the overflow area it is f. Derive an expression for the average search length just after initial loading.

6. Write a new version of the program UPDATE from Section 3.3.3 which, in addition to modification and deletion, also carries out insertion of new records.

7. List the relative performance merits of direct versus sequential loading of hash files with progressive overflow.

8. A hash file is loaded as a REGIONAL(1) file, but without an accompanying calculation of the average search length. The file extends over 100,000 regions and the region

(or address) capacity is unity. Among other fields, each record in the hash file contains a field TAG, indicating possible deleted status, a field SKEY, containing the record source key, and a field REG containing the record's home address, which is the region number resulting from hashing the field SKEY. Write a short program that reads only the hash file and outputs the average search length. The overflow system is progressive.

9. Repeat Exercise 8, but this time the program should output the maximum search length for the file.

10. A hash file has 75,000 records hashed to 100,000 addresses. Each address can hold only 1 record, the overflow system is progressive, and the hash routine is a radix transformation.

   a. Applying the curves of Figure 3.7, estimate the average search length for the file just after initial loading.

   b. Give an estimate for the average search length when the file comes to a state of dynamic equilibrium.

11. In a certain hash file, 100,000 records are assigned to 50,000 addresses by means of a radix transformation of the source key. The capacity of each address is 4 records.

   a. Using Table 3.2, compute the total number of records in the home address just after initial loading.

   b. If the overflow records from this file are placed in a separate overflow file with a block factor of 1 and chained together, use Table 3.2 to compute the total number of accesses required to access all of these overflow records in random order.

   c. From the correct answers to (a) and (b), compute the average search length for this file.

12. As in Exercise 11, 100,000 records are assigned to 50,000 addresses by means of a radix transformation of the source key. Overflow records from a given address are placed in a separate overflow file and chained together. The block factor for both the home-address file and the overflow file is 4. Using Table 3.2, compute the total number of accesses required to access the overflow records in random order just after initial loading of the file.

13. Rewrite the hash file loading program LOADHASH with the address capacity equal to 1 using chained progressive overflow.

14. Redesign the structure variable BLOCK from the hash file loading program, LOAD-HASH, to allow for chained progressive overflow to be used instead of progressive overflow.

15. A variation of the progressive overflow technique is to combine it with the use of two hashing routines, such as HASHA and HASHB. HASHA is applied first; if the address generated has no empty space, then HASHB is applied. Only if the new address generated contains no empty space is the progressive overflow technique applied.

Assume that **LOADHASH** is to be rewritten with an address capacity of 1, but using **HASHA** and **HASHB**, and progressive overflow as described above.

a. Design a suitable structure variable from which the hash file records will be transmitted.

b. Write the loading program, with the hash file open for **DIRECT OUTPUT**.

16. Rewrite the programs **LOADHASH** and **UPDATE** to allow for the growth of the hash file by means of an increasing address capacity or block factor.

REFERENCES

Bratbergsengen, K., K. Hofstad, and K. Wibe, 1973, *Filsystemer og Databaser,* Tapir Publishing Co., Trondheim, Norway (in Norwegian).

Fagin, R., and others, 1979, "Extendible Hashing—A Fast Access Method for Dynamic Files," *ACM Trans. on Data Base Systems,* **4**(3):315–44.

Horowitz, E., and S. Sahni, 1977, *Fundamentals of Data Structures,* Pitman Press, London, England.

IBM, 1976a, *OS PL/1 Optimizing Compiler, Programmer's Guide,* Order Form GC33–0009.

IBM, 1976b, *OS PL/1 Optimizing Compiler, Language Reference Manual,* Order Form FC33–0006.

Knuth, D. E., 1973, *The Art of Computer Programming 3, Sorting and Searching,* Addison-Wesley, Reading, Mass.

Lum, V. Y., P. S. J. Yuen, and M. Dodd, 1971, "Key-to-Address Transform Techniques, A Fundamental Performance Study on Large Existing Formatted Files," *CACM,* **14**(4):228–39.

Lum, V. Y., 1973, "General Performance Analysis of Key-to-Address Transformation Methods Using an Abstract File Concept," *CACM,* **16**(10):603–12.

Maurer, W. D., and T. G. Lewis, 1975, "Hash Table Methods," *Computing Surveys,* **7**(1):5–19.

Peterson, W. W., 1957, "Addressing for Random Access Storage," *IBM J. R&D,* **1**(2):130–46.

Rindfleisch, D. H., 1978, *Utilizing System 360/370 OS and VS Job Control Language and Utility Programs,* Prentice-Hall, Englewood Cliffs, N.J.

Tainiter, R., 1963, "Addressing for Random Access Storage with Multiple Bucket Capacities," *J. ACM,* **10**(3):307–15.

Index
Sequential
Files

4

As we have seen from our study of hash files, one of their major disadvantages is the impossibility of processing them sequentially in key sequence order. Hash files may be read in addressable region number sequence but not in key sequence.

This problem is solved by the use of *index sequential files* [Gotlieb, 1978; Ghosh, 1977; Rus, 1979; Tremblay, 1976]. Such files also have the advantage of easily permitting growth, which—as we have seen—is another difficulty with hash files. Unfortunately, they are also slower than hash files.

4.1 BASIC PRINCIPLES

4.1.1 Basic File Organization

In principle, index sequential organization is very simple, but in practice there are often many details to consider before such a file can be created. The principle of this file organization is illustrated in Figure 4.1. We could imagine that 40 records with keys ranging from 0 to 99 are written in ascending key sequence order into 20 addresses going from 0 to 19. To keep the example realistic, we might suppose that the REGIONAL(1) file organization described in the last chapter was used, so that the 20 addresses are the first 20 region numbers in the file. We further imagine the block factor to be 2.

There is no relationship present between the record keys and the addresses. However, it is possible to arrange the regions or data blocks into *block intervals;* for instance,

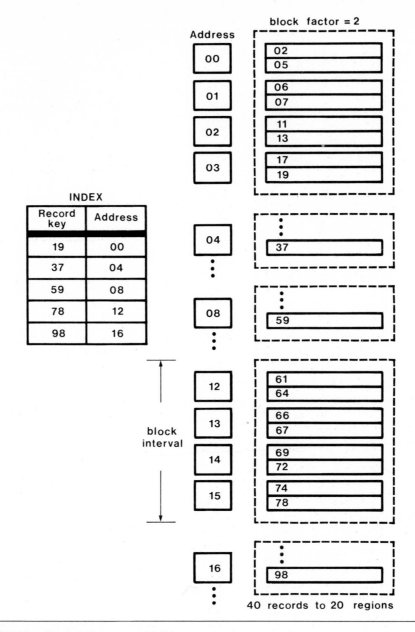

FIGURE 4.1. *Simple index sequential file constructed using* REGIONAL(1) *file organization and an index table. The records are blocked and the blocks grouped into block intervals. The index contains the address and largest key for each block interval.*

intervals of 4 data blocks each. If a table is made from the highest key in an interval and the address of the first data block in the same interval, as shown in Figure 4.1, we can call this table an *index* to the file.

This index could be easily constructed when the file is first created. It can then be used to retrieve records directly. Suppose we wish to retrieve the record with key 74. From a search of the index, the required record is found to be in block interval 4, which has 4 regions, and the first of these regions is at region number 12. Regions 12, 13, 14, and 15 can then be read and the record obtained.

In our simple example above, the index could be in main memory when being used, so that it may be quickly searched. However, if the index were very large, it could pay to construct an index to the index; that is, a second and higher-level index. The (lower-level) index could then be stored in an external storage device as a direct-access file. In practice, up to 4 levels of index are used. A theory of indexes is given in Section 4.4.

There is a major problem as far as this simple example is concerned. We can see that the file can be processed sequentially, and—by means of the index—also directly. The big problem is what to do with insertions. There are two main techniques for dealing with the problem: *separate overflow area technique* and *block interval splitting technique*. These methods distinguish the two main types of index sequential file in use today.

The Separate Overflow Area Technique   The separate overflow area technique involves placing overflow records in an overflow area, in such a way that key sequence order is maintained. The records overflowing from a given block interval are chained together, and the index is expanded to permit reference both to the highest key in an interval and the highest key in the overflow chain for the interval. To avoid having too many records in the overflow area, on initial loading of the file the block intervals are sometimes not completely filled to allow space for additions. This overflow area usually necessitates a third, or overflow, file, with the accompanying overhead of additional details. (Thus an indexed sequential file can in reality consist of three physical storage files or *datasets:* an *index* dataset, a *prime-data area* dataset, and an *overflow area* dataset.)

A major disadvantage of this method of handling insertions is that the performance of the file decreases drastically as records are placed in the overflow chains; that is, the search length increases. Partial or sparse filling of the prime data area on loading cannot wholly solve this problem, as it may frequently be necessary to insert a large clump of records with keys in between existing consecutive keys in the file. An additional problem with such sparse files is that the increased size of the prime data area will increase the size of the index, which may increase the number of index levels and reduce overall performance.

The Block Interval Splitting Technique   The other method of handling the insertion problem involves what is known as splitting of the block intervals. When the file is first created, empty space is left in each block interval, as with the first method. However, in addition, empty space is left in the file for empty block intervals. When a block interval is filled by insertions, half the records from the full interval are placed in an empty interval. The full interval is thus split in two. The two intervals are chained so that sequential order is maintained, and an extra element is placed in the index to allow for the new interval. This method is also used for manipulating B-trees (see Section 4.4).

With this method, performance is quite good as far as retrieval is concerned, and there is little deterioration as a result of insertions. However, insertions can be time consuming, especially when interval splitting takes place.

System/370 Index Sequential File Organizations   With the System/370, we have two types of index sequential file [IBM, 1976a; 1976b], and both may be used with PL/1 and COBOL. They are based on the two major methods of handling overflow discussed above. We have ISAM (*Index Sequential Access Method*) files in which overflow records are placed in chains in an overflow area, which may be a separate file. We also have VSAM (*Virtual Sequential Access Method*), which allows insertions to be handled by permitting the block intervals of the file (known in VSAM files as *control intervals*) to be split when full. We shall first look at these two types of index sequential file in some detail, then consider indexes, and finally investigate the PL/1 language for manipulating an index sequential file.

4.2 ISAM FILE ORGANIZATION

The structure of an ISAM file is shown in Figure 4.2. When an ISAM file is created, records are written out in ascending order by key sequence in the prime data area. The file is specified in cylinder sizes and the minimum file occupies one cylinder [IBM, 1976b; Tremblay, 1976].

The records may be blocked, with fixed or variable length. However, the format of a data block is count-key data, as described in Chapter 1. The highest key in a data subblock, that is, the key of the last record in the data subblock, is accordingly placed in the key subblock.

The *block interval* (see Figure 4.1) referenced by an index entry is always a disk track. Thus the entries of the lowest level index reference complete tracks; this lowest level index is called a *track index*. When the file is in use, the track index remains in external storage, and—to limit seeks—a separate track index is built for each cylinder of the file. Each track index is placed on the first track of the cylinder which it serves, as may be seen from Figure 4.2.

We see, therefore, that in each cylinder of prime data area, we first have a track index immediately followed by the records. Last of all, there may be a cylinder overflow area which is used for overflow records from the tracks of that cylinder.

Thus the simplest ISAM file we could build would occupy one cylinder, with a part of the first track being used for a track index, the last few tracks for an overflow area, and the remaining tracks for the data blocks of the prime data area [Rindfleisch, 1978]. The DD statement for such a simple file would be as follows.

```
//BETA   DD   DSN = BETA(PRIME),UNIT = 3350,VOL = SER = 123,
//                SPACE = (CYL,(1,,0)),DISP = (NEW,CATLG),
//                DCB = (DSORG = IS,RECFM = FB,LRECL = 80,BLKSIZE = 2000,[1]
```

---

[1]*Readers are reminded that block size* (BLKSIZE) *specified in JCL is actually the length of the data subblock.*

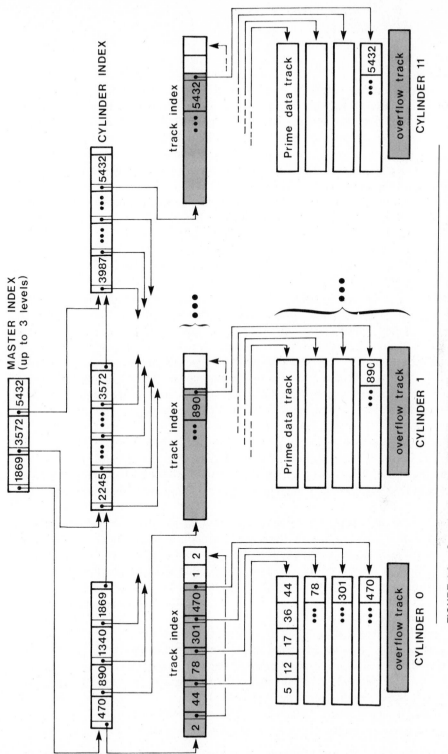

FIGURE 4.2. *Organization of an ISAM file. Overflow records are handled by overflow tracks in each cylinder and may also be handled by a separate overflow-record cylinder (not shown). The diagram assumes no overflow records. While not shown, the track index has an additional component to deal with overflow records (see Figure 4.3).*

```
//                    KEYLEN = 6,RKP = 10,
//                    OPTCD = YL,
//                    CYLOFL = 2)
```

The statement specifies a PRIME data area for the file BETA, which occupies one cylinder in which there are 2 overflow tracks (CYLOFL = 2). The file organization is ISAM, as specified by DSORG = IS. Within a record the length of the key (KEYLEN) is specified to be 6, and the key starts at byte number 11 of the record (RKP = 10). The DCB parameter OPTCD = YL specifies that the (2) overflow tracks are to be in the same cylinder as the other records, and that dummy records are handled automatically by the access methods (for example, a delete statement in a PL/1 program would result in (8)'1'B being placed in the first byte of the record specified).

However, an ISAM file is normally more complex than that specified above. For a large file, a cylinder index can be built in addition to the track index to shorten the time required to search through all the track indexes. In addition, a higher-level index can be built (the *master index* with up to three levels) to facilitate a faster search of the cylinder index. These additional indexes can be incorporated in the PRIME data area or in a separate dataset requiring a separate DD statement.

Furthermore, in addition to having overflow tracks for each cylinder of PRIME data area, it is possible to have a separate overflow area for records from all cylinders on another cylinder or on another dataset. Thus, depending on the options chosen, the file may require 1, 2, or 3 DD statements to specify it fully. The reader will now appreciate the earlier statement that many details may have to be dealt with before an index sequential file can be set up. We shall not concern ourselves further with these specification details, except where they reflect overall processing strategy. However, we still need to consider the method of handling overflow to appreciate the problems it causes.

4.2.1 Overflow Records

As we have seen (Figure 4.2), the overflow records are placed in cylinder overflow tracks and possibly in a separate overflow area in another cylinder as well, depending on the file specification.

Regardless of which kind of overflow area is used, records that overflow from a given track are chained together in the overflow area. Normally when a file is created, some space for insertions is left on each track (by writing out dummy records). When a record is inserted, the other records on the track are moved up to allow for the inserted record, so that sequential key order is maintained. If, on moving up, a valid record (but not a dummy) is forced off the track, it is placed in the overflow area as part of a chain of records forced off the track earlier.

This situation is depicted in Figure 4.3, which shows a track of (prime) records and the associated overflow records. The track index relating to this track is also shown. The overflow records are not physically contiguous in the overflow area (which is not shown). They are normally dispersed among other records belonging to other overflow chains; they also tend to be spread over different overflow tracks. For overflow records the block factor is always unity.

To permit direct retrieval of both the overflow records and prime records, the index

---

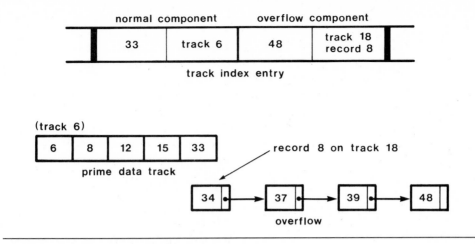

FIGURE 4.3. ISAM *track index entry for a track of prime-data records and associated overflow chain. The records of the chain are physically distributed throughout either the cylinder overflow area or the separate overflow area. The chain above starts at record 8 on track 18.*

entry for a track has two components, usually referred to as the *normal* and *overflow* components. Each component is a count-key data block. The normal component of the index gives the track number and the key of the last record on the track. The overflow component gives the key of the last record of the chain of overflow records (the first record of the chain has the lowest key in the chain), together with the track number and relative position of the first record of the chain. This is illustrated in Figure 4.3.

As already mentioned, the records of the overflow chains have a block factor of unity so that it can cost up to n accesses to traverse n records along a chain in search of an overflow record. However, it is a continuously executing channel program that carries out the search, so that several records of the chain may well be searched in one access. Nevertheless, performance will deteriorate with the size of the overflow chains.

To see this more clearly, let us consider the following example. Suppose the file has on average $5N$ records assigned to a track, of which N are in the overflow area. To retrieve the N overflow records in any order can require

$$\frac{N(N + 1)}{2}$$

accesses altogether. To retrieve the $4N$ prime records in any order can require $4N$ accesses. Thus the total accesses to retrieve all the records can be

$$4N + \frac{N(N + 1)}{2} \quad \text{or} \quad \frac{N^2 + 9N}{2}$$

Thus the search length for a track can be

$$\frac{N^2 + 9N}{10N} \quad \text{or} \quad \frac{N + 9}{10}$$

obtained by dividing the total number of accesses by the total number of records.

To get a typical value for N, let us further imagine that the records are each 120 bytes long with a block factor of 25, and that the disk is a 3350 unit. Since the format is count-key data, we need the key length too; let us assume it is 10 bytes. Then the number of data blocks to a track is the quotient

$$\frac{19,254}{[267 + (10 + 3000)]}$$

using the expression for 3350 track utilization developed in Chapter 1 (we could also use a table such as Table 1.1). From this we can determine that there can be a maximum of 5 data blocks per track, or 125 records to a track. Out of these 125 records, it would be realistic to assume that 25 were dummy or deleted, so that there are 100 records on the track.

Thus with 120 byte records and a block factor of 25, we could assume 100 records on a track. But in the search length calculation above, we assumed $4N$ records on a track. Therefore we could use $N = 25$ in the expression for search length above.

This gives a search length of 3.4; that is, it is the search length for a track where one-fifth of the records assigned to the track are in an overflow chain and one-fifth of the available record space on the track is filled by deleted or dummy records. This search length may appear large, but we must remember that it is a worst-case figure, since an ISAM channel program searching the overflow chain may actually undertake fewer accesses. It is difficult to estimate a realistic best-case figure for the search length, because this will depend very much on the character of the overflow chains. However, in some rare cases when the records of an overflow chain are on one track in the right order, it may be possible for the channel to search the chain in one access.

The above calculation of search length can be repeated for different proportions of records in the overflow area. The results used to produce the worst-case curves for search length are shown in Figure 4.4.

In the above calculations, we have ignored the effect of the necessity to access the index before the actual records are accessed. Since the cylinder and track indexes are normally not in main memory (the highest-level index can be in main memory in an ISAM file), there will be at least one, and often two, extra accesses associated with each retrieval. However, it is difficult to put a precise figure on the effect of accessing the indexes; with ISAM, in order to improve performance as much as possible, a continuously executing channel program controls processing of the index levels in external storage. This is possible with ISAM because pointers in index entries point to disk addresses, which may be used directly by a channel program to efficiently manage the operation of a disk controller.

Nevertheless, it is clear that performance will deteriorate rapidly with increasing overflow chain lengths. This disadvantage requires careful monitoring of ISAM file performance and quite frequent reorganization, whenever performance drops below acceptable levels for the application. However, the problem may be avoided by using the block-interval splitting method of handling insertions. With System/370, VSAM files are a well-known example of this method.

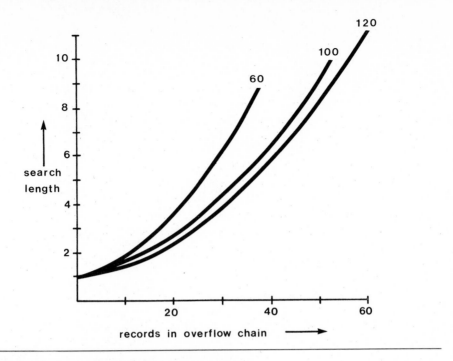

FIGURE 4.4. *The curves show how the worst-case search length for an* **ISAM** *prime-data track increases with the number of records from the track in the overflow chain. The three curves are for the cases of 60, 100, and 120 records on a disk unit track. The curves are the worst cases because the channel program searching an overflow chain with* n *records may in some cases require fewer than the* n *accesses assumed by the curves. The contribution of the index accesses to the search length is not included. On a 3350 track, there can be at most one hundred and twenty-five 120-byte records with a block factor of 25.*

4.3 VSAM FILE ORGANIZATION

There are, in fact, two kinds of **VSAM** file structure: *key-sequenced structure* and *entry-sequenced structure* [IBM, 1976]. Only the key-sequenced structure is an index sequential file; we shall confine our discussion to this structure. (For tutorial purposes, we ignore the **VSAM** facility for multiple indexes, mentioned in Section 5.1.2.)

The structure of a (key-sequenced) **VSAM** file is shown in Figure 4.5. The block interval discussed in the first section of this chapter is now called a *control interval* (CI) and—unlike the case of **ISAM** files—is not necessarily a track. Thus **VSAM** files are to a large degree device independent [IBM, 1976c; Martin, 1977].

The records in a control interval are physically maintained in key sequence by means of the record key. When the file is created initially, records are thus written out in ascending key sequence, just as with an **ISAM** file.

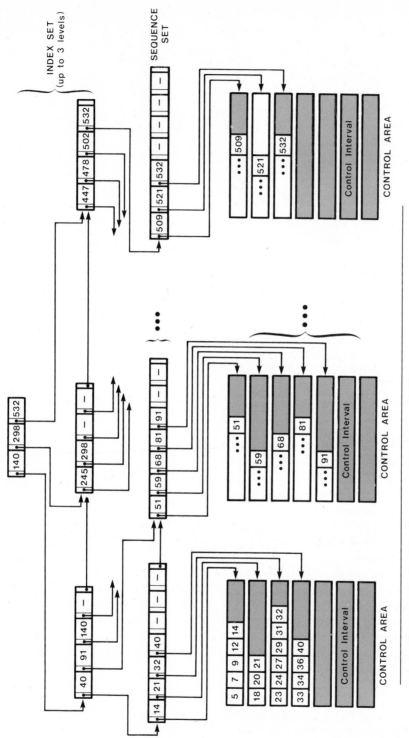

FIGURE 4.5. VSAM *file structure. The records (numbered) reside in control intervals, and a group of control intervals constitutes a control area. Shaded parts of control intervals are empty. The structure of a control interval is shown in Figure 4.9. In addition to the control areas containing records, there will normally also be empty control areas (three are implied in the diagram). Note that the number of entries per index block at any index level may vary, as in a B-tree.*

The control intervals are grouped together into *control areas*. A control area is quite often a cylinder; however, it may be specified to be smaller. The lowest-level index is associated with a control area and is called a *sequence set*. The sequence set corresponds to the track index with ISAM files, and the entries contain the highest keys in the control intervals of the control area associated with the particular sequence set [Wagner, 1973].

As can be seen from Figure 4.5, the higher-level indexes consist of *index blocks*[1] of key-pointer pairs. A key-pointer pair contains the highest key in the index block pointed to in the next lowest index level, where the block pointed to is another index block or control interval in the file.

So far, except for the fact that control intervals do not correspond to a track, the VSAM key-sequenced file is superficially similar to the ISAM file. However, when a VSAM file is loaded, free space is left to allow for insertions. The precise amount and character of the space is specified in the JCL for the file. Two parameters are required: One gives the fraction of each loaded control interval to be left free and the other gives the fraction of control intervals in each control area to be left free [Keehn, 1974].

4.3.1 Insertions and Splitting

When a record is inserted into the file, it is physically placed in key sequence in the correct control interval; if necessary, all the records in that control interval with higher keys are moved up. To do this, the control interval is first read and then rewritten.

If, on an attempt to insert a record, there is no free space in the correct control interval, then the control interval is split. Half the records (those with highest keys) in the control interval are placed in one of the free control intervals in the control area. In addition, the affected sequence set (that is, lowest index level) entry is updated, and a new entry (for the new control interval) is inserted by moving up existing entries.

Were there no free control intervals available for control interval splitting, then the control area itself is split, and half the control intervals in the old control area are written into the new control area. At the same time, a new sequence set for the new control area is created, and the higher-level indexes and old sequence set are adjusted accordingly.

Because splitting is a time-consuming operation, one consequence of this method of handling insertions is that insertion is, on the average, slowed down. However, retrieval is not slowed, compared with the overflow chain method (ISAM), and because normally there will be more retrievals than insertions, it is reasonable to assume that the block-interval (that is, control interval) splitting method (as in VSAM) is superior. One consequence is that VSAM is widely used with data base files.

It is not difficult to carry out some useful calculations on the effect of block-interval splitting on insertion time [Keehn, 1974]. To make the calculations relevant, we may imagine that we have a VSAM file with R control intervals that are partly filled, just after initial loading. Furthermore, we imagine that each of these R control intervals has room for b records before a control interval split is necessary. We shall ignore the less-common need for a control area split.

---

[1]*Readers should note that the term* block *is used in three senses in this chapter. We have a* data *block, which exists on a track in count-key data format. We have a* block *interval, which is a collection of data blocks and is referenced by an index entry. Finally, we have an* index *block, which is a collection of index entries referenced by a higher-level index entry.*

We can now consider the insertions to take place randomly; the situation is precisely analogous to the hash file example of records being assigned randomly to R addresses that can hold b records. The only difference is that assignment of more than b records results in a control interval split. Hence we can use the Poisson distribution to find the number of splits as a function of the number of records (r) inserted (that is, assigned in the hashing case). The problem is thus the same as finding the number of addresses that give rise to overflow as a function of the number of records assigned; we apply the Poisson distribution function $F(x)$ (see Figure 4.6).

When r records have been inserted, the number of original control intervals which, without splits, would have been assigned x records is $F(x)$. Hence the number that will have to be split is

$$\sum_{x=b+1} F(x)$$

which we may write as $S(r, R, b)$. Thus S gives us the number of splits as a function of r, R, and b.

This function is illustrated graphically in Figure 4.7. The curve gives the percentage of the original partly filled control intervals which have been split, as a function of the average number of insertions per original control interval. As we should expect, the number of completed splits rises steeply at relatively low insertion levels when b is small; that is, when insufficient free space has been specified for the original control intervals. For the user who needs to keep splitting to a minimum, a good rule of thumb might be to leave about 40% more free space in each control interval at loading than will actually be needed to accommodate insertions. This can be seen from the curves in Figure 4.7.

Let us now suppose that the time for a normal insertion is t and that for a control interval split is T. During a period when we have a small number, dr, of insertions, we shall have a small number, dS, of splits. Thus dS/dr is the split rate, in splits per insertion, and can be obtained from the slopes of the curves in Figure 4.7. It can thus be seen that

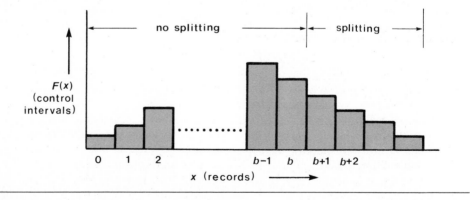

FIGURE 4.6. *Application of the Poisson distribution function to determine the number of split control intervals after insertion of* r *records. After initial loading, there is assumed to be space for* b *records unused in each control interval.*

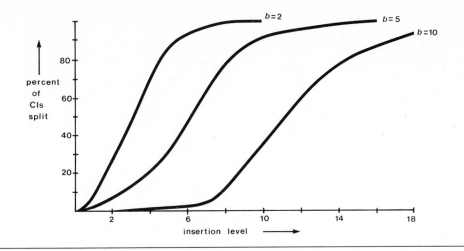

FIGURE 4.7. *The curves show the percentage of the original (partly filled) control intervals that have been split as a function of the average number of insertions per original control interval. The curves cover the three cases where the original free space per control interval has room for 2, 5, and 10 records. Insertions are assumed to occur randomly, and the curves are deduced from the Poisson distribution.*

the split rate starts out at zero at low insertion levels, climbs to a maximum as the original control intervals are filled up, and then falls off to zero again. Of course, we are considering only first-generation splits; the possibility of a second-generation split is ignored.

The total time to insert dr records is therefore

$$TdS + tdr \quad \text{or} \quad \left(T\frac{ds}{dr} + t\right)dr$$

so that the average insertion time per record is

$$T\frac{dS}{dr} + t$$

From this expression, the curves in Figure 4.8 are derived.

These curves give the average insertion time per record plotted against the insertion level expressed in terms of records inserted per original control interval. The insertion time without splitting (t) is assumed to be 50 milliseconds, and the time to split a control interval is assumed to be 300 milliseconds. As would be expected from the fact that the split rate reaches a maximum and then falls off again, the average insertion time, as a function of insertion level, does the same.

The three curves are for different values of free space in the original control intervals, expressed in terms of the number of remaining records b which can be inserted without a split. It is clear that low values for b cause the insertion time to climb rapidly at low

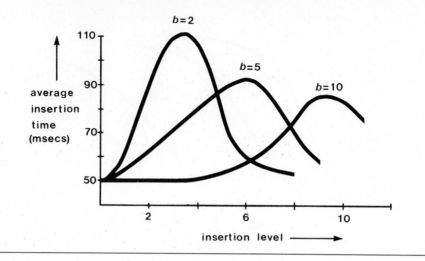

FIGURE 4.8. *Average insertion time per record versus insertion level expressed in terms of records inserted per original control interval. The curves cover the cases where the original free space per control interval has room for 2, 5, and 10 records. Only first-generation splitting is assumed. The curves assume values of 50 and 300 milliseconds for t and T, respectively (see text).*

insertion levels. In addition, it should be remembered that these curves are the result of a theoretical analysis that neglects both control-area splitting and second-generation control-interval splitting, so that in practice the situation will probably be worse. It is therefore important to specify the free space carefully to optimize performance for a given application.

4.4 THEORY OF INDEXES

So far in our discussion of ISAM and VSAM, we have concentrated on overflow techniques, since the two access methods are excellent examples of the two main methods of handling overflow in an index sequential file. We have not discussed the indexes of these index sequential files in any detail, although there is considerable difference between them. In the following discussion of indexes, we treat the subject from a more theoretical point of view, and look at some of the considerations involved in the design of indexes. To begin with, we can usefully distinguish between two kinds of indexes, *one-level indexes* and *multiple-level indexes*. Multiple-level indexes are most commonly used.

4.4.1 One-Level Indexes

The simple index given in the example in Section 4.1 and illustrated in Figure 4.1 is a one-level index. As we saw, to retrieve a record from the file, the index must be searched to obtain the address of the block interval containing the record.

We are always interested in keeping the average search length as low as possible; and since at least with VSAM, only one file access will be necessary to retrieve a record once we have obtained its address from the index, the number of accesses needed to search the index becomes the important design parameter that must be minimized. The simplest way to reduce the time spent searching the index would be to keep the index in main storage, but if we assume we are dealing with fairly large files, this must be ruled out, either because of limitations in main memory space or because it would give rise to excessive paging (see Chapter 1).

This means that the index has to be stored either as a sequential file or as a hash file. We take the sequential file layout first and assume that the records of the (index) file are blocked. There are three main ways of searching through a sequential file to obtain just one record.

a. *Linear search*

The *linear search* simply involves accessing the data blocks in the index one after another. If N is the number of data blocks in the index, the average number of accesses T required will be:

$$T = \frac{N}{2} \qquad (1)$$

b. *Step search*

With the *step search*, we step through the index several data blocks at a time until we come to a data block where the largest key value is greater than the value of the search key. The preceding blocks in the step are then searched sequentially until the desired data block is retrieved.

Let Z be the step size, and suppose that N is the number of data blocks in the index. The total number of steps T required will then be:

$$T = \frac{1}{2}\left(\frac{N}{Z} + 1\right) + \frac{Z - 1}{2}$$

The first term gives the average number of accesses while stepping forward Z data blocks at a time, while the second gives the average number of accesses stepping backward one data block at a time. There is clearly a minimum value for T at some value of Z, so taking

$$\frac{dT}{dZ} = \frac{-N}{2Z^2} + \frac{1}{2} = 0$$

we see that T is least when $Z = \sqrt{N}$, and that the minimum value of T is

$$T_{min} = \sqrt{N} \qquad (2)$$

This result is better than that obtained using a linear search, but if the index had 100 data blocks, we would still need 10 file accesses to search the index. Of course, for the method to be used at all, the index would have to be stored on a direct-access device, for example, as a PL/1 **REGIONAL(1)** file.

c. *Binary search*

The *binary search* method entails accessing the index at the halfway point. Then, if the key value here is less than the search key, a new access is made halfway between this point and the end of the index, otherwise halfway from this midpoint to the beginning of the file. This halving process is continued until only one data block is left, which must be the required data block if the index is in sequential order. Obviously, the required data block may be found prior to the end of the halving process.

If we assume that the halving process goes all the way to the end, if there are T halving operations

$$\frac{N}{2^T} = 1$$

where N is the total number of blocks. Solving for T gives

$$T = \log_2(N)$$

Because we check for equality of the search key with the index key during the halving process, there is a possibility that the process will not go all the way to the end. If we take this probability into account, we get as an approximate value

$$T = \log_2(N) - 1 \tag{3}$$

This result is well known [Martin, 1977; Gotlieb, 1978], and while it is more encouraging than that obtained for step searching of the index, it is hardly acceptable for larger indexes. Even an index of about 130 data blocks would require 6 file accesses to retrieve a given key. As with the case of a step search, the index would have to be on a direct-access device.

We are thus forced to conclude that storing a one-level index as a sequential file is not going to result in a low average search length. The remaining possibility is to store the index as a hash file. As we saw in the previous chapter, a well-designed hash file can have a search length close to unity. The reader may wonder what advantage an index sequential file with a hash index file has over a straight hash file. After all, the hash index file will, at best, have a search length close to 2, while the hash file could have search length close to 1.

The answer is that the hash file cannot be processed sequentially, while the hash index file can be. The hash index file is still quite fast, and sometimes it can pay to use this almost hybrid file organization.

However, the standard solution to the problem of fast access to the index is the multiple-level index, which we shall now examine.

4.4.2 Multiple-Level Indexes

There are two main types of multiple-level index: the type based on the (e-order) *balanced tree* and the type based on the *B-tree*. The ISAM index is a balanced tree, while the VSAM index is based to a considerable extent on the B-tree. We look at them in turn.

Balanced-Tree Indexes   In Figure 4.9a we have a small-scale example of an index with a structure widely referred to as a balanced tree [Augenstein, 1979; Gotlieb, 1978; Knuth, 1973]. The index has E entries with address pointers that point directly to the

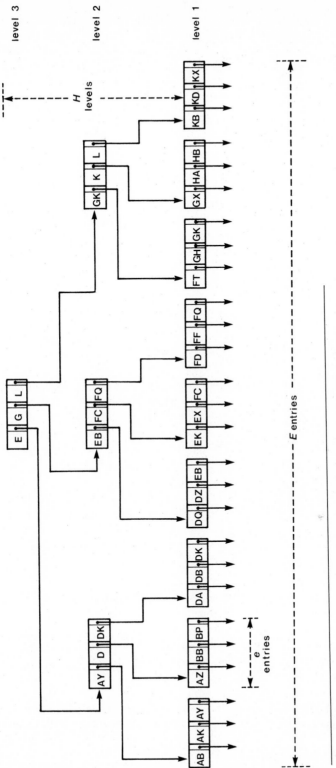

FIGURE 4.9a *Balanced H-level index tree. The total number of index entries (E) is 27, the number of index entries per index block (e) is 3, and the height (H) or number of levels in the index is 3. To reduce the size of the index entries, right-compression of the keys is being used.*

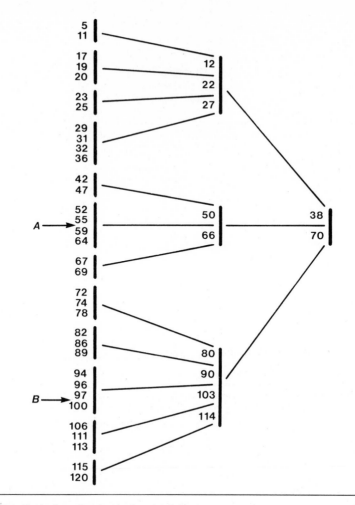

FIGURE 4.9b. *Illustration of a simple 5-order B-tree.*

addresses of block intervals of records (see Figure 4.1). Thus E is the number of index entries at the first level.

If we consider the first level of index entries as a sequential file, the second level is a one-level index to the first level, the third level is a one-level index to the second level, and so on. In each level, the index entries are grouped into *index blocks* of length e, where in this case $e = 3$. Thus the index tree in Figure 4.9a is a 3-order balanced tree. Note that in an implementation of such an index, the index block length has nothing to do with a data block on a disk track, and *an index block stored on disk may be made up of more than one storage block* (as with ISAM).

The index is used for retrieval in a straightforward manner. Suppose we need to retrieve the record with key FORD from the file for which Figure 4.9a is the index. We note that the key in an index entry is the same as or higher than the highest key in the "child" entries for that entry. Accessing level 3, we select the index entry with key G. The pointer takes us to the second index block in level 2 and, searching this index block, we select the entry with key FQ. This entry points to the sixth index block in level 1, and, searching it, we select the entry with key FQ. The key in this entry references the desired block interval of records in a sequential file (see Figure 4.1).

Updating gives us the problem already discussed. If we wish to insert a record in the block interval of data records when it is full, then a record must move to an overflow area, and the only thing to do with the index is to replace the single index entry per block interval with two index entries, one for the block interval and one for the overflow chain. The double-entry system is required only at the first level of the index, however, as with ISAM (see Figure 4.3).

It is clear that the time to search the index will be equal to the height of the tree multiplied by the time to search an index block or *node* of the tree. In practice, the analysis is complicated by the fact that the top levels may be in main memory, while lower levels are searched by the disk controller using a continuously executing channel program. We take this question up again in Section 4.4.3.

B-Trees   The B-tree is a relatively recent invention due to Bayer, McCreight, and Kaufman [Bayer, 1972; Knuth, 1973] and is clearly superior to the balanced tree. A B-tree of order 5 is shown in Figure 4.9b; it may be taken as an index to a file. Thus, as before, the pointers of the lowest level index blocks point to the block intervals of records in a sequential file.

The reader should study the diagram carefully, as the inherent elegance of the structure is not apparent at first glance. First, we note that the number of keys per index block varies between 2 and 4. It is a property of a B-tree that the order of the tree is $e + 1$, where e is the maximum number of keys per index block. The minimum number is required to be $\lfloor e/2 \rfloor$. (But the final *root* or top-level index block may have as few as 1 key.)

Next we note that with 4 keys, we have 5 pointers; with 3 keys, 4 pointers; and with 2 keys, 3 pointers (Figure 4.9b). It is a property of a B-tree that we have $p + 1$ pointers for p keys in an index block. These pointers are used in an original way. Take the first index block in the second level. The first pointer points to the index block which has keys that are less than 12 (but none of them have to *be* 12), the next points to an index block with keys greater than 12 and less than 22, and so on. Note that the first pointer in the top-level index block points to the level-2 index block, which points to level-3 index blocks all of whose keys are less than 38.

With this structure, both searching and insertion of new keys can be carried out quite simply. Searching the index is clearly a straightforward affair, requiring that we start at the root and choose the pointer which has a position matching the relative position of our search key with respect to the index entry keys in the root.

Insertion is clearly reminiscent of VSAM. Just to keep things in perspective, we could imagine that the lowest level of the index in Figure 4.9b was a sequence set as in VSAM. Now suppose that we have to insert an additional key 57 (at A) perhaps because of a block interval (*control interval* in VSAM) split. There is no room in the index for key 57. But since an index block can have as few as $e/2$ keys, it may be split; this gives

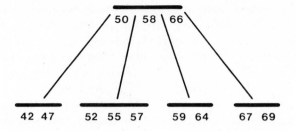

with no changes at the top level. All the index blocks again have between $e/2$ and e keys. An insertion can, in fact, propagate changes all the way to the top of the index. For example, suppose we need to insert key 99 at B. The (level-1) index block needs to be split, but so does the parent index block; the top-level index block requires the additional entry

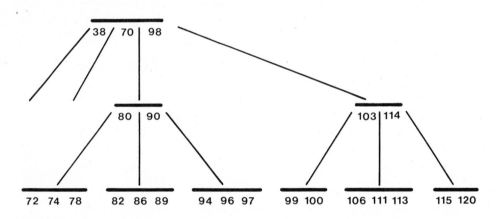

Thus the structure can multiply itself endlessly.[1] It is this structure that—in adapted form— is being used in VSAM. The difference is that the number of VSAM keys is equal to the number of pointers, and the key in an index block, as in ISAM, is greater than or equal to the keys in the lower-level block it points to.

As with the balanced tree, the number of accesses required to search the index is equal to the height of the index. It is clear that a B-tree index will, on the whole, tend to be higher than a balanced-tree index of the same order, simply because there will on the average be fewer keys in an index block. An expression (Expression 4) for the height of an index is derived in the next section.

4.4.3 Index Design Considerations

There are two main considerations in the design of an index, namely, its size and the search length. We want to keep the size as small as possible to reduce the consumption

---

[1] *Deletion of a key is slightly more complicated, as it will sometimes be necessary to merge two index blocks that are children of the same parent index block.*

of storage and also to reduce the search length. We want to keep the search length low for purposes of performance. An additional design consideration is whether the index should be based on a balanced tree or a B-tree, but we shall not consider this much broader question here. We merely assume in our analysis that the size of an index block can vary as in a B-tree or VSAM.

Index Size   The size of an index depends on the height of the index, and at first glance the obvious thing to do is reduce the height (H) of the tree. However, we cannot arbitrarily reduce H: If we reduce it to unity, we are back to the problems of the 1-level index. Instead, we reduce the size of the index by compressing the keys in the index, the height of the index being optimized to give a minimum search length, as we shall see shortly.

The balanced tree index in Figure 4.9a incorporates key compression. Here the keys are right-compressed; that is, the unnecessary rightmost characters are removed from the record key. Thus we assume that two (leftmost) key characters are sufficient in the first level of the index. In the second level, further compression is attempted. For example, the second entry of the first index block contains D instead of BP. It should be apparent that D is sufficient. In the third level, compression continues. For example, E replaces DK, which is sufficient.

Left-compression of the keys may also be used. For example, suppose an index block contains the keys

BRADFORD   BRADLEY   BRADSON

They could be replaced by

BRADFORD   4LEY   4SON

The digit indicates that the first 4 characters are the same as the previous 4.

Another technique involves omitting characters appearing at a lower level which already appear at a higher level. Thus since L is in the third top-level entry, it could safely be omitted from the last entry of the second level.

Combinations of these techniques may also be used, and the resulting key-compression routines can be quite complex. ISAM does not have a key-compression facility, but VSAM does [Martin, 1977].

Optimization of Index Searching   We now consider the main methods for minimizing the search length for a multiple-level index. We can use Figure 4.9 to guide our thinking. For any tree index, we take E as the total entries, e as the *average* number of entries per index block (we take an average to allow for the case of a B-tree), and H as the index height.

It is clear that the larger we make e, the smaller H will be and the fewer the accesses to the index required to search the index. But although we gain from a reduction in the number of accesses to the index, as e becomes larger more time will be required both to transmit a complete index block from disk storage, and to search it. (We note that in the case of the VSAM B-tree index, the average index block size will probably be three-fourths of the maximum size.) Thus there must be some optimum value for e, at the point where the increased time to transmit and search an index block begins to offset the gains made by reducing H and having fewer accesses. We therefore need to deduce an expression for the search time.

First we need to know how many index levels result from given values of e and E. It is clear that the number of times we have to divide e into E to obtain a quotient equal to or just less than unity is the required value of H, so that

$$\frac{E}{e^H} \leq 1$$

Hence[1]:

$$H = \left\lceil \frac{\log_2 E}{\log_2 e} \right\rceil \tag{4}$$

Since in a B-tree of order k, e will be $3k/4$ on average, a B-tree index is higher than a balanced-tree index of the same order.

To obtain a search time for a single index block, we assume it will be brought into main storage (this is not necessarily the case in practice, since with ISAM the controller searches the lower levels of an index under the control of a continuously executing channel program). We let D be the sum of the seek and rotational delay (latency) times for the disk on which the index is stored. If B is the length in bytes of an index *block* as stored on a disk track (we again remind the reader that an index block can be stored as a number of storage blocks) and if s is the disk transmission rate, then the time to transmit an index block will be B/s.

Finally, let us assume that when in main memory, the index block is placed in an array such that each index entry becomes an element of the array. The array could be searched by either linear, step, or binary searching, and with e instead of N, we use Expressions 1, 2, and 3 for the number of *array* (instead of file) accesses, T. If a is the time for an array access (and associated processing), then the time to search the array in internal memory is Ta.

Hence we have the following expression for the time t to search the index.

$$t = H\left(D + \frac{B}{s} + Ta \right) \tag{5}$$

That is,

$$t = \left\lceil \frac{\log_2 E}{\log_2 e} \right\rceil \left(D + \frac{eK}{s} + Ta \right) \tag{6}$$

where we substitute for H using Expression 4 and where B is replaced by eK, where K is the average length of an index *entry* in storage.

---

[1] $\lceil x \rceil$ *means the nearest integer above x, so that* $\left\lceil \frac{5}{2} \right\rceil$ *is 3. Similarly,* $\left\lfloor \frac{5}{2} \right\rfloor$ *is 2.*

Substituting Expressions 1, 2, and 3 for T gives the search times for internal linear, step, and binary processing of each index block accessed. Assuming that E is 50,000, the three expressions may be illustrated by the curves in Figure 4.10, for IBM 3350 and IBM 3380 disk drives. The curves are strongly affected by seek and latency times and disk transmission rate. We have assumed a to be 10 microseconds; the result is that the curves are not particularly affected by the choice of index block search technique. Nevertheless, binary searching is the fastest, although VSAM uses step searching since the compression of VSAM keys prevents binary searching [Martin, 1977]. The optimum value for e lies between about 20 and 150, so that 3 is the optimum height of the index for $E = 50,000$. In the case of VSAM, e is an average; the maximum value is about 33% higher. Note that K is assumed to be 200 bytes, a figure that could vary a lot with the design of the index.

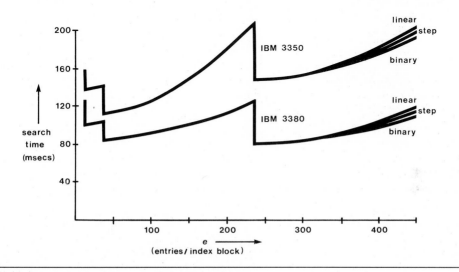

FIGURE 4.10. *Time to search an index of 50,000 entries versus average number of entries per index block. The curves are for IBM 3350 and 3380 disks, and an index block is assumed processed internally by linear, step, or binary searching at a cost of 10 microseconds per entry. An index entry is assumed to occupy 200 bytes on a disk track.*

4.5 PROCESSING OF INDEX-SEQUENTIAL FILES WITH PL/1

In this section, we examine the PL/1 sublanguage for index-sequential files and its application to the creation and manipulation of such files.

4.5.1 PL/1 SUBLANGUAGE FOR INDEX-SEQUENTIAL FILES

The PL/1 sublanguage for index-sequential files was originally designed for ISAM files [IBM, 1976a], and the sublanguage employs READ and WRITE statements. With the advent of VSAM, an additional and similar language using PUT and GET statements was designed. However, the facility is not as yet widely used, because many installations do not have compilers that provide for it. Fortunately the file sublanguage for ISAM files may also be employed with VSAM files, so we shall restrict our discussion of sublanguages in this section to the ISAM file sublanguage.

It is worth recalling that the access method must be able to inspect the record key, so that the user must specify its position and length in a record by means of the accompanying JCL. (With ISAM files it is also possible to have the key redundantly attached to the beginning of each record in a data block.) As already mentioned (see Section 4.2), the data blocks in an ISAM file are stored in count-key-data format, with the *highest key in the block redundantly stored in the key subblock*. As with CONSECUTIVE and REGIONAL(1) file organizations, a data block length specified in a DD statement is actually the length of the data subblock (see Chapter 1).

In a VSAM file, a control interval can contain one or more data blocks, but the data block size is chosen by VSAM [Keehn, 1974] to be one of 512, 1024, 2048, or 4096 bytes. As can be seen from Figure 4.11, a control interval contains records, free space, and control information. A control interval may also be regarded as a "train" of data blocks [Wiederhold, 1977].

File Declaration   Useful statements are

DCL BETA FILE RECORD ENV (INDEXED);

for ISAM files and

DCL BETA FILE RECORD ENV (VSAM);

for VSAM files.

OPEN Statement   As with REGIONAL(1) files, we must distinguish between how a file is organized and how it is to be processed.

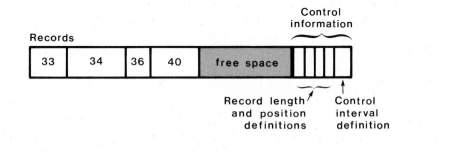

FIGURE 4.11.   *Format of a VSAM control interval. The control information contains record length and position data, whether or not the records have varying length.*

OPEN FILE (BETA)
$$\left\{ \begin{array}{l} \text{SEQUENTIAL OUTPUT KEYED} \\ \text{SEQUENTIAL INPUT [KEYED]} \\ \text{SEQUENTIAL UPDATE [KEYED]} \\ \text{DIRECT INPUT KEYED} \\ \text{DIRECT UPDATE KEYED} \end{array} \right\}$$

The file can only be output sequentially, as we would expect. However, it may be read in and updated either sequentially or by direct access. We now look at the statements that may be used with the various modes of processing.

File Creation   To create the index-sequential file, we open with

OPEN FILE (BETA) SEQUENTIAL OUTPUT KEYED:

Using the following WRITE statement, records are written out in ascending key order; if there is an error in the sequence the KEY condition is raised.

WRITE FILE (BETA) FROM (S) KEYFROM *(record-key);*

Here S is the usual structure variable or string variable, while *record-key* is the key of the record (of type string). Since in the accompanying JCL, the key position in the record and length of the key are specified, if there is a mismatch between the value in the record (that is, in S) and the value following KEYFROM, then the KEY condition is raised.

Sequential Processing of Index-Sequential Files

a.   *Opened for input*
We open the file with

OPEN FILE (BETA) SEQUENTIAL INPUT KEYED:

The KEYED option is used when we want to use the key of the record with retrievals; that is, when we need to use the KEY or KEYTO options in the following READ statements.
The file may be read as with a CONSECUTIVE file.

READ FILE (BETA) INTO (S);
   /* First record read */
READ FILE (BETA) IGNORE (6);
   /* Next 6 records ignored */

However, we may skip backward or forward from the last position to read a record which has a key that has been presented with the KEY option.

READ FILE (BETA) INTO (S) KEY (T);

To retrieve the record with a key which is the value of T, the access method uses the index, so that we skip to a new position in the file. We may now resume sequential processing from this new position with, for example,

READ FILE (BETA) INTO (S);

The above statement causes the record following the one with key T to be read. However, if we now code

READ FILE (BETA) INTO (S) KEYTO (R);

the next record is read and its key (which the access method can extract because of the information provided by the DD statement) is placed in the program variable R.

In the above, with ISAM files, deleted records (that is, with $(8)'1'B$ in the first byte) are read unless otherwise specified in the accompanying JCL. When we have specified that deleted records are not to be read but attempt to read them with a KEY option, as shown above, then the KEY condition will be raised.

b. *Opened for update*

All of the statements that may be used when a file is open for SEQUENTIAL INPUT KEYED can also be used when we open the file with

OPEN FILE (BETA) SEQUENTIAL UPDATE KEYED;

where, as before, KEYED permits use of KEY and KEYTO with READ statements.

We may not use a WRITE statement, but REWRITE and DELETE may be used in the context

```
READ FILE (BETA) INTO (S);   /* Next record read, placed in S */
..................;   /* Record fields, but not key field, updated in S */
..................;
REWRITE FILE (BETA) FROM (S);
```

The REWRITE statement causes the record in S to be written out in the same location that the previous READ statement accessed. If, later in the program, we encounter

DELETE FILE (BETA);

the next record is deleted, and with ISAM, deletion consists of having $(8)'1'B$ placed in the first byte of the record. Note that with VSAM files, the other records are moved up, so that the deleted record is physically removed from the file.

Direct Processing of Index-Sequential Files

    a.   *Opened for input*
        To open the file we code

        OPEN FILE (BETA) DIRECT INPUT KEYED;

        To read any record we write

        READ FILE (BETA) INTO (S) KEY (T);

        where the record key for the record we wish to retrieve is in the string variable T.

    b.   *Opened for update*
        To open the file we code

        OPEN FILE (BETA) DIRECT UPDATE KEYED;

        As with direct input processing, we may read any record with

        READ FILE (BETA) INTO (S) KEY (T);

        where T has the record key. To write out a record, since the access is direct, we must supply a key here too.

        WRITE FILE (BETA) FROM (S) KEYFROM (R);

        However, if the key specified (in R above) is that of an existing record, then the KEY condition will be raised.
            To overwrite an existing record, the record is first read in with a READ statement.

        READ FILE (BETA) INTO (S) KEY (Q);

        and then rewritten

        REWRITE FILE (BETA) FROM (S) KEYFROM (Q);

        To delete a record, the key must be supplied.

        DELETE FILE (BETA) KEY (W);

        The result is that an ISAM record is marked with $(8)'1'B$ in the first byte, and a VSAM record is physically removed. For the DELETE statement to be valid with ISAM files, a specification to this effect must be made in the file JCL when the file is first created.

4.5.2 Creation of an Index-Sequential File

A program to create a VSAM file is quite simple and consists of little more than a simple WHILE loop in which records are read in from a sequential file and written out in the index-sequential file. The access method sees to it that the free space specified in the JCL is provided for.

If the file organization is ISAM, as we have seen, it can often pay to leave empty space at the end of each data track, so that insertions can take place without the special overflow areas (and thus the slow overflow chains) having to be used, at least in the beginning.

It is important to understand that with an ISAM file, even if dummy records (programmer-made free space) are distributed throughout a track, if the last record on the track is a valid one then an insertion anywhere on that track may cause the record to be moved to an overflow chain. Thus the dummy records or free space should be at the end of each track on initial loading.

It is clear, therefore, that the loading of an ISAM file to minimize the length of future overflow chains is more complex. Let us consider a cylinder that contains overflow tracks, data tracks, and space for a track index. The track index starts on track 1 and continues onto track 2 if necessary. *The prime data area starts where the track index stops,* so that—in general—the first data track will have fewer records than ensuing data tracks. The number of records on the first and remaining tracks must therefore be incorporated into the loading program for the dummy records to be at the end of each track.

To illustrate these points, we shall take the loading of the file TAPEDRIL from the previous chapter. The record format is as shown in Figure 3.10. The file TAPEDRIL will be loaded as the ISAM file ISDRIL. The loading program will be (unfortunately) dependent on the disk unit, so we shall assume an IBM 3350 unit; its parameters are discussed in Chapter 1 (see also Appendix 1).

The IBM 3350 unit has 30 tracks per cylinder, and we shall assume that 1 track is left as an overflow track, leaving 29 for the data and track index. For each prime data track there is an index entry with two components, the *normal* and the *overflow* component. Each component is a count-key data block, with a 10-byte data subblock containing a pointer, and with the key subblock the key of a record in the prime data area. Since the keys in ISDRIL are 10 bytes long (see the record structure in the loading program), each index component will therefore take up $267 + 10 + 10$ bytes, or 287 bytes on a track. Since we have 2*29 index components in the track index, the index takes up 2*29*287 bytes in all, or 16,646 bytes (see Section 1.4.2).

Because a track has 19,254 bytes available altogether, after allowing for the index there will be $19,254 - 16,646$, or 2608, bytes left on the first track for records from the data area.

Hence the prime-data area of the file (on a given cylinder, except possibly the last) will have 1 track with 2608 bytes and 28 tracks with 19,254 bytes. Since each data record is 22 bytes long, if we take a block factor of 100, we get 2200 bytes in each data subblock of the count-key data block used in the prime data area. Since the record key is 10 bytes, the total length of a count-key data block is $267 + 10 + 2200$, or 2477, bytes.[1]

---

[1] *But in the DD statement we specify* BLKSIZE = 2200.

There is thus room for 1 such block, that is, 100 records, in the index track, which has 2608 bytes available. In each of the other tracks, there is room for 7 such blocks or 700 records. Thus the cylinder can hold 100(28*7 + 1), or 19,700, records.

If the file were such that a cylinder index was built into one of the cylinders, this would have to be taken into account in the calculation above. However, the principle should be clear; to keep things simple, we shall assume that there is only a track index to take care of. Let us therefore assume that TAPEDRIL has 17,000 records—not quite enough to fill the cylinder—so that a cylinder index is unnecessary.

We shall, therefore, write out 19,700 records altogether; of these, 17,000 are genuine and the remaining, 2700 are dummies. Since about 15% of the records are dummies, it seems reasonable to distribute the dummies proportionally among the available tracks: The first track has space for 100 records, so that it could get 12 dummies, and each of the remaining tracks could get 96 dummies. The cylinder is illustrated in Figure 4.12.

We shall now look at a program to load the file.

ISLOAD: PROC OPTIONS (MAIN);
/*

1. Program loads a 1-cylinder ISAM file with 17,000 genuine and 2700 dummy records.

2. Each record describes a drill-hole, key length 10 bytes, record length 22 bytes, and block factor 100.

3. Track index occupies 16,646 bytes on first track, and overflow area occupies the last track.

4. Dummy records are placed at the end of each track, 12 dummies at the end of the index track, and 96 dummies at the end of each remaining track. Thus there are 88 genuine records on the index track and 604 genuine records on each remaining track.

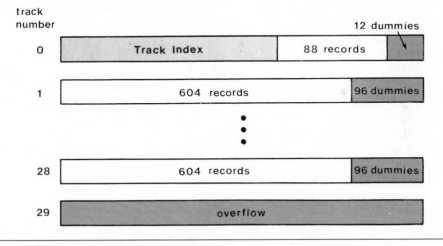

FIGURE 4.12. *The cylinder of the index-sequential (ISAM) file used in the example. Dummy records are loaded at the end of each data track, including the index track. The device is an IBM 3350.*

5. Records are taken from the CONSECUTIVE file TAPEDRIL, and placed on the ISAM file ISDRIL.

6. Record key HOLE in TAPEDRIL is 6 bytes long, but corresponding key in ISDRIL is 10 bytes long, to allow for output of dummy records in ascending sequential order.   */

```
DCL TAPEDRIL FILE RECORD ENV (CONSECUTIVE),
    1 TPAREA,
        2 HOLE CHAR (6),                        /* Assume this key is numeric */
        2 REC,
            3 DEPTH FIXED BIN (15),
            3 COST FIXED DEC (8),
            3 LOC CHAR (4);


DCL ISDRIL FILE RECORD ENV (INDEXED),          /* ISAM file */
    1 ISAREA,
        2 TAG BIT (8),
        2 HOLE PIC (10) '9',                    /* Extended key */
        2 ISREC LIKE REC;                       /* 22 bytes altogether */

OPEN FILE (TAPEDRIL) INPUT,
     FILE (ISDRIL) SEQUENTIAL OUTPUT KEYED;


        /* Main loading loop */

DO I = 1 TO 29;
    IF I = 1 THEN L = 88;                       /* 88 genuine on index track */
            ELSE L = 604;                       /* 604 genuine on other tracks */
                                                /* Loading of genuine records */
    TAG = '00000000'B;
    DO J = 1 TO L;
        READ FILE (TAPEDRIL) INTO (TPAREA);
        ISAREA.HOLE = TPAREA.HOLE;
        ISAREA.HOLE = ISAREA.HOLE*10000;        /* Key lengthened */
        ISREC = REC;
        WRITE FILE (ISDRIL) FROM (ISAREA) KEYFROM (ISAREA.HOLE);
        END;


                /* Loading of dummy records */
    IF I = 1   THEN M = 12;                     /* 12 dummies on index track */
            ELSE M = 96;                        /* 96 dummies on each other track */
    TAG = '11111111'B;
    DO J = 1 TO M;
        ISAREA.HOLE = ISAREA.HOLE + 1;          /* Sequential order preserved */
        WRITE FILE (ISDRIL) FROM (ISAREA) KEYFROM (ISAREA.HOLE);
        END;
END;
```

```
END;
/*
//GO.TAPEDRIL   DD   DSN = TAPEDRIL,DISP = OLD
//GO.ISDRIL    DD   DSN = ISDRIL(PRIME),UNIT = 3350,VOL = SER = 123
//                  SPACE = (CYL,(1,0)),DISP = (NEW,CATLG),
//                  DCB = (DSORG = IS,RECFM = FB,LRECL = 22,BLKSIZE = 2200,
//                  KEYLEN = 10,RKP = 1,OPTCD = YL,CYLOFL = 1)
```

4.5.3 Updating of Index-Sequential Files

There are three basic methods of processing an index-sequential file: *sequential, skip sequential,* and *direct processing*. We shall take them in turn. To make the analysis as relevant as possible to practical conditions, we shall assume we have an ISAM file with 80-byte records, with 100,000 records in the file. We shall consider the effect of the block factor (using values of 25 and 12) on the average time to access a record for updating, using the three processing methods. We assume that the file is on a 3380 disk unit, with the timing parameters given in Appendix 1. We further assume that there are no overflow records, and that no other job is using the disk concurrently.

Sequential Processing   With sequential processing, we open the file with the attributes SEQUENTIAL UPDATE. Since the parameter KEYED is not specified, the access method will not use the index for retrievals. The average time to retrieve a record will depend on how many records have to be accessed.

Suppose that 100%, or 100,000, of the records are to be accessed. The time to retrieve a block will be half the rotation time, that is, 8.4 milliseconds, plus the block transmission time, which—with a block factor of 25—will be 0.66 milliseconds, and—for a block factor of 12—about 0.32 milliseconds. Thus with block factors 25 and 12, the average record retrieval times are 0.36 and 0.73 milliseconds, respectively.

If only 8% of the records are to be accessed, with a block factor of 25 only 2 records per block are required, on the average. It takes 9.05 milliseconds to read a 25-record block, the average record access time thus being 4.5 milliseconds. A block factor of 12 would double this to 9.1 milliseconds.

If we calculate again when only 1% of the records are to be accessed, we get about 36 and 73 milliseconds access time per record for block factors 25 and 12, respectively. Thus with a low percentage retrieval or *hit rate,* the processing becomes very inefficient.These calculations are illustrated in Figure 4.13. We now compare this with skip sequential processing.

Skip Sequential Processing   With skip sequential processing the file is opened with the attributes SEQUENTIAL UPDATE KEYED. Specification of KEYED permits use of the record key while reading through the file in a sequential manner. Thus we may skip from a record with one key to the next desired record without having to read all the records in between.

However, use of the record key means that the index may have to be used, in which case total block-access time is the sum of the index-access time and the block direct-access and transmission time.

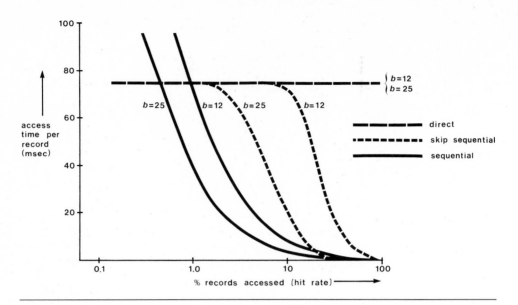

FIGURE 4.13. *Average access time per record against hit rate for direct skip sequential, and sequential processing of an **ISAM** file on an IBM 3380 disk. There are curves for block factors 25 and 12. The curves are purely theoretical, derived for a file of 100,000 80-byte records. It is assumed that an index access takes 50 milliseconds and that there are no overflow records.*

Let us take a round figure of 50 milliseconds for the time to access the index (this figure could vary a lot with the design of the file). If the index is being used, there will be a seek time associated with each data-block access (16 milliseconds). Thus the total time to access a block will be about 50 + 16 + 8.4 + 0.66 milliseconds, where 0.66 milliseconds is from the transmission time for a 2000 byte block, giving a total of 75.06 milliseconds.

If the hit rate is only 1%, we can be sure that the index is used in every retrieval. Thus for a block factor of 25, the average access time per record will be 75.06 milliseconds, since an average of only one block will be retrieved per record. The same will be true when the block factor is reduced to 12, giving an average retrieval time per record of 50 + 16 + 8.4 + 0.32, or 74.72 milliseconds.

When the hit rate is 100%, it will clearly not be necessary to make use of the KEYED attribute, and thus of the index. Thus the average record retrieval times should be the same as with ordinary sequential retrieval. We saw that this was 0.36 and 0.73 milliseconds for block factors 25 and 12, respectively.

It is a substantially more difficult matter to deduce the retrieval time per record for the case where the hit rate is about 8%, for here the index may be used advantageously with some retrievals but not with others. However, it is probably reasonable to assume that the index will be used in this case most of the time. It should be noted that if a block is retrieved using the index and this block subsequently contains more than one of the records to be retrieved, then a new access does not have to be made for the second and third (or other later) records.

Thus the access time per record with a block factor of 25 and an 8% hit rate will be close to

$$\frac{(50 + 16 + 8.4 + 0.66)}{2} = 37.5 \text{ milliseconds}$$

When the block factor is 12, it will be 74.72*50/48, or 77.83 milliseconds. These results are displayed in Figure 4.13.

Direct Processing With direct processing, the file is opened with the attributes DIRECT UPDATE KEYED, and the record key is always necessary to retrieve a record. Use of the key requires access to the index, and as before we shall assume this costs about 50 milliseconds.

Since records are typically retrieved in random order, a block will have to be retrieved for each record in nearly all cases, regardless of the hit rate. (This is not strictly true for high hit rates as there is always a small probability that two consecutively required records will be retrieved in a single block.)

Thus the access times per record will be 75.06 and 74.72 for block factors of 25 and 12, respectively, as computed for the case of skip sequential processing. This result is also depicted graphically in Figure 4.13.

Selection of a Processing Strategy The curves in Figure 4.13 are purely theoretical. They assume an index access time of 50 milliseconds, a 3380 disk unit, and no overflow records. They do, however, give a reasonable indication of what can be expected.

The conclusion that can be drawn from these curves is in agreement with common experience; that is, that unless the hit rate is very low, sequential processing is the most efficient for ISAM files, and indeed for all index sequential files. However, it is clear from the foregoing analysis that block factor and device type will have an effect on the relevant trade-offs, so that an individual analysis is necessary in each case.

EXERCISES

1. Prepare a small file of company records, where company name is the unique key. From these records an index sequential read-only file is to be constructed using REGIONAL(1) file organization. The creation program will construct the index for the file and store it in the REGIONAL(1) file. Write the file creation program.

2. Suppose that, just after creation, an ISAM file has g genuine records per track and d dummy records at the end of each track. During later processing an average of k records per track are inserted randomly (but with the preservation of sequential order), and no deletions take place. Use the Poisson distribution function from Chapter 3 to estimate the minimum number of records the overflow area should be able to hold.

3. Create a single cylinder ISAM file along the lines suggested by the program CREATE in Section 4.3.1, but where no dummy records are output. Determine which records are at the start of each track immediately after loading. Delete about 10 records distributed over a given track, and then insert about 10 new records with key values between the highest and lowest initial key values on the track. Obtain a printout of both the genuine and dummy records now on this track, together with a printout of the records in the overflow area. Explain your results.

4. An ISAM file of 80 byte records is to be placed on a single 3350 cylinder. If one track is reserved for overflow records, determine how many records the file can hold for (a) a block factor of 25, and (b) a block factor of 10. Assume that the record key is 15 bytes long.

5. Assume a VSAM file with R partially full control intervals, each capable of holding f records and each with room for b more records following loading. Assuming that there are enough empty control intervals to render control area splits unnecessary, if r records are inserted randomly into the file, use the Poisson distribution function to deduce an expression for the number of second generation splits as a function of r.

6. In a VSAM file there are e empty control intervals in each control area just after initial loading; there are also R partially full control intervals in each control area with b empty record spaces in each such control interval. When r records are inserted randomly, derive an expression for the number of resulting first generation control area splits as a function of r. Assume that $e < R$.

7. An access method for index sequential files is being constructed. The access method is to cater for files that typically have 10,000 index entries. If an index entry takes up 300 bytes on a disk track and step searching of index blocks in main memory is to be used, estimate the optimum number of entries in an index block. Assume an IBM 3350 disk.

8. The following simple exercise is designed to demonstrate how an index sequential file can maintain sequential order, even when a clump of records is inserted.

   Create an index sequential file ALPHA containing about 300 records with keys (perhaps randomly generated) ranging from 0 to 1000, each record with a field containing 'ORIGINAL RECORD'. ALPHA is then updated by inserting 100 records with keys ranging from 200 to 299. For these inserted records, if the key is new then the records should have a field containing 'NEW RECORD'; otherwise the field should contain 'UPDATED RECORD'. Finally the complete file should be printed out.

9. Suppose that in addition to the index sequential file ISDRIL created in this chapter, we have an additional sequential file PERSON, which contains records describing drilling workers. The fields of a PERSON record are SOCSECNUMB (social security number, the key field), AGE, WAGE, NATIONALITY (these three with obvious semantics), and HOLE (the number of the hole on which a worker is active). Write a creation program for PERSON, where the keys are in ascending order and each HOLE value is checked (by direct access) against the value in the ISDRIL file. ISDRIL should also be created.

10. Assuming that we can get a version of PERSON (from Exercise 9) sorted on HOLE, write a report program to print out the cost per foot of holes on which the majority

of the workers are under 25 years old. ISDRIL from Exercise 9 is assumed to be available.

11. Write a report program to give the nationalities of workers on holes currently deeper than 15,000 feet. ISDRIL and PERSON from Exercise 9 should be used.

12. With reference to the B-tree in Figure 4.9*b,* draw out the altered parts of the tree when key 35 is added to the lowest level.

13. Again referring to Figure 4.9*b,* how would the tree look if key 115 were deleted?

14. Suppose keys 55, 59, 42, and 69 are consecutively deleted from the B-tree in Figure 4.9*b.* Draw the affected parts of the index following each deletion.

REFERENCES

Augenstein, M. J., and A. M. Tenenbaum, 1979, *Data Structures and PL/1 Programming,* Prentice-Hall, Inc., Englewood Cliffs, N.J.

Bayer, R., and E. McCreight, 1972, "Organization and Maintenance of Large Ordered Indices," *Acta Informatica,* **1**(3):173–89.

Gotlieb, C. C., and L. R. Gotlieb, 1978, *Data Types and Structures,* Prentice-Hall, Inc., Englewood Cliffs, N.J.

Ghosh, S. P., 1977, *Data Base Organization for Data Management,* Academic Press, New York.

IBM, 1976*a, OS PL/1 Optimizing Compiler, Programmer's Guide,* Order Form GC33–0009.

IBM, 1976*b, OS PL/1 Optimizing Compiler, Programmer's Guide,* Order Form FC33–0006.

IBM, 1976*c, Introduction to IBM Direct Access Storage Devices and Organization Methods,* Student Text, Order Form GC20–1649.

Keehn, D. G., and J. O. Lacy, 1974, "VSAM Data Set Design Parameters," *IBM Sys. J.,* **13**(3):186–212.

Knuth, D. E., 1973, *The Art of Computer Programming,* vol. 3, Addison-Wesley, Reading, Mass.

Martin, J., 1977, *Computer Data Base Organization,* Prentice-Hall, Inc., Englewood Cliffs, N.J.

Rindfleisch, D. H., 1978, *Utilizing System 360/370 OS and VS Job Control Language and Utility Programs,* Prentice-Hall, Inc., Englewood Cliffs, N.J.

Rus, T., 1979, *Data Structures and Operating Systems,* John Wiley, New York.

Tremblay, J. P., and P. G. Sorenson, 1976, *Introduction to Data Structure with Applications,* McGraw-Hill, New York.

Wagner, R. E., 1973, "Indexing Design Considerations," *IBM Sys. J.,* **12**(4):351–67.

Wiederhold, G., 1977, *Data Base Design,* McGraw-Hill, New York.

Hybrid and Merge Files

5

It is possible to extend, vary, or modify the basic file structures presented in the previous chapters. The resulting files are generally known as *hybrid files*. So large is the possible number of hybrid files that it is probably true to state that many of them have been invented, forgotten, and later reinvented to fulfill the needs of a particular system [Ghosh, 1977; Martin, 1977; Pfaltz, 1977; Wiederhold, 1977].

However, in this chapter we shall study what are undoubtedly the two most important types:

    a.   Inverted files;

    b.   Multiple key or multiple-access method files.

We shall also study *sorted partition* or *merge* files, which find wide application in sorting large quantities of data. They have a special structure and may in fact be regarded as hybrid files. We shall also see how they are used in merging.

5.1 INVERTED FILES (SECONDARY INDEXES)

Inverted files are normally used to greatly improve the retrieval power of a system. They are of fundamental importance. However, as is usually the case, increased retrieval power is gained at the expense of increased updating overhead [Gotlieb, 1977; Pfaltz, 1977].

5.1.1 Basic Principles

The principles involved are quite simple, but we must distinguish clearly between the structure of an inverted file and the use to which it may be put.

Structure of an Inverted File We shall illustrate the structure of an inverted file with an example. Consider the file DRILHOLE[1] with contents as shown in Figure 5.1*b*. The records of DRILHOLE describe bore-holes. HOLE is the key field, COMPANY is the name of the oil company which owns the hole, COST is the cost of the hole, LOC is its location, and DRILL_FIRM is the name of the drilling company which drills the hole.

From the contents of the file we see that an oil company can own many holes and that a drilling firm drills many holes for different oil companies.

An inverted file may be constructed for any nonkey field in a file (such as DRILHOLE), although normally, because of the overhead involved, only a few fields will be selected for inversions. We shall take an inversion of the field COMPANY.[2]

We construct a new file INVER_CO. This file is called the *inverted* or *inversion file* for COMPANY; it is also sometimes called the *inversion index* for COMPANY. The contents of INVER_CO are shown in Figure 5.1*a*. We see that the file contains all the COMPANY values in DRILHOLE, and since there are no duplicate COMPANY values in INVER_CO, the field COMPANY in INVER_CO can be used as the prime key.

The remaining fields in an INVER_CO record are pointer fields, which point to a group of records in DRILHOLE with the same COMPANY value as the INVER_CO record. In the diagram, the pointer fields contain the physical address of the DRILHOLE records and are called *physical* pointers. They could be replaced by the keys to the DRILHOLE records, in which case they would be called *symbolic* pointers.

Inversion Aided Retrievals Let us suppose that we have an inversion for the COMPANY field in DRILHOLE called INVER_CO, and also an inversion for the DRILL_FIRM field called INVER_DF. Consider the following retrieval.

Retrieval:

> **Find the hole numbers for holes drilled by** 'DRILLPETE' **for the company** 'WESTGAS'.

Method 1, without use of inversions:

1. Retrieve next DRILHOLE record.

2. If COMPANY = 'WESTGAS' and DRILL_FIRM = 'DRILLPETE', then print out HOLE value and repeat Step 1; otherwise, just repeat Step 1.

Method 2, with use of inversions:

1. Retrieve INVER_CO record with key 'WESTGAS', placing pointers in an auxiliary variable P_CO.

2. Retrieve INVER_DF record with key 'DRILLPETE', placing pointers in an auxiliary variable P_DF.

3. If pointers are symbolic, print out pointer values that are in both P_CO and P_DF.

---

[1] *PL/1 file names can have at most 8 characters.*

[2] *Some authors refer to the complete set of inversions as an inverted file.*

COMPANY	ADDRESS	ADDRESS	ADDRESS	...
EASTPETE	150	342	—	—
MULTOIL	204	782	—	—
WESTGAS	106	389	089	—

(a) Inverted file INVER_CO with physical pointers.

ADDRESS
106
204
150
389
782
089
342

HOLE	COMPANY	COST	LOC	DRILL_FIRM
23	WESTGAS	1000	ALASKA	DRILLPETE
39	MULTOIL	800	YUKON	DEEPDRILL
41	EASTPETE	900	MEXICO	BOREFIRM
47	WESTGAS	600	TEXAS	GASRIG
58	MULTOIL	1000	ALASKA	DRILLPETE
62	WESTGAS	1200	N. SEA	DEEPDRILL
74	EASTPETE	400	TEXAS	GASRIG

(b) The file DRILHOLE showing record addresses.

FIGURE 5.1. *Inversion of the field* COMPANY *in the file* DRILHOLE.

4. If pointers are physical, access the DRILHOLE records pointed to in both P_CO and P_DF, printing out HOLE values.

The advantage of the inverted files should be clear. Without them, we would have to process every record in DRILHOLE to carry out the retrieval. With the inversions, the job can be done in 2 retrievals if the pointers are symbolic; if the pointers are physical, it can be done in $2 + x$ retrievals, where x is the number of holes satisfying the retrieval conditions.

5.1.2 Creation and Use of an Inverted File

In this section we shall create the two inverted files INVER_CO and INVER_DF from the previous subsection. Unfortunately, unless we use a system such as VSAM, which has a built-in facility for inverted files [IBM, 1976], such files are somewhat difficult to set up.

File Design Considerations

1. *Index sequential or hash*
    The first question is whether to have the inversion organized as an index sequential or a hash file. Hash files have better performance, but we cannot avoid variable length records in the inversion, and these are more easily handled in an index sequential file. With PL/1 and OS/MVT or OS/MVS, there is no facility for easily constructing hash files with blocked records of variable length. Index-sequential organization is therefore more suitable for inversions. Under OS/MVS, we have VSAM and ISAM file organizations. However,

an inverted file is really a special kind of index, and **VSAM** has a built-in facility for the creation and maintenance of inverted files (or *alternate indexes,* in **VSAM** terminology), thus shielding the user from most of the difficulties. This is very convenient in a practical situation; but to give the reader a clear idea of what is involved, we shall apply **ISAM**.

2. *Pointer and record insertions in* **INVER_CO**
   The usual problem with **ISAM** files is what to do with insertions. With an inverted file, furthermore, there are two types of insertions to take into account. Consider the files **DRILHOLE** and **INVER_CO**. An insertion in **DRILHOLE** will of necessity affect **INVER_CO**. If the value of the **COMPANY** field in the new record is one that already occurs elsewhere in the file, then an additional pointer has to be attached to a record in **INVER_CO**. This is one type of insertion.

   However, if insertion of a new record in **DRILHOLE** also results in a new **COMPANY** value, then a new record must be inserted in **INVER_CO**. Thus the inverted file design must be able to accommodate insertion of both additional pointers and additional records.

3. *Maximum size of* **INVER_CO** *records*
   If pointer insertions result in the record size exceeding the maximum record size, the file will have to be reorganized. To postpone this problem, we could load the file with some dummy pointers in each record to allow for insertions. An additional advantage of dummy pointers is that many pointer insertions could be carried out without record insertions, the inserted pointer replacing a dummy. (The alternative is to delete the record and insert a new, longer record with the extra pointer.)

   Since normally the number of pointer insertions will reflect the number of valid pointers per record at loading time, the number of dummy pointers per record should be a fixed percentage of the number of valid pointers. In other words, if a large company in possession of 5000 holes comes into possession of 50 more holes in the course of a period of time, it is reasonable to assume that a small company with 500 holes could get 5 extra holes in the same period.

   Reasoning in this way, we could give the **INVER_CO** records a format for implementation purposes as shown in Figure 5.2. In addition to the key field **COMPANY**, the fields **TP** and **VP** give the total pointer fields and the valid pointer fields. Thus **TP** − **VP** gives the number of dummies, and the value for each record is such that we have approximately the same value of k for each record, where

$$k = (TP - VP)/VP$$

4. *Calculation of maximum record length*
   To get the maximum record length, the file **DRILHOLE** must be processed separately. This is clearly best done after the file is sorted on the field **COMPANY**. We require a value for **MAX**, the maximum occurrences of any **COMPANY** field in **DRILHOLE**. The file **DRILHOLE** must be so sorted to permit loading of the inverted file **INVER_CO** anyway. The maximum record length is the sum of the following.

1. **TAG** field   1 byte

2. **COMPANY** field   11 bytes

(a) Fixed part of record; TP gives total pointers and VP gives valid pointers.

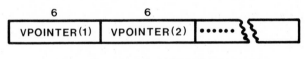

(b) First variable part of record: valid pointer array.

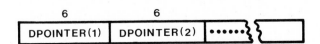

(c) Second variable part of record: dummy pointer array.

FIGURE 5.2. *Format of a record in the inverted file INVER_CO as used in file creation program. The record has a fixed and two variable length parts. The byte length of fields appears above field names.*

3. **TP, VP** fields	4 bytes
4. Maximum occurrences of any **COMPANY** field in **DRILHOLE**	MAX*(DRILHOLE key length) bytes
5. Dummy pointers	k*(DRILHOLE key length)*MAX bytes
6. **ISAM** record length field	4 bytes

We may thus use as block size in the DD statement a multiple of the maximum record length plus 4 bytes for **ISAM** block length control.

5. *Creation of dummy records to reduce overflow*
By far the simplest way of dealing with whole record insertions is to write out the records with some well-dispersed dummy records. This will mean that the dummies are not at the end of the track. However, placing the dummies at the end of a track when the records have variable length would require that the program find the sum of the block lengths and, on the basis of the data for count-key data format and the available space per track, compute the points where the dummy-record output should start and stop. Since this more effective method will involve our loading program in device-dependent data and calculations, we shall omit them in the interests of clarity. It may also be argued that it is pointer insertions that predominate, so that not too many records will end up in the overflow area with an inverted file anyway.

Inverted File Loading Program   In order to be able to have the key values (COMPANY values) for INVER_CO available in ascending order together with the corresponding key values in DRILHOLE (that is, HOLE values), a version of DRILHOLE should be available that has been sorted with COMPANY as primary sort key and HOLE as secondary sort key (see Figure 5.3). Sorting DRILHOLE with HOLE as secondary sort key ensures that pointers in each pointer array are in ascending HOLE (key) value.

```
LOADINV: PROC OPTIONS (MAIN);
/*
```

1. Program loads the inverted file INVER_CO as an index sequential file. The inversion is based on inversion of the field COMPANY in the CONSECUTIVE file DRILHOLE (see Figure 5.1).

2. The file DRILHOLE is assumed sorted on COMPANY value, with HOLE value as secondary sort key.

3. The format of INVER_CO records is shown in Figure 5.2. Symbolic pointers are used, and loading also incorporates dummy pointers in each record to allow for insertion of new records in the file DRILHOLE.

4. The variable MAX gives the maximum number of valid pointers in a record on loading; the variable K gives the number of dummy pointers as a fraction of number of valid pointers. One dummy record is written out for every VAL valid records. MAX, K, and VAL are read in as control parameters.   */

```
DCL DRILHOLE FILE RECORD ENV(CONSECUTIVE),
        1 DHAREA,                          /*   Holds DRILHOLE record   */
            2 HOLE CHAR (6),               /*   Key   */
            2 COMPANY CHAR (10),           /*   Inversion field   */
            2 COST FIXED BIN (15),
            2 LOC CHAR (3),
            2 DRILL_FIRM CHAR (10);
```

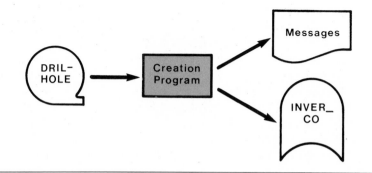

FIGURE 5.3. *System for creation of the inverted file* INVER_CO.

HYBRID AND MERGE FILES

```
DCL INVER_CO FILE RECORD ENV (INDEXED);
                    /*   The program structure to hold an INVER_CO record is declared in the
                    inner block BLOCKB as it has a dynamic structure    */

DCL COUNTER FIXED BIN (31);                    /*   Counts records   */
DCL (MAX,                                      /*   Maximum valid pointers in a
                                               record   */

     VAL)                                      /*   Number of genuine records per
                                               dummy   */

     FIXED BIN (15);
DCL K FIXED BIN (31,15);                       /*   Fraction of dummy pointer fields
                                               in an INVER_CO record   */

DCL INVCOMP CHAR (10);                         /*   Auxiliary variable to hold
                                               COMPANY value   */

DCL BEOF BIT (1);                              /*   Logical variable   */
GET LIST (MAX, VAL, K);                        /*   Control parameters   */

BLOCKA: BEGIN;
    DCL POINTER (MAX) CHAR (6);                /*   Holds pointers for an INVER_CO
                                               record   */
    OPEN FILE (DRILHOLE) INPUT,
        FILE (INVER_CO) SEQUENTIAL OUTPUT KEYED;
    BEOF = '1'B;
    ON ENDFILE (DRILHOLE) BEOF = '0'B;

    READ FILE (DRILHOLE) INTO (DHAREA);
    COUNTER = 0;
    DO WHILE (BEOF);
        INVCOMP = COMPANY:                     /*   We now obtain all DRILHOLE
                                               records with this COMPANY
                                               value   */


        J = 1;
        DO WHILE (INVCOMP = COMPANY & BEOF);
            IF J > MAX THEN DO;
                PUT SKIP LIST (2) ('POINTER TOTAL EXCEEDS MAX');
                PUT SKIP LIST ('HOLE VALUE', MAX);
                STOP; END;
            POINTER(J) = HOLE;
            READ FILE (DRILHOLE) INTO (DHAREA);
            J = J + 1;
        END;
                    /*   Pointers for INVCOMP value are now in POINTER   */

        BLOCK B: BEGIN;
            DCL 1 INVAREA,                     /*   Holds INVER_CO record   */
```

```
              2 TAG BIT (8),
              2 COMPANY CHAR (11),
              2 TP FIXED BIN (15),         /*   Total pointer number   */
              2 VP FIXED BIN (15),         /*   Valid pointer number   */
              2 VPOINTER(J − 1) CHAR (6),              /*   Valid pointers   */
              2 DPOINTER((J − 1)*K) CHAR (6)           /*   Dummies   */
                         INIT(((J − 1)*K)(1)'');

         DO I = 1 TO J − 1;
              VPOINTER(I) = POINTER(I);
         END;
         TAG = '00000000'B;
         INVAREA.COMPANY = INVCOMP;
         TP = (J − 1) + (J − 1)*K;
         VP = J − 1;

         WRITE FILE (INVER_CO) FROM (INVAREA)
                   KEYFROM (INVCOMP);
         COUNTER = COUNTER + 1;

         /*   A dummy INVER_CO record is written out after every VAL valid records   */
         IF MOD(COUNTER,VAL) = 0 THEN DO;
         TAG = '11111111'B;
         SUBSTR(INVAREA.COMPANY, 11, 1) = '9';
         /*   Dummy COMPANY value produced in ascending sequential order   */
         WRITE FILE (INVAR_CO) FROM (INVAREA)
         KEYFROM (INVAREA.COMPANY);
         END;
         END BLOCKB;
         END;   /*   End of DO WHILE (BEOF) loop   */
END BLOCKA;
END;
/*
//GO.SYSIN DD   *
    < MAX >, < VAL >, < K >
/*
//GO.DRILL_HOLE DD DSN = SORTDRIL,DISP = (OLD,KEEP)
//GO.INVER_CO DD DSN = ...
```

We do not include a DD statement or statements for the inverted file INVER_CO, because such statements would of necessity be arbitrary owing to the fact that we have not carried out a full-file design to the extent necessary to completely specify an ISAM file. For example, we have not discussed the length of this file, so we are not in a position to specify the amount and type of overflow space or the type of index required. The size of the prime-data area for the file may be computed from the dimensions of the original file DRILHOLE. The reader familiar with Job Control Language should complete the design and DD statement as an exercise.

Referring again to Figure 5.2, it can be seen that the above program, with only minor modification, could be used to load an implementation of the inverted file INVER_DF. Let us assume this has also been done, so that the two inverted files can be used to facilitate retrievals.

Retrievals   Using these two inverted files, we may now attempt a typical retrieval. Retrieval:

> ***Find the hole numbers for drill holes owned by the company*** 'WESTGAS' ***and drilled by the company*** 'DRILLPETE'.

If HOLE is any one of the required set of holes, the retrieval may be expressed as

$$S = \{(HOLE) : COMPANY = 'WESTGAS' \ \& \ DRILL\_FIRM = 'DRILLPETE'\}$$

where S is the required set of hole numbers. It is clear that S is dependent on the HOLE subsets S_c and S_d as follows.

$$S = S_c \cap S_d$$

where

$$S_c = \{(HOLE) : COMPANY = 'WESTGAS'\}$$

and

$$S_d = \{(HOLE) : DRILL\_FIRM = 'DRILLPETE'\}$$

The retrieval procedure consists in retrieving the subset S_c from the inverted file INVER_CO, retrieving the subset S_d from the inverted file INVER_DF, and taking the set intersection of the two sets.

The program to carry out this retrieval is therefore quite simple, and will consist of reading in two variable length records and carrying out an intersection operation on two 1-dimensional arrays.

```
FIND: PROC OPTIONS (MAIN);
/*
```

1. This retrieval program uses two inverted files INVER_CO and INVER_DF organized as ISAM files. INVER_CO is an inversion of DRILHOLE (Figure 5.1) on COMPANY, and INVER_DF is an inversion on DRILL_FIRM.

2. Structure of INVER_DF is same as that of INVER_CO (shown in Figure 5.2).

3. Retrieval involves finding HOLE values for records in DRILHOLE where COMPANY = 'WESTGAS' & DRILL_FIRM = 'DRILLPETE'.   */

```
DCL (INVER_CO, INVER_DF) FILE RECORD INV (INDEXED);
DCL TEST CHAR (616) VAR;                            /*  Records read into this string,
                                                    which we assume can hold longest
                                                    record. See Section 2.3.3 for
                                                    explanation   */

DCL 1 OVERLAY BASED (PT),                           /*  Gets overlaid on TEST   */
    2 TAG BIT (1),
    2 COMPANY CHAR (11),
    2 TP FIXED BIN (15),
    2 VP FIXED BIN (15),
    2 POINTER (100) CHAR (6);                       /*  Maximum pointers expected   */

DCL BOOL BIT (1);                                   /*  Logical variable   */
DCL CPOINTER (100) CHAR (6);                        /*  Auxiliary pointer array   */
DCL CVP FIXED BIN (15);                             /*  Used to hold number of
                                                    pointers   */
DCL (X,Y) CHAR (20);                                /*  Holds search parameters   */

OPEN FILE (INVER_CO) DIRECT INPUT KEYED,
     FILE (INVER_DF) DIRECT INPUT KEYED;
PT = ADDRESS (TEST);                                /*  Overlay set up   */

GET LIST (X, Y);
READ FILE (INVER_CO) INTO (TEST) KEY (X);
CVP = VP;                                           /*  OVERLAY is coincident with
                                                    TEST   */
DO J = 1 TO CVP;
    CPOINTER(J) = POINTER(J);
END;
    /*  Valid pointers from INVER_CO record in CPOINTER   */

READ FILE (INVER_DF) INTO (TEST) KEY (Y);
    /*  Pointers from INVER_DF are now in array OVERLAY.POINTER   */
    /*  Perform intersection of arrays CPOINTER and POINTER   */

PUT SKIP LIST ('LIST OF DESIRED HOLES');
DO K = 1 TO CVP;
    BOOL = '1'B;
    DO J = 1 TO VP WHILE (BOOL);
        IF CPOINTER (K) = POINTER(J) THEN DO;
            BOOL = '0'B;
            PUT SKIP LIST (POINTER(J));
        END;
    END;
END;
END;
```

```
/*
//GO.SYSIN DD   *
    'WESTGAS' 'DRILLPETE'
/*
//GO.INVER_CO DD ...
//GO.INVER_DF DD ...
```

5.1.3 Multiple-Linked Lists

An important alternative to the inversions or secondary indexes described in this section is the *multiple-linked list* (or *multi-list*) file organization. Multi-list files can do much the same job as inverted files and are much easier to set up; unfortunately, they are also less efficient on the whole.

Figure 5.4 depicts the multi-list equivalent of an inversion on the field LOC for the file DRILHOLE from Figure 5.1. All DRILHOLE records with the same LOC value are chained together, so that DRILHOLE contains as many chains as there are distinct LOC values. In addition, an index is used to point to the first record of each chain or list. The pointers can be either physical or symbolic.

Comparison with Inversions   The first important point is that the index in this case is composed of entries of fixed length, compared with the variable entries of the inversion. This means that the multi-list file will be easier to set up. But if the multi-list aspect of the file is going to be subjected to intense use, as will often be the case, ease of initial creation is not a deciding factor.

In the case of retrievals, suppose that we use physical pointers with both inversions and multi-list files. Retrieval efficiency is the same for both techniques, provided we are

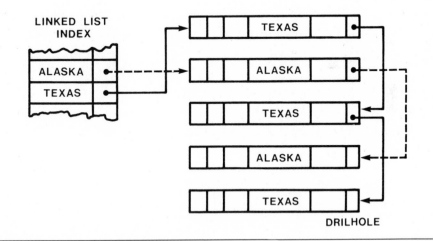

FIGURE 5.4.   *The multiple linked list alternative to an inversion or secondary index. The index points to the start of each linked list of records in* **DRILHOLE.**

dealing with an inversion and multi-list *for just one field*. Every record in the list or referenced in an inversion record must be accessed. However, if we have to deal with inversions and multi-lists for more than one field, then—with inversions—we can minimize the accesses to the main file by taking set intersections, unions, and differences of the keys in the inversion records. With multi-lists, we would have to traverse all the lists involved. The inversion approach is thus superior here. If we have symbolic pointers, with retrievals the inversion approach is better even when we are using an inversion on only one field. This is because with inversions, no accesses to the main file are required when we are retrieving information about the prime keys.

With updating, unless we use 2-way chains, insertions of new records with multi-list files will require chain traversals to allow for chain repair. Even with 2-way chains, insertion will be slightly slower with the multi-list file organization.

5.2 MULTIPLE-KEY FILES

This is really a special case of file inversion, where we have two or more unique key fields in each record; an inversion is carried out on one of these fields. This is illustrated in the following example.

5.2.1 File with Two Unique Keys

In Figure 5.5*a*, we have a file called DRILHOLE, which is the same as that used in the previous section, except that we have an additional field HOLENAME containing the name of the bore hole. Recall that HOLE is the prime key and contains the (unique) number of the bore hole. Let us suppose that HOLENAME contains unique values, so that it also is a candidate for prime-key status.

However, we suppose further that DRILHOLE is created as, for example, a hash file using HOLE as the prime key. How then can we access the file DRILHOLE using the HOLENAME value? The answer, of course, would be to "invert" on the field HOLE-NAME.

The result of this inversion is shown in Figure 5.5*b*. Of course this inverted file would almost always be referred to as an index, and in this case we give it the name H_INDEX.

(a) *File with two candidate prime key fields.*

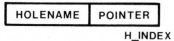

(b) *Index file for the candidate key field* **HOLENAME**.

FIGURE 5.5.

Since for each HOLENAME value in H_INDEX there can only be one corresponding DRILHOLE record, each H_INDEX record contains only one pointer, which may be either physical or symbolic.

Thus the way to achieve access through another candidate prime key is to create an index for the field involved.

5.3 SORTED PARTITION OR MERGE FILES

Sorted partition or *merge* files are probably the simplest kind of hybrid file. However, they are of fundamental importance and find wide use as intermediate files for sorting large quantities of data resident on external devices such as disk or tape.

A sorted partition file may be implemented as a PL/1 CONSECUTIVE file; records are grouped into groups or partitions, where the records in each partition are sorted in ascending key sequence. The partitions have variable numbers of records, and the smallest partition may contain one record. This is illustrated by

16   23   29   56   68   /   49   52   /   14   58   72   88   91   94   /   42   /

36   39   47   55   61   69

where the numbers represent the keys in a sorted partition file with 20 records and 5 sorted partitions. Going from left to right, the 5 partitions each contain records sorted in ascending key order.

Note that when such a file is implemented on disk or tape, no pointers or indicators of any kind are included in the file to mark the boundaries of the partitions. The partitions are distinguished in a processing program simply by the fact that between the end of one partition and the start of another (for example, the first and second above), the key sequence reverses order; in this case, we go from 68 down to 49. This key sequence reversal is often called a *stepdown* [Gotlieb, 1978].

As mentioned earlier, these files are used for completely sorting large files. These large files are in almost all cases partially sorted into one or more sorted partition files; the final sorting is completed by a process of merging the sorted partitions. In the next subsection, we shall look at how sorted partition files are generated from an unsorted file. In later sections, we shall look at four well-known methods for merging sorted partition files, namely, *balanced k-way merge*, *polyphase merge*, *cascade merge*, and *oscillating merge*.

Before we proceed, a note on terminology is necessary. There is no accepted terminology for the sorted partitions of the files being described in this section. Some authors refer to them as *strings*, which may be confused with data strings. Others [Knuth, 1973; Gotlieb, 1978] refer to them as *runs*, although Knuth does admit that this can cause confusion when we need to refer to programming runs. For the purpose of a presentation that is as simple as possible, and given the inherent complexity of the subject [Knuth, 1973], we have decided to use the almost self-explanatory term *sorted partition*. The term *sorted partition file* is also our invention. There appears to be no other widely used name for these files, although the term *merge file* is sometimes used.

5.3.1 Generation of Sorted Partition Files from Unsorted Files

Sorted partition files are used to produce a file with a single sorted partition, or a sorted file, by means of merging processes to be described later. Merging requires a great deal of file accessing; this accessing can be greatly minimized by starting the merging process with partitions containing as many records as possible. Thus in the generation of a sorted partition file, the resulting partitions should be as large as possible.

Simple Sorted Partition Generator A simple method of generating a sorted partition file from an unsorted file would be to process the unsorted file sequentially by reading a collection of records into main memory and sorting them, with the resulting sorted collection then output as a sorted partition in a sorted partition file. The collection of records being sorted in main memory would be as large as the limitations of the computer would permit, in order that the resulting partition would be as large as possible. Of course, the resulting partitions would all be the same size, limited by the number of records we could have in main storage for sorting. The sorting routine chosen could be one of the standard internal sorts [Knuth, 1973; Lorin, 1974].

We note that the size of our resulting sorted partition is limited by the number of records that can be held in main memory. It is this that makes this simple method unsatisfactory, because there exists a method, known as *replacement selection,* that permits sorted partitions to be formed that are much larger than the number of records that can be held in main memory.

The Replacement Selection (Snowshovel) Sorted Partition Generator The principle behind the replacement selection sorted partition generator is quite straightforward, if considered in the right way. The analogy of a snowplow plowing a circular road in a never-ending snowfall [Knuth, 1973] has been used to derive the size of the sorted partitions produced by the method; however the author has found that the principle behind the generator is easily explained by using the analogy of a snowshovel clearing a path through a layer of snow. Here the records of the unsorted file are the snow, and the capacity of the snowshovel is the maximum number of records the main memory can hold. Figure 5.6 illustrates the mechanism.

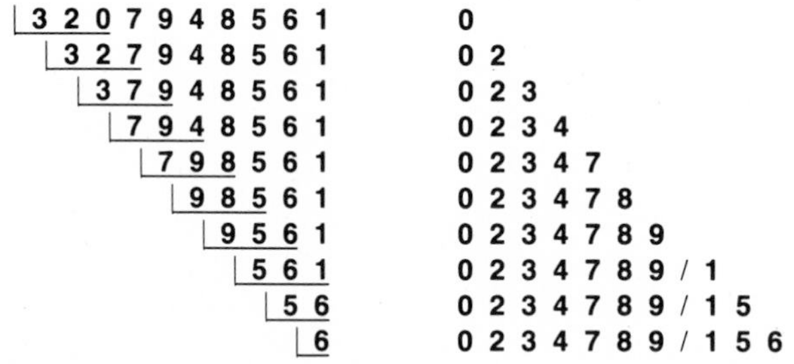

```
3 2 0 7 9 4 8 5 6 1      0
  3 2 7 9 4 8 5 6 1      0 2
    3 7 9 4 8 5 6 1      0 2 3
      7 9 4 8 5 6 1      0 2 3 4
        7 9 8 5 6 1      0 2 3 4 7
          9 8 5 6 1      0 2 3 4 7 8
            9 5 6 1      0 2 3 4 7 8 9
              5 6 1      0 2 3 4 7 8 9 / 1
                5 6      0 2 3 4 7 8 9 / 1 5
                  6      0 2 3 4 7 8 9 / 1 5 6
```

FIGURE 5.6. *Replacement selection generator.*

For the sake of the illustration, suppose that we have 10 unsorted records with keys 3 2 0 7 9 4 8 5 6 1 going from the start to the end of the file (left to right in the diagram). This initial file is shown at the top left of the diagram.

The file is processed sequentially and we suppose that the main memory (the snow-shovel) can only hold 3 records. The first 3 records are loaded into main memory (line 1) and the one with the lowest key is output at the right; that is, record key 0. This record with key 0 is also supposed to have been removed from the main memory and is replaced by the next record in sequence, that is, record key 7 (exactly where the new record is placed on the shovel is immaterial as far as the basic principle is concerned). The contents of the shovel are now searched for the smallest key *greater* than that previously output, in this case 2. The record with key 2 is placed in the output file and the shovel moved to the right, with key 2 replaced on the shovel by key 9. The process of moving the shovel to the right and outputting a record is continued until the state of affairs on the shovel is the one shown on the third line from the bottom.

This marks the completion of the creation of a sorted partition. The previous record output had key 9, but the latest movement of the shovel resulted in keys on the shovel, *all* of which are less than 9. This marks a stepdown, and the whole process begins again: we select the minimum key on the shovel just as was done on line 1, or key 1, and output it, starting a new sorted partition.

We see that we get two sorted partitions in the output file, the first with 7 records, which is more than twice the capacity of the main memory or shovel (3 records). In general, the replacement selection generator produces sorted partitions that are an average of at least twice as long as the number of records contained in the shovel [Knuth, 1973]. It is not difficult to see why.

Consider a shovel that can contain x records, and let us imagine that, for convenience in selecting the record with the smallest suitable key, the records on the shovel are maintained in ascending key order. This is shown in Figure 5.7, where the shovel at the top left (containing 4 records) illustrates the situation at the start of the generation of a new sorted partition. Records to the left of the star in the shovel cannot be output to the sorted partition because the key value is too small. As the records are output to the sorted partition, the star moves from the extreme left to the extreme right of the shovel, at which point all the keys in the shovel are too small and the sorted partition is complete. In the diagram, it is assumed that the probability of a replacement record entering the shovel to the right of the star is exactly the same as that of entering the shovel to the left of the star.

*15	21	45	56		15								
	*21	45	47	56	15	21							
	17*	45	47	56	15	21	45						
		17*	47	56	72	15	21	45	47				
		17	32*	56	72	15	21	45	47	56			
		17	32*	61	72	15	21	45	47	56	61		
		17	27	32*	72	15	21	45	47	56	61	72	
		17	27	32*	96	15	21	45	47	56	61	72	96
		17	27	32	69*	15	21	45	47	56	61	72	96 / 17

FIGURE 5.7. *Replacement selection with sorted records in shovel.*

When the star has migrated all the way to the right of the shovel, the original records in the shovel—those with keys 15, 21, 45, and 56—will all have been transferred to the sorted partition, that is, x records. But, in addition, the shovel now contains x records that have entered to the left of the star. Therefore x records must also have been added to the right of the star in the course of its migration. But since these records were inserted to the right of the star, they would all have been output to the sorted partition, that is, an additional x records. Thus the total records output will on average be $2x$ if the keys are random in the unsorted file. As pointed out by Knuth [Knuth, 1973], the unsorted records will not in general be random but will have some inherent order, so that in practice the number output will exceed $2x$.

Practical Considerations   Since a replacement selection generator is likely to be used a great deal with large files, there are two main practical questions relating to its construction.

   a.   How many bytes should the shovel contain?

   b.   Since the shovel has to be continually searched for the record with the smallest key greater than that previously output, how should the shovel be searched, and how should its contents be structured to minimize the search time?

The answer to the first question used to be fairly straightforward, before the advent of virtual operating systems (see Chapter 1). Then it was simply a matter of using the largest portion of main memory available. With virtual operating systems, we should like to avoid substantial paging of the pages making up the shovel. The minimum size of the shovel would clearly be 1 page (4K bytes), and the maximum size would be the main memory available when no other jobs were using the machine (an unlikely possibility). The optimum lies somewhere in between; the exact size probably depends on the type and number of concurrent jobs. We are not aware of any investigations of this problem.

The usual technique for efficient searching of the shovel is to construct a balanced tree, usually a binary tree, as shown in Figure 5.8a. Here the shovel contains 4 records, and the root of the tree is the key with the minimum value. When a record in the shovel is replaced by another, the tree is modified, as shown in Figure 5.8b. The tree can also be regarded as describing a tournament between pairs of keys, with the winner, the lowest key, occupying the next node in the tree. When the winner (15) is output to the sorted partition, the new insertion (47) makes key 21 the subsequent winner. This type of tree can clearly be searched in the order of $\log_2 x$ accesses, where x is the number of records in the shovel.

Another method for searching is to keep the keys of the records in *sorted order* in a dense one-level index to the records (see Section 4.4). A new record would be inserted in

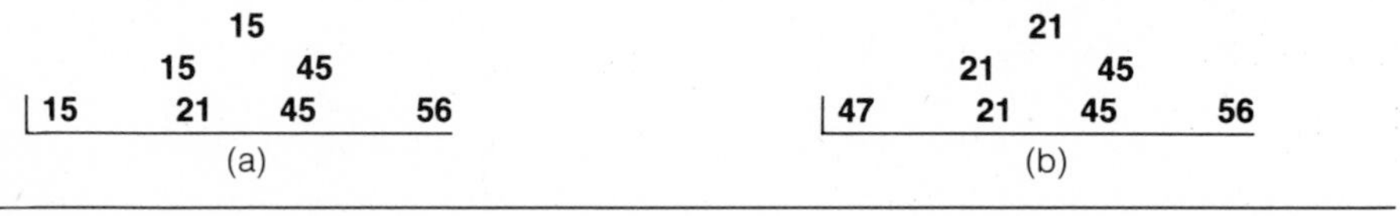

```
        15                              21
    15      45                      21      45
| 15   21   45   56             | 47   21   45   56
        (a)                             (b)
```

FIGURE 5.8. *Tournament structure for keys in the replacement selection shovel.*

the position vacated by the old one, while a new key (and pointer) would be inserted in the one-level index by moving up the index entries (a constant amount of distributed free space being used for this purpose). Insertion would thus involve a binary search of the index; retrieval of the next record to be output to the sorted partition would involve no search, because—as in Figure 5.7—an indicator (the star) could be used to locate the correct position. Searching for an insertion location would thus involve accesses of the order of $\log_2 x + n/4$, where n is the average number of index entries between consecutive free space slots. In practice, n would be between 4 and 10.

Apart from the size and structure of the shovel in main memory, the replacement selection or snowshovel generator is a straightforward example of a file processing routine, with one input file and one (or more, as we shall see) output files. We now turn to merging the file or files output from the replacement selection generator.

5.4 THE BALANCED MERGE

The balanced merge is easily the simplest method available for merging the sorted partition files resulting from processing an unsorted file. The method is quite effective but, as we shall see, it may be improved on. For convenience we shall distinguish between balanced 2-way and higher order k-way merges.

5.4.1 The Balanced 2-Way Merge

For the balanced 2-way merge, we need 4 storage files and up to 4 storage devices. There are usually a considerable number of processing stages involved, and 2 files are used for input and 2 for output. We shall assume 4 tapes on 4 drives.

The first stage (Figure 5.9) is the generation of two sorted partition files on tapes T1 and T2 from an unsorted file (on tape T3) using the generator described in the previous section. The generator produces, for example, 8 sorted partitions P1, P2, ..., as shown in the diagram, and placed alternately on T1 and T2 to insure that these files receive approximately the same number of partitions. We note that the partitions will be of varying length.

Generation of the initial sorted partition files is then followed by as many merge stages as are necessary to merge all the partitions. In the first merge stage (MERGE_1), tapes T1 and T2 are merged giving two new sorted partition files, with half as many partitions, on tapes T3 and T4. Note that T3 needs to be rewound before this stage can begin. In more detail, referring to Figure 5.9, the first pair of partitions from T1 and T2 are merged to give the first partition on T3; then the second pair of partitions on T1 and T2 are merged to give the first partition on T4. The process continues with consecutive pairs of partitions on T1 and T2 merged to give new partitions, output alternately on T3 and T4.

At the beginning of the next stage (MERGE_2) all the tapes are rewound, and the merge described for the first stage is now applied to the files on tapes T3 and T4. The result is two tapes, T1 and T2, each with only one partition. In the final stage, all the tapes may be rewound, and T1 and T2 are merged to give the sorted file output on T3.

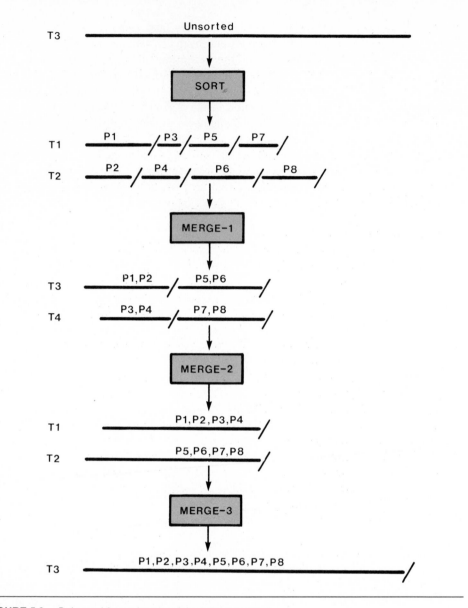

FIGURE 5.9. *Balanced 2-way merge of the sorted partition files initially on tapes* T1 *and* T2 *following generation from the unsorted file initially on* T3.

In case the reader has not completely grasped the details of a merge of two partitions, we give a simple numerical example further illustrating MERGE_1 from Figure 5.9, as follows.

TAPE T1 Contents: 14 16 22 / 18 / 17 29 35 / 23 31 /
TAPE T2 Contents: 20 27 / 21 26 / 25 / 11 15 28 /

$$\downarrow$$

TAPE T3 Contents: 14 16 20 22 27 / 17 25 29 35 /
TAPE T4 Contents: 18 21 26 / 11 15 23 28 31 /

Both T1 and T2 are processed sequentially, left to right, one record at a time. The keys of the two records are compared, and the record with the lesser key output and removed from consideration and replaced with the next consecutive record of the same type. The comparison process then takes place again. We shall be examining the process in more detail later, in the program MERGE.

General 2-Way Merge Algorithm   We can see that the process of merging in general involves taking two tapes, T1 and T2, and merging them, and then distributing the partitions onto two other tapes, T3 and T4. Following a rewind, T3 and T4 are merged and distributed onto T1 and T2. This continues alternately until we have only one output partition on one tape. Omitting the details, the following is a general algorithm.

1.   Merge sorted partitions on T1, T2.

2.   Distribute merged partitions alternately to T3, T4.

3.   If only one partition is distributed, then stop.

4.   Rewind all tapes.

5.   Merge sorted partitions on T3, T4.

6.   Distribute merged partitions alternately to T1, T2.

7.   If only one partition is distributed, stop.

8.   Rewind all tapes.

9.   Repeat from Step 1.

Since the number of sorted partitions is cut in half at each merge, it is clear that in general the process will require $\lceil \log_2 S \rceil$ merges. This means that the contents of each of the original S partitions have to be read $\lceil \log_2 S \rceil$ times, so that the total number of partitions read is

$$S\lceil \log_2 S \rceil \tag{1}$$

Thus if we had 64 partitions originally, each containing 1000 records on the average (or approximately 64,000 records), then the 2-way merge would be equivalent to reading in and writing out $64{,}000 * \log_2 64$ of these records, or 384,000 records. If instead of 64,000 records in 64 partitions, we had 64,000 records in 16 partitions, each containing an average of 4000 records, the 2-way merge process would be equivalent to reading in and writing out $64{,}000 * \log_2 16$, or 256,000, records, a clear improvement. This may be taken as proof of the assumption used in the previous section, namely, that the partitions of sorted partition files should be as large as possible.

Practical Considerations   So far we have assumed that the files were on tapes, thus making at least four tape drives mandatory. However, with the very large capacity disk

---

packs available today (for example, one drive of an IBM 3380 disk unit has a storage capacity of about 16 million card images, see Appendix 1), it is more than likely that all four files could easily reside on a single drive. Although the files would be processed sequentially, time-consuming seeks would necessarily and unfortunately occur as the disk controller switches from reading a block from one file on one cylinder to writing a block for another file on another cylinder.

However, a single IBM 3380 disk unit has two drives, with two independently addressable read/write head assemblies (actuators) per drive or disk pack. Thus, if such a unit were available, it would be possible to carry out an efficient 2-way merge with large files. We could eliminate seeks by having one file per actuator.

An advantage of using disk files is that tape rewinds can be avoided between merges. Of course it is clear that with most tape drives today, it is usually possible for the records on a tape to be read in reverse order. Following a merge in which the input tapes (for example, T1 and T2) are read forwards, if we now can read the new input tapes T3 and T4 backwards, then, provided the tapes T1 and T2 are replaced with fresh empty reels, all rewinding at the end of a merge can thus be avoided. The reader will recall that a PL/1 CONSECUTIVE file, which is directly applicable to the merging process, can be opened with:

OPEN FILE (BETA) INPUT BACKWARDS

if BETA is a tape file with standard System/370 drives. However, if we read the tapes in reverse instead of rewinding, we cannot use the same merge routine as for forward processing. With reverse reading, we output the record with the larger key when two records are compared.

We shall now give a practical example of a 2-way balanced merge on disk, where we assume that we initially have two disk files on which the sorted partitions generated from an unsorted file have been distributed. We do not assume, as in the example in Figure 5.9, that the two files have equal numbers of sorted partitions. For purposes of continuity, our initial files will be A and B, and in the first merge they will be merged and the resulting sorted partitions distributed onto C and D. Since in alternate merges, we shall be merging from C and D to A and B, we can use the PL/1 TITLE facility to accomplish switchovers in a simple way. The TITLE facility permits us to use an alias in all file manipulation statements defined as follows in an OPEN statement.

```
OPEN FILE (T1) TITLE ('A') INPUT,
     FILE (T3) TITLE ('C') OUTPUT;
.......;
READ FILE (T1) INTO ....;            /*  Physical file A read   */
........;
WRITE FILE (T3) FROM ....;           /*  Physical file C written   */
.......;
CLOSE FILE (T1), FILE (T3);          /*  End of first merge, physical files A, C closed   */
OPEN FILE (T1) TITLE ('C') INPUT,
     FILE (T3) TITLE ('A') OUTPUT;
........;
```

```
READ FILE (T1) .....;              /*  Physical file C read   */
WRITE FILE (T3) FROM .....;        /*  Physical file A written   */
..........;
CLOSE FILE (T1), FILE (T3);        /*  End of second merge, physical files C, A
                                   closed   */
```

In the first merge, we therefore use T1, T2, T3, and T4 as aliases for the underlying files A, B, C, and D, respectively (note that we require DD names A, B, C, and D). In the second merge, we can switch the aliases so that T1, T2, T3, and T4 correspond to the files C, D, A, and B, respectively. Thus in our routine, we have to have logic only for merging from T1 and T2 to T3 and T4. (Users of MULTICS PL/1 will note that this use of TITLE under IBM differs only in detail, not in principle.)

```
MERGE: PROC OPTIONS (MAIN);
/*
```

1. Program merges two initial sorted partition files A and B by a balanced 2-way merge using initial empty output files C and D.

2. All files are assumed to be on disk, preferably with separate read/write head assemblies, eliminating seeks if no other users are processing other files on same disk unit concurrently.

3. In the program the logical file names or aliases T1, T2, T3, and T4 are used to correspond alternately to the files A, B, C, and D, respectively, and the files C, D, A, and B, respectively. The merging is then always from T1 and T2 to T3 and T4.

4. Current merge records from T1 and T2 are held in structure variables S1 and S2, respectively. Current merge keys are in variables S1.KY and S2.KY. Most recently output keys from T1 and T2 are held in variables R1 and R2, respectively.

5. Raising of flags EOP1 and EOP2 indicates the end of current T1 and T2 sorted partitions, respectively. EOF1 and EOF2 are flags for end of T1 and T2, respectively.

6. Initially A and B do not necessarily have the same number of sorted partitions.

7. Program indicates in which file the final sorted version lies.   */

```
DCL (T1,T2,T3,T4) FILE RECORD ENV (CONSECUTIVE);

DCL 1 S1,                          /*  Holds T1 record   */
    2 KY CHAR (10),                /*  Record key   */
    2 DESCRIPTION CHAR (190),      /*  Remainder of record   */
    R1 CHAR (10);                  /*  Holds key prior to S1.KY   */

DCL 1 S2 LIKE S1,                  /*  Holds T2 record   */
    R2 CHAR (10);                  /*  Holds key prior to S2.KY   */

DCL (M,                            /*  Counts number of merges or passes   */
    P) FIXED BIN (15);             /*  Counts new partitions formed in a given
                                   merge   */
```

```
DCL (EOP1, EOP2,                    /*  End of T1, T2 partition flags   */
    EOF1, EOF2) BIT (1);            /*  End of T1, T2 flags   */


ON ENDFILE (T1) EOF1 = '1'B;
ON ENDFILE (T2) EOF2 = '1'B;


M = 0; P = 0;
DO WHILE (P⌐ = 1);
```

/*   This major loop controls merges or passes; when the number of sorted partitions output
from a merge is equal to 1, no further merges will be required   */

```
M = M + 1;                          /*  First or next merge starts   */
IF MOD(M,2) = 1                     /*  M is odd; A and B used for input   */
THEN   OPEN      FILE (T1) TITLE ('A')          INPUT,
                 FILE (T2) TITLE ('B')          INPUT,
                 FILE (T3) TITLE ('C')          OUTPUT,
                 FILE (T4) TITLE ('D')          OUTPUT;
ELSE                                /*  M is even; C and D used for input   */
     OPEN
                 FILE (T1) TITLE ('C')          INPUT,
                 FILE (T2) TITLE ('D')          INPUT,
                 FILE (T3) TITLE ('A')          OUTPUT,
                 FILE (T4) TITLE ('B')          OUTPUT;
```

`P = 1;  /*  First sorted partition in this merge will now be generated   */`

```
EOP1,EOP2,EOF1,EOF2 = 'O'B;         /*  Flags all down initially   */
READ FILE (T1) INTO (S1);
READ FILE (T2) INTO (S2);
DO WHILE ( ⌐ EOF1|⌐ EOF2);
```

/*   In this loop T1 and T2 records are read until the end of both files are reached. The
internal logic is complicated by the fact that we must watch out for ends of generated
partitions and distribute them between T3 and T4   */

```
IF (S1.KY < S2.KY & ⌐ EOP1) | EOP2 THEN
BEGIN;
```

/*   FIRST ACTION BLOCK   */

/*   T1 record in S1 will be written on T3 or T4 and replaced by a new T1 record. If
EOP2 flag is raised then a key comparison is not necessary since we have reached the
end of the current T2 partition   */

```
R1 = S1.KY;     /*  Retain current key for stepdown check   */
IF MOD(P,2) = 1  /*  Odd numbered partition   */
```

```
              THEN WRITE FILE (T3) FROM (S1);
              ELSE WRITE FILE (T4) FROM (S1);
READ FILE (T1) INTO (S1);  /*   Replace current record   */


      /*   We may have reached the end of the file, but   */
IF ⌐EOF1 THEN   /*   If not end of file   */
/*   Maybe end of current partition?   */
      IF (S1.KY < R1) THEN   /*   Stepdown confirmed, end of partition   */
          IF   EOP2  THEN   /*   If we are also at end of T2 partition   */
                          /*   Maybe also at end of T2 file?   */
              IF EOF2   THEN   P = P + 1;  /*   Generation of fresh sorted partition
                                              indicated   */
                      ELSE                 /*   Not also end of T2 file   */
                    DO;
                        EOP2 = 'O'B;  /*   Permits start of generating fresh
                                          partition   */
                        P = P + 1;  /*   Generation of fresh partition
                                        indicated   */
                    END;
          ELSE   /*   Not end of T2 partition   */
              EOP1 = '1'B;  /*   Raise end of T1 partition flag   */
      ELSE;   /*   Not stepdown   */
      /*   But suppose it had been the end of T1 file   */


ELSE   /*   End of file T1 confirmed   */
    IF EOP2 THEN   /*   If we are also at end of T2 partition   */
        IF EOF2  THEN;   /*   If also at end of T2 file, do nothing   */
            ELSE DO;   /*   Not at end of T2 file   */
                EOP2 = '0'B;  /*   Permits generation of fresh partition from
                                  T2 records only   */
                P = P + 1;  /*   Generation of fresh partition indicated   */
                EOP1 = '1'B;  /*   End of T1 partition flag raised   */
          END;
    ELSE   /*   Not also end of T2 partition   */
        EOP1 = '1'B;  /*   End of T1 partition flag raised   */
END;  /*   End of FIRST ACTION BLOCK   */

ELSE IF S1.KY = S2.KY   /*   This shouldn't happen   */
              THEN CALL ERROR;   /*   ERROR prints a message and stops
                                     program   */
ELSE IF (S1.KY > S2.KY &  ⌐EOP2) | EOP1 THEN

BEGIN;
```

                      /*   SECOND ACTION BLOCK   */
      /*   The FIRST and SECOND ACTION BLOCKS are symmetrical. The SECOND
          BLOCK may be obtained by substituting the digits 2 and 1 for 1 and 2,

respectively, in all variable and file names in the FIRST ACTION BLOCK. Thus EOP2 would read EOP1, and T1 would read T2.

We could have used a subroutine for both the FIRST and SECOND ACTION BLOCKS, but the increased number of variables caused by the introduction of the subroutine parameters would have decreased readability. The reader might construct the necessary subroutine as an exercise.   */

```
END;  /*  End of SECOND ACTION BLOCK  */

END;  /*  Of WHILE ( ⌐ EOF1 or ⌐ EOF2) loop  */

    /*  We can now start next merge  */

CLOSE FILE (T1), FILE (T2), FILE (T3), FILE (T4);
    /*  Note that if we forget to close the files (i.e., A, B, C, and D), the system cannot open
       them with new aliases for the next merge */
END;  /*  Of WHILE (P ⌐ = 1) loop  */

    /*  We need to determine on which file the result lies  */
IF MOD (M,2) = 0 THEN PUT SKIP LIST ('RESULT IS ON FILE A');
                ELSE PUT SKIP LIST ('RESULT IS ON FILE C');
PUT SKIP LIST (M, 'PASSES REQUIRED');
END;
/*
//GO.A DD DSN = A, ...
//GO.B DD DSN = B, ...
//GO.C DD DSN = C, ...
//GO.D DD DSN = D, ...
```

The equivalent program for sorting tape files is a little trickier to write, if in alternate merges we have to read the tapes in reverse. This would give us four versions of the ACTION BLOCK to worry about, two with forward merging and two with backward merging.

5.4.2 The *k*-Way Merge

In a k-way merge, we merge from k files and distribute onto k files, so that we use $2k$ files in all. Thus the k-way merge is a simple extension of the 2-way merge.

The logic of a higher-order merge can easily be depicted in a table, provided we agree on notation. We shall use the notation $n(j)$ to mean that a tape has n partitions, each partition being j IPLs long. An *IPL* (Initial Partition Length) is the length of an initial partition on average. Thus in the 2-order merge depicted in Figure 5.9, tape T1 had initially 4(1) partitions; that is, 4 partitions each the length of an initial partition. At the end of the first merge, T3 had 2(2) partitions; that is, 2 partitions each twice the length of an initial partition, or simply 2 IPLs long.

In the example of a 3-way merge shown in Table 5.1, we have 27 partitions initially distributed on the three tapes T1, T2, T3. These tapes are merged giving 3 partitions each

SIMPLE 3-WAY MERGE						
Stage	T1	T2	T3	T4	T5	T6
Initial	9(1)	9(1)	9(1)	—	—	—
MERGE_1	—	—	—	3(3)	3(3)	3(3)
MERGE_2	1(9)	1(9)	1(9)	—	—	—
MERGE_3	—	—	—	1(27)		

TABLE 5.1

3 IPLs long on each of tapes T4, T5, and T6. These tapes are then rewound (instead of rewinding T1, T2, and T3, we could replace them with fresh empty reels) and the merging continues as depicted in the diagram.

It is clear that if m is the order of the merge and S is the total number of partitions, the total number of passes through the data is

$$\left\lceil \frac{\log_2 S}{\log_2 m} \right\rceil$$

At first glance, then, it would appear that the bigger we make m, the better. This is true in theory, but in practice, limitations of storage devices and main memory place practical upper limits of between 3 and 5 on the merge order, as we shall now see.

Practical Considerations   We shall, in practice, use either disks or tapes for a higher-order merge. Let us first consider briefly the main factors that come into play for both these types of devices, and then derive some useful expressions for the time to merge a large file as a function of merge order and type of device.

With tapes, two factors will limit the order of the merge. The first is obvious. Tape drives are complicated and expensive, and more than 10 in working order is an uncommon occurrence. This would immediately limit the merge order to 5. However, a more subtle limitation is at work. It is clear that the amount of main memory we can use for buffers for an application without excessive paging is limited. We had this problem with the amount of main memory we could use for the shovel in the replacement selection generator. In practice, the amount will be some fairly small multiple of the page size. Thus increasing the merge order will mean smaller buffers for each tape. Smaller buffers will mean a smaller block size, which will cause the block size to become comparable with the inter-block gap. We recall from Chapter 1 that the interblock gap can be quite large; on a 1600-bpi industry tape, it is 12 card-images, or 960 bytes. This will mean that the data transmission rate will deteriorate rapidly with increasing merge order. Thus, although there are few passes, each pass becomes a lot slower.

An additional consideration is the possibility of improved efficiency due to overlapped I/O. Since the files are on separate tape drives, I/O could be overlapped by the operating system using different channels concurrently, as described in Chapter 1. Nevertheless the amount of overlapping will be limited by the number of channels, with close to $2k$ channels being required to completely overlap I/O in a k-order merge. Thus 100% I/O overlap will be most unlikely in practice.

With disk files we can distinguish two distinct possibilities. The latest disk drives have very large capacity, so that one possibility is to have all the files on a single disk drive with one read/write head assembly for all of them (thus ensuring no I/O overlap). The other possibility is to place the files on sufficient disk drives to ensure that each file has a read/write head assembly (thus ensuring the possibility of 100% I/O overlap, if sufficient channels are available).

In the case of a single read/write head assembly for *all* files, processing time will be dominated by seeks, since when one file is read, the next READ will be for a different block on a different cylinder, and so on. Thus there will be a seek associated with every block transmitted. As with tapes, because of limited main memory buffer space, we can expect that the block size will fall with increasing merge order; that is, the number of blocks will increase. Thus the number of seeks per file increases with increasing merge order, but the number of passes through the data decreases. To see what will happen, we must resort to mathematics, and we shall see that the losses from the seeks exceed the gains from the reduced number of passes.

In the case of one read/write head assembly for *each* file, processing time will be dominated by rotational delay. However, increasing merge order will again be associated with decreasing block size and increasing number of blocks per file. Thus we will have increasing rotational delay losses per file processed with increasing merge order, and—as we shall see—this exceeds the gains from having to process the data fewer times. However, in this case we have the possibility of I/O overlap if there are sufficient channels available. We now give a more detailed analysis of these three important cases.

Mathematical Analysis   We need the following parameters.

Total initial sorted partitions	S	
Average length of an initial partition	i	(bytes)
Maximum main memory buffer space	$2X$	(bytes)
Merge order	m	
Storage device nominal transmission rate	s	(bytes/millisecond)
Average seek time	P	(milliseconds)
Disk rotation time	R	(milliseconds)
Tape interblock gap	g	(bytes)

There will be X bytes of buffer space for input files. To prevent CPU delays, we shall have to assign two buffers for each file (double buffering is described in Chapter 2), so that the buffer size and, therefore, the block size will be

$$\frac{X}{2m} \quad \text{bytes}$$

The total length of the unsorted file is Si bytes, so that the total number of blocks in the input files will be:

$$\frac{2mSi}{X} \quad \text{blocks}$$

There will be an equal number in the output files. (This will be true even for the last file; that is, the result file.)

The number of passes through the data is

$$\left\lceil \frac{\log_2 S}{\log_2 m} \right\rceil \quad \text{passes}$$

Hence the total number of blocks written and read in the complete merging process will be

$$\frac{4mSi}{X} * \left\lceil \frac{\log_2 S}{\log_2 m} \right\rceil \quad \text{blocks} \tag{2}$$

This expression tells us how many blocks we have to process (input and output), regardless of the type of storage device we are using. We now continue for each type of storage device in turn, making use of Expression 2.

1. *Disk, with one R/W head assembly for all files*
    The time to transmit a single block will be (as shown in Chapter 1)

    $$\left(P + \frac{R}{2} + \frac{X}{2ms} \right) \quad \text{milliseconds}$$

    Hence, using Expression 2, the time to transmit all the blocks will be

    $$\left(P + \frac{R}{2} + \frac{X}{2ms} \right) * \frac{4mSi}{X} * \left\lceil \frac{\log_2 S}{\log_2 m} \right\rceil \quad \text{milliseconds} \tag{3}$$

    and, assuming that I/O is overlapped with internal memory processing time, this expression gives us the total merging time. Because of the single R/W head, there is no possibility of I/O overlap for the different files.

2. *Disk, R/W head assembly for each file*
    We may assume that seeks will have a negligible impact, so that we may assert that the processing time is Expression 3 with $P = 0$. Thus the time is

    $$\left(\frac{R}{2} + \frac{X}{2ms} \right) * \frac{4mSi}{X} * \left\lceil \frac{\log_2 S}{\log_2 m} \right\rceil \quad \text{milliseconds} \tag{4}$$

    Because each file has its own R/W head assembly, there is the possibility of 100% overlap of I/O, always provided there are enough channels. Such overlap is not very likely, but it represents a best-case result, just as Expression 4, which assumes no I/O overlap, represents a worst-case result. Because we have *2m* files being read and written at any given time (except when the last file is being written, which we neglect), then if there is 100% overlap of I/0, the processing time will be as in Expression 4, divided by *2m*.

$$\left(\frac{R}{2} + \frac{X}{2ms}\right) * \frac{2Si}{X} * \left\lceil \frac{\log_2 S}{\log_2 m} \right\rceil \quad \text{milliseconds} \tag{5}$$

3. *Tape*

Taking the large tape interblock gap into account, the time to transmit a block will be

$$\left(\frac{X}{2m} + g\right)\frac{1}{s} \quad \text{milliseconds}$$

Combining this with the number of blocks processed, as given by Expression 2, the expression for the total processing time is

$$\left(\frac{X}{2m} + g\right) * \frac{4mSi}{sX} * \left\lceil \frac{\log_2 S}{\log_2 m} \right\rceil \quad \text{milliseconds} \tag{6}$$

This expression assumes no I/O overlap and thus represents a worst case. The corresponding best-case expression for 100% I/O overlap, which is unlikely, may be obtained by dividing Expression 6 by *2m:*

$$\left(\frac{X}{2m} + g\right) * \frac{2Si}{sX} * \left\lceil \frac{\log_2 S}{\log_2 m} \right\rceil \quad \text{milliseconds} \tag{7}$$

Note that in both Expressions 6 and 7, we have assumed that no rewinds are involved, which may be achieved by using fresh empty reels and reading tapes backwards.

Merging with Current Storage Devices   We may apply Expressions 2 through 7 to a practical merge problem on current media. We use the following figures.

$$S = 1024 \text{ partitions}$$

$$2X = 32,000 \text{ bytes}$$

$$i = 8000 \text{ bytes} \quad \text{(about twice an IBM page)}$$

Thus we assume that we have an initial unsorted file about 8 million bytes long. (Note that the length of a record has no effect on our processing time expressions, since record lengths affect only internal processing time.)

We use parameters for three storage media.

a.   IBM 3380 disk (1980).

$$P = 16 \text{ milliseconds}; \quad \frac{R}{2} = 8.3 \text{ milliseconds}; \quad s = 3000 \text{ bytes/millisecond}$$

b.   IBM 3350 disk (1976).

$$P = 25 \text{ milliseconds}; \quad \frac{R}{2} = 8.3 \text{ milliseconds}; \quad s = 1198 \text{ bytes/millisecond}$$

c. 1600-bpi industry tape.

$g = 960$ bytes; $s = 160$ bytes/millisecond

We note that our (8 million byte) file will not be too large to reside on a single reel (2400 feet of tape) when finally sorted.

These parameters and Expressions 3 through 7 have been used to compute the curves in Figure 5.10. Curves *Da* and *WDa* describe the case for 3350 and 3380 disks, respectively, where there is only one read/write head assembly for all the files. This, of course, is probably the most inefficient way to carry out a *k*-way merge. Nevertheless, despite the excessive seeks, on a 3380 disk the low order merge is competitive with the industry tape merge. As the merge order is increased, the processing time increases quite rapidly. There is clearly little to be gained from a merge order much above 2.

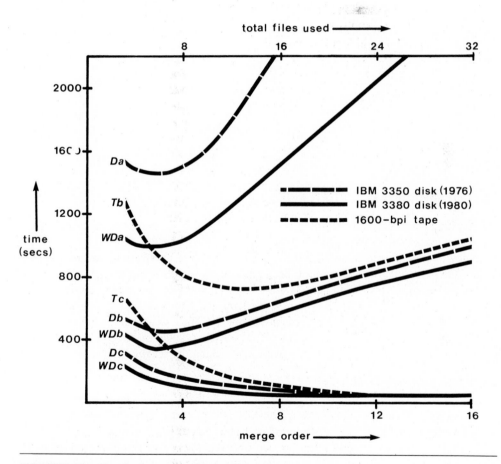

FIGURE 5.10. *Time for k-way merging 8 million bytes of data. For full explanation, see text. The total number of merge files used will always be twice the merge order. Buffer area is assumed limited to 32,000 bytes.*

THE BALANCED MERGE

Giving each disk file its own R/W head assembly cuts the time to less than half of the previous case, as can be seen from curves Db and WDb. The time increases slowly with m, and $m = 2$ is probably the optimum in practice. If we have 100% overlap of I/O, then the processing time is further reduced, and only now do we find that the time falls with increasing merge order (curves Dc and WDc). Thus Db/WDb and Dc/WDc represent the worst and best cases, respectively, where each disk file has its own read/write head assembly, and there is no interference from other jobs (causing extra seeks).

With the industry tape, and assuming no I/O overlap, the processing time initially falls with increasing merge order, because the time to process the data is not initially dependent on the length of a block. However, with higher-order merges, the block size becomes comparable with the gap width (for $m = 16$ and block size $= 1000$, with $g = 960$) and the processing time begins to increase again (curve Tb). There is little to gain from having the merge order much above 5. If 100% I/O overlap is allowed, the processing time will decrease with increasing merge order, but again there is little to be gained from a merge order above 5 (curve Tc). Curves Tb and Tc clearly represent worst and best cases for the industry tape. We note that, in general, processing on disk with a read/write head assembly per file is faster.

These curves must be taken with a grain of salt, however. We have used average quantities a great deal and have not been able to incorporate the effect of interference from other jobs. Furthermore, they would change substantially were different buffer sizes to be used. Nevertheless they do give some idea of the relative processing times involved in what is clearly a complex situation. The reader is referred to Knuth [Knuth, 1973] or Lorin [Lorin, 1974] for additional analysis.

5.5 POLYPHASE AND OTHER MERGES

Close examination of k-way merging indicates that it may be improved on in principle. For example, consider once more the simple 2-way merge illustrated in Figure 5.9. Suppose now that instead of allowing MERGE-2 to proceed to completion, we instead stop it after the first pair of partitions have been merged, as shown in Figure 5.11. The result of this partial merge is now on tape T1 while tape T2 is empty. We could now rewind T1 and start a different MERGE-3, this time merging the unprocessed parts of T3 and T4 together with T1, producing the final result on tape T2. Thus we save the input and output of four initial partitions, the equivalent of the initial contents of T1 or T2, which is a substantial saving. This leads us to the basic idea behind the *polyphase merge*.

5.5.1 The Polyphase Merge

A short polyphase merge with 4 storage devices is depicted in Table 5.2. As before, we use the convention that 4(5) means 4 sorted partitions, each 5 IPLs in length, an IPL being the average length of an initial partition. We start out with 13 partitions on device A, 11 on B, and 7 on C. The length of each of the partitions on A, B, and C is 1 IPL.

At the end of the first merge (merge 1 in Table 5.2), we have merged until the smallest file C has been exhausted; the result is on the initially empty file D, which now contains 7 partitions, each 3 IPLs in length, because 3 files were merged to produce them.

POLYPHASE MERGE WITH FOUR INITIAL FILES **A, B, C,** and **D,** CONTAINING 31 IPLs							
Merge	A	B	C	D	Total IPLs	Total Current Partitions	IPLs Processed
—	13(1)	11(1)	7(1)	—	31	31	0
1	6(1)	4(1)	—	7(3)	31	17	7*3
2	2(1)	—	4(5)	3(3)	31	9	4*5
3	—	2(9)	2(5)	1(3)	31	5	2*9
4	1(17)	1(9)	1(5)	—	31	3	1*17
5	—	—	—	1(31)	31	1	1*31

TABLE 5.2

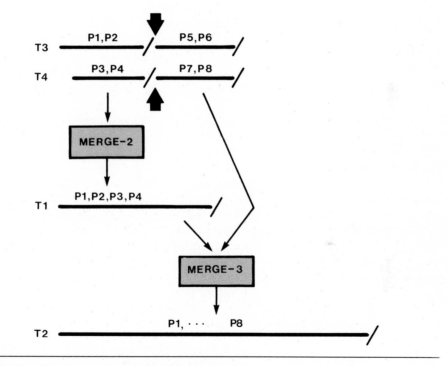

FIGURE 5.11. *The diagram illustrates how the balanced 2-way merge from Figure 5.9 can be made more efficient by employing a 3-way merge onto* **T2** *in the final merge. The second merge must be stopped (heavy arrows) when the first two partitions on* **T3** *and* **T4** *have been merged onto* **T1.**

In the second merge, A and B are processed forward from the point at which they were stopped at the end of the previous merge, and they are now merged with D; the result is placed on the empty file C. However, this merge is stopped when B is exhausted, and because we are merging two files with partitions that are each 1 IPL long with a file that has partitions which are 3 IPLs long, partitions in C must be 5 IPLs long. Because B had 4 partitions at the start of this merge, C will have 4 partitions at the end of it.

The next merge proceeds in the same way. The smallest file is merged to exhaustion, and the output is placed on the empty file, exhausted in the previous merge. Finally, we come to the situation where each of the three files has only one partition. Merging of these files gives the final result.

The polyphase merge is effective because in every merge we have the highest-order merge possible, just as in the improved merge described in Figure 5.11. However, the merge depicted in Table 5.2 went smoothly *only because we choose the initial distribution of sorted partitions on A, B, and C, so that in the final merge we were merging three files, each with a single sorted partition.* Thus in order to get the polyphase merge to work, we must start out with certain "perfect" distributions of sorted partitions on the files initially, as we shall now see.

Polyphase Merge Patterns and Perfect Distributions Table 5.2 is full of (3rd order) Fibonacci numbers arranged in a very intricate pattern. To understand the nature of this pattern and how to make use of it, let us begin by rearranging Table 5.2 as shown in Table 5.3. Here and at all stages in the merge, we have arranged the intermediate files as logical files T1, T2, and T3 in such a way that the largest file is always T1 and the smallest T3.

We now see that the initial number of partitions on T1, 13, is the sum of the number on T1 at the end of the first, second, and third merges, or $7 + 4 + 2$. Furthermore, the number of partitions at the end of the first merge, 7, is the sum of the numbers at the ends of the next three merges, $4 + 2 + 1$, and so on. It turns out that the column for T1 is part of the 3rd-order Fibonacci sequence, in which each number is the sum of its 3 (because it is 3rd order) predecessors. Thus to find a suitable perfect number for the number of partitions on T1 initially, we must generate the correct Fibonacci sequence.

The general situation for merging with 4 files (that is, merging from 3 files, distributing on 1 file) is shown in Table 5.4. To completely describe the sequence for T1, we must use the exact Fibonacci sequence together with start values. When we have a polyphase merge with $p + 1$ files, then the pth-order Fibonacci sequence applies, where for each element $F_n^{(p)}$, we have

$$F_n^{(p)} = F_{n-1}^{(p)} + F_{n-2}^{(p)} + \cdots + F_{n-p}^{(p)}$$

where

$$F_{p-1}^{(p)} = 1, \quad \text{and for } n < p - 1, \quad F_n^{(p)} = 0$$

Thus for $p = 3$, the case in hand, $F_2^{(3)} = 1$, $F_1^{(3)} = 0$, and $F_0^{(3)} = 0$. The first 3 elements on the sequence are, therefore, 0, 0, and 1; by summing the 3 predecessors we can generate the rest, that is, 1, 2, 4, 7, 13, 24, . . . and so on.

				Total	Total Current	IPLs
Merge	T1	T2	T3	IPLs	Partitions	Processed
—	13(1)	11(1)	7(1)	31	31	0
1	7(3)	6(1)	4(1)	31	17	7*3
2	4(5)	3(3)	2(1)	31	9	4*5
3	2(9)	2(5)	1(3)	31	5	2*9
4	1(17)	1(9)	1(5)	31	3	1*17
5	1(31)	0( )	0( )	31	1	1*31

THIS TABLE IS THE SAME AS TABLE 5.2, EXCEPT THAT WE EMPLOY LOGICAL FILES T1, T2, AND T3 TO HOLD SUCCESSIVE MERGE FILES IN ORDER OF SIZE, THE LARGEST IN T1, AND THE SMALLEST IN T3.

TABLE 5.3

GENERALIZATION OF TABLE 5.3, TO ALLOW FOR DIFFERENT INITIAL PARTITION TOTALS (t_n). THE TABLE MAY BE GENERATED FROM THE 3RD-ORDER FIBONACCI SEQUENCE.

3rd-order Fibonacci Subscript	T1	T2	T3	Total Current Partitions	IPLs Processed
n	a_n	b_n	c_n	t_n	0
$n-1$	a_{n-1}	b_{n-1}	c_{n-1}	t_{n-1}	$a_{n-1}*t_3$
⋮	⋮	⋮	⋮	⋮	⋮
7	13	11	7	31	a_7*t_{n-5}
6	7	6	4	17	a_6*t_{n-4}
5	4	3	2	9	a_5*t_{n-3}
4	2	2	1	5	a_4*t_{n-2}
3	1	1	1	3	a_3*t_{n-1}
2	1	0	0	1	a_2*t_n
1	0	0	0	Initial 3rd-order Fibonacci values	
0	0	0	0		

TABLE 5.4

So much for the number of initial partitions on the largest file T1; however, we still need a way of generating the numbers for the other two files. Now using Table 5.4 (and perhaps also Table 5.2), if we take $n = 7$ and $n = 6$ to guide us, from the nature of the merging process we must have

$$a_n = a_{n-1} + b_{n-1} \qquad \text{(for example, } 13 = 7 + 6)$$

$$b_n = a_{n-1} + c_{n-1} \qquad \text{(for example, } 11 = 7 + 4)$$

$$c_n = a_{n-1} \qquad \text{(for example, } 7 = 7)$$

Combining these three expressions, it is simple to obtain the following defining relationships.

$$a_n = a_{n-1} + a_{n-2} + a_{n-3}$$

$$b_n = a_{n-1} + a_{n-2}$$

$$c_n = a_{n-1}$$

The first of these three expressions is proof of what we have already observed; that is, that the 3rd-order Fibonacci sequence governs the number of sorted partitions on T1. The remaining two expressions enable the other columns to be generated. Thus the values of a_8, b_8, and c_8 should be 24, 20, and 13, respectively.

Of course, this analysis applies to the case of 4 storage devices; if we have 3 devices, then the 2nd-order Fibonacci sequence applies, giving the pattern in Table 5.5a. Here the defining relationships will be:

$$a_n = a_{n-1} + a_{n-2}$$

$$b_n = a_{n-1}$$

If we have 6 devices, then the 5th-order Fibonacci sequence applies, as illustrated in Table 5.5b. Here the defining relationships will be

$$a_n = a_{n-1} + a_{n-2} + a_{n-3} + a_{n-4} + a_{n-5}$$

$$b_n = a_{n-1} + a_{n-2} + a_{n-3} + a_{n-4}$$

$$c_n = a_{n-1} + a_{n-2} + a_{n-3}$$

$$d_n = a_{n-1} + a_{n-2}$$

$$e_n = a_{n-1}$$

2nd-order Fibonacci Subscript	T1	T2	5th-order Fibonacci Subscript	T1	T2	T3	T4	T5
n	a_n	b_n	n	a_n	b_n	c_n	d_n	e_n
⋮	⋮	⋮	⋮	⋮	⋮	⋮	⋮	⋮
7	13	8	10	31	30	28	24	16
6	8	5	9	16	15	14	12	8
5	5	3	8	8	8	7	6	4
4	3	2	7	4	4	4	3	2
3	2	1	6	2	2	2	2	1
2	1	1	5	1	1	1	1	1
1	1	0	4	1	0	0	0	0
0	0	0	3	0	0	0	0	0
(a)			2	0	0	0	0	0
			1	0	0	0	0	0
			0	0	0	0	0	0
			(b)					

Table title: PARTITION DISTRIBUTION FOR THE CASE OF 3 FILES (a) AND THE CASE OF 6 FILES (b)

TABLE 5.5

It should now be clear how we can determine the perfect numbers for the initial distribution of sorted partitions. But if we use the replacement selection generator, how can we ensure that it will generate the correct perfect distribution? The answer is that we cannot, but we can round off the distributions by using dummy-sorted partitions; that is, partitions each with a single dummy key. Thus the replacement generator for 4 devices would be programmed to distribute according to the pattern in Table 5.4, starting with the bottom rows. If generation was completed with the distribution 10, 10, and 7 on T1, T2, and T3, respectively, then 3 dummy partitions would be added to T1 and 1 to T2. Unfortunately, in this simple generation, the dummies are at the ends of the files. Closer examination of the merging process (Table 5.2) reveals that sorted partitions at the start of the files are processed most often, so that it is best if these are short. Thus dummy partitions are best placed near the beginning of the files. Algorithms for doing this have been described by Knuth [Knuth, 1973]. We now look at the efficiency of the polyphase merge, assuming that we can always use perfect initial distributions.

Polyphase Merge Efficiency   In this analysis, we wish to find how many initial partitions are read in during all the merges of the complete merge process. Dividing this by the number of initial sorted partitions gives us what corresponds to the number of passes through the data.

Consider the merge in Table 5.2 again. In the first merge, 7 partitions from 3 files are read in; that is, 7*3 IPLs in all. In the second merge, 4 partitions from 3 files are read, but in 2 of the files the partitions are each 1 IPL long, while in the third file, the partitions are 3 IPLs long. Thus 4*(1 + 1 + 3), or 4*5, IPLs are processed. We can continue in this way, as indicated in the last column of Table 5.2. The number of passes through the data will be

$$\frac{7*3 + 4*5 + 2*9 + 1*17 + 1*31}{31}$$

where 31, or 13 + 11 + 7, is the total number of initial partitions. The result in this case is 3.45, which incidentally gives us a point on the graph in Figure 5.12. Had we used a 2-way balanced merge, we would have had 5 passes.

The method outlined above for obtaining the number of passes using Table 5.2 is rather tedious. However, referring to Table 5.3, we notice that the products in the last column use the number of partitions on T1 at each merge (7, 4, 2, 1, 1) and the total partitions on T1, T2, and T3 at each merge, as given in the column under *Total Current*

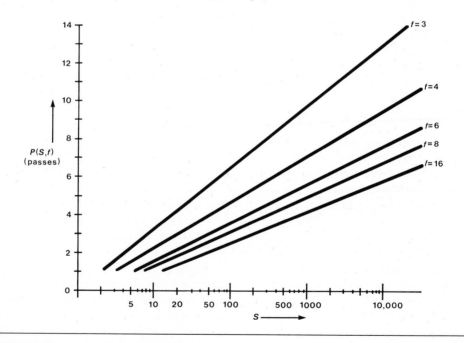

FIGURE 5.12.   *Approximate number of passes versus number of initial partitions (S) for a standard polyphase merge for different numbers of files (f) employed.*

Partitions; that is, 31, 17, 9, 5, 3 (but not 1). Thus we do not have to concern ourselves with the length of current partitions in IPLs, as given in parentheses in the table. Turning now to Table 5.4, we see that the products may be expressed generally in terms of a_n values and t_n values, where the total current partitions is t_n given by

$$t_n = a_n + b_n + c_n$$

It is useful to note that the t_n values may be obtained even more simply, since it follows from the defining relations for the 4-device case given earlier, that

$$t_n = a_n + b_n + c_n = t_{n-1} + 2a_{n-1}$$

and in the general case with $p + 1$ devices,

$$t_n = t_{n-1} + (p - 1)a_{n-1}$$

The general expression for the number of passes through the data in a complete polyphase merge is therefore

$$\frac{a_{p-1}*t_n + a_{p-1+1}*t_{n-1} + a_{p-1+2}*t_{n-2} + \cdots + a_{n-1}*t_p}{t_n} \tag{8}$$

where t_n is the total initial sorted partitions and a_n is the nth p-order Fibonacci sequence number. We leave it to the interested reader to devise a summation expression for Expression 8. If we let $S = t_n$ and $f = p + 1$, so that S is the number of sorted partitions and f is the number of files or devices, we can replace 8 by

$$P(S, f) \tag{9}$$

indicating that the number of passes is a function of the number of initial sorted partitions and number of files employed. With the help of the Fibonacci numbers, we can express $P(S, f)$ graphically, as shown in Figure 5.12. The curves are only an approximation, connecting total passes for cases where the total initial distributions are perfect. When the distributions are not perfect, the number of passes will depend on how the merging routine treats the necessary dummy partitions. Nevertheless, the curves do give a picture that is accurate to within a few percentage points in most cases. We notice that $P(S, f)$ increases with log S. More detailed curves have been deduced by Knuth [Knuth, 1973].

If we carefully compare the curves of Figure 5.12 with the number of passes for the k-way merge, we find that for small f, the polyphase merge can be up to 30% faster, but for f greater than about 8, depending on S, there is little difference in the number of passes required.

Practical considerations   We have much the same kind of device factors coming into play with the polyphase merge as with the k-way merge. Thus we could have all the files

---

served by a single R/W head assembly or have each file with its own R/W head assembly. Or we can have the files on tape. Thus we can apply relationships of the kind developed for k-way merging; that is, Expressions 3 through 7, which give processing times with the amount of buffer space $2X$ fixed regardless of the number of files $(2m)$, not an unreasonable condition. To use Expressions 3 through 7 for a polyphase merge, we need to replace the number of k-way passes,

$$\left\lceil \frac{\log^2 S}{\log_2 m} \right\rceil$$

by $P(S, f)$, which is based on Expression 8 and displayed in Figure 5.12. In addition, we must replace m by $f/2$. We then have the following cases.

1. *Disk, one R/W head assembly for all files.*
   The processing time is

$$\left(P + \frac{R}{2} + \frac{X}{fs} \right) * \frac{2fSi}{X} * P(S, f) \qquad \text{milliseconds} \qquad (10)$$

2. *Disk, R/W head assembly for each file.*
   The processing time with no I/0 overlap is

$$\left(\frac{R}{2} + \frac{X}{fs} \right) * \frac{2fSi}{X} * P(S, f) \qquad \text{milliseconds} \qquad (11)$$

Overlapping I/O 100% seems to be a theoretical impossibility with the polyphase merge. Unlike the k-way merge case, the length of partitions in different files will vary a great deal, requiring much more I/O with one file than another (see Table 5.2).

3. *Tape.*
   Neglecting rewind time, processing time with no I/O overlap is

$$\left(\frac{X}{f} + g \right) * \frac{2fSi}{sX} * P(S, f) \qquad \text{milliseconds} \qquad (12)$$

Again 100% I/O overlap is a theoretical impossibility with the standard polyphase merge.

Polyphase Merging with Current Storage Devices   As in the case of the k-way merge, we may apply Expressions 10 and 11 to IBM 3350 and 3380 disks and 12 to the 1600-bpi tape. The parameters chosen ($S = 1024$, $2X = 32{,}000$, and $i = 8000$) are the same as before to facilitate comparison. The resulting curves are shown in Figure 5.13. It can be seen that there is a significant improvement only for $f<8$. See page 179–80.

Although we have no curve for the best case of I/O overlap, some I/O overlap is theoretically possible, so that curves Db, WDb, and Tb must be taken as worst case. Of course, with Tb, we have assumed no rewind or mount/demount time of significance, which will only be valid with special processing algorithms [Knuth, 1973].

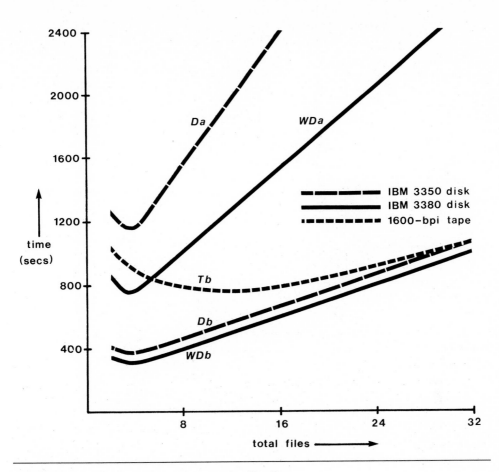

FIGURE 5.13. *Time for polyphase merging 8 million bytes of data. Curves should be compared with those in Figure 5.10. Buffer area is assumed limited to 32,000 bytes. For full explanation, see text.*

5.5.2 Other Merges

We shall conclude this chapter with a brief look at *cascade merging* and a mention of the *oscillating merge* and *sort/merge packages* for large files.

The Cascade Merge   Cascade merging requires perfect initial distributions of the sorted partitions, as with polyphase merging. However, the generating pattern is different but simpler. Table 5.6 depicts a simple cascade merge with 4 files. We have distributed 14, 11, and 6 IPLs onto A, B, and C, with D empty. The first merge is as with the polyphase case and we merge until the smallest file is exhausted, the result being placed on D. In the next merge, that is, 1*b*, we do not use D, but merge the remaining files A and B until B is exhausted, the result being placed on C. We now repeat the two merges above this time starting with D, C, and A, and so on.

CASCADE MERGE WITH 4 FILES				
Merge	A	B	C	D
1a	14(1)	11(1)	6(1)	—
1b	8(1)	5(1)	—	6(3)
2a	3(1)	—	5(2)	6(3)
2b	—	3(6)	2(2)	3(3)
3a	2(5)	3(6)	—	1(3)
3b	1(5)	2(6)	1(4)	—
4a	—	1(6)	1(14)	1(11)
4b	1(41)	0( )	0( )	0(0)

TABLE 5.6

If there were 4 initial files, we would merge in groups of 3, and so on. The perfect distribution numbers for starting a cascade merge are displayed in Table 5.7. The defining relationships for the table are

$$a_n = a_{n-1} + b_{n-1} + c_{n-1}$$

$$b_n = a_{n-1} + b_{n-1}$$

$$c_n = a_{n-1}$$

$$a_1 = 1 \qquad b_1 = 0 \qquad c_1 = 0$$

Similar rules are valid for other numbers of files.

To determine the number of passes as a function of initial number of sorted partitions and number of files used, we proceed essentially as with the polyphase merge. It turns out that the pass function $P(S, f)$ is very close to that for polyphase merges, and for practical purposes we could use Figure 5.12. It might be added that the cascade merge tends to be slightly slower than polyphase for $f < 6$, but for $f > 6$ it tends to be slightly faster. The readers are invited to carry out an analysis for themselves.

The Oscillating Merge/Distribution The oscillating merge/distribution was designed for tapes that can be read backward and is more efficient generally than either the polyphase or cascade merges. The method is unique in that we oscillate between distribution of a new partition to each file and merging.

Imagine that all of the *sorted partitions* reside in a file X *as yet undistributed* and that we have 4 other files A, B, C, and D available for merging. First of all, 3, *and only 3*, sorted partitions are distributed from X, so that A, B, and C each get one. A, B, and C are

PERFECT NUMBERS FOR A CASCADE MERGE WITH 4 FILES			
Sequence Number	T1	T2	T3
n	a_n	b_n	c_n
⋮	⋮	⋮	⋮
5	14	11	6
4	6	5	3
3	3	2	1
2	1	1	1
1	1	0	0

TABLE 5.7

then merged, the result being on D. But A, B, and C were merged backward from their position at the end of the initial distribution, and the result was placed forward on D. Thus all the partitions so far distributed have been merged on D. The reader should attempt to draw this out, noting that R/W head positions.

Next 3 more partitions arrive from X, this time going to B, C, and D. The same procedure as before is applied and these 3 new partitions are merged onto A. (We do not touch the partition on D that is 3 IPLs long because of the initial positions of the R/W heads.) The next three partitions from X are merged onto B.

Now A, B, and D each have a partition 3 IPLs long. These are then merged onto C, so that C now has a fully merged partition 9 IPLs long. Thus at this stage all partitions emitted from X have been sorted and reside on C. We could then proceed so that the next 9 from X end up sorted on D and the next 9 on A. These can then be merged, giving 27 sorted on B, and so on. Readers are advised to attempt to draw this process out for themselves. Tables are not very useful, and the position of the read/write heads is all-important. No rewinds are ever necessary. It should become clear that when S is the number of partitions on X, the number of total passes (excluding the distribution pass) will be $\log_3 S$. This is the number of passes for a balanced merge with 6 tapes.

Sort/Merge Packages   It is not common for a programmer to have to write a sort/merge program for a large file today (unless he or she happens to be taking a course in file techniques). Commercial sort/merge packages embody most of the techniques for merging described in this chapter. They normally accept a specification of the file to be sorted and then fabricate a suitable sort/merge routine from sort/merge modules. Because sorting of large files is a frequent requirement in commercial data processing and because sorting and merging have been intensively studied, we may safely state that the sort/merge packages in use today are highly effective in a wide range of circumstances.

5.6 ORDER, RETRIEVAL, AND UPDATING

Before we end Part 1 of this book and go on to data-base management, it is appropriate to point out a relationship that the careful reader will already have noticed. There is a relationship between the inherent order in a collection of files and the time to retrieve information from them, as well as the time to update them.

This relationship is illustrated qualitatively in Figure 5.14. Let us try to apply it to the file DRILHOLE from Figure 15.1*b* and two of its inversions, INVER_CO and INVER_DF. These 3 files contain no more information than the file DRILHOLE alone, but it is clear that there is a greater inherent order in them.

Thus we have that the time required for information retrieval in the high-order case (that is, basic file plus inversions) is low, while that for updating is necessarily high, since the inversions also require updating.

Conversely, the time for retrieval in the low-order case (that is, no inversions) is high, while that for updating is low, since there are no inversions to update.

It is difficult to make this relationship quantitative, but it makes itself evident in all situations where files are employed, and especially in integrated collections of files or data bases. Decisions relating to how much inherent order to incorporate always hinge on the extent to which a file will be used for information retrieval as opposed to updating.

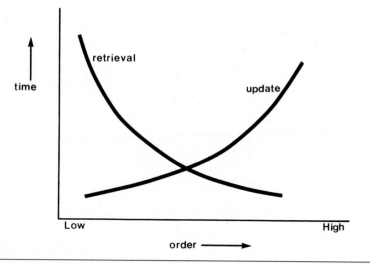

FIGURE 5.14. *Qualitative relationship between file order and retrieval and updating times.*

EXERCISES

1. Assume that the inverted file INVER_CO has been created as an ISAM file with the record structure of Figure 5.2. Write a program that updates INVER_CO following insertion and deletion of records in the file DRILHOLE (Figure 5.1).

2. Create a hybrid file that would permit the hash file DRILHASH (created by the program LOADHASH in Section 3.3.2) to be accessed directly by means of the hashing routine, and sequentially by means of the record key HOLE.

3. Create the equivalent of an inversion on COMPANY for the file DRILHOLE, by loading a multi-list version of DRILHOLE. This new version of DRILHOLE, and the index to the multiple chains, should be index-sequential files.

4. Using the multi-list version of DRILHOLE from Exercise 3, write a retrieval program to retrieve the hole numbers for holes owned by the company 'WESTGAS' and drilled by 'DRILLPETE'.

5. Using the multi-list version of DRILHOLE from Exercise 3, repeat Exercise 1.

6. Assume again that the inverted file INVER_CO has been created as an ISAM file with the record structure of Figure 5.2. Write a report program that outputs the name of each oil company together with the number of its most expensive hole.

7. Assuming that INVER_CO is as in Exercise 6, write a report program to give the name of each oil company together with the average cost of a hole in each location in which the company operates.

8. Assuming that INVER_CO is as in Exercise 6, write a report program to find the names of oil companies that have at least one hole in Alaska. (This illustrates *existential quantification,* to be introduced in Chapters 11 and 14.)

9. Assuming again that INVER_CO is as in Exercise 6, write a report program to find the names of oil companies that have all their holes, if any, in Alaska. (This illustrates *universal quantification.*)

10. Write a simple replacement selection generator program in which the shovel can hold only 5 records. Use internal linear searching.

11. Write a replacement selection generator in which the shovel is about 100 records long and is structured into a binary tree, as described in the text.

12. Write a replacement selection generator in which the shovel is large and is accompanied by a one-level index to the records it contains.

13. Draw a table or diagram for a 3-way balanced merge of 31 records. How many passes through the data are employed?

14. Write a merge program for a 2-way balanced merge on tape. The tape can be read backwards (but not written backwards), and logical files should be employed as in the program MERGE. Assume that fresh empty reels are available.

15. Rewrite the program MERGE to handle a 3-way balanced merge.

16. Modify Expression 6 to take rewind time into consideration, assuming that the tape cannot be read backwards.

17. Modify Expression 6 to take rewind time into consideration, assuming the tape is read backwards (it cannot be written backwards).

18. Derive curve *WDa* in Figure 5.10 for $S = 4096$ and 16,000 bytes of buffer space. Assume that initial sorted partitions are approximately 8000 bytes long.

19. A 3380-disk drive is occupied by an unsorted file with 4000-byte data blocks. How long would it take to sort the file using a 4-way balanced merge on disk if we have a replacement selection generator that has a shovel 32,000 bytes long and the maximum buffer size available for the merge and initial sort operation is 16,000 bytes? We may assume that during the sort, the files each have their own R/W head assemblies and there is no interference from other jobs.

20. In a 6-file polyphase merge, the initial sorted partition distributions are 16, 15, 14, 12, and 8. Describe the merge by a table similar to Table 5.3.

21. Derive the curve for $f = 5$ in Figure 5.12.

22. Rewrite the program MERGE using a polyphase merge (with 4 files).

23. Generate the merge pattern table for $f = 8$, using a table similar to Table 5.4.

24. What are the cascade merge expressions corresponding to Expressions 10, 11, and 12?

25. Describe a cascade merge with 6 files and initial distributions 55, 50, 41, 29, and 15. The result should be displayed as in Table 5.6.

26. In Exercise 25, what is the number of passes required?

27. Referring to Figure 5.12, derive the curve for $f = 4$ for the cascade merge.

28. Draw a diagram clearly describing the oscillating merge described in the text; R/W head positions should be clearly indicated.

REFERENCES

Ghosh, S. P., 1977, *Data Base Organization for Data Management,* Academic Press, New York.

Gotlieb, C. C., and L. R. Gotlieb, 1978, *Data Types and Structures,* Prentice-Hall, Inc., Englewood Cliffs, N.J.

IBM, 1976, *Introduction to IBM Direct Access Storage Devices and Organization Methods,* Order Form GC20–1649.

Knuth, D., 1973, *The Art of Computer Programming,* vol. 3; *Sorting and Searching,* Addison-Wesley, Reading, Mass.

Lorin, H., 1974, *Sorting and Sort Systems,* Addison-Wesley, Reading, Mass.

Martin, J., 1977, *Computer Data Base Organization,* Prentice-Hall, Inc., Englewood Cliffs, N.J.

Pfaltz, J., 1977, *Computer Data Structures,* McGraw-Hill, New York.

Weiderhold, G., 1977, *Data Base Design,* McGraw-Hill, New York.

PART 2

DATA-BASE TECHNIQUES

"Ideas, both when they are right and when they are wrong, are more powerful than is commonly understood. Indeed, the world is ruled by little else."

John Maynard Keynes, in The General Theory of Employment, Interest, and Money, *1936.*

Data-Base Concepts

6

In this chapter we examine the basic concepts connected with data bases, which, as we have seen, are *integrated collections of computer files*. The idea of integrating computer files has been fruitful; it largely originated in the 1960s mainly as the result of practical work to solve two fundamental problems in the use of files, namely, the *data independence problem* and the *data redundancy problem* [Date, 1977; Fry, 1976; Senko, 1977*b*].

1. *The data independence problem*

   The data independence problem is the problem of attaining the ideal of application programs that will still run regardless of changes to file storage organizations (for example, changes from hash to index sequential) or of changes to record structure (for example, addition or removal of a field from a record should not affect a program that does not use that field).

2. *The data redundancy problem*

   The data redundancy problem is the problem of ensuring that each item of information appears only once in a collection of master files. When an item of data appears in more than one file or more than one place in a single file, there is not only a waste of storage space but a high risk of inconsistency in the stored data.

We shall begin by studying these two problems, and then look at the various types of structures that data bases can have. Subsequently, we shall examine the associated software for managing a data base.

6.1 DATA INDEPENDENCE

To fully appreciate the problem of data independence and its solution, we need consider only a single file, not a data base. However, we need to distinguish clearly between three types of files: *storage* or *internal* files, *conceptual* files, and *external* files [Jardine, 1977; Senko, 1977b].

All the files we have been dealing with until now have been storage files. The other two types are new.

6.1.1 Storage and Conceptual Records and Files

We first clarify the concepts of storage and conceptual records and files and introduce the concept of *physical data independence*. Let us consider a program X, which manipulates the conceptual records of a conceptual file C_FILE, as depicted in Figure 6.1*a*.

C_FILE conceptual records contain the fields A, B, and C used by the program X, but the actual storage C_FILE records contain extra fields FLAG and P. Thus what is stored is something quite different, which we call S_FILE, the storage file corresponding to the conceptual file C_FILE.

S_FILE is a hash file and overflow records are chained together, starting with the home-address record. P points to the next overflow record and FLAG tells whether the record is or is not in its home address.

However, X does not manipulate S_FILE directly, but only indirectly through a subroutine STOR_SYS. It is this subroutine that issues the (PL/1) READ and WRITE statements, of the type studied in earlier chapters. It is for this reason that we refer to S_FILE as the *storage file,* made up of *storage records.* Thus it should be clear that the files and records studied in previous chapters were storage files and records.[1]

The file C_FILE, on the other hand, is a *conceptual file,* containing *conceptual records.* A conceptual record is a storage record with implementation fields or "clutter" removed. We may regard the main routine X as manipulating this conceptual file by issuing suitable calls to STOR_SYS (Figure 6.1*a*).

Referring again to Figure 6.1, suppose that for reasons of system performance, we now decide it would be an improvement to replace the old hashing routine HASH by HASHHASH, and that, furthermore, the overflow pointer chain system should be replaced by progressive overflow.

As we saw in Chapter 3, pointers and flags are unnecessary with progressive overflow, so the storage file is (in this case) the same as the conceptual file. If we still want the program X to run, it is only necessary to change the storage file S_FILE and the subroutine STOR_SYS (Figure 6.1*b*).

The main consequence of this change is that if there had been many programs such as X, all manipulating C_FILE through STOR_SYS and S_FILE, then we escape having to change all of these programs. We just change STOR_SYS and S_FILE; all these programs continue to carry out their logical function unaffected, except that the performance of some of them will be altered.

We say that these programs such as X enjoy *physical data independence,* that is, they

---

[1]*Strictly, we should distinguish between logical* storage *files and physical* storage files. *The former are made up of the records manipulated by PL/1 or COBOL* READ/WRITE *commands, while the latter consist of the storage blocks manipulated by the access methods and channel programs. Thus a physical storage file corresponds to an IBM dataset.*

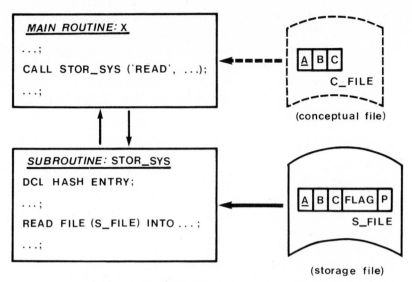

(a) The main routine **X** reads a conceptual record from the conceptual file **C_FILE** by means of the subroutine **CON_SYS** and the storage file **S_FILE**.

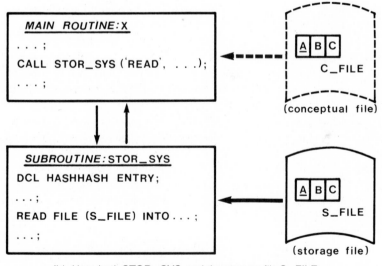

(b) Here both **STOR_SYS** and the storage file **S_FILE** have been changed, but **X** and **C_FILE** remain unaltered.

FIGURE 6.1 *How the use of a conceptual and underlying storage file gives rise to physical data independence.*

---

are independent of the physical method of storing the file C_FILE [Date, 1977; Jardine, 1977; Tsichritzis, 1977]. *Storage data independence* might have been a better term.

Finally, we note that a conceptual file may be implemented in storage by more than one storage file, usually with a minimum of overlapping fields. For example, if one storage file for C_FILE is a hash file and the other an index sequential file, we could have very fast direct access and yet acceptable sequential access. Hybrid files (see Chapter 5) are thus often useful as storage files.

6.1.2 Conceptual and External Records and Files

Suppose that we have two different users of the conceptual file C_FILE from Figure 6.1. User U1 needs fields A and B, while user U2 needs fields A and C. Furthermore, suppose user U1 writes programs in FORTRAN, while U2 employs PL/1.

We can deal with this situation by introducing an even higher level conceptual file known as an *external file*, as illustrated in Figure 6.2. Here we have two external files E1_FILE and E2_FILE, for users U1 and U2, respectively. Both external files contain *external records*, with fields that are subsets of the set of fields in the underlying conceptual C_FILE records.

However, U1's application program manipulates its external file E1_FILE by issuing calls to a routine CON_SYS. CON_SYS accepts and delivers A- and B-field values for E1_FILE and carries out an appropriate manipulation of the underlying conceptual file C_FILE. C_FILE is manipulated by CON_SYS by means of STOR_SYS and the underlying storage file S_FILE as described in Section 6.1.1. The external file E2_FILE is manipulated by U2's program in like manner.

Another advantage to the further distinction between external and conceptual files as illustrated in Figure 6.2 is that it gives rise to *logical data independence*.

Logical Data Independence Suppose that a new user needed to use a file with the field A and B from C_FILE together with a new field D. We have two possibilities.

First, we could set up an entirely new storage file N_FILE containing the three fields. However, since two of the three fields are already in S_FILE, it is likely that values in S_FILE and N_FILE will get out of step with each other because of factors such as different updating schedulles. Thus we will have an undesirable data redundancy, as well as a probable lack of consistency.

It is interesting to note that this type of data redundancy is very common in computer installations. One user group with an existing file will rarely agree to have a new field tagged on to accommodate a new user group, the excuse always being that they would have to rewrite all their existing programs. Thus a new file is inaugurated, later to be followed by another, and so on.

However, if we are following the three-tier system illustrated in Figure 6.2, a much better alternative is to alter the conceptual file C_FILE to one containing fields A, B, C, and D, the corresponding change being made in the underlying storage file S_FILE. We can then make the necessary changes in CON_SYS and STOR_SYS so that they can manipulate these new files. We can now introduce a new external file E3_FILE, which the new user (U3) can manipulate with his or her application programs by means of CON_SYS.

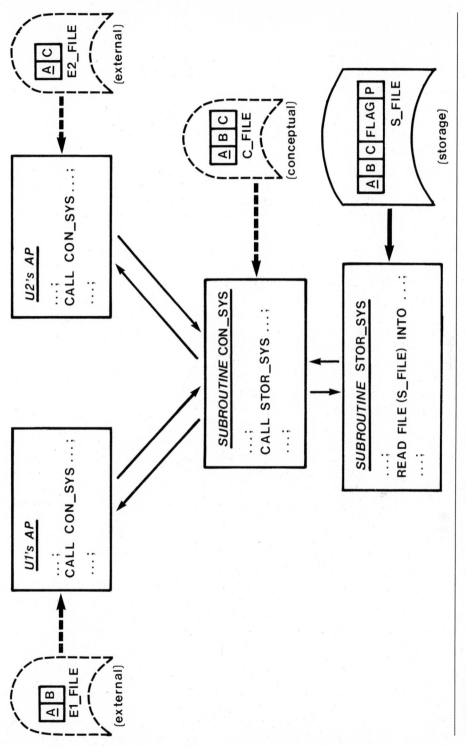

FIGURE 6.2. *How systems based on the use of external files and common conceptual file give rise to logical data independence.*

The point of this discussion is that the application programs of users U1 and U2 are not affected by these changes, except perhaps for a small decrease in performance. The application programs are said to be *logical data independent;* that is, they are independent of the logical makeup of the underlying records being manipulated [Date, 1977; Senko, 1977a; Tsichritzis, 1977]. *Conceptual data independent* might have been a better term.

The Conceptual File   The importance of the conceptual file in this kind of three-tier system cannot be overemphasized. We can look at it in three ways.

1. The conceptual file is the same as the stored file stripped of its implementation pointers, flags, and so on.

2. The conceptual file is a common denominator logical file for all users, such as U1, U2, U3, as just described.

3. The conceptual file is a collection of conceptual records, each of which describes an entity (in the widest sense) of the real world.

The last way of looking at such a file takes some getting used to, but a little thought will show its utility.

We shall find it convenient to deal with conceptual files after this. For example, we can regard a *conceptual data base* as a collection of conceptual files, where—for each conceptual file—there are many possible external files to suit a wide variety of users. For each conceptual file in the conceptual data base there is also an underlying storage file, which may be altered from time to time to improve performance.

6.2 DATA REDUNDANCY

Here we are concerned with *data redundancy* mainly due to duplicated data *within* a file. We saw in the previous section that data redundancy caused by the use of identical field types in several conceptual files can be largely overcome by the use of external files based on a single conceptual file. It is redundancy within a conceptual file that now interests us.

We shall make use of the conceptual file EXPLORATION shown in Figure 6.3*a*. The file describes holes drilled in search of hydrocarbons. The key field is HOLE, containing the hole number; the other fields describe the hole, some directly and some only indirectly.

Those fields describing the hole directly are COMPANY, the company that owns the hole; LOC, the hole's location; and DRILL_FIRM, the company that drilled the hole.

Those fields describing the hole *indirectly* are HQ, the headquarters location of an owning company, and CHIEF, the director of an owning company. It is clear from the semantics of the situation that HQ and CHIEF describe a company *directly.* However, if that company owns a hole, then these fields may be said to describe that hole indirectly.

We see that there is redundancy in the file; it has its origin in those fields that describe a hole only indirectly. If 'HOUSTON' and 'JONES' are the location and chief of the company 'WESTGAS', then these field values must appear in every record describing a hole owned by 'WESTGAS'.

COMPANY	HQ	CHIEF	HOLE	LOC	DRILL_FIRM
WESTGAS	HOUSTON	JONES	23	ALASKA	DRILLPETE
MULTOIL	CALGARY	SMITH	39	YUKON	DEEPDRILL
EASTPETE	CHICAGO	HIND	41	MEXICO	BOREFIRM
WESTGAS	HOUSTON	JONES	47	TEXAS	GASRIG
MULTOIL	CALGARY	SMITH	58	ALASKA	DRILLPETE
WESTGAS	HOUSTON	JONES	62	N. SEA	DEEPDRILL
EASTPETE	CHICAGO	HIND	74	TEXAS	GASRIG

(a) Contents of the conceptual file EXPLORATION.   EXPLORATION

COMPANY	HQ	CHIEF
WESTGAS	HOUSTON	JONES
MULTOIL	CALGARY	SMITH
EASTPETE	CHICAGO	HIND

PETROFIRM

COMPANY	HOLE	LOC	DRILL_FIRM
WESTGAS	23	ALASKA	DRILLPETE
MULTOIL	39	YUKON	DEEPDRILL
EASTPETE	41	MEXICO	BOREFIRM
WESTGAS	47	TEXAS	GASRIG
MULTOIL	58	ALASKA	DRILLPETE
WESTGAS	62	N. SEA	DEEPDRILL
EASTPETE	74	TEXAS	GASRIG

DRILL_HOLE

(b) Contents of the conceptual files PETROFIRM and DRILL_HOLE, formed from EXPLORATION by removing redundant descriptions of each oil company.

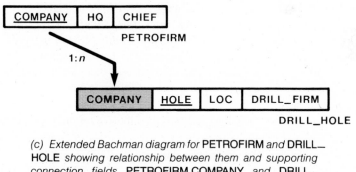

(c) Extended Bachman diagram for PETROFIRM and DRILL_HOLE showing relationship between them and supporting connection fields PETROFIRM.COMPANY and DRILL_HOLE.COMPANY. Key fields are underlined.

FIGURE 6.3. Formation of two related conceptual files by elimination of redundancy.

This redundancy is undesirable. Apart from the ensuing waste of storage space with the corresponding storage file, there are updating and consistency problems (described in detail in Chapter 7). Suppose 'WESTGAS' changes its headquarters to 'NEW YORK'. Many records have to be updated and, while the job is being done, the file is internally inconsistent. The redundancy may be eliminated, either partially or wholly. We take each case in turn.

6.2.1 Partial Redundancy Elimination

To partially remove the redundancy, we make two new files PETROFIRM and DRILL_ HOLE. DRILL_HOLE is simply the old file EXPLORATION with the HQ and CHIEF fields removed. Thus all the remaining fields in DRILL_HOLE now describe a hole *directly* (Figure 6.3*b*).

On the other hand, PETROFIRM is formed by removing the fields HOLE, LOC, and DRILL_FIRM from EXPLORATION and eliminating duplicates from the remaining records (incidentally, as we shall see in Chapters 7 and 16, this process is called *projection*). Thus in PETROFIRM, each record describes an oil company that owns some of the holes described in DRILL_HOLE. COMPANY will be the prime key in PETROFIRM, and both HQ and CHIEF values describe a company directly.

However, it is now quite clear that these two conceptual files are related. For each company in PETROFIRM, there are many holes in DRILL_HOLE. For example, 'WESTGAS' has holes 23, 47, and 62. Also, for a given hole, there is a full description in PETROFIRM of the company that owns the hole.

The conceptual files and their 1:*n* (one to many) relationship are depicted in Figure 6.3*c*. The arrow points from the one to the many. This general type of diagram is called a *Bachman diagram* after its inventor [Bachman, 1969]. Since the files are related and both conceptual, the diagram in fact describes a simple conceptual data base [Kent, 1978; Senko, 1977].

Connection Fields   The fields PETROFIRM.COMPANY and DRILL_HOLE.COM-PANY deserve closer attention. It is these fields that determine the relationship between the two files at the conceptual level. They may be called *connection fields*, since they serve to connect the two conceptual files together. The 1:*n* relationship between the two files is in fact equivalent to a parent-child relationship. Thus PETROFIRM.COMPANY can be called the *parent-connection field*, and DRILL_HOLE.COMPANY the *child-connection field*.

In an *extended* Bachman diagram (Figure 6.3*c*), the 1:*n* relationship arrow goes from the parent-connection field to the child-connection field. Because 1:*n* relationships are the most common kind in conceptual data bases, connection fields will never be very far from our attention in the remainder of this book. They play a dominating role in the relational approach to data-base management (Section 6.4.8) and an important role in the CODASYL approach (Section 6.4.8). In extended Bachman diagrams in this book, the child-connection fields are lightly stippled.

6.2.2 Full Redundancy Elimination

We see that the formation of DRILL_HOLE shown in Figure 6.3a and 6.3b only partially eliminates the redundancy in EXPLORATION caused by the group of fields COMPANY, HQ, and CHIEF.

Suppose that the company 'WESTGAS' changes its name. The 'WESTGAS' record in PETROFIRM will, of course, have to be updated. In addition, however, all the records in DRILL_HOLE describing holes owned by 'WESTGAS' will also have to be updated.

This remaining redundancy could be eliminated by simply removing the field type COMPANY from DRILL_HOLE, as shown in Figure 6.4. However, this elimination exacts a price. We can no longer determine *at the conceptual level alone* which holes belong to a given company. The 1:*n* relationship between PETROFIRM and DRILL_ HOLE still exists, however, but it is not available from an examination of the records of the conceptual files. Information has therefore been lost.

What we have in fact done is eliminate the child-connection field, as is indicated by the shaded field in Figure 6.4. Such an elimination is not permitted in the relational approach to data-base management; the resulting redundancy is tolerated. In the CODA-SYL approach to data-base management the elimination is allowed, but a new grouping of conceptual records called an *owner-coupled set* is necessary to preserve the 1:*n* relationship at the conceptual level. We introduce the approaches to data-base management and owner-coupled sets in Section 6.4.8.

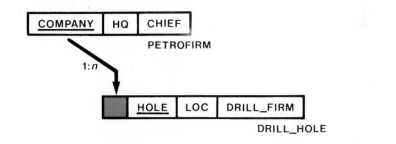

FIGURE 6.4. *Extended Bachman diagram for the conceptual files* PETROFIRM *and* DRILL_HOLE, *where the connection field in* DRILL_HOLE *that could support the 1:n relationship between the two files is omitted. This is indicated by the shaded field. Key fields are underlined.*

6.3 CONCEPTUAL DATA-BASE STRUCTURES

A conceptual data base can be regarded as a collection of conceptual records of one or more different types. A conceptual file, formed by grouping together all conceptual records of a given type, will usually be related to other conceptual files of the data base. Thus Figure 6.3c depicts a simple conceptual data base.

The relationships between the conceptual files of a data base impart structure to the data base [Bachman, 1969; Fry, 1976; Senko, 1977].

6.3.1 Example of a Larger Conceptual Data Base

Figure 6.5 shows an extended Bachman diagram for a data base called RESOURCE. The data base has six conceptual files.

a. PETROFIRM: Each record describes an oil company.

b. CONCESSION: Each record describes a drilling concession.

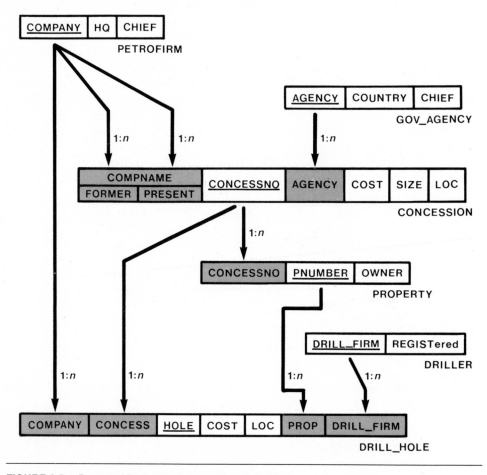

FIGURE 6.5. *Extended Bachman diagram of a related file collection or data base called* RESOURCE. *The data-base files describe entities involved in the search for hydrocarbons. Key fields are underlined. (For tutorial purposes, the data base is not in fourth normal form (4NF), as explained in Chapter 7.)*

c.   GOV_AGENCY: Each record describes a government granting agency.

d.   PROPERTY: Each record describes a registered property.

e.   DRILL_HOLE: Each record describes a hole owned by a company.

f.   DRILLER: Each record describes a drilling firm.

Most of the fields have self-evident semantics; for example, COUNTRY clearly gives the name of the country in which a government agency is located. In fact, with the exception of the key and connection fields, the semantics of the fields are irrelevant just now (see glossary for full semantics). The key and connection fields are involved in the relationships between the files of the data base. We can distinguish between 1:n (one to many) and n:m (many to many) relationships. The 1:n relationships are explicit.

1:n Relationships in the Data Base RESOURCE   We examine these relationships in turn.

1.   Between PETROFIRM and CONCESSION: There are two relationships, supported by the child-connection fields CONCESSION.PRESENT and CONCESSION.FORMER. The key field PETROFIRM.COMPANY holds the name of an oil company; PRESENT gives the oil company holding the concession at present, while FORMER gives a company formerly holding the concession. For one PETROFIRM record, there are many CONCESSION records, but in two relatinships.

2.   Between GOV_AGENCY and CONCESSION: CONCESSION.AGENCY is the child-connection field holding the name of the agency (GOV_AGENCY.AGENCY) granting the concession.

3.   Between PETROFIRM and DRILL_HOLE: A company has many bore-holes. DRILL_HOLE.COMPANY is the child-connection field giving owning company.

4.   Between CONCESSION and DRILL_HOLE: On a concession, there are many bore-holes. DRILL_HOLE.CONCESS is the child-connection field giving concession number.

5.   Between CONCESSION and PROPERTY: A concession consists of many properties. PROPERTY.CONCESSNO is the child-connection field giving the containing concession number.

6.   Between PROPERTY and DRILL_HOLE: On a property there are many bore-holes. DRILL_HOLE.PROP is the child-connection field giving containing property.

7.   Between DRILLER and DRILL_HOLE: A drilling contractor drills many holes. The DRILL_HOLE.DRILL_FIRM child-connection field gives the name of the drilling contractor.

n:m Relationships in the Data Base RESOURCE   The n:m relationships are only implicitly evident.

1.   An oil company (PETROFIRM record) deals with many government agencies (GOV_AGENCY records), and vice versa.

---

2. An oil company deals with many drilling contractors (DRILLER records), and vice versa.

3. A concession (CONCESSION record) is drilled by many drilling contractors (DRILLER records), and vice versa.

4. A property (PROPERTY record) is drilled by many drilling contractors (DRILLER records), and vice versa.

From the foregoing, it is clear that an *n:m* relationship exists between the records of files A and B, if for a given A-record there are many B-records, and if for a given B record there are many A records. Thus, according to the extended Bachman diagram in Figure 6.5, there is *not* an implicit *n:m* relationship between the files PETROFIRM and PROPERTY; for a given oil company there are many properties, but for a given property there is just one oil company with the right to drill.

Redundant Relationships The file collection also contains some redundant relationships. One we could consider as redundant is the relationship (3) between PETROFIRM and DRILL_HOLE based on the connection field DRILL_HOLE.COMPANY. This relationship could be used when we need the holes belonging to a given oil company. However, this information could be obtained using relationship (1) between PETROFIRM and CONCESSION and relationship (4) between CONCESSION and DRILL_HOLE. Thus to find the holes belonging to a given oil company, we could use relationship (1) to find the concessions belonging to the company; for each concession, using relationship (4), we could find the holes it contained. This type of redundancy can also cause inconsistency with storage operations: Consider the situation if a new DRILL_HOLE record is stored with COMPANY and CONCESS values that do not identify the same PETROFIRM record.

There is an additional redundant relationship in RESOURCE, which the reader should find. (While instructive, these redundant relationships mean that the data base RESOURCE, as it stands, is not in fourth normal form, as explained in Chapter 7.) We continue with an examination of the basic conceptual data structures that can occur in a conceptual data base.

6.3.2 Hierarchical Data-Base Structures

Referring to Figure 6.6, we can see that the three files CONCESSION, PROPERTY, and DRILL_HOLE form a simple *hierarchical structure* or *hierarchy*. In such a structure the files are connected by 1:*n* relationships. However, for a given parent file there can be many child files, while for a given child file there can be only one parent file. (Note this terminology: With files A and B, such that for one A-record there are many B-records, we may say that A is the *parent file* and B is the *child file*.)

The Connection Trap Care needs to be taken with hierarchical structures when they occur in a data base. For example, with the file collection in Figure 6.6, there is no relationship between the files PROPERTY and DRILL_HOLE. However, it is a common mistake (widely known as the *connection trap*) to assume that there is a relationship. We cannot, in fact, find out from this structure what holes are on a given property. But we are

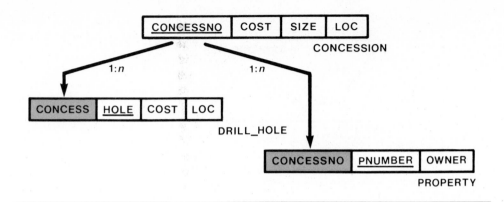

FIGURE 6.6. *Related file collection or data base with hierarchical structure; that is, for a given parent file there is more than one child file, and for a given child file there is only one parent file. Key fields are underlined.*

tempted to take the given PROPERTY key, and from the 1:*n* relationship between CONCESSION and PROPERTY, determine the CONCESSION number for the concession in which the property is located. We might then use the concession number and the 1:*n* relationship between CONCESSION and DRILL_HOLE to find the holes on this concession. It is clearly wrong to take these holes as those on the given property. However, when the hierarchical structure is buried in a much more complex data base, this is not so easy to see. The same basic error can also arise with multiple-level hierarchies (see Chapter 17).

6.3.3 Multiple Relationships between Two Files

Referring to the conceptual data base in Figure 6.7, we see that there are two distinct 1:*n* relationships between the two files PETROFIRM and CONCESSION. This reflects the fact that for a given oil company (PETROFIRM record) there are those concessions held at present and those formerly held.

The structure in Figure 6.7 does not describe a hierarchy, since a child record in CONCESSION will have two distinct parent records in PETROFIRM, one for the PETROFIRM company that presently has the concession, and one for the company that formerly held the concession. This structure is, in fact, an example of a *network*.

Observe that the existence of more than one relationship between PETROFIRM and CONCESSION makes it ambiguous to refer to *the* relationship between the two files. To be able to refer explicitly to the relationships, we shall either have to introduce arbitrary relationship names or invent a naming technique that utilizes the fact that the relationships are supported by distinct connection fields.

We could name the relationships RELA and RELB, as shown in Figure 6.7. Alternatively, we could use something like PETROFIRM'S PRESENT CONCESSIONS and PETROFIRM'S FORMER CONCESSIONS, as an example of nonarbitrary names.

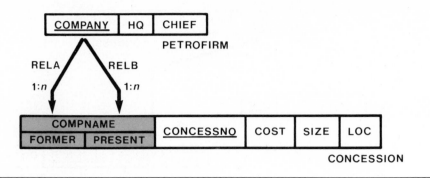

FIGURE 6.7. *Related file collection with network, as opposed to hierarchical structure. There are two 1:n relationships connecting the files* **PETROFIRM** *and* **CONCESSION**.

6.3.4 Simple Network Data Base

We now refer to the conceptual data base in Figure 6.8a. Here we have the simplest and most common network structure. Study it carefully. An oil company (PETROFIRM record) has many bore-holes (DRILL_HOLE records). However, a drilling contractor (DRILLER record) also has (drilled) many bore-holes.

Thus for a given bore-hole, there are two parents: the record for the company that owns the hole and the record for the firm that drilled the hole. This little network is so important that we give examples of some records for the three files. The full files are shown twice, in Figure 6.8b and Figure 6.8c.

In 6.8b, the DRILL_HOLE child records are grouped according to PETROFIRM parent value, so that the holes owned by a given company are all grouped together. In 6.8c, the child records are grouped instead after their DRILLER parent.

6.3.5 A Many to Many or *n:m* Relationship

Many to many relationships occur only in network structures and are often specified at the conceptual level by means of an auxiliary file (such as HELPFILE in Figure 6.9), which links the two files involved in the relationship. However, even the auxiliary file alone may be regarded as exhibiting an *n:m* relationship.

Figure 6.9 illustrates the *n:m* relationship between PETROFIRM and DRILLER. An oil company deals with *n* drilling firms, while a drilling firm deals with *m* oil companies. The connection fields COMPANY and DRILL_FIRM in HELPFILE support the 1:*n* relationship between PETROFIRM and HELPFILE and the 1:*m* relationship between DRILLER and HELPFILE, respectively.

The auxiliary file HELPFILE contains all possible pairs of COMPANY and DRILL_FIRM values, where the organizations in the pair deal with each other. Thus if oil company 'A' deals with drilling firms 'V' and 'W', and oil company 'B' deals with drilling firms 'X' and 'V', we would have the following in the auxiliary file.

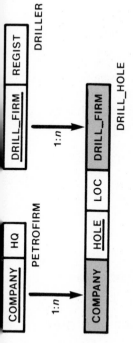

(a) Simple network data base. Key fields are underlined.

PETROFIRM

COMPANY	HQ
WESTGAS	HOUSTON
MULTOIL	CALGARY

DRILL_HOLE

COMPANY	HOLE	LOC	DRILL_FIRM
WESTGAS	23	ALASKA	DRILLPETE
WESTGAS	62	N. SEA	DEEPDRILL
WESTGAS	47	TEXAS	GASRIG
MULTOIL	39	YUKON	DEEPDRILL
MULTOIL	58	ALASKA	DRILLPETE

DRILLER

DRILL_FIRM	REGIST
DRILLPETE	ALBERTA
DEEPDRILL	TEXAS
GASRIG	TEXAS

(b) Records from the simple network data base. DRILL_HOLE records are grouped together according to PETROFIRM parent (or COMPANY child-connection field).

PETROFIRM

COMPANY	HQ
WESTGAS	HOUSTON
MULTOIL	CALGARY

DRILL_HOLE

COMPANY	HOLE	LOC	DRILL_FIRM
MULTOIL	58	ALASKA	DRILLPETE
WESTGAS	23	ALASKA	DRILLPETE
WESTGAS	62	N. SEA	DEEPDRILL
MULTOIL	39	YUKON	DEEPDRILL
WESTGAS	47	TEXAS	GASRIG

DRILLER

DRILL_FIRM	REGIST
DRILLPETE	ALBERTA
DEEPDRILL	TEXAS
GASRIG	TEXAS

(c) Same as (b), but DRILL_HOLE records are grouped according to DRILLER parent (or DRILL_FIRM child-connection field).

FIGURE 6.8. Anatomy of a simple network (conceptual) data base.

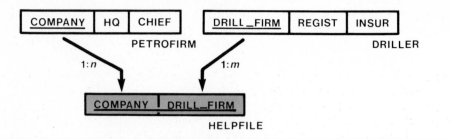

FIGURE 6.9. *The* n:m *relationship between the files* PETROFIRM *and* DRILLER *is implicit and explicitly represented by a 1:n relationship between* PETROFIRM *and* HELPFILE, *and a 1:m relationship between* DRILLER *and* HELPFILE. *However, the file* HELPFILE *may be regarded as (internally) exhibiting an* n:m *relationship. Key fields are underlined.*

COMPANY	DRILL_FIRM
A	V
A	W
B	X
B	V

Thus given a company record in PETROFIRM (for company 'A', for example), the $1:n$ relationship between PETROFIRM and HELPFILE enables us to ascertain which pairs of COMPANY and DRILL_FIRM values are applicable to company 'A'. The pairs would be 'A' 'V' and 'A' 'W'. Making use of the $m:1$ relationship between HELPFILE and DRILLER, the DRILLER records for the firms dealing with PETROFIRM company 'A' can be obtained from the parent records in DRILLER of these two HELPFILE records.

In a similar manner, the PETROFIRM records for companies dealing with the drilling firm 'V' can be obtained.

6.3.6 Recursive 1:*n* Relationship

To illustrate this kind of relationship, we assume that any oil company in PETROFIRM is capable of

1. Being a fully (and legally) owned subsidiary of another company in PETROFIRM;

2. Wholly (and legally) owning one or more companies in PETROFIRM.

To specify the relationship exactly, we introduce a new connection field PARENTCOMP in the file PETROFIRM. In a given record describing company 'A', for example, the value of the PARENTCOMP field will be the name of the legal parent company of 'A'. Conversely, if we extract from the file all those records with PARENTCOMP value 'A', then these records describe the companies that are wholly owned subsidiaries of 'A'. The relationship is illustrated in Figure 6.10, assuming the 14 companies, 'A', 'B', . . . , 'N'.

It is therefore clear that the connection field PARENTCOMP is adequate to specify the relationship. The relationship is said to be *recursive* because any record can participate in it in two ways, first as a child record belonging to a parent and then as a parent record in possession of one or more child records.

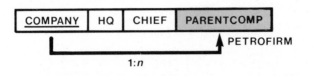

FIGURE 6.10. *Recursive 1:n relationship. It is assumed that any company in* **PETROFIRM** *can be the legal outright owner of one or more other* **PETROFIRM** *companies. For a record for a company in* **PETROFIRM,** *the field* **PARENTCOMP** *contains the name of the legal parent company.*

We may also regard the recursive 1:*n* relationship as being the generator of an implicit hierarchy of files. If we take a given company 'A', it may have subsidiaries 'E', 'F', and 'G'; 'F' in turn may have subsidiaries 'L', 'M', and 'N', and so on through many hierarchical levels. Thus the relationship can also be illustrated by the diagrams in Figure 6.11*a* and 6.11*b*.

Here we introduce multiple versions of the file PETROFIRM, all identical and all connected by 1:*n* relationships in a hierarchical manner. Thus if we take any company 'A' in PETROFIRM, the first 1:*n* relationship gives us the child records in the (subsidiary) file X_PETROFIRM that describe the subsidiaries of 'A'. Any one of these subsidiaries in X_PETROFIRM may itself have subsidiaries in Y_PETROFIRM as given by the next 1:*n* relationship, and so on.

Another method of illustrating this recursive relationship involves using an auxiliary file, such as the auxiliary file LINK shown in Figure 6.11*c*. LINK contains one connection field COMPANY and is really a list of the keys of all the companies in PETROFIRM. Hence there must be a 1:1 relationship between PETROFIRM and LINK and, because for a company in LINK there are many subsidiary companies in PETROFIRM, there must be a 1:*n* relationship between LINK and PETROFIRM. For one of these subsidiaries, there will in turn be a LINK record for which there will be further subsidiary companies in PETROFIRM, and so on.

6.3.7 Recursive *n:m* Relationships

The recursive *n:m* relationship is often referred to as the *bill of materials* relationship because it is present in bills of materials, which basically describe parts, each of which may contain other parts, and so on. However, there are other useful examples of *n:m* recursive relationships. Relationships of this kind are of fundamental importance, but a

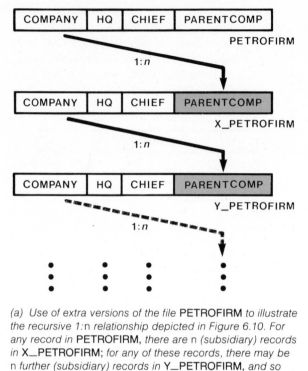

COMPANY	HQ	CHIEF	PARENTCOMP

PETROFIRM

1:*n*

COMPANY	HQ	CHIEF	PARENTCOMP

X_PETROFIRM

1:*n*

COMPANY	HQ	CHIEF	PARENTCOMP

Y_PETROFIRM

1:*n*

(a) *Use of extra versions of the file* **PETROFIRM** *to illustrate the recursive 1:n relationship depicted in Figure 6.10. For any record in* **PETROFIRM,** *there are* n *(subsidiary) records in* **X_PETROFIRM;** *for any of these records, there may be* n *further (subsidiary) records in* **Y_PETROFIRM,** *and so on, in hierarchical fashion.*

FIGURE 6.11.

full treatment would take us beyond the scope of this book. We first look at an organizational example, dealing with the ownership of joint stock companies.

A joint stock company is legally owned by the holders of its shares or stock. The holders of the stock in a company may be private individuals, other companies, or other nonincorporated organizations. Thus any company may be legally owned by more than one other company. Further, any company may legally own one or more other companies.

We consider an arbitrarily simple example, as shown in Figure 6.12. We have 10 companies, 'A', 'B', . . . , 'K'. The solid line between 'A' and 'D', for example, indicates that 'A' (at the left) legally owns stock in 'D' (at the right). We can thus see that company 'B' legally owns part of companies 'E', 'F', and 'J'. However, company 'F' also legally owns a part of 'J', as well as owning part of 'H' and 'K'. Furthermore, in addition to being legally owned partly by company 'B', company 'F' is also partly legally owned by company 'C', and so on.

The companies in the diagram are thus divided into three levels: those that are not legally owned by other companies (such as 'A', 'B', and 'C'), those that do not legally own any other companies (such as 'H', 'I', 'J', and 'K'), and those that are legally owned by top level companies and can also themselves legally own bottom level companies (such

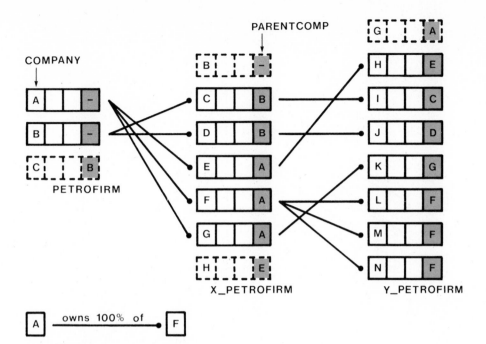

(b) Selected records from the three versions of
PETROFIRM *showing the 1:n relationships between them.*
Thus company 'A' is outright owner of companies 'E', 'F',
and 'G'; 'F', in turn, is the outright legal owner of
companies 'L', 'M', and 'N'.

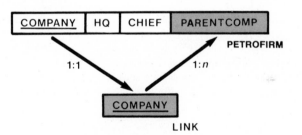

(c) Alternatively, an additional and auxiliary file **LINK** *can*
be used to illustrate the recursive 1:n relationship from
Figure 6.10. For each company in **PETROFIRM**, *there is*
one record in **LINK**; *for that* **LINK** *record, there are* n
subsidiary records in **PETROFIRM**. *For any of these*
PETROFIRM *records, there is again one* **LINK** *record, and*
for that **LINK** *record* n **PETROFIRM** *records, and so on*
recursively.

FIGURE 6.11.   *(continued)*

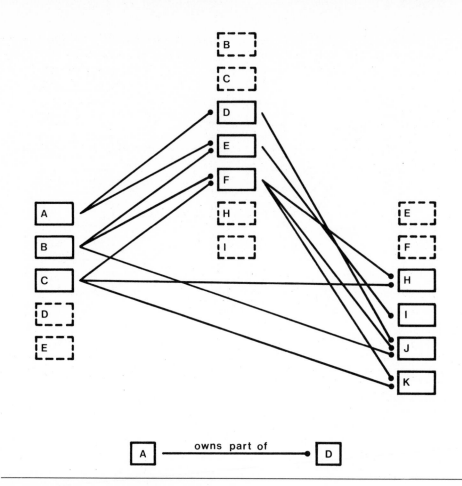

FIGURE 6.12. *The file* PETROFIRM *is assumed to describe companies* 'A', 'B', 'C', . . . , 'K'. *The companies in the above example can be segregated into those which are not subsidiaries* ('A', 'B', 'C'), *those which are both subsidiaries and parents* ('D', 'E', 'F'), *and those which are only subsidiaries* ('H', 'I', 'J', 'K'). *The line between (for example)* 'A' *and* 'D' *(left to right) indicates that* 'A' *legally owns a part of* 'D'. *Thus* 'F' *is partly legally owned by both* 'B' *and* 'C', *but is itself a parent of* 'H', 'J', *and* 'K'. PETROFIRM *records thus participate in an* n:m *relationship with themselves.*

as 'D', 'E', and 'F'). Let us refer to these three groups as *top, bottom,* and *intermediate.* Between top and intermediate, there is an *n:m* relationship; such relationships also exist between top and intermediate and between intermediate and bottom.

Now let us suppose that all the companies 'A', 'B', . . . , 'K' are placed in one file PETROFIRM. Since different groups of PETROFIRM records enter into *n:m* relationships with other groups of PETROFIRM records, it follows that the PETROFIRM file is participating in an *n:m* relationship with itself; that is, a recursive *n:m* relationship.

When a substantial degree of complexity is involved, display of the relationships by means of diagrams such as Figure 6.12 is not practical. We may, however, usefully employ an extended Bachman diagram as shown in Figure 6.13. Here we introduce an auxiliary file LINK, which *links* PETROFIRM with itself. We assume that all the company records are in the file PETROFIRM.

The file LINK has two connection fields PARENT and SUBSIDIARY, each of which supports a 1:*n* relationship between PETROFIRM and LINK. To understand how this works, let us first consider any LINK record. It will contain the name of a parent company such as 'B' and a subsidiary company such as 'F'. (The reader could find it useful also to refer back to Figure 6.12.) For this LINK record, there is one parent record in PETROFIRM in the 1:*n* relationship (describing company 'B') and also one parent record in the 1:*m* relationship (describing company 'F'). Thus the LINK file links a parent company with its subsidiary.

Explosions with Recursive *n:m* Relationships Consider the PETROFIRM record for oil company 'B', and let us additionally take all the LINK records in which the PARENT connection field has the value 'B'. The member LINK records are as follows, if we assume the relationships from Figure 6.12.

PARENT	SUBSIDIARY
B	E
B	F
B	J

If we then access PETROFIRM with the keys 'E', 'F', and 'J', we get the records for the subsidiaries of 'B'; that is, we take the parent records in PETROFIRM for the above LINK records, but using the 1:*m* relationship supported by the SUBSIDIARY child-connection field.

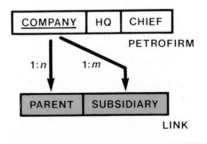

FIGURE 6.13. *Extended Bachman diagram of a recursive n:m relationship involving the companies of* PETROFIRM. *The introduction of the auxiliary file* LINK *permits the precise specification of the relationship in terms of the simpler 1:n type relationships.*

Let us now take one of these parent records 'F' and its child records in LINK using the 1:n relationship supported by the PARENT field. The following LINK records are obtained.

PARENT	SUBSIDIARY
F	H
F	J
F	K

If we now take the parent records in PETROFIRM for these LINK records using the relationship supported by the SUBSIDIARY connection field, we have the subsidiary companies for the subsidiary company 'F'. In this way we can find the subsidiary companies for company 'B' and the subsidiaries for each of these companies.

The result of this process is known as a *record explosion* or, in this case, a *company explosion*. The opposite process leads to an *implosion,* where for a company we obtain its parent companies, and then their parents, and so on.

Complexity Considerations   The example used in this section was deliberately chosen to have three distinct organization levels for the companies described, namely, the top, intermediate, and bottom levels. These three levels give rise to three distinct $n:m$ subrelationships. In general, if there are N organizational levels, there are $N(N - 1)/2$ subrelationships between the companies of the N levels. The proof is elementary and is left to the reader.

When $N = 4$, this means a maximum of four levels, from the parent companies which are not subsidiaries of other companies, down to the subsidiary companies which are not parents of any other companies. With $N = 4$, the reader should be able to see that there are two types of intermediate companies.

An Additional Use of the LINK File   Let us suppose that we need to have information about the exact percentage of stock that one company owns in another. We need to introduce a PERCENT field to contain this information, but we must place this field in the LINK file, as shown in Figure 6.14.

PERCENT is thus an attribute of a pair of companies, parent and subsidiary. PERCENT cannot be in PETROFIRM, since it informs about a pair of companies and not just one company, as do the fields of PETROFIRM records. In LINK, PERCENT gives the percentage of SUBSIDIARY that is owned by PARENT.

Display of LINK File Contents   If we assume that the relationships displayed in Figure 6.12 are still valid for Figure 6.14, it is possible to show the contents of the individual PETROFIRM and LINK records, as in Figure 6.15. Of course the diagram is practicable here only because of the low degree of complexity involved. A LINK record holds a parent name, a subsidiary name, and the percentage of the subsidiary owned by the parents.

Component Bill of Materials   As mentioned at the beginning of this section, recursive $n:m$ relationships occur in bills of materials, as used in manufacturing. As an example, we give a conceptual data base for components (see Figure 6.16a). For a given component,

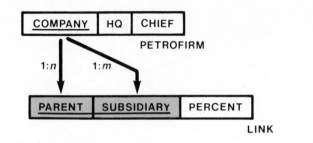

FIGURE 6.14. *Referring to the data base in Figure 6.12, if we wish to include information about what percentage of a given company's stock is owned by another company, a new field PERCENT must be incorporated in the LINK file. The field PERCENT contains the percentage of the stock of the SUBSIDIARY company owned by the PARENT company.*

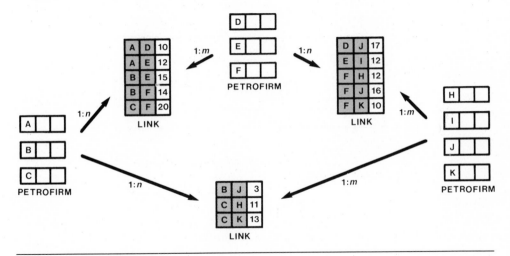

FIGURE 6.15. *Record-by-record display of the possible relationships between the records LINK and PETROFIRM in Figure 6.14. There are only three levels in the implicit network formed by the records of PETROFIRM as shown above. Thus company 'K' at the lowest level is 10% legally owned by company 'F' at the intermediate level.*

we have an *explosion* which gives the hierarchy of components contained within that component. The reverse implosion gives the components in which a given *type* of component is contained.

As in the case of the company-organization data base, the bill-of-materials data base may be described using an auxiliary file LINK. Both CONTAINS and CONTAINED_IN hold a value for a part number. The CONTAINS part contains the CONTAINED_IN part, located as specified in WHERE. If we assume that Figure 6.12 now applies to components instead of companies, the explosion for part 'B' would be as in Figure 6.16*b*.

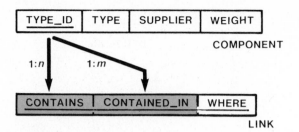

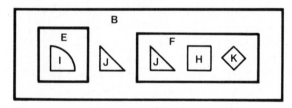

COMPONENT

LINK

(a) Bill of materials for components. A given component contains several components, giving one 1:n relationship between **COMPONENT** and **LINK**; this type of component also occurs in several other components, giving a second 1:n relationship between **COMPONENT** and **LINK**. The **WHERE** field in **LINK** specifies the geometrical coordinates of the position of the component referenced by **CONTAINED_IN** in the component referenced by **CONTAINS**.

(b) Assuming that Figure 6.12 now describes components instead of companies, this structure could match the explosion of 'B'.

FIGURE 6.16.

6.4 ANSI/SPARC DATA-BASE SYSTEM ORGANIZATION

A data base requires a software system for its manipulation and maintenance and, taken as a whole, such a system is referred to as a *Data-Base Management System* (DBMS).

At the present time, there is quite broad agreement about the organization of these systems, although there are only a few commercial systems (at the time of writing) that conform completely to this agreed organization. This agreement is reflected in the ANSI/SPARC [Jardine, 1977] proposal of 1975. The ANSI/SPARC study group was established by the Standards Planning and Requirements Committee (SPARC) of the American National Standards Institute (ANSI). Our treatment of the organization of data-base systems will closely follow the ANSI/SPARC proposal.

6.4.1 ANSI/SPARC Levels of Data-Base Abstraction

The ANSI/SPARC study group proposes that there be three levels of abstraction for a data base. These three levels more or less conform to the three levels of abstraction we have been using for files in this chapter; that is, the *external file*, the *conceptual file*, and the *storage file*.

Thus we distinguish between the conceptual-level data base and the external-level data base. Since the external-level data base contains external files and the conceptual-level data base contains conceptual files, this distinction (with the appropriate management software) will promote logical data independence.

We also distinguish between the conceptual-level data base and the internal- (or storage) level data base. This will promote physical data independence. Thus we have the three levels of abstraction.

1. *Internal-level data base*
   At the internal level, we have the storage records of the data base, containing user-relevant data fields and implementation flags and pointers.

2. *Conceptual-level data base*
   At the conceptual level, we have the conceptual records of the data base. Their fields describe only user-relevant entities. The records will form conceptual *groupings*, the most common being the conceptual file for conceptual records of the same type. However, other and additional groupings may also be present, such as the owner-coupled sets of records (usually not all of the same type) of the CODASYL approach to data-base management (see Chapter 8). (Owner-coupled sets reflect the relationships between conceptual files.)

3. *External-level data base*
   There may be an external-level data base for each user of the data base. An external-level data base is a collection of those fields of conceptual-level records which a user needs. External records are normally grouped in a manner which corresponds closely to the way conceptual records are grouped. However, in the relational approach to data-base management, entirely new and derived groupings of external records may be employed (see Chapter 16).

6.4.2 Data-Base Management Software

The important software components for data-base management are shown on Figure 6.17. An application program interacts with the *data-base control system*, which further interacts with a conceptual schema, an external schema, and an internal schema. With the information obtained from these schemas, the data-base control system accesses the data base.

The Data-Base Control System (DBCS) The DBCS receives retrieval, storage, updating, or deletion commands from an application program and initiates appropriate action. The statements an application program can use to communicate with the DBCS make up a *Data-Manipulation Language* (DML). Data-manipulation languages may vary widely in power. Some permit the specification of only fairly simple commands such as

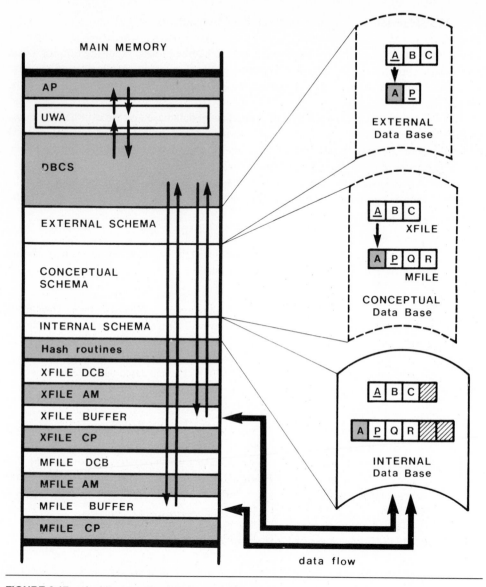

FIGURE 6.17. *Architecture of a data-base management system, consistent with the ANSI/SPARC study group report. The architecture is illustrated by a data base consisting of the files* **XFILE** *and* **MFILE**. *Pointer fields are shaded. The connection field is stippled.*

those involved in retrieving a single record from a file given the record key or a combination of field values. Others can carry out highly complex retrievals involving related records in many different files. As we will see in Section 6.4.8, DMLs may be classified as procedural or nonprocedural depending on retrieval power.

The Conceptual Schema The *conceptual schema* is the specification of the conceptual (common denominator) data base. We should distinguish between a *source schema* (the manual specification) and the *object schema,* which is used by the DBCS. However, we shall not often do so, as it is usually clear from the context whether a schema is a source or object schema. The conceptual schema describes the conceptual records of the data base, together with how they are to be grouped together. For example, conceptual records might be grouped into conceptual files and owner-coupled sets.

The External Schema The *external schema* is the description of that (derived) part of the conceptual data base that a given application program or user needs. We have source and object schemas and, as before, the type to which we refer is usually clear from the context.

The Internal or Storage Schema The *internal or storage schema* is a specification of the files used to implement the conceptual data base. Again, we have the source and object schema; again, the type to which we refer is usually clear from the context. More than one storage file may be required to implement a conceptual file.

Since some of the storage files will be hash files, the appropriate hashing routines will have to be present in the system. They are normally specified in the internal schema.

Operation of the System Suppose we have an application program that issues a command to retrieve a record from the data base. We have the following sequence.

1. The DBCS analyzes the command and selects the proper action routine.

2. The DBCS checks with the object schemas to obtain the information necessary to access and manipulate the required records.

3. The DBCS accesses the storage record or records and places the required field values at the disposal of the application program.

6.4.3 Data-Base Administrator

The *data-base administrator* (DBA) is sometimes a person but is usually a team of experts, and is a necessary part of the overall setup. The main function of the DBA is the prevention and resolution of conflicts. As such, the DBA will need to interact with higher management, user departments, and the operating departments [Jardine, 1977].

The ANSI/SPARC study group has identified three basic roles for the DBA.

1. *Enterprise administration:* In this role, the DBA is responsible for providing a specification or definition of the conceptual level data base. Here the DBA must be oriented primarily towards the needs of the organization setting up the data base.

2. *Application administration:* In this role, the DBA provides specifications of the external data bases used by the various user departments and as such must be familiar with the individual needs of these users.

3. *Implementation administration* (for tutorial purposes the terminology for naming this

role differs here from that used by ANSI/SPARC[1]): In this role, the DBA is responsible for the implementation of the files and relationships between them. The DBA is primarily computer-system oriented, and the main task is to specify and maintain the internal schema.

6.4.4 The Data Dictionary

A *data dictionary* contains information *about* a data base. We may identify at least four overlapping categories of information that may be stored in a data dictionary.

a. Information required by the data-base management system (for example, external, internal, and conceptual schema information).

b. Information of use to the general user (for example, the organizational source of a data-field value).

c. Information of use to the data-base administrator (for example, frequency of use of a data field).

d. Information of use to an auditor (for example, the times at which certain sensitive fields were updated).

The data dictionary is made up of files and, depending on the data base, these files may support quite complex interfile relationships. Thus a data dictionary is a data base in its own right, and is also useful for designing data bases [Teory, 1980].

ANSI/SPARC identifies category (a) as the minimum data dictionary, so that any data-base management system employing external, conceptual, and internal schemas may be said to employ a data dictionary. However, that does not mean that the DBMS has a *data dictionary facility*. Many current DBMSs have no data dictionary facility. A DBMS equipped with such a facility would need a subsystem (which we might call the *data dictionary control system*) roughly corresponding to the data-base control system. As we have seen, the DBCS manipulates the *data base* in response to user requests. In contrast, the data dictionary control system would manipulate the *data dictionary* in response to requests from the data-base administrator, authorized users, and auditors.

A DBCS equipped with a full data dictionary facility would also provide a language for the specification of data dictionary information belonging to categories (b), (c), and (d) above. It would also provide a subsystem for translation of the source version of such a specification into the object version in the data dictionary.

At the time of writing, there are a considerable number of *data dictionary systems* available commercially. Such systems are designed to interface with an existing DBMS and thus provide it with a data dictionary facility. However, we can expect that in the future most data-base management systems will incorporate some limited data dictionary facility. Unfortunately, no standards for such a facility have yet been proposed. Since a data dictionary facility is not an essential component of a data-base management system, and since the subject is still under development and somewhat controversial, it will not be dealt with further here. Appendix 3 has additional details.

(It is interesting to consider integrating a data dictionary with the data base it describes.

---

[1] *The term ANSI/SPARC uses is* data-base administration, *which we find confusing.*

This would allow user programs to manipulate the two data bases by means of just the DBMS. It could also allow us to do away with distinct schema-specification languages (see the next section) if it were permitted to use data-base loading programs (Chapters 9, 13, and 18) to load system-required data dictionary files (such as the three types of schema) from source files that have a standard format.)

6.4.5 Creation of a Data Base

To create a data base we require the following.

1. A data-base management system.
2. A data-base design; that is, a conceptual and internal schema for the data base and one or more external schemas.
3. A collection of source-data files from which the data base will be constructed.
4. A collection of data-base creation or loading programs.

The source schemas are written in data-base languages that will normally depend on the data-base system being employed. Thus we have the following languages.

1. Data-base conceptual schema language.
2. Data-base internal schema language.
3. Data-base external schema language.

However, the external-schema language is strictly a sublanguage of the application program (or host) programming language. Thus for a given DBMS, we expect external-schema sublanguages for COBOL, PL/1, and so on.

Preparation for Loading the Data Base   Referring to Figure 6.18, the conceptual schema is first of all read in by a translator, which is a component of the data-base system. The output is shown as an object module for the conceptual schema. However, many systems have translators that merely output a higher or assembly language program, which is then further compiled or assembled by the appropriate compiler or assembler, which then outputs the required object module.

Similarly, the internal schema is next translated to produce either directly or indirectly the object module for the internal schema. Next the hashing routines are compiled and output as object modules. We note that, depending on the internal schema, hashing routines may not be required at all.

Next, a data-base manipulation system object module is prepared, if one is not already available. The system linkage editor is then used to link-edit together:

a. The conceptual-schema object module;
b. The internal-schema object module;
c. The hash-routine object modules;
d. The DBCS object module.

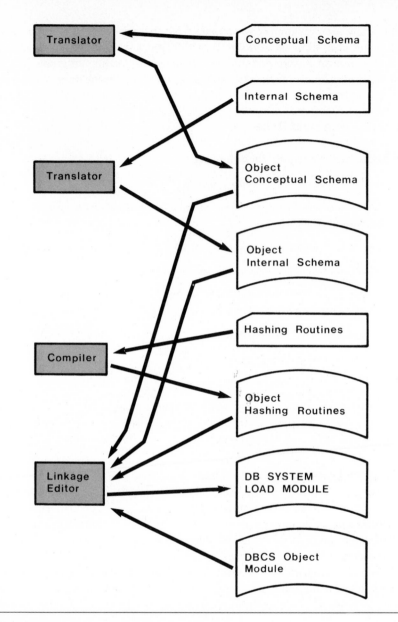

FIGURE 6.18. *First steps in the creation of a data base. The basic data-base system load module is created from object modules for the conceptual and internal schemas, the hashing routines, and the DBMS.*

The result is a load module, sometimes referred to as the *data-base system-load module*. This basic module will be made use of by every application program using the data base.

Loading the Data Base   Referring now to Figure 6.19, the next step is the compilation of the loading program that will load the data base; the result is the loading-program object module. In practice, it is unlikely that there will be one loading program to load the data base. The data base is loaded from data in existing data files, and there is rarely a 1:1 correspondence between the data in the original files and the new data-base files. Thus to load a large data base with many files and relationships, it is most likely that the job will be done in steps with more than one loading program. (Writing these loading programs is one of the major expenses connected with establishing a data base. The loading programs are based on the original non-data-base files. Once the data base is constructed, they will never be used again. This is true even though the data base will be reloaded periodically during its lifetime. This will be necessary for many reasons, such as damage to or extension of the data base. However, these reloadings will be based on the old data-base files, since it is now these that hold the most up-to-date data. Thus to reload the data base after a period of use, we need reload programs, which can be reused often with little or no modification. The original loading programs are thus expensive.)

Referring again to Figure 6.19, the next step is the preparation of the external-schema object module. As with the other schemas, a translator reads in the source schema. The object-external schema, object-load program, and data-base system load module are then link-edited and loaded for execution.

6.4.6 Using the Data Base

The data base may be used in either batch or on-line mode. We defer the discussion of the on-line mode until later and consider only a simple batch situation.

A new user of the data base (in the batch mode) will require:

1.   A suitable application program;

2.   The proper external schema;

3.   Transaction files, if the data base is to be updated.

In most organizations, the external schema is drawn up with the permission and participation of the data-base administrator. The appropriate external-schema object module is then created. This external schema will then be used in conjunction with many, if not all, of the user's data-base application programs.

An application program is first compiled to give the object module, which is then linked to the external schema and the data-base system load module created when the data base was first loaded. The resulting load module is then executed, the transaction files area read in, and the data base updated.

6.4.7 Implementation Strategies

The implementation of a data base represents a major investment for an organization. It also means a new style of data processing, as compared to data processing based on

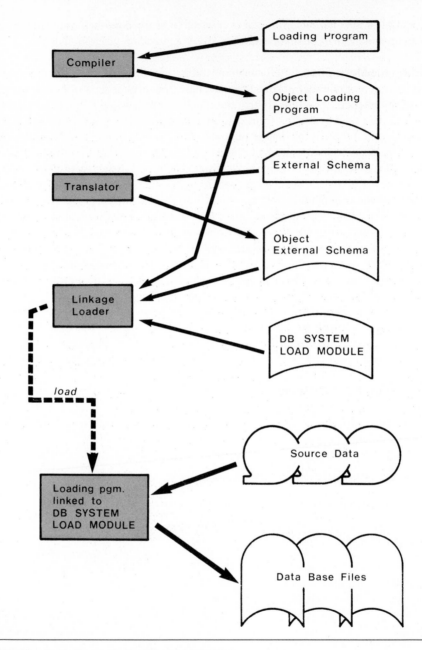

FIGURE 6.19. *Final steps in the creation of a data base. The loading program is linked to the basic data-base system-load module and executed. Source-data files are read in and the data-base files are written out.*

individual files, with all the accompanying problems caused by lack of data-independent application programs and use of redundant data.

Given the expense of constructing a data base and accompanying application programs and considering the organizational effect of such a step, the construction or implementation strategy chosen is of critical importance. A detailed discussion of this area is beyond the scope of this book; there are, however, two overall strategies that may be considered.

1. *The all-or-nothing strategy*

    The all-or-nothing strategy involves designing a data base that will replace all the essential data files in the organization. At the same time, all the file-oriented application programs are replaced by the new data-base application programs.

2. *The core-data-base strategy*

    The core-data-base strategy involves designing a smaller or core-data base, which will replace a portion of the conventional files. A limited number of application programs are written for the core-data base. In the course of time, the number of files in the data base is gradually increased to the point where all the essential conventional files of the organization have been replaced. At the same time, the old conventional file-oriented application programs are gradually eliminated in favor of data-base-oriented application programs.

Both methods have their advantages and disadvantages. With the all-or-nothing method, the risk of an expensive failure is high; if successful, this method will lead to reduced costs and a better utilization of the data resource in a short time. Because of the high risk, it is not likely to be used very often, however.

The core strategy reduces the risk of failure and, if applied to the right set of data files initially, it can demonstrate the advantages of the data-base approach for a relatively small investment. On the other hand, the user organization will have to live with some data in the data base and some in conventional files for a long time, and this will inevitably lead to problems of data redundancy and data independence.

6.4.8 The Main Approaches to Data-Base Management Systems

Data-base management systems may be classified according to the type of conceptual schema and the type of data-manipulation language they use. However, it is common practice to use the type of (conceptual) schema to distinguish between the approaches [Date, 1977; Tsichritzis, 1977; Wiederhold, 1977].

The Main Types of Conceptual Schema or Data Model   There are three main types of schema or *data model:* the *hierarchical* type of schema, the *network or owner-coupled set* type of schema, and the *relational* type of schema. The three basic approaches that they identify will be dealt with in detail in the remaining chapters of this book. However, a brief summary of their various characteristics is useful.

a. *The hierarchical schema*   The conceptual records of this type of (conceptual) schema can be grouped together in two distinct ways. First, the records can be grouped into files, each of which contains records of the same type. Secondly, the records can be grouped into *hierarchy types,* where a hierarchy type is made up of *hierarchy occurrences.*

A hierarchy type is a collection of conceptual files with mutual relationships that form a hierarchical structure. Figure 6.20*a* shows an extended Bachman diagram for six conceptual files of a given hierarchy type. In this particular hierarchy type, an AFILE parent record will have BFILE and CFILE child records. Each of these child records may also be parents of child records (DFILE and EFILE records, or FFILE records).

An occurrence of the hierarchy type from Figure 6.20*a* is an AFILE (or root) record together with all its descendents, as shown in Figure 6.20*b*. Some writers refer to the hierarchy type as a *tree type* and a hierarchy occurrence as a *tree occurrence*. Information Management System (IMS) from IBM is the most widely known hierarchical DBMS. Present versions of IMS follow the ANSI/SPARC recommendations to a considerable degree. However, the internal and conceptual schemas are combined in IMS.

b. *Network or owner-coupled set schema*

We shall consider the CODASYL (conceptual) schema, since the CODASYL DBMS contains what is probably the most important example of a network schema. The CODASYL DBMS is the proposal of the voluntary body responsible for developing COBOL, and the latest version follows the ANSI/SPARC recommendations quite closely (see Chapter 8).

In a CODASYL conceptual schema, the conceptual records are grouped into records of the same type, that is, conceptual files.[1] However, records may also be grouped into what are known as *owner-coupled sets,* which reflect 1:*n* relationships between files. This additional type of grouping is very important. To better understand it, consider the simple conceptual data base with extended Bachman diagram shown in Figure 6.21 and some of the conceptual records shown in Figure 6.22.

Any record from PETROFIRM is grouped with its child records from DRILL_HOLE. This subgrouping is called an *owner-coupled set occurrence,* the PETROFIRM record being the *owner record* and the DRILL_HOLE records being the *member records.*

All such owner-coupled set occurrences are grouped together into an *owner-coupled set* which is given a name; in this case, it is PETEHOLE. It is clear that PETEHOLE embodies the 1:*n* relationship between PETROFIRM and DRILL_HOLE as supported by the parent connection field PETROFIRM.COMPANY and the child-connection field DRILL HOLE.COMPANY. The occurrences of PETEHOLE are shown in Figure 6.22.

Similarly, we can have an owner-coupled set D_HOLE, which embodies the 1:*n* relationship between DRILLER and DRILL_HOLE. It should be clear that a conceptual DRILL HOLE record can take part in three conceptual groupings, because it is (a) a record in the conceptual file DRILL_HOLE; (b) a member record in PETEHOLE; and (c) a member record in D_HOLE. The reader should draw the occurrences of D_HOLE as an exercise.

There are a substantial number of CODASYL systems in commercial use, although, at the time of writing, some are based on earlier CODASYL recommendations that did not incorporate the ANSI/SPARC recommendations.

---

[1]File *is not a CODASYL term; see Chapter 8.*

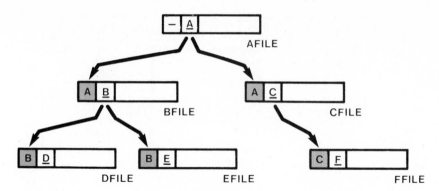

(a) Extended Bachman diagram for the conceptual files of a hierarchy type.

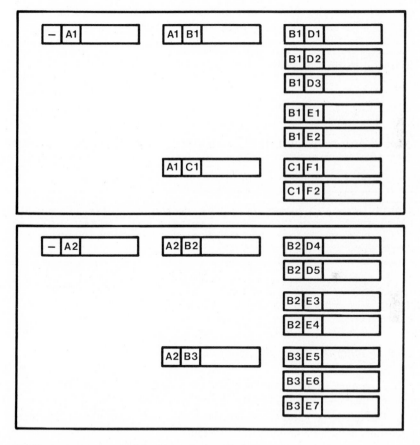

(b) Some occurrences of the hierarchy type in (a).

FIGURE 6.20. Record groupings in a hierarchical schema.

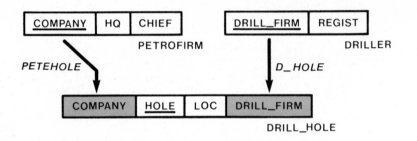

FIGURE 6.21. *Extended Bachman diagram for a* CODASYL *conceptual data base. The owner-coupled sets* PETEHOLE *and* D_HOLE *embody the 1:n relationships between* PETROFIRM *and* DRILL_HOLE *and between* DRILLER *and* DRILL_HOLE, *respectively.*

WESTGAS	HOUSTON	JONES

WESTGAS	23	ALASKA	DRILLPETE
WESTGAS	47	TEXAS	GASRIG
WESTGAS	62	N. SEA	DRILLPETE

MULTOIL	CALGARY	SMITH

MULTOIL	39	YUKON	DEEPDRILL
MULTOIL	58	ALASKA	DEEPDRILL

EASTPETE	CHICAGO	HIND

EASTPETE	41	MEXICO	BOREFIRM
EASTPETE	74	TEXAS	GASRIG

FIGURE 6.22. *Some occurrences of the owner-coupled set* PETEHOLE *from Figure 6.21. Each occurrence has a* (PETROFIRM) *owner record and can have any number, including zero, of* DRILL_HOLE *member records.*

c. *Relational schema*   With this approach, conceptual records (termed *tuples* in the relational approach) have a restricted structure and may be grouped into what may be called *relational files*. In the hierarchical and owner-coupled set approaches, the relationships between files are embodied in the hierarchy and owner-coupled set groupings, respectively. The relational approach is unique in that there are no groupings that embody the relationships between relational files explicitly.

Thus the relational file is the only grouping employed. The relationships between such files are always determined by the connection-field values. Hence the child-connection fields must not be omitted from the relational files, as can be done in the other two approaches. A relational file contains unique, fixed format *conceptual* records, and is often called simply a *relation*. By definition, a relational file cannot contain duplicate tuples (or records), nor two different kinds of tuple.

The relational approach has been the subject of intense research and development for most of the past decade, and the introduction of a full-scale relational DBMS by a major vendor cannot be too far in the future.

Types of Data-Manipulation Languages   Data-manipulation languages for data-base management systems are best distinguished by the retrieval sublanguage; that is, the part of the data-manipulation language concerned with retrieval of data from the data base. We distinguish between two main types.

1. *Procedural sublanguages*

   In a typical retrieval, the required data may be located in more than one record in any file and in more than one file. Thus a language that permits retrieval of only one record (or part of a record) at a time will necessitate the writing of a procedure for any given retrieval. Such a procedure retrieves a record, processes it, and—on the basis of this processing— retrieves another record that would also be processed, and so on. This sequence of retrievals continues until the required data for the retrieval are assembled.

   This process of retrieving a sequence of records from a data base has been termed *navigation,* since the user's application program "navigates" through the files of the data base selecting appropriate records.

   Thus a *procedural sublanguage* retrieves data by means of a procedure or, more metaphorically, by means of *navigation*. The retrieval sublanguage in the CODASYL proposal is *procedural* or *navigational*.

2. *Nonprocedural sublanguages*

   With *nonprocedural sublanguage,* the required data may be specified in a *single* retrieval expression, which in general has a degree of complexity corresponding to the complexity of the retrieval. The data-base manipulation system will be capable of translating the retrieval expression into a procedure that retrieves the required records one at a time.

   For example, referring to the data base in Figure 6.5, we might have the following retrieval:

   For all holes costing more than $500,000, find the name of the head of the company owning them, the owner of the property on which they are drilled, and the head of the agency granting the concessions on which they are drilled.

   Such a retrieval could be specified in a single expression, just as in English it may be expressed in a single sentence. It should be clear that it will require the access of the files PETROFIRM, GOV_AGENCY, CONCESSION, PROPERTY, and DRILL_HOLE.

   The relational data base systems that have been proposed have all included a non-procedural language for retrievals. The term *nonnavigational* may be used instead of *nonprocedural*.

The fact that the CODASYL proposal used a procedural retrieval language and that relational proposals used a nonprocedural language should not be interpreted as meaning that owner-coupled set schema types intrinsically require a procedural language, while relational schema types require a nonprocedural language.

EXERCISES

1. Consider the file TAPEDRIL from Figure 3.15 as a conceptual file. Make up a flowchart of a system that would permit this file to be loaded and manipulated independently of whether the underlying storage file was a hash or index-sequential file.

2. Construct an extended Bachman diagram of a data base describing trade between three American states. The data-base files should at least describe the following entities:

    (a) Companies.

    (b) Types of products.

    (c) Board chairpersons.

3. In a bill of materials for components, the *maximum* number of levels is four; that is, a component can be contained in another component which itself may be contained in another component, which itself may be contained in a fourth component.

    (a) Taking about three or four components at each level, make a diagram of the type shown in Figure 6.12.

    (b) From the diagram, generate some explosions and implosions.

4. Draw a system flowchart along the lines of that in Figure 6.19 for loading and running a program to update an existing data base from some transaction files.

5. Suppose that the files in Figure 6.3c have been implemented as index-sequential files, and that we have an inversion for the field company in DRILL_HOLE. Give a flowchart (omitting technical detail) of a method for retrieving the headquarters of companies with at least six holes in Alaska.

6. Suppose the files in Figure 6.7 have been implemented as index-sequential files, with inversions for the fields FORMER and PRESENT. Give a flowchart of a method for retrieving the cost of holes on concessions presently owned by Houston-based companies, but formerly owned by New York-based companies.

7. Suppose that the three files in Figure 6.9 have been implemented as index-sequential files. Give a flowchart for retrieving the names of the chiefs of oil companies that deal only with drilling firms registered in Colorado.

8. Suppose that PETROFIRM in Figure 6.10 has been implemented as an index-sequential file. Give a flowchart for a retrieval of the ultimate owners of all companies headquartered in Miami. An inversion of PARENTCOMP is available as an index-sequential file.

9. Suppose that the files in Figure 6.14 are implemented as index-sequential files, with inversions for the fields PARENT and SUBSIDIARY. Let us suppose further that there are three organization levels as shown in Figure 6.15. Give a flowchart for retrieving all the subsidiaries of company 'X'.

10. Using the files for Exercise 9, give a flowchart for retrieving Denver-based companies that are more than 50% owned by Houston-based companies.

11. Suppose we have the files of Exercise 9, but where the number of organization levels is not known. Give a flowchart for the retrieval of the subsidiaries of company 'X' (an explosion).

REFERENCES

Bachman, C. W., 1969, "Data Structure Diagrams," *Data Base, J. ACM SIGBDP,* **1**(2):4–10.

Date, C. J., 1977, *Introduction to Database Systems,* Addison-Wesley, Reading, Mass.

Fry, J. P., and E. H. Sibley, 1976, "Evolution of Data Base Systems," *ACM Comp. Surveys,* **8**(1):7–42.

Jardine, D. A. (ed.), 1977, "The ANSI/SPARC DBMS Model," *Proc. 2nd SHARE Conf. Montreal,* 1976, North-Holland, New York.

Kent, W., 1978, *Data and Reality,* North-Holland, New York.

Senko, M. E., 1977a, "Conceptual Schemas, Abstract Data Structures, and Enterprise Descriptions," *Proc. ACM International Computing Symposium,* Liege, Belgium, North-Holland, New York, pp. 85–102.

Senko, M. E., 1977b, "Data Structures and Data Accessing in Data Base Systems: Past, Present, Future," *IBM Sys. Journal,* **16**(3):208–57.

Teory, T. J., and Fry, J. P., 1980, "The Logical Record Access Approach to Database Design," *ACM Comp. Surveys,* **12**(2):179–212.

Tsichritzis, D. C., and F. H. Lochovsky, 1977, *Data Base Management Systems,* Academic Press, New York.

Wiederhold, G., 1977, *Data Base Design,* McGraw-Hill, New York.

Data-Base Design and Normal-Form Files

7

This chapter deals with the design of the records of files of the conceptual schema. The techniques described here were developed largely as a result of pioneering research on relational data bases by E. F. Codd [Codd, 1972], but they may be applied to most conceptual schemas. The essence of the design technique is to ensure that each file is in what is called *fourth normal form* (4NF). A 4NF file has unique, fixed-format *conceptual* records and the key field (or field combination) of a record identifies some entity; for most purposes each field directly describes only that entity (see Section 6.2).

A 4NF file thus has very simple semantics. With the one exception of DRILL_HOLE, conceptual files from the RESOURCE data base (Figure 6.5) are in 4NF. It is the simplicity of 4NF files that makes them desirable. Files that are not 4NF, that is, files with more complex semantics, can give rise to serious updating problems, as we shall see.

This chapter requires some new concepts. They are the concept of *normal form,* the concept of *functional dependence,* and the concept of *binary-join dependence.*[1] We consider normal form and functional dependence first and later develop the concept of binary-join dependence [Fagin, 1977; Delobel, 1978]. The following treatment is nonmathematical, with emphasis placed on a diagrammatic approach [Date, 1977; Bradley, 1978]. Readers should note, however, that there exists an extensive mathematically oriented literature on the subject [Ullman, 1980]. If desired, readers may skip the rest of this chapter until they have studied the remainder of the book, particularly the chapter on relational algebra (Chapter 16); however, they should understand that a 4NF file is simple, and has no complex semantics.

---

[1]*This was formerly called* multivalued dependence. *Recent research has shown that this term is inappropriate.*

7.1 NORMAL FORMS AND FUNCTIONAL DEPENDENCIES

7.1.1 Normal-Form Files

A normal-form file is merely a relational file, or simply a *conceptual* file with fixed-format unique records. Thus such a file is in the form of an *N* by *M* table, with *N* unique records and *M* fields per record.

The files used in all the extended Bachman diagrams in the previous chapter have been in normal form. As we shall see, there are five different categories of normal-form files, depending on the complexity of the allowed semantics for the file. However, all normal-form files have a simple table-like structure, which is attractive in itself.

7.1.2 Functional Dependence

The concept of functional dependence applies to normal-form files and informs about the internal semantics or *semantic infrastructure* of a file. Hence this is a concept of fundamental importance for the data-base designer.

A normal-form file has by definition unique conceptual records, so that there exists some one field (or combination of fields) that may serve as a record identifier at the conceptual level. We refer to such a field (or field combination) as the *prime key*. If the prime key is a combination of fields, the key is said to be *composite*.

Another way of looking at this is to regard each record as describing some unique prime entity, with the prime key being a unique identifier of that entity. It is convenient to refer to such an entity as the *prime entity*. (It may be noted that there can be more than one prime key identifying the prime entity.)

In the normal-form file PETROFIRM in Figure 7.1, we see that each record describes an oil company. The prime key is the field COMPANY, which is the unique identifier of the prime entity, *oil company*. The file has two other fields HQ (headquarters of an oil company) and CHIEF (chief of an oil company). These fields each describe the prime entity *oil company*. For the file PETROFIRM, we may state that these fields HQ and CHIEF are both *functionally dependent* on the field COMPANY. Thus we may write HQ = f(COMPANY), and CHIEF = f′(COMPANY). This means that for a given COMPANY value, there is just one HQ value and just one CHIEF value. But for a given HQ value, there may be more than one COMPANY value; for a given CHIEF value there may also be more than one COMPANY value. This dependence is illustrated in the instance of PETROFIRM in Table 7.1.

Dependency Diagrams   The two functional dependencies HQ = f(COMPANY) and CHIEF = f′(COMPANY) may be illustrated diagrammatically by a minor modification of

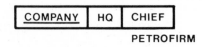

PETROFIRM

FIGURE 7.1.   *The records of* PETROFIRM *describe oil companies, the prime entities.*

PETROFIRM

COMPANY	HQ	CHIEF
WESTGAS	HOUSTON	JONES
ROCKYPETE	HOUSTON	SMITH
QUIKOIL	HOUSTON	BROWN
MULTOIL	CALGARY	SMITH
BOWOIL	CALGARY	JONES
EASTPETE	CHICAGO	BROWN
MICHGAS	CHICAGO	JONES

P(HQ)

HQ
HOUSTON
CALGARY
CHICAGO

TABLE 7.1

the extended Bachman diagrams we have been using to illustrate 1:*n* relationships between different conceptual files. We can do this because *functional dependencies describe 1:*n *relationships between fields in the records of a file*. Thus if we can create what may be called a *projection* or *virtual* file made up of records containing the fields involved in a dependency, we could apply the extended Bachman-diagram technique.

To see this clearly, we must consider what is known as the *projection*[1] from a file on a single field or any group of fields. For example, if we have a file F with fields A, B, and C, the projection on the field A is a file with single field records containing all the unique field A values from F. This projection or virtual file may be referred to as PROJ(A), or P(A). As an example, in Table 7.1, P(HQ) is the projection of PETROFIRM on the field HQ. Similarly, P(A,B) would contain all the unique combinations of the values of A and B in F. The projection operation has its origins in relational algebra (Chapter 16).

It is now clear that there must be a 1:*n* relationship between P(HQ) and PETROFIRM and between P(CHIEF) and PETROFIRM, as shown in the dependency diagram in Figure 7.2. Since HQ = f(COMPANY), for a given HQ value such as 'HOUSTON' there will be several COMPANY values such as 'WESTGAS', 'ROCKYPETE', and 'QUIKOIL', using the

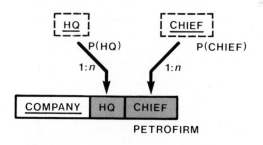

FIGURE 7.2. *Dependency diagram for the file* PETROFIRM.

[1]*A useful description of* projection *is also given in Section 16.1.1, and might be referred to if that given here is not understood.*

instance of PETROFIRM in Table 7.1. But for each value of HQ, there is a unique P(HQ) record, and for each value of COMPANY, there is a unique PETROFIRM record (since COMPANY is the prime key). Hence there must be a 1:n relationship between P(HQ) and PETROFIRM. Similarly, there is a 1:n relationship between P(CHIEF) and PETROFIRM. The fields HQ and CHIEF are the (child) connection fields in PETROFIRM supporting these relationships.

The dependency diagram in Figure 7.2 thus bares the semantic infrastructure of the simple file PETROFIRM. The projection files P(HQ) and P(CHIEF) do not exist, of course, even at the conceptual level. They are merely used here to illustrate functional dependencies. In the example given, the diagrams are almost trivial, but that is because the semantics of PETROFIRM are very simple. It is possible to have normal-form files with very complex semantics, and correspondingly complex functional (and perhaps more elaborate) dependencies. We shall now examine normal-form files more closely and classify these files in accordance with the complexity of the allowed semantic infrastructure.

7.1.3 The Higher Normal Form

We may isolate categories of files that are said to be in *higher normal forms*. We do this by placing increasing restrictions on the allowed dependencies, going to a higher normal-form file with each increase in the number of restrictions. This is depicted diagrammatically in Figure 7.3. We start with the universe of all possible files, whether in normal form or not. A subset of this universe contains the *first normal-form files* (1NF files), which includes all files in normal form. By placing restrictions on 1NF files, we arrive at 2NF, 3NF, BCNF, and 4NF files. We shall first state what these restrictions are, *with limited explanation,* and afterwards illustrate with some examples.

Second Normal-Form (2NF) Files   A second normal-form (2NF) file is subject to the following restrictions.

1. A 2NF file is also a 1NF file.

2. Each nonkey field is functionally dependent on the prime key, but not on any subfields of the key if the key is a composite.

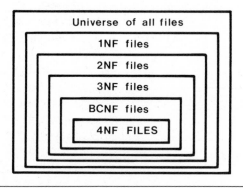

FIGURE 7.3.   *By a process of progressive restriction, we arrive at 4NF files that are the simplest possible.*

Thus 2NF files are semantically simpler than some 1NF files, since they do not permit the complexity of having a nonkey field functionally dependent on a subkey field. An example of a 2NF file is given in the following section. However, a 2NF file is not semantically simple enough. A serious defect is the fact that functional dependence of a nonkey field on another nonkey field is permitted.

Third Normal-Form (3NF) Files

A third normal-form (3NF) file is subject to the following restrictions.

1. A 3NF file is also a 2NF file.

2. A nonkey field may not be functionally dependent on any other nonkey field.

For a while it was thought that 3NF files were ideal for designing data bases, as their allowed dependencies appeared very simple and restrictive. The following is an alternative definition of such a file:

> A 3NF file is a normal-form file which allows nonkey fields to be functionally dependent only on the prime key.

However, examples in which subkey fields were functionally dependent on nonkey fields were soon uncovered. Such dependencies are not simple, but are allowed by the 3NF definition. The concepts of 1NF, 2NF, and 3NF were originally identified by Codd [Codd, 1972].

Boyce-Codd Normal-Form (BCNF) Files

A Boyce-Codd normal-form (BCNF) file is subject to the following restrictions.

1. A BCNF file is also a 3NF file.

2. A subkey field can be functionally dependent only on the prime key.

The following is an alternative definition of a BCNF file.

> A BCNF file is a normal form file in which all fields are functionally dependent only on the prime key.

This very restricted file with very simple functional dependencies appeared to be the ultimate in semantic simplicity until it was realized that there was another type of dependency, called a binary-join dependency [Fagin, 1977]. We saw that a functional dependency basically involves a 1:n relationship between fields; a binary-join dependency basically involves a special kind of n:m relationship among fields. Furthermore, since a 1:n relationship is a special case of an n:m relationship, we can say that all functional dependencies are also (trivial) binary-join dependencies, but the converse is not true. We shall not explain binary-join dependencies further at this stage; they are discussed in Section 7.2. As it turned out, BCNF files permitted binary-join dependencies, which, as we shall see, have anything but simple semantics.

Fourth Normal-Form (4NF) Files

A fourth normal-form (4NF) file is subject to the following restrictions.

1. A 4NF file is also a BCNF file.

2. No binary-join dependency is allowed that does not also imply functional dependency.

The prohibition of nontrivial binary-join dependencies from 4NF files gives these files the simple semantics we desire. (A fifth normal form has recently been revealed however; it prohibits a complex but unlikely type of join dependency from 4NF files.) We may give an alternative definition of a 4NF file.

> A 4NF file is a normal-form file in which every field is functionally dependent only on the prime key and any binary-join dependency also implies functional dependency.

Binary-join dependencies that do not also imply functional dependencies are very subtle. However, they are not common, are readily recognizable, and even appear somewhat contrived. Thus for most practical purposes we can take a BCNF file as being in 4NF. In addition, since a single-field key 3NF file must be a BCNF file, *we may also take a single-field key 3NF file as being in 4NF*. This simplification is useful in practice.

7.1.4 Functional Dependencies and Decomposition to 4NF Files

We now give examples of files that violate the 4NF rule. We show also the consequences of the files not being in 4NF, usually as far as updating or insertion of a new record is concerned. In addition, a decomposition of each file into semantically equivalent 4NF files is illustrated. In the examples in this section we deal only with functional dependencies. An example involving a nontrivial binary-join dependency is given in the next section.

Violation 1: Functional Dependence on a Subkey Field

Example Consider the file SEISMIC_TEST in Figure 7.4. The file describes seismic tests carried out by an oil company; the prime entity is thus a seismic test. The semantics of the file are as follows.

1. CONCESSNO gives the number of the drilling concession on which the test is carried out. Many tests are performed on a concession, so this field cannot be used as the prime key.

2. TIME gives the point in time at which a test is carried out. No two tests on a given concession may be carried out at the same time. (In a seismic test, sound waves from an explosion are recorded by surface detectors following reflection or refraction from under-

SEISMIC_TEST

FIGURE 7.4. *The file* SEISMIC_TEST, *which describes seismic tests, is not in 4NF. Note that the prime key is a composite.*

SEISMIC_TEST

CONCESSNO	TIME	GEOPHYS	LOC
99X9	1245 01011980	FINDERS	TEXAS
99X9	1345 01011980	CORNELIUS	TEXAS
2001	0945 09091979	FINDERS	YUKON
256K	1100 10031981	CORNELIUS	TEXAS
2001	1100 10031981	CORNELIUS	YUKON

TABLE 7.2

ground formations. Tests carried out on the same concession at the same time could interfere with each other.)

3. GEOPHYS gives the geophysicist responsible for the test. A geophysicist may be responsible for more than one test at a given time.

4. LOC gives the location of the concession on which the test was carried out, such as Texas or the Yukon. In a given location, there may be many concessions.

We have an instance of the file SEISMIC_TEST in Table 7.2. It is obvious that we could use the fields CONCESSNO and TIME as a composite prime key and as an identifier of the prime entity (a seismic test). GEOPHYS is clearly functionally dependent on the prime key, since for a given test there is just one geophysicist and a geophysicist may conduct many tests. LOC is clearly also functionally dependent on the prime key, because a test is carried out in one location (such as a state) and in a given location more than one test may be carried out. However, LOC is also functionally dependent on CONCESSNO, since a concession has one location and a location many concessions. This last functional dependency means that the file SEISMIC_TEST is not even in 2NF, and this is illustrated in Figure 7.5. Assuming the instance of SEISMIC_TEST in Table 7.2, the projection file P(CONCESSNO,LOC) will be as in Table 7.3.

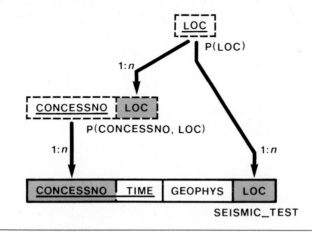

FIGURE 7.5. *Dependency diagram for the conceptual file* SEISMIC_TEST. *The problem is that* LOC *is functionally dependent on the subkey field* CONCESSNO.

P(CONCESSNO,LOC)

CONCESSNO	LOC
99X9	TEXAS
2001	YUKON
256K	TEXAS

TABLE 7.3

P(LOC)

LOC
TEXAS
YUKON

TABLE 7.4

The relationship between P(CONCESSNO,LOC) and SEISMIC_TEST is 1:n and reflects the functional dependency between CONCESSNO and the SEISMIC_TEST prime key; that is, for a concession there are many seismic tests. The 1:n relationship between P(LOC) and SEISMIC_TEST, reflecting the functional dependency between LOC and the prime key, is also shown in Figure 7.5. The contents of P(LOC) are in Table 7.4. However, it is clear from Figure 7.5 that there is also a relationship between P(LOC) and P(CONCESSNO,LOC), and it is this relationship that reflects the functional dependency between the field LOC and the subkey field CONCESSNO. If it were not for this dependency, all the fields would be dependent only on the prime key and the file would be 4NF.

Consequences   Suppose a new concession, on which as yet no seismic tests have been performed, is acquired by the company. It is likely that we should wish to store this data in the data base. Specifically, we should like to store the concession number and the location of the concession. However, we cannot because we cannot place a record in the file SEISMIC_TEST without a key. A further consequence is that there is nothing to prevent us from updating SEISMIC_TEST in such a way that a given concession would have two different LOC values in two different records, thus making the file inconsistent.

Remedy   The remedy is suggested by the dependency diagram in Figure 7.5. We decompose SEISMIC_TEST into CONCESSION and S_TEST, as shown in Figure 7.6. These two files are both in 4NF, and taking the 1:n relationship between them into account, they are consistent with the semantic rules for SEISMIC_TEST. The reader should be able to see that with CONCESSION and S_TEST, the undesirable consequences mentioned above are avoided.

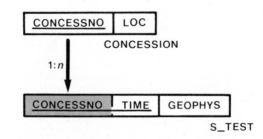

FIGURE 7.6. *The remedy is to create two distinct 4NF files* CONCESSION *and* S_TEST.

Violation 2: Functional Dependence on a Nonkey Field

Example   Consider the file DRILL_HOLE in Figure 7.7. The file describes drill-holes owned by an oil company. The semantics for the file are as follows.

1. The prime entity is a drill-hole identified by the prime key HOLE.

2. LOC gives the location of a drill-hole, and we may have many holes in one location.

3. COMPANY names the oil company owning the drill-hole. A company may own many holes.

4. HQ gives the headquarters location of the oil company owning the hole. More than one company can have its headquarters in a given location.

Here we see that the fields COMPANY, LOC, and HQ are each functionally dependent on the prime key HOLE because, given a HOLE value, the other field values are determined. However, HQ is also functionally dependent on the nonkey field COMPANY, since when a COMPANY value is given, the HQ value is determined. Alternatively, for a given LOC value we have many possible COMPANY values. It is clear, therefore, that the file is in 2NF but not in 3NF.

DRILL_HOLE

FIGURE 7.7.   *The conceptual file DRILL_HOLE is not in 4NF.*

We can display the undesirable functional dependency by means of the dependency diagram in Figure 7.8. The 1:*n* relationships between P(HQ) and DRILL_HOLE and between P(COMPANY,HQ) and DRILL_HOLE reflect the functional dependencies between HQ and DRILL_HOLE and between COMPANY and DRILL_HOLE. The 1:*n* relationship between P(HQ) and P(COMPANY,HQ) reflects the undesirable dependency between HQ and COMPANY.

Consequences   First of all, if a new company is incorporated with a certain headquarters location, this information cannot be stored until the company owns at least one drill-hole. Furthermore, if the headquarters location of a company is changed, many DRILL_HOLE records will have to be updated. During the updating process, the file is not consistent, which will give problems if there are retrieval programs operating concurrently with the updating program. Lastly, there is nothing to prevent the file from being permanently inconsistent if the HQ field has two different values for two records, each containing the same COMPANY value.

Remedy   The remedy is again suggested by the dependency diagram in Figure 7.9. It involves decomposing the DRILL_HOLE file into the two 4NF files OILFIRM and BOREHOLE. Together with the 1:*n* relationship between them, these two files are consistent with the semantic rules for the file DRILL_HOLE.

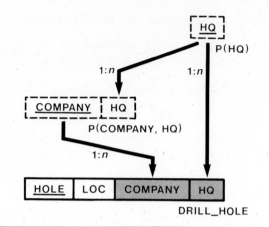

FIGURE 7.8. *Dependency diagram for the conceptual file* DRILL_HOLE. *The problem is that* **HQ** *is functionally dependent on the secondary entity oil company.*

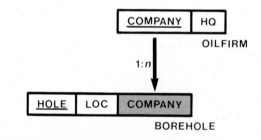

FIGURE 7.9. *The remedy is to create two distinct 4NF files from* DRILL_HOLE.

7.2 BINARY-JOIN DEPENDENCIES

In this section, we study an apparently simple file that contains both functional dependencies and a binary-join dependency (BJD). We first look at the semantics of this file and isolate the functional dependencies. We then examine the BJD that it exhibits.

7.2.1 Semantics and Functional Dependencies

Consider the file ASSIGNMENT in Figure 7.10. The file describes assignments (the prime entity) involving the placement of consulting engineers by a company to company-operated locations. We have the following semantic rules.

1. COMPANY is the name of the company that employs the consulting engineer and has operations in an operating location.

ASSIGNMENT

FIGURE 7.10 *The conceptual file* **ASSIGNMENT** *which includes a binary-join dependency.*

2. CON_ENG is the consulting engineer employed by a company. A company has many consulting engineers working for it.

3. A consulting engineer works for just one company.

4. LOC is the name of a location in which a company has operations (for example, drilling or exploration). There are many locations in which a company carries on operations.

5. Only one company carries on operations in a given location.

6. Each engineer is assigned to *all* of *his or her* company's operating locations at all times.

We give an instance of the file ASSIGNMENT in Table 7.5, where we are dealing with two companies, each with two engineers and two operating locations.

We can see that the file is all key; that is, a record may be identified by a composite key with the fields CON_ENG, COMPANY, and LOC. We see also that the file contains two undesirable functional dependencies, for COMPANY is functionally dependent on CON_ENG and COMPANY is functionally dependent on LOC. More concisely, we may state that COMPANY = f(CON_ENG), or CON_ENG determines COMPANY, and COMPANY = f'(LOC), or LOC determines COMPANY. These two dependencies exist because of the semantic rules in (3) and (5). However, there is a far more elaborate dependency in ASSIGNMENT that has nothing to do with the two functional dependencies caused by the rules in (3) and (5). In fact, this elaborate dependency would still be there even if rules (3) and (5) were removed.

7.2.2 The Binary-Join Dependency in ASSIGNMENT

Analysis   The elaborate dependency to which we are referring is binary-join dependency, originally discovered by Fagin [Fagin, 1977]. (Fagin used the term *multivalued dependency*.) This dependency exists because of rules (2), (4), and (6) acting together. The following definition of a binary-join dependency closely follows the one given by Fagin; however, we have introduced some minor modifications for tutorial purposes:

If Y, X, and Z are fields (or field composites) in a normalized conceptual file F, then F is said to contain a binary-join dependency (so that Y and Z are both *binary-join dependent*[1] on X), provided that whenever we have two F records with field values

---

[1] *Fagin has a difficult terminology here. According to him,* Y *multidetermines* X, *thus implying that* Z *also* multidetermines X.

ASSIGNMENT

CON_ENG	COMPANY	LOC
WRIGHT	WESTGAS	HIGHVALLEY
WRIGHT	WESTGAS	DEEPLAKE
DERRICK	WESTGAS	HIGHVALLEY
DERRICK	WESTGAS	DEEPLAKE
SMART	MULTOIL	STEEPHILL
SMART	MULTOIL	DRYRIVER
QUIKLEY	MULTOIL	STEEPHILL
QUIKLEY	MULTOIL	DRYRIVER

TABLE 7.5

('Y1', 'X1', 'Z1') and ('Y2', 'X1', 'Z2'), F is required as a consequence to contain the records ('Y2', 'X1', 'Z1') and ('Y1', 'X1', 'Z2').

That the requirement in the above definition applies to the file ASSIGNMENT is clear from rules (2), (4), and (6). From rules (2) and (4) we can have the following records:

WRIGHT   WESTGAS   HIGHVALLEY
DERRICK   WESTGAS   DEEPLAKE

However, because rule (6) requires that an engineer be assigned to all company locations (with the implication that a location must be assigned all company engineers), we must also have the records:

WRIGHT   WESTGAS   DEEPLAKE
DERRICK   WESTGAS   HIGHVALLEY

We note that even if rules (3) and (5) were removed, rules (2), (4), and (6) would still cause ASSIGNMENT to contain a binary-join dependency (see Exercise 1).

(There is a trivial case of binary-join dependency, which is merely equivalent to a case of functional dependency. This would occur in ASSIGNMENT if we removed rules (3) and (5), and then modified rules (2) and (4) as follows:

(2) A company may have only one engineer working for it.

(4) A company may operate in only one location.

In this case, only one record containing the COMPANY field 'WESTGAS' would be possible, so that COMPANY would become the prime key. In addition, CON_ENG and LOC (corresponding to Y and Z in the definition) would be functionally dependent on COMPANY. However, because of rule (6), CON_ENG and LOC would still be binary-join dependent on COMPANY, but in a trivial and inconsequential manner. Hence only a binary-join dependency that does not also reduce to functional dependencies is of any consequence.)

Diagrammatic Display of a Binary-Join Dependency   We notice that there is a symmetry in the definition of a binary-join dependency. Both CON_ENG and LOC (Y and Z) are binary-join dependent on COMPANY (X). This symmetry is apparent from the dependency diagram in Figure 7.11, which displays the important dependencies in ASSIGNMENT. The functional dependencies resulting from rules (3) and (5) are reflected by the 1:n relationships between P(COMPANY) and P(CON_ENG, COMPANY) and between P(COMPANY) and P(COMPANY, LOC). These projection files are further illustrated in Tables 7.6, 7.7, and 7.8.

The binary-join dependency is illustrated by the rather special relationship between P(CON_ENG, COMPANY) and P(COMPANY, LOC), which in fact is an n:m relationship of a special kind, one that might be called a *partitioned Cartesian product n:m relationship*.

Consider the n:m relationship between P(CON_ENG, COMPANY) and P(COMPANY, LOC), as shown in the diagram. What is unusual is the fact that for the first time we come across a case where both connection fields supporting the relationship are child-connection fields. This means that *each* of the P(CON_ENG, COMPANY) records with a COMPANY value 'WESTGAS' is connected to *each* P(COMPANY, LOC) record with a COMPANY value 'WESTGAS', and vice versa, because of the partitioned Cartesian product n:m relationship between P(COMPANY, LOC) and P(CON_ENG, COMPANY). This relationship is denoted by the 2-way arrow enclosing an "*".

We can look at this in another way. Suppose we partition both P(CON_ENG, COMPANY) and P(COMPANY, LOC) into *subfiles* for each COMPANY value. The file ASSIGNMENT is then the result of taking the Cartesian product of each subfile from P(CON_ENG, COMPANY) with a corresponding subfile from P(COMPANY, LOC) that has the same COMPANY field value. (A Cartesian product of subfiles A and B concatenates all possible pairs of A and B records. See also Chapter 13.)

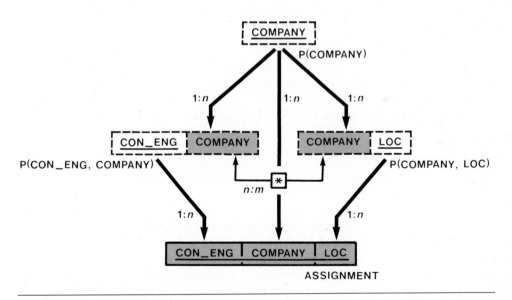

FIGURE 7.11. *Dependency diagram for* ASSIGNMENT *showing the binary-join dependency.*

P(CON_ENG,COMPANY)

CON_ENG	COMPANY
WRIGHT	WESTGAS
DERRICK	WESTGAS
SMART	MULTOIL
QUIKLEY	MULTOIL

TABLE 7.6

P(COMPANY, LOC)

COMPANY	LOC
WESTGAS	HIGHVALLEY
WESTGAS	DEEPLAKE
MULTOIL	STEEPHILL
MULTOIL	DRYRIVER

TABLE 7.7

P(COMPANY)

COMPANY
WESTGAS
MULTOIL

TABLE 7.8

Consequences of the BJD   The file ASSIGNMENT is in 3NF; it is not in BCNF because of the functional dependencies due to semantic rules (3) and (5). If these rules were removed, it would be in BCNF but not in 4NF because of the binary-join dependency. It is clear that the binary-join dependency is not desirable, as it leads to insertion and deletion difficulties. For example, if we insert a new record into the ASSIGNMENT instance in Table 7.5, with the fields

WRIGHT   WESTGAS   SALTCREEK

we would also have to have the insertion

DERRICK   WESTGAS   SALTCREEK

Similarly, deletion of one record would require deletion of other records.

Remedy   The remedy is suggested by the dependency diagram in Figure 7.12. We decompose ASSIGNMENT into the two 4NF files ENGINEER and OPERATION, which are connected together by means of the partitioned Cartesian product $n:m$ relationship (Figure 7.12). (Note that this relationship cannot be embodied in an owner-coupled set.)

7.2.3 Functional and Join Dependencies in Data-Base Design

It should now be clear that a data base should be made up of simple 4NF conceptual files. However, this ideal of simplicity is not easy to achieve in an actual design situation. In practice, with a complex data base there are a multitude of dependencies to consider, and it is easy to overlook obscure or hidden dependencies. A great deal of painstaking work is required to design a semantically acceptable 4NF conceptual data base.

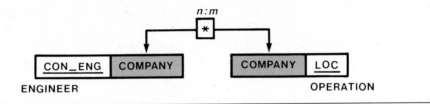

FIGURE 7.12. *The 3NF file* ASSIGNMENT *may be decomposed into two 4NF files,* ENGINEER *and* OPERATION.

It should nevertheless be understood that a dependency as complex (and perhaps as contrived) as a BJD is not likely to occur very often, and cannot occur in a file with a single field as the prime key. Thus the designer who attempts to avoid composite prime keys will automatically avoid many obscure and complex dependencies. We recall that a 3NF file with a single field as prime key is automatically in 4NF. Thus functional dependencies are by far the most important in practice.

Having made these encouraging statements, for the sake of completeness we must now inform the reader that recent research indicates that a BJD is but a particular case of a more general (but still obscure and perhaps contrived) dependency called a *join dependency* [Rissanen, 1978]. A brief study of join dependencies helps to put binary-join dependencies in a better perspective.

Join Dependencies A join dependency may be of order n, where n is a positive integer; thus the binary join dependency discussed in the previous section is the join dependency of order 2. To gain a practical understanding of the general concept of join dependency, we shall now examine an example of a join dependency of order 3.

Suppose that we have three files A_FILE, B_FILE, and C_FILE, as shown in Figure 7.13a. These files are in 4NF, as they have only simple dependencies; in A_FILE, for example, P and Z are both functionally dependent on the key field A. The three files have a field in common, the Z field. This indicates that there may be a relationship among the three files. Finally, let us suppose that we have partitioned each file, so that in any partition in a given file, the records all have the same Z value.

We now take a group of partitions with the same Z value (there will normally be three in any group) from the three files. We then form records of a new file J_FILE (Figure 7.13b) by taking the *expanded Cartesian product* of the three partitions; that is, omitting duplicate Z fields, we concatenate every group of three records, one from each partition, that may be formed. Thus if the three partitions had each p, q, and r records, the expanded Cartesian product would give pqr J_FILE records. An expanded Cartesian product is carried out for each group of partitions with the same Z value from each of the three files in Figure 7.13a; the result of each operation is additional J_FILE records. We can call the whole process a *join* of A_FILE, B_FILE, and C_FILE based on the *join field* Z (join operations are further discussed in Chapter 16), or we can call it the *expanded partitioned Cartesian product* of the three files based on the field Z.

If it were a semantic property of J_FILE that it was always required to consist of an expanded partitioned Cartesian product of A_FILE, B_FILE, and C_FILE, then we may say that C_FILE has a join dependency of order 3. Furthermore, A_FILE, B_FILE, and

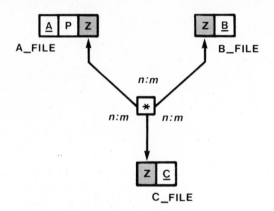

A_FILE   B_FILE

n:m

n:m   *n:m*

C_FILE

(a) *These three files are related by a third order partitioned Cartesian product n:m relationship depicted by the three-headed arrow.*

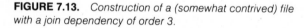

J_FILE

(b) *Since J_FILE is formed from an expanded partitioned Cartesian product of the files, it contains a join dependency of order 3.*

FIGURE 7.13. *Construction of a (somewhat contrived) file with a join dependency of order 3.*

C_FILE may be regarded as virtual or projection files of J_FILE, since each of them may be formed by taking an appropriate projection of the fields of J_FILE. Accordingly, the three files in Figure 7.13a are connected by a special relationship, which may be termed a *third order expanded partitioned Cartesian product n:m relationship*. It is depicted in Figure 7.13a by a three-headed arrow with the (join) "∗" in the middle. Z may be taken as a connection field for each file. This special relationship clearly implies also that for any *two* of the files in Figure 7.13a, there exists a (second order) partitioned Cartesian product *n:m* relationship, of the kind shown in Figures 7.11 and 7.12. This means that the join dependency of order 3 in J_FILE implies three binary join dependencies. Thus J_FILE is clearly not in 4NF.

In practice it would be difficult to maintain the semantic properties of J_FILE. If for Z and A values 'Z1', 'A2', we have respectively *s* and *t* distinct B and C values including 'B1' and 'C1', there must always be *st* records with these A, B, C and Z values. If we then inserted a record with values 'A1', 'B1', and 'C1' for the fields A, B,and C, respectively, we would be required to insert *st-1* additional records, each with the 'A1' value for A, assuming that the 'A1' value were new. It is clear that the join dependency in J_FILE is best removed, and this may be done by decomposing J_FILE into its projection files A_FILE, B_FILE, and C_FILE. (Note that the special *n:m* relationship between these three decomposition files could not be embodied in an owner-coupled set of the CODASYL approach.) A related join dependency is prohibited in 5NF files.

Application of Functional and Join Dependencies in Practice We believe that files exhibiting join dependencies are somewhat contrived, and that such files, together with their 4NF decomposition files that are related by special *n:m* relationships (Figures 7.12 and 7.13*a*), are not likely to occur often in practice. It is obscure *functional* dependencies that are likely to cause the most trouble in practice. For example, the functional dependencies of the otherwise simple file DRILL_HOLE in Figure 6.5 complicate its semantics. The semantics may be simplified and the file brought into 3NF (and hence automatically into 4NF) simply by removing the fields COMPANY and CONCESS from the file (see Exercise 3).

EXERCISES

1. Analyze the dependencies for the file ASSIGNMENT in Section 6.5 for the case where semantic rules (3) and (5) are omitted.

2. Analyze ASSIGNMENT in Section 6.5.5 when semantic rule (6) is changed to:

   > 6. An engineer may be assigned to more than one of the company's operating locations, and such a location may have several engineers assigned to it.

3. In which normal form is the file DRILL_HOLE in RESOURCE in Figure 6.5? Why is the remedy to remove the fields COMPANY and CONCESS?

4. Alter the file PETROFIRM in RESOURCE in Figure 6.5 so that the file is no longer in 3NF. Draw a diagram of the dependency you have introduced.

5. Devise a version of LINK in Figure 6.14 that is not 3NF, giving a diagram of the dependency.

REFERENCES

Bradley, J., 1978, "An Extended Owner-Coupled Set Data Model and Predicate Calculus for Data Base Management," *ACM Trans. on Database Systems*, **3**(4):385–416.

Codd, E. F., 1972, *Further Normalization of the Data Base Relational Model*, vol. 6, *Courant Computer Science Symposia Series*, Prentice-Hall, Inc., Englewood Cliffs, N.J.

Date, C. J., 1977, *Introduction to Database Systems*, Addison-Wesley, New York.

Delobel, C., 1978, "Normalization and Hierarchical Dependencies in the Relational Data Model," *ACM Trans. on Database Systems*, **3**(3):201–22.

Fagin, R., 1977, "A New Normal Form for Relational Data Bases," *ACM. Trans. on Database Systems*, **2**(3):262–79.

Rissanen, J., 1978, "Theory of Relations for Data Bases," *Lect. Notes in Computer Science*, **64**:536–51.

Ullman, J. D., 1980, *Principles of Data Base Systems*, Computer Science Press, Potomac, Maryland.

The CODASYL Conceptual-Schema Data-Description Language

8

We saw in Chapter 6 that the best-known example of a network or owner-coupled set data-base management system was that proposed by CODASYL. In Chapters 8, 9, 10, and 12, we shall look at the CODASYL proposals in some detail. But before we begin our study, it is well to point out that the CODASYL set of proposals have been undergoing continued extension and improvement since the original CODASYL Data Base Task Group Report in 1969 [CODASYL, 1969]. The CODASYL proposals are the work of different committees, and major reports are issued periodically. (There are about ten of them at the time of writing.)

Accordingly, we shall begin by looking at the structure of the CODASYL organization as it relates to data-base management and attempt to present an overview of its many activities in a historical perspective. This should enable the reader to appreciate the significance of future CODASYL reports or the formation of additional CODASYL committees and task groups.

8.1 CODASYL IN PERSPECTIVE

The Conference on Data System Languages (CODASYL) is a voluntary organization representing user groups and manufacturers and was originally responsible for the COBOL programming language. In the 1960s, CODASYL had a number of committees; one of these was the *Programming Language Committee* (PLC), which was responsible for approving all changes to the COBOL language. The PLC had its own publication, the *CODASYL COBOL Journal of Development* (JOD).

As interest in data-base management grew, PLC set up, in 1965, what was first known as the *List Processing Task Force;* its aim was to investigate complex data structures for possible inclusion in COBOL. In 1967 its name was changed to the *Data Base Task Group* (DBTG), to reflect the fact that the "complex data structures" being studied were widely being called *data bases*.

The first major DBTG report in 1969 was widely distributed [CODASYL, 1969]. This report contains specifications for a data-base manipulation language and for a schema-(combined internal and conceptual schema) specification language or data-description language (DDL). The report caused considerable controversy, and several IBM researchers issued a highly critical report of their own. However, with the encouragement of the parent committee (PLC), DBTG continued its work and in 1971 issued a revised report [CODASYL, 1971], which contained a subschema DDL for specifying external schemas in addition to the schema DDL. At a meeting in Washington in 1971, this report was accepted by PLC, but not by four leading computer manufacturers, who voted against acceptance [Engles, 1971].

Following acceptance of the DBTG 1971 report, the CODASYL executive committee agreed to place in the hands of the programming language committee the task of incorporating the DBTG data-manipulation language (DML) and subschema DDL into COBOL. It was hoped that the subschema DDL would become part of the COBOL data division language and the DML would become part of the COBOL procedure division language.

At the same time, CODASYL set up a new committee known as the *Data Description Language Committee* (DDLC). This was done because it was felt that the schema DDL, which would be used in the design and administration of a data base, had no place in COBOL and consequently needed to be developed as a separate language. Hence the new DDLC committee was formed (Figure 8.1).

Thus the situation in 1971 was that PLC was responsible for getting the subschema DDL and DML into COBOL, while the DDLC was responsible for an entirely new language, namely the CODASYL schema DDL.

To expedite its work, the PLC set up a new task group, the *Data Base Language Task Group* (DBLTG), in 1971, whose purpose was to put the DBTG 1971 proposal in a form that would permit its incorporation in COBOL. In 1973 the DBLTG came up with a widely distributed proposal, which was approved by the parent PLC and incorporated in CODASYL COBOL in the 1976 *CODASYL COBOL Journal of Development* [CODASYL, 1973; CODASYL, 1976*a*].

At the same time, the DDLC was also busy with the schema DDL, and the result was published in the *CODASYL DDLC Journal of Development* in 1973 [CODASYL, 1973]. A revised working document appeared in 1976 [CODASYL, 1976*b*].

So much for the schema DDL and data-base facilities for COBOL. However, there still remained the problem of data-base facilities for other major programming languages, such as FORTRAN and PL/1. In 1975 a start was made by CODASYL, and the *FORTRAN Data-Base Manipulation Language Committee* was formed; its function was to incorporate the 1971 DBTG proposal into FORTRAN. This committee has its own *Journal of Development,* first published in 1976.

While all this was going on, as mentioned in Chapter 6, the ANSI/SPARC study group report was released in 1975, recommending—as we have seen—the three fundamental levels of abstraction for the definition or specification of a data base: the external

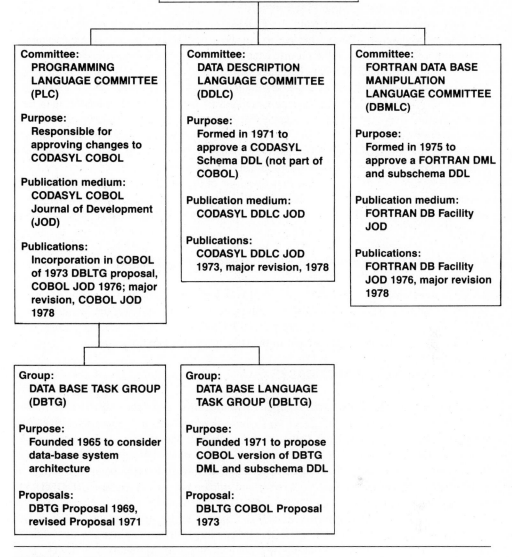

FIGURE 8.1. *History of CODASYL committees and task groups. Note that DDLC and DBTG did not coexist, nor did DBLTG and DBTG.*

level, the conceptual level, and the internal level. The ANSI/SPARC report received a mostly positive reception, and opened the way for further criticism of the CODASYL DDL, in which it was possible to specify many properties of a data base that properly belonged in an internal schema [Tsichritzis, 1977].

However, the latest report from the CODASYL DDLC has made a first attempt at rectifying this state of affairs. This report, in the 1978 *DDLC Journal of Development,* is a major revision of the 1973 report. Many capabilities have been removed from the schema DDL and placed in a new language called the *data storage description language* (DSDL), which is described for the first time [CODASYL, 1978*b*].

In 1978 there also appeared a major revision of the CODASYL COBOL data-base facility from the Programming Language Committee [CODASYL, 1978*a*]; this is published in the *COBOL JOD*. However, the COBOL DML specifications have been running behind the schema DDL specifications, particularly with respect to recursive structures. A major FORTRAN revision was also published in 1978 in the *FORTRAN JOD*.

In the future, we may expect further revisions of the work of the existing CODASYL committees and the setting up of additional CODASYL committees with new data-base assignments. (Note that in 1977 the name of the PLC was changed to the *COBOL Committee*.)

8.1.1 CODASYL and American National Standards (ANSI)

At the present time the CODASYL proposal is being considered as a possible American National Standard. The ANSI COBOL committee (X3J4) is studying the latest COBOL DML (1978), while a different committee (X3H2) is studying the schema DDL. Their reports are awaited with great interest in the data-processing communities.

8.1.2 Implementation of CODASYL

At the time of writing, many major computer manufacturers and data-base software houses are engaged in implementing CODASYL systems that conform to the new specifications. Some systems already available conform quite closely. Sperry Univac [Sperry Univac, 1980*a*, 1980*b*] have a three-level system (DMS1100), which not only supports COBOL but also PL/1. Since no PL/1 DML specifications have currently been developed by CODASYL, Sperry Univac had to develop and implement an unofficial PL/1 DML. (In this book, an unofficial PL/1 CODASYL DML is also used, but without a tedious Call Syntax. This PL/1 DML has traditional PL/1 syntax style, and semantics that mirror precisely those of the CODASYL COBOL DML, except for some minor and unavoidable deviations; COBOL DML commands are also included in Appendix 2.) DMIV from Honeywell [Honeywell, 1978] also conforms closely to the new CODASYL specifications. IDMS is a CODASYL system from Cullinane Corporation [Cullinane, 1978] which runs on IBM machines. Digital Equipment Corporation has a CODASYL system for their VAX machines. TOTAL is a widely used data-base system from Cincom Corporation [Cincom, 1978], and a CODASYL version was due to appear in 1980. In this book we assume that a CODASYL system based on the 1978–1980 specifications has been implemented. This implementation is assumed to incorporate the proposed CODASYL DDL and DSDL (see below), and a PL/1 DML that is very much in the spirit (if not the letter) of the CODASYL COBOL DML.

8.1.3 The CODASYL 1978 DDL

The CODASYL schema data-description language (DDL) described in this chapter is based on the 1978 *DDLC Journal of Development* specifications. These specifications differ radically from the earlier (1973) specifications because of the introduction of a new and entirely separate internal schema DDL, officially referred to as the *data storage description language* (DSDL). This is, of course, in keeping with the spirit of the 1975 ANSI/SPARC proposal.

This DSDL, which is still a draft specification, contains many former schema DDL facilities that had to do with fine tuning details properly belonging in an internal schema [CODASYL, 1978; Manola, 1978]. In this chapter, we consider only the CODASYL conceptual schema, however [Yeh, 1978]. The DSDL is considered in Chapter 12.

Technical Note   The reader familiar with CODASYL will notice that the CODASYL concept of an AREA (or REALM) is not used in this book. We have chosen to omit AREAs, confident that the concept will not be included in the ANSI version of CODASYL when it appears. The latest version of CODASYL had practically rendered the concept redundant. Where a REALM appeared in a DML command, it was omitted by assuming it to be capable of holding no more than records of the same type, that is, at most one file, so that a file and an area become synonymous. This assumption permits a systematic simplification of related CODASYL semantics.

8.2 THE CODASYL CONCEPTUAL DATA BASE

The reader is reminded that a conceptual schema is a specification or exact description of a conceptual data base (or *data model*), and that the conceptual schema is written in a special language. This language is known as the (conceptual) *schema data description language* (DDL).

8.2.1 Conceptual Record Groupings

The distinguishing feature of the CODASYL approach is that it permits and requires that the conceptual records be grouped in two quite different ways. These are

    a.   Groupings of records of the same type into what we shall call *conceptual files*. (Note that CODASYL does not make use of the terms *file* or *conceptual file* in the schema DDL. It refers only to *named* (conceptual) *record types*. However, in the interests of a consistent and uniform terminology, in this book we shall normally refer to CODASYL conceptual records of type X as records from a conceptual file X. This difference is merely one of terminology, and introduces no deviation from the semantics or syntax of the CODASYL DDL.)

    b.   Groupings of records not necessarily of the same type into *owner-coupled sets*. An owner-coupled set is a named grouping made up of set occurrences, each of which consists of an owner record together with zero or more member records, as we have

---

already seen in Section 6.4.8. An owner-coupled set embodies a 1:*n* relationship between two conceptual files.[1]

8.2.2 FORESTRY Conceptual Data-Base Example

To illustrate a typical CODASYL conceptual data base, schema, and DDL, we shall employ a 4NF conceptual data base called FORESTRY, depicted in an extended Bachman diagram in Figure 8.2. The data base contains data pertaining to an experimental forestry program lasting over many years and involving many different trees of different species, in different forests; in addition many measurements are carried out on these trees.

We now examine the semantics underlying this conceptual data base. (Additional semantic details are available in the glossary.)

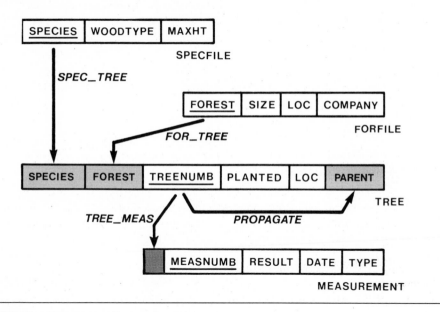

FIGURE 8.2. *Experimental forestry data base* (FORESTRY). *Data is accumulated in the* MEASUREMENT *file about trees (described in the* TREE *file) that are geographically distributed throughout different forests (described in the* FORFILE *file). The different tree species involved are described in the* SPECFILE *file. The conceptual files are in 4NF.*

---

[1]*CODASYL refers to* set type *instead of* owner-coupled set. *Unfortunately the term* set *has traditionally denoted a* mathematical set, *and mathematical sets are basic to the relational approach to data-base management. In the interests of clarity, we shall normally refer to a CODASYL* set type *as an* owner-coupled set, *a term that is fairly widely used. The term* structure set *is also sometimes used.*

FORESTRY Conceptual Files   The conceptual files are as follows.

a.   TREE file: Each record describes a tree, identified by TREENUMB (tree number), the prime key. PLANTED and LOC tell when and where the tree was planted. The connection fields SPECIES and FOREST give the tree species and the name of the forest containing the tree.

b.   SPECFILE file: Each record describes a species, identified by SPECIES value. WOODTYPE gives the type of wood obtainable from the species, and MAXHT gives the maximum height to which a tree of that species can grow.

c.   FORFILE file: Each record describes a forest identified by the forest name in FOREST. SIZE gives the forest's size, LOC gives its location, and COMPANY gives the name of the company owning the forest.

d.   MEASUREMENT file: Each record describes a measurement carried out on a tree, the record identifier being MEASNUMB or measurement number. RESULT is the result of a measurement, DATE is its date, and TYPE gives the type of measurement involved.

FORESTRY Owner-Coupled Sets   The FORESTRY owner-coupled sets are the following.

a.   FOR_TREE set: This embodies the 1:n relationship between FORFILE and TREE, which reflects the fact that a given forest has many trees. FORFILE is the owner file, TREE is the member file, and the member-connection field supporting the relationship is TREE.FOREST.

b.   SPEC_TREE set: This reflects the fact that for a given species there are many trees described in the data base. SPECFILE is the owner file and TREE is the member file, with TREE.SPECIES being the member-connection field for the relationship.

c.   TREE_MEAS set: This reflects the fact that many measurements are carried out on a given tree. The TREE file is the owner and MEASUREMENT file is the member. The member-connection field is omitted from the conceptual MEASUREMENT file. This is permitted in CODASYL.

d.   PROPAGATE set: This is a special type of owner-coupled set known as a *recursive set;* it embodies a recursive 1:n relationship of the type described earlier in Section 6.3.6.

In the experimental program, new trees may be propagated from an existing tree; the number of this parent tree is contained in the PARENT field of each tree record. (The propagation takes place by means of a shoot taken from the parent tree, so that a given tree can have only one parent. If propagation were by means of seeds, there would be two parents, one of them usually unknown.) There thus exists a recursive 1:n relationship between a parent tree and its child trees. TREE.PARENT is the supporting child-connection field. It is this relationship that is embodied in the set PROPAGATE. Some set PROPAGATE occurrences are shown in Figure 8.3.

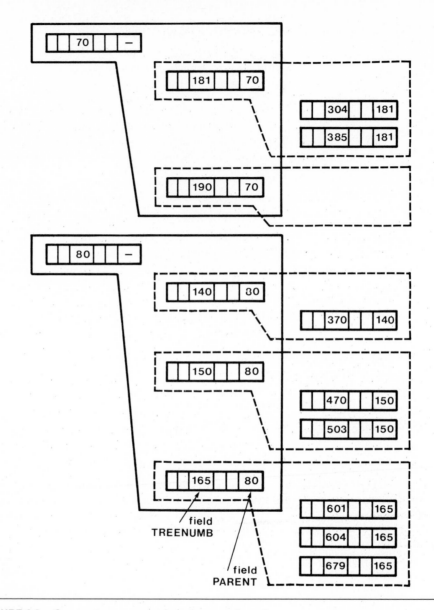

FIGURE 8.3. *Some set occurrences from the recursive set* PROPAGATE. *The conceptual records are from the file* TREE, *but only the key field* TREENUMB *and connection field* PARENT *are shown as having values.*

Tree 80 is the owner of a **PROPAGATE** occurrence with trees 140, 150, and 165 as member records. However, for example, tree 150 is also the owner of a set occurrence with trees 470 and 503 as member records. Thus tree 150 is a member record in one set occurrence and an owner in another.

8.2.3 The Major Schema Components or Entry Types

There are two major entries in the schema.

1. The file entry, which specifies the conceptual files of the data base.

2. The set entry, which specifies the owner-coupled sets of the data base.

Syntax Formalism Note From time to time in this chapter, we shall give DDL syntax; in the remaining chapters, we shall give syntax for other languages. In all cases, we shall use the formalism used in CODASYL reports, with the following rules.

1. The language is in upper case, while user-provided words are in italics.

2. Required words are underlined; other words are included to improve readability.

3. $\begin{bmatrix} A \\ B \end{bmatrix}$ means that at least nothing and at most A or B is to be included.

4. $\begin{Bmatrix} A \\ B \end{Bmatrix}$ means that either A or B is to be included.

5. $\left\|\begin{matrix} A \\ B \end{matrix}\right\|$ means that A, B, A B, or B A is to be included.

6. Three dots (…) following a subclause means that the subclause may be repeated as many times as required.

8.3 FILE (OR RECORD) ENTRY SPECIFICATION

A *file entry* consists of a collection of *file subentries,* one for each conceptual file in the data base. At this point we again note that the CODASYL DDLC does not refer to conceptual files as such, but simply to different types of conceptual records. Hence CODASYL uses the terminology *record entry* and *record subentry,* a trait that is probably inherited from a close association with COBOL. In this book, as in the previous chapters, we shall continue to refer to a collection of records of the same type as a file. We also stress that we are dealing with the specification of *conceptual* records and files.

In the file subentry we specify

a. The file name;

b. Information relating to the key for the file;

c. The record fields.

We take (a) and (c) first, and then (b).

8.3.1 Filename and Field Specifications

This specification is quite straightforward, and we omit a syntax specification. We might have the following for the file SPECFILE from Figure 8.2.

```
RECORD NAME IS SPECFILE
KEY .....
    02  SPECIES         PIC X(20).      /*  20 characters long  */
    02  WOODTYPE        PIC X(25).
    02  MAXHT           PIC 9(3).       /*  3 digits long  */
```

The first line specifies the name of the conceptual file. However, we notice that this specification explicitly states that SPECFILE is the name of a type of *record*. As explained earlier, we may interpret this as a specification of a conceptual *file* called SPECFILE. The next line specifies the key for the conceptual file. We give a syntax specification for the KEY clause in the next section. Finally, the *data items* or fields for the conceptual records of SPECFILE are listed, together with their respective *data types* and *precisions*. The data type for WOODTYPE is PICTURE, and we have specified that conceptual WOODTYPE fields can hold 25 characters of data, the precision specification.[1]

8.3.2 The KEY Clause

If the file has no key, the KEY clause may be omitted. However, the syntax is as follows.

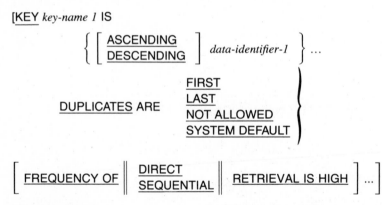

We shall first give some examples of the application of this syntax to the specification of the file SPECFILE.

Example 1

KEY SPECKEY IS ASCENDING SPECIES
DUPLICATES ARE NOT ALLOWED

Example 2

KEY SPECKEY IS DESCENDING SPECIES
DUPLICATES ARE NOT ALLOWED

---

[1]*Data items may be aggregated into multiple-level and repeating structures as in a PL/1 structure variable or COBOL record. This may encourage files which are not in 4NF, however (see also Section 9.1.1).*

FREQUENCY OF DIRECT RETRIEVAL IS HIGH
    KEY AUXIL_KEY IS ASCENDING WOODTYPE
    DUPLICATES ARE LAST
    FREQUENCY OF SEQUENTIAL RETRIEVAL IS HIGH

Now we can give the semantics or the meaning of syntax.

In Example 1, we specified that the field SPECIES is a key, and that if we wish we can refer to it elsewhere as SPECKEY. ASCENDING means that the records of SPECFILE are available to the user in ascending SPECIES order. The fact that duplicate key values are not allowed means that each key value is unique and that the key SPECIES may serve as a prime key. Such a key is referred to as a *record key* in CODASYL. *There may be more than one record key for a file.* A record key may be made up of more than one data item. The key name *key-name-1* is mainly used for referring to composite keys.

In Example 2, SPECIES is again the prime or record key, but the records are available in descending SPECIES order. As a guide to the internal schema designer, we have stated that, with this key, there will be a lot of direct-access retrieval.

However, this time we have additionally specified a *secondary or order key,* WOODTYPE, so that the records of SPECFILE will also be available in WOODTYPE ascending order. There may be more than one record with the same WOODTYPE value, so that the order in which records with these *duplicate* key values are to be available must also be specified. Here we have specified LAST, which means that each new record placed in the file—with a duplicate WOODTYPE value—will be placed conceptually or logically as the last of a group of records with this key value. Specification of FIRST would mean that instead the record with a duplicate key value would be placed as the first of such a group of records. Specification of SYSTEM_DEFAULT would mean that placement was left to the system. (Retrieval of records with duplicate key values is described in Section 9.3.3.) Note that a secondary key implies the existence of an inverted file in the internal data base.

Finally, as a guide to the designer of the internal schema, we have stated that there will be a lot of sequential retrieval using this secondary key.

8.3.3 File Entry for the FORESTRY Data Base

We can now create a file-entry specification for the FORESTRY data base for Figure 8.2. The first line of the specification is a minor entry giving the name of the schema.

```
03   SCHEMA NAME IS FORESTRY.
04
05   RECORD NAME IS SPECFILE
06       KEY SPECKEY IS ASCENDING SPECIES
07           DUPLICATES ARE NOT ALLOWED
08           FREQUENCY OF DIRECT RETRIEVAL IS HIGH.
09   02   SPECIES          PIC X(20).
10   02   WOODTYPE         PIC X(25).
11   02   MAXHT            PIC 9(3).
12
13
```

```
14   RECORD NAME IS FORFILE
15       KEY FORKEY IS ASCENDING FOREST
16           DUPLICATES ARE NOT ALLOWED.
17       FOREST, SIZE, LOC, COMPANY ...   /*   Data types omitted   */
18
19
20   RECORD NAME IS TREE
21       KEY TREEKEY IS ASCENDING TREENUMB
22           DUPLICATES ARE NOT ALLOWED
23           FREQUENCY OF DIRECT RETRIEVAL IS HIGH
24       KEY SPECKEY IS ASCENDING SPECIES
25           DUPLICATES ARE LAST
26       KEY LOCKEY IS ASCENDING LOC
27           DUPLICATE ARE LAST.
28       SPECIES, FOREST, TREENUMB, PLANTED, LOC, PARENT ...   /*   Data types
                                                                   omitted   */
29
30
31   RECORD NAME IS MEASUREMENT
32       KEY MEASKEY IS ASCENDING MEASNUMB
33           DUPLICATES ARE NOT ALLOWED
34           FREQUENCY OF SEQUENTIAL RETRIEVAL IS HIGH.
35       MEASNUMB, RESULT, DATA, TYPE ...   /*   Data types omitted   */
```

We note the following.

a. The above specification is not to be interpreted as a solution to a data-base design problem. The options are selected on tutorial grounds.

b. Full specifications of the data types for each field, of no concern at present, are omitted (except in the case of **SPECFILE**).

c. All the files have a record key, and, in addition, the file **TREE** (lines 24, 26) has two secondary or order keys.

d. The specification of somewhat peripheral facilities (described in Section 8.5) has been omitted on tutorial grounds.

We now look at the next part of the schema specification, which has to do with the 1:n relationships in the data base.

8.4 SPECIFICATION OF OWNER-COUPLED SETS

The reader should be familiar by now with the concept of an owner-coupled set (see Sections 6.4.8 and 8.2.2). Examples of owner-coupled set occurrences comprising an owner-coupled set are given in Figures 6.22 and 8.3. We shall now give a definition of an owner-coupled set.

Definition: An *owner-coupled set occurrence* is an ordered pair in which the first component of the pair is a conceptual record, called the *owner record,* and the second component of the pair consists of a mathematical set of unique conceptual records, none of which can be the owner record, called the *member records;* an *owner-coupled set* is then a mathematical set of owner-coupled set occurrences where all the owner records are of the same type (belong to the same conceptual file) and where no two occurrences of the owner-coupled set have either a common owner record, or any member records in common.

We notice the following.

a. Owner and member records in a set can be either from the same conceptual file, giving rise to recursive sets (see Figure 8.3), or from different conceptual files, giving rise to nonrecursive sets.

b. With nonrecursive sets, the owner records must all be from one conceptual file, the *owner file,* while the member records may either be from a single file—giving rise to the single member-file set (as exemplified in Figure 6.22), or the member records may be from several files—giving rise to the multiple member-file set.

Thus the most common example of an owner-coupled set occurs when we have two conceptual files A and B, each containing unique and distinct records, with a $1:n$ relationship between A and B. Thus for a given A-record, there will be a group of B-records, and this A-record and the corresponding B-records form a set occurrence. All the set occurrences that can be constructed on the basis of the $1:n$ relationship make up the set.

In passing, we observe that sets with member records from more than one file are not common; we shall therefore not discuss them in this book, except to mention that in one application—namely, the construction of a data base for operations or processes—we have found them quite useful [Bradley, 1978].

It should thus be clear that an owner-coupled set is a conceptual grouping, just as a mathematical set is a conceptual grouping. In the CODASYL schema, the owner-coupled sets are specified at a logical or conceptual level; the specification of how a given set is to be implemented at the storage level will have no effect on the validity of the code used in an application program that manipulates the set. The simplest way of looking at an owner-coupled set is to consider it as just another grouping of conceptual records, but embodying a $1:n$ relationship.

The specification of the owner-coupled sets in CODASYL is much more complex than the specification of the conceptual files, so we shall take it in steps. These steps will describe (a) the simple *set declaration,* (b) *set storage and removal class,* (c) *set selection,* and (d) *set order.*

8.4.1 Simple Set Declaration

In the simple set declaration, the set is given a name and the owner and member files are pointed out.[1] Whether the member-connection field (connection field is not a CODASYL term) will determine membership in a set must also be specified.

---

[1] *Note that CODASYL does not refer to* owner *and* member files, *but to* owner *and* member records.

This last point requires some explanation. Referring to Figure 8.2, let us contrast the two sets FOR_TREE and TREE_MEAS. In the FOREST field of a given TREE record, there appears the name of the forest to which the tree belongs. The FOREST field in a TREE record thus gives the key field FOREST of the FORFILE owner record for the TREE member record in the set FOR_TREE. It would not, therefore, be reasonable to couple a TREE record with FOREST value 'X' into a set occurrence of FOR_TREE with a FORFILE owner record with FOREST value 'Y'. The connection-field value (FOREST value) in TREE thus should determine in which set occurrence a TREE member record should participate. This kind of set is referred to by the CODASYL DDLC as a *value-based set*.

As far as the set TREE_MEAS is concerned, the member file MEASUREMENT has no connection field to indicate which TREE owner record a given MEASUREMENT record should have. CODASYL permits sets with such member files, and member records are coupled to their owners in the internal or storage data base *only* by the implementation-pointer system. In the case of the value-based set, the members are coupled to their owner records at the conceptual level of the connection-field values *and* at the internal level by some pointer system. In order for the system to be able to maintain consistency between the conceptual-level coupling and the implementation-level coupling of member records to their owner records, when the set is value-based, the system will have to be informed and the relevant member connection-field specified. Specifically, an attempt to couple a member record with connection-field value 'X' to an owner record with key value 'Y' must be rejected by the system.

In most cases, it would in theory be sufficient to specify the following for value-based sets.

SET IS VALUE_BASED
    MEMBER CONNECTION_FIELD IS *data-identifier-1*

However, the CODASYL DDLC covers the general case.

STRUCTURAL CONSTRAINT IS
    data-identifier-1 EQUAL TO *data-identifier-2* ...

where *data-identifier-1* must be a data item in the member file and *data-identifier-2* is a data item in the owner file.

Usually *data-identifier-1* will be the member-connection field, while *data-identifier-2* will be the owner-connection field, which is always a record key of the owner record (provided the member file is in 4NF; see Exercise 1).

We are now in a position to give the simple set declarations for some sets from the FORESTRY data base, and we take the sets FOR_TREE and TREE_MEAS as examples.

SET NAME IS FOR_TREE
    OWNER IS FORFILE
    MEMBER IS TREE
    STRUCTURAL CONSTRAINT IS
    FOREST EQUAL TO FOREST

```
SET NAME IS TREE_MEAS
    OWNER IS TREE
    MEMBER IS MEASUREMENT
```

In the above example, the set FOR_TREE is value based.

The STRUCTURAL specification may also be used to prevent inconsistency due to redundancy of the type discussed in Section 6.3.1, that is, due to a file not being in 4NF. (The reader is urged to study Exercise 1.)

8.4.2 Set Removal and Storage Class

Taken together, the *removal* and *storage classes* form the basis for the *membership class* of a record in a set.

Set Removal Class   We illustrate this concept by means of the set FOR_TREE from the FORESTRY data base in Figure 8.2. The removal class for a member record in a set has to do with whether and how a record may be removed from a set. For the set FOR_TREE, we can distinguish three cases that could occur in practice and are provided for by the removal class specification.

1. *Removal class* FIXED

    Consider tree 10 in forest 'X'. If tree 10 and all other trees are large, then tree 10 would be fixed in its forest, as would all other trees in their forests. Thus tree 10 could not be taken out of forest 'X' and placed in forest 'Y'.

    Removal class FIXED reflects this physical situation. A record that is a member in a given set cannot be uncoupled from the set and placed in another set when it has this removal class.

2. *Removal class* MANDATORY

    Suppose now that many trees in the forests are small and can easily be transplanted. It would now be physically possible to move tree 10 from forest 'X' to forest 'Y'. It may also be a common feature of the forestry program that trees are allowed to grow some years in a forest with, for instance, one type of climate and then are moved to a forest with another type, perhaps to study growth rate. However, a tree must be in some forest.

    Removal class MANDATORY reflects this physical situation. A member record with this removal class can be moved from one set occurrence to another, but membership in some set occurrence is mandatory; that is, the record cannot be in the member file without it also being a member of some set occurrence.

3. *Removal class* OPTIONAL

    We shall again suppose that the trees in the forests can be quite small and are sometimes transplanted from one forest to another. Let us further suppose that some trees, instead of being replanted at once in another forest, are taken to the forestry program's laboratory where they are allowed to grow under controlled conditions for some time and where further measurements (to be entered into the MEASUREMENT file) are performed.

    Removal class OPTIONAL reflects this situation. A member record cannot only be moved from one set occurrence to another, but it can also be removed from a set occurrence and not placed in another while still remaining in the member file in the data base.

We note that we have earlier reasoned that the set FOR_TREE should be specified as a value-based set. An additional small detail needs to be remembered when dealing with value-based sets with removal class MANDATORY or OPTIONAL. Suppose a TREE record with connection-field FOREST value 'X' is being removed from a set occurrence with owner key 'X' and placed in another set occurrence with owner key 'Y'. The connection-field FOREST value of the TREE record would first have to be changed from 'X' to 'Y' before it could be coupled into a new set occurrence.

Set Storage Class   *Set storage class* involves the means by which a member record can be stored in an owner-coupled set.

To illustrate it, we shall again make use of the set FOR_ TREE from the FORESTRY data base in Figure 8.2. We shall also need to introduce briefly two DML commands, STORE and CONNECT. STORE is used to place a record in the data base, and CONNECT can couple a record already in the data base to a specified owner-coupled set.

1. *Record groupings and placement operations*

    We recall that the conceptual records of a CODASYL data base may be regarded as participating in two types of groupings, namely, conceptual files and owner-coupled sets.

    A record can be in only one file at any given time, but it can be in many different owner-coupled sets. As an example, consider the FORESTRY conceptual data base in Figure 8.2. A TREE record belongs to the conceptual file grouping TREE; but it is a member in three owner-coupled sets, FOR_TREE, SPEC_TREE, and PROPAGATE.

    Thus placing a record in a CODASYL data base is a relatively complex affair, since a record not only has to be placed in a conceptual file in accordance with its declared key values, but also in the owner-coupled sets in which it is declared to be capable of participating.

    The question naturally arises as to the relative timing of the placement of a record in a file and its sets; that is, is it possible to place a record in a file and then place it in one or more of its sets later, or is it necessary to place the record in its file and its sets in one storage operation, and so on? These questions are taken care of by the storage class specification. We may specify either storage class AUTOMATIC or MANUAL.

2. *Storage class* AUTOMATIC

    When a set is specified to be AUTOMATIC and whenever a record capable of being a member in the set is being placed in the data base, the record must be placed both in its file and in that set in the same operation. As we shall see later, a variation of the STORE command enables this to be done.

3. *Storage class* MANUAL

    With MANUAL sets, whenever a record capable of being a member is placed in the data base, it is first placed in the proper file and also in any AUTOMATIC sets. The STORE command is used for this purpose. Later, in a separate operation, the record may be placed in MANUAL sets using a CONNECT command.

As we shall see, the concepts of AUTOMATIC and MANUAL storage class for sets are quite useful, as they reflect aspects of the physical world. However, storage class AUTOMATIC requires that the DBCS executing a STORE command have some way of selecting the occurrence of the AUTOMATIC set to which a record is to be coupled. In very simple terms, we need a key to tell the system where to put a record in a file, and we need a set *occurrence* to tell the system where to put a record in a set. This requirement could be fulfilled either by a *set selection* specification in the schema, valid for all STORE commands with that set, or by a set selection specification in the STORE command. CODASYL chose set selection specification in the schema.

Utility of the Storage Class Concept Suppose a new and strategically important tree species known as Species-X has been developed. Users need to be informed about its progress in order to make important decisions. Suppose further that programs retrieving information about Species-X trees do so by means of the forest involved and the set FOR_TREE; that is, typically a forest and then the trees in that forest are accessed to see which of them are Species-X trees. If FOR_TREE is AUTOMATIC, then when a new Species-X TREE record is placed in the data base, it will be retrieved by these (concurrent) retrieval programs at once; otherwise it might be missed.

Membership Class Syntax The full syntax for membership class involves an extension to the MEMBER IS ... statement used in Section 8.4.1. The CODASYL syntax is

$$\text{INSERTION IS } \left\{ \begin{array}{l} \underline{\text{AUTOMATIC}} \\ \underline{\text{MANUAL}} \end{array} \right\} \text{ RETENTION IS } \left\{ \begin{array}{l} \underline{\text{FIXED}} \\ \underline{\text{MANDATORY}} \\ \underline{\text{OPTIONAL}} \end{array} \right\}$$

Thus the set declaration for FOR_TREE shown in Section 8.4.1 might be more correctly written

```
SET NAME IS FOR_TREE
    OWNER IS FORFILE
    MEMBER IS TREE
        INSERTION IS MANUAL
        RETENTION IS OPTIONAL
```

and so on. Here we assume that it is not important that a new TREE record be immediately obtainable through FOR_TREE, and that the tree may well be removed after planting from a forest to a nursery or laboratory growth environment for further measurements.

8.4.3 Set Selection

We have seen in the previous section that when a set has storage class AUTOMATIC, execution of a STORE command on a member file record results in the record being automatically coupled or connected to the correct set occurrence. The necessary *set selection* technique is specified in CODASYL in the set subentry for the set involved.

Readers who are not familiar with the CODASYL data-manipulation commands (covered in both Chapters 9 and 10) should consider skipping this section until Chapter 9 has been studied. The problem is that while SET SELECTION specifications are part of the schema, they are intimately connected with certain DML commands, particularly the STORE command. Thus the ideas behind set selection can be *fully* grasped only when these DML commands are also understood.

There are three main methods of automatic set selection. The first one involves presenting the owner record of the correct set occurrence to the DBCS, the second involves presenting the whole set occurrence to the system, and the third involves telling the system to use the record member connection field. We shall examine these methods in turn.

Set Selection by Presentation of the Owner Record   The following syntax is used in the set specification, to indicate that the owner record is to be used for automatic set selection.

SET SELECTION IS THRU *set-name* OWNER
    IDENTIFIED BY KEY *key-name*

Thus for the set TREE_MEAS from the FORESTRY data base in Figure 8.1, we could have specified

SET NAME IS TREE_MEAS
    OWNER IS TREE
MEMBER IS MEASUREMENT
    INSERTION AUTOMATIC
    RETENTION FIXED
SET SELECTION IS THRU TREE_MEAS OWNER
    IDENTIFIED BY KEY TREENUMB

and so on.

In an applications program using the FORESTRY data base, if we wish to store a new MEASUREMENT record in the data base, the DBCS will have to select the correct TREE_ MEAS set occurrence following execution of the STORE command because the insertion is specified in the schema to be AUTOMATIC.

The DBCS will get at the correct set occurrence by obtaining the TREENUMB key of the owner from the *User Working Area* (UWA; see Figure 6.17), where it should have been placed by the programmer prior to execution of the STORE command. To see this in practice, suppose the user working area contains PL/1 structure variables, corresponding to the structures of the records of the conceptual files SPECFILE, FORFILE, TREE, and MEASUREMENT in the data base. Let us further imagine that the MEASUREMENT record to be stored has to do with tree 13. If TREEREC and MEASREC are structure variables for TREE and MEASUREMENT records, and if the PL/1 variable NEWDATA initially contains the new record, then we would code in the application program

TREEREC.TREENUMB = 13;   /*   Structure variable TREEREC in UWA now contains key
                               value   */
MEASREC = NEWDATA;   /*   New record now in UWA structure variable MEASREC   */
STORE FILE (MEASUREMENT);   /*   PL/1 STORE command   */

The DBCS fetches the MEASUREMENT record from MEASREC in the UWA and, from the KEY specification for the MEASUREMENT file in the schema, uses the field MEASNUMB to place the record in the file. It then looks up the SET SELECTION clause in the schema for the set or sets in which MEASUREMENT is a member file. In this case, set selection is by means of the owner record in the file TREE and the record key to use is TREENUMB. It then fetches the TREENUMB value from TREEREC in the UWA and proceeds with the job of coupling the MEASUREMENT record into the TREE_MEAS set occurrence thus identified. (For the STORE command, see Section 9.3.6.)

PL/1 and COBOL Syntax Note   At the time of writing, there are official CODASYL DML commands only for COBOL and FORTRAN. The reader is reminded that in this book unofficial syntax for PL/1 DML commands is used. These PL/1 commands are given in full in Chapters 9 and 10. Their semantics are almost identical to those of the COBOL DML commands. The PL/1 command syntax merely reflects the style of PL/1; it is also intended for further readability. The COBOL DML commands are given in Appendix 2.

Set Selection by Presenting the Current of Set   As we shall see in more detail in the next chapter, the DBCS maintains what is known as a *table of currencies* or *current indicators*. Among other things, the currency table contains indicators for the most recently accessed records for each kind of set in the data base. These are referred to as the *current of set indicators*.

Thus for the FORESTRY data base in Figure 8.2, there will be a current SPEC_ TREE set indicator, a current FOR_TREE set indicator, and so on. The indicator is really the address of a record in the storage data base (for the concept of the data-base key, see Section 9.1.1), and the record to which the indicator points is known as the *current record of set*.

The current (record) of set is the most recently accessed owner or member record in a given set, and thus identifies the most recently accessed occurrence of the set (if the set is not recursive). For a full discussion of currencies, see Sections 9.2.1 and 9.5.1.

The record occurrence identified by the set currency indicator is widely referred to as the *current of set*. Thus if we specify in the schema that automatic set selection is by means of the current of set, then before a STORE command for storage of a member record in an AUTOMATIC set is executed, the owner or a member of the correct set occurrence must have been accessed to make it the current of set.

The syntax for the schema specification of this type of set selection is

SELECTION IS THRU *set-name* OWNER
   IDENTIFIED BY APPLICATION

It might have been better if APPLICATION had been replaced by CURRENT OF SET, but evidently the DDLC thought that APPLICATION better brought home the fact that the application program must ready the owner of the set by accessing the correct set occurrence, thus making it current of set. The original DBTG (1971) syntax for this set selection is relevant here. It was

SET OCCURRENCE <u>SELECTION</u> IS <u>THRU</u> <u>CURRENT</u> OF <u>SET</u>

However, in the majority of cases, the set occurrence will be made ready for the STORE command by prior access of the owner and rarely by a member. This further explains the DDLC (1978) syntax.

If in the FORESTRY data base we change the set selection clause for the set TREE_ MEAS to

SET SELECTION IS THRU TREE_MEAS OWNER
    IDENTIFIED BY APPLICATION

then we need a new procedure for storing a MEASUREMENT record in the data base as a member record in a TREE_MEAS set occurrence.

As in the previous case, we assume that the MEASUREMENT record to be stored is available in the PL/1 structure variable NEWDATA. If the key to the TREE owner record is 13, we have:

TREEREC.TREENUMB = 13; /* UWA TREEREC structure variable contains key */
FIND FILE (TREE) KEY (TREEREC.TREENUMB);
    /* This DML FIND command (see Section 9.3.2 for details) causes the TREE record with
    record-key value 13 to be accessed and thus to become the current of set TREE_MEAS,
    which then identifies the required TREE_MEAS set occurrence */
MEASREC = NEWDATA; /* New record now in UWA structure variable MEASREC */
STORE FILE (MEASUREMENT); /* The record is placed in the TREE file in accordance
    with its record-key value. The current of set TREE_MEAS is used by the DBCS to select
    the correct TREE_MEAS occurrence */

The comments explain the sequence of events.

Set Selection by Means of the Connection Fields Use of connection fields is probably the simplest method of set selection and is conceptually the most natural. However, it applies only to value-based sets. The syntax is

SET SELECTION IS BY STRUCTURAL CONSTRAINT

Consider the set FOR_TREE from Figure 8.2, and let us have the following schema declaration.

SET NAME IS FOR_TREE
    OWNER IS FORFILE
    MEMBER IS TREE
        INSERTION AUTOMATIC RETENTION FIXED
    STRUCTURAL CONSTRAINT IS

```
          FOREST EQUAL TO FOREST
      SET SELECTION IS BY STRUCTURAL CONSTRAINT
```

We see that the storage class is AUTOMATIC, so that execution of a STORE command in an application program will requiire the use of the set selection specification. Since FOR_ TREE is specified as a value-based set, set selection can be specified to be by means of the connection fields supporting the set.

All this means that when a TREE record is being stored in the data base, the DBCS will use the member connection field FOREST to obtain the value of the key of the owner record of the set occurrence the record is to be coupled to.

Thus if we assume the new TREE record is available in the PL/1 structure NEWTREE, we need only code

```
TREEREC = NEWTREE;  /*  New TREE record now in UWA  */
STORE FILE (TREE);  /*  Record placed in file according to record key, and the connection
     field is used to obtain the owner of the required set occurrence  */
```

8.4.4 Set Order

It is possible to specify for each set exactly how the member records of a set occurrence will be ordered. The reader should understand that we are not dealing here with the physical order of the member records of a set occurrence in the data base. We are dealing instead with the logical or conceptual order of the member records in a set occurrence. If the programmer retrieves the member records from a set occurrence in sequential fashion, it is in the *set order* that they will appear. Thus the applications programmer must be aware of the internal ordering of member records in a set occurrence.

Following Olle, we can distinguish between two types of set ordering [Olle, 1978]. These two types are *sorted* and *chronological*. We first look at these two types of set ordering. Then we examine the relevant schema syntax, and give some examples of its use.

Sorted Order In sorted order, the members of a set occurrence are maintained in a logical order, usually determined by a set *sort key,* that is, a key specified in the schema set specification.

Chronological Order In *chronological order,* the member records of a set occurrence are maintained in a logical order determined by the time of their first insertion in (or coupling to) the set occurrence. We can distinguish between a number of different possibilities.

1. Insertion is FIRST: In this case, the member records will form a *stack;* that is, the record chronologically last in will be in logical order the first retrieved, if the member records are retrieved sequentially. Thus a new record inserted becomes FIRST in logical order.

2. Insertion is LAST: Here the member records form a *queue*. A new record inserted becomes the last in logical order.

3. Insertion is **PRIOR**: Here a new record is placed in logical order before the member record that identifies the current set in the current set occurrence indicator for that particular set. (The current of set concept is introduced in Section 8.4.3 in connection with set selection.)

4. Insertion is **NEXT**: Here a new member is placed in logical order after the member record identifying the current of set.

Schema Syntax   The above possibilities are reflected in the schema syntax. It should be noted that set order may be specified in two different parts of the schema set specification, first as part of the OWNER subentry and secondly as part of the MEMBER subentry. We take the OWNER subentry first (for an explanation of OWNER IS SYSTEM, see Section 10.1.5).

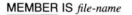

OWNER IS $\left\{ \begin{array}{l} \textit{file-name} \\ \underline{\text{SYSTEM}} \end{array} \right\}$

<u>ORDER</u> IS <u>PERMANENT</u>

INSERTION IS $\left\{ \begin{array}{l} \underline{\text{FIRST}} \\ \underline{\text{LAST}} \\ \underline{\text{PRIOR}} \\ \underline{\text{NEXT}} \\ \underline{\text{SORTED}} \text{ BY } \underline{\text{DEFINED}} \text{ KEYS} \end{array} \right\}$

If the set is specified with the INSERTION subentry as a SORTED set, then the actual set sort keys may be specified in the member subentry, using the following syntax.

<u>MEMBER</u> IS *file-name*

....

....

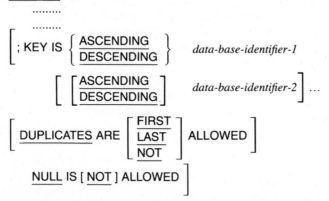

$\left[\text{; } \underline{\text{KEY}} \text{ IS } \left\{ \begin{array}{l} \underline{\text{ASCENDING}} \\ \underline{\text{DESCENDING}} \end{array} \right\} \textit{data-base-identifier-1} \right.$

$\left[\left[\begin{array}{l} \underline{\text{ASCENDING}} \\ \underline{\text{DESCENDING}} \end{array} \right] \textit{data-base-identifier-2} \right] \dots$

$\left[\underline{\text{DUPLICATES}} \text{ ARE } \left[\begin{array}{l} \underline{\text{FIRST}} \\ \underline{\text{LAST}} \\ \underline{\text{NOT}} \end{array} \right] \text{ ALLOWED} \right]$

$\left. \underline{\text{NULL}} \text{ IS } [\underline{\text{NOT}}] \text{ ALLOWED} \right]$

Both of the syntax expressions above are incomplete, in the sense that they are subsets of the DDLC syntax. However, most of the omitted syntax has only marginal value and is unlikely to be commonly implemented. The explanation for the clause ORDER IS PERMANENT in the owner subentry is that we have specified that the user cannot temporarily change the order in his or her application program. (The DDLC syntax also allows the specification of ORDER IS TEMPORARY, with the implication that under some circumstances the user could change the set order temporarily.)

Set Order Examples   As an example of the use of the set order specification, we take the set FOR_TREE; we also suppose that it is desirable to have the trees in a given forest available in the order in which they were entered into the data base. We would specify

```
SET NAME IS FOR_TREE
    OWNER IS FORFILE
        ORDER IS PERMANENT INSERTION IS LAST.
    MEMBER IS TREE .....
```

On the other hand, suppose we require that for a given forest the trees will be available in the order in which they were planted; in that case, we shall have to use the member field PLANTED as the set sort key. The relevant portion of the set specification would be

```
SET NAME IS FOR_TREE
    OWNER IS FORFILE
        ORDER IS PERMANENT INSERTION IS SORTED BY DEFINED KEYS.
    MEMBER IS TREE
        INSERTION IS MANUAL
        RETENTION IS OPTIONAL
    KEY IS ASCENDING PLANTED
        DUPLICATES ARE LAST
        NULL IS NOT ALLOWED
    STRUCTURAL CONSTRAINT .....
```

Here we have specified in the owner subentry that the set is SORTED. Then in the member subentry, we specify the set sort key PLANTED, as well as what to do with duplicates. LAST here has the meaning described earlier, that is, a record with a duplicate set sort key is inserted as the last of a group of duplicates. We also have specified that the set sort key PLANTED must have a nonnull value, as is reasonable in this case.

8.4.5 Summary of Set Specification Requirements

We may summarize the requirements for the schema specification of an owner-coupled set as follows.

1. *Set name*

2. *Owner name*

   a.   Set order specification.

3. *Member name*

   a.   Storage and removal class.

   b.   If set order is SORTED, then specification of set sort key is made.

   c.   If a value-based set is involved, then specification of structural constraint is made.

4. *Set selection specification*

The syntax and semantics for all of the above specification parts has been dealt with in Sections 8.4.1 through 8.4.4. We can now continue the schema specification for the FORESTRY data base from Figure 8.2, which was started in Section 8.3.3. We now specify all the sets except the recursive set **PROPAGATE**.

```
37
38
39   SET NAME IS SPEC_TREE
40   OWNER IS SPECFILE
41       ORDER IS PERMANENT SORTED BY DEFINED KEYS.
42   MEMBER IS TREE
43       INSERTION IS AUTOMATIC
44       RETENTION IS FIXED
45       KEY IS ASCENDING PLANTED IN TREE
46           DUPLICATES ARE LAST NULL IS NOT ALLOWED
47       STRUCTURAL CONSTRAINT IS SPECIES OF TREE
48           EQUAL TO SPECIES OF SPECFILE
49   SET SELECTION IS BY STRUCTURAL CONSTRAINT.
50
51
52   SET NAME IS FOR_TREE
53   OWNER IS FORFILE
54       ORDER IS PERMANENT INSERTION IS LAST.
55   MEMBER IS TREE
56       INSERTION IS MANUAL
57       RETENTION IS OPTIONAL
58       STRUCTURAL CONSTRAINT IS FOREST OF TREE
59       EQUAL TO FOREST OF FORFILE
60   SET SELECTION IS BY STRUCTURAL CONSTRAINT.
61
62
63   SET NAME IS TREE_MEAS
64   OWNER IS TREE
65       ORDER IS PERMANENT SORTED BY DEFINED KEYS.
66   MEMBER IS MEASUREMENT
67       INSERTION IS AUTOMATIC
68       RETENTION IS FIXED
69       KEY IS ASCENDING DATE IN MEASUREMENT
70           ASCENDING TYPE IN MEASUREMENT
71           DUPLICATES ARE LAST
72           NULL IS NOT ALLOWED
73       SET SELECTION IS THRU TREE_MEAS OWNER
74           IDENTIFIED BY APPLICATION.
75
```

We note the following.

---

a. Sets SPEC_TREE and FOR_TREE have been declared as value based (lines 47 and 58), consistent with the extended Bachman diagram in Figure 8.2.

b. Set order for set FOR_TREE is chronological (line 54), while for the others it is sorted. Two set sort keys are specified for the set TREE_MEAS (line 69).

8.4.6 Specification of Recursive Sets

The 1978 DDLC specification permits specification of recursive sets for the first time in a CODASYL schema. Because recursive sets are much more complex to deal with than nonrecursive sets and because the DDLC for fundamental reasons found it necessary to impose certain restrictions on their specification, we shall deal with them separately. In particular, we shall consider the specification of the recursive set PROPAGATE in the FORESTRY data base.

MANUAL Insertion   With recursive sets, we may not have AUTOMATIC storage class. To see why, consider the set PROPAGATE, for which examples of set occurrences are given in Figure 8.3. We see that not every TREE record is a member record in PROPAGATE. In fact, there are some TREE records that are only owners (for example, tree numbers 70 and 80), some that are both owners and members (for example, 181 and 150), and some that are only members (for example, 304 and 370).

It should thus be clear that from time to time it will be necessary to store records in TREE that are not members of PROPAGATE. Accordingly, AUTOMATIC storage class is impossible, at least in the way in which it applies to nonrecursive sets.

On the other hand, MANUAL storage class permits a TREE record to be stored in the file without being a member of PROPAGATE. The applications program will then have to determine if the new record is a member record of a PROPAGATE set occurrence, and if so, carry out a connection operation to that set occurrence.

Value-Based Recursive Sets   We may specify recursive sets as value based if desired. However, since the manipulation of recursive sets is at best a complex affair, any measure that would tend to ease the difficulties is to be recommended. The fact that a member record in a value-based recursive set occurrence carries the key of its owner record in the connection field is certain to simplify storage and retrieval operations involving this type of set.

Accordingly, the STRUCTURAL CONSTRAINT clause can be expected to be commonly used in the specification of recursive sets.

Set Selection   As we shall see in Chapters 9 and 10, some subtle problems can arise with the application of the standard set selection clause involving the current of set indicator to recursive sets. The problems also appear with a FIND command (see Section 10.1.6).

Nevertheless, there are no problems involved in using the simplest type of set selection, namely, that using the connection fields or set selection by STRUCTURAL CONSTRAINT. The fact that this type of set selection can only be used with value-based sets is a further indication of the utility of declaring all recursive sets as value based, as recommended in the previous subsection.

Specification of the Recursive Set PROPAGATE We are now in a position to complete the specification of the FORESTRY schema. A reasonable PROPAGATE set specification would be as follows.

```
76   SET NAME IS PROPAGATE
77        OWNER IS TREE
78            ORDER IS PERMANENT SORTED BY DEFINED KEYS.
79        MEMBER IS TREE
80            INSERTION IS MANUAL
81            RETENTION IS FIXED
82            KEY IS ASCENDING PLANTED IN TREE
83                DUPLICATES ARE LAST
84                NULL IS NOT ALLOWED
85            STRUCTURAL CONSTRAINT IS PARENT OF TREE
86                EQUAL TO TREENUMB OF TREE
87        SET SELECTION IS BY STRUCTURAL CONSTRAINT.
```

We note the following.

    a.   We specify removal class as FIXED since a set occurrence describes a tree (owner) and the trees (members) propagated from it. It would not be reasonable to move a tree from one set occurrence to another.

    b.   There are no significant problems in specifying the member record order within a set occurrence. Here the order is sorted, based on the set sort key PLANTED (lines 78, 82).

8.5 DATA VALIDATION

This short section briefly describes an important but peripheral facility that may be specified in the schema. The section may safely be omitted on first reading.

We deal here with *data validation,* which affects the long-term maintenance of the data base. Data validation involves the means by which only valid data is permitted to enter the data base, and thus contributes to the *integrity* of the data in the data base.

8.5.1 Data Validation

The specification of each data item in the schema may be accompanied by a data validation, or CHECK clause. This clause places limits on the values the data item concerned may take on and thus will prevent the storing of some (but not all) invalid data in the data base. It thus helps to ensure the integrity of the stored data.

The syntax for the CHECK clause is:

CHECK IS VALUE [NOT] *literal-1* [THROUGH *literal-2*]
    [, *literal-3* [THROUGH *literal-4*]]...

Thus we would specify the following for the file SPECFILE in the FORESTRY data base.

```
RECORD NAME IS SPECFILE
      WITHIN TREE_AREA
      KEY SPECKEY IS ASCENDING SPECIES
         DUPLICATES ARE NOT ALLOWED.
      SPECIES       PIC X(20).
      WOODTYPE    PIC X(25)    CHECK IS VALUE NOT 'TROPICAL HARDWOOD'.
      MAXHT FIXED PIC 9(3)     CHECK IS VALUE 0 THROUGH 300.
```

Thus the field WOODTYPE cannot have the value 'TROPICAL HARDWOOD' in any SPEC-FILE record, and the field MAXHT (maximum tree height) cannot be less than zero or greater than 300 units. Data types have also been included in the above SPECFILE specification for the sake of completeness (see Section 8.3.1).

Note on the Internal CODASYL Schema   As already mentioned, it is only since 1978 that the CODASYL schema more or less corresponded to the ANSI/SPARC conceptual schema. Before that date, the CODASYL schema encompassed the equivalent of the combined ANSI/SPARC conceptual and internal schemas [Manola, 1978].

The specification of the internal schema is an important part of the design process, as it will have a significant effect on the performance of the total system. However, in the interests of a simpler presentation of the subject, we shall leave a detailed discussion of the internal schema until Chapter 12 [Yeh, 1978]. The reader is asked to assume that this task of internal schema specification has been carried out correctly so that we can move to specification of external schemas and the writing of loading programs to load the FORESTRY data base in the next chapter.

EXERCISES

1.   Consider the data base RESOURCE depicted in Figure 6.5. We can reduce the chance of inconsistency if in the schema we specify as value based the set connecting PETRO-FIRM and DRILL_HOLE and the set connecting CONCESSION and DRILL_HOLE. What fields should we use? Note that the inconsistency can arise because DRILL_HOLE is not in 4NF.

2.   Taking the data base RESOURCE, consider the use of value-based sets with the relationships between CONCESSION and DRILL_HOLE and between PROPERTY and DRILL_HOLE.

3.   Make up a conceptual schema for the RESOURCE data base and justify each entry, having first converted DRILL_HOLE to 4NF by removing fields COMPANY and CONCESSION (see Section 7.2.3).

4.   Make up a conceptual schema for the data base in Figure 6.14 in which PETROFIRM records are involved in a recursive *n:m* relationship. Consider your choice of entries carefully.

REFERENCES

Bradley, J., 1978, "Operations Data Bases," *Proc. ACM Conf. on Very Large Data Bases,* Berlin, pp. 164–76.

Cincom Systems Inc., 1978, *TOTAL/8 Data Base Administration User Manual,* Cincinnati, Ohio.

CODASYL, 1969, "Data Base Task Group Report," *ACM,* New York, October.

CODASYL, 1971, "Data Base Task Group Report," *ACM,* New York, April.

CODASYL, 1973a, "Data Base Language Task Group Proposal," *ACM,* New York, February.

CODASYL, 1973b, "Data Description Language Committee," *Journal of Development,* Department of Supply and Services, Canadian Federal Government, Hull, Quebec, Canada.

CODASYL, 1976a, "Programming Language Committee," *COBOL Journal of Development,* Department of Supply and Services, Canadian Federal Government, Hull, Quebec, Canada.

CODASYL, 1976b, "Data Description Language Committee," *DDLC Journal of Development* (current working version), Department of Supply and Services, Canadian Federal Government, Hull, Quebec, Canada.

CODASYL, 1978a, "COBOL Committee," *Journal of Development* (with updates to 1981), Department of Supply and Services, Canadian Federal Government, Hull, Quebec, Canada.

CODASYL, 1978a, "COBOL Committee," *Journal of Development* (with updates to 1981), Department of Supply and Services, Canadian Federal Government, Hull, Quebec, Canada.

Cullinane Corporation, 1978, *IDMS Utilities, Release 5.0,* Boston, Mass.

Engles, R. W., 1971, "An Analysis of the April 1971 DBTG Report—IBM Position Paper," *Workshop on Data Description, Access and Control, ACM SIGFIDET, ACM,* New York.

Honeywell Information Systems, 1978, *Data Management IV, Data Base Administration Reference Manual,* Order Number DF 77.

Manola, F., 1978, "Review of the 1978 CODASYL Data Base Specifications," *Proc. ACM Conf. on Very Large Data Bases,* Berlin, pp. 232–40.

Olle, T. W., 1978, *The CODASYL Approach to Data Base Management,* John Wiley, London.

Sperry Univac, 1980a, *Data Management System (DMS 1100) Level 8R2: Schema Definition,* Order Number UP–7909.

Sperry Univac, 1980b, *Data Management System (DMS 1100) Level 8R2: PL/1 Data Manipulation Language,* Order Number UP—7908.

Tsichritzis, D., and A. Klug (eds.), 1977, *The ANSI/X3/SPARC DBMS Framework: Report of the Study Group on Data Base Management Systems,* AFIPS Press, Montvale, N.J.

Yeh, R. T., P. Chang, and C. Mohan, 1978, "A Multi-level Approach to Data Base Design," *IEEE Software & Applications Conf.,* Chicago, Ill.

Loading The CODASYL Data Base

9

Data bases are normally loaded in steps: First one part is loaded, then another part, and so on. A loading applications program is required for each of the loading steps. As mentioned in Chapter 6, these loading programs are expensive because they rarely are required or used again once the data base has been loaded.

A loading program can be considered as a data-base manipulations program, so that it can run only if there is an external schema available. With CODASYL data bases, the external schema is usually called a *subschema* [CODASYL, 1978a].

Thus we must study the methods for specification of subschemas, and the DML commands required to write loading programs. We now take these subjects in turn using the FORESTRY data base from Chapter 8.

9.1 THE CODASYL SUBSCHEMA

The subschema is closely connected to the *host* procedural language used in manipulating the data base, such as COBOL or PL/1. As mentioned in Chapter 7, there are official *subschema* specification languages for use with COBOL and FORTRAN, but at the time of writing, there is none for PL/1 [Manola, 1978].

The subschema language has to be closely connected to the host procedural language, since the (record) structure variables and field data types should reflect those available in the host language. If we wish, we should be able to specify MEASNUMB as FIXED DECIMAL in a PL/1 subschema, this data type being available in PL/1.

The fact that MEASNUMB is declared as FIXED DEC in a subschema does not necessarily mean that the value for the internal data base field is assigned 4 bits of machine storage per digit, as is the case with the PL/1 variable. How MEASNUMB is actually mapped to machine storage is specified in the storage schema, or at an even lower spec-ification level. It is up to the DBCS to ensure that for a given field, proper conversion is carried out between a subschema data type and the corresponding storage data type.

Apart from these considerations of record structure and data type, the subschema is (largely) a subset of the original schema. Thus if we take the required schema subset, in which the data types for the record fields have been declared as PL/1 data types and in which subschema record structures are consistent with the structure variables used in PL/1, then we can be satisfied that we have a reasonable, albeit unofficial, PL/1 sub-schema. It is difficult to envisage any other kind of basic PL/1 CODASYL subschema.

9.1.1 The PL/1 Subschema

We have stated that the subschema is not entirely a subset of the schema. This of course is true for the official COBOL and FORTRAN subschemas; for the same reasons, it is also true for the PL/1 subschema presented here.

That the subschema is a subset of the schema is consistent with the fact that we can omit from the subschema the specification of any of the conceptual files, sets, and data items that have been specified in the schema. Nevertheless, we may in addition use different names or aliases, such as file or set names, for schema declared names. We may also change the relative order of fields in their records and, if desired, we may have set selection clauses that are different from and override the ones declared in the schema [CODASYL, 1978a, 1978b].

PL/1 Subschema Record Structures   The requirement that the structure of sub-schema records reflect those of PL/1 structure variables could present some difficulties, because the use of structure and structure array variables in PL/1 can give rise to a wide variety of record structures.

A generally acceptable solution to this problem should be left to an appropriate CODASYL committee. Fortunately, a simple though somewhat restrictive solution is avail-able. We have seen that it is desirable to have only files that are in 4NF, and that records in 4NF files always have a key (which may be composite) that corresponds to some unique entity, and nonkey fields that directly describe this entity (Chapter 7).

Thus since the fields of a PL/1 record substructure usually describe the entity corre-sponding to the substructure, records with structures corresponding to PL/1 structure variables with level greater than 2 are not likely to be from a 4NF file.

As a simple example of this, consider a file of records describing people, where each record has the structure corresponding to the following PL/1 structure variable PERSON.

```
DCL 1 PERSON
      2  SOC_SEC_NUMBER FIXED DEC (15),   /*  Key  */
      2  WEIGHT FIXED BIN (15),
      2  EYE_COLOR CHAR (10),
      2  EMPLOYER,  /*  Substructure  */
         3  NAME CHAR (20),
         3  NUMBER_EMPLOYED FIXED BIN (31),
         3  PAYROLL FIXED BIN (31);
```

Each record describes a unique entity, a person; the person's social security number is used as the key. Thus WEIGHT and EYE_COLOR describe the person directly; that is, they are both directly functionally dependent on the entity person. EMPLOYER.NAME, the name of the person's employer, also describes the person directly, but NUMBER_EMPLOYED and PAYROLL describe the person *only indirectly*. NUMBER_EMPLOYED and PAYROLL are functionally dependent on the employer. PERSON records are therefore not in 4NF; they are in 2NF.

Thus if we encourage only record structures in the subschema that correspond to level-2 PL/1 structure variables, we shall at any rate discourage records that are not in 4NF. That this would not prevent such records can be seen from the fact that the above structure PERSON could be changed to the following level-2 structure and still be able to hold a record from a 2NF file.

```
DCL 1 PERSON,
    2   SOC_SEC_NUMBER FIXED DEC (15),
    2   WEIGHT FIXED BIN (15),
    2   EYE_COLOR CHAR (10),
    2   EMPLOYER_NAME CHAR (20),
    2   NUMBER_EMPLOYED FIXED BIN (31),
    2   PAYROLL FIXED BIN (31);
```

Therefore, for the purpose of this book, we shall use PL/1 subschema record structures that correspond to level-2 PL/1 structure variables. This is also very convenient, since we have already used such record structures in the schema for the FORESTRY data base. The files of the FORESTRY data base are in 4NF.

Keep-Lists and Data-Base Keys   In the subschema, CODASYL also permits declaration of lists or arrays of variables known as *keep-lists* that may not be declared in the schema. (This further demonstrates the truth of the statement made earlier that a subschema is not entirely a subset of the schema.)

Keep-lists are related to *data-base keys*. At this point, it would be well to point out that we have already dealt with three other types of keys in the schema. These were the *record key* (requiring unique values), declared with the KEY clause in the file specification (for example, line 6 in the FORESTRY schema), the *set sort key*, declared as part of a set order specification (for example, line 45 in the FORESTRY schema), and a *secondary key* (permitting duplicate values) declared with the KEY clause in the file specification.

The data-base key is a fourth type of key and can be considered to correspond to the address of a record in storage. Such a key can be of use to the applications programmer. For example, suppose an application program retrieves a SPECFILE record from the FORESTRY data base using the SPECFILE record key SPECIES with value 'SPRUCE'.

The average search length for the physical SPECFILE version may be high; if it is a well-designed hash file, it will probably lie between 1 and 1.5; if it is an index-sequential file, it may be considerably higher depending on the location of indexes and overflow system (see Chapters 3 and 4). In general, there will be more than one file access required to retrieve the SPECFILE record with key 'SPRUCE'. However, following this initial access, if the program could keep the storage address of the record just retrieved or equivalent—that is, the data-base key—this address could be used for later accesses instead of the record key 'SPRUCE'. In most cases, use of the data-base key would give a search length of near unity. Thus data-base keys can lead to improved performance.

Of course, the programmer may well access more than one SPECFILE record which is to be accessed later, so that for each file a list or *keep-list* for the data-base keys will be necessary. Since the data-base keys are delivered to the keep-list by the DBCS, the keep-list must be known to the DBCS. For this reason, the keep-list for each file is declared in the subschema [Manola, 1978]. The keep-list specification in the subschema will depend on the implementation, but for a PL/1 subschema, we might use the syntax

DCL *keep-list name* KEEPLIST FILE (*file-name*):

More than one keep-list can be declared for a given file.

It should be noted that the DBCS will undertake to keep the data-base key for a record constant during a run-unit; that is, as long as an application program using it is running.[1] Thus data-base keys cannot be kept from one run-unit to the next, and they certainly cannot be kept by storing them in the data base. Note that a keep-list variable can only be used with DML commands and not with ordinary (PL/1 or COBOL) host-language statements. As we shall see in Section 10.1.9, keep-lists have an additional use in concurrency control.

9.1.2 PL/1 Subschema for the FORESTRY Data Base

To load the FORESTRY data base, we need at least one subschema, that is, that which describes the whole data base. In practice data bases are loaded in steps, and it is often useful to have a subschema that more or less corresponds to that part of the data base being loaded. However, more than one loading program may employ the same subschema.

Data bases are normally loaded from the top down. This means that files which are owner files only, such as SPECFILE and FORFILE, are loaded first. Then the member files for these owner files, such as TREE, are loaded next, their records being coupled to the proper set occurrences. The member files for these files, such as MEASUREMENT, are loaded next, and so on.

This loading method may vary considerably, however, depending on whether the sets have storage class AUTOMATIC or MANUAL. If the sets are all AUTOMATIC, no variation is possible because when a member file record is loaded into the data base, it must be immediately coupled to the proper set occurrences; this is possible only if the correct owner records have already been loaded.

Thus we may select our initial subschema designs to reflect the usual top-down loading technique. We take two subschemas, TOP_FORESTRY, and BOT_FORESTRY; the parts of the data base described are shown in Figures 9.1 and 9.2, respectively.

The TOP_FORESTRY **Subschema** In the subschema that follows, *the schema entries for the files and sets specified in the subschema are assumed to have been specified by default in the subschema, unless overridden by a specific subschema specification.*

---

[1]*Run-units are explained in Section 9.2.2.*

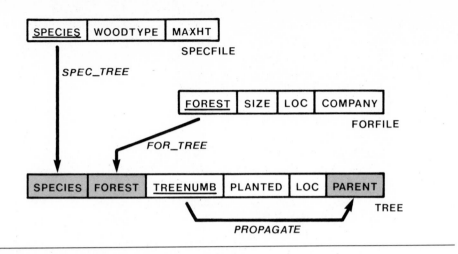

FIGURE 9.1. *Extended Bachman diagram for that part of the* **FORESTRY** *data base (see Figure 8.2) specified in the* **TOP_FORESTRY** *subschema.*

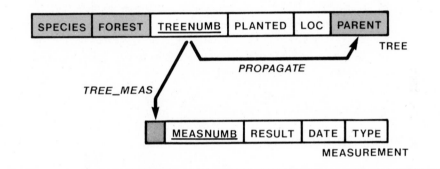

FIGURE 9.2. *Extended Bachman diagram for that part of the* **FORESTRY** *data base specified in the* **BOT_ FORESTRY** *subschema.*

```
DCL TOP_FORESTRY SUBSCHEMA FOR (FORESTRY):
    DCL SPECFILE FILE,
        1 SPECREC,
            2   SPECIES CHAR (20),
            2   WOODTYPE CHAR (25),
            2   MAXHT FIXED BIN (15);
    DCL FORFILE FILE,
        1   FORREC
            2   FOREST CHAR (15),
            2   SIZE FIXED BIN (31),
            2   LOC CHAR (10),
            2   COMPANY CHAR (20);
```

THE CODASYL SUBSCHEMA

```
DCL TREE FILE,
    1   TREEREC,
            2   SPECIES CHAR (20),
            2   FOREST CHAR (15),
            2   TREENUMB FIXED BIN (31),
            2   PLANTED FIXED DEC (8),
            2   LOC FIXED BIN (15),
            2   PARENT FIXED BIN (31);
DCL (SPEC_TREE, FOR_TREE, PROPAGATE) SET;
```

You should be aware that the above PL/1 CODASYL subschema is unofficial. It is written in the style of PL/1 language, but semantically it is very close to the official CODASYL COBOL subschema.[1] However, we note the following.

  a.   We make only occasional use of keep-lists in the loading and manipulation programs presented in this book, so none are specified in the subschema.

  b.   As in CODASYL COBOL, data types and precisions are specified for the fields of the files. However, we have included three structure variables, SPECREC, FORREC, and TREEREC corresponding to records from the three files SPECFILE, FORFILE, and TREE, respectively. This is not done in the CODASYL COBOL subschema, but it is in PL/1 tradition to distinguish between the file (for example, SPECFILE) and the name of a program structure (for example, SPECREC) which may contain a record from the file.

  c.   In the interests of encouraging only 4NF records, PL/1 subschema structures are restricted to two levels.

The BOT_FORESTRY **Subschema**   This is also an unofficial PL/1 CODASYL subschema.

```
DCL BOT_FORESTRY SUBSCHEMA FOR (FORESTRY);
    DCL TREE FILE,
        1   TREEREC,
                2   SPECIES CHAR (20),
                2   FOREST CHAR (15),
                2   TREENUMB FIXED BIN (31),
                2   PLANTED FIXED DEC (8),
                2   LOC FIXED BIN (15),
                2   PARENT FIXED BIN (31);
    DCL MEASUREMENT FILE,
        1   MEASREC,
                2   MEASNUMB FIXED BIN (15),
                2   RESULT FLOAT DEC (6),
```

---

[1] *See discussion in Section 9.1.1.*

```
    2   DATE FIXED DEC (8),
    2   TYPE CHAR (10);
DCL (PROPAGATE, TREE_MEAS) SET;
```

We note that the file TREE and the set PROPAGATE are specified in both subschemas.

9.2 DML COMMAND AUXILIARY CONCEPTS: CURRENCY AND UWA

There are two important auxiliary DML command concepts with which we must deal before looking at the DML commands in detail. These two concepts are the *currency concept* and the *user working area* (UWA) concept. Both concepts were introduced in Chapter 8. We now examine them further, in their proper perspective.

9.2.1 The CODASYL Currency Concept

The currency concept is fundamental to CODASYL. However, because it is closely related to the concept of a run-unit, we shall deal with this concept first.

The Run-Unit Concept   A data-base management system is normally used as a sub-component of some larger system. Let us suppose that in such a system there are two applications programs A and B, each of which can interact with a user via a terminal and a data base via the DBCS.

In a batch environment, a user *A1* might run program A linked to the DBCS and be the only user interacting with the data base. However, in a real-time environment, there could be two users *A1* and *A2*, each of which needs to run program A at the same time, but for different purposes. Similarly, there could be two users *B1* and *B2* for program B who wish to run program B independently of each other and at the same time *A1* and *A2* wish to run A. This situation can be managed in two ways.

1. *Batch partition method*
    Two versions of A, each linked to a copy of the DBCS, are each loaded into separate partitions of the operating system (see Chapter 1). Similarly, we load two versions of B. The result is four partitions, each with an applications program and a linked DBCS. This method is rarely used because of the enormous waste of memory, but it is conceptually useful for understanding the alternative method.

2. *Real-time partition method*
    A special operating system component known as a *teleprocessing monitor* is allowed to run in and control the activities of a single operating system partition. The teleprocessing monitor interacts with the four users *A1, A2, B1,* and *B2* (see Figure 9.3).

    The teleprocessing monitor loads a single copy of the DBCS (and associated internal, conceptual, and external schemas) into the single operating system partition, which is widely referred to as a *real-time* or *on-line partition.*

The teleprocessing monitor also loads two application programs, namely, A and B; the monitor ensures that each program has two different program data areas so that there is one for each user. The DBCS used will probably be able to support separate sets of buffers for each user.

The monitor is able to control execution of programs A and B in such a way that user *A1* is largely unaware of user *A2*. Thus at any instant we have two execution positions for program A, that for user *A1* and that for user *A2*. The same is true for program B. We say that program A has two run-units, one processing the data for *A1* and one processing the data for *A2*. Similarly, program B has two run-units. The situation is illustrated in Figure 9.3. Programs that may be executed in this way are said to be *reentrant*.

This arrangement saves memory and permits overlap of I/O both for data-base and nondata files. The amount of I/O overlap achieved depends on the type of teleprocessing monitor used. Unfortunately, a full account of real-time partitions and teleprocessing monitors is beyond the scope of this book [Cypser, 1978; Taylor, 1979].

The real-time partition technique is widely used, so that—in general—for any given applications program interfacing with a data base, there will be more than one run-unit. However, each user will not be entirely unaware of concurrent run-units (see concurrency control in Section 10.4).

The Current-Record Concept   The most recently accessed record belonging to a given category is given a name in CODASYL. For *each run-unit,* we have the following.

1. *The current (record) of run-unit*
    The *current record of run-unit* (CRU) is the most recently accessed record in the data base. At any instant, there can only be one such record for a run-unit. It plays a dominant role in many DML commands.

2. *The current (record) of file*
    There is a *current record of file* for every file in an external data base. For a given external file, it is the most recently accessed record in the file, unless special circumstances are involved (as we shall see shortly).

3. *The current (record) of set*
    There is a *current record of set* for every set in the external data base. For a given set, it is the most recently accessed owner or member record participating in the set, unless the same kind of special circumstances, as in (2), are involved.

4. *The current occurrence of set*
    We sometimes need to refer to the *current occurrence of set*. This is not a record but is the most recently accessed occurrence of a set, where we regard a set occurrence as accessed if either a member or the owner record has been accessed. *Thus the current record of set identifies the corresponding current* occurrence *of a set*. The expression *current of set* is widely used, but in this book it must always be assumed to mean current record of set, unless otherwise stated. We must be careful with the idea of the current occurrence of a set, for it is meaningful only with nonrecursive sets, as we shall discuss further in Section 9.5.1 on recursive set currency problems.

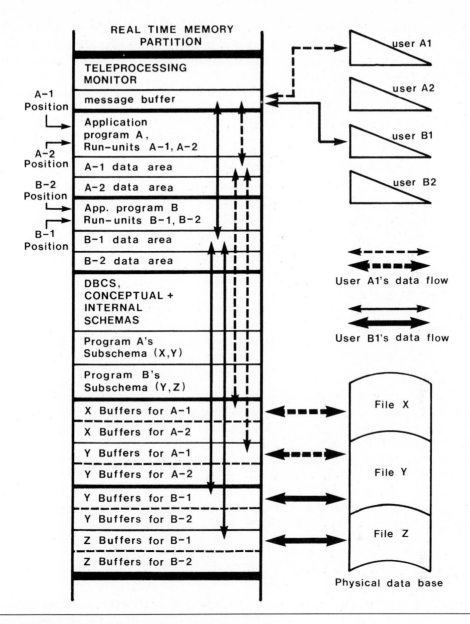

FIGURE 9.3. *Relationship between applications programs A and B and their run-units. The subschema for A uses files X and Y, while that of B uses files Y and Z.*

For every current record, there exists what is referred to as a *currency indicator*. The reader is advised to attempt to distinguish carefully between current records and currency indicators.

We now look at currency indicators.

Currency Indicators For each run-unit, the DBCS maintains a special currency table that is not accessible to manipulation by host-language statements. The currency table contains a list of *currency indicators. A currency indicator will normally be a data-base key for a record in the data base.*

There is a currency indicator corresponding to every current record in the external data base. Thus we have the following.

1. *The CRU indicator*
   The *CRU indicator* is the data-base key of the current record of run-unit. It is updated following each record retrieval. There is only one CRU indicator.

2. *The current-of-file indicator*[1]
   The *current-of-file indicator* is the data-base key for the current record of file. It is normally updated after each retrieval of a record from a file. However, such updating can be permanently suppressed by a run-unit. In such circumstances, the current of file indicator will not reference the most recently accessed record in the file involved. There is a current of file indicator for each file.

3. *The current-of-set indicator*
   The *current-of-set indicator* is the data-base key for the current record of set. It is normally updated after each retrieval of an owner or member in the set involved. As with the current-of-file indicator, updating can be permanently suppressed by the run-unit, so that in such circumstances the current-of-set indicator will not reference the most recently accessed record of the set. There is a current-of-set indicator for each set.

The fact that updating of currency indicators for files and sets may be suppressed by a run-unit complicates our definitions somewhat. Such suppressions are the special circumstances mentioned earlier in the definitions of current records. Thus we can more precisely state that the current record of a file is that record with the data-base key that is the current indicator for that file. The current record for a file is, therefore, not always the most recently accessed record. The same is true for sets.

Currency Table for the TOP_FORESTRY **Data Base** For a run-unit employing the TOP_FORESTRY subschema, the DBCS would maintain the currency table shown as Table 9.1.

9.2.2 The User Working Area

Many of the DML commands directly or indirectly involve the user working area (UWA). As we have seen from Chapter 8, the UWA is that part of the data area of a run-unit which can be accessed by the DBCS. Thus, in practice, the UWA for a PL/1 run-unit might consist of a list of variables declared with the EXTERNAL attribute, with variable names already known to the DBCS.

For convenience, we shall divide the variables of the run-unit UWA into two categories, namely, *record variables* and *special registers*.

---

[1] *CODASYL uses the term* current of record type X, *when referring to the current of file* X.

CURRENCY TABLE FOR **TOP_FORESTRY** SUBSCHEMA	
Current Record	**Allowed Indicator (Data-Base Key)**
Current record of run-unit.	SPECFILE TREE FORFILE
Current record of file **SPECFILE**.	SPECFILE }
Current record of file **TREE**.	TREE }
Current record of file **FORFILE**.	FORFILE }
Current record of set **SPEC_TREE**.	SPECFILE TREE
Current record of set **FOR_TREE**.	FORFILE TREE
Current record of set **PROPAGATE**.	TREE }

TABLE 9.1

UWA Record Variables   Each record variable serves as a loading/unloading point for data being moved to and from the data base. There will be a UWA record variable for each file described in the subschema, and its name will be the same as that of the structure variable used in the subschema to specify the record structure for a given file.

Thus with reference to the **BOT_ FORESTRY** subschema, we could declare the following UWA record variables in a PL/1 application program using this subschema.

```
DCL 1 TREEREC EXTERNAL,          /*   Holds a TREE record   */
    2 SPECIES .....;
DCL 1 MEASREC EXTERNAL,          /*   Holds a MEASUREMENT record   */
    2 MEASNUMB .....;
```

The UWA record variables are known to the DBMS because their names are used in the subschema. The UWA record variables in this case are PL/1 structure variables.

Instead of declaring the UWA in the application program using structures corresponding exactly to those of the subschema, however, CODASYL permits us to issue the INVOKE DML command in the application program.

INVOKE SUBSCHEMA (BOT_FORESTRY):

This would result in an implicit declaration of the **BOT_FORESTRY** subschema in the application program. For the reader's convenience, we shall usually list the UWA variables in application program examples.

Special Registers   The following is the most useful special register.

DB_STATUS   Following each execution of a DML command, the DBCS places a seven-digit exception code in DB_STATUS. The first two digits (statement code) indicate the command involved, while the last five digits (status code) indicate the type of exception or error involved.

We shall not list the command and status codes in this book. However, we shall frequently have use for two exception codes. We will need that which indicates that the DML command has been executed normally. This is always '0000000' for all commands. We also need one with the FIND command to indicate that no record has been found. It is assumed to be '0502400' [CODASYL, 1978b].

9.3 DML COMMANDS FOR LOADING A CODASYL DATA BASE WITH PL/1

The semantics of the CODASYL DML commands are fairly complex, and the commands are therefore best studied in steps. In the following sections we shall confine our attention to those commands needed for loading a data base. In the examples we use the commands with the FORESTRY subschemas (Section 9.1.2).

As pointed out in Chapter 8, at the time of writing there is no official CODASYL PL/1 DML. In Section 9.3.1 and in Chapter 10, we give syntax and semantics for unofficial PL/1 DML commands. The syntax used is in the tradition of PL/1 and is as suggestive of the underlying semantics as possible. The underlying semantics are *exactly equivalent* to the semantics of the corresponding COBOL DML commands, except for a few cases. In these few cases, some extra semantics with corresponding syntax are incorporated into the commands, the purpose being to include extra facilities that would be expected in PL/1. The equivalent and official COBOL DML commands are described in Appendix 2. Readers are cautioned that the material in this section has the character of reference material. Semantic rules and contextual examples might well be skipped on first reading. (Note that peripheral semantic descriptions are omitted for many commands. Readers who are interested in the full description of the CODASYL commands should consult the original CODASYL specifications.)

9.3.1 READY **Command**

This command informs the DBCS of the intention of the run-unit to process one or more subschema data-base files in a specified manner. In certain cases permission to process may be denied and the run-unit placed in a wait queue (see Section 10.4).

1.   *PL/1 syntax*

READY[FILE   *(file-name-1* [, *file-name-2*] ...)] $\begin{bmatrix} \underline{RETRIEVAL} \\ \underline{UPDATE} \end{bmatrix}$

2. *Command examples*

READY FILE (SPECFILE) RETRIEVAL;
READY FILE (TREE, MEASUREMENT);
READY UPDATE;

3. *Semantics*

a. All files (and owner-coupled sets based on them) that are specified in the command are made available for manipulation, provided they are specified in the subschema. Default value is *all* subschema files and sets.

b. If RETRIEVAL is specified, then only DML commands that cause data to be retrieved from the data base, such as FIND and GET, may be used.

c. If UPDATE is specified, then all other DML commands may be used in addition.

d. If the final clause is omitted, the default is RETRIEVAL.

4. *Remarks*
The syntax presented above is not complete. We have deliberately omitted that part which specifies how update and retrieval will take place in an environment of concurrently executing run-units. This subject will be discussed in Section 10.4 on concurrent processing.

9.3.2 Record Key FIND Command, First Version (JOD Format 2)

There are seven basic FIND commands, each given a format number by the *CODASYL Journal of Development* (JOD). Several of these basic commands may have different versions. The command we now describe is one of the simplest FIND commands, and has two versions. (The second involves retrieval of records with duplicate key values.) The first version of the *record-key* FIND command is one of the most commonly used FIND commands, and is a file-access command, permitting a record to be retrieved from a file directly using a record or secondary key. The reader should recall that a record key has unique values, while a secondary key may have duplicate values.

1. *PL/1 syntax*

FIND FILE (*file-name*) KEY ([,] … *variable-name*);

2. *Command examples*

FIND FILE (TREE) KEY (TREENUMB);
FIND FILE (TREE) KEY (X);
FIND FILE (TREE) KEY (, , Z);

3. *Semantics*

a. A record from the file specified is retrieved and becomes the CRU, the current of file for the file specified and the current record of set for all the sets in which it participates. (Thus, as is the case with all FIND commands, the currency table is merely updated,

---

an additional GET command (see Section 9.3.4) being necessary to bring the record to the UWA.[1])

b. If *variable-name* is one of the record or secondary keys specified in the subschema,[2] the key value is fetched by the DBCS from the appropriate UWA structure element, which should have been initialized.

c. If *variable-name* is an arbitrary program variable, its value is used as a key. If more than one key has been specified in the subschema[2] for the file (as we have arbitrarily done in the case of the TREE file), the number of commas in the KEY clause indicates to the DBCS which of the keys is *intended*. Thus, referring to the command examples above, X must contain a TREENUMB value, while Z must contain a LOC value.

d. If duplicate values can occur for the key used or intended (that is, if the key is a secondary key), the system retrieves the first record with the specified key value, in the order specified in the subschema for retrieval with that type of key. To retrieve the remaining records with that duplicate key value, the second version of the record-key FIND command must be used.

4. *Remarks*

Use of the KEY clause to permit a key value to be fetched directly from a program variable preserves the traditional flexibilty of PL/1 in a simple manner. This is not available in the COBOL version (see Appendix 2).

5. *Contextual example*

Referring to the TOP_FORESTRY schema, let us suppose we wish to retrieve the TREE record where the record-key TREENUMB value is in the program variable X. The value of X may be assigned to the appropriate UWA variable corresponding to the record key field, before the FIND command is used.

```
DCL 1   TREEREC EXTERNAL,   /*   UWA structure variable   */
     2   SPECIES ......,
     2   FOREST .......,
     2   TREENUMB FIXED BIN (31),   /*   Holds record key   */
     2   PLANTED .....,
     .....;

TREENUMB = X;   /*   Record key to UWA   */
FIND FILE (TREE) KEY (TREENUMB);   /*   TREE record becomes CRU   */
```

---

[1]*However, in 1980, CODASYL introduced FETCH commands. A FETCH command functions like a FIND command followed by a GET command. Essentially the syntax of a FETCH command is that of its corresponding FIND command, except that the word "FIND" has been replaced by "FETCH." A FETCH command has essentially the same semantics as its corresponding FIND command, except that in addition, the record retrieved is placed in the appropriate UWA structure. The RETAIN and FOR UPDATE clauses may also be used (Sections 9.5.3 and 10.4.2).*

[2]*Schema entries for subschema files and sets may be specified in the subschema by default (see Section 9.1.2).*

9.3.3 Record-Key FIND Command, Second Version

This version of the FIND command is mainly used for retrieving records with duplicate key values, that is, with secondary keys.

1. *PL/1 syntax*

    FIND FILE (*file-name*) DUPLICATE KEY ([,] ... *variable-name*);

2. *Command examples*

    FIND FILE (TREE) DUPLICATE KEY (LOC);
    FIND FILE (TREE) DUPLICATE KEY (,Y);
    FIND FILE (TREE) DUPLICATE KEY (,,Z);

3. *Semantics*

    a. Semantic Rules 1, 2, and 3 for the first version also apply to the second version.

    b. The key used with the command does not have to be specified as allowing duplicate values to occur, that is, it does not have to be a secondary key.

    c. On execution of the command, the DBCS first checks the CRU. If the record type and key value of the CRU match that of the record to be retrieved, the file is accessed and the *next* record in the file with a duplicate key value is retrieved. *Next* is in the order specified in the subschema for records with duplicate values of that type of key. If the record type or key value do not match that of the CRU, the file is accessed and the system retrieves the first record with the specified key value, in the order specified in the subschema for retrieval with that type of key.

4. *Contextual example*

    With reference to the FORESTRY schema and TOP_FORESTRY subschema, suppose we wish to retrieve the TREENUMB values for all trees in the location contained in the variable L. We would code as follows.

    ```
    DCL  1   TREEREC EXTERNAL,  /*  UWA structure variable  */
         2   SPECIES ....,  /*  Holds secondary key, duplicates allowed  */
         2   TREENUMB ....,  /*  Holds record key, no duplicates  */
         2   PLANTED ....,
         2   LOC FIXED BIN (15),  /*  Holds secondary key, duplicates allowed  */
         2   PARENT .....;
    TREEREC.LOC = L;       /*  Secondary key to UWA  */
    FIND FILE (TREE) DUPLICATE KEY (LOC)  /*  First duplicate becomes
                                                CRU  */
    DO WHILE (DB_STATUS ¬ = '0502400')
         /*  If none left stop loop  */
         GET INTO (TREEREC, TREENUMB);  /*  This command moves CRU to
                                               UWA; see Section 9.3.4  */
         PUT SKIP LIST ('TREE NUMBER', TREENUMB);
         FIND FILE (TREE) DUPLICATE KEY (LOC);
    ```

```
                        /*   Next duplicate becomes CRU   */
END;
```

9.3.4 The GET Command

It is this command which moves data from the CRU to the UWA, where it may be manipulated by the application program.

 1. *PL/1 syntax*

GET [CRU (*file-name*)] INTO (*identifier-1* [, *identifier-2*] ...);

 2. *Command examples*

```
GET CRU (TREE) INTO (TREEREC);      /*   Record to UWA   */
GET INTO (PLANTED, PARENT);         /*   Fields to UWA   */
GET CRU (TREE) INTO (PLANTED);      /*   Field to UWA    */
```

 3. *Semantics*

 a. The identifier must identify either the record or a field of the record presently the CRU.

 b. The record or data items so identified are assigned to the corresponding UWA structure or variables, respectively.

 4. *Contextual example*

The example in Section 9.3.3 demonstrating the use of **FIND DUPLICATE** also illustrates the use of the **GET** command.

We might note that in practice the execution of **GET** will be accompanied by type conversions. Consider the TREE file. Different (for example, PL/1 and COBOL) subschemas based on this file may have different data types declared for the TREE fields in the structure TREEREC or equivalent. On the other hand, the TREE record retrieved by the DBCS will have fields with data types declared in the internal schema by the data-base administrator; hence the need for type conversions.

9.3.5 The CONNECT Command

This command is used to couple or connect a record already in the data base to one or more set occurrences as a new member record.

 1. *PL/1 syntax*

$$\text{CONNECT} \left[\begin{array}{l} \underline{\text{CF}}\ (\textit{file-name}) \\ \underline{\text{CRU}}\ (\textit{file-name}) \end{array} \right] \underline{\text{TO CS}} \left\{ \begin{array}{l} (\textit{set-name-1}\ [,\ \textit{set-name-2}]\ .\ .\ .) \\ \underline{(\text{ALL})} \end{array} \right\} ;$$

 2. *Command examples*

```
CONNECT TO CS (FOR_TREE);
CONNECT CRU (TREE) TO CS (FOR_TREE);
```

---

3. *Semantics*

    a.   If **CF** is specified, the record to be connected is the current record of the file specified; otherwise it is the CRU.

    b.   If a set name is specified, it must be a set that has been specified in the subschema.

    c.   If **ALL** is specified, the connection operation will be attempted on *all* subschema sets for which the record affected is a potential member.

    d.   For each set involved, the record is coupled to the current of set (**CS**) occurrence, in accordance with the ordering criteria for the set (see Section 8.4.4).

    e.   For each set to which the record is coupled, the record becomes the current of set. It also becomes the CRU. Other currency indicators are not updated.

4. *Contextual example*

Let us suppose we wish to couple a **TREE** record, available in the UWA structure **TREEREC** but also stored in the data base, to the **MANUAL** set **FOR_TREE**.

First we must make the desired **FOR_TREE** set occurrence the current of set **FOR_TREE**. Next we make the **TREE** record the CRU. Only then can we apply the **CONNECT** command. We note that the order of these operations is important.

```
FORREC.FOREST  =  TREEREC.FOREST;   /*   Record key of FORFILE owner
                                          record in correct UWA variable
                                          for use of FIND command   */
FIND FILE (FORFILE) KEY (FOREST);   /*   Owner FORFILE record becomes CRU
                                          and current of set FOR_TREE   */
FIND FILE (TREE) KEY (TREENUMB);    /*   TREE record to be coupled becomes
                                          CRU   */
CONNECT TO CS (FOR_TREE);
```

We see that the **FOR_TREE** owner (a **FORFILE** record) must be retrieved and made current of set **FOR_TREE** before the **TREE** record is retrieved and made CRU. If we reverse these operations, then at the time the **CONNECT** command is executed, the **FORFILE** owner record is both the CRU and the current of set **FOR_TREE**.

CONNECT Command with Recursive Sets   There are some fundamental problems associated with applying the **CONNECT** command to recursive sets. Although there are a number of proposed solutions to these problems, there is, at the time of writing, no official CODASYL resolution of the difficulties [Manola, 1978].

The heart of the problem lies not with the **CONNECT** command itself, but with the application of the current of set concept to recursive sets. Thus similar problems appear in every DML command using the current of set concept.

With reference to Figure 8.3, we can see that a **TREE** record could participate in two quite different **PROPAGATE** set occurrences, in one as an owner record and in the other as a member record. Thus a **TREE** record retrieved by a **FIND** command could represent two set occurrences and not one, as with nonrecursive sets. We shall look at an effective solution to this problem in Section 9.5.1.

9.3.6 The STORE Command

As we saw in Section 8.4.3, the STORE command can store a record in a file and at the same time connect it to one or more set occurrences.

1. *PL/1 syntax*

    STORE FILE (*file-name*) [FROM (*variable*)] ;

2. *Command examples*

    STORE FILE (TREE);
    STORE FILE (TREE) FROM (XTREEREC);

3. *Semantics*

    a. When the FROM subclause is omitted, the semantics are as given in Rules b to g.

    b. The command stores in the specified file, the record available in the corresponding UWA structure.

    c. The record is stored consistent with the ordering criteria for record and secondary keys specified in the subschema. These key values should be available in the UWA structure involved.

    d. The command also couples the UWA record to all AUTOMATIC sets for which it can be a member.[1]

    e. The set occurrences of these AUTOMATIC sets are selected on the basis of the SET SELECTION specifications in the subschema.

    f. UWA data items or variables required by the DBCS in following a SET SELECTION specification should be initialized in the UWA.

    g. Following successful execution of a STORE command, the record stored becomes the current of run unit, current of the file in which it was stored, and current of all sets to which it was coupled.

    h. Inclusion of the FROM clause means that the record to be stored is available as the value of the specified identifier. The structure of this identifier should be compatible with that of the UWA structure variable for records of the file specified.

4. *Remarks*
    Use of the FROM subclause to permit records to be fetched from program variables directly contributes to the preservation of the traditional flexibility of PL/1. The FROM facility is not in the COBOL version.

5. *Contextual example*
    Let us suppose we wish to store a TREE record in the data base. We note that the TREE

---

[1]*The data-base administrator will need to ensure that an updating run-unit has a subschema which includes all the schema AUTOMATIC sets for which a subschema file can be a member file.*

---

file is an AUTOMATIC member of the set SPEC_TREE. We assume for convenience that the TREE record is available in the UWA structure TREEREC.

With the set SPEC_TREE, SET SELECTION is by means of the structural constraint, that is, the TREE connection field SPECIES. Thus, as long as the SPECIES value in TREEREC is not null, the DBCS will be able to select the proper SPEC_TREE set occurrences. Thus we need only code

```
STORE FILE (TREE);   /*   1.  TREE record fetched from UWA TREEREC.
                          2.  SPEC_TREE set occurrence selected by means of
                              SPECFILE record key in TREEREC.SPECIES   */
```

9.4 FILE AND NONRECURSIVE SET LOADING

9.4.1 Loading Programs

We shall load the FORESTRY data base in three stages with the following three loading programs.

1. A program referencing the TOP_FORESTRY subschema, which loads the files SPEC-FILE, FORFILE, and TREE and the sets FOR_TREE and SPEC_TREE.

2. A program referencing the BOT_FORESTRY subschema, which loads the file MEA-SUREMENT and the set TREE_MEAS.

3. A program to load the recursive set PROPAGATE. This program will be given in Section 9.5.4, following resolution of the current of set problem for recursive sets.

9.4.2 Loading Program for the TOP_FORESTRY Subschema

The data base is loaded from data in existing files. If the data base is being loaded for the first time, it is likely that a data-base record must typically be constructed from data in more than one of the existing files. Before such a newly constructed record is stored, further validation checks using other existing files may be required.

However, for the sake of a clear presentation, we shall assume here that the data to be loaded is in three existing files, namely, XSPECFILE, XFORFILE, and XTREE; their record structures are the same as those for SPECFILE, FORFILE, and TREE, respectively, in the conceptual schema. Thus the loading program can read in an XTREE record and, without further manipulation of the record, store it in the data-base file TREE. The system diagram for this simple loading scheme is shown in Figure 9.4.

We use the following program.

```
TOPLOAD: PROC OPTIONS (MAIN);

    /*   User working area   */
```

```
DCL  1   SPECREC EXTERNAL        /*  Holds SPECFILE records   */
     2   SPECIES CHAR (20),       /*  Record key   */
     2   WOODTYPE CHAR (25),
     2   MAXHT FIXED BIN (15);

DCL  1   FORREC EXTERNAL,        /*  Holds FORFILE records   */
     2   FOREST CHAR (15),        /*  Record key   */
     2   SIZE FIXED BIN (31),
     2   LOC CHAR (10),
     2   COMPANY CHAR (25);

DCL  1   TREEREC EXTERNAL,       /*  Holds TREE records   */
     2   SPECIES CHAR (20),       /*  Connection field   */
     2   FOREST CHAR (15),        /*  Connection field   */
     2   TREENUMB FIXED BIN (31), /*  Record key   */
     2   PLANTED FIXED DEC (8),
     2   LOC FIXED BIN (15),
     2   PARENT FIXED BIN (31);

DCL  DB_STATUS CHAR (7) EXTERNAL; /*  Special register   */

                    /*   End of UWA   */

DCL  (XSPECFILE,   /*   9-character file name tolerated to improve readability   */
      XFORFILE,
```

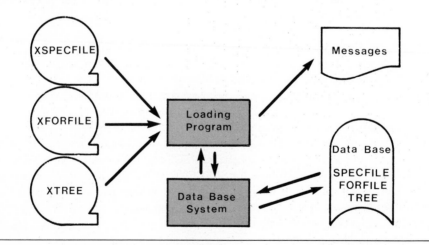

FIGURE 9.4. *System diagram for loading that part of the*
FORESTRY data base covered by **TOP_FORESTRY**
subschema. This is the simplest possible loading
configuration. In practice, a data-base record may need to
be constructed from several source file records and then
validated against data in other files.

```
             XTREE) FILE RECORD ENV (CONSECUTIVE);  /*   Source data files   */
DCL BEOF BIT (1);   /*   Logical variable; Before End Of File   */
ON ENDFILE (XSPECFILE) BEOF = '0'B;
ON ENDFILE (XFORFILE) BEOF = '0'B;
ON ENDFILE (XTREE) BEOF = '0'B;
OPEN FILE (XSPECFILE) INPUT,
       FILE (XFORFILE) INPUT,
       FILE (XTREE) INPUT;
READY UPDATE;   /*   DML command, see Section 9.3.1
                           (empty) data base ready for processing    */


                     /*   First Step: Loading of file SPECFILE   */


READ FILE (XSPECFILE) INTO (SPECREC);   /*   First source record in UWA   */
BEOF = '1'B;
DO WHILE (BEOF);
     STORE FILE (SPECFILE);   /*   DML command, see Section 9.3.6   */
     IF DB_STATUS = '0000000'   /*   If command executed OK   */
        THEN READ FILE (XSPECFILE) INTO (SPECREC);
           ELSE DO; PUT DATA (SPECREC, DB_STATUS); STOP; END;
END;
PUT SKIP LIST ('SPECFILE LOADED');


                     /*   Second Step: Loading of file FORFILE   */


/*   This step is just as simple as Step 1. We simply read XFORFILE records into the UWA
     structure FORREC, and load them into the data base file FORFILE using the STORE
     command as in Step 1.   */


      /*   Third Step: Loading of file TREE and sets FOR_TREE and SPEC_TREE   */


READ FILE (XTREE) INTO (TREEREC);   /*   XTREE source record in UWA   */
BEOF = '1'B';
DO WHILE (BEOF);
     /*   We first access the FORFILE owner of the UWA TREE record to be STOREd. This
           FORFILE record then becomes the current of set FOR_TREE (and the CRU)   */
     FIND FILE (FORFILE) KEY (TREEREC.FOREST);
                          /*   DML command, Section 9.3.2   */
        IF DB_STATUS ⌐= '0000000'   /*   Something wrong?   */
           THEN DO;
                   PUT DATA (TREEREC.FOREST, DB_STATUS);
                   STOP; END;
           ELSE;
     STORE FILE (TREE);      /*   DML command, Section 9.3.6   */
     /*   1. TREE record in UWA is fetched and stored in TREE file.
           2. Since set SPEC_TREE is AUTOMATIC and SET SELECTION in the schema
```

requires use of the connection field, the TREE record is connected to the SPEC_
TREE set occurrence whose owner SPECFILE record key is TREEREC.SPECIES
value.   */

```
IF DB_STATUS ¬ = '0000000'  /*  Something wrong?  */
     THEN DO;
          PUT DATA (TREEREC, DB_STATUS);
          STOP; END;
CONNECT CRU (TREE) TO CS (FOR_TREE);  /*  DML command, Section 9.3.5  */
```

```
          /*  1. The STORE command has made the TREE record the CRU.
               2. The FIND command above made this TREE record's FORFILE owner the
                  current of set FOR_TREE.
               3. The CONNECT command can therefore now couple the TREE record to the
                  correct FOR_TREE occurrence.   */
IF DB_STATUS ¬ = '0000000'  /*  Something wrong?  */
     THEN DO;
          PUT DATA (TREEREC, DB_STATUS);
          STOP; END;
     ELSE;
          READ FILE (XTREE) INTO (TREEREC);  /*  Next source record  */
END;
     PUT SKIP LIST ('FILE TREE, SETS SPEC_TREE, FOR_TREE LOADED   ')
                         /*  End of Step 3  */
END;
/*
//GO.XSPECFILE DD .....
```

The program could be much more robust (see Chapter 2). As it is, if something goes
wrong, it does not attempt to isolate the cause and continue; instead it merely stops and
prints relevant data and the error code.

The heart of the program is in the third step. As each TREE member record is stored
in the TREE file, it is connected to the AUTOMATIC set SPEC_TREE automatically, and
then by means of the CONNECT command to the MANUAL set FOR_TREE.

9.4.3 Loading Program for the BOT_FORESTRY Subschema

This program loads the file MEASUREMENT and the set TREE_MEAS. A glance at Figure
9.2 shows that in the file MEASUREMENT there is no member connection field to indicate
which TREE owner any particular record in the set TREE_MEAS belongs to.

This information must come from the source file or files. Here we shall assume that
the data base is loaded from a source file called XMEAS which has the same fields as
MEASUREMENT plus an extra field TREENUMB indicating the tree number for the tree
on which the measurement has been carried out.

Thus we program the following.

```
BOTLOAD:   PROC OPTIONS (MAIN);

               /*   User working area   */


DCL 1 MEASREC EXTERNAL,   /*   UWA structure   */
    2   MEASNUMB FIXED BIN (15),   /*   Record key   */
    2   RESULT FLOAT DEC (6),
    2   DATE FIXED DEC (8),
    2   TYPE CHAR (10);
DCL DB_STATUS CHAR (7);   /*   Special register   */

                        /*   End of UWA   */


DCL XMEAS FILE RECORD ENV (CONSECUTIVE);   /*   Source file   */
    1 XMEASREC,                          /*   Holds XMEAS record   */
        2   TREENUMB FIXED BIN (31),
        2   SUBSTRUCT LIKE MEASREC; /*   Holds MEASUREMENT record   */


DCL BEOF BIT (1);
ON ENDFILE (XMEAS) BEOF = '0' B;
OPEN FILE (XMEAS) INPUT;
READY UPDATE;                          /*   DML command, Section 9.3.1   */


          /*   Loading of MEASUREMENT and TREE_MEAS   */


READ FILE (XMEAS) INTO (XMEASREC);   /*   Source record in SUBSTRUCT   */
BEOF = '1'B;
DO WHILE (BEOF);
    FIND FILE (TREE) KEY (XMEASREC.TREENUMB);
                              /*   DML command, Section 9.3.2   */
    /*   Source MEASUREMENT record's owner becomes current of TREE_MEAS   */
    IF DB_STATUS ⌐ = '0000000'
        THEN DO; PUT DATA (XMEASREC, DB_STATUS);
                STOP; END;
    STORE FILE (MEASUREMENT) FROM (SUBSTRUCT);
                              /*   DML command, Section 9.3.5   */
    /*   1. This time the source MEASUREMENT record is fetched directly from SUBSTRUCT
           and STOREd and not from the UWA.
        2. TREE_MEAS is an AUTOMATIC set, and SET SELECTION is specified in the
           schema as requiring a MEASUREMENT member record to be connected to the
           TREE_MEAS set occurrence which is current of set. Thus the MEASUREMENT
           record is connected to the TREE_MEAS set occurrence whose owner was accessed
           by the FIND command above.   */
    IF DB_STATUS ⌐ = '0000000'        /*   Something wrong?   */
        THEN DO; PUT DATA (XMEASREC, DB_STATUS);
                STOP; END;
```

```
            ELSE DO; READ FILE (XMEAS) INTO (XMEASREC); END;
END;
PUT SKIP LIST ('FILE MEASUREMENT, SET TREE_MEAS LOADED');
END;
/*
//GO.XMEAS DD etc.
```

This program is similar to the third part of the first loading program. As before, it could be made much more robust. We note that the UWA structure MEASREC is not used at all. Because the records of the existing file XMEAS have an extra field (TREENUMB) attached, we do not read XMEAS records into MEASREC but into XMEASREC instead. The STORE command for PL/1 allows us to *store* a record from XMEASREC directly, although this is not a UWA structure. The COBOL version (see Appendix 2) would require use of the UWA structure.

We have yet to couple the TREE records to the set PROPAGATE, but first we must closely examine the current-of-set concept with recursive sets.

9.5 RECURSIVE SET LOADING

9.5.1 Recursive Sets and the Current-of-Set Concept

The remaining sections of this chapter deal with a more advanced topic, which may be omitted on first reading. As described in Chapter 8, the 1978 DDLC specifications for the conceptual schema permit recursive sets for the first time. However, the corresponding COBOL DML specifications from the PLC do not as yet allow for their manipulation (see Figure 8.1, which depicts the CODASYL organization), since there are some fundamental problems still to be resolved. In this section, we shall examine these problems. There are a limited number of solutions available within the general framework of the existing CODASYL proposals. We shall select what appears to be the simplest and most effective one, and then go on to make use of our choice in the manipulation of the recursive set PROPAGATE in the FORESTRY data base.

Current-of-Set Concept for Nonrecursive Sets   Strictly speaking, with nonrecursive sets, when we refer to the current of set SETX, we are referring to

    a.   The current *record* of the set SETX, where

    b.   The current record is the most recently accessed record participating in SETX, and where

    c.   The most recently accessed record is either an owner record or a member record of the set SETX.

However, since an owner or member record of SETX can at most participate in one SETX set occurrence, the current record of SETX also points to or identifies the most recently accessed SETX set occurrence. We call the most recently accessed SETX set occurrence the *current occurrence* of the set SETX. We may therefore distinguish between two closely related concepts, namely, the concepts of

    a.   The current record of set SETX;

    b.   The current occurrence of set SETX.

For convenience, we shall refer to (a) as the CRS and (b) as the COS.

For nonrecursive sets, there is no currency indicator for the COS. It is not necessary, since the COS is uniquely identified by the CRS. However, both concepts are being used in the DML for nonrecursive sets. In a FIND command, the record found becomes the CRS for all sets in which it participates, and each CRS entry in the currency table identifies a corresponding COS.

Further, when we use a CONNECT command, we are coupling the CRU into the COS, as identified by the CRS. The STORE command for AUTOMATIC sets with the set selection clause ' . . . . . IDENTIFIED BY APPLICATION' also couples a record to the COS.

With nonrecursive sets, it is clear that no harm is done by not distinguishing very clearly between the COS and the CRS. There is a 1:1 relationship between them for any set, and a single entry in the currency table for the CRS is sufficient. This is the situation at the time of writing for CODASYL COBOL. Unfortunately, the simple 1:1 relationship between the COS and the CRS breaks down when we deal with recursive sets.

Difficulties with Recursive Sets   The set PROPAGATE is a typical example of a recursive set, and its internal structure is illustrated in Figure 8.3. It is clear that a given TREE record can be both the owner of a set occurrence and a member in another set occurrence. Let us now apply the CRS and COS concepts to the set PROPAGATE.

Suppose that we access the file TREE by means of a FIND command and retrieve a record 'T1'. The record 'T1' then becomes the CRU. However, since the record 'T1' also participates in the set PROPAGATE, it also becomes the current of set PROPAGATE, or more precisely the CRS for PROPAGATE. This must be so since 'T1' is the most recently accessed record participating in PROPAGATE.

However, there is not a single most recently accessed PROPAGATE set occurrence. The record 'T1' participates in two PROPAGATE set occurrences, one in which it is the owner record and one in which it is a member record. We refer to these two occurrences as 'P1_OWN' and 'P1_MEM', respectively. Thus the CRS 'T1' identifies two COS values, 'P1_OWN' and 'P1_MEM'.

As we have seen, the CONNECT command couples a record to the COS for a set, and the COS used is identified by the corresponding CRS. However, with the set PROPAGATE, for a CRS such as 'T1' there are two COS values, 'P1_OWN' and 'P1_MEM'. Thus the CONNECT command and some others, including some FIND commands, as structured at the time of writing cannot be used without ambiguity with recursive sets such as PROPAGATE.

Resolution of Difficulty   Since for a given recursive set we can have one CRS value and two COS values, it might be useful to give names to the two types of COS values. The two types of COS values are in fact

---

a. The current occurrence of a set (COS) where the current record of the set (CRS) is an *owner record* in the set;

b. The COS where the CRS is a *member record* in the set.

We shall refer to (a) as CS_OWN and to (b) as CS_MEM.

It seems desirable that the solution to the problem of the two COS values for recursive sets should be such that no changes need to be made to the DML commands for nonrecursive sets, and that the changes for recursive sets should merely involve simple extensions to the syntax and semantics.

If this is acceptable, there are only three possible solutions to the problem. In every DML command that uses the COS concept (as distinct from the CRS concept) either explicitly or implicitly,

a. The DBCS will automatically assume that the type of COS value required is CS_OWN;

b. The DBCS will automatically assume that the type of COS value required is CS_MEM;

c. The user must specify in the command either CS_OWN or CS_MEM according to which of the two types of COS values is to be used.

We are of the opinion that the solution in (c) is to be preferred because it is the most flexible. It is never a simple matter to manipulate a recursive set, so that the more flexibility the manipulation language has, the better. However, it is quite possible that the CODASYL PLC will settle for either (a) or (b), although in the last analysis it may well be up to the implementor.

9.5.2 CONNECT **Command with Recursive Sets**

So far the only command we have dealt with that requires extension before it can manipulate recursive sets is the CONNECT command. Consistent with the solution in (c) above, we give suitable syntaxes for both the COBOL and PL/1 versions. We illustrate using the file TREE and the set PROPAGATE.

COBOL Version

```
CONNECT TREE TO CS_OWN PROPAGATE
CONNECT TREE TO CS_MEM PROPAGATE, FOR_TREE
CONNECT TREE TO CS_MEM ALL
```

The syntactical change simply involves inserting the qualifier CS_OWN or CS_MEM before a set name or before ALL. If the set so specified is not recursive, the qualifier would be ignored. In the first command we are coupling the CRU, which is a TREE record, to the current occurrence of the set (COS) PROPAGATE for which the current record of the set (CRS) PROPAGATE is an owner record.

PL/1 Version

```
CONNECT CRU (TREE) TO CS_OWN (PROPAGATE);
CONNECT CRU (TREE) TO CS_MEM (ALL);
CONNECT CRU (TREE) TO CS (FOR_TREE), CS_MEM (PROPAGATE);
```

The syntactic extension additionally permits us to qualify a set, list of sets, or ALL with either CS_OWN or CS_MEM. As with the COBOL version, if a nonrecursive set is qualified by either CS_OWN or CS_MEM, then CS will be assumed by the DBCS.

9.5.3 The RETAIN Clause in DML Commands

With each FIND command and with the STORE command, it is possible to attach a RETAIN clause. This clause prevents specified currency indicators (but not the CRU) from being updated by the execution of the commands (see also Section 9.2.1).

1. *PL/ syntax*

$$
\text{RETAIN CURRENCY} \quad \left(\left\{ \begin{array}{l} \text{ALL} \\ \| \text{ RECORD} \\ \| \text{ set-name-1 \{, set-name-2\} ...} \end{array} \right. \| \right\});
$$

2. *Examples*

```
FIND FILE (TREE) KEY (TREEREC.TREENUMB) RETAIN (RECORD);
STORE FILE (TREE) RETAIN (ALL);
FIND FILE (TREE) KEY (X) RETAIN (SPEC_TREE, FOR_TREE);
```

3. *Semantics*

   a. If ALL is specified, only the CRU is updated.

   b. If RECORD is specified, the currency for the file specified in the FIND or STORE command is not updated.

   c. For each set specified, the currency is held unchanged.

4. *Contextual example*
   See the loading program for the recursive set PROPAGATE in Section 9.5.4.

9.5.4 Loading Program for the Recursive Set PROPAGATE

We notice that with the two previous loading programs, TOPLOAD and BOTLOAD, as each member record (such as TREE or MEASUREMENT records) is loaded, it is also coupled to the appropriate nonrecursive set occurrences. This is possible because the loading method is top-down.

However, it is not possible to load TREE records into the TREE file and at the same time couple them to the recursive set PROPAGATE. The TREE file must be loaded first, and only then can the records be coupled to PROPAGATE. If all the TREE records have

---

not been loaded when we try to couple a TREE record to a PROPAGATE occurrence, the set occurrence may not exist because the owner record is yet to be loaded.

We load the set as follows.

a. We may use either the TOP_FORESTRY or BOT_FORESTRY subschema.

b. We read in the TREE records sequentially from the existing nondata base file XTREE. We use XTREE here primarily because we have not yet introduced the DML command for reading the existing data-base TREE file sequentially; however, it would be more efficient normally to use XTREE, since the DBMS overhead is avoided.

c. We use the PARENT field for each record read from XTREE to make the owner record CRU, current of TREE and current of set (CRS) PROPAGATE.

d. We then use the TREENUMB field for the same XTREE record (that is, the member record) to make this record the CRU, and current of TREE, avoiding making it current of set PROPAGATE by means of the RETAIN clause.

e. We now couple the XTREE record to the PROPAGATE set using the extended CONNECT command (Section 9.5.2). We must specify that the current of set (CRS) be used as a pointer to the current occurrence of the set (COS) for which the CRS is an owner record.

The loading program follows.

```
RECSET: PROC (OPTIONS) MAIN;

                        /*   User working area   */

DCL 1 TREEREC EXTERNAL
     2  SPECIES CHAR (20),
     2  FOREST CHAR (15),
     2  TREENUMB FIXED BIN (31),  /*   Record key   */
     2  PLANTED FIXED DEC (8),
     2  LOC FIXED BIN (15),
     2  PARENT FIXED BIN (31);  /*   Connection field for set PROPAGATE   */
DCL DB_STATUS CHAR (7);  /*   Special register   */

                        /*   End of UWA   */

DCL XTREE FILE RECORD ENV (CONSECUTIVE);
     /*   Source XTREE file contains the same records as data base TREE file loaded earlier   */
DCL BEOF BIT (1);
ON ENDFILE (XTREE) BEOF = '0'B;
OPEN FILE (XTREE) INPUT;
READY FILE (TREE) UPDATE;  /*   DML command, Section 9.3.1   */
ERROR : PROC;  /*   Used after DML commands   */
     PUT SKIP DATA (XTREE, DB_STATUS );
```

LOADING THE CODASYL DATA BASE

```
        STOP;
END;


                    /*   Connection operation begins   */

READ FILE (XTREE) INTO (TREEREC);
BEOF = '1'B;
DO WHILE (BEOF)
    IF PARENT ¬ = 0 THEN DO;   /*   If PARENT value is zero then the TREE record has
                                      no owner in PROPAGATE   */
        FIND FILE (TREE) KEY (TREEREC.PARENT);   /*   DML, Section 9.3.2   */
        /*   TREE owner of (source) TREE record becomes CRS PROPAGATE   */
        IF DB_STATUS ¬ = '0000000' THEN CALL ERROR;
                                        ELSE;
        FIND FILE (TREE) KEY (TREEREC.TREENUMB)   /*   DML, Section 9.3.2   */
            RETAIN CURRENCY (PROPAGATE);   /*   DML, Section 9.5.3   */
    /*   Source TREE record becomes CRU but not CRS PROPAGATE   */
        IF DB_STATUS ¬ = '0000000' THEN CALL ERROR;
                                        ELSE;
        CONNECT CRU (TREE) TO CS_OWN (PROPAGATE);   /*   DML, Sections
                                                        9.3.5, 9.5.2   */
            /*   The CRU is coupled to the PROPAGATE set occurrence which has owner
                  record that is the CRS for PROPAGATE   */
        IF DB_STATUS ¬ = '0000000' THEN CALL ERROR;
                                        ELSE;
        END;
        ELSE;
        READ FILE (XTREE) INTO (TREEREC);
END;
PUT SKIP LIST ('RECURSIVE SET PROPAGATE LOADED');
END;
/*
//GO.XTREE   DD etc.
```

We note again that the program could be made more robust. The utility of the PL/1 FIND command version compared to the COBOL version is clearly illustrated in this program. We have to deal with two TREE records, the member record and its owner, at all times. In a COBOL version of this program, an auxiliary structure to hold TREE records would be necessary.

EXERCISES

1. Using the conceptual schema for the RESOURCE data base from Exercise 3 in Chapter 8, prepare external schemas and programs suitable for loading the data base.

2. For the data base with schema prepared in Exercise 4 in Chapter 8, prepare an external schema and loading program.

3. Prepare conceptual and external schemas for the bill of materials data base shown in Figure 6.16a. Then write a program to load the data base.

4. Consider the problem of applying the CONNECT command to recursive sets. Show how the considerations involved also apply to one type of automatic SET SELECTION. Recommend a solution.

REFERENCES

CODASYL, 1978a, "Data Description Language Committee," *DDLC Journal of Development,* Dept. of Supply and Services, Canadian Federal Government, Hull, Quebec, Canada.

CODASYL, 1978b, "COBOL Committee," *Journal of Development* (with updates to 1981), Dept. of Supply and Services, Canadian Federal Government, Hull, Quebec, Canada.

Cypser, R. J., 1978, *Communications Architecture for Distributed Systems,* Addision-Wesley, Reading, Mass.

Manola, F., 1978, "A Review of the 1978 CODASYL Data Base Specifications," *Proc. ACM Conference on Very Large Data Bases,* Berlin, pp. 232–40.

Taylor, F. E., 1979, *Teleprocessing Monitor Packages,* NCC Publications, Oxford Road, Manchester, U.K.

Manipulating The CODASYL Data Base

10

In this chapter we shall first examine the remaining CODASYL DML commands [CODASYL, 1978] and then give some examples of how they may be used to manipulate a data base. We divide the remaining commands into two categories, namely, the FIND commands and the remaining updating commands. We look first at the FIND commands.

10.1 THE FIND COMMANDS WITH PL/1

The FIND commands are fundamental to the CODASYL DML. The COBOL JOD classifies them into seven formats, three of which have two significant versions. The FIND commands are often referred to by their COBOL JOD format number. Thus the record-key FIND command introduced in the previous chapter can be referred to as the *format-2* FIND *command* and, as we have seen, has two versions.

The COBOL JOD classification appears somewhat arbitrary; it is certainly not helpful for tutorial purposes, so little use will be made of it in this book. A much simpler classification would divide them into those which deal exclusively with files, and those which deal with both files and owner-coupled sets. We shall present the commands according to this classification, and in addition to giving their JOD format numbers, we shall refer to them by suggestive names, such as the record-key FIND command already discussed.

As in the previous chapter, we shall present the PL/1 commands with the COBOL equivalents listed in Appendix 2. With some FIND commands, we have the same problem with recursive sets that occurred with the CONNECT command. The problem may be solved in the same way as before, and both PL/1 and COBOL versions suitable for use with recursive sets are described. Readers are cautioned that the material in this and the

---

following section has the character of reference material. Semantic rules and contextual examples might well be skipped on first reading. (Note that peripheral semantic descriptions are omitted for many commands. Readers interested in a full description of the commands should consult the original CODASYL specifications.)

10.1.1 Classification of the FIND Commands

The main classification of FIND commands is by those that deal with files and those that deal with sets and files. Those which deal with files are further classified as those which permit direct access and those which permit sequential access. The commands dealing with files and sets are classified into those which permit retrieval of members of a set occurrence, those which permit retrieval of the owner of a set occurrence, and those which deal with updating of currencies and keep-lists. The classification follows.

File FIND Commands

1. *Direct-access commands*

   a. Record-key FIND: The record is retrieved on specification of a record key. The first version is for record keys; the second is for secondary keys (Section 9.3.2, JOD format 2)

2. *Sequential access commands*

   a. Sequential FIND command: The command permits sequential or skip sequential processing of a file in a record-key order (Section 10.1.2, JOD format 1).

   b. Data-base key-order FIND command: The records of a file may be processed in data-base key order (Section 10.1.3, JOD format 4).

File/Set FIND Commands

1. *Set-scan commands*

   a. Controlled set-scan FIND command: Each member of a set occurrence may be retrieved in the order of the set member records. When used with a system set, the member file is processed sequentially (Section 10.1.5, JOD format 4).[1]

   b. Set-scan target FIND command: The first member of a set occurrence with field values satisfying a target specification is retrieved (Section 10.1.6, JOD format 7).

   c. Set-scan duplicate target FIND command: The next member record of a set occurrence with field values satisfying a target specification is retrieved (Section 10.1.7, JOD format 3).

2. *Owner retrieval command*

   a. Owner FIND command: The owner record of the current of set is retrieved (Section 10.1.8, JOD format 6).

---

[1]*System sets are described in Section 10.1.5.*

3. *Currency commands*

    a. Currency **FIND** command: The record reference by a currency indicator or keep-list data-base key is retrieved (Section 10.1.11, JOD format 5).

    b. **KEEP** command: This command is best classified with the **FIND** commands. The data-base key for a currency indicator is assigned to a keep-list (Section 10.1.10).

10.1.2 Sequential FIND Command (JOD Format 1)

This command permits sequential or skip sequential processing of a data-base file in record-key order. With skip sequential retrieval, records satisfying specified target conditions are retrieved.[1] Processing is superficially similar to processing an ISAM or VSAM file opened for SEQUENTIAL INPUT (see Chapter 4).

1. *PL/1 syntax*

$$\underline{\text{FIND}} \left\{ \begin{array}{c} \underline{\text{FIRST}} \\ \text{NEXT} \end{array} \right\} \underline{\text{FILE}} \ (\textit{file name}) \ [\underline{\text{WHERE}} \ (\textit{logical-expression})];$$

2. *Command examples*

```
FIND NEXT FILE (TREE);
FIND NEXT FILE (TREE) WHERE (SPECIES = 'SPRUCE');
FIND FIRST FILE (TREE) WHERE ((SPECIES = 'SPRUCE') & (FOREST =
    'XFOR') );
FIND NEXT FILE (TREE) WHERE (PLANTED>19000101);
```

3. *Semantics*

    a. When **FIRST** is specified, the first record in the specified file is retrieved in prime key order. If **WHERE** is also specified, the first record in record-key order which satisfies the target conditions is retrieved.

    b. Target conditions are specified by the logical expression in the **WHERE** clause.

    c. Each relation in the logical expression must contain a UWA data item corresponding to a field in the record being retrieved.

    d. When **NEXT** is specified, the next record in record-key sequence following the current of file is retrieved. If **WHERE** is also specified, the DBCS retrieves the next record following the current of file which satisfies the target conditions.

    e. The record retrieved becomes the CRU, the current of file, and the current of set for all sets in which it participates.

4. *Contextual example*
We retrieve all the tree numbers for 'SPRUCE' trees. (All examples in this chapter deal with the **FORESTRY** data base and associated conceptual and external schemas.)

---

[1] *As mentioned in the previous chapter, **FIND** commands do not actually retrieve records, they merely update the currency indicators.*

```
BEOF = '1'B; N = 1;
DO WHILE (BEOF);
      IF N = 1 THEN FIND FIRST FILE (TREE) WHERE (SPECIES =
                'SPRUCE');
                ELSE FIND NEXT FILE (TREE) WHERE (SPECIES =
                'SPRUCE');
      IF DB_STATUS = '0502400'   /*  None left   */
         THEN BEOF = '0'B;
         ELSE IF DB_STATUS = '0000000'   /*  Normal return   */   THEN DO;
               GET CRU (TREE) INTO (TREEREC.TREENUMB);   /*  DML, Sec-
                                                           tion 9.3.4   */

         PUT SKIP LIST (TREENUMB);
         N = N + 1; END;
               ELSE CALL ERROR;
      END;
```

5. *Remarks*

It is difficult to see how search condition specifications as primitive as those of the COBOL version could be acceptable in PL/1 (see Appendix 2). The PL/1 command above is semantically very close to the simplest EOS (nonnavigational) retrieval command (see Chapter 11).

10.1.3 Data-Base Key-Order FIND Command (JOD Format 4)

The data-base key-order command may be used for processing a data-base file in data-base key order. It is reasonably useful and resembles the PL/1 READ command for reading a REGIONAL(1) file in region-number sequence (see Chapter 3). We have found it quite useful for loading recursive sets, because here it is necessary to read all records efficiently. Since records are retrieved in data-base key order, we may expect a search length of unity (see Chapter 3) for each retrieval with this command.

1. *PL/1 syntax*

$$\underline{\text{FIND FILE}} \; \textit{(file-name)} \; \underline{\text{DB\_KEYSEQ}} \quad \left(\left\{ \begin{array}{l} \underline{\text{NEXT}} \\ \text{PRIOR} \\ \text{FIRST} \\ \underline{\text{LAST}} \\ \textit{integer} \\ \textit{identifier} \end{array} \right\} \right);$$

2. *Command examples*

FIND FILE (TREE) DB_KEYSEQ (FIRST);
FIND FILE (TREE) DB_KEYSEQ (LAST);

---

3. *Semantics*

    a.   The record is retrieved from the file specified and becomes the CRU, the current of file, and the current of set for all sets in which it participates.

    b.   The records in the file may be considered to be available in ascending or descending data-base key order.

    c.   Specification of **FIRST** or **LAST** respectively retrieves the first or last of the records from the file specified.

    d.   If n is the value of *integer* or if n is the value of the program variable specified by *identifier*, then the nth record is retrieved. With negative n, we process backwards through the file.

    e.   If the current of file record was the nth, specification of **NEXT** or **PRIOR** causes the $(n + 1)$th or $(n - 1)$th record, respectively, to be retrieved.

4. *Contextual example*

We could use this command to rewrite the main loop of the program **RECSET** from Section 9.5.4, which was used for loading the recursive set **PROPAGATE**.

    In the original version of the program **RECSET**, the **TREE** records were already stored in the data base **TREE** file before processing began. Instead of reading the file **TREE** sequentially, we read the **TREE** records from the sequential (tape) file **XTREE**, whence the file **TREE** had originally been loaded.

    If the file **XTREE** is not available in easily accessible form (more than one original file could have been used to produce the data-base file **TREE**, for example), then the data-base file **TREE** has to be processed sequentially. We have two basic choices.

    a.   Process sequentially in record-key order.

    b.   Process sequentially in data-base key order.

The second method will generally be more efficient because we can be sure of an average search length close to one with most implementations. We can thus use the data-base key-order **FIND** command.

```
BEOF = '1'B; N = 1;
FIND FILE (TREE) DB_KEYSEQ (N);
DO WHILE (BEOF);
                /*   File TREE will be processed in data-base key order   */
    GET CRU (TREE) INTO (TREEREC);   /*   DML, Section 9.3.4; Nth record to
                                                    UWA   */
IF TREEREC.PARENT ¬= 0   /*   If TREE record has a parent   */
    THEN DO;
            /*   Make parent TREE the CRS for PROPAGATE   */
    FIND FILE (TREE) KEY (TREEREC.PARENT);
                    /*   DML record key FIND command, Section 9.3.2   */
    /*   Parent TREE now CRU and CRS for PROPAGATE   */
```

```
       FIND FILE (TREE) DB_DEYSEQ (N)
               RETAIN CURRENCY (PROPAGATE);   /*  See Section 9.5.3   */
       /*  TREE record to be coupled is now CRU but not CRS PROPAGATE   */
       /*  We can now CONNECT the CRU to the PROPAGATE occurrence for which the
           CRS is the owner   */
       CONNECT CRU (TREE) TO CS_OWN (PROPAGATE);   /*  DML, Section
                                                        9.3.5   */
   END;
   ELSE;   /*  If TREE record has no parent in PROPAGATE   */
   N = N + 1;
   FIND FILE (TREE) DB_KEYSEQ (N);
       IF DB_STATUS ⌐ = '0000000'              /*  Something wrong   */
           THEN IF DB_STATUS = '0502400'       /*  No more TREE records   */
           THEN BEOF = '0'B;
           ELSE CALL ERROR;
END;
```

10.1.4 Record-Key FIND Command (JOD Format 2)

The record-key FIND command is the workhorse FIND command introduced in Section
9.3.2. We mention it again here for the sake of completeness.

10.1.5 Controlled Set-Scan FIND Command (JOD Format 4)

The controlled set-scan FIND command is fundamental and involves retrieval from a set
occurrence. The command permits the member records of a set occurrence to be retrieved
sequentially in the order specified for member records in the subschema set specification.
The members are thus scanned in a controlled manner. It is one of the most frequently
used FIND commands.

If a set occurrence has as members all the records in a file, as is the case with *system
sets* (as we shall see later in this section), then the command may also be used to retrieve
all the records of the file sequentially in secondary key order (as opposed to data-base key
order).

1. *PL/1 syntax*

```
FIND FILE (file-name) IN CS (set-name) MEMBER ( { NEXT
                                                  PRIOR
                                                  FIRST
                                                  LAST     } );
                                                  integer
                                                  identifier
```

2. *Command examples*

```
FIND FILE (TREE) IN CS (FOR_TREE) MEMBER (N);
FIND IN CS (FOR_TREE) MEMBER (FIRST);
```

MANIPULATING THE CODASYL DATA BASE

3. *Semantics*

   a. The record is retrieved from the file specified and becomes CRU, current of file, and the current of set for all sets in which it participates.

   b. The records of a set occurrence for the set specified are retrieved in the order specified for member records in the subschema set specification.

   c. The required set occurrence is selected by means of the current (record) of set for the set specified.

   d. FIRST retrieves the first member record, and LAST retrieves the last member record.

   e. If *n* is the value of *integer* or if *n* is the value of the program variable specified by *identifier,* then the *n*th record in the set occurrence is retrieved. If *n* is negative, the order of retrieval is from last to first.

   f. If the current of set record is the *n*th, specification of NEXT or PRIOR retrieves the $(n + 1)$th or $(n - 1)$th member, respectively, of the set occurrence.

4. *Contextual example*

   Let us suppose we wish to retrieve all the measurement data for tree 13. We code:

```
TREEREC.TREENUMB = 13;          /*  Record key to UWA  */
FIND FILE (TREE) KEY (TREENUMB);  /*  DML, Section 9.3.2  */
                /*  TREE 13 becomes CRS for TREE_MEAS  */
N = 1;  /*  N is identifier in syntax specification  */
FIND FILE (MEASUREMENT) IN CS (TREE_MEAS) MEMBER (N);
BEOS = '1'B;  /*  BEOS is a logical variable: Before End Of Set  */
DO WHILE (BEOS);
    GET CRU (MEASUREMENT) INTO (MEASREC);  /*  DML, Section 9.3.4  */
    PUT SKIP LIST (MEASREC);
    N = N + 1;
    FIND FILE (MEASUREMENT) IN CS (TREE_MEAS) MEMBER (N);
        IF DB_STATUS ¬ = '0000000'  /*  Something wrong?  */
            THEN IF DB_STATUS = '0502400'  /*  No members left  */
            THEN BEOS = '0'B;
            ELSE CALL ERROR;
END;
```

5. *Remarks*

   Neither the PL/1 nor the COBOL version of the command can be used with recursive sets without modification. This is discussed later in this section.

Application to Sequential Data-Base File Processing—System Sets In the schema, we may specify *system* or *singular sets*. These are owner-coupled sets with only *one* set occurrence and whose owner record is some imaginary system record. The member records of such an owner-coupled set are normally all the records in a single file. We can specify a system set for each file in the data base (owner subentry syntax, Section 8.4.4). The topic is peripheral, however, and could be skipped on first reading.

The following is a schema specification for the system set SYS_TREE for the member file TREE.

```
SET NAME IS SYS_TREE
     OWNER IS SYSTEM
          ORDER IS PERMANENT SORTED BY DEFINED KEYS.
     MEMBER IS TREE
          INSERTION IS AUTOMATIC
          RETENTION IS FIXED
     KEY IS ASCENDING LOC IN TREE
          DUPLICATES ARE LAST
          NULL IS NOT ALLOWED.
```

The important point to grasp is that we may specify as the system-set sort-key (see Section 8.4.4), the same key field as we have specified as the member file secondary key. Furthermore, the order of the records (ascending or descending, and so on) may also be specified to be the same in both system set and member file. Thus in the above specification, the order for the set sort-key LOC is the same as that for the secondary key LOC (see schema, lines 26 and 27) in the member file TREE.

It is thus possible to use the set-scan FIND command with a system set to process all the records in a file in any secondary key order. As an example, let us assume a schema specification of the system set SYS_ TREE for the file TREE as given above, together with a subschema declaration. We shall use this set with the FIND command to print out all the records in TREE in secondary key (LOC) sequence, as illustrated in the following program excerpt.

```
N = 1;
FIND FILE (TREE) IN CS (SYS_TREE) MEMBER (FIRST);
     /*   There is only one occurrence of SYS_TREE   */
BEOF = '1'B;
DO WHILE (BEOF);
     GET CRU (TREE) INTO (TREEREC);   /*   DML, Section 9.3.4   */
     PUT SKIP LIST (TREEREC);
     N = N + 1;
     FIND FILE (TREE) IN CS (SYS_TREE) MEMBER (N);
     IF DB_STATUS ¬ = '0000000'   /*   Something wrong?   */
          THEN IF DB_STATUS = '0502400'   /*   None left in the set, that is, in the
                                                                 file   */
               THEN BEOF = '0';
               ELSE CALL ERROR;
          ELSE;
END;
```

Recursive Sets and the Controlled Set-Scan FIND Command   The same fundamental problem occurs with the controlled set-scan command as with the CONNECT command (see the discussion in Section 9.3.8). To see the problem as it affects this FIND command, consider the illustration of two of the owner-coupled set occurrences in PROP-AGATE (Figure 10.1). We have tree 7 as the owner of trees 50, 75, and 80, where tree 75 in turn is the owner of trees 106, 150, and 208.

Let us now suppose that tree 75 is the current (record) of set PROPAGATE. When the statement

FIND FILE (TREE) IN CS (PROPAGATE) MEMBER (NEXT);

is executed, there are two possible set occurrences from which the "next" number can be retrieved. If the set occurrence is that with owner tree 7, then tree 80 is retrieved; if it is that with owner 75, tree 106 is retrieved.

Thus we have the problem identified already: There is one current record of set (CRS) for a recursive set, but two current occurrences of set. The two current occurrences are the one for which the CRS is the owner (which we refer to as CS_ OWN) and the one for which the CRS is a member (which we refer to as CS_MEM).

As before, the solution is to be able to specify precisely in the command to which of the two set occurrences we are referring; this may be accomplished by inserting CS_OWN or CS_MEM in the FIND command.

1. *PL/1 syntax*

$$\text{FIND [\underline{FILE} (\textit{file-name})] IN } \begin{Bmatrix} \text{CS} \\ \text{CS\_OWN} \\ \text{CS\_MEM} \end{Bmatrix} \text{(\textit{set-name}) MEMBER } (\begin{Bmatrix} \text{FIRST} \\ \text{LAST} \\ \vdots \end{Bmatrix});$$

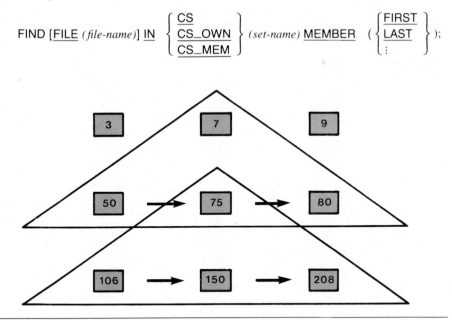

FIGURE 10.1. *Two set occurrences containing* TREE *records in the recursive set* PROPAGATE. *One set has owner record with tree number 7, and members with tree numbers 50, 75, and 80. The other has owner 75 and members 106, 150, and 208. The arrows show order of member records; thus in the top set, occurrence 50 is* FIRST *and 80 is* LAST.

2. *Command examples*

    FIND FILE (TREE) IN CS_OWN (PROPAGATE) MEMBER (N);
    FIND IN CS_MEM (PROPAGATE) MEMBER (LAST);

3. *Semantics*

    a. The semantics are the same as with the nonrecursive set version, but with the following additional rules.

    b. With a recursive set, **CS_OWN** means that the set occurrence selected is that for which the current (record) of set (CRS) is the owner record.

    c. With a recursive set, **CS_MEM** means that the set occurrence selected is that for which the CRS is a member record.

    d. If either **CS_MEM** or **CS_OWN** is specified with a nonrecursive set, they are ignored.

    e. If neither **CS_MEM** nor **CS_OWN** is specified with a recursive set, then **CS_MEM** is assumed by default.

4. *Remarks*

    A default specification of **CS_MEM** is the most useful, since most commonly **FIND** commands of this type are retrieving member records in a set where the CRS is a member record. **CS_OWN** and **CS_MEM** are also required in the COBOL version (see Appendix 2).

5. *Contextual example*

    Referring again to Figure 9.5, let us retrieve records for trees immediately propagated from tree 75. For convenience, let us further assume we know that there are 3 trees. We code as follows.

    ```
    TREEREC.TREENUMB = 75;
    FIND FILE (TREE) KEY (TREENUMB);  /*  Record key FIND, Section 9.3.2  */
                    /*  TREE 75 is now CRS for PROPAGATE  */
    DO N = 1 TO 3;
        IF N = 1 THEN
            FIND FILE (TREE) IN CS_OWN (PROPAGATE) MEMBER (N);
            ELSE
            FIND FILE (TREE) IN CS_MEM (PROPAGATE) MEMBER (N);
        GET CRU (TREE) INTO (TREEREC);  /*  DML, Section 9.3.4  */
        PUT SKIP LIST (TREEREC);
    END;
    ```

10.1.6 Set-Scan Target FIND Command (JOD Format 7)

The set-scan target FIND command causes the DBCS to scan through the members of an owner-coupled set occurrence until it comes to a "target" record, with fields as specified in the command.

There are two versions of the command, depending on how the set to be scanned is selected. In the first version, the set selected is by means of the current (record) of set. In the second version, the set is selected in accordance with the SET SELECTION clause in the subschema. However, this second version is subtle and is not likely to be commonly implemented. We shall not include it in this section [CODASYL, 1978].

As was the case with the previous command (the controlled set-scan FIND command), the usual problems with recursive sets are in evidence because the set-scan target FIND command employs the current (occurrence) of set. These problems may be solved in the same way as before, and we include from the beginning the necessary CS_OWN/CS_MEM extension to the command syntax.

1. *PL/1 syntax*

$$\text{FIND [\underline{FILE} (\textit{file-name})] IN} \left\{ \begin{array}{l} \underline{\text{CS}} \\ \underline{\text{CS\_OWN}} \\ \underline{\text{CS\_MEM}} \end{array} \right\} (\textit{set-name}) [\underline{\text{WHERE}} (\textit{logical-expression})];$$

2. *Command examples*

   FIND FILE (TREE) IN CS (FOR_TREE) WHERE (LOC = 1001)
   FIND IN CS (SPEC_FILE) WHERE ((LOC = 12) & (FOREST = 'YFOR'))

3. *Semantics (nonrecursive sets)*

   a. The set occurrence is selected by means of the current record of set for the set specified.

   b. The record retrieved becomes the CRU, current of file for the file specified, and the current of set for all the sets in which it participates.

   c. The member records of the selected set occurrence are scanned in the order specified for member records in the subschema set specification until the first member record satisfying the logical expression is found. In all cases the scan starts with the first member record of the set occurrence.

   d. The WHERE clause contains a PL/1 logical expression. Each relation in the expression must contain a UWA data item corresponding to a field in the record being retrieved.

4. *Semantics (recursive set)*

   a. Rules b, c, and d for nonrecursive sets still hold.

   b. If CS_OWN is specified, the set occurrence selected has the CRS as its owner. If CS_MEM is specified, the set occurrence selected has the CRS as a member. If neither is specified, CS_MEM is assumed by default.

5. *Contextual examples*

   a. Nonrecursive set: Let us retrieve the first electrical measurement carried out on tree 56. We code

```
TREEREC.TREENUMB = 56;
FIND FILE (TREE) KEY (TREENUMB);
                    /*   Record key FIND, Section 9.3.2   */
/*   TREE 56 is now CRS TREE_MEAS   */
FIND FILE (MEASUREMENT) IN CS (TREE_MEAS)
    WHERE (TYPE = 'ELECTRICAL');
GET CRU (MEASUREMENT) INTO (MEASREC);   /*   DML, Section 9.3.4   */

PUT LIST (MEASREC);
```

b. Recursive set: Find the first tree which is (1) propagated from the same tree as tree number 50, and (2) planted in location 1001. We may refer to Figure 10.1, where we see that tree 50 was propagated from tree 7. The tree we are seeking must also be propagated from tree 7. We code

```
TREEREC.TREENUMB = 50;
FIND FILE (TREE) KEY (TREENUMB);   /*   DML, Section 9.3.2   */
   /*   TREE 50 is now CRS PROPAGATE   */
FIND FILE (TREE) IN CS_MEM (PROPAGATE)
        WHERE (LOC = 1001);
GET CRU (TREE) INTO (TREEREC);   /*   DML, Section 9.3.4   */
PUT LIST (TREEREC);   /*   Action for "not found" is omitted   */
```

10.1.7 Set-Scan Duplicate Target FIND Command (JOD Format 3)

In the previous set-scan command, the member records of an occurrence are scanned until a record with fields matching the WHERE specification is found. The scan is in the order for the member records specified in the subschema set specification. However, there may be another record in the set occurrence which also satisfies the WHERE specification. We may refer to such a record as a *duplicate* record.

This duplicate record cannot be retrieved by the previous set-scan target FIND command. A first execution of the command will retrieve the first record satisfying the WHERE conditions; however, a second execution of the command will also retrieve this record.

The set-scan duplicate target FIND command can retrieve the first record satisfying the WHERE conditions in the first execution; if the retrieved record is still the current of set for the set involved, a second execution will retrieve the next duplicate satisfying the same WHERE conditions, and so on.

We shall insert in the syntax of the PL/1 version, the CS_OWN/CS_MEM extensions necessary for recursive sets.

1. *Syntax*

$$\text{FIND [\underline{FILE} (\textit{file-name})] \underline{DUPLICATE} IN} \left\{ \begin{array}{l} \underline{\text{CS}} \\ \underline{\text{CS\_OWN}} \\ \underline{\text{CS\_MEM}} \end{array} \right\} (\textit{set-name})$$

WHERE (*logical-expression*);

2. *Command example*

FIND FILE (TREE) DUPLICATE IN CS (FOR_TREE) WHERE (LOC = 1001);

3. *Semantics*

   a. The search is carried out in the order specified for member records in the subschema set specification for the set specified in the command.

   b. The search starts at the member record following the record which is current of set. However, if the current of set is the owner, the search starts at the first member record.

   c. As with the previous command, the WHERE clause defines the target record.

   d. The set occurrence is selected by means of the current record of set; if the set is recursive, the CS_OWN/CS_MEM specification pinpoints which set occurrence is to be used, the default value being CS_MEM.

   e. The record retrieved becomes the CRU, and so on.

4. *Contextual examples*

   a. Nonrecursive set: Let us retrieve all the records for measurements of type 'ELEC-TRICAL' carried out on tree 56. We code as follows.

```
TREEREC.TREENUMB = 56;
FIND FILE (TREE) KEY (TREENUMB);  /*  DML, Section 9.3.2  */
BEOS = '1'B;
FIND IN CS (TREEMEAS) WHERE (TYPE = 'ELECTRICAL');
                    /*  DML, Section 10.1.6  */
             /*  Next, assume there are duplicates  */
DO WHILE (BEOS);
GET CRU (MEASUREMENT) INTO (MEASREC);  *  DML, Section 9.3.4  */

PUT SKIP LIST (MEASREC);
FIND DUPLICATE IN CS (TREEMEAS)
             WHERE (TYPE = 'ELECTRICAL');
IF DB_STATUS ⌐ = '0000000'  /*  Problem?  */
      THEN IF DB_STATUS = '0502400'
           THEN BEOS = '0'B;  /*  No duplicates left  */
           ELSE CALL ERROR;
      ELSE;
END;
```

   b. Recursive set: We now consider an example very similar to (a) above, but with recursive sets. Let us suppose we need to retrieve trees immediately propagated from tree 75, but which are all in location 1001. Referring to Figure 10.1 we code as follows.

```
TREEREC.TREENUMB = 75;
FIND FILE (TREE) KEY (TREENUMB);  /*  DML, Section 9.3.2  */
```

```
/*   TREE record is owner of desired PROPAGATE occurrence   */
BEOS = '1';
FIND FILE (TREE) in CS_OWN (PROPAGATE)
                    WHERE (LOC = 1001);   /*   DML, Section 10.1.6   */
          /*   TREE record just accessed becomes new CRS for PROPAGATE   */
DO WHILE (BEOS);
      GET CRU (TREE) INTO (TREEREC);   /*   DML, Section 9.3.4   */
      PUT SKIP LIST (TREEREC);
      FIND DUPLICATE IN CS_MEM (PROPAGATE)
                    WHERE (LOC = 1001);
      IF DB_STATUS ⌐ = '0000000'   /*   Something wrong?   */
          THEN IF DB_STATUS = '0502400'
                THEN BEOS = '0'B;   /*   No duplicates left   */
                ELSE CALL ERROR;
          ELSE;
END;
```

10.1.8 Owner FIND Command (JOD Format 6)

The previous three scan commands have all been concerned with retrieving a member record in a set occurrence. In contrast, the owner FIND command permits the owner record of a set occurrence to be retrieved. Since a set occurrence may have only one owner, the command is very simple. We specify a set and the owner of the current (occurrence) of set is retrieved.

Since the current (occurrence) of set is involved, the usual problems with recursive sets are in evidence with the standard syntax. As with the other commands, the problem may be solved by the CS_OWN/CS_MEM extension, which we include in the syntax.

1. *Syntax*

$$\text{FIND [FILE (\textit{file-name})] OWNER IN} \left\{ \begin{array}{l} \text{CS} \\ \text{CS\_OWN} \\ \text{CS\_MEM} \end{array} \right\} \textit{(set-name)};$$

2. *Command examples*

    FIND OWNER IN CS (TREE_MEAS);
    FIND FILE (TREE) OWNER IN CS_MEM (PROPAGATE);

3. *Semantics*

    a. The set occurrence is selected by means of the current record of set for the set specified.

    b. For recursive sets, the proper set occurrence is specified using CS_OWN or CS_MEM, with the usual meaning. The default value is CS_MEM.[1]

    c. The owner record of the set specified becomes the CRU, and so on.

    ---

    [1]*Use of* CS_OWN *is almost redundant with this simple command.*

4. *Contextual example*

We wish to find the record for the tree on which measurement 306 was carried out. We code the following.

```
MEASREC.MEASNUMB = 306;
FIND FILE (MEASUREMENT) KEY (MEASNUMB);   /*   DML, Section 9.3.2   */
     /*   Member MEASUREMENT record is current record of TREE_MEAS   */
FIND OWNER IN CS (TREE_MEAS);
GET CRU (TREE) INTO (TREEREC);   /*   DML, Section 9.3.4   */
PUT LIST (TREEREC);
```

10.1.9 The Currency Indicator Commands—KEEP and Currency FIND

The KEEP and currency FIND commands are so closely interrelated that from an expositional point of view, it is best to deal with them together.

Both commands manipulate currency indicators and keep-lists. We saw in Section 9.2.1 that a currency indicator is the data-base key of a current record of file or current record of set or current record of run-unit.

In Section 9.1.1, we saw that a keep-list is a subschema declared list that can hold currency indicators or data-base keys that are not available for manipulation by a host-language statement.

KEEP Command   This command is new; simply stated, it can assign the currency indicator for a specified current record to a keep-list. The currency indicator, which is a data-base key, is assigned to the end of the list of currency indicators in the keep-list.

Currency FIND Command   The semantics of the currency FIND command are also new (JOD format 5). This command makes the record retrieved the CRU, current of file, and current of set for all sets involved, in the same way as with the other FIND commands.

However, to do this the DBCS takes the currency indicator for the specified file or set or the first currency indicator in the specified keep-list and treats it as the currency indicator for the most recently accessed record. This currency indicator is thus used to update the currency table in the usual way. *Thus the command does not involve an access of the data base but merely a readjustment of the currency table, using indicators either from the currency table or from keep-lists.*

The KEEP and currency FIND commands will normally be used together. When a run-unit needs to save a currency indicator for future use, the KEEP command is used to place it in a keep-list. Later this currency can be quickly retrieved using the currency FIND command.

As also mentioned in Section 9.1.1, keep-lists have an additional use in the 1978 CODASYL proposal, in connection with concurrency control. In this connection, another new command has been introduced, namely, the FREE command; it is capable of removing (or deleting) a data-base key from a keep-list. The FREE command is new. This command is discussed in Section 10.4.2 on record-level concurrency control.

We now examine the KEEP and currency FIND commands in more detail.

10.1.10 The KEEP Command

The KEEP command permits a data-base key value corresponding to a currency indicator to be assigned to a keep-list.

1. *PL/1 syntax*

    <u>KEEP</u> [DB_KEY (*data-base-key-identifier*)] <u>IN</u> (*keep-list-name*);

2. *Command examples*

    KEEP IN (TREEKEEP);
    KEEP DB_KEY (TREE) IN (TREEKEEP);

3. *Semantics*

    a. The data-base key is placed at the end of the list of keys in the specified keep-list.

    b. If the DB_KEY clause is omitted, the data-base key assigned is that of the CRU currency indicator.

    c. When *data-base-key-identifier* denotes a file or set, the data-base key from the corresponding currency indicator is assigned to the keep-list. A keep-list may also be denoted by *data-base-key-identifier*.

4. *Contextual example*
    See the next section.

10.1.11 The Currency FIND Command (JOD Format 5)

The currency FIND command retrieves the record whose data-base key is either of the following.

a. That of the currency indicator for the specified file or set.

b. That which is first in the specified keep-list.

1. *PL/1 syntax*

    <u>FIND</u> CURRENT (*data-base-key-identifier*);

2. *Command examples*

    FIND CURRENT (TREE)
    FIND (TREEKEEP); /* Keep-list name */

3. *Semantics*

    a. The record retrieved becomes the CRU, current of file and current of set for all sets in which it participates.

    b. When a file name or set name is denoted by *data-base-key-identifier*, the record referenced by the data-base key of the corresponding currency indicator is retrieved.

---

c. When a keep-list is denoted by *data-base-key-identifier,* the record referenced by the first data-base key in the keep-list is retrieved.

4. *Contextual example*

In this example, we shall illustrate the use of both the KEEP and currency FIND commands. The commands may be employed in the main loop of the program RECSET for loading the recursive set PROPAGATE. We have already had two versions of this program, originally in Section 9.5.4 and later in Section 10.1.3, as an illustration of the data-base key-order FIND command.

In the version shown below, we continue to use the data-base key-order FIND command, but we use it only half as many times as in Section 10.1.3. The saved data-base key-order FIND commands are replaced by KEEP and currency FIND commands, thus reducing the number of data-base accesses.

```
N = 1; BEOF = '1'B;
FIND FILE (TREE) DB_KEYSEQ (N);   /*   DML, Section 10.1.3   */
                /*   Sequential processing in data-base key order   */
DO WHILE (BEOF);
    GET CRU (TREE) INTO (TREEREC);   /*   DML, Sections 9.3.4   */
    IF TREEREC.PARENT ¬ = 0   /*   If parent exists   */
    THEN DO;
        KEEP DB_KEY (TREE) IN (TREEKEEP);   /*   DML, Section
                                    10.1.10   */
        /*   Data-base key of TREE record to be coupled to a PROPAGATE set
        occurrence is in the keep-list TREEKEEP. TREEKEEP is assumed to be
        initially empty   */
        FIND FILE (TREE) KEY (TREEREC.PARENT);
                        /*   DML, Section 9.3.1   */
                /*   Parent TREE record is now both CRU and CRS for
                PROPAGATE   */
        FIND CURRENT (TREEKEEP)
                RETAIN CURRENCY (PROPAGATE);
                    /*   DML, Section 9.5.3   */
        /*   Nth TREE record is now CRU, while its TREE parent record is still
        CRS for PROPAGATE   */
        CONNECT CRU (TREE) TO CS_OWN (PROPAGATE);
        FREE (TREEKEEP);   /*   DML, Section 10.4.2   */
        /*   Simple command, keep-list emptied   */
    END;
    ELSE;   /*   No parent, do nothing   */
    N = N + 1;
    FIND FILE (TREE) DB_KEYSEQ (N);
                    /*   DML, Section 10.1.3   */
    IF DB_STATUS ¬ = '0000000'   /*   Not OK   */
        THEN IF DB_STATUS = '0502400'
```

```
                    THEN BEOF = '0'B;   /*   End of TREE file   */
                    ELSE CALL ERROR;
            ELSE;
    END;
```

10.2 THE UPDATING DML COMMANDS WITH PL/1

We now have four remaining commands to consider, namely, MODIFY, RECONNECT, DISCONNECT, and ERASE commands. These commands are used only for updating. Since the MODIFY, RECONNECT, and DISCONNECT (and CONNECT) commands can be considered as a group, we shall first examine the relationship between them.

10.2.1 The Relationship between the MODIFY, RECONNECT, DISCONNECT, and CONNECT Commands

The MODIFY command basically permits one or more fields of a record in any file to be changed or updated. The command might thus appear to have very simple semantics. The opposite is the case—the command has very complex semantics.

However, the MODIFY command in the 1978 CODASYL proposal is significantly simpler than that in earlier specifications. The earlier command not only permitted fields to be updated, it also permitted the updating of the set membership of a record under a wide variety of circumstances.

The latest MODIFY command still permits set membership to be updated but only in a limited way, as we will see. For more general updating of a record's set membership, a new command has been introduced for the first time. This is the RECONNECT command, which permits a record to be disconnected from one set occurrence and placed in another.

The DISCONNECT command allows a record to be uncoupled from a set occurrence and still remain in a data-base file. By using the CONNECT command, which we have already studied (Section 9.5.2), the record can later be coupled to a different set occurrence.

The reader may well wonder why the MODIFY command should be able to change a record's set occurrence membership or why we need a RECONNECT command for the same purpose, when a combination of DISCONNECT and CONNECT would apparently do just as well. The answer is that the DISCONNECT and CONNECT commands are not always sufficient. In the case of the MODIFY command, let us suppose we wish to update the FOREST (connection) field of a TREE record. Since the FOR_TREE set (see Figure 8.2 and Section 8.4.5) is value based, such an update would invalidate the current set occurrence membership of the record. There are two possibilities. Either such a MODIFY should be rejected, or the MODIFY should be accepted and the record's set membership updated. The second alternative is the one chosen by CODASYL.

If the first alternative were chosen, however, we would have to use DISCONNECT and CONNECT instead. This would be possible in the example outlined above, since retention class for FOR_TREE is OPTIONAL, so that a record may be disconnected from the set and later connected to another set occurrence of FOR_TREE after updating of the FOREST field has been carried out using a MODIFY command.

However, suppose that FOR_TREE were a MANDATORY set. In that case, the DISCONNECT/CONNECT approach could not be used, for while member records may switch set occurrences in a MANDATORY set, they may not be disconnected out of a set occurrence. Thus for MANDATORY value-based sets, a MODIFY command that will update set membership on update of a member connection field is essential.

We also need the RECONNECT command with MANDATORY sets that are not value based. With a set that is not value based, the MODIFY command would never require update of set-occurrence membership, since there are no connection fields to be updated. However, if we did want to update a record's set-occurrence membership, we could not use the DISCONNECT/CONNECT approach, because DISCONNECT is still not allowed. In this case we use the RECONNECT command, which takes a record from one set occurrence and places it in another.

10.2.2 The MODIFY Command

The MODIFY command permits update of one or more fields in a record which is either CRU or current of file. If a connection field in a value-based set is updated, then the record's set-occurrence membership is also updated, consistent with the updated value of the connection field.

1. *PL/1 syntax*

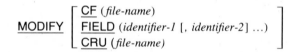

2. *Command examples*

   MODIFY FIELD (TREE.FOREST,PLANTED);
   MODIFY CRU (TREE);
   MODIFY;

3. *Semantics*

   a. When CF is specified, the record being updated is the current record of the file (CF) specified.

   b. When FIELD is specified, one or more fields of the current record of the file so identified are to be updated.

   c. When CRU or just MODIFY is specified, the CRU is updated.

   d. The fields specified by the identifiers are updated using the corresponding UWA values. When FIELD is not specified, all the fields of the target record are updated using the UWA field values.

   e. If an updated field is either a set sort key, or a secondary or order key, the record is repositioned in either its set occurrence or its file, respectively.

---

f. If an updated field is a member connection field in a value-based set, then the record's set-occurrence membership is updated consistent with the new value of the connection field and criteria for set ordering. However, whenever the set involved has retention class **FIXED**, then a request to update the connection field will be rejected.

g. The execution of a **MODIFY** makes the record modified the CRU, and

(1) If the current of set indicator points to the record being modified, it will be set to null whenever a record's position in or membership of a set occurrence of that set is updated;

(2) If the current of file indicator points to the record being modified, it will be set to null whenever a record's position in the file is changed because an order key is updated.

4. *Contextual examples*

a. We wish to change the location of tree 56 to location 101:

```
TREEREC.TREENUMB = 56;
FIND FILE (TREE) KEY (TREENUMB);   /*   DML, Section 9.3.2   */
              /*   Required record is CRU and current of TREE   */
TREEREC.LOC = 101;
MODIFY FIELD (TREE.LOC);
          /*   Corresponding data-base record updated, current of TREE set to null   */
```

b. TREE 56 is being moved from forest 'XFOR' to forest 'YFOR'; the new location of the tree in 'YFOR' is 201. We wish to update the data base to reflect these changes.
    We can see that the FOR_TREE membership of the TREE record is going to be affected. We could also use a sequence of **DISCONNECT**, **MODIFY**, and **CONNECT** commands here (see the example in Section 10.2.4). However, we can manage with a single **MODIFY** command.

```
TREEREC.TREENUMB = 56;
FIND FILE (TREE) KEY (TREENUMB);   /*   DML, Section 9.3.2   */
              /*   Required record is CRU, and current of TREE   */
TREEREC.FOREST = 'YFOR';   /*   New connection field   */
TREEREC.LOC = 201;
MODIFY FIELD (TREE.FOREST, TREE.LOC);
/*   1. Corresponding data-base record altered
     2. Record placed in new FOR_TREE set occurrence
     3. Current of FOR_TREE set to null   */
```

10.2.3 The RECONNECT Command

The RECONNECT command updates a record's set-occurrence membership for one or more specified sets in which it participates. The record affected is the CRU or current of file, and the new set occurrences into which it is coupled are selected by means of SET SELECTION as specified in the subschema. Recursive sets may be handled by the proposal in (f) of semantics statement 3. The command is not used with value based sets.

1. *PL/1 syntax*

$$\underline{\text{RECONNECT}} \quad \left[\begin{array}{l} \underline{\text{CF}} \ (\textit{file-name}) \\ \underline{\text{CRU}} \ (\textit{file-name}) \end{array} \right] \ \underline{\text{TO}} \ \underline{\text{SS}} \ (\textit{set-name-1} \ [, \ \textit{set-name-2}] \ ...);$$

2. *Command examples*

   RECONNECT TO SS(TREE_MEAS)
   RECONNECT CRU (MEASUREMENT) TO SS(TREE_MEAS)

3. *Semantics*

   a. If **CF** is specified, it is the current of the file specified that is affected, otherwise it is the CRU.

   b. For each set referenced in the command, the record is effectively uncoupled from the set occurrence in which it occurs and then coupled to a new set occurrence in accordance with the set-ordering criteria.

   c. For each set referenced, the new set occurrence is that selected in accordance with the **SET SELECTION (SS)** specification in the schema or subschema, and required UWA values must be initialized accordingly.

   d. For a referenced set with **FIXED** retention class, **SET SELECTION** must select the same set occurrence as that in which the record is currently a member.

   e. The execution of a **RECONNECT** command makes the record affected the CRU, and if the current of set indicator for a referenced set identifies the record affected, it will be set to null.

   f. For recursive sets, when set selection involves the current of set, **CS_OWN** or **CS_MEM** should be specified in the **SET SELECTION** clause.[1]

4. *Contextual example*

   If we suppose set **TREE_MEAS** is **MANDATORY**, change the **TREE_MEAS** set occurrence for measurement 100 to that owned by tree 1000.

   TREEREC.TREENUMB = 1000; /* Owner key ready for SET SELECTION */
   MEASREC.MEASNUMB = 100;
   FIND FILE (MEASUREMENT) KEY (MEASNUMB); /* DML, Section 9.3.2 */
   RECONNECT CRU (MEASUREMENT) TO SS (TREE_MEAS);
   /* Current of set TREE_MEAS set to null */

---

[1] *The current of set for which the CRS is the owner (that is,* **CS_OWN***) could be assumed by default, no syntax extension of the* **SET SELECTION** *clause being required.*

10.2.4 The DISCONNECT Command

The DISCONNECT command is used to uncouple a member record from one or more set occurrences. The record being uncoupled must be the CRU or current of file. Since this record is uncoupled from a set occurrence identified by a record, we must give recursive sets special consideration. Fortunately, no special syntactic extensions are required.

1. *PL/1 syntax*

$$\text{DISCONNECT} \left[\begin{array}{l} \underline{\text{CF}}\ (\textit{file-name}) \\ \underline{\text{CRU}}\ (\textit{file name}) \end{array} \right] \underline{\text{FROM SETS}}$$

$$(\left\{ \begin{array}{l} \textit{set-name-1}\ [,\ \textit{set-name-2}] \dots \\ \underline{\text{ALL}} \end{array} \right\});$$

2. *Command examples*

   DISCONNECT CRU (TREE) FROM SETS (FOR_TREE);
   DISCONNECT FROM SETS (ALL);

3. *Semantics*

   a. If **CF** is specified, the current of the file specified is to be uncoupled, otherwise it is the CRU.

   b. The sets from which the record is to be uncoupled are specified using the set-name identifiers. If **ALL** is specified, the record is to be uncoupled from all sets for which it is a member record.

   c. For a set so specified, the set occurrence required is identified by the record being uncoupled. For recursive sets, this record points to two set occurrences, and we propose that the one used be that for which this record is a member record.

   d. A record can be uncoupled only from a set that has the **OPTIONAL** retention class.

   e. Following the execution of the command, the record uncoupled becomes the CRU, and for each set from which the record has been uncoupled, the current of set indicator is set to null, if it identified the record affected.

4. *Contextual example*

   We can repeat (b) of contextual example 4 from Section 10.2.2 (MODIFY), in which we have to move tree 56 in 'XFOR' to location 201 in 'YFOR'. This time we uncouple the record for tree 56 from FOR_TREE, update it using the MODIFY command, then couple it to the set occurrence containing the records for trees in the forest 'YFOR'.

   TREEREC.TREENUMB = 56;
   FIND FILE (TREE) KEY (TREENUMB); /* DML, Section 9.3.2 */
                    /* Required record is CRU and current of TREE */
   DISCONNECT CRU (TREE) FROM SETS (FOR_TREE);
   TREEREC.FOREST = 'YFOR'; /* Connection field updating */
   TREEREC.LOC = 201;

MODIFY FIELD (TREE.FOREST, TREE.LOC);
/*   Modified record in data base but not
coupled to any set   */
KEEP DB_KEY (TREE) IN (TREEKEEP);
/*   DML, Section 10.1.10; record needed later   */
FIND FILE (FORFILE) KEY (TREEREC.FOREST);   /*   DML, Secton 9.3.2   */
/*   New FORFILE owner is now CRU and CRS FORFILE   */
FIND CURRENT (TREEKEEP);
/*   DML, Section 10.1.11; TREE record again CRU   */
CONNECT CRU (TREE) TO CS (FOR_TREE);   /*   DML, Section 9.3.5   */

10.2.5 The ERASE Command

The ERASE command is used to delete records from the data base. The semantics of the command are complicated by the consequences of deleting a record which is the owner of a set occurrence.

1.   *PL/1 syntax*

2.   *Command examples*

ERASE FILE (TREE);
ERASE ALL FILE (FORFILE);

3.   *Semantics*

   a.   If **CF** is specified, the record affected (the object record) is the current of the file specified, otherwise it is the CRU.

   b.   When **ALL** is omitted and if the object record has members, the object record is erased if the members have **FIXED** or **OPTIONAL** membership. **FIXED** members are also erased, while **OPTIONAL** members are disconnected.

   c.   When **ALL** is specified, the object record is erased. Furthermore, regardless of set retention class, all member records for which the object record is the owner are also erased.

   d.   Members of erased members are erased except if **ALL** is omitted, when Rule b then applies to such members as well as to the object record.

   e.   Currency indicators identifying an erased record are set to null, as is that for a set occurrence whose owner has been erased.

4.   *Contextual examples*

   a.   Measurement 78 on tree 56 is unreliable and is to be deleted.

      TREEREC.TREENUMB = 56;
      FIND FILE (TREE) KEY (TREENUMB);   /*   DML, Section 9.3.2   */

```
                    /*   Check that MEASUREMENT 78 is for TREE 56   */
          FIND FILE (MEASUREMENT) IN CS (TREE_MEAS)
                    WHERE (MEASNUMB = 78);   /*   DML, Section 10.1.6   */
          IF DB_STATUS = '0000000'   /*   No problems   */
                    THEN ERASE CRU (MEASUREMENT);
```

b. A forest fire has wiped out forest 'YFOR'. All trees propagated from trees from 'YFOR' forest are no longer of interest to the experimental program, nor are measurements on these propagated trees or the trees that were in 'YFOR'. The relevant records are to be deleted.

```
          FORREC.FOREST = 'YFOR';
          FIND FILE (FORFILE) KEY (FOREST);   /*   DML, Section 9.3.2   */
          ERASE ALL CRU (FORFILE);
                    /*   FORFILE record deleted.
                         Its TREE members in FOR_TREE set also deleted. Their TREE
                         members in PROPAGATE set also deleted, their TREE members
                         in PROPAGATE deleted, and so on, recursively.
                         Measurement records in all TREE_MEAS occurrences for which
                         owner TREE has been deleted are also deleted   */
```

It should be clear from this last example that the **ERASE ALL** command can delete a very large part of a data base. (However, the above program would require a subschema covering **FORFILE, TREE, MEASUREMENT, FOR_TREE, PROPAGATE,** and **TREE_MEAS.**) It should be used with great care.

10.3 RETRIEVALS WITH THE CODASYL DML

A common function of data-base application programs is the retrieval of data from a data base. In many cases these retrievals are of a relatively simple nature, of the kind used to illustrate DML commands in previous subsections.

However, in some cases the retrievals are complex and involve a great many file accesses. In such cases the application program (or programmer) is said to *navigate* through the data base from one file to another and from one record to another, by means of set occurrences. Such programs can be called *navigational* programs and form the basis for complex retrievals with the present CODASYL DML [Bachman, 1973].

It is difficult to classify retrievals in general,[1] but for expositional purposes we find it useful to distinguish between those involving nonrecursive sets and those involving recursive sets. Because complex retrievals can involve many accesses of the files involved, it is important that the number of them be kept to a minimum. As we shall see in Chapter 12, an important contribution can be made here by a low average search length for the files, brought about by a proper internal level data-base design.

---

[1]*A classification system is used in Chapter 11.*

It is in the design of the retrieval routine that a very large contribution can be made to system performance. For any required retrieval, there are normally many different methods that can be used, all equally good as far as the end result is concerned but varying widely in the number of file accesses required. It is thus necessary to consider the different ways a retrieval could be carried out and to select that which is most likely to minimize the number of file accesses. Only then should coding of the retrieval begin (we assume a production environment where a retrieval program can expect a long lifetime).

For each retrieval discussed in the following sections, we first analyze it and describe competing alternatives. We then select and code what appears to be the most efficient method as far as minimizing file accesses is concerned. In the programs, we use PL/1 DML commands. Following each command is a short comment referencing the number of the section in which the command is discussed. The COBOL alternative is given in Appendix 2.

10.3.1 Retrievals with Nonrecursive Sets

Retrieval 1

Request   **Find the species names and their maximum heights for trees in forests owned by company 'C'.**

Analysis   Refer to Figure 9.2. There are two basic methods for carrying out the retrieval.

1. Process FORFILE sequentially, selecting records for forests owned by company 'C'. For each such selected FORFILE record, process the member TREE records of FOR_TREE set.

   For each TREE record retrieved, take the SPECFILE owner record in SPEC_TREE set.

   For each such SPECFILE record retrieved, select the SPECIES and MAXHT field values.

2. Process SPECFILE sequentially, selecting each record in turn. For each such SPECFILE record, take each of the member TREE records in the current SPEC_TREE set occurrence.

   For each such TREE record, take the FORFILE owner record.

   If this FORFILE owner record has COMPANY field value C, then take SPECIES and MAXHT values from current SPECFILE record.

   Retrieve next SPECFILE record, and so on.

From the foregoing, it is clear that we need the files SPECFILE, TREE, and FORFILE, as well as the sets FOR_TREE and SPEC_TREE, so that the retrieval program can use the subschema TOP_FORESTRY.

The choice of method here will clearly hinge on which of the two methods will access the most TREE records, for there must be far more TREE records than either SPECFILE or FORFILE records. In the first method, only some of the FOR_TREE set occurrences are processed; in the second method, all of the SPEC_TREE occurrences are processed.

The first method appears to be more efficient, and we therefore select it. However, in case of doubt—and where performance is critical—testing may be necessary.

Program   A closer examination of Method 1 reveals that duplicate SPECIES values are likely to be retrieved. Since we do not want to print out duplicate values, the species values will have to be stored in an array XSPECIES, to which duplicate values are not assigned.

A not insignificant programming problem is the number of elements there should be in XSPECIES: we must also decide whether there should be an overflow array, in case there are more retrievals than XSPECIES can hold. We ignore these considerations in the following program and assume that (for instance) 100 elements will be sufficient.

```
R1: PROC OPTIONS (MAIN);

            /*   UWA declarations for TOP_FORESTRY subschema here   */

DCL DB_STATUS CHAR (7) EXTERNAL;  /*   Special register   */
DCL XSPECIES (100) CHAR (20) INIT((100)(1)");   /*   Holds results   */
DCL XCOMPANY CHAR (20);  /*   Holds search parameter   */
DCL (BEOF, LOGICAL, CHECK) BIT (1);  /*   Logical variables   */
DCL (M, N, P) FIXED BIN (31);  /*   For scanning   */
ERROR: PROC;
    PUT SKIP DATA (DB_STATUS, SPECREC, FORREC, TREEREC);
    STOP; END;
READY FILE (FORFILE, TREE, SPECFILE) RETRIEVAL;  /*   DML, Section 9.3.1   */

            /*   FORFILE now processed sequentially in data-base key order   */

GET LIST (XCOMPANY);  /*   Read in search parameter 'C'   */
N = 1; BEOF = '1'B;
DO WHILE (BEOF);
    FIND FILE (FORFILE) DB_KEYSEQ (N);  /*   DML, Section 10.1.3   */
    IF DB_STATUS = '0502400'  /*   Endfile   */   THEN BEOF = '0'B;
    ELSE DO;
        IF DB_STATUS ¬ = '0000000' THEN CALL ERROR;  /*   Stop, abnormal
                                                          completion   */
                            ELSE;
        GET CRU (FORFILE) INTO (FORREC);  /*   DML, Section 9.3.4   */
                        /*   Nth FORFILE record in UWA   */
        IF XCOMPANY = FORREC.COMPANY THEN DO;

            /*   Search member TREE records of this FORFILE record's FOR_TREE set
                occurrence   */

            M = 1; LOGICAL = '1'B;
            DO WHILE (LOGICAL);
```

```
                                    /*   Retrieval of FOR_TREE member records   */
          FIND FILE (TREE) IN CS (FOR_TREE) MEMBER (M);   /*   DML, Section
                                                          10.1.5   */
          IF DB_STATUS = '0502400' THEN LOGICAL = '0'B;   /*   End of set   */
          ELSE DO;
               IF DB_STATUS ¬ = '0000000' THEN CALL ERROR;   /*   Stop   */
                                    ELSE;
               /*   Let us now examine the SPECIES value in this TREE record   */
               GET CRU (TREE) INTO (TREEREC);   /*   DML, Section 9.3.4   */
                    /*   Before accessing the owner of this TREE record in SPECFILE, we
                    can determine beforehand if this is necessary, by checking to see if the
                    SPECIES value in question is already in the array XSPECIES containing
                    SPECIES values already retrieved   */

               P = 1; CHECK = '1'B;
               DO WHILE ((XSPECIES(P) ¬ = ' ') & (CHECK = '1'B));
                    /*   We loop through results array as long as (not last entry) and
                    (duplicate not found)   */
                    IF XSPECIES(P) = TREEREC.SPECIES THEN CHECK = '0'B;
                    P = P + 1;
               END;   /*   If CHECK is false there is a duplicate   */

               IF CHECK = '1'B THEN DO;   /*   Assuming no duplicate SPECIES
                                           value   */
                    /*   Retrieve owner in SPECFILE   */
                    FIND FILE (SPECFILE) OWNER IN CS (SPEC_TREE);
                                                  /*   DML, Section 10.1.8   */
                    GET CRU (SPECFILE) INTO (SPECREC);   /*   DML, Section
                                                         9.3.4   */
                    /*   Add SPECIES value to results array XSPECIES   */
                    XSPECIES(P) = SPECREC.SPECIES;
                    PUT SKIP DATA (SPECREC.SPECIES, MAXHT);
                    IF P = 100 THEN DO;   /*   Results array full   */
                         PUT SKIP (2) LIST (N, 'RESULTS ARRAY FULL');
                         STOP; END;
               END;
               M = M + 1;
          END;
     END;   /*   End of searching FOR_TREE occurrence   */
     END;
     N = N + 1;
  END;
END;   /*   End of searching FORFILE records   */
END;   /*   End of program   */
```

Navigational programs can be tricky to write. We must always check with DB_STA-TUS after each DML command and arrange for appropriate action. In a few cases in the above program (with GET and FIND . . . OWNER) we have omitted the action to be taken in order to make the program more readable. This action would involve calling up ERROR if DB_STATUS indicated trouble. In addition we must watch out for the values in the DBMS currency table. New FIND commands can wipe out currency values essential for processing major file or set occurrence loops initiated earlier. In the next retrieval example, we are forced to use the RETAIN clause to maintain desired currency values.

Another consideration concerns the effect on performance of the choice of DML commands, especially FIND commands, which in practice means the effect on the number of file accesses carried out by DBCS. In the program, we chose to go through the file FORFILE sequentially in data-base key order using the command

FIND FILE (FORFILE) DB_KEYSEQ (N);

where N is incremented each time the command is executed. Each execution should result in one (or very close to one) access of the storage file FORFILE (assuming it is physically implemented as one storage file, and not two) for each block of FORFILE records retrieved.

Alternatively, we could have used the sequential FIND command

FIND NEXT FILE (FORFILE) WHERE (COMPANY = XCOMPANY); /* DML, Section 10.1.2 */

Each execution of the command would extract a required record, but the whole file would probably still be processed. We would have to consult the data-base administrator responsible for the storage data base to find out whether this command would be just as efficient in this case. If FORFILE were implemented as a hash or ISAM file, it would probably be less efficient, but if it were implemented as a VSAM file, it might well be somewhat more efficient (see Chapters 3 and 4).

Another alternative is to use a system set SYS_FOR with FORFILE. We could then use the set scan duplicate target FIND command:

FIND FILE (FORFILE) DUPLICATE IN CS (SYS_FOR)
                WHERE (COMPANY = XCOMPANY); /* DML, Section 10.1.7 */

dispensing with the scanning variable N. Each execution would extract a FORFILE record with the required company value. We would again need to consult the data-base administrator to find out if this command would be more efficient. It is indeed probable that a sequential search of FORFILE would still be carried out, this time by the DBCS, so that nothing would be gained. On the other hand, the SYS_FOR set may have been implemented with an index for the field COMPANY, so that a required FORFILE record could be extracted in a few accesses, giving rise to a large increase in performance. Such an index would be equivalent to an inversion of FORFILE on COMPANY (see Chapters 5 and 12).

From these considerations, it should be clear that while changes to the internal or

---

storage level data-base schema will not impair a program's ability to run (physical data independence), such changes can drastically affect a program's performance.

Retrieval 2

Request **Find the forest records for forests that do not have species 'X' but do have species 'Y'.**

Analysis   Refer again to Figure 9.2. As with the previous example, we can identify two promising methods for carrying out the retrieval.

1. Process the FORFILE file sequentially, selecting each record in turn. For each FORFILE record, investigate the member TREE records in FOR_TREE set. If at least one member TREE record has SPECIES value 'Y' and none have SPECIES value 'X', then select the FORFILE record for output.

2. Retrieve the SPECFILE record for key SPECIES value 'Y'.

    Examine the member TREE records in the SPEC_TREE set occurrence owned by this SPECFILE record, taking each TREE record in turn.

    For each TREE record so retrieved, take the FORFILE owner record in set FOR_TREE.

    Examine all the TREE member records of this FORFILE owner record. If none of them have SPECIES value 'X', then select the FORFILE owner record for output.

The first method is certainly the simplest to grasp. However, it involves processing all the FORFILE records and all their TREE member records. Thus it involves processing all the TREE records as well. It may thus be considered a method of brute force.

The second method involves processing no more FORFILE records than there are TREE members in the SPEC_TREE set occurrence. For these limited FORFILE records, we then process the TREE member records in set FOR_TREE. We thus process a small fraction of the FORFILE records and a small fraction of the TREE records.

We see again that the subschema TOP_FORESTRY may be used with the application program.

Program   The currencies in the following program are not easy to keep track of, but the problems involved are typical of those encountered in complex retrievals. To illustrate more clearly, in Figure 10.2 we have a diagram for the SPEC_TREE set occurrence owned by the SPECFILE record for species Y. We call this record S(Y), and show it as owning the three TREE records T(12), T(13), and T(14). We also show that FORFILE record F(80), which owns T(12) and which also owns T(10) and T(15) in the set FOR_TREE.

In the processing we first access S(Y) and then its first member T(12). We then find the owner of T(12) in FOR_TREE, that is, F(80). We then go through the members of F(80) in FOR_TREE—that is, T(10), T(12), and T(15)—to determine if any of them have a SPECIES value 'X'. If not, F(80) is printed out.

Then, going back to the set SPEC_TREE, we move to the next SPEC_TREE member

---

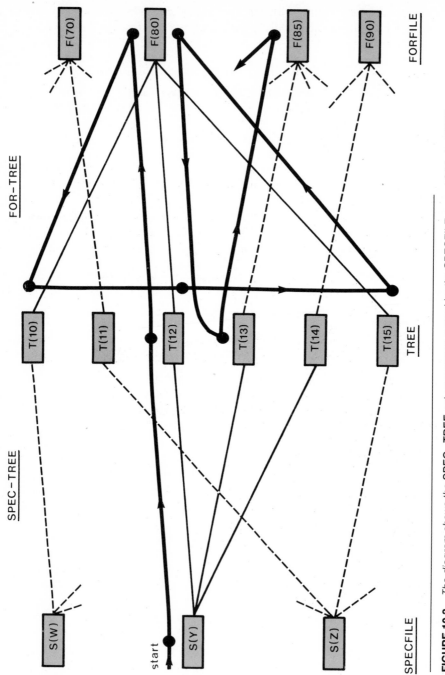

FIGURE 10.2. *The diagram shows the SPEC—TREE set occurrence owned by the SPECFILE record S(Y); its TREE members are T(12), T(13), and T(14). T(12) is also a member record in a FOR_TREE set occurrence owned by the FORFILE record F(80). The FOR_TREE members owned by F(80) are T(10), T(12), and T(15). The solid line with arrows shows the navigational route taken by the retrieval program R2 through the data base. The circles give the sequence of CRUs. Refer to the user currency tables in Figure 9.7. Note that the navigational route taken assumes that F(80) satisfies the retrieval conditions.*

T(13) and repeat as before; that is, find its FORFILE owner and investigate their TREE members for a SPECIES value 'X'.

In order for the program to navigate correctly through the data base, the currency table must accurately reflect the program's assumed data-base position. Failure to do so will lead to an otherwise correct DML command causing the program to navigate to an incorrect destination. This aspect of CODASYL has been criticized, but there is nothing unusual about it. It is merely an aspect of any situation in which navigation is required. A ship can hardly be expected to reach the correct destination if its otherwise competent navigator has faulty information as to the ship's position.

A useful navigational aid is what is sometimes called a user-currency table. This table is prepared by the programmer and gives the record referenced by each currency indicator following execution of each program DML command.

For the retrieval program below, we shall set up two tables. The first (Figure 10.3a) shows what happens if we forget to include the RETAIN clause (command C4). The second (Figure 10.3b) shows what happens to the routine below with the RETAIN clause included. While the tables can best be understood in association with the program, they may also be understood if the retrieval path shown in Figure 10.2 is examined carefully.

```
R2: PROC OPTIONS (MAIN);

        /*   UWA declarations for TOP_FORESTRY subschema here   */

DCL DB_STATUS CHAR (7) EXTERNAL;    /*   Special register   */
DCL (YESSPECIES,                    /*   Holds 'Y' value   */
       NOSPECIES) CHAR (20);        /*   Holds 'X' value   */
DCL (BEOS, LOGICAL, CHECK) BIT (1); /*   Logical variables   */
DCL (N,M) FIXED BIN (15);           /*   For scanning sets   */


ERROR: PROC;                        /*   Action on abnormal return from DBCS   */
       PUT SKIP DATA
          (DB_STATUS, SPECREC, FORREC, TREEREC);
       STOP;
END;


READY FILE (FORFILE,
              TREE,
              SPECFILE) RETRIEVAL;  /*   DML, Section 9.3.1; DB files ready for
                                         input   */
GET LIST (YESSPECIES, NOSPECIES);   /*   Read in search parameters   */
SPECREC.SPECIES = YESSPECIES;       /*   Search key in UWA   */

C1: FIND FILE (SPECFILE) KEY (SPECREC.SPECIES);  /*   DML, Section 9.3.2   */
      /*   SPECFILE record for species 'Y', that is, S(Y), is CRU and CRS SPEC_TREE   */
      /*   We now scan S(Y)'s member records in SPEC_TREE   */
N = 1; BEOS = '1'B;
```

N M COMMAND	C1	N=1 C2	N=1 C3	N=1 M=1 C4	N=1 M=2 C4	N=1 M=3 C4	N=1 C5	N=2 C2	N=2 C3
CRU	S(Y)	T(12)	F(80)	T(10)	T(12)	T(15)	F(80)	T(11)	F(70)
SPECFILE	S(Y)	S(Y)	S(Y)	S(Y)	S(Y)	S(Y)	S(Y)	S(Y)	S(Y)
TREE	—	T(12)	T(12)	T(10)	T(12)	T(15)	T(15)	T(11)	T(11)
FORFILE	—	—	F(80)	F(80)	F(80)	F(80)	F(80)	F(80)	F(70)
SPEC_TREE	S(Y)	T(12)	T(12)	T(10)	T(12)	T(15)	T(15)	T(11)	T(11)
FOR_TREE	—	T(12)	F(80)	T(10)	T(12)	T(15)	F(80)	T(11)	F(70)

(a) Currency table when **RETAIN** clause in command C4 is omitted. Program starts to go wrong the first time C4 is executed, but the error only becomes serious at the end of the first looping of the inner loop (N = 1, M = 3). From this point onward, it goes completely wrong (underlined).

N M COMMAND	C1	N=1 C2	N=1 C3	N=1 M=1 C4	N=1 M=2 C4	N=1 M=3 C4	N=1 C5	N=2 C2	N=2 C3
CRU	S(Y)	T(12)	F(80)	T(10)	T(12)	T(15)	F(80)	T(13)	F(85)
SPECFILE	S(Y)	S(Y)	S(Y)	S(Y)	S(Y)	S(Y)	S(Y)	S(Y)	S(Y)
TREE	—	T(12)	T(12)	T(10)	T(12)	T(15)	T(15)	T(13)	T(13)
FORFILE	—	—	F(80)	F(80)	F(80)	F(80)	F(80)	F(80)	F(85)
SPEC_TREE	S(Y)	T(12)	T(12)	T(12)	T(12)	T(12)	T(12)	T(13)	T(13)
FOR_TREE	—	T(12)	F(80)	T(10)	T(12)	T(15)	F(80)	T(13)	F(85)

(b) Currency table for correctly executing program R2. The CRU values give the navigational path taken by the program. Refer to Figure 10.2.

FIGURE 10.3.

```
DO WHILE (BEOS);
    C2: FIND FILE (TREE)
        IN CS (SPEC_TREE) MEMBER (N);   /*DML, SECTION 10.1.5   */
    IF DB_STATUS = '0502400' THEN BEOS = '0'B;   /*   End of set   */
    ELSE DO;
        IF DB_STATUS ˥ = '0000000' THEN CALL ERROR;   /*   Abnormal return   */
                            ELSE;

        /*   Now find FORFILE owner of the Nth
        TREE record in this S(Y)'s SPEC_TREE set occurrence   */
    C3: FIND FILE (FORFILE) OWNER
            IN CS (FOR_TREE);   /*   DML, Section 10.1.8   */
        /*   We now find its TREE members in FOR_TREE; prepare to scan current
            FOR_TREE set occurrence   */
    M = 1; LOGICAL = '1'B;
```

```
        CHECK = '1'B;   /*   Stays '1'B unless 'X' value found   */
    DO WHILE (LOGICAL);
        C4: FIND FILE (TREE)
                IN CS (FOR_TREE) MEMBER (M)   /*   DML, Section 10.1.5   */
                RETAIN CURRENCY (SPEC_TREE);   /*   DML, Section 9.5.3   */
        /*   Navigational trap: for example for N = 1, M = 1, without RETAIN clause
             CRS SPEC_TREE becomes T(10), but for N = 1 and M = LAST, CRS
             SPEC_TREE becomes T(15), which is quite wrong. See Figure 10.2   */

        IF DB_STATUS = '0502400' THEN LOGICAL = '0'B;
                                                    /*   End of set   */
    ELSE DO;
        IF DB_STATUS ¬ = '0000000' THEN CALL ERROR;
                                                /*   Abnormal return   */
                            ELSE;

                    /*   We need to examine this TREE record   */
        GET CRU (TREE) INTO (TREEREC);   /*   DML, Section 9.3.4   */
        IF TREEREC.SPECIES = NOSPECIES
        THEN DO;   /*   If record is 'X' species   */
            LOGICAL = '0'B;
            CHECK = '0'B;
        END;
        ELSE M = M + 1;   /*   Proceed with scan   */
    END;
END;                                    /*   End of FOR_TREE scan   */

        /*   Since all of the members of the FORFILE record have now been scanned, if
             CHECK is still '1'B then this forest has at least one species 'Y' but no
             species 'X'. We therefore retrieve the FORFILE record and print it out   */
    IF CHECK THEN DO;                           /*   Forest has no species 'X'   */
        C5: FIND CURRENT (FORFILE);  /*   DML, Section 10.1.11   */
        /*   Current record of FORFILE becomes CRU   */
        GET CRU (FORFILE) INTO (FORREC);
        PUT SKIP LIST (FORREC);
    END;
            ELSE;   /*   Forest has an 'X' species   */
        N = N + 1;                          /*   Proceed with scan of S(Y)'s members   */
    END;
END;                                    /*   Scan of S(Y)'s members completed   */
END;
```

From the user-currency table, we see that the RETAIN clause in FIND command C4 keeps the program from navigating astray. Note that command C4 and the whole FOR_TREE set occurrence scan carried out in the DO WHILE (LOGICAL) loop could be replaced by the set-scan target FIND command (Section 10.1.6); nevertheless, for the same reason we still need the RETAIN clause (see Exercise 13).

10.3.2 Retrievals with Recursive Sets

Retrieval 3

Request **Retrieve all TREE records on which 'ELECTRICAL' measurements have been carried out, and which are descended from tree 56.**

Analysis The descendents of tree 56 are those trees propagated from tree 56, and the trees propagated from these trees, and so on. It is thus clear that the recursive set PROPAGATE is involved. As before, we identify two possible methods.

1. Access the TREE file at tree 56.

    For this tree record, process each TREE member in PROPAGATE in sequential fashion. For each such tree member, do the following.

    Step 1. Search the MEASUREMENT members in TREE_MEAS for an 'ELECTRICAL' value for the field TYPE. If found, print out the TREE record.

    Step 2. Process each TREE record in the next lower level PROPAGATE set occurrence. For each of these TREE records, repeat Steps 1 and 2.

2. Process the TREE file sequentially

    For each TREE record search MEASUREMENT member records for a record with TYPE value equal to 'ELECTRICAL'. If found, select TREE owner record. For such TREE records, progress up PROPAGATE owner chain until the top or last owner is found. If an owner is tree 56, then print out the TREE record.

The second method will clearly require more accesses than the first. In the second method, the whole of the TREE file and a great deal of the MEASUREMENT file will have to be processed. Indeed, some parts of the TREE file have to be processed several times. Since the TREE file can be expected to have more than one record for each record in FORFILE, we can only conclude that it will be large. Similarly, MEASUREMENT is likely to be even larger than TREE.

We therefore select the first method, which involves processing a limited number of TREE records with their MEASUREMENT member records. We note that the routine is recursive. This is unavoidable, since we have no way of knowing the structure of a hierarchy of set occurrences in PROPAGATE. In Figure 10.4, we show a *typical* hierarchical structure for PROPAGATE recursive set occurrences.

Program In the following retrieval program, we make extensive use of the recursive procedure SETSCAN. Since SETSCAN is recursive, it can call another and nested version of SETSCAN, which can in turn call another nested version, and so on. We first make TREE 56 the CRU. We then call SETSCAN, which goes through the TREE members of TREE 56. For each TREE record so processed, a nested version of SETSCAN is called that processes the TREE member records of that TREE record. This process is continued with further recursive SETSCAN calls until the bottom of the structure is reached. The program should thus function regardless of the structure of the PROPAGATE hierarchy.

In the program we need the files TREE and MEASUREMENT, and the sets PROPAGATE and TREE_MEAS. Thus we can use the BOT_FORESTRY subschema. Again it is not

---

MANIPULATING THE CODASYL DATA BASE

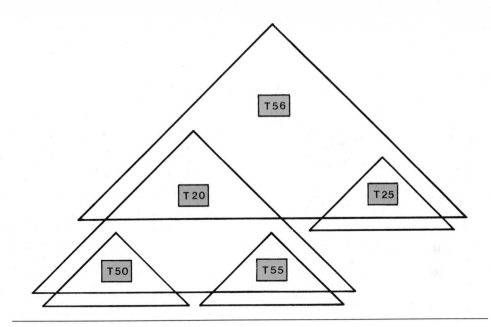

FIGURE 10.4. *Hierarchy formed by the descendants of tree 56 and investigated by the retrieval program R3. The currency table for the above hierarchy is given in Figure 10.5, in which the CRU values give the navigational path taken by the program through the hierarchy. Note there are five PROPAGATE set occurrences in the above hierarchy.*

easy to keep track of the currencies, and the reader is urged to examine the currency table in Figure 10.5, constructed for the hierarchy in Figure 10.4.

```
R3: PROC OPTIONS (MAIN);

              /*   UWA declarations for BOT_FORESTRY subschema here   */

DCL DB_STATUS CHAR (7);                                /*   Special register   */
DCL XNUMB FIXED BIN (31);                    /*   Holds target TREENUMB value   */
READY RETRIEVAL;                          /*   BOT_FORESTRY ready for input   */
GET LIST (XNUMB);                            /*   We read in TREE number 56   */
FIND FILE (TREE) KEY (XNUMB);        /*   TREE 56 is CRU and CRS PROPAGATE   */
                                                   /*   DML, Section 9.3.2   */


CALL SETSCAN;   /*   SETSCAN retrieves all the acceptable descendants and prints them
                   out   */
                   /*   End of main procedure   */


SETSCAN: PROCEDURE RECURSIVE;
```

RECURSION NEST LEVEL		01		02		03				01		01	
DML COMMAND	Entry (R3)	C1a	C3	C1a	C3	C1a	C1b	C3	C1a	C2	C1b	C3	C1a	C2
CRU	T56	T20	T20	T50	T50	T50	T55	T55	T55	T20	T25	T25	T25	T56
Current of TREE	T56	T20	T20	T50	T50	T50	T55	T55	T55	T20	T25	T25	T25	T56
Current Record of PROPAGATE	T56	T20	T20	T50	T50	T50	T55	T55	T55	T20	T25	T25	T25	T56

FIGURE 10.5. *Currency table for the recursive routine SETSCAN embedded in the retrieval program* **R3.** *The descendants of tree 56 (as shown in Figure 10.4) are being investigated.*

```
DCL N FIXED BIN (15);                              /*  For scanning  */
DCL (CHECK,
     BEOS) BIT (1);                                /*  Logical variables  */
DCL 1 XTREEREC LIKE TREEREC;                        /*  Holds TREE record  */

ERROR: PROC;                                        /*  For abnormal returns  */
    GET CRU (TREE) INTO (XTREEREC);
    GET CRU (MEASUREMENT) INTO (MEASREC);           /*  DML, Section 9.3.4  */
    PUT SKIP DATA
        (DB_STATUS, TREEREC, MEASREC);
    STOP;
END;

              /*  We now go through the members of the CRU TREE record  */

N = 1; BEOS = '1'B;
DO WHILE (BEOS);
    C1: IF N = 1
    THEN                                            /*  First member  */
    FIND FILE (TREE) IN CS_OWN (PROPAGATE)          /*  C1a  */
                        MEMBER (FIRST);
    ELSE                                            /*  Other member  */
    FIND FILE (TREE) IN CS_MEM (PROPAGATE)          /*  C1b  */
                        MEMBER (N);       /*  DML, Section 10.1.5  */
              /*  Notice use of CS_OWN and CS_MEM  */
```

/*   There are two possibilities.

   a. There are no members left, in which case we return from this version of SETSCAN, making certain before we leave that the TREE owner of the set occurrence being investigated is the CRU.

b. There is a member left, in which case we investigate its MEASUREMENT member records and then call a nested version of SETSCAN to investigate its TREE members   */

```
IF DB_STATUS = '0502400' THEN DO;   /*  (a) No members left   */
    BEOS = '0'B;                                       /*  No more looping   */
    C2: IF N > 1                       /*  If owner of set being scanned is not CRU   */
    THEN FIND FILE (TREE) OWNER
                         IN CS_MEM (PROPAGATE);   /*  DML, Section 10.1.8   */
END;

ELSE DO;                                              /*  (b) There is a member left   */
    IF DB_STATUS ⌐ = '0000000' THEN CALL ERROR;   /*  Abnormal return   */
                                    ELSE;
    /*  Now we check current TREE's members in TREE_MEAS set   */
    FIND FILE (MEASUREMENT) IN CS (TREE_MEAS)
              WHERE (TYPE = 'ELECTRICAL');   /*  DML, Section 10.1.7   */
        /*  The above command scans the members looking for an electrical
        measurement   */
    IF DB_STATUS = '0502400' THEN CHECK = '0'B;
                         /*  No such member found   */
    ELSE IF DB_STATUS = '0000000' THEN CHECK = '1'B;
                         /*  Electrical measurement found   */
                                    ELSE CALL ERROR;
    IF CHECK = '1'B THEN DO;   /*  Current TREE record should be retrieved   */
            C3: FIND CURRENT TREE;   /*  Current TREE becomes CRU; DML, Section
                           10.1.11   */
            GET CRU (TREE) INTO (XTREEREC);   /*  DML, Section 9.3.4   */
            PUT SKIP LIST (XTREEREC);
    END;
        /*  Regardless of whether or not current TREE record had electrical
        measurements, we must now investigate its PROPAGATE members   */
    CALL SETSCAN;   /*  Looks after lower level processing   */
    N = N + 1;
    END;
END;                                    /*  End of scanning current PROPAGATE
                                        set   */

END;                                    /*  End of SETSCAN   */
END;                                    /*  End of R3   */
```

As explained in the previous chapter, at the time of writing the capability of manipulating recursive owner-coupled sets has not been included in the CODASYL DML. However, as we saw in Chapter 6, such conceptual structures may be replaced by nonrecursive sets and an extra file LINK, which does not necessarily have to have any data fields.

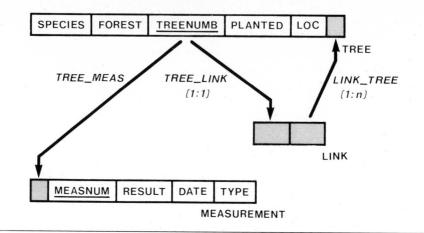

SPECIES | FOREST | TREENUMB | PLANTED | LOC

TREE

TREE_MEAS

TREE_LINK
(1:1)

LINK_TREE
(1:n)

LINK

MEASNUM | RESULT | DATE | TYPE

MEASUREMENT

FIGURE 10.6. *Extended Bachman diagram for a new version of the* **BOT_FORESTRY** *subschema, in which we replace the recursive set* **PROPAGATE** *by the file* **LINK** *(without conceptual fields) and the two sets* **TREE_LINK** *and* **LINK_TREE**. *None of the sets in the diagram are value based.*

Figure 10.6 shows a diagram of a second conceptual data base for that part of the FORESTRY data base covered by the BOT_FORESTRY external schema. Here we have the auxiliary file LINK, without fields, and the owner-coupled sets LINK_TREE and TREE_LINK. Figure 10.7 shows the hierarchy of descendants of tree 56, this time using LINK records instead of recursive sets as in Figure 10.4. Note that TREE_LINK embodies a 1:1 relationship. The situation is clearly more complex than with the recursive set PROPAGATE.

Let us now assume that we have a subschema to cover this conceptual data base, with TREEREC and MEASREC capable of holding TREE and MEASUREMENT records, as with the BOT_FORESTRY subschema. If we now attempt the above retrieval with this data base, we need only modify the recursive procedure SETSCAN. The basic structure of SETSCAN is little changed, as is the basic navigational path taken through the data base. We could have the following procedure (omitting ERROR for brevity).

SETSCAN: PROC RECURSIVE;

```
DCL N FIXED BIT (31);            /*  For scanning   */
DCL (CHECK, BEOF) BIT (1)        /*  Logical variables   */
DCL 1 XTREEREC LIKE TREEREC;     /*  Holds TREE record   */

       /*  We now find the LINK record belonging to the CRU TREE and scan through this
              LINK record's TREE member records   */

C1: FIND FILE (LINK) IN CS (TREE_LINK)
                  MEMBER (FIRST);   /*  DML, Section 10.1.5   */
```

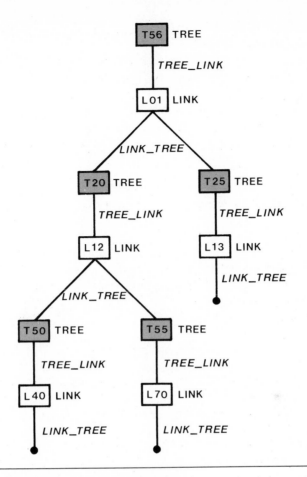

FIGURE 10.7. *Sample hierarchy formed by* **TREE** *and*
LINK *records in the sets* **TREE_LINK** *and* **LINK_TREE**.
*The hierarchy gives the trees descended from tree 56. The
path taken by procedure* **R3** *through this hierarchy can be
traced from the CRU values in the currency table in Figure
10.8. This diagram should be contrasted with that in Figure
10.4.*

```
N = 1; BEOF = '1'B;
DO WHILE (BEOF);   /*   We search a LINK_TREE set occurrence   */
    C2:
    FIND FILE (TREE) in CS (LINK_TREE) MEMBER (N)   /*   DML, Section 10.1.5   */
```

/*   As with previous version, we have now two courses open.
  a. There are no members left, in which case we return from this version of SETSCAN,
     making sure that the TREE owner of the current LINK record is CRU   */
  b. There is a member left, in which case we investigate its MEASUREMENT member
     records, and then call SETSCAN to investigate the descendant TREE records   */

```
IF DB_STATUS = '0502400' THEN DO   /*   Course (a), no more members   */
    BEOF = '0'B;                              /*   No more looping   */
    C3a: FIND FILE (LINK) OWNER IN CS (LINK_TREE);
    C3b: FIND FILE (TREE) OWNER IS CS (TREE_LINK);   /*   DML, Section
                                                          10.1.8   */
    /*   We use these commands to establish the TREE owner of the LINK record, that
    owns the LINK_TREE set occurrence being processed, as CRU and CRS LINK_
    TREE, in preparation for return to an outer SETSCAN version   */

END;
ELSE DO;                                        /*   (b) There is a member left   */
    IF DB_STATUS ⌐ = '0000000' THEN CALL ERROR;
                                    ELSE;

    /*   Now we check this TREE's members in TREE_MEAS   */
    FIND FILE (MEASUREMENT) IN CS (TREE_MEAS)
              WHERE (TYPE = 'ELECTRICAL');   /*   DML, Section 10.1.7   */
    IF DB_STATUS = '0502400'
    THEN CHECK = '0'B;
                          /*   No such member found   */
    ELSE IF DB_STATUS = '0000000' THEN CHECK = '1'B;
                          /*   Electrical measurement found   */
                              ELSE CALL ERROR;
    IF CHECK = '1'B THEN DO;   /*   Current TREE record should be retrieved   */
        C4: FIND CURRENT TREE;   /*   Current TREE becomes CRU; DML, Section
                                      10.1.11   */
        GET CRU (TREE) INTO (XTREEREC);
        PUT SKIP LIST (XTREEREC);
    END;
    /*   We now investigate this TREE's LINK record and its members by calling a nested
    version of SETSCAN   */
    CALL SETSCAN;
    N = N + 1;
END;
END;                              /*   End of scanning at this level   */
END;                              /*   End of SETSCAN   */
```

It is worth pointing out that it is in fact much simpler to write SETSCAN using the recursive set PROPAGATE. When the LINK file is used, the currency situation is not at all simple, and there are more currencies of which we must keep track.

In Figure 10.8 is a currency table for an investigation of the hierarchy from Figure 10.7. The table is clearly more complex than that in Figure 10.5. If we tried to write either version of SETSCAN without the help of a currency table, however, it is probably fair to state that the chances of doing it correctly are close to zero.

DML COMMAND	Entry (R3)	01			02			03			02	
RECURSION NEST LEVEL		C1	C2	C4	C1	C2	C4	C1	C3a	C3b	C2	C4
CRU	T56	L01	T20	T20	L12	T50	T50	L40	L40	T50	T55	T55
Current of TREE	T56	T56	T20	T20	T20	T50	T50	T50	T50	T50	T55	T55
Current of LINK	—	L01	L01	L01	L12	L12	L12	L40	L40	L40	L40	L40
Current of TREE_LINK	T56	L01	T20	T20	L12	T50	T50	L40	L40	T50	T55	T55
Current of LINK_TREE	—	L01	T20	T20	L12	T50	T50	L40	L40	T50	T55	T55

(continues below)

DML COMMAND	03			02		01		02			01	
RECURSION NEST LEVEL	C1	C3a	C3b	C3a	C3b	C2	C4	C1	C3a	C3b	C3a	C3b
CRU	L70	L70	T55	L12	T20	T25	T25	L13	L13	T25	L01	T56
Current of TREE	T55	T55	T55	T55	T20	T25	T25	T25	T25	T25	T25	T56
Current of LINK	L70	L70	L70	L12	L12	L12	L12	L13	L13	L13	L01	L01
Current of TREE_LINK	L70	L70	T55	L12	T20	T25	T25	L13	L13	T25	L01	T56
Current of LINK_TREE	L70	L70	T55	L12	T20	T25	T25	L13	L13	T25	L01	L01

FIGURE 10.8. *Currency table for the execution of the second version of the recursive procedure* SETSCAN *embedded in the retrieval program* R3. *The hierarchy of* TREE *records being investigated is shown in Figure 10.7. This time the recursive set* PROPAGATE *is not being used.*

10.4 CONCURRENT PROCESSING

This section deals with the situation when two or more run-units are competing for access to the same file or record. It may be omitted on first reading without loss of continuity. It is, nevertheless, an important topic. We may distinguish between two kinds of run-unit, namely *retrieval* run-units and *updating* run-units. As the term implies, in an updating run-unit a file or files have been opened for update, while in a retrieval run-unit, no file is open for update and all files are thus opened only for retrieval.

If we have two or more retrieval run-units executing concurrently, they will not interfere with each other's retrieval of data from the data base. However, if one or more concurrent run-units is an update run-unit, serious interference can occur. As an example of such interference, consider the TOP_FORESTRY subschema. Suppose that we have two run-units R1 and R2 running concurrently, and that each is updating the file FORFILE.

a.   Update for R1: A forest 'THISFOR' of the company 'XCO' has been increased in size to 30 square miles. The FORFILE.SIZE field is to be updated in the FORFILE record with the key value 'THISFOR'.

b.   Update for R2: The name of company 'XCO' has been changed to 'YCO'. The field COMPANY is to be updated in all FORFILE records with field value 'XCO'.

Let us now see what happens when the two programs execute. We assume that the teleprocessing monitor (see Figure 9.3) switches control from one run-unit to another as illustrated below.

R1: Find FORFILE record with key value 'THISFOR'.

R1: GET command used to place retrieved *record* (not just the SIZE field) in the UWA for R1.

R2: Find next FORFILE record with COMPANY field value 'XCO'. This record happens to have key value 'THISFOR'.

R2: GET command places record in the UWA for R2.

R2: 'XCO' changed to 'YCO'.

R2: MODIFY command places updated record back in data base file FORFILE.

R1: SIZE field value changed to 30.

R1: MODIFY command places whole UWA record back in data-base file FORFILE.

We see that R1 has seriously interfered with the updating by R2; as a result, the COMPANY field value 'XCO' is not changed to 'YCO' in the FORFILE record with key value 'THISFOR'. Further processing would probably compound this error.

It is clear that for concurrent processing of the data in a data base, some kind of concurrency control is necessary. This concurrency control is exercised at two different levels in the CODASYL approach, namely, at the file level and at the record level. We shall examine these two control techniques in turn.

10.4.1 File-Level Concurrency Control

The file-level concurrency control to be exercised is specified in the READY command for the file or files involved. We have already dealt with the READY command in Section 9.2.1, but as mentioned then, we did not deal with the aspects of the command involving concurrency control.

We shall start by looking at the full READY command.

1. *PL/1 syntax*

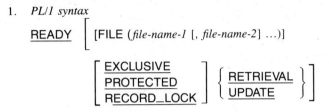

2. *Command examples*

    READY FILE (FORFILE) EXCLUSIVE UPDATE:
    READY RECORD_LOCK UPDATE;

3. *Semantics*

    a. We have a concurrency-control clause that allows us to specify EXCLUSIVE, PRO-TECTED, RECORD_LOCK, or nothing.

    b. Nothing is semantically the same as RECORD_LOCK.[1]

    c. The detailed semantics for these three possible specifications are discussed in the following subsections.

The EXCLUSIVE Option   A run-unit running with the EXCLUSIVE option for a given file prevents any other run-unit from accessing the file involved. Thus as long as this run-unit is running and the file involved is open or "ready," then no other run-unit will be able to have a READY command involving this file executed. Thus there is exclusive control over the file.

However, in order for a run-unit to get EXCLUSIVE control over a file, not only does the READY EXCLUSIVE command have to be issued, but the run-unit will have to wait until all other run-units are finished with the file; that is, until all other run-units have "closed" the file. While we have not discussed it so far, this is the reason for the existence of a command for closing files. In COBOL it is very simple, namely, FINISH *file-name;* a suitable PL/1 version is possibly FINISH FILE *(file-name).* With this command, a run-unit can relinquish control of a file but still continue to process some other file. By so doing, another run-unit could perhaps begin processing the relinquished file.

It is clear that if all run-units used the EXCLUSIVE option, the performance of the

---

[1]*CODASYL COBOL does not use the syntax element RECORD_ LOCK; in COBOL, the option was orignially indicated by specifying nothing. In 1980 it was named SHARED by CODASYL, an inappropriate terminology in the author's opinion.*

system would be greatly reduced. Run-units using the same file would effectively be forced to operate in series instead of concurrently.

The PROTECTED Option   When a run-unit is running in the PROTECTED mode, there may not be any concurrent EXCLUSIVE or update run-units for the file involved. There may be concurrent retrieval run-units, but if the run-unit involved is PROTECTED UPDATE, there may not be a concurrent PROTECTED RETRIEVAL. This is true because it would mean that this second run-unit was running with a concurrent PROTECTED update run-unit, in clear violation of the main rule. Thus a run-unit with this option is protected against updating by other run-units while it is processing a given file. However, this option also reduces system performance.

Consider a file with, for example, 100,000 records, and a PROTECTED run-unit involved in processing at most 10 of them. Only these 10 records, not the whole 100,000, need to be protected against outside updating. The next option permits this refinement.

The RECORD_LOCK Option   The term RECORD_LOCK is unofficial, introduced by the author to describe the case, clearly defined by CODASYL, where neither EXCLUSIVE nor PROTECTED are specified in the COBOL version of the READY command. It is a distinct option and we believe that it is better given a name and specified explicitly, as is proposed with the PL/1 version of the command (see footnote on page 357).

When a run-unit is running in this mode, as we would expect there may be no concurrent EXCLUSIVE run-units. There may be any other run-units, except in the case where the RECORD_LOCK run-unit is also an updating run-unit, in which case there may not be any concurrent PROTECTED run-unit (this is consistent with the properties of the PROTECTED option).

It is thus possible for two RECORD_LOCK run-units to be running concurrently in the UPDATE mode for a given file, and thus run the risk of interfering with each other's data-base activities. However, in the record-lock mode, as the name suggests, it is possible for a run-unit to apply locks to individual records for a period of time and thus prevent their updating by a competing run-unit. This is done by means of the DML KEEP, COMMIT and FREE commands, as we shall see shortly (Section 10.4.2).

Interrelationships between Concurrency-Control Modes   It is instructive to attempt to get an overall view of the situation where several programs are operating concurrently. We can do this with the aid of a concurrency table. An early version of this type of table is given in the 1971 DBTG report [CODASYL, 1971]. In this table we consider two run-units, one which already has control of a file, called the *active run-unit,* and another which is attempting to gain control of a file, called the *inactive run-unit.* We consider what happens to a READY command from the inactive run-unit for different concurrency-mode specifications, in relation to different concurrency-mode specifications issued earlier by the active run-unit. The table is shown in Figure 10.9. If the READY command of the inactive run-unit is accepted by the DBCS, a "YES" appears in the table; otherwise a "NO" appears.

INACTIVE RUN-UNIT'S READY REQUEST		ACTIVE RUN-UNIT's USAGE MODE					
		EXCLUSIVE		PROTECTED		RECORD_LOCK	
		UPDATE	RETRIEVAL	UPDATE	RETRIEVAL	UPDATE	RETRIEVAL
EXCLUSIVE	RETRIEVAL	NO	NO	NO	NO	NO	NO
EXCLUSIVE	UPDATE	NO	NO	NO	NO	NO	NO
PROTECTED	RETRIEVAL	NO	NO	YES	YES	NO	YES
PROTECTED	UPDATE	NO	NO	NO	NO	NO	YES
RECORD_LOCK	RETRIEVAL	NO	NO	YES	YES	YES	YES
RECORD_LOCK	UPDATE	NO	NO	YES	NO	YES	YES

FIGURE 10.9. *File-level concurrency table for active/inactive run-units. The active run-unit has control of a file and the inactive run-unit issues a READY command to attempt to gain control of it. The result is a "YES" or "NO", depending on the usage mode of the active run-unit and that specified in the READY command issued by the inactive run-unit.*

Deadlock   If there are two run-units A and B, each of which has to get control of two files F1 and F2, and if one of the run-units has either the EXCLUSIVE or PROTECTED mode, then we have a chance of a *deadlock* developing.

Deadlock occurs when each of two run-units cannot run because each is waiting on the other to relinquish control of a file. Thus if A first gets control of F1 and then B gets control of F2, when A subsequently attempts to get control of F2, this is denied until B relinquishes F2. Then B tries to get control of F1, but this is also denied until A relinquishes F1. We could have coded in the two run-units

```
run-unit A:    READY FILE (F1) PROTECTED UPDATE;  /*   Granted   */
run-unit B:    READY FILE (F2) PROTECTED RETRIEVAL;  /*   Granted   */
run-unit A:    READY FILE (F2) PROTECTED UPDATE;
                              /*   Denied; program enters wait state   */
run-unit B:    READY FILE (F1) PROTECTED RETRIEVAL;
                              /*   Denied; program enters wait state   */
```

A simple solution to the problem lies in prohibiting multiple READY commands. Thus if the above code had been replaced by

```
run-unit A:    READY FILE (F1, F2) PROTECTED UPDATE;  /*   Granted   */
run-unit B:    READY FILE (F1, F2) PROTECTED UPDATE  /*   Denied   */
```

then A would run; when A eventually finished, B could run. However, a more general solution is an *activity monitor*, which monitors run-units in waiting states and detects and breaks deadlocks.

10.4.2 Record-Level Concurrency Control

We saw in the previous section that two concurrently executing run-units with the RECORD_LOCK concurrency or usage mode are protected from mutual interference only by the use of special concurrency commands, namely KEEP, COMMIT and FREE. We shall now see how these may be used. The reader might note, however, that a CODASYL specification for these facilities first appeared in the 1980 CODASYL specifications. The CODASYL specification is to a large extent based on a solution originally used by UNIVAC in an earlier CODASYL DMS 1100 system (see Section 8.1.2).

The system is somewhat complex and is best understood in relation to the concurrency table in Figure 10.10. The previous concurrency table dealt with control over a file; however, this table deals with control over a record. As before, we imagine two run-units: One is active with respect to the record involved and has partial, complete, or no control over it. We also have what we still call an inactive run-unit that is trying to gain control. The table gives the result of each attempt.

Associated with each record in the data base are two locks, known as the *update* and *selection* locks. As we might expect, to carry out an updating operation on a record, the run-unit must first hold the update lock. To carry out a retrieval of a record, the run-unit must hold the selection lock.

		LOCKS HELD BY ACTIVE RUN-UNIT			
		Selection, update	Update	Selection	No locks
INACTIVE	**Updating**	NO (U)	NO (U)	NO (U)	YES (U)
RUN-UNITS	**Retrieval**	NO (S)	NO (S)	YES (S)	YES (S)
COMMANDS	**(1) Retrieval**	NO (S)	NO (S)	YES (S)	YES (S)
	(2) Updating			NO (U)	YES (U)

FIGURE 10.10. *Record-level concurrency table for active/inactive run-units. The active run-unit has control, partial control, or has just relinquished control of a record. Full control means it possesses update and selection locks, while partial control means possession of update or selection locks. The inactive run-unit tries to gain some control by issuing update, retrieval, or a sequence of update/retrieval commands. The result is shown as a "YES" or "NO," followed by the lock granted or denied, symbolized by U or S.*

Let us now imagine that, for a given record, the active run-unit is in possession of both the update and selection locks, the update lock alone, the selection lock alone, or no locks, as illustrated in Figure 10.10. We then watch the efforts of a competing or inactive run-unit (the run-unit is inactive as far as the record involved is concerned) to gain control of the selection and update locks, both individually and together. The rules for gaining control are as follows.

1*a*. Control of an update lock for a given run-unit A for record R is granted when A issues an update command for R, provided no other record is holding the update or selection lock for the record. (An update command is a STORE, MODIFY, CONNECT, DISCONNECT, RECONNECT, ERASE, or FIND FOR UPDATE command. This last command is simply any FIND command with FOR UPDATE inserted after FIND to signal intended subsequent updating of the record retrieved.)

b. Possession of a record's selection lock prevents other run-units from acquiring the record's update lock. (This rule is also implicit in Rule 1*a*, but is restated explicitly for tutorial purposes.)

c. Only one run-unit at a time can hold a record's update lock. (This rule is also implicit in Rule 1*a*.)

2*a*. Control of a selection lock is given to run-unit A for record R when A issues a retrieval command (FIND) for R, provided no other run-unit is holding the record's update lock.

b. Possession of a record's update lock prevents other run-units from acquiring the record's selection lock. (This rule is implicit in Rule 2*a*.)

c. Many run-units can hold a record's selection lock at the same time. (This rule is implicit in Rule 2*a*.)

We can thus see that possession of a record's update lock by a run-unit corresponds at the file level exactly to a usage mode of EXCLUSIVE. No other run-unit can gain control of the update or selection locks and thus modify or retrieve the record; that is, the record may not be used in any way by a concurrent run-unit.

On the other hand, possession of a record's selection lock permits other run-units to carry out retrievals of the record involved (since other run-units may hold the selection lock), but no other run-unit can carry out updating operations (since the update lock may not be held by other run-units).

Referring now to Figure 10.10, suppose the inactive run-unit issues an update command, requiring that it be given the update lock for the record involved. We see that the request is granted only when the active run-unit is no longer in possession of either update or selection locks. This follows from Rules 1*b* and 1*c*.

Let us now suppose that the inactive run-unit tries a retrieval command. We see that the request is granted, with the run-unit gaining control of the record's selection lock, when the active run-unit is either in possession of the selection lock or has relinquished all locks for the record involved. This follows from Rules 2*b* and 2*c*.

Finally, consider the case when the inactive run-unit attempts a retrieval command followed by an update command. The reader should confirm the results in the table as an exercise.

The KEEP, FREE, and COMMIT DML Commands   So far we have discussed only how a run-unit may gain control over a selection or update lock, together with the consequences of possession. We shall now investigate the period for which a lock may be held and how it may be relinquished.

We have seen (Section 9.1.1) that for each file, keep-lists may be defined in the subschema. A keep-list is essentially a queue (FIFO) of data-base keys; however, it is empty at the initiation of a run-unit, and keep-lists for different (concurrent) run-units are quite distinct.

Data-base keys are placed in keep-lists in the order in which they are assigned, that is, chronological order. They may be assigned by the KEEP command, which has the following simple (PL/1) syntax (as we have seen in Section 10.1.10).

KEEP [DB_KEY (*data-base-key-identifier*)] IN (*keep-list-name*)

The data-base key for the specified currency indicator is placed in the keep-list. Note that we may assign the same currency twice or more to a keep-list, with the corresponding data-base key occupying as many elements of the list.

It is also possible to delete a data-base key from a keep-list by means of the simple FREE command with the following COBOL syntax.

$$\text{FREE} \left\{ \begin{array}{l} \textit{data-base-key-identifier} \\ \text{ALL} \quad [\text{FROM } \textit{keep-list-names}] \end{array} \right\}$$

The syntax rules are as follows.

1. If *data-base-key-identifier* references a currency indicator in a currency table, it is set to null.

2. If *data-base-key-identifier* references a keep-list, the first data-base key in the list is deleted.

3. If **ALL** and not **FROM** is specified, all keep-list contents are deleted.

4. If **ALL** and **FROM** are specified, the contents of the specified keep-lists are deleted.

A **COMMIT** command is also involved. This command's syntax consists simply of the word **COMMIT**. The **COMMIT** command defines a *quiet point* in the execution of a run-unit. When issued by a run-unit

1. All update and selection locks held by the run-unit are released.

2. All data-base changes made by the run-unit since the previous quiet point become available to concurrent run-units.

3. The run-unit's keep-lists are emptied and its currency indicators set to null.

The rules for retaining and relinquishing selection and update locks are dependent on the **KEEP**, **FREE**, and **COMMIT** commands, and are as follows.

1. A run-unit retains a selection lock for a record as long as the record's data-base key appears either in a keep-list or in the run-units currency table, but a **COMMIT** command at any time causes the lock to be released.

2. A **COMMIT** command causes an update lock to be released.

Thus a programmer who lets a currency be updated for a record being processed without first placing it in a keep-list is running the risk of finding it changed next time it is retrieved. On the other hand, a programmer who places all currencies encountered in a keep-list without ever freeing any of them, just to be on the safe side, is reducing system performance and should be prevented from so doing by the data-base administrator.

Deadlock   We have the possibility of deadlock at the record level with this system. Let us suppose we have two concurrent run-units, R1 and R2, which both need to process two records A and B; R1 is a retrieval run-unit and R2 an updating run-unit. Consider now the following sequence of events, assuming there are no other competing run-units.

R1: Retrieval command for A (selection lock granted).

R2: Updating command for B (update lock granted).

R1: Retrieval command for B (selection lock denied, Rule 2a; R1 placed in wait queue).

R2: Updating command for A (update lock denied, Rule 1a; R2 placed in wait queue).

Programmer discipline cannot solve this problem. Furthermore, this type of deadlock could be a common occurrence. However, CODASYL has proposed an additional command to solve the problem, namely, ROLLBACK.

First of all, a new data-base exception code will be assigned to the run-unit's DB_ STATUS variable to indicate a deadlock situation. Thus the run-unit's programmer can code to test for deadlock. If deadlock is detected, the program can issue a ROLLBACK command, which will have the run-unit rolled back to the previous quiet point, undoing all data base updates since the quiet point and releasing all record locks and emptying all keep-lists. From this point, the program can continue, this time, it is to be hoped, not entering a deadlock situation.

A quiet point to which a run-unit can be rolled back is specified by means of a COMMIT command. The ROLLBACK command's syntax consists of the single word ROLLBACK [CODASYL, 1978].

10.5 CRITICISM OF THE CODASYL PROPOSAL

The CODASYL proposal is of great importance. However, during its developmental period, the past 12 years, it has been subjected to severe criticism [Clemons, 1979; Engles, 1971; Olle, 1977; Waghorn, 1975]. Most of this criticism has been constructive, and the latest specifications, which are a decided improvement over the earlier specifications, have rendered a lot of this earlier criticism irrelevant [Metaxides, 1979]. Nevertheless, the CODASYL proposal can still be criticized; taken constructively, this will lead to further improvement. In this section we shall deal briefly with some useful criticism relevant to the latest proposal.

10.5.1 The Currency Concept

The currency concept, which is still a central part of the proposal, has been subject to criticism. The following criticisms are common.

1. Execution of DML commands, such as FIND commands, gives rise to side effects, such as updating of currency indicators. Language specialists prefer to have no side effects as this reduces the chance of error.

2. DML commands are dependent on the currency-table values. If a value is wrong, a program will continue to execute without any indication of failure. An example of this was given in Retrieval 2 in Section 10.3.1.

This criticism is probably valid. However, it is difficult to see what can be done about it in a navigational retrieval language. A data base is a complex data structure, and if the retrieval language permits selection of only one record at a time in sequential fashion, there must be a way of recording the position of the program with respect to the structure [Bachman, 1973].

There appear to be only two possibilities: Either the DBCS will maintain a record of the program's position in each file (and set) of the data base, or the programmer must do it. As mentioned in Section 10.3.1, the problem is inherent in all situations where navigation is required. The navigator must know his or her position; otherwise there is the risk of navigating "onto the rocks."

10.5.2 The Complexity of the FIND Commands

The seven FIND command formats are sometimes considered to be too many and too complex. We are inclined to agree. Let us consider what is really necessary:

1. A command to access a file sequentially in record-key order.

2. A command to access a file directly using a record key.

3. A command to access a file sequentially in data-base key order.

4. A command to access a file directly using a data-base key.

5. A command to search the members of a set occurrence.

6. A command to retrieve the owner record of a set occurrence.

7. A command to update currency indicators.

It could be argued that (3) could well be omitted. However, the availability of this command will undoubtedly lead to improved system performance, and because data-base systems are notorious for relatively poor performance, it is clear that the command must be retained. Note that (4) is implicit in (7).

We need a command to search a set occurrence. However, CODASYL gives us three, the three set-scan commands (Sections 10.1.5, 6, and 7). Some rationalization could be applied here. The three set-scan commands could well be replaced by the following command, which—to a large extent—has the same capability. We give a PL/1 version.

$$\text{FIND [FILE (\textit{file-name})] \underline{IN CS} (\textit{set-name}) \underline{MEMBER}} \left\{ \begin{array}{l} \text{FIRST} \\ \text{LAST} \\ \text{NEXT} \\ \text{PRIOR} \\ \text{N} \end{array} \right\}$$

$$\text{[\underline{WHERE} (\textit{logical-expression})]}$$

The logical expression identifies a target member record or records. We may thus retrieve the Nth, first, or last *target* record in a set occurrence identified by the current of set indicator. We may also retrieve the next *target* record after, or prior *target* record before, the current of set record. When the WHERE clause is omitted, *all member records are considered targets*. Of course, if we wish to manipulate a recursive set, then CS will have to be replaced by either CS_OWN or CS_MEM.

10.5.3 Set Selection

The way in which set selection is handled in CODASYL is not acceptable to many. The main command involved with set selection is the STORE command, and we shall deal with it first.

It is clear that the twin groupings of conceptual records into conceptual files and owner-coupled sets is fundamental to CODASYL. The owner-coupled set grouping, while relatively new, is both useful and powerful and will undoubtedly survive. This being the case, we must accept the fact that when a record is placed in the data base, it will be placed in a file and in one or more sets. We have seen that when a set is AUTOMATIC, such a record must be placed in the file and the set following execution of the STORE command. The trouble is that we cannot specify in the command into which set occurrence the record should go. This is done in a very roundabout fashion using the SET SELECTION clause in the schema. It also means that, as the reader will certainly have noticed, use of set selection in an applications program makes the program hard to read, because of the need to reference the schema. The author believes that it would simplify the schema, improve the readability of loading programs, and reduce the likelihood of error if SET SELECTION were entirely removed from the schema, and the STORE command instead equipped with set selection capability.

Let us see what would be required in such a STORE command. We need to identify the file into which the record is to be placed. We also need to specify the following.

    a.   Record keys, so that the system knows where to place the record in relation to other records.

    b.   For each set to which the record is to be connected, the set name and either an identification or identification method for the correct set occurrence.

    c.   The record to be stored.

With this in mind, we can construct a new STORE command.

STORE FILE (*file-name*) [FROM (*variable*)] [{*set-clause*} ...]

Let us defer the syntax for the set clause until later. When *set-clause* is omitted, the record contained in the variable is stored in the file specified. The system uses the subschema key specification to extract the keys from the record. This is simple enough and so far is not new. (When FROM is omitted, the record is taken from the UWA.)

Now we give the following syntax specification for *set-clause*.

$$
\left\{
\begin{array}{l}
\underline{\text{IN}} \quad
\left\{
\begin{array}{l}
\text{CS} \\
\text{CS\_OWN} \\
\text{CS\_MEM}
\end{array}
\right\}
(\textit{set-name}) \\[2em]
\underline{\text{IN}} \quad \text{SET } (\textit{set-name}) \; [\underline{\text{OWN\_KEY}} \quad (\textit{variable})]
\end{array}
\right\}
$$

There must be a *set-clause* for every AUTOMATIC set, while for other sets we can specify one if we wish.

We illustrate the syntax with some examples.

1. STORE FILE (TREE) FROM (NEWDATA) IN CS (FOR_TREE);
   A TREE record in the variable NEWDATA is stored in the file TREE and coupled to the set FOR_TREE set occurrence that is current of set.

2. STORE FILE (TREE) FROM (NEWDATA) IN (FOR_TREE) OWN_KEY (FOR-REC.FOREST)
   This time the record in NEWDATA is coupled to the FOR_TREE occurrence which has owner record key that is in FORREC.FOREST, that is, in the UWA.

3. STORE FILE (TREE) FROM (NEWDATA) IN (FOR_TREE); This time the FOR_TREE occurrence chosen has an owner record key the same as the connection field value of the record in NEWDATA.

Thus this new command clearly permits us to do what was possible with the present SET SELECTION specification in the schema. The default connection field method (example 3) is to be preferred, and its adoption would bring CODASYL more in line with TOTAL (section 8.1.2.). Another advantage is that we can store records in MANUAL sets in a single STORE command. However, such a STORE command would not permit us to remove SET SELECTION from the schema. The RECONNECT command depends on SET SELECTION. We could remove this difficulty by permmitting the specification of the method of set selection in the command, using *set-clause* from the new STORE command. (The CONNECT command could be improved in the same way.)

$$\underline{\text{RECONNECT}} \left[\frac{\underline{\text{CF}}\,(\textit{file-name})}{\underline{\text{CRU}}\,(\textit{file-name})} \right] \left\{ \{\textit{set-clause}\} \ldots \right\}$$

Thus when we code

RECONNECT CRU (MEASUREMENT) IN SET (TREE_MEAS) OWN_KEY (K);

we wish to remove the MEASUREMENT record that is CRU from its present TREE_MEAS occurrence and place it in that which has owner key in the variable K.

Finally, there is a FIND command that employs SET SELECTION. It is a version of the set-scan target FIND command (Section 10.1.6). It would be better to scrap this subtle command, which is not likely to find much use, rather than attempt to incorporate a set-clause, as with STORE and RECONNECT. It is thus clearly possible to do away with the SET SELECTION specification in the schema.

10.5.4 Repeating Groups in CODASYL Records

The CODASYL proposal says nothing about the desirability of 4NF relational files (Chapter 7). In fact, it includes a facility which encourages the designer not to have 4NF files. This facility permits the specification of repeating groups of fields in records in much the same way as it is possible to include an array in a PL/1 structure variable (see Section 8.3.1). As an example, consider the following.

```
DCL 1 FORREC,   /*   Describes a forest   */
    2 FOREST ......,   /*   Key field   */
    2 SIZE ......., /*   Size of forest   */
    2 TREESUBREC (1000),   /*   1000 repeating groups of 3 fields (1000 trees)   */
        3 TREENUM ......,   /*   Number of a tree   */
        3 SPECIES ......,
        3 PLANTED .....;
```

Such records are clearly undesirable, as it is widely agreed that simple 4NF files are superior. The author believes the facility should be removed from CODASYL. Fortunately, implementors do not have to implement it, and if they go to the (unnecessary) trouble of doing so, designers do not have to make use of it.

10.5.5 Lack of a Nonnavigational Retrieval Language

In the CODASYL DML, it is possible to specify the retrieval of a record based on specified field values for the file involved. However, in the relational approach to data-base management (Chapter 13), the retrieval languages are nonnavigational; that is to say, a record can be retrieved based on very complex search parameters involving different records from many different files without it being necessary for the user to specify the necessary navigation through these different files (Chapter 14).

Such relational retrieval languages may thus be regarded as high-level languages, compared with the CODASYL language. However, it has been shown to be possible to have nonnavigational retrieval languages with owner-coupled set data bases; in the next chapter, we shall describe an enhancement to CODASYL which would give it nonnavigational capability.

The lack at the present time of an efficient nonnavigational retrieval language in the CODASYL proposal is not a serious disadvantage, especially when there are as yet no fully equipped commercial relational data-base systems available. However, there is no doubt that such a language would be useful.

EXERCISES

1. Referring to the FORESTRY data base, devise a routine to retrieve the names of companies that own hardwood trees. The retrieval is similar to Retrieval 1.

2. Referring to the RESOURCE data base in Chapter 6, devise a routine to retrieve the names of property owners (PROPERTY.OWNER) whose properties are on concessions granted to Houston-based (HQ = 'HOUSTON') oil companies.[1]

---

[1]*In the RESOURCE data base the 4NF version of DRILL—HOLE should be used (see Chapter 7). This may be obtained by removing the CONCESSION and COMPANY fields from DRILL—HOLE.*

3. Referring to the RESOURCE data base, devise a routine to retrieve the names of the heads of agencies (GOV_AGENCY.CHIEF) who have granted North Sea (CONCESSION.LOC = 'NORTH SEA') concessions under 100,000 dollars (CONCESSION.COST < 100000).[1]

4. Referring to the RESOURCE data base, devise a routine to retrieve the heads of oil companies (PETROFIRM.CHIEF) that have never drilled a hole in any of their Texas (CONCESSION.LOC = 'TEXAS') concessions.[1]

5. Referring to Retrieval 1, devise a user-currency table for the routine R1.

6. Referring to the RESOURCE data base, if Exoil Company sells all its concessions to Zedoil Company, devise a routine to update the data base to reflect such transactions.[1] How does the retention class of the sets involved affect the routine?

7. Refer to the data base in Figure 6.10. Devise a routine to retrieve all the companies with headquarters in Calgary that are either immediate or lower level subsidiaries of Zedoil.

8. Repeat Exercise 7, using the data base in Figure 6.11*b*.

9. Referring to the data base in Figure 6.11*b,* if the company Kayoil buys the company Westoil from the company Exoil, devise a routine to update the data base.

10. Referring to the data base in Figure 6.14, devise a routine to produce an "explosion" of the subsidiaries of Zedoil.

11. Referring to the data base in Figure 6.16*a,* devise a routine to produce an "implosion" of the part 2001.

12. Referring to the data base in Figure 6.14, if company Kayoil buys half the shares of company Westoil from company Exoil, devise a routine to update the data base.

13. Rewrite the retrieval routine R2 using the set-scan target FIND command.

REFERENCES

Bachman, C. W., 1973, "The Programmer as Navigator," *CACM,* **16**(11):653–58.

Clemons, E. K., 1979, "Rational Data Base Standards, An Examination of the 1978 CODASYL Proposal," *Information Systems,* **4**(3):235–39.

CODASYL, 1971, "Data Base Task Group Report," *ACM,* New York, April.

CODASYL, 1978, *COBOL Committee, Journal of Development* (with updates to 1981), Dept. of Supply and Services, Canadian Federal Government, Hull, Quebec, Canada.

Engles, R. W., 1971, "An analysis of the 1971 DBTG report—IBM position paper," *Workshop on Data Description, Access and Control, ACM SIGFIDET, ACM,* New York.

Metaxides, A., 1979, "Reply to a paper by E. K. Clemons," *Information Systems,* **4**(3):247–49. (Deals with second paper above.)

Olle, T. W., 1977, *The CODASYL Approach to Data Base Management,* John Wiley, New York.

Waghorn, W. J., 1975, "The DDL as an Industry Standard," B. C. M. Douque, G. M. Nijssen (eds.), *Proc. IFIP; TC-2 Special Working Conference on Data Base Description* (January, 1975) North-Holland.

A Nonnavigational CODASYL Enhancement 11

The present CODASYL specifications support only navigational or procedural retrieval of data from a data base. Thus all of the retrieval routines given in the previous chapter are navigational, the term *navigational* being used—as explained earlier—in the sense of the programmer charting a course through the data base from record to record and from file to file, as registered by a succession of CRU values.

We are thus forced to conclude that the CODASYL retrieval sublanguage is very low level. However, as mentioned in Chapter 6, it is possible to have higher-level data-base retrieval sublanguages that are nonnavigational or nonprocedural. Although primitive non-procedural retrieval language prototypes were not uncommon in the 1960s, development really got under way with the conception by Kuhns [Kuhns, 1969, 1971] of mathematically based nonprocedural languages for use with relational data bases (Chapter 13), a concept later significantly developed by Codd [Codd, 1971, 1972; Date, 1977].

In recent years, there has been considerable interest in the development of a nonnavigational retrieval sublanguage as an enhancement to the CODASYL DML. Such a language would permit the expression of complex retrievals, which would be carried out by a DBCS which also employed the standard CODASYL schemas, DML commands, UWA, and currencies [Bradley, 1978a, 1978b; Deheneffe, 1976; Ernest, 1975; Haseman, 1975; Parsons, 1974; Whinston, 1975]. The GPLAN CODASYL enhancement, described in detail in a data-base text by Haseman and Whinston [Haseman, 1977] is a significant example.

In this chapter we shall describe a later (and possibly simpler) enhancement, known as the EOS CODASYL enhancement. The reader should not infer that this enhancement will be incorporated into the CODASYL specifications; however, the incorporation of some kind of nonnavigational enhancement is unlikely to be postponed for too long. If desired, the reader may delay reading this chapter until after relational data bases have been studied (Chapter 13).

11.1 AN EOS CODASYL ENHANCEMENT SUBLANGUAGE

The EOS (Extended Owner-coupled Set) retrieval sublanguage was originally developed to manipulate a conceptual schema which employed relational files and owner-coupled sets [Bradley, 1978a]. The adaptation of this original sublanguage that is used in this chapter is designed to interface with a DBMS conforming to the present CODASYL specifications and can thus manipulate a CODASYL conceptual data base.

11.1.1 The EOS Sublanguage Syntax

From a syntactic point of view, the sublanguage consists of one basic and very flexible command. The syntax for this command is expressed (recursively) in Figure 11.1. (The reader familiar with the Chomsky hierarchy of grammars [Chomsky, 1959] will find that the sublanguage forms a context-free grammar.) Simply stated, the command retrieves a target record, the *target-file-name* record, for which we may not only specify field or key values, but also properties of other records (often in other files) that are related to the target record in some way. It is the ability of the EOS CODASYL enhancement to permit expression of these relationships by means of owner-coupled sets, which is its distinguishing feature. However, as we shall see, it is usually possible to avoid naming the owner-coupled sets involved in such expressions.

The fundamental semantics behind the EOS syntax will be explained in later sections using retrieval examples. However, we must first examine that elementary part of the syntax and semantics that governs the interface to CODASYL.

11.1.2 Interface to CODASYL

From the syntax expressions in (1) and (2) in Figure 11.1, we can assert that a typical EOS statement applied to the FORESTRY data base is

FIND NEXT : TREE RECORD (*logical-expression-1*);

Essentially, the DBCS is asked to retrieve the next record in the TREE file that satisfies the search conditions in *logical-expression-1*. Here some TREE record is the target record of the retrieval, and the TREE file is the *target-file-name* file.

The logical expression can be complex, involving many files and sets, depending on the complexity of the retrieval. However, in this section we are not concerned with *logical-expression-1*, and the reader for the moment should regard it simply as a collection of conditions that a target TREE record must satisfy before it can be retrieved.

There will be many TREE records in general that satisfy the conditions in *logical-expression-1*, and it is in the selection of one of these records that the interface to CODASYL is involved. We have the following semantic rules.

1. When FIRST is specified (after FIND), the record retrieved is the first in record-key order in the *target-file-name* file that satisfies the search conditions specified in *logical-expression-1*.

(1) An EOS statement has the syntax

FIND $\left\{\begin{array}{l}\underline{\text{FIRST}}\\\underline{\text{LAST}}\\\underline{\text{NEXT}}\\\underline{\text{PRIOR}}\end{array}\right\}$: *EOS-predicate*;

(2) *EOS-predicate* has the syntax

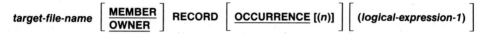

target-file-name $\left[\begin{array}{l}\underline{\text{MEMBER}}\\\underline{\text{OWNER}}\end{array}\right]$ **RECORD** $\left[\begin{array}{l}\underline{\text{OCCURRENCE}}\ [(n)]\end{array}\right]$ $\left[\begin{array}{l}\text{(logical-expression-1)}\end{array}\right]$

(3) An element of *logical-expression-1* has the syntax

$\left\{\begin{array}{l}\textit{condition-term}\\\textit{xreference}\end{array}\right\}$

(4) The element *xreference* (a cross reference via an owner-coupled set) has the syntax

$\left[\ [\neg]\ \right]$ $\left\{\begin{array}{l}\underline{\text{MEMBER}}\\\underline{\text{OWNER}}\\\textit{quant}\end{array}\right\}$ $\underline{\text{SET}}$ *(set-name)* $\left[\begin{array}{l}\underline{\text{OCCURRENCE}}\ [(n)]\end{array}\right]$ $\left[\begin{array}{l}\text{(logical-expression-2)}\end{array}\right]$

(5) An element of *logical-expression-2* has the syntax

$[\ \neg\ ]$ *[quant] [adj-expression] **file-name*** (continued on next line)

$\left[\begin{array}{l}\underline{\text{MEMBER}}\\\underline{\text{OWNER}}\end{array}\right]$ $\left[\begin{array}{l}\underline{\text{RECORD}}\\\underline{\text{RECORDS}}\end{array}\right]$ $\left[\begin{array}{l}\underline{\text{OCCURRENCE}}\ [(n)]\end{array}\right]$ $\left[\begin{array}{l}\text{(logical-expression-1)}\end{array}\right]$

(6) The adjectival expression *adj-expression* has the syntax

(logical-expression-1)

FIGURE 11.1. *EOS CODASYL Enhancement Syntax.*

2. Similarly, LAST indicates the last record in record-key order that satisfies the search conditions specified in *logical-expression-1*.

3. When NEXT is specified, if a *target-file-name* record is the CRU, the record retrieved is the next after the CRU (in the *target-file-name* file) that satisfies the search conditions in *logical-expression-1*. If the CRU is not a *target-file-name* record, NEXT is interpreted as being the same as FIRST.

4. Similarly, when a *target-file-name* record is the CRU, PRIOR indicates retrieval from the specified file of the record prior to the CRU (in record-key order) that satisfies the retrieval conditions in *logical-expression-1*. When the CRU is not a *target-file-name* record, PRIOR is interpreted as LAST.

5. A *target-file-name* record that is retrieved becomes the CRU, the current of the *target-file-name* file, and the current of all sets in which it participates. *No other currencies are*

---

affected, no matter how many files are accessed by the DBCS in the course of carrying out a retrieval.

The interface to CODASYL is thus quite simple and makes it possible to process a file sequentially in record-key order, retrieving records that satisfy the (often complex) search conditions in *logical-expression-1*. The currency indicators keep track of our position in the file being investigated in the usual way.[1] Thus having used the EOS FIND to arrive at a certain position in the data base, we may continue processing with the conventional CODASYL DML commands, and vice versa.

11.2 RETRIEVALS INVOLVING NONRECURSIVE SETS

In this section we shall illustrate the EOS FIND command by a series of retrievals of increasing complexity using the FORESTRY data base. The EOS FIND command can manage many varied and complex retrievals. Accordingly, in an effort to classify these retrievals in an orderly manner, we make use of the concept of *retrieval level*.

11.2.1 The Concept of Retrieval Level

We classify retrievals in accordance with the maximum distance from the target record that the DBCS must navigate in order to determine if the target record satisfies the conditions in *logical-expression-1*. Thus the *retrieval level* of a retrieval is $(h + 1)$, where h is the maximum number of serial hops from an owner file to a member file, or vice versa, made by the DBCS. Thus in a level-1 retrieval, h is zero and no owner-coupled sets are involved. We start with a single level-1 retrieval. This retrieval is elementary, and the reader might use it to clarify his or her understanding of the interface to CODASYL.

11.2.2 Level-1 Retrieval

The command here is really quite similar to the PL/1 version of the CODASYL sequential FIND command as described in Section 10.1.2. No owner-coupled sets are involved.

Retrieval 1   *Find the **TREENUMB** and **SPECIES** field values for those **TREE** records which have **FOREST** field value 'XFOR' and **LOC** field value 1001.*
We process the TREE file by means of a PL/1 DO WHILE loop, examining each TREE record in turn using the EOS FIND command. If a TREE record satisfies the search conditions (that is, satisfies *logical-expression-1*) it is selected as the target record and becomes the CRU. A conventional CODASYL DML GET command is then used to place the required field values in the UWA (user working area).

---

[1]However, as with the conventional CODASYL FIND commands (see Section 9.3.2.), the FIND command in the EOS CODASYL enhancement could be supplemented by a corresponding FETCH command. Thus the effect of replacing the word "FIND" by "FETCH" would be that the retrieved record would in addition be placed in the appropriate UWA structure.

```
BEOF = '1'B;
DO WHILE (BEOF);
FIND NEXT:
              TREE RECORD ((FOREST = 'XFOR') & (LOC = 1001));
IF DB_STATUS = '1502400'   /*   None left in file   */   THEN BEOF = '0'B;
    ELSE DO;
        GET CRU (TREE) INTO (TREEREC.TREENUMB, TREEREC.SPECIES);
        PUT SKIP LIST (TREEREC.TREENUMB, TREEREC.SPECIES);
            END;
END;
```

Examining the FIND command in the light of syntax expressions in (1), (2), and (3) from Figure 11.1, we see that TREE is substituted for *target-file-name*, and that *logical-expression-1* has two constituent elements. These elements are the *condition-term* elements

(FOREST = 'XFOR'),

and

(LOC = 1001)

A *condition-term* element is simply a logical relation involving a field from a record and a value. In the above FIND command *logical-expression-1* has no elements that are *xreference* specifications (that is, cross references to files, usually other files). If it did it would not constitute a level-1 retrieval. We now look at some level-2 retrievals.

11.2.3 Level-2 Retrievals and the Basic Quantifiers

In level-2 retrievals, we deal not only with the target file (the file containing target records) but also with files which have records that are either owners or members of sets involving target records. The relevant syntax is to be found using Expressions (1), (2), (3), (4), (5), (6), and (3) in Figure 11.1. We see that *xreference* specifications are involved.

We also have to involve something called a *quantifier,* denoted by *quant* in Figure 11.1. There are two *basic* quantifiers, the *existential* and *universal* quantifiers [Kuhns, 1971]. These are well known and are used in DSL ALPHA, a relational nonnavigational retrieval sublanguage (see Chapter 14).

We denote the existential quantifier in the EOS FIND command by EXISTS and the universal quantifier by FOR ALL. As we shall now see, we use the existential quantifier in level-2 retrievals, when, for example, we wish to retrieve a target record that is owner of a (specified) set occurrence, in which there *exists* at least one member record with specified properties.

Similarly, we use the universal quantifier when we wish to retrieve a target record that is owner of a specified set occurrence, in which *for all* member records, if any, specified conditions are satisfied. Thus we use the universal quantifier when specified conditions are universally true for all members of a set occurrence for which the target record is the owner.

In addition to the basic quantifiers, a large number of other quantifiers may be used. We refer to these quantifiers as the *natural quantifiers* because they are commonly used in everyday language. The application of the basic quantifiers is illustrated in the following retrievals.

Retrieval 2: Existential Quantifier   *Retrieve the names of companies owning forests larger than 1000 acres and containing 'SPRUCE' trees.*

We place the following EOS FIND and DML GET commands in a suitable DO loop.

```
FIND NEXT:
        FORFILE OWNER RECORD ((SIZE > 1000) &
        OWNER SET (FOR_TREE) OCCURRENCE
        (EXISTS TREE MEMBER RECORD (SPECIES = 'SPRUCE') ));
        .........
GET INTO (FORREC.COMPANY);
```

A literal translation of the EOS FIND command above would be:

> Find the next FORFILE record (following the CRU) with SIZE field value greater than 1000 that is the owner of a FOR_TREE set occurrence, in which there EXISTS a TREE member record with SPECIES field value equal to 'SPRUCE'.

It is also useful to analyze the syntax of the above command in terms of the general syntax given in Figure 11.1. Here *logical-expression-1* has two constituent elements. One of them is the *condition-term* element

(SIZE > 1000)

The other is the *xreference* element

OWNER SET (FOR_TREE) OCCURRENCE (*logical-expression-2*)

In this particular case, *logical-expression-2* is

EXISTS TREE MEMBER RECORD (*logical-expression-1*)

where the second *logical-expression-1* has only one constituent element, namely, the *condition-term* element

(SPECIES = 'SPRUCE')

If this second *logical-expression-1* were to contain an *xreference* element, the retrieval level would be greater than two.

Retrieval 3: Universal Quantifier

Find the locations of cedar trees on which all measurements, if any, have been electrical.

We place the following in a suitable DO loop:

```
FIND NEXT:
    TREE OWNER RECORD ((SPECIES = 'CEDAR') &
    OWNER SET (TREE_MEAS) OCCURRENCE
    (FOR ALL MEASUREMENT MEMBER RECORDS (TYPE = 'ELECTRICAL') ));
```

For a TREE record to be retrieved, *all* of its member records in TREE_MEAS must have TYPE value 'ELECTRICAL', but if there are no member records, the TREE record will still be retrieved.

Retrieval 4: No Quantifier

Find the locations of all hardwood trees in the forest 'XFOR'.

We place the following in a suitable DO loop:

```
FIND NEXT:
    TREE MEMBER RECORD ((FOREST = 'XFOR') &
    MEMBER SET (SPEC_TREE) OCCURRENCE
    (SPECFILE OWNER RECORD (WOODTYPE = 'HARDWOOD') ));
..........
GET INTO (TREEREC.LOC);
```

When we navigate from a target member record to an owner record, a quantifier is not required, because for a given target member record, there is only one owner record in a given set occurrence.

Retrieval 5: Two Quantifiers with One Set

Find the tree numbers for cedar trees on which there are measurements with a result greater than 500 millivolts and on which all measurements are electrical.

We place the following in a suitable DO loop:

```
FIND NEXT:
    TREE OWNER RECORD ((SPECIES = 'CEDAR') &
    OWNER SET (TREE_MEAS) SET OCCURRENCE
    ((EXISTS MEASUREMENT MEMBER RECORD (RESULT > 500))
    & (FOR ALL MEASUREMENT RECORDS (TYPE = 'ELECTRICAL'))));
........
GET INTO (TREEREC.TREENUMB);
```

The reader should study this retrieval carefully. We have specified that within a TREE_MEAS set occurrence owned by a target TREE record, two conditions must hold.

    a.   At least one MEASUREMENT record has a result greater than 500 millivolts.

    b.   All MEASUREMENT records must have a type value 'ELECTRICAL'.

Thus referring to the syntax expressions in Figure 11.1, *logical-expression-2* has two constituent *xreference* elements, namely, (EXISTS ... 500) and (FOR ALL ... 'ELECTRI-CAL').

Retrieval 6: Two Sets   *Find the tree numbers for trees that are either in location 1001 and are hardwoods or are in location 2002 and belong to company 'XFIRM'.*

In this and many subsequent retrievals, we omit the accompanying DML GET statement. We place the following in a suitable DO loop.

```
FIND NEXT: TREE MEMBER RECORD (
    ((LOC = 1001) & MEMBER SET (SPEC_TREE) OCCURRENCE
                (SPECFILE OWNER RECORD (WOODTYPE = 'HARDWOOD' )))

  | ((LOC = 2002) & MEMBER SET (FOR_TREE) OCCURRENCE
                (FORFILE OWNER (COMPANY = 'XFIRM')))   );
```

Referring to the syntax expressions in Figure 11.1, we see that *logical-expression-1* has two *condition-term* elements, and also two *xreference* elements. One of the *xreference* elements involves the set SPEC_TREE, while the other involves the set FOR_TREE.

It should be noted that this is still a level-2 retrieval. Although two sets are involved, the involvement is "parallel"; that is, the DBCS must navigate from the target TREE record to the owner of its SPEC_TREE set occurrence, and then from the TREE target record to the owner of its FOR_TREE set occurrence. Therefore the maximum distance in set hops is one, so that the level is two.

11.2.4 Retrieval Diagrams

It is possible to construct diagrams to represent nonnavigational retrievals. In line with the complexity of the retrieval, nonnavigational expressions (such as the EOS expressions and DSL ALPHA expressions, as we shall see in Chapter 14) can be very complex, so that retrieval diagrams can be a useful aid to communication. Such diagrams have been little used to date, but this can probably be ascribed to the fact that, as yet, nonnavigational retrieval has been little used in the commercial world.

Diagram Principles   Retrieval diagrams begin to be useful with level-2 retrievals, and we shall therefore use the retrievals 2 through 6 from the previous subsection to illustrate them.

Figure 11.2*a* illustrates retrieval 2. The OWNER file can be taken as FORFILE and the MEMBER file as TREE, connected by the set FOR_TREE. The target (FORFILE) record is denoted by an arrow with a small circle at the end of it. The vertical arrow means that this target is related to a TREE record by means of an *xreference* element. This vertical arrow points to another horizontal arrow, which points to a TREE record; the latter has a small square at the end of it representing the existential quantifier. Thus a target FORFILE

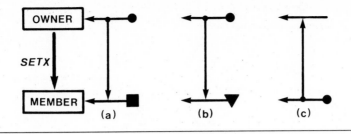

FIGURE 11.2. *Diagrammatic representation of nonnavigational retrievals with a single owner-coupled set and (a) the existential quantifier, (b) the universal quantifier, and (c) no quantifier. An arrow with a small square represents an existentially quantified record, while an arrow with a small triangle represents a universally quantified record. An arrow with a small circle represents a target record.*

record is depicted as being related to an existentially quantified TREE record by means of the set FOR_TREE.

In Figure 11.2*b*, retrieval 3 is represented; this time the OWNER is a TREE record and the MEMBER is a MEASUREMENT record. The target record is connected to a universally quantified record, denoted by an arrow with a small triangle at the end of it. Retrieval 4, with no quantifiers, is depicted in Figure 11.2*c*. Here the OWNER is a SPECFILE record, and the MEMBER is a TREE record. However, the target TREE record is connected to an unquantified SPECFILE record, denoted simply by an arrow.

Figure 11.3, representing retrieval 5, shows a target TREE record connected through the set TREE_MEAS to member MEASUREMENT records, which are both existentially *and* universally quantified. When a connecting arrow forks, logical AND is assumed unless OR appears in the diagram.

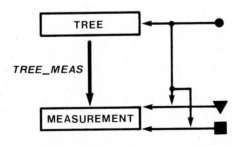

FIGURE 11.3. *Retrieval 5 representation.*

In retrieval 6, shown in Figure 11.4, a target TREE record is connected either to a SPECFILE owner record *or* to a FORFILE owner record. Here we have an explicit use of logical OR.

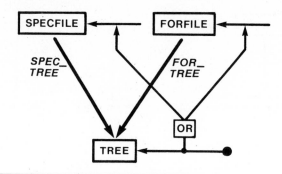

FIGURE 11.4. *Retrieval 6 representation. Unless* **OR** *is explicitly shown, as in this case, logical* **AND** *is assumed.*

11.2.5 Retrieval 7: Bench-Mark Retrieval

We very tentatively single out this retrieval for use as a bench-mark, or measure, of the ease of use of different sublanguages. Retrievals of this type are very common and often occur embedded in more complex retrievals. Furthermore, the retrieval has reasonable inherent complexity and has the advantage of being capable of expression with either the universal or existential quantifiers. We return to this retrieval again in Chapter 14. The retrieval is

> **Find the tree numbers and locations of spruce trees on which no electrical measurements have been carried out.**

For this retrieval we give two commands, the first with the universal quantifier and the second with the existential quantifier. Of course, both commands would be inserted in DO loops:

1. Universal quantifier

```
FIND NEXT:  TREE OWNER RECORD ((SPECIES = 'SPRUCE')
                OWNER SET (TREE_MEAS) OCCURRENCE
                (FOR ALL MEASUREMENT MEMBER RECORDS
                                (TYPE ¬ = 'ELECTRICAL'))  );
```

2. Existential quantifier

```
FIND NEXT:  TREE OWNER RECORD ((SPECIES = 'SPRUCE')
                & OWNER SET (TREE_MEAS) OCCURRENCE
                (¬ EXISTS MEASUREMENT MEMBER RECORD
                                (TYPE = 'ELECTRICAL')  ));
```

In the universal quantifier version, we are looking for the next TREE record of species spruce that is owner of a TREE_MEAS set occurrence in which every measurement record does not have TYPE value 'ELECTRICAL', while in the existential version, we specify that in the TREE_MEAS set occurrence there cannot exist an 'ELECTRICAL' member.

11.2.6 The Natural Quantifiers

So far, we have made use in our expressions only of the basic quantifiers EXISTS and FOR ALL. These basic quantifiers are in many cases sufficient, and increased convenience is the main reason for introducing any other quantifiers. Thus the mathematically based relational sublanguage DSL ALPHA uses only the basic quantifiers. However, as we shall see the natural quantifiers increase the ease of use of a nonnavigational retrieval sublanguage, and in this section we shall illustrate some of them.

Quantifier Syntax   We are now in a position to give an extended syntax for a quantifier as it may be used in the syntax expression in Figure 11.1. We have the following syntax for *quant* in Figure 11.1.

$$
\left\{
\begin{array}{l}
\text{FOR ALL} \\
\text{EXISTS} \\
\\
\text{FOR ONE AND FOR ALL} \\
\text{FOR ALL BUT ONE} \\
\text{FOR ALL BUT N} \\
\text{FOR NO} \\
\text{FOR MAJORITY OF} \\
\text{FOR AT LEAST X PERCENT OF} \\
\\
\text{EXISTS} \left\{
\begin{array}{l}
\text{MORE THAN} \\
\text{LESS THAN} \\
\text{EXACTLY} \\
\text{AT LEAST} \\
\text{AT MOST}
\end{array}
\right\} \text{N}
\end{array}
\right\}
$$

This list is not exhaustive, and the reader will probably be able to "invent" a few more natural quantifiers. Note that N can be either an integer or a program variable with a value that is an integer, and that X is either a numerical value between 0 and 100 or a program variable containing a numerical value between 0 and 100.

Quantifier Semantics   The first two quantifiers on the list are the basic quantifiers. The next six quantifiers are natural quantifiers based on the universal quantifier; the remaining quantifiers are also natural and based on the existential quantifier. We illustrate their semantics with three variations of retrieval 8:

Retrieval 8a   **Find tree numbers for cedar trees on which 10 measurements were electrical.**

FIND NEXT:

```
        TREE OWNER RECORD ((SPECIES = 'CEDAR') &
        OWNER SET (TREE_MEAS) OCCURRENCE
(EXISTS EXACTLY 10 MEASUREMENT MEMBER RECORDS
                                        (TYPE = 'ELECTRICAL')))
```

In retrieval 8*a* the quantifier is a natural quantifier that is based on the existential quantifier. In the following versions of retrieval 8, the retrievals use natural quantifiers that are based on the universal quantifier.

Retrieval 8b   **Find tree numbers for cedar trees on which the majority of measurements were electrical.**

```
FIND NEXT:
      TREE OWNER RECORD ((SPECIES = 'CEDAR') &
OWNER SET (TREE_MEAS) OCCURRENCE
      (FOR MAJORITY OF MEASUREMENT MEMBER RECORDS
                                        (TYPE = 'ELECTRICAL' )));
```

Retrieval 8c   **Find tree numbers for cedar trees on which electrical and only electrical measurements have been carried out.**

```
   FIND NEXT:
        TREE OWNER RECORD ((SPECIES = 'CEDAR') &
        OWNER SET (TREE_MEAS) OCCURRENCE
(FOR ONE AND FOR ALL MEASUREMENT MEMBER RECORDS
                                        (TYPE = 'ELECTRICAL')));
```

With retrieval 8c, a TREE record will not be retrieved if there are no member records in TREE_MEAS.

It can be seen that the natural quantifiers are convenient to use with the EOS CODASYL enhancement sublanguage, the main application being to the members of a set occurrence. The fact that the relational retrieval sublanguages do not have a grouping equivalent to the owner-coupled set with which to work probably explains why the natural quantifiers are not used in the relational approach [Date, 1977].

11.2.7 Level-3 and Higher-Level Retrievals

In level-3 retrievals, we have to navigate serially across two owner-coupled sets. Referring to the EOS syntax expressions in Figure 11.1, we see that this involves the recursive structure of the command syntax. We first take a simple level-3 retrieval, which incidentally will use the natural quantifiers.

Retrieval 9: Natural Quantifiers   *Find the names of companies with forests which contain a majority of cedar trees, on each of which more than 10 electrical measurements have been carried out.*

We place the following in a suitable DO loop.

FIND NEXT:
    FORFILE OWNER RECORD
    (OWNER SET (FOR_TREE) OCCURRENCE
    (FOR MAJORITY OF TREE MEMBER RECORDS
       ((SPECIES = 'CEDAR') & OWNER SET (TREE_MEAS) OCCURRENCE
         (EXISTS MORE THAN 10 MEASUREMENT MEMBER RECORDS
            (TYPE = 'ELECTRICAL')))))

Thus for a FORFILE record to be selected it must be the owner of a FOR_TREE occurrence where the majority of member trees each

1. Have species "cedar"; and

2. Have had more than 10 electrical measurements carried out.

It is useful to consider the syntax of the command in the light of the general syntax expression in Figure 11.1. In the command, *logical-expression-1* has one constituent element, an *xreference* element. This *xreference* element is

(OWNER SET (FOR_TREE) .... (TYPE = 'ELECTRICAL')))))

Thus the *xreference* element uses the set **FOR_TREE** and *logical-expression-2* given by:

(FOR MAJORITY OF .... (TYPE = 'ELECTRICAL'))))

The quantity *logical-expression-2* contains a new *logical-expression-1*, made up of the *condition-term* element

(SPECIES = 'CEDAR')

and another *xreference* element

OWNER SET (TREE_MEAS) .... (TYPE = 'ELECTRICAL'))

This *xreference* element makes use of another *logical-expression-2*

(EXISTS MORE THAN 10 MEASUREMENT RECORDS (TYPE = 'ELECTRICAL'))

In this *logical-expression-2*, we have a final *logical-expression-1*, made up of a single element which is a *condition-term* element

(TYPE = 'ELECTRICAL')

The recursive structure of the syntax expression in Figure 11.1 should thus be apparent. A further recursive cycle would generate a level-4 command.

    The retrieval diagram for this retrieval is given in Figure 11.5. We now take a more complex level-3 retrieval.

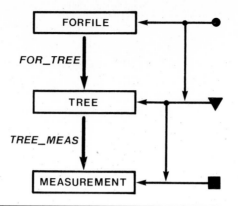

FIGURE 11.5. *Retrieval 9.*

Retrieval 10: Complex Retrieval *Find the names of the companies for which, in each of their Oregon forests,*

a. *Most trees are spruce, on which no biological measurements have ever been carried out; and*

b. *At least 5% of the trees are cedar, on which at least one electrical and one chemical measurement have been carried out.*

The reader might well study the retrieval diagram in Figure 11.6 before studying the EOS command, which would be placed in a suitable loop.

```
FIND NEXT:
    FORFILE OWNER RECORD ((LOC = 'OREGON') &
    OWNER SET (FOR_TREE) OCCURRENCE
        ((FOR MAJORITY OF TREE MEMBER RECORDS
            ((SPECIES = 'SPRUCE') & OWNER SET (TREE_MEAS) OCCURRENCE
                (FOR NO MEASUREMENT MEMBER RECORDS
                                (TYPE = 'BIOLOGICAL'))))
    & (FOR AT LEAST 5 PERCENT OF TREE MEMBER RECORDS
        ((SPECIES = 'CEDAR') & OWNER SET (TREE_MEAS) OCCURRENCE
            ((EXISTS MEASUREMENT MEMBER RECORD
                        (TYPE = 'ELECTRICAL'))
        & (EXISTS MEASUREMENT MEMBER RECORD
                    (TYPE = 'CHEMICAL')))))));
```

It goes without saying that most level-3 requests will be rather lengthy. It is also uncertain that it would be economic to implement an enhancement that would permit them. They are not likely to be frequently used. This is even more likely to be the case for retrieval levels greater than three.

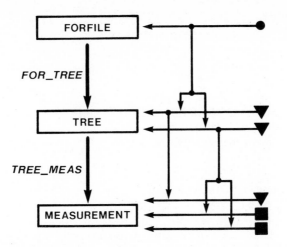

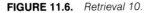

FIGURE 11.6. *Retrieval 10.*

11.2.8 Use of the OCCURRENCE (*n*) Facility in Complex Retrievals

The OCCURRENCE(*n*) facility is likely to be used only in complex retrievals. It is used to distinguish between different occurrences of sets or records. We shall illustrate its use by means of two retrievals, retrieval 11, and retrieval 12. Retrieval 11 is trivial, while retrieval 12 is fundamentally complex.

Retrieval 11: Trivial Use of OCCURRENCE Facility *Find the location of cedar trees on which at least two electrical measurements have been carried out.*

FIND NEXT:
      TREE OWNER RECORD (SPECIES = 'CEDAR') &
      OWNER SET (TREE_MEAS) OCCURRENCE
            ((EXISTS MEASUREMENT MEMBER OCCURRENCE (1)
                                          (TYPE = 'ELECTRICAL'))
            & (EXISTS MEASUREMENT MEMBER OCCURRENCE (2)
                                          (TYPE = 'ELECTRICAL')));

In the above expression we have used the basic quantifier EXISTS to specify that in order for a TREE record to be selected, in its TREE_MEAS set occurrence there must exist one (OCCURRENCE (1)) member record with TYPE value 'ELECTRICAL' and a different (OCCURRENCE (2)) member with TYPE value 'ELECTRICAL'. That is, there must be at least two members with TYPE value 'ELECTRICAL'.

We could have used the natural quantifier EXISTS AT LEAST 2 instead.

FIND NEXT:
      TREE OWNER RECORD ((SPECIES = 'CEDAR') &

OWNER SET (TREE_MEAS) OCCURRENCE
(EXISTS AT LEAST 2 MEASUREMENT RECORDS (TYPE = 'ELECTRICAL')))

The use of OCCURRENCE (*n*) in this retrieval thus appears to be trivial. This is not true for the next retrieval, however.

Retrieval 12: Need for OCCURRENCE (*n*) Facility   *Find the sizes of forests that contain all the species listed in the data base.*

We place the following in a suitable DO loop.

FIND NEXT:
    FORFILE RECORD OCCURRENCE (1)
    (FOR ALL SET (SPEC_TREE) OCCURRENCE
    (EXISTS TREE MEMBER RECORD (MEMBER SET (FOR_TREE) OCCURRENCE
                 (EXISTS FORFILE OWNER RECORD OCCURRENCE (1)))));

The retrieval diagram is shown in Figure 11.7. The retrieval is level-3, but it is unusual in that the DBCS has two entry points to the data base or, in other words, a main target and a subsidiary target.

The main target is a FORFILE record, labeled OCCURRENCE (1) and labeled (*m*) in the retrieval diagram. We then enter the data base at the set SPEC_TREE, labeled *s* in the diagram. We take each set occurrence of SPEC_TREE, and for at least one TREE member from each of these occurrences, the owner in FOR_TREE must be the target FORFILE record already labeled OCCURRENCE (1).

We see that it was necessary to use a FORFILE record twice in the expression, the occurrence label signifying that it is the same record in both cases. We could introduce a default rule here. Thus the system could take two record occurrences as being the same unless OCCURRENCE (*n*) was used to specify that they were different, or vice versa.

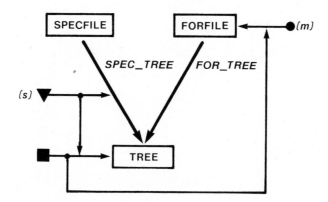

FIGURE 11.7. *Retrieval diagram for retrieval 12.*

11.2.9 Use of Simplified Syntax

Referring to the syntax expressions in Figure 11.1—and in particular to Expression 4—it may be seen that the subclause involving a set

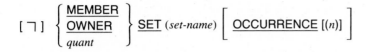

$$[\neg] \left\{ \begin{array}{l} \text{MEMBER} \\ \text{OWNER} \\ quant \end{array} \right\} \underline{\text{SET}}\ (set\text{-}name)\ \left[\underline{\text{OCCURRENCE}}\ [(n)] \right]$$

may be omitted from EOS commands. This can be done in many cases, thus shortening and simplifying the commands. We shall illustrate this possibility by means of some examples. However, we shall first give the syntactic rule governing omission of the set subclause from syntax Expression 4.

> The set subclause may be omitted from syntax Expression 4 whenever there is only one set connecting the owner and member files of the set, provided the quantifier is not required.

This definition applies both to recursive and nonrecursive sets, and because more than one set connecting two files is not too common, the set subclause may usually be omitted. For example, in the FORESTRY data base we have no files connected by two sets. In all the examples of retrievals given so far, except in the case of retrieval 12 in which the set is quantified, we could have omitted the set subclause.

To see why we may so frequently omit the set subclause, let us take retrieval 2 again. It was as follows.

Retrieve the names of companies owning forests larger than 1000 acres and containing 'SPRUCE' trees.

The simplified EOS command would be

```
FIND NEXT:
        FORFILE OWNER RECORD ((SIZE > 1000) &
        (EXISTS TREE MEMBER RECORD (SPECIES = 'SPRUCE'));
```

Here *logical-expression-1* has two elements, namely, a *condition-term* element and an *xreference* element involving the TREE file. From the expression, the DBCS can determine that it has to deal with TREE records that are related to a potential FORFILE target record. Using the external schema, the DBCS can determine that there is only one set FOR_TREE connecting FORFILE and TREE; it will therefore use the FOR_TREE occurrence with the owner that is the potential target record. The set subclause is thus superfluous. However, had there been two or more sets connecting FORFILE and TREE, the DBCS could not determine which group of member records to use unless the set subclause were also included.

As an example of a case where we could not omit the set subclause, consider the data

---

base in Figure 6.7 involving oil companies and drilling concessions. We suppose that we have two sets RELA and RELB, where RELA connects a company to some former concessions and RELB connects it to its present concessions; consider the following retrieval in which the full EOS syntax must be used.

Find the names of companies with present concessions all in Texas.

```
FIND NEXT:
        PETROFIRM OWNER RECORD
        (OWNER SET (RELB) OCCURRENCE
(FOR ONE AND FOR ALL CONCESSION MEMBER RECORDS (LOC = 'TEXAS')))
```

11.2.10 Use of Adjectival Expressions

Referring to the syntax expressions in Figure 11.1, we notice that in Expression 5 provision is made for the use of what we call *adjectival expressions (adj-expression)*. Furthermore, from Expression 6 we see that an adjectival expression has the same structure as *logical-expression-1,* which, as we have seen, consists of *condition-term* and *xreference* elements. However, we have so far made no use of the adjectival expression facility.

To understand the use to which adjectival expressions may be put, we must first turn back and consider the way in which we used quantifiers in the EOS CODASYL enhancement. It will help if we develop the discussion around a simple EOS predicate involving the universal quantifier, such as the following.

```
        FORFILE OWNER RECORD ((LOC = 'CALIFORNIA') &
        OWNER SET (FOR_TREE) OCCURRENCE
(FOR ALL TREE MEMBER RECORDS (PLANTED < 19600101)))
```

Here we are specifying California forests in which all the trees, if any, were planted before 1960.

In this very typical example of the use of the universal quantifier, the quantifier quantifies not all the records of the file TREE, but only those records which are the members of a specified owner-coupled set occurrence. This use of quantifiers is quite natural and mirrors their use in natural languages. When we say "all the trees in the forest X," we mean "all the tree member entities belonging to the forest owner entity X." (In contrast, as we shall see in Chapter 14, in the well-known relational nonnavigational sublanguage DSL ALPHA, the quantifiers quantify a complete file of records, thus making quantifiers more difficult to use.)

However, natural language has a further refinement and permits quantification of subsets of the group of member entities belonging to a single owner entity. For example, when we state "all the cedar trees in forest X," we mean "all of a certain subset (that is, cedars) of the tree member entities of the forest owner entity X." In such a case, the natural language quantifier *all* quantifies only those tree members qualified by the adjective *cedar*. It is this further refinement that is permitted by the adjectival expression of the EOS CODASYL enhancement. When the adjectival expression is used, the preceding quantifier quantifies that subset of the member records of a set occurrence specified by the adjectival expression.

We now illustrate the use of the adjectival expression with two examples, one simple and the other complex, which for convenience employ the simplified syntax described in the previous section. We take the simple example first.

Retrieval 13: Simple Adjectival Expression   *Find the names of California forests in which most of the cedar trees were planted before 1960.*

We place the following expression in a suitable DO loop.

```
FIND NEXT:
        FORFILE OWNER RECORD ((LOC = 'CALIFORNIA') &
        (FOR MAJORITY OF (SPECIES = 'CEDAR') TREE MEMBER RECORDS
                                        (PLANTED < 19600101) ))
```

The adjectival expression is underlined. Here the natural quantifier FOR MAJORITY OF specifies what quantity of a certain subset of the members of each FOR_TREE set occurrence are to satisfy the condition (PLANTED < 19600101), and that subset consists of cedar trees as specified in the adjectival expression. In the following retrieval, we consider a more involved adjectival expression.

Retrieval 14: Complex Adjectival Expression   *Find the names of California forests in which the majority of electrically measured cedar trees were planted before 1960.*

Note this is not the same as retrieving the names of California forests in which the majority of trees are cedars that have had electrical measurements, and that were planted before 1960. We place the following in a suitable DO loop.

```
FIND NEXT:
        FORFILE OWNER RECORD ((LOC = 'CALIFORNIA') &
        (FOR MAJORITY OF   (SPECIES = 'CEDAR' &
                            OWNER SET (TREE_MEAS) OCCURRENCE
                    (EXISTS MEASUREMENT MEMBER (TYPE = 'ELECTRICAL')))
                            TREE MEMBER RECORDS (PLANTED < 19600101) ))
```

The rather involved adjectival expression is underlined. Here the natural quantifier FOR MAJORITY OF quantifies a subset of the TREE members of each FOR_TREE set occurrence, and that subset consists of member records that are cedar and have had electrical measurements performed on them.

The reader may have noticed that the real need for adjectival expressions becomes apparent only when the natural quantifiers are used. Had the previous two retrievals involved the basic quantifier FOR ALL, then it would have been possible to find an alternative construction not involving the use of the adjectival expression. We can see this from the following modified version of retrieval 13.

Retrieval 13a: Basic Quantifier   *Find the names of the California forests in which all of the cedar trees, if any, were planted before 1960.*

We place the following in a suitable DO loop.

FIND NEXT:

             FORFILE OWNER RECORD ((LOC = 'CALIFORNIA') &
    (⌐EXISTS TREE MEMBER RECORD (SPECIES = 'CEDAR
                              & PLANTED > = 19600101))

A similar construction could have been used with retrieval 14, had it involved the basic quantifier FOR ALL. As an exercise, the reader might attempt to express retrieval 14 without the use of an adjectival expression.

11.3 RETRIEVALS WITH RECURSIVE SETS

We saw in earlier chapters that in many cases special versions of the CODASYL DML commands are required with recursive sets. With these commands the trouble was invariably due to the fact that the current record of set could be taken as pointing either to the set occurrence in which it was the owner or to the set occurrence in which it was a member.

We have a somewhat related difficulty with the EOS sublanguage. Fortunately, since the language makes almost no use of the concept of current of set, the problem is not serious and the solution almost trivial. As we shall see, it is necessary merely to *require* the inclusion of MEMBER and OWNER in EOS expressions involving recursive sets.

11.3.1 Necessity of OWNER/MEMBER Specifications

We may not omit the OWNER/MEMBER specification when dealing with recursive sets. If we do, we risk ambiguity. We illustrate this in the two following retrievals.

Retrieval 15: Level-2 with Universal Quantifier   *Find the date of planting for those trees for which all immediate descendants, if any, are in the forest 'XFOR'.*
We use the following in a suitable DO loop.

FIND NEXT:
    TREE OWNER RECORD
    (OWNER SET (PROPAGATE) OCCURRENCE
        (FOR ALL TREE MEMBER RECORDS (FOREST = 'XFOR')));
........;
GET INTO (TREEREC.PLANTED);

Here we select a TREE record if all of its members in PROPAGATE have FOREST value 'XFOR'. Figure 11.8a gives the retrieval diagram.

Retrieval 16: Level-2 with Universal Quantifier   *Find the date of planting for each tree which is the immediate descendant of a tree for which all immediate descendants are in the forest 'XFOR'.*
We place the following in a suitable loop.

FIND NEXT:
    TREE MEMBER RECORD

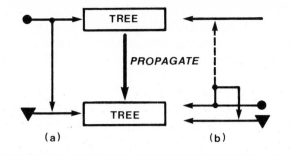

(a) (b)

FIGURE 11.8. *Retrievals with the recursive set*
PROPAGATE, *shown for convenience as connecting*
together two separate TREE *files. Retrievals 15 and 16 are*
shown in (a) and (b), respectively.

      (MEMBER SET (PROPAGATE) OCCURRENCE
      FOR ALL TREE MEMBER RECORDS (FOREST = 'XFOR')));
.......;
GET INTO (TREEREC.PLANTED);

Thus we select a TREE record if it is a member of a PROPAGATE occurrence in which all member records have a FOREST field value 'XFOR'. The retrieval diagram is given in Figure 11.8*b*.

Prevention of Ambiguity   If, in the previous two retrievals, we omit OWNER and MEMBER, the retrieval expressions become identical. However, since the two retrievals are clearly quite different, it is the correct use of OWNER and MEMBER that prevents ambiguity.

    The solution to the problem is thus the inclusion of a syntactic rule to the effect that OWNER/MEMBER syntax may not be omitted when a *file-name,* that is, a *target-file-name,* record is specified in a capacity either as owner or member of a recursive set. However, in the next section we turn to the real limitations of the EOS enhancement.

11.4 LIMITATIONS OF THE EOS ENHANCEMENT

11.4.1 Performance Optimization

In the previous chapter we saw that it is the responsibility of the applications programmer to write retrieval programs employing the CODASYL DML so as to optimize performance. In practice this usually means that the program should have a minimum of accesses to the data base. We saw also that with a more complex retrieval, more than one retrieval strategy may be identified, and that optimization of the performance of the retrieval program to a large extent depends on selection of the right retrieval strategy.

    The same considerations apply to the use of the EOS CODASYL enhancement. The reader should be aware that the enhancement is limited in capability. While powerful, it permits merely sequential search of a file, with search arguments dependent not only on field values in the file being searched but also on the relationships of the file to other files in the data base. Thus the applications programmer has possibilities for optimizing applications programs by means of the choice of files to be searched using the enhancement. An example should clarify this important point.

Let us suppose that we wish to carry out retrieval 2 from Chapter 10 using the EOS enhancement. The optimization of this retrieval with standard CODASYL commands was discussed in Section 10.3.1. The retrieval was as follows.

Find the forest records for forests which do not have species 'X' but do have species 'Y'.

The simplest method of carrying out this retrieval with the EOS enhancement would involve sequentially searching the FORFILE file with appropriate search conditions. We could place the following in a suitable WHILE loop.

```
FIND NEXT:
        FORFILE OWNER
        (OWNER SET (FOR_TREE) OCCURRENCE
        ((FOR ALL TREE MEMBER RECORDS
                        (SPECIES ⌐ = 'X'))
        & (EXISTS TREE MEMBER RECORD
                        (SPECIES = 'Y')));
        ........;
GET CRU (FORFILE) INTO (FORREC);
PUT LIST (FORREC);
```

This retrieval could be very inefficient, however, as it might require searching each FORFILE record together with all of its TREE members—that is, all of the FORFILE and TREE records. (Of course, depending on the internal data-base structures, this retrieval could be very efficient.)

A better method could involve searching the TREE file for records with SPECIES value 'Y' and retrieving the corresponding FOREST value. Using this FOREST value the FORFILE owner record could be accessed and its TREE members searched; since FOREST is the record-key field for FORFILE the system would always be able to access the file directly for such a record. A check can then be made to see if all the members in FOR_TREE are not of species 'X'. We could place the following in a suitable WHILE loop.

```
FIND NEXT:
        TREE RECORD (SPECIES = 'Y');
        .........;
        GET INTO (TREEREC.FOREST);
        FIND FIRST:
            FORFILE OWNER RECORD ((FORFILE.FOREST = TREEREC.FOREST) &
```

```
OWNER SET (FOR_TREE) OCCURRENCE
(FOR ALL TREE MEMBER RECORDS (SPECIES ⌐ = 'X')));
.......;
GET CRU (FORFILE) INTO (FORREC);
PUT LIST (FORREC);
```

It is clear that performance optimization can sometimes require more complex coding, as in this case. However, the above program excerpt would be a lot easier to write than the conventional CODASYL retrieval in Section 10.3.1. The reader should easily see that the retrieval strategy is almost the same in both cases.

11.4.2 Advanced CODASYL Enhancements

The CODASYL enhancement described in this chapter is also limited in another very important way. While nonnavigational as far as search conditions are concerned, it still retrieves only one record at a time. A step forward would be an enhancement that could retrieve all the records from a file that satisfied the conditions specified in a predicate. One problem with such an enhancement would be the placement of the data-base keys of the retrieved records. A solution might be special keep-lists, from which the program could fetch the data-base keys of the retrieved records as required.

However, not all the problems connected with such an advanced enhancement have been solved, although there is every reason to believe that such an enhancement is possible. A great benefit would be the possibility of automatic performance optimization. The system would merely use the retrieval expression as a specification of the records to be retrieved and use a software component known as an *optimizer* to determine the best retrieval strategy. Such optimizers have been developed for prototypes of relational data-base management systems (see Chapter 16).

11.4.3 Status of the EOS CODASYL Enhancement

At the time of writing, the EOS CODASYL enhancement is purely demonstrative of what can be constructed in the way of powerful retrieval sublanguages capable of manipulating a CODASYL schema and based on conceptual records and owner-coupled sets. It also demonstrates the fundamental importance of the otherwise pragmatic concept of the owner-coupled set.

The reader should be aware, however, that in the past decade research and development on nonnavigational retrieval sublanguages has been to a large extent devoted to relational sublanguages (see the relational approach to data-base management in Chapters 13, 14, 15, and 16).

It is probably fair to state that the proponents of the relational approach have had a head start in this particular race, mainly because it was possible to adapt previously developed set theoretical expressions and in this way construct relational retrieval sublanguages such as DSL ALPHA and SQL. We may therefore expect that it will be some time before a nonnavigational retrieval sublanguage is incorporated in the CODASYL specifications; nevertheless, in our opinion, such an incorporation is in the long run inevitable.

EXERCISES

1. Referring to the 4NF version of the data base in Figure 6.5, construct an EOS CODASYL enhancement expression for the following retrievals. The reader should first remove **CONCESSION** and **COMPANY** from **DRILL_HOLE** and then devise owner-coupled sets for the relationships involved in this data base.

   a. Find the name of the agencies that have granted drilling concessions costing less than $100,000.

   b. Find the headquarters of oil companies at present holding drilling concessions on properties owned by **'X'**.

   c. Find the place of registration of drilling firms that have drilled holes now owned by Texas oil companies.

   d. Find the locations and concession numbers for concessions on which all holes drilled so far have cost more than $100,000 each.

   e. Find the headquarters of oil companies at present holding at least one Texas concession formerly held by Texoil.

   f. Find the chiefs of the agencies that have granted concessions to oil companies with headquarters in Calgary.

   g. Find the names of the drilling firms that drilled the holes now on concessions formerly held by Texoil.

   h. The semantics of the data base prevent us from retrieving the names of all the companies for which the drilling firm Testdrill has drilled holes. Why?

2. Referring to the data base in Figure 6.10, devise an EOS expression to retrieve the names of the chiefs of those oil companies with immediate subsidiaries that all have their headquarters location in Denver.

3. Referring to the data base in Figure 6.14, devise an EOS expression to retrieve the headquarters and names of companies that are themselves more than 5% owned by immediate subsidiaries of Texoil.

REFERENCES

Bradley, J., 1978a, "An Extended Owner-coupled Set Data Model and Predicate Calculus for Data Base Management," *ACM Trans. on Database Sys.,* **3**(4):385–416.

Bradley, J., 1978b, "Operations Data Bases," *Proc. ACM Conference on Very Large Data Bases,* Berlin, pp. 164–76.

Chomsky, N., 1959, "On Certain Formal Properties of Grammars," *Inf. and Control,* **2**(2):113–24.

Codd, E. F., 1971, "A Data Base Sublanguage Founded on the Relational Calculus," *Proc. ACM SIGFIDET Workshop on Data Description, Access and Control,* pp. 35–78.

Codd, E. F., 1972, "Relational Completeness of Data Base Sublanguages," in *Courant Computer Science Symposium Series,* vol. 6, Prentice-Hall, Englewood Cliffs, N.J., pp. 65–98.

Date, C. J., 1977, *Introduction to Data Base Systems,* Addison-Wesley, Reading, Mass.

Deheneffe, C., and H. Hennebert, 1976, "NUL: A Navigational User's Language for a Network Structured Data Base," *Proc. ACM SIGMOD,* pp. 135–42.

Ernest, C., 1975, "Selection and Higher Level Structures in Networks," in *Data Base Description,* B. C. M. Douque and G. M. Nijsson (eds.), North-Holland, N.Y., pp. 215–37.

Haseman, W. D., and A. B. Whinston, 1975, *Structure of a Query Language for a Network Data Base*, Purdue University, Lafayette, Ind.

Haseman, W. D., and A. B. Whinston, 1977, *Introduction to Data Management,* Irwin, Inc., Homewood, Ill.

Kuhns, J. L., 1969, "Logical Aspects of Question Answering by Computer," *Proc. of the Third Int. Symposium on Computer and Information Sciences,* Miami Beach, Florida, Academic Press, New York.

Kuhns, J. L., 1971, "Quantification in Query Systems," *Proc. ACM Symp. on Information and Retrieval,* available from *ACM,* New York.

Parsons, R. G., A. G. Dale, and C. V. Yurkanan, 1974, "Data Manipulation Requirements for Data Base Management Systems," *Comptr. J.,* **17**(2):99–103.

Whinston, A. B., 1975, "Water Quality Management and Information Systems," Tech. Rep. No. 68, Wateces Res. Ctr., Purdue University, W. Lafayette, Ind. (NTIS No. PG-247-142).

The Internal CODASYL Schema

12

In order to load the FORESTRY data base in Chapter 9 with the conceptual schema given in Chapter 8, we assumed that a data-base administrator had prepared and link-edited a suitable internal schema. In this chapter, we shall look at the techniques involved in the specification of internal schemas.

12.1 THE DATA STORAGE DESCRIPTION LANGUAGE (DSDL)

An internal CODASYL schema is specified by means of a data storage description language (DSDL). The DSDL with which we shall be dealing in this chapter is quite new and is still a draft of a proposed standard. It was prepared by a working group responsible jointly to the British Computer Society and the CODASYL Data Description Language Committee (DDLC). It was published in 1978 in the DDLC Journal of Development along with the new conceptual schema DDL, which we describe in Chapter 8 [CODASYL, 1978].

Readers are reminded that the DSDL is very much a draft language and may well undergo significant modification in years to come. This chapter should merely be taken as an illustration of the kinds of features (and perhaps difficulties) to be found in such a language. We illustrate the language by means of the FORESTRY data base and refrain from giving an exact specification of its syntax.

12.1.1 Capabilities of the DSDL

The DSDL permits the data structures described in the conceptual schema to be further specified in terms of an idealized external storage environment. We use the term *idealized storage environment* to underline the fact that this environment is independent of both operating systems and physical devices.

Thus the internal schema is not sufficient to fully specify the physical data base. Some of the requirements listed in the internal schema must be made known to the operating system, and it is expected that this will be done by means of implementation-dependent facilities. If the operating system were OS/MVS, we could use IBM Job Control Language for this purpose.

As an example of this dependence, and as we shall see later, in the internal schema an internal file takes up a specified number of pages of storage space, and a page has a fixed size in characters.[1] Let us suppose that the number of characters in a record of an internal file is constant. In the internal schema specification, we could have

```
INITIAL SIZE IS 80 PAGES
PAGE SIZE IS 2000 CHARACTERS
```

Using OS JCL, we could then specify a DD statement with

```
//ddname      DD      .......SPACE = (TRK,10),...,DISK = 3350,
                             DCB = (RECFM = FB,BLKSIZE = 2000,...)
```

This would give us 10 tracks, each containing eight 2000-byte blocks.

Two other important capabilities of the DSDL are worth mentioning. These are the capability of permitting *performance tuning* of the data base and the capability of promoting physical-data independence. The two are quite closely related. (Physical-data independence has already been introduced in Chapter 6.)

Performance Tuning and Physical Data Independence   Although the internal schema is specified in terms of an idealized storage environment, the specification will, with the help of the implementation Job Control Language, determine the physical implementation of the data base. However, the physical data base can be structured in different ways without affecting the results of the execution of an application program.

For example, suppose that in an application program we issue a DML command

```
FIND FILE (TREE) KEY (TREENUMB);
```

This is the record-key FIND command, permitting retrieval of a TREE record on presentation of its record key TREENUMB, and if the internal file corresponding to the conceptual schema TREE file is organized as a hash file, the record will be retrieved in a few internal file accesses. However, if it is organized as a sequential file, the number of internal file accesses required to retrieve it will be very much dependent on the kind of index available for the file. But no matter how the internal file is organized, the record will be retrieved.

When the results of execution of a program are independent of the physical data base

---

[1]*These do not necessarily have anything to do with pages of memory in virtual operating systems (see Chapter 1).*

in this way, the program is said to be *physical-data independent* (see Chapter 6). The *performance* of the program will be very much dependent on the physical data base, however.

A data-base administrator could change the internal schema for a data base to permit one group of programs to perform more efficiently, which often causes another group to run less efficiently. This function of the data-base administrator is known as *performance tuning,* and an internal schema is one of the required tools.

12.1.2 DSDL Terminology

Since the DSDL is used to specify schema structures in an idealized storage environment, the introduction of some new terminology is unavoidable. We need the following terms.

1. Storage schema: The internal schema is referred to as a *storage schema* to distinguish it from the conceptual schema, which is simply referred to as the *schema.*

2. Storage area: The *storage area* is a portion of external storage media space and may be regarded as corresponding to a disk pack. It may thus contain one or more storage files, together with indexes.

3. Page: A *page* is a numbered (or addressable) subdivision of a storage area and is the unit of transfer between storage area and DBCS buffers. In a given storage area, all pages have the same size. A page thus corresponds reasonably well to an IBM data block. (But see criticism, Section 12.3.1.)

4. Storage record: A *storage record* is a record in a storage area. It may contain data fields corresponding to schema record-data fields. A storage record will normally also contain pointer fields. A given schema record may be mapped onto (that is, implemented by) more than one type of storage record, and these storage records may have overlapping data fields. We shall refer to a collection of storage records corresponding to a schema file as a *storage file.*

5. Index: This is an *index* in the most general sense. It is a sequence of elements each containing either a pointer or a pointer and a key.

12.1.3 Structure of a Storage Schema

A storage schema has the structure shown in Figure 12.1. There are five kinds of entry, two of them introductory and three of them repeating. (In reading this section, readers should frequently refer to Figure 12.1, and also to Figure 12.2.)

Storage-Schema Entry   In the storage-schema entry we may specify

1. The name of the storage schema and relevant (conceptual) schema;

2. The schema files and sets covered by the storage schema.

It has to be possible for a storage schema to contain a useful specification of only a part of the structures specified in the schema in order to facilitate testing and development.

```
*   STORAGE SCHEMA entry
*   MAPPING DESCRIPTION entry

    *   STORAGE AREA entry
        **  Storage Record entry
        **  Storage Record entry
            ..................
        **  Storage Record entry
            Index entry
            Index entry
            ...........
            Index entry

    *   STORAGE AREA entry
        **  Storage Record entry
            ..................
            Index entry
            ...........
    *   STORAGE AREA entry
            ..................
```

FIGURE 12.1. *Structure of a CODASYL internal or storage schema.*

Mapping-Description Entry   The *mapping-description entry* consists of mapping subentries, and there is a subentry for each schema file covered by the storage schema.

A mapping subentry names the storage file or files for each schema file. As mentioned earlier, there may be one or more storage files for a given schema file. For example, if we needed to access a schema file very fast, then the file could have a corresponding storage file structured as a hash file. However, if reasonably fast sequential access were also required, an additional storage file could be named. This file might have just a key field and a pointer to the corresponding record in the hash file but have sequential organization in key order.

Storage-Area Entry   There will be many storage areas in the physical data base, each one taking up space on our idealized storage medium. In the storage-area entry we may specify

1. The name of the storage area;

2. The initial number of pages it contains, together with the size of increments by which this number can increase and maximum allowed number of pages;

3. The page size in characters (or words).

The storage area can contain one or more storage files, but they are not specified here. The storage area is roughly equivalent to a disk pack.

Storage-Record Entry   There is a storage-record entry for each of the storage files in a storage area and named in the mapping-description entry above. In this entry we can

---

THE INTERNAL CODASYL SCHEMA

1. Name the storage file or record type involved;

2. Define the contents of the records of the file;

3. Specify how the records are to be stored or placed in the data base.

The storage-record entry is fairly complex, as might be expected. It has four subentries, three of which may be repeated. The subentries are the *storage-record subentry,* the *placement subentry,* the *set-pointer subentry*, and the *data subentry*. The structure of a storage-record entry is displayed in Figure 12.2. We take each subentry in turn.

Storage-record subentry   The storage-record subentry permits us to specify the following.

1. The name of the storage file involved.

2. The name of another storage file with records to which the records of the specified storage file are linked. This will be used when a schema file is specified in the mapping-description entry as having more than one storage file. The storage files involved must then be linked together, either by direct or indirect (that is, by means of an index) pointers.

3. The number of pointers needed in the storage-file records.

Placement subentry   The placement subentry permits us to specify the following.

1. The load factor, in terms of the number of records allowed per page (or block).

2. The access or placement method. There are three possibilities.

    a. Hashed, by specifying a hashing routine and a hashing key.

    b. Clustered; the record is placed physically as close as possible to its owner record in a specified owner-coupled set.

    c. Sequential, in specified ascending or descending key order.

3. The name of the storage area to which a storage file is assigned, together with the designation (in page numbers) of the part of the storage area that may be used.

```
**   Storage Record Entry:
          Storage record subentry
          Placement subentry
          Placement subentry
          ..................
          Set Pointer subentry
          Set Pointer subentry
          ...................
          Data subentry
          Data subentry
          .............
```

FIGURE 12.2.   *Structure of a storage-record entry for a storage schema.*

Set-pointer subentry   The set-pointer subentry permits us to specify one of the following types of pointer.

1.   INDEX pointer. This points to an index or pointer array and can be used if the corresponding schema file is an owner file.

2.   FIRST and LAST pointers. These point to the first and last members of a set occurrence and may be used if the corresponding schema file is an owner file.

3.   NEXT and PRIOR pointers. These point to the next and prior members of a set occurrence and may be used if the corresponding schema file is a member file.

4.   OWNER pointer. This points to the owner record of a set occurrence and may be used if the corresponding schema file is a member file.

By means of multiple set-pointer subentries, the pointer systems for the sets in which the corresponding schema record participates may be specified. There are two types of pointer system allowed, as shown in Figures 12.3*a* and 12.3*b*. The set pointer or representation systems are known as the *member chain* and *set index* or *set pointer array*. We take them in turn.

1.   Member-chain representation.
     The simplest specification allows an owner record to point to the first member using a FIRST pointer and a member to point to the next member using a NEXT pointer. This permits the set occurrence to be processed in "clockwise" fashion. An OWNER pointer may also be specified, thus permitting fast retrieval of the owner of any member.
         Anticlockwise processing of the set occurrence is possible if there is a LAST pointer in the owner record and a PRIOR pointer in the member record.

2.   Set-index representation
     Here we specify an INDEX pointer in an owner record that points to all of the member records. Each member record may have an OWNER pointer, as in the case of member-chain representation.

It is worth observing here that sets are not specified directly in the storage schema. What we specify are the set pointers needed by a storage record. The choice will, of course, depend on whether the schema record corresponding to the storage record in question is an owner, a member, or an owner and a member.

Data subentry   With the *data subentry*, we specify a data field from the schema record that will be included in the storage record in question. With the specified data field, the data type (format), precision and alignment may be specified.

Index Entry   For a given storage-area entry, there will be an index entry for each index used with the storage files in that storage area. The index entry thus defines the characteristics of an index.
     There are three kinds of index, shown diagrammatically in Figures 12.3*b* and 12.4.

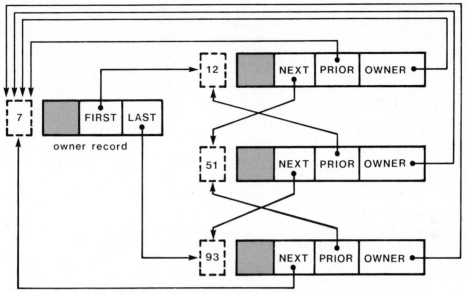

(a) Member-chain pointer system for owner-coupled set representation. The pointers shown are direct, that is, they reference the address of a record. Thus the **PRIOR** pointer field in member-1 record contains the owner address 7. Indirect pointers may also be used.

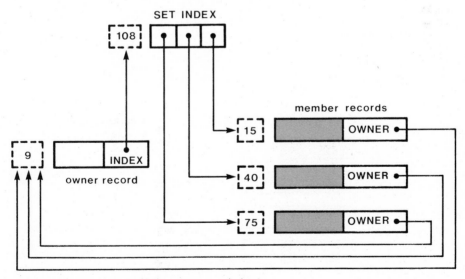

(b) Set index or pointer array for owner-coupled set representation. The **OWNER** pointers may be direct or indirect.

FIGURE 12.3.

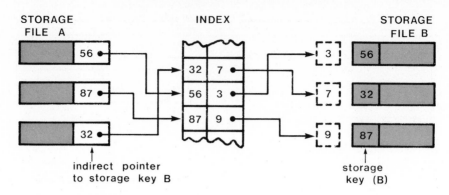

(a) Use of storage-key index.

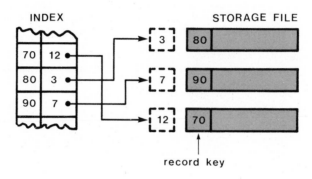

(b) Use of record-key index.

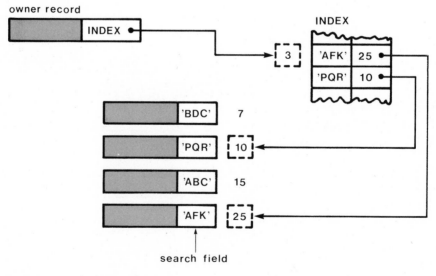

(c) Use of a search-set index.

FIGURE 12.4. Storage-schema indexes.

1. Storage-key indexes: These are used as indirect pointers to connect two storage records together (Figure 12.4a). Each index element consists of a *storage key* and a *pointer*. The storage key is a unique key assigned by the system to each storage record. (The storage-record subentry contains the storage key specification.)

2. Record-key indexes: These are used to permit direct and sequential access to storage records by means of secondary or record keys declared in the schema. Each index element consists of a pointer to the storage record and the schema key value (Figure 12.4b).

3. Set indexes: These are used with owner-coupled sets. There are two kinds.

   a. Set representation indexes: These are used to represent owner-coupled sets, as illustrated in Figure 12.3b. Each index element consists of a pointer. The order of the pointers coincides with the member record order as specified in the schema.

   b. Search-set indexes: These are for searching for records with certain field values in set occurrences with very large numbers of member records. Each entry in the index consists of a pointer to a member record, together with the value of a search field (or fields). See Figure 12.4c.

The use of a so-called storage key in the storage-key index does not seem altogether satisfying. It was clearly introduced because the freedom to specify storage records with any of the fields from the corresponding schema necessarily results in the possibility of storage records without the unique record-key field. Furthermore, storage records without a unique record-key field would always result if the corresponding schema record were declared without a unique record key. An alternative might be to require that all schema and storage records contain a unique record key, as specified in the schema. This would also satisfy one of the requirements for a 4NF file.

12.2 FORESTRY DATA-BASE STORAGE SCHEMA

We shall now give an example of a storage schema as applied to the FORESTRY database schema from Chapter 8. However, we shall not give a specification for the whole schema, as this would involve a great deal of repetition. The reader is invited to complete the storage schema below as an exercise. We restrict this storage schema to a specification for the schema TREE and MEASUREMENT files and the TREE_MEAS and PROPAGATE sets; that is, that corresponding to the BOT_FORESTRY subschema from Chapter 9. In addition, we make the assumption that there are 100,000 records in the MEASUREMENT file and 10,000 in the TREE file; we assume also that there are four characters in a pointer field and that the loading factor for the storage file MAIN_TREE is close to 75%.

We shall take the specification in steps, explaining the choice of structures used and discussing DSDL syntax and semantics where useful. Specification lines are numbered.

12.2.1 Storage-Schema Entry

```
01        STORAGE SCHEMA NAME IS STORFOR
02                      FOR FORESTRY SCHEMA
03            REPRESENT ONLY TREE
```

```
04              MEASUREMENT RECORDS
05              AND ONLY TREE_MEAS
06                  PROPAGATE SETS
```

If we specify ALL instead of ONLY after REPRESENT, all the schema records are assumed to be included. We may also specify ALL EXCEPT, in which case all the files are included except those specified. The same alternatives are available instead of ONLY after AND.

12.2.2 Mapping Description Entry

```
07          MAPPING FOR TREE
08              STORAGE RECORDS ARE MAIN_TREE
09                              SUBSID_TREE
10
11          MAPPING FOR MEASUREMENT
12              STORAGE RECORD IS STOR_MEAS
```

We have chosen two storage files to represent the TREE files. We would like to have fast, direct, and sequential access to the TREE file. The storage file MAIN_TREE will have the same fields as TREE and will have a hash-file organization. The other (subsidiary) storage file SUBSID_TREE will have just the record key field TREENUMB and be organized as a sequential file, but with each SUBSID_TREE record having a (direct) pointer to the corresponding MAIN_TREE record. The situation is illustrated in Figure 12.5. Had we intended to have an indirect link between these two storage records, a storage-record index would need to be specified (in the index entry).

12.2.3 First Storage-Area Entry

```
13          STORAGE AREA NAME IS S_A_TREE
14              INITIAL SIZE IS 400 PAGES
15              PAGE SIZE IS 3300 CHARACTERS
```

After the INITIAL clause, we may specify by how much we intend to allow the storage area to grow in size. However, this storage area will contain the TREE storage files, and we assume that we do not have a requirement for extra space in the short run. MAINTREE is a hash file and we shall have a load factor initially near 75%, which allows for some growth in the size of the TREE file without requiring a larger storage area. The page size of 3300 characters permits 50 storage MAIN_TREE records per page, each with 4 pointers (see end of Section 12.2.4).

12.2.4 First Storage-Record Entry

Storage-Record Subentry

```
16          STORAGE RECORD NAME IS MAIN_TREE
17              RESERVE 4 POINTERS
```

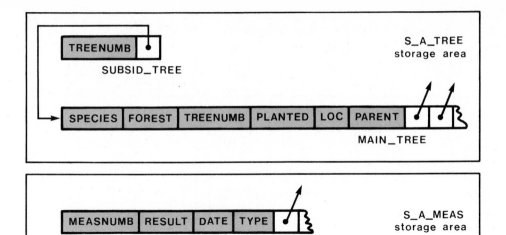

FIGURE 12.5. *Storage files and areas used to map the* TREE *and* MEASUREMENT *schema files and the* TREE_MEAS *and* PROPAGATE *schema sets. The* TREE *file is mapped by the two storage files* SUBSID_TREE *and* MAIN_TREE.

We shall place all the set pointers in the MAIN_TREE storage file and none in the SUBSID_TREE file.

Placement Subentry

18	DENSITY IS 50 STORAGE RECORDS PER PAGE
19	
20	PLACEMENT IS CALC TREEHASH USING TREEKEY /* See schema line 21 */
21	WITHIN S_A_TREE
22	FROM PAGE 0 THRU 280

With the FROM clause, we allocate the space in the storage area S_A_TREE that can accept MAIN_TREE records. If this space is 75% full, 10,000 MAIN_TREE storage records will occupy about 280 pages. TREEHASH is a hashing routine.

Set-Pointer Subentry

| 23 | SET TREE_MEAS |
| 24 | POINTER FOR FIRST LAST IS DIRECT |

We have specified owner to member pointers as being direct. See Figures 12.3*a* and 12.6.

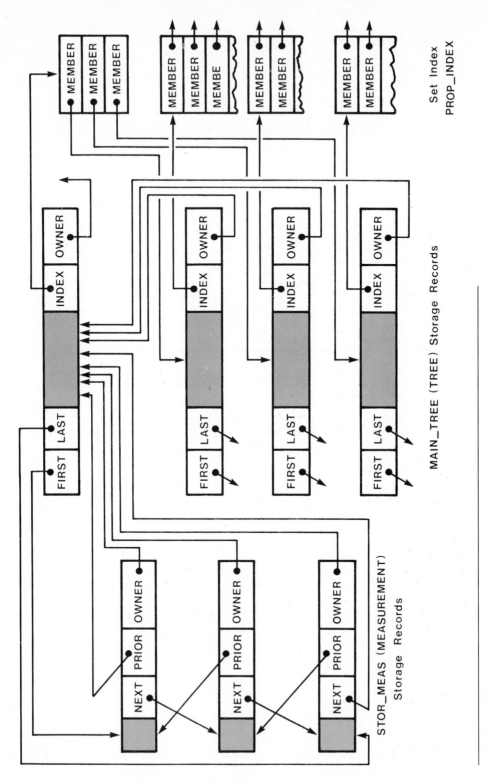

FIGURE 12.6. *Showing the pointer systems for the sets PROPAGATE and TREE_MEAS as specified in the storage schema STORFOR. PROPAGATE is a recursive set.*

408

Set-Pointer Subentry

25	SET PROPAGATE
26	POINTER FOR INDEX IS PROP_INDEX

A MAIN_TREE record in its capacity as owner of a PROPAGATE occurrence will point to its MAIN_TREE members via the index PROP_INDEX.

Set-Pointer Subentry

27	SET PROPAGATE
28	POINTER FOR OWNER IS DIRECT

A MAIN_TREE record in its capacity as member of a PROPAGATE occurrence will point to the MAIN_TREE owner record.

The last two set-pointer subentries could have been combined into a shorter, single subentry. In addition, the pointer system in which MAIN_TREE records participate as owners of TREE_MEAS and as owners and members in PROPAGATE is shown in Figure 12.6. We see that MAIN_TREE records each contain 4 pointers.

Data Subentries

29	SPECIES CHARACTER SIZE 20 CHARACTERS
30	FOREST CHARACTER SIZE 15 CHARACTERS
31	TREENUMB FIXED BINARY SIZE 32 BITS
32	PLANTED PACKED DECIMAL SIZE 40 BITS
33	LOC FIXED BINARY SIZE 16 BITS
34	PARENT FIXED BINARY SIZE 32 BITS

Thus, including the 4 pointers, which are each 4 characters long, each storage record is 66 characters long.

12.2.5 Second Storage-Record Entry

Storage-Record Subentry

35	STORAGE_RECORD NAME IS SUBSID_TREE
36	RESERVE 1 POINTER

Placement Subentry, Data Subentry

37	DENSITY IS 412 STORAGE RECORDS PER PAGE
38	
39	PLACEMENT IS SEQUENTIAL ASCENDING TREEKEY
40	WITHIN S_A_TREE PAGE 280 THRU 310
41	TREENUMB FIXED BINARY SIZE 32 BITS

We have no set-pointer subentry for SUBSID_TREE, since MAIN_TREE records carry all the set pointers (see also Section 12.3.1).

12.2.6 Index Entry

We have specified that an index is being used with PROPAGATE to connect an owner to its members.

```
42          INDEX NAME IS PROP_INDEX
43              USED FOR SET PROPAGATE MEMBER TREE KEY PLANTED
44              WITHIN S_A_TREE
45              FROM PAGE 310 THRU 326
```

From the FORESTRY schema (line 82), we see that members of a PROPAGATE set occurrence are available in set sort-key order; the set sort key is PLANTED. We therefore specify PLANTED (see also Section 12.3.1).

12.2.7 Index Entries

In the schema (lines 24 and 26), we specified that the fields SPECIES and LOC were secondary record keys, duplicates being allowed. It would therefore be useful to specify record-key indexes for these two secondary keys.

```
46          INDEX NAME IS SPEC_INDEX
47              USED FOR RECORD KEY
48                  KEY SPECKEY
49
50          INDEX NAME IS LOC_INDEX
51              USED FOR RECORD TREE
52                  KEY LOCKEY
```

The WITHIN clauses may be omitted, and we leave it to the system to find space for these indexes in S_A_TREE storage area.

12.2.8 Second Storage-Area Entry

```
53          STORAGE AREA NAME IS S_A_MEAS
54              INITIAL SIZE IS 1250 PAGES
55
56                      EXPANDABLE BY STEPS OF 50 PAGES
57                                      TO 2000 PAGES
58              PAGE SIZE IS 2640 CHARACTERS
```

This storage area will initially hold 10,000 records from the STOR_MEAS storage file (corresponding to the schema MEASUREMENT file). We are assuming that the file will grow. Hence we use the EXPANDABLE clause, which specifies the increments and extent of the desired growth. The page size of 2640 permits 80 records per page, each record with 3 pointers (see the end of Section 12.2.9).

12.2.9 Storage-Record Entry

```
59      STORAGE RECORD NAME IS STOR_MEAS
60          RESERVE 3 POINTERS
61
62      DENSITY IS 80   STORAGE RECORDS PER PAGE
63
64      PLACEMENT IS SEQUENTIAL ASCENDING MEASKEY
65          WITHIN S_A_MEAS
66
67      SET TREE_MEAS
68      POINTER FOR NEXT PRIOR IS DIRECT
            OWNER IS DIRECT
```

We make the MEASUREMENT file sequential, since in the schema (line 34) there is a guidance specification that informs the data-base administrator that the frequency of sequential retrieval is high. We also assume that direct retrieval is by means of the owner file.

Because we specified that the owner-to-member pointers were FIRST/LAST in a set-pointer subentry for MAIN_TREE, we are now required to specify NEXT/PRIOR pointers for the file STOR_MEAS in the set TREE_MEAS. In the schema we declared two set sort keys for member records in TREE_MEAS (FORESTRY schema, line 69). The member records in a set occurrence will thus be kept sorted with DATE and TYPE as major and minor sort keys, respectively.

We end the storage-record entry with the data subentries.

```
69      MEASNUMB FIXED BINARY SIZE 16 BITS
70      RESULT FLOAT BINARY SIZE 32 BITS
71      DATE PACKED DECIMAL SIZE 40 BITS
72      TYPE CHARACTER SIZE 10 CHARACTERS
```

Thus, including the 3 pointers, each storage record is 33 characters long.

12.2.10 Index Entries

We have no need for any index entries. There is only one storage file for the schema file MEASUREMENT and all pointers are direct, so that no storage-record indexes are required. In addition, there is no index being used with the set TREE_MEAS, either for the owner-to-member pointers or to facilitate a possible set index. However, because MEASURE-

---

MENT is organized as a sequential file, a direct-access capability could be incorporated, if desired, by specifying a record-key index for the prime key MEASNUMB (Figure 12.4*b*).

12.3 LIMITATIONS OF THE CODASYL DSDL

In this section, we look briefly at a few of the more obvious limitations of the CODASYL DSDL. We use the storage schema specification from the previous section to illustrate some of these limitations.

12.3.1 The S_A_TREE Storage-Area Specification

Here we must give at least the size of a page and the size of the area. The area must be big enough to hold all the files and indexes belonging to it. In this case it will contain the following.

a. The storage file MAIN_TREE.

b. The storage file SUBSID_TREE.

c. The set-representation index PROP_INDEX.

d. The record-key index SPEC_INDEX.

e. The record-key index LOC_INDEX.

The page size (block size) is going to be the same for all of these files and indexes. The largest file in the area will clearly be MAIN_TREE, and so we have chosen the page size that suits this file as that for the whole area.

We can see from the MAIN_TREE storage record-data subentries that the useful data portion of a MAIN_TREE record is 52 characters long. A MAIN_TREE record is specified to have 4 pointers as well, so that the total length of a record is 66 characters. Using this figure and drawing on Chapter 1 for an indication of reasonable block sizes and on Chapter 3 for block factors likely to minimize overflow with hash files, a block factor of 50 was chosen, giving a block size of 3300 characters.

As was explained in part in the previous section, because the MAIN_TREE storage records each have length 66 with a page size of 50, a total of 280 pages will be required for the 10,000 records if the space is to be only 75% full. Similarly, we allot 50 pages to the other storage file SUBSID_TREE, 15 pages to PROP_INDEX, and 30 pages each to SPEC_INDEX and LOC_INDEX. We thus need 400 pages in the storage area S_A_TREE.

The block size of 3300 characters was chosen to meet the needs of the hash file MAIN_TREE. But this block size is the block size for the whole S_A_TREE storage area, which also contains the file SUBSID_TREE and 3 indexes. There is no reason to assume that this block size will suit this file or any of the indexes. However, the DSDL does not permit us to give each file or index in a storage area its own block size. This limitation could hinder the optimization of performance, especially when there are several hash files in the same storage area.

There is no provision in the DSDL for specifying what kind of overflow system is to be used or where the overflow records will go. It does seem reasonable to give the data-base administrator some choice here, especially when a hash file is being used (see Chapter 3).

12.3.3 The Performance Control Module

The reader may have noticed that if the data-base administrator wishes to tune a CODASYL data base, he or she needs to dump the data bases onto (for example) auxiliary tapes, modify the internal schema, have it compiled and link-edited to the DBCS, and so on, and then reload the data base.

A better way is by means of what is known as a *Performance Control Module* (PCM). The PCM is simply a program that can read in changes to an internal schema, carry out the updating of the object internal schema, output an updated source internal schema, and reload the parts of the storage data base affected by the changes. This is illustrated in Figure 12.7.

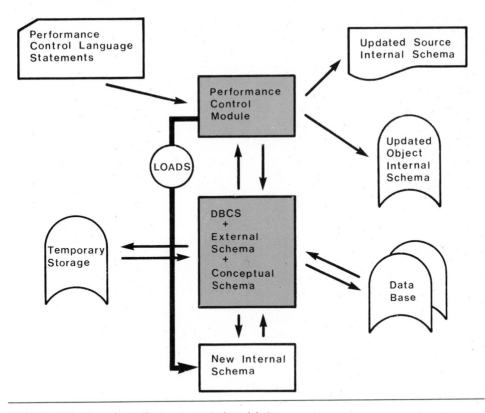

FIGURE 12.7. *Use of a performance control module to tune an existing data base.*

A performance control language will be necessary with the PCM so that tuning changes can be simply specified. It is clear that this language will be closely related to the DSDL. At the time of writing, no specifications for such a language have been proposed.

EXERCISES

1. Make up a CODASYL internal schema for the whole FORESTRY data base.

2. With reference to the RESOURCE data base in Figure 6.5, make up an internal schema for that part of the data base dealing with the files PETROFIRM, CONCESSION, and GOV_AGENCY.

3. Make up a CODASYL internal schema for the data base in Figure 6.10.

REFERENCE

CODASYL, 1978, "Data Description Language Committee," *DDLC Journal of Development,* Dept. of Supply and Services, Canadian Federal Government, Hull, Quebec, Canada.

The Relational Approach to Data-Base Management

13

Since the first CODASYL report in 1969, comprehensive implementations of the CO-DASYL proposals have found widespread use in commercial and government data-processing installations. At the time of writing, some such implementations are to a considerable extent based on the older CODASYL specifications. Furthermore, the retrieval sublanguages used with these implementations are mainly navigational, and no retrieval facility that is as high level as the EOS CODASYL enhancement illustrated in Chapter 11 is commonly provided for.

In contrast, the relational approach to a large extent involves only nonnavigational sublanguages [Chamberlin, 1976], but experience since Codd [Codd, 1970, 1971] proposed the relational approach in the early 1970s has shown that the implementation of a high-performance relational data-base system involves a major research and development effort [Blasgen, 1977].[1]

During the past 10 years, there have been many experimental implementations of relational systems in universities and industries, particularly at IBM. Initial projects were aimed at proving the feasibility of a relational data-base system supporting high-level nonprocedural retrieval sublanguages. Of these projects, the best known are probably MADAM (MACAIMS Data Management System) at MIT [Strand, 1971; Whitney, 1977], RDMS (Relational Data Management System) at General Motors Research [Whitney, 1977], and SQL (Structured Query Language) at IBM [Astrahan, 1975a, 1975b].

Later projects involved more comprehensive relational data-base systems; the most important are probably the System R project at IBM [Astrahan, 1976] and the INGRES

---

[1]*This should not be interpreted as criticism of the relational approach. The comparable problem of implementing a high-performance nonnavigational enhancement for CODASYL has hardly been investigated.*

(Interactive Graphics and Retrieval System) project at the University of California at Berkeley [Held, 1975; Stonebraker, 1976]. System R is implemented on an IBM 370 machine running under VM/370 and using PL/1 as an implementation language, while INGRES is implemented on a PDP-11 minicomputer.[1] Both projects are still active at the time of writing and Appendix 3 contains details of the System R prototype.

Because relational retrieval sublanguages are nonprocedural in general, the relational DBCS must be capable of translating the relational retrieval commands into lower-level procedures. However, as we saw in the retrievals in Chapter 10, there is almost always more than one procedure that can be used to carry out a given retrieval. Accordingly, a high-performance relational system requires what is known as an *optimizer* [Chamberlin, 1976; Kim, 1979] to insure that the procedure resulting from the translation of a retrieval command will perform as efficiently as possible. Both System R and INGRES (as well as other major prototypes) are equipped with optimizers [Blasgen, 1977; Stonebraker, 1976]. Optimizers are mentioned briefly in Chapter 11 and are discussed in more detail in Chapter 16.

A further difference between the relational and CODASYL approach lies in the external schema. We saw in Chapter 9 that the CODASYL external schema is more or less a simple subset of the conceptual schema. In the relational approach, a retrieval command specifies the retrieval of a new and derived *relation* (a relation is a relational file as discussed in Chapters 6 and 7), and it is thus natural to permit an external schema consisting of any of the relations that may be derived from the relations of the conceptual schema. Both System R and INGRES (as well as other major prototypes) permit these *derived external schemas* [Stonebraker, 1976; Chamberlin, 1975].

At the time of writing, no fully comprehensive relational system is available commercially. However, some more specialized relational systems, such as IBM's Query-by-Example [IBM, 1978; Zloof, 1977] and Honeywell's MRDS [Honeywell, 1978] are available. Although it is widely agreed that the appearance of a comprehensive commercial relational data-base system is inevitable, difficulties with the performance of such systems seem to be delaying their introduction.

The relational approach is based on mathematical relations, and in this chapter we shall look at the concept of a relation and see how relations may be used to define a conceptual and external schema. Where appropriate, we compare relational and CODA-SYL concepts.

13.1 FUNDAMENTALS OF RELATIONS

The concept of a relation has its origin in the mathematical theory of sets (not to be confused with the owner-coupled sets of CODASYL). However, relations may also be explained in terms of the conceptual files which we have been using until now. We therefore draw on the reader's knowledge of conceptual files in our initial discussion of relations; however, in Section 13.1.2, we shall discuss relations in terms of conventional set theory. Some of the following concepts have already been introduced in Chapter 7.

---

[1]*VM/370 is a special type of virtual operating system from IBM, not unlike Honeywell's MULTICS.*

13.1.1 The Concept of a Relation

There are two kinds of relation, *normalized* and *unnormalized*. It is normalized relations that are of interest in the relational approach. We may explain these concepts in very simple terms.

1. Normalized relation

   This is a conceptual file, where the conceptual records have a unique key and are of the same type, having fixed record length and fixed-format fields, which may not be further decomposed. Thus a normalized relation can also be regarded as a table with nondecomposable values.

   The conceptual files FORFILE, SPECFILE, TREE, and MEASUREMENT from the FORESTRY (Figure 8.2) data base can all be considered normalized relations. The normalized relation SPECFILE is displayed in Figure 13.1*a*.

2. Unnormalized relation

   Any relation can be considered to be a table, and an unnormalized relation is one in which the elements of at least one column of the table can be further decomposed. The normalized relation SPECFILE is restructured as an unnormalized relation in Figure 13.1*b*.

We can thus see that a normalized relation is a conceptual file of a restricted type. It is fairly common to refer to a normalized relation as a *relational file* (see Chapter 7). Thus the files from Figures 8.2 are all relational files.

The Degree of a Relation   The *degree of a relation* is the number of columns in the relation when it is considered as a table. Thus SPECFILE is of degree 3 and TREE is of degree 6, if these conceptual files are considered as relations.

The Attributes of a Relation   An *attribute of a relation* is the name of a column when the relation is considered as a table. If in addition to a row we specify an attribute, then we have isolated a value of the relation. The attribute concept corresponds closely to the field (type, not occurrence) concept in conventional data processing.

SPECIES	WOODTYPE	MAXHT
OAK	HARD	40
MAHOGANY	HARD	60
PINE	SOFT	60
SPRUCE	SOFT	40

(a) Normalized relation

TREE		
SPECIES	WOODTYPE	MAXHT
OAK SPRUCE	HARD SOFT	40
MAHOGANY PINE	HARD SOFT	60

(b) Unnormalized relation

FIGURE 13.1.   *Relations corresponding to the relational file* SPECFILE *from the* FORESTRY *data base.*

The Domains of a Relation   The concept of a domain has never been employed in conventional data processing, but it could well be. A *domain* is the set of values from which the set of attribute values of a relation may be taken; that is, from which a column of a table may be formed.

Thus the domain D_SPECIES could contain the set of names of all known species of tree. However, the set of attribute values of SPECIES in the SPECFILE relation is that subset of D_SPECIES that occurs in the forests described in the data base.

More than one column or set of attribute values may be drawn from a single domain. Consider the relation TREE, and let us suppose that D_TREENUMB is the set of tree numbers for all the trees in the forests described in the data base. Not all the trees in these forests are part of the experimental program for which our illustrative data base is constructed. Thus the set of TREENUMB attribute values will be a subset of the set D_TREENUMB. However, the attribute PARENT also lists tree number values. Thus the PARENT attribute values are a subset of the same underlying domain D_TREENUMB.

A practical consequence of two different attributes that take their values from the same domain is that it becomes meaningful to compare their values for equality. We return to this point later.

Domains with values that are noncomposite are said to be *simple*. If the attributes of relations are drawn from simple domains, the relations will thus be normalized. Relations formed from nonsimple domains are unnormalized.

The Tuples of a Relation   We may consider a relation as being a mathematical set of *tuples*. When we consider a relation as a table, a *tuple* is a row in the table. Thus a tuple corresponds to a conceptual record in a conventional conceptual file, but the correspondence is exact only when the conceptual file is a relational file. *Each tuple in a relation is unique,* since it is an element in a mathematical set.

Relational Keys   Since each tuple in a relation is unique, there will always be some combination of attributes with values that may be used to uniquely identify a tuple. A minimum collection of attributes that can function as a unique identifier is called a *candidate key*. Since it is possible for more than one collection of attributes to function as a unique identifier, a relation may have more than one candidate key.

The term *candidate* is used since each of these candidate keys is a candidate for selection as the prime key of the relation. Choice of prime key is arbitrary, but usually a candidate key involving only one attribute will be chosen if possible. Such a prime key is said to be *noncomposite*.

Thus in the relation TREE, TREENUMB is a noncomposite key. The other keys in the FORESTRY data base are also noncomposite. Another reason for choosing noncomposite keys is that by doing so, we avoid the possibility of functional dependence between the composite attributes of the key and the key itself, as explained in Chapter 7, and also the possibility of join dependencies.

13.1.2 Mathematical Foundation

Most of what has been said in the section above can be more concisely formulated on the basis of conventional set theory. In this chapter, the term *set* is taken to mean a mathematical set. The owner-coupled set of the preceding chapters is something quite different, and we shall use the adjective *owner-coupled* to distinguish it from a mathematical set.

Consider the special case of two sets A and P, where

$$A = \{a, b\} \quad \text{and} \quad P = \{p, q, r\}$$

We may define a *Cartesian product* $A \times B$ on these sets as follows.

$$A \times P = \{ (x, y) : x \, \varepsilon \, A \wedge y \, \varepsilon \, P\}$$

Thus $A \times P$ is the set:

$$\{ (a, p),$$
$$(a, q),$$
$$(a, r),$$
$$(b, p),$$
$$(b, q),$$
$$(c, r) \}$$

The elements (x, y) of this set are called *2-tuples*, and any subset of $A \times P$, such as

$$\{ (a, q),$$
$$(b, p),$$
$$(c, r) \}$$

is a *binary relation*, or a relation of degree 2. The sets A and P are the underlying domains for any relation formed on them.

We now take the general case of a relation of degree n. Consider n sets $D_1, D_2, \ldots, D_n$. The expanded Cartesian product of these n sets is given by

$$D_1 \times D_2 \times \ldots \times D_n = \{(d_1, d_2, \ldots, d_n) : d_1 \, \varepsilon \, D_1; d_2 \, \varepsilon \, D_2, \ldots, d_n \, \varepsilon \, D_n\}$$

Any subset R of this expanded Cartesian product is a relation of degree n, formed on the domains $D_1, D_2, \ldots, D_n$. These domains do not have to be distinct, so that we might have

$$D_r = D_s$$

An element $(d_1, d_2, \ldots, d_n)$ of R is an n-tuple, usually shortened to just *tuple* in discussions on the relational approach. Thus a relation is a mathematical set of tuples, and when these tuples are displayed as rows in a table, the columns are subsets of the underlying domains from which the relation is formed. The columns are usually called attributes, as we have seen.

Order   The concept of order is not fundamental to the concept of a relation. A relation is a set of tuples and sets are not ordered. However, in the relational approach, in practice a relation is usually considered to have an order, based on values of some attribute of the relation.

13.2 THE RELATIONAL SCHEMAS

13.2.1 The Conceptual Schema

We shall now use the relational concept to construct a relational conceptual schema for the FORESTRY data base depicted in Figure 8.2. Since the conceptual files used in the data base in Figure 8.2 were all relational files, only a minor change is required. An extended Bachman diagram of a slightly modified FORESTRY data base, which better reflects our relational view, is shown in Figure 13.2.

We notice that a new attribute TREENUMB has been added to the MEASUREMENT relation. A TREENUMB occurrence for a given MEASUREMENT tuple contains the prime key value for the TREE tuple describing the tree on which the measurement was carried out. However, it must be understood that the new attribute TREENUMB in the MEASUREMENT relation is in no way necessary to make the old MEASUREMENT conceptual file from Figure 8.2 into a relational file. The old MEASUREMENT file was a relational file as well. The reason for the new attribute is much more fundamental and highlights the difference between the CODASYL and relational approaches.

Relationships between Relations   Relationships between relations are not explicitly specified at the conceptual level in the relational approach, and the concept of an owner-coupled set is absent.

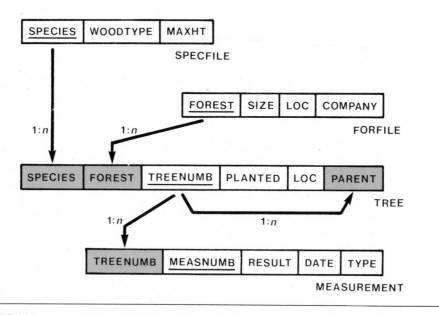

FIGURE 13.2.   *A modified version of the experimental* FORESTRY *data base. Semantically, the only difference between this data base and that shown in Figure 8.2 is the new attribute* TREENUMB *in the* MEASUREMENT *relation.*

Relationships are implicitly supported by the equivalent of the connection field. In relational terminology, a connection field has been called a *foreign key* [Date, 1977], since it contains a key "foreign" to the relation. However, *connection key* is a much more expressive term, and we shall use it in this book.

The reason for introducing the new TREENUMB attribute in the MEASUREMENT relation should now be clear. It is only by means of this MEASUREMENT attribute and the prime-key attribute of the TREE relation is that it is possible to determine which measurements were carried out on which tree.

Thus we have the following.

1. The prime key SPECIES in SPECFILE and the connection key SPECIES in TREE determine the 1:*n* relationship between tuples of these two relations.

2. FOREST in FORFILE and FOREST in TREE support the 1:*n* relationship between FORFILE and TREE tuples.

3. TREENUMB in TREE and PARENT in TREE support the recursive 1:*n* relationship inherent in the TREE relation.

4. TREENUMB in TREE and TREENUMB in MEASUREMENT support the 1:*n* relationship between TREE and MEASUREMENT tuples.

In the CODASYL approach, the connection keys (or fields) play only a secondary role and are, strictly speaking, unnecessary; they are often convenient, though, as we have seen, and can contribute to improved performance.

On the other hand, the connection keys play a dominant role in the relational approach. Relationships between relations cannot be modeled without them, and they are in constant use in retrieval sublanguage expressions [Codd, 1971; Date, 1977].

Extended Bachman Diagrams Since the relational approach uses connection keys to model relationships, extended Bachman diagrams are directly applicable to displaying a given conceptual schema, particularly as far as relationships are concerned. It is therefore surprising to discover that most writers on the subject of relational data bases go to great lengths to avoid Bachman-type diagrams [Date, 1977; Tsichritzis, 1977].

However, in the author's opinion, there is no good reason to avoid Bachman-type diagrams. Experience indicates particularly that extended Bachman diagrams are a useful communications tool. The important point is that they are just as applicable to the relational approach as to the CODASYL approach, and this is the main reason why the author is strongly in favor of them.

Domains and Connection Keys It is clear that it must be possible to match values of prime keys with associated connection keys. It therefore follows that matching prime and connection-key attributes must be drawn from the same domain. In a relational schema, the domain to which an attribute belongs must be specified.

It is in this indirect way that the existence of a connection key is revealed to the database system. If a non-prime-key attribute is drawn from the same domain as a prime-key attribute, then it must be a connection-key attribute.

13.2.2 FORESTRY **Relational Schema**

We shall now construct a schema for the FORESTRY data base from Figure 13.2. Since no widely used relational system is available at the time of writing, we shall employ an idealized schema (Date, 1977).

The structure of the schema is simply a series of domain entries, one for each domain employed, followed by a series of relation entries, one for each relation.

```
01   RELATIONAL SCHEMA_NAME   FORESTRY
02
03   DOMAIN      D_SPECIES      CHARACTER (20)
04   DOMAIN      WOODTYPE       CHARACTER (25)
05   DOMAIN      MAXHT          NUMERIC (3)
06
07   DOMAIN      D_FOREST       CHARACTER (15)
08   DOMAIN      SIZE           NUMERIC (10)
09   DOMAIN      F_LOC          CHARACTER (10)
10   DOMAIN      COMPANY        CHARACTER (20)
11
12   DOMAIN      D_TREENUMB     NUMERIC (10)
13   DOMAIN      PLANTED        NUMERIC (8)
14   DOMAIN      T_LOC          NUMERIC (6)
15
16   DOMAIN      MEASNUMB       NUMERIC (6)
17   DOMAIN      RESULT         FLOATING POINT (6)
18   DOMAIN      DATE           NUMERIC (8)
19   DOMAIN      TYPE           CHARACTER (10)
20
21   RELATION    SPECFILE     ( SPECIES          DOMAIN  D_SPECIES,
22                               WOODTYPE,
23                               MAXHT)
24        KEY (SPECIES)
25
26   RELATION    FORFILE      ( FOREST           DOMAIN  D_FOREST,
27                               SIZE,
28                               LOC              DOMAIN  F_LOC,
29                               COMPANY)
30        KEY (FOREST)
31
32   RELATION    TREE         ( SPECIES          DOMAIN  D_SPECIES
33                               FOREST           DOMAIN  D_FOREST,
34                               TREENUMB         DOMAIN  D_TREENUMB,
35                               PLANTED,
36                               LOC              DOMAIN  T_LOC,
37                               PARENT           DOMAIN  D_FOREST)
```

```
38        KEY (TREENUMB)
39
40  RELATION   MEASUREMENT   (TREENUMB       DOMAIN  D_TREENUMB,
41                            MEASNUMB,
42                            RESULT,
43                            DATE,
44                            TYPE)
45        KEY (MEASNUMB)
```

In the relational entries, an attribute is assumed to be drawn from a domain of the same name when no domain is specified. We notice that LOC, the location of a tree in a forest, is drawn from the domain T_LOC, while LOC, the location of a forest, is drawn from an entirely different domain F_LOC.

Since PLANTED and DATE attributes both contain date values, it might have been desirable for certain types of query to have them both drawn from the same domain. This would permit the comparison of DATE and PLANTED values for equality in certain (complex) retrieval expressions.

All the relations specified are in 4NF. As explained in Chapter 7, this reduces the chance of inconsistency under updating.

13.2.3 FORESTRY Relational Subschema or External Schema

A *relational subschema* is composed of entries that describe relations and domains, as is a schema. However, the domains and relations that may be employed are any which may be derived from the schema domains and relations. Thus a subschema is a subset of a schema only in the very widest sense [Chamberlin, 1975; Kim, 1979].

Since we have not yet studied the art of deriving new relations from old ones, we shall assume for the time being that the subschema for the FORESTRY data base is identical to the schema. This assumption in no way restricts our discussion of the relational manipulation sublanguages. Derived subschemas are discussed in Section 16.4.3.

13.2.4 FORESTRY Internal Schema

We shall not discuss an internal relational data-base facility in this book. We shall merely assume that such a schema may be implemented. (A relational internal schema for a System R data base is covered briefly in Appendix 3.)

13.2.5 Comparison of Relational and CODASYL Schemas

In both schemas, collections of forest, species, tree, and measurement entities are modeled. For any of these entities—for example, a tree—in the relational case there will be a tuple and, in the CODASYL case, a conceptual record. For the same type of entity—again, a tree—the corresponding tuples are grouped into relations, while the corresponding records are grouped into conceptual files.

A primary key is specified for each relation, and a record key is specified for each conceptual file. However, in the relational case we specify the domains from which the attributes are drawn. The equivalent is absent in the CODASYL case. But in the CO-DASYL case, we specify an order for the records (record-key order) and we may also specify secondary keys with associated secondary key order. The equivalent is absent in the relational case, at least in theory.[1]

Because it would not be difficult, and would even be desirable, to introduce the domain concept to CODASYL, and because tuple prime- and secondary-key order could easily be incorporated into a relational schema, we may conclude that no far-reaching difference can be discerned between the use of relations in a relational schema and relational files in a CODASYL schema.

When we look at the owner-coupled set specifications of the CODASYL schema, the difference between the two approaches is quite apparent. The conventional relational approach has no equivalent grouping of tuples. Conceptual records in a CODASYL conceptual data base are not only grouped into conceptual files, they are also grouped into one or more owner-coupled sets. The CODASYL groupings are reflected in the physical world. Entities not only participate in a grouping of entities of the same type, they also participate in other groupings involving other entities. Thus trees participate in the grouping of all the trees under consideration. However, they may also be grouped in a more-or-less physically fixed manner in accordance with which forest they grow in, in accordance with which species they belong to, in accordance with which trees they are propagated from, and so on. It is the absence of an explicit declaration in the relational schema of these additional groupings that is the fundamental difference between the two approaches.

As we shall see in the following chapters, there is no logical necessity for the concept of an owner-coupled set in relational retrieval sublanguages; the specification of connection keys is all that is required. This is clearly demonstrated in DSL ALPHA and relational algebra, the two original relational retrieval sublanguages. But a later important relational sublanguage, SQL (see Chapter 15), has a facility (GROUP BY facility) which in effect permits an implicit specification of an owner-coupled set occurrence. This is an important development, for it shows (a) that an owner-coupled set may be specified implicitly in the relational approach, and (b) that implicit owner-coupled sets may well be a desirable convenience, although not a necessity, in relational retrieval sublanguages. We shall return to the subject of implicit owner-coupled sets in the relational approach in Chapter 15, following a discussion of SQL. We conclude with a mention of a recent proposal to extend the relational model, to provide for additional groupings of tuples.

Surrogates and the RM/T Model   Examples of relational data bases may occur where the simple relational model cannot adequately describe the inherent semantics. A common example is the data base with two relations, EMPLOYEE and SHAREHOLDER, each describing a category of entities belonging to the entity class *person*. The EMPLOYEE and SHAREHOLDER relations list the employees and shareholders of a company, respectively. However, suppose an employee may be a shareholder. In such a data base, if different sets of keys are used in the two relations—for example, employee number and social security number—it may be impossible for the system to ascertain that a given employee and a given shareholder are the same *person* entity.

---

[1]*In practice, the relations of a conceptual schema are ordered, so that they are not strictly relations in a mathematical sense.*

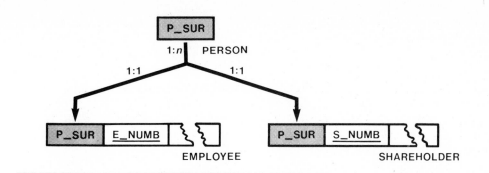

FIGURE 13.3. *The extended Bachman diagram shows how a secret or surrogate attribute* **P_SUR** *(shaded) is used to permit the system to keep track of entities of the same class in different relations. The surrogate values are not revealed to a user. There is in fact a 1:n relationship between the surrogate relation* **PERSON** *and the other relations. To be able to handle insertions the system must be aware of the relationship.*

A proposal by E. F. Codd [Codd, 1979] to extend the relational model is an attempt to rectify such inadequacies. Codd's new model, called the RM/T model, is quite complex, but it indirectly provides for additional groupings of tuples. The basic idea is that every entity of the same class (not category) should be identified to the system by a unique and secret key value or *surrogate* value. A tuple in SHAREHOLDER and a tuple in EMPLOYEE could be identified by the system as describing the same *person* entity by means of a common surrogate value, as is illustrated by the extended Bachman diagram in Figure 13.3. Thus tuples with a common surrogate value form a grouping which must be known to the system, but which is definitely not a relation.

EXERCISES

1. Draw up a relational conceptual schema for the RESOURCE data base in Figure 6.5, having converted DRILL_HOLE to 4NF (see Section 7.2.3).

2. Draw up a relational conceptual schema for the data base in Figure 6.10.

3. Draw up at least two different but equivalent conceptual schemas for the data base in Figure 6.14.

4. List the differences between a conventional conceptual file and a relation.

5. Give an example of a conceptual file which is not a relation.

REFERENCES

Astrahan, M. M., and D. D. Chamberlin, 1975*a*, "Implementation of a Structured English Query Language," *Comm. ACM*, **18**(10):580–88.

Astrahan, M. M., and R. A. Lorie, 1975*b*, "SEQUEL-XRM, A Relational System," *Proc. ACM Pacific Regional Conf.*, pp. 34–38.

Astrahan, M. M., and others, 1976, "System R. Relational Approach to Data Base Management," *ACM Trans. Database Sys.*, **1**(2):97–137.

Blasgen, M. W., and P. K. Eswaran, 1977, "Storage and Access in Relational Data Bases," *IBM Sys. J.*, **16**(4):363–77.

Chamberlin, D. D., J. N. Gray, and I. N. Traiger, 1975, "Views, Authorization, and Locking in a Relational Data Base System," in *Proc. AFIPS Nat. Computer Conf.*, vol. 44, AFIPS Press, Montvale, N.J., pp. 425–30.

Chamberlin, D. D., 1976, "Relational Data Base Management Systems," *Comput. Surv.*, **8**(1):43–46.

Codd, E. F., 1970, "A Relational Model for Large Shared Data Banks," *Comm. ACM*, **13**(6):377–87.

Codd, E. F., 1971, "A Data Base Sublanguage Founded on the Relational Calculus," *ACM SIG-FIDET Workshop on Data Description, Access and Control*, pp. 35–68.

Codd, E. F., 1979, "Extending the Data Base Relational Model to Capture More Meaning," *ACM Trans. on Database Sys.*, **4**(4):397–434.

Date, C. J., 1977, *An Introduction to Data Base Management Systems*, Addison-Wesley, Reading, Mass.

Goldstein, R. C., and A. J. Strand, 1974, "The MacAIMS Data Management System Proc.," *SIGFIDET Workshop on Data Description, Access and Control*, pp. 201–29.

Held, G. D., and M. Stonebraker, 1975, "Storage Structures and Access Methods in the Relational Data Base System INGRES," *Proc. ACM Pacific Regional Conf.*, pp. 26–33.

Honeywell, 1978, *MRDS Reference Manual*, Order Number AW53, Rev. 2.

IBM, 1978, *Query-by-Example Terminal User's Guide*, Order Form SH20-2078-0.

Kim, W., 1979, "Relational Data Base Systems," *ACM Comput. Surv.*, **11**(3):185–213.

Stonebraker, M., E. Wong, P. Kreps, and G. Held, 1976, "The Design and Implementation of INGRES," *ACM Trans. Database Sys.*, **1**(3):189–222.

Strand, A. J., 1971, "The Relational Approach to the Management of Data Bases," *Proc. IFIP Cong.*, North-Holland, New York, pp. 901–4.

Tsichritzis, D. C., and F. H. Lochovsky, 1977, *Data Base Management Systems*, Academic Press, New York.

Whitney, V. K. M., 1974, "Relational Data Management Implementation Techniques," *ACM SIG-MOD Workshop on Data Description, Access and Control*, pp. 321–48.

Zloof, M. M., 1977, "Query-By-Example: A Data Base Language," *IBM Sys. J.*, **16**(4):324–43.

Relational Predicate Calculus

14

In this chapter we study DSL ALPHA, which is a powerful and fundamental nonprocedural sublanguage based on relational predicate calculus [Kuhns, 1969; Codd, 1971, 1972]. In subsequent chapters we shall introduce SQL, another nonprocedural sublanguage, and then relational algebra, a very high-level procedural language. All three languages require a special relational user working area, and we cannot begin our study of the relational retrieval sublanguages without looking first at its structure. In addition, since we shall use the FORESTRY data base from Figure 13.2 throughout, we shall also show how this data base can be initially loaded.

14.1 USER WORKING AREA AND LOADING PROGRAMS

14.1.1 The Relational User Working Area

The relational UWA is imagined to consist of many different *relational workspaces,* each of which may be dynamically given a name in a retrieval expression. A (relational) workspace is capable of holding any relation from the subschema or derivable from those in the subschema. A relation in a workspace may be used in retrievals on an equal footing with the relations of the subschema.

Normally, a retrieval expression retrieves a relation which is placed in a workspace (although pseudo-relations with duplicate tuples may be allowed with some implementations). Thus if a new user has relational workspaces $W_1, W_2, \ldots, W_n$ and has subschema relations $R_1, R_2, \ldots, R_n$, he or she may initially express a retrieval involving any of the subschema's relations, the resulting relation being placed in, for example, W_1.

However, the user may now specify a retrieval involving any of W_1, R_1, ..., R_n, the result being placed in, for instance, W_2. The next retrieval could involve the relations W_1, W_2, R_1, R_2, ..., R_n, and so on.

Thus the ideal relational UWA is quite different from the simple CODASYL UWA, and—as mentioned in Chapter 11 on the subject of retrieving more than one record at once—the CODASYL UWA concept could usefully be extended. However, in practice, system limitations will probably constrain the relational UWA somewhat.

14.1.2 Loading a Relational Data Base

Relational data bases are by far the easiest to load. Since the only groupings of tuples in a relational data base are the relations themselves, loading consists of reading in the records from each source file in turn and storing them as tuples in the corresponding relations. Of course, as mentioned in discussing loading the CODASYL data base in Chapter 9, we may have more than one source file with the data from which a relation is to be constructed. In that case, we read in records from the source files concerned and form the tuples in main memory before storing them in the data base, in a manner similar to the program **CREATE** in Chapter 2. Again, while the loading technique is simple in principle, extensive cross-checking of the data entering a data base may need to be carried out; furthermore, we may need to write robust loading programs, as exemplified by the robust version of **CREATE** in Chapter 2.

We shall merely give an example of a nonrobust loading program for one of the **FORESTRY** relations, as the other relations would in principle be loaded in a similar manner. The loading program we shall use requires the equivalent of the CODASYL **STORE** command, namely the relational **STORE** command. However, the relational command is simpler. We use the following command with PL/1 (although many variations are possible).

STORE RELATION *(relation-1)* FROM WORKSPACE *(workspace-relation);*

The tuples to be stored are in the workspace relation, which would typically be a two-level structure array. The tuples will, in most implementations, be stored in accordance with their prime key values. In our case, we shall take a workspace relation that can hold exactly one tuple for loading purposes. The loading program is a follows.

RELLOAD: PROC OPTIONS (MAIN);
/* 1. Program loads the relation SPECFILE in the relational data base FORESTRY using records from the source CONSECUTIVE file XSPECFILE. XSPECFILE records have the same structure as SPECFILE tuples.
2. The workspace W1 holds 1 SPECFILE tuple.
3. We use the variable STATUS to return completion messages from the DBCS.
4. We ready the relation SPECFILE for update, using a READY command, which, with extended syntax and semantics, could be used to manage concurrent processing (see Section 10.4 for corresponding CODASYL command).
5. Other relations in FORESTRY are loaded in a similar manner   */
   /*   Workspace   */

```
DCL 1 W1 EXTERNAL,  /*  Known to relational DBCS through external schema  */
    2 SPECIES CHAR (20),  /*  Prime key  */
    2 WOODTYPE CHAR (25),
    2 MAXHT FIXED BIN (15);
DCL STATUS CHAR (20) EXTERNAL;
DCL (BEOF) BIT (1) INIT ('1'B);
DCL XSPECFILE FILE RECORD ENV (CONSECUTIVE);  /*  Source file  */
ON ENDFILE (XSPECFILE) BEOF = '0'B;  /*  Note name XSPECFILE too long for PL/1
                                           compiler  */
READY (SPECFILE) UPDATE:
OPEN FILE (XSPECFILE) INPUT;
/*  Storage operation begins  */
READ FILE (XSPECFILE) INTO (W1);
DO WHILE (BEOF);
    STORE RELATION (SPECFILE) FROM (W1);
    IF STATUS ⌐ = 'OK' THEN CALL ERROR;  /*  ERROR prints message and stops
                                               program.  */
    ELSE READ FILE (XSPECFILE) INTO (W1);
END;
END RELLOAD;  /*  Relation loaded  */
```

Thus in the simplest case, loading a relational data base is nothing more than a copying operation.

14.2 DSL ALPHA RETRIEVALS

In the remainder of this chapter we shall study Data Sublanguage (DSL) ALPHA, developed by E. F. Codd at IBM. In its basic form, it consists of mathematical expressions for defining relations [Codd, 1971]. (Some readers may find it convenient to skip DSL ALPHA on first reading, and go on to study the more user-friendly sublanguage SQL in Chapter 15.)

We recall that a relation is a set of tuples. Thus an ALPHA expression defines a set of tuples as follows.

$$\{tuple : predicate\}$$

where *tuple* lists the attributes required in a typical tuple, and *predicate* lists the requirements that a selected tuple must satisfy. However, in addition, we need to use what are usually called *range variables* [Codd, 1971; Date, 1977].

14.2.1 Range Variables

A range variable closely corresponds to a PL/1 level-1 structure variable. However, its use in DSL ALPHA is somewhat more abstract.

A range variable can hold a tuple of the relation over which it is (dynamically) declared capable of ranging. Thus the value of a range variable T for the relation TREE could range over all the tuples in TREE. Since T is a tuple and TREE is a set of tuples, we also can write:

T ε TREE

However, in addition, T.TREENUMB is understood to be the value of the attribute TREE-NUMB in the tuple T. Since the attribute TREENUMB is a set of values, we could write

T.TREENUMB ε TREENUMB

The concept of a range variable is simple, but it is easily confused with the concept of a relation. Range variables are extensively employed in ALPHA expressions, so it is important to be clear about the underlying concept.

In the following retrievals, we shall assume a range variable S for the relation SPECIES, F for FORFILE, T for TREE, and M for MEASUREMENT. Figure 14.1 illustrates the SPECIES relation and the range variable S; while apparently trivial, it may help the reader to firmly grasp the concept.

14.2.2 Full DSL ALPHA Expressions

We shall refrain from giving a syntax for DSL ALPHA. Many different versions are possible. The most fundamental version, and also the clearest, is the mathematical, or set theoretical, version [Codd, 1971].

There are also versions with more of a computer language syntax [Date, 1977]. These are usually abbreviated in relation to the mathematical version, and a great deal is not stated explicitly. We shall therefore start with the full mathematical version. This should clarify the techniques for the reader. We can then continue with an abbreviated version.

Retrieval 1   *Find the names of companies which have forests larger than 1000 acres.*

{(F.COMPANY) : F ε FORFILE ∧ F.SIZE > 1000}

SPECIES	WOODTYPE	MAXHT	
OAK MAHOGANY	HARD MAHOGANY	40 60	↑
PINE	SOFT	60	range variable S
SPRUCE	SOFT	40	↓

FIGURE 14.1.   *Relation* SPECFILE *and range variable* S.
S *can contain any tuple in* SPECFILE.

This may be read "the relation composed of tuples, each of which is the COMPANY component of a range variable F, where F is a tuple in FORFILE, and where the SIZE component from F is greater than 1000."

Retrieval 2   *Find the names of companies and the names of the forests owned when the forests are located in California.*

{(F.COMPANY, F.FOREST) : F ε FORFILE ∧ F.LOC = 'CALIFORNIA'}

This may be read "the relation composed of tuples, each containing the COMPANY and FOREST components of a range variable F, such that (or where) F is a tuple in TREE and where the LOC component from F is equal to 'CALIFORNIA'.

Retrieval 3: Use of Existential Quantifier   *Find the size and location of forests containing cedar trees.*

{(F.SIZE, F.LOC) : F ε FORFILE ∧
                              ∃T ε TREE (T.SPECIES = 'CEDAR' ∧ T.FOREST = F.FOREST)}

This may be read "the relation composed of tuples, each containing the SIZE and LOC components of the range variable F, such that F is a tuple in FORFILE, and there exists, or is to be found, a T tuple, where T is a tuple in TREE, such that the FOREST component of T is equal to the FOREST component of F and the SPECIES component of T is equal to 'CEDAR'.

In this expression, the connection-key attribute FOREST from the TREE relation is used to link an F tuple from the FORFILE relation to the T tuple from the TREE relation. The existential quantifier ∃ is not used in quite the same way as was EXISTS in the EOS enhancement. The expression ∃T means "there exists a T tuple in the *whole* relation TREE." (In the EOS CODASYL enhancement, EXISTS was used to indicate that a record with specified properties existed in an owner-coupled set *occurrence*.)

Retrieval 4: Relation Formed from Two Relations   *Find the tree numbers for cedar trees, and the size of the forests containing them.*

{(F.SIZE, T.TREENUMB) : F ε FORFILE ∧ T ε TREE ∧
        T.FOREST = F.FOREST ∧ T.SPECIES = 'CEDAR'}

The reader should attempt to rewrite the above expression without symbols as an exercise.

Note that there is an important restriction in at least the basic version of DSL ALPHA. Range variables from the target lists (that is, which will be used to construct the relation to be retrieved) cannot be quantified (by either the universal or existential quantifiers). Additional range variables are used instead.

14.2.3 Abbreviated Version of DSL ALPHA

In this version a retrieval expression has the general form

GET *workspace* (*target-list*) : *predicate*

and the *predicate* expression will be more abbreviated than the mathematical version. For example, if T occurs in the target list, we shall usually omit T ε TREE in the predicate. If T is existentially quantified, we shall just write ∃ T instead of ∃ T ε TREE.

The workspace is assumed to be capable of holding any relation and can itself take part in further retrievals, as explained in Section 14.1. The target list may contain either or both tuples and tuple attributes. Examples of valid target lists follow.

GET W1 (T) : *predicate*
GET W1 (T.TREENUMB, T.LOC, M.MEASNUMB) : *predicate*
GET W1 (F, T.TREENUMB) : *predicate*

We shall use the range variables F, S, T, and M as introduced in Section 14.2.1. Sometimes we need more than one range variable for a given relation. These may be declared dynamically along with a retrieval.

RANGE TREE TX
GET ......

We shall now illustrate the sublanguage by a series of retrievals of increasing complexity. The concept of retrieval level, as introduced with the EOS enhancement sublanguage, may also be used with DSL ALPHA for classifying retrievals. Informally, a retrieval involving a tuple in one relation and either parent or one or more child tuples in another relation would be a level-2 retrieval, and so on. We shall use the retrieval level concept to classify each retrieval studied.

The retrieval diagrams introduced in Chapter 11 may also be usefully employed with DSL ALPHA, and we shall include such diagrams where they can help to clarify a retrieval specification. We first repeat the retrievals 1 through 4 from Section 14.2.2.

Retrieval 1 (Level 1)   *Find the names of companies with forests larger than 1000 acres.*

GET W1 (F.COMPANY) : F.SIZE > 1000

Retrieval 2 (Level 1)   *Find the names of companies and the forests owned when the forests are located in California.*

GET W1 (F.COMPANY, F.FOREST) : F.LOC = 'CALIFORNIA'

Retrieval 3 (Level 2): Use of Existential Quantifier   *Find the size and location of forests containing cedar trees.*

GET W1 (F.SIZE, F.LOC);
            ∃ T TUPLE (T.FOREST = F.FOREST ∧ T.SPECIES = 'CEDAR')

Notice again how the connection key T.FOREST is employed to link the child T tuple to the parent F tuple.

Retrieval 4 (Level 2): Relation Formed from Two Relations   *Find the tree numbers for cedar trees, and the size of the forests containing them.*

GET W1 (F.SIZE, T.TREENUMB) :
   T.FOREST = F.FOREST ∧ T.SPECIES = 'CEDAR'

Notice again the use of the connection key T.FOREST.

Retrieval 5 (Level 2): Bench-mark Retrieval   *Find the tree numbers and locations of spruce trees on which no electrical measurements have been completed.*

This is the bench-mark retrieval already used with the EOS sublanguage in Section 11.2.5. We have two versions, a universal-quantifier version and an existential-quantifier version. We note that the universal quantifier ∀ is not used like FOR ALL in the EOS enhancement; the expression ∀T means "for all T tuples, if any, from the *whole* relation TREE."

1. Universal-quantifier version

   GET W1 (T.TREENUMB, T.LOC) : T.SPECIES = 'SPRUCE'
              ∧ ∀M TUPLES (M.TREENUMB ⌐ = T.TREENUMB
                                 ∨ M.TYPE ⌐ = 'ELECTRICAL')

2. Existential-quantifier version

   GET W1 (T.TREENUMB, T.LOC) : T.SPECIES = 'SPRUCE'
              ∧ ⌐∃M TUPLE (M.TREENUMB = T.TREENUMB
                                 ∧ M.TYPE = 'ELECTRICAL')

The predicates should be studied carefully. The universal quantifier in DSL ALPHA quantifies *every* tuple in a quantified relation. Thus the expression following ∀M must be true for every M tuple for a T tuple to be retrieved.

The predicate for (1) partitions the MEASUREMENT relation into two kinds of tuples. One kind describes M tuples that have a connection key (TREENUMB) different from the key of the T tuple under consideration. The second kind describes M tuples that have a connection key equal to the key of the T tuple under consideration. For the T tuple to be selected, the TYPE value from the second group of M tuples must not be 'ELECTRICAL'. The retrieval diagram is given in Figure 14.2.

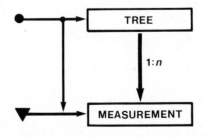

FIGURE 14.2.   *Retrieval 5, universal quantifier version.*

Retrieval 6 (Level 2): Two Quantifiers, Single Relationship   *Find the tree numbers and locations of spruce trees on which only electrical measurements have been carried out, at least one of which gave a result greater than 200 millivolts.*

This retrieval involves only one relationship, namely the parent/child relationship between T and M tuples as determined by the connection-key attribute M.TREENUMB. However, we must deal with MEASUREMENT tuples twice in the retrieval expression.

RANGE MEASUREMENT MX
GET W1 (T.TREENUMB, T.LOC):
   ∃M TUPLE (T.TREENUMB = M.TREENUMB
     ∧ M.RESULT > 200)
  ∧ ∀MX TUPLES (MX.TREENUMB ¬ = T.TREENUMB
    ∧ MX.TYPE = 'ELECTRICAL')

Here we see that the 1:*n* relationship between TREE and MEASUREMENT is expressed twice and in two quite different ways. For this reason we need an additional range variable MX. The retrieval diagram is shown in Figure 14.3.

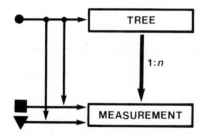

FIGURE 14.3.   *Retrieval 6.*

Retrieval 7 (Level 2): Retrieval Involving Two Relationships   *Find the tree numbers for trees that either (a) are in location 1001 and are hardwoods; or (b) are in location 2002 and belong to the company 'XFIRM'.*

Here we must make use of both the relationship between SPECFILE and TREE and between FORFILE and TREE.

GET W1 (T.TREENUMB) :
   (T.LOC = 1001 ∧ ∃S TUPLE (S.SPECFILE = T.SPECIES ∧
            S.WOODTYPE = 'HARDWOOD'))
∨ (T.LOC = 2002 ∧ ∃F TUPLE (F.FOREST = T.FOREST ∧
            F.COMPANY = 'XFIRM'))

The retrieval diagram in Figure 11.4 is applicable here. (The EOS CODASYL enhancement expression for this retrieval is described under retrieval 6 in Chapter 11.)

Retrieval 8 (Level 3): Two Relationships, Both Quantifiers   *Find the names of companies with at least one California forest in which there is at least one cedar tree, on which (1) at least one electrical measurement has been carried out; and (2) no chemical measurements at all have been carried out.*

We see that we need the 1:*n* relationship between FORFILE and TREE and the 1:*n* relationship between TREE and MEASUREMENT.

```
RANGE MEASUREMENT MX
GET W1 (F.COMPANY)
      F.LOC = 'CALIFORNIA' ∧ ∃T TUPLE (F.FOREST = T.FOREST
                                        ∧ T.SPECIES = 'CEDAR'
            ∧ ∃M TUPLE (T.TREENUMB = M.TREENUMB
                         ∧ M.TYPE = 'ELECTRICAL')
            ∧ ∀MX TUPLES (T.TREENUMB ⌐ = MX.TREENUMB ∨
                          MX.TYPE ⌐ = 'CHEMICAL'))
```

The retrieval diagram is shown in Figure 14.4. We notice that it is necessary to link tuples from different relations by means of connection keys. F is first linked to T, and then T is linked to M twice, requiring the use of the extra range variable MX.

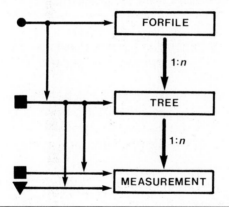

FIGURE 14.4. *Retrieval 8.*

Retrieval 9 (Level 3)   *Find the names and sizes of forests that contain all species.*

```
GET W1 (F.FOREST, F.SIZE) :
      ∀S TUPLES (∃T TUPLE (T.SPECIES = S.SPECIES
                            ∧ T.FOREST = F.FOREST))
```

The retrieval diagram is shown in Figure 14.5. This retrieval is somewhat special in that it may be regarded as having two "entry points" (see the retrieval diagram). These entry points are labeled *m* (main) and *s* (subsidiary) in the retrieval diagram. First we take a

FORFILE tuple F and hold it (main entry point). Then for every possible S tuple value (subsidiary entry point) we check that there is a linking T tuple that may be linked to the F tuple originally held. It is useful to compare the DSL ALPHA expression with the EOS CODASYL enhancement expression (retrieval 12, Chapter 11).

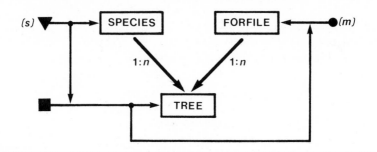

FIGURE 14.5. *Retrieval 9.*

Retrieval 10 (Level 2): Recursive Relationship   *Find the date of planting for those trees whose immediate descendants, if any, are all in the forest* 'XFOR'.

RANGE TREE TX
GET W1 (T.PLANTED) : ∀ TX TUPLES (T.TREENUMB ¬ = TX.PARENT
                                ∨ TX.FOREST = 'XFOR')

Here we must have two range variables for use with the TREE relation. We note that it is necessary to use the connection key PARENT to connect a TX tuple to a T tuple. (In Chapter 11, the EOS CODASYL enhancement expression for this retrieval is found under retrieval 15.) Readers should consider the effect of removing *if any* from the retrieval request.

Retrieval 11 (Level 2): Recursive Relationship   *Find the date of planting for the trees that are immediately propagated from those trees that have all their immediate descendants in the forest* 'XFOR'.

This retrieval is very similar to the previous one, at least superficially. The two must be compared carefully.

RANGE TREE TX
GET W1 (T.PLANTED) : ∀ TX TUPLES (T.PARENT ¬ = TX.PARENT
                                ∨ TX.FOREST = 'XFOR')

Here the PARENT connection key is used differently. We must group the TX tuples according to whether they have the same parent as the tree described by tuple T. (The retrieval diagram is in Figure 11.8*b,* and the EOS CODASYL enhancement version is under retrieval 16 in Chapter 11.)

Retrieval 12: Two-Stage Retrieval We may break retrieval 8 into two separate retrievals using the working spaces W1 and W2.

Find the names of companies with at least one California forest in which there is at least one cedar tree; and for each such company, also retrieve the tree numbers for any such cedar trees.

We need to form a new relation W1, with attributes COMPANY and TREENUMB; W1 will therefore be formed from the two relations FORFILE and TREE. Remembering that target attributes cannot be quantified in DSL ALPHA, we retrieve

```
GET W1 (F.COMPANY, T.TREENUMB) :
            F.LOC = 'CALIFORNIA'
∧ F.FOREST = T.FOREST ∧ T.SPECIES = 'CEDAR'
```

Find the names of companies in W1 with trees on which (a) at least one electrical measurement has been carried out; and (b) no chemical measurements have been carried out.

We employ the relation W1 from the previous retrieval. The primary key in W1 must be TREENUMB. Thus W1 tuples can be linked to MEASUREMENT tuples by means of the connection key MEASUREMENT.TREENUMB:

```
RANGE W1    W
RANGE MEASUREMENT MX
GET W2 (W.COMPANY) :
            ∃M TUPLE (W.TREENUMB = M.TREENUMB
                                    ∧ M.TYPE = 'ELECTRICAL')
      ∧     ∀ MX TUPLES (W.TREENUMB ¬ = MX.TREENUMB
                                    ∨ MX.TYPE ¬ = 'CHEMICAL')
```

14.2.4 Status of DSL ALPHA

DSL ALPHA is often used as retrieval standard against which the retrieval power of other retrieval sublanguages may be compared [Codd, 1971]. An arbitrary relational retrieval sublanguage L is said to be *relationally complete* if L expressions may be used to specify any retrieval that may be specified by DSL ALPHA expressions.

DSL ALPHA has earned this status primarily for the following reasons.

a. The sublanguage is solidly based on set-theoretical expressions.

b. Its noncomputational retrieval power (see Section 16.4.1) is probably in excess of what would be required in practice.

On the other hand, the sublanguage is difficult to use for those not trained in mathematics. The fact that relationships between relations must be formulated in a predicate tends to complicate the expressions. This is quite apparent when quantifiers are used, especially the universal quantifier.

It seems reasonable to assume that DSL ALPHA will retain its position as a retrieval sublanguage standard but will find only limited use in the world of commercial data processing. Nevertheless, for users with the necessary mathematical background, the sublanguage is both easy and convenient to learn. Consequently it has a very wide following in academic circles and, for this reason alone, we may expect that implementations incorporating it will not be uncommon. However, it is acknowledged that DSL ALPHA has disadvantages for the typical user; largely in an effort to overcome these disadvantages, a different nonprocedural sublanguage, SQL, was developed. We shall study SQL in the next chapter.

EXERCISE

Use DSL ALPHA to express each of the retrievals listed in the exercises for Chapter 11.

REFERENCES

Codd, E. F., 1971, "A Data Base Sublanguage Founded on the Relational Calculus," *Proc. ACM SIGFIDET Workshop on Data Description, Access and Control,* pp. 35–78.

Codd, E. F., 1972, "Relational Completeness of Data Base Sublanguages," in *Courant Computer Science Symposium Series,* vol. 6, Prentice-Hall, Englewood Cliffs, N.J., pp. 65–98.

Date, C. J., 1977, *Introduction to Data Base Systems,* Addison-Wesley, Reading, Mass.

Kuhns, J. L., 1969, "Logical Aspects of Question Answering by Computer," *Proc. of the Third Int. Symposium on Computer and Information Sciences,* Miami Beach, Florida, Academic Press, New York.

SQL   15

Structured Query Language (SQL) was developed as part of the SQL project at IBM and later incorporated into the System R prototype [Astrahan, 1976].[1] It is an English-like version of a more fundamental relational sublanguage known as SQUARE (Specifying Queries As Relational Expressions), which employs a mathematical notation and is based on mathematical set-theory concepts [Boyce, 1975; Chamberlin, 1974; Kim, 1979]. The language is relationally complete; that is, it may be used to specify any retrieval that can be expressed by DSL ALPHA. Nevertheless, it is more user-friendly than DSL ALPHA and does not make use of either the existential or universal quantifiers in any explicit manner. From a user standpoint, SQL is probably the most important relational retrieval sublanguage at the time this is being written. (SQL under System R is described in Appendix 3.)

15.1 THE MECHANICS OF SQL

For the nonmathematician, the main problem with DSL ALPHA is that when a quantifier is applied to a relation, it quantifies every tuple in that relation, with the result that DSL ALPHA predicates that are logically correct do not always appear intuitively to be correct. In attempting to find a solution to this problem it is clear that there are two possible avenues of development. One avenue might be called the *SQUARE-SQL avenue* and involves the development of languages in which quantifiers are not needed. Another avenue, which might be called the *natural-quantifier avenue*, involves the development of languages in which quantifiers are used in a more intuitively appealing manner. In the early

---

[1]*Until quite recently SQL was known as SEQUEL.*

1970s, the second avenue was not apparent and the designers of SQL decided that the solution to the quantifier problem was a relational retrieval sublanguage that did not use quantifiers at all. To uncover a suitable language, researchers turned to the very foundations of the relational approach once again, the mathematical theory of sets, and came up with SQUARE, on which SQL is based.

The basic idea behind SQL is quite simple and is straight out of set theory. For example, using the relation TREE we can easily specify selection of the relation SUBTREE containing all the TREE tuples with SPECIES value 'SPRUCE'. Similarly, we could easily select a relation SUBMEAS from MEASUREMENT with all the MEASUREMENT tuples containing the TYPE value 'ELECTRICAL'. Now suppose we wish to specify those TREE tuples for spruce trees on which one or more electrical measurements have been performed. We could do this by specifying that we want those SUBTREE tuples for which the TREEN-UMB value is a member of the mathematical set of TREENUMB values obtainable from SUBMEAS. In this simple way we avoid the use of the existential quantifier. As we shall see in retrieval 5, another set theoretic technique may be used to avoid the universal quantifier.

15.1.1 SQL Syntax

In contrast to DSL ALPHA, the syntax of SQL is not at all obvious, and readers should familiarize themselves with the structure of an SQL expression. A (useful) SQL expression has the following form.

SELECT [UNIQUE] *attribute-1, attribute-2, ...*
FROM *relation-1 [label-1], relation-2 [label-2], ...*
      [WHERE *requirement*]
      [GROUP BY (*attribute*) HAVING *requirement*]

1. The *requirement* clause has the form

$$\left\{ \begin{array}{l} \textit{requirement} \left\{ \begin{array}{l} \text{AND} \\ \text{OR} \end{array} \right\} \textit{requirement} \\ \textit{logical-relation} \end{array} \right\}$$

2. The *logical-relation* clause has the form

$$\left\{ \begin{array}{l} \textit{attribute} \left\{ \begin{array}{l} \lnot = \\ = \\ > \\ \lnot > \\ < \\ \lnot < \end{array} \right\} \left\{ \begin{array}{l} \textit{constant} \\ \textit{attribute} \end{array} \right\} \\ \textit{attribute} \left\{ \begin{array}{l} \text{IS IN} \\ \text{IS NOT IN} \end{array} \right\} \left\{ \begin{array}{l} \textit{(SQL-expression)} \\ \textit{set} \\ \text{SET } \textit{(attribute)} \end{array} \right\} \\ \left\{ \begin{array}{l} \textit{(SQL-expression)} \\ \textit{set} \\ \text{SET } \textit{(attribute)} \end{array} \right\} \left\{ \begin{array}{l} \text{CONTAINS} \\ \text{DOES NOT CONTAIN} \\ \lnot = \\ = \end{array} \right\} \left\{ \begin{array}{l} \textit{(SQL-expression)} \\ \textit{set} \\ \text{SET } \textit{(attribute)} \end{array} \right\} \end{array} \right\}$$

We see that the syntax specification is recursive, permitting SQL expressions to be nested within outer SQL expressions. In the vast majority of SQL retrievals we have to construct one or more SELECT_FROM_WHERE blocks, and such a block specifies a set of tuples, that is, a relation. To handle relationships, we typically specify that a tuple from one such block IS IN another nested block, or that a block contains the tuples of another block. While not shown in the syntax above, a *requirement* may be enclosed in parentheses; where parentheses are not used, logical AND will take precedence over logical OR.

15.2 SQL RETRIEVALS

15.2.1 Level Concept

The level concept, as used with the EOS CODASYL enhancement and DSL ALPHA retrieval sublanguage examples, is not quite as useful or obvious with SQL retrievals. However, we shall give the level number for each retrieval for purposes of comparison.

15.2.2 Retrieval Examples

Retrieval 1 (Level 1) *For forests in California, find the sizes and the names of the companies owning them.*

```
SELECT SIZE, COMPANY
FROM    FORFILE
WHERE LOC = 'CALIFORNIA'
```

In this retrieval, we have a very simple *requirement* clause, namely, LOC = 'CALIFORNIA'. Conceptually, we scan down the LOC column until we come to a tuple with LOC = 'CALIFORNIA'. This tuple is extracted and the scan of the LOC column continues. We see that there is a possibility of retrieving duplicate tuples here. However, in SQL the requirement that the retrieved data form a relation is relaxed. Duplicate tuples are removed only if UNIQUE is specified following SELECT. Thus SQL may retrieve a conceptual file which is not a relation.

Retrieval 2 (Level 1) *Retrieve all details about forests in California.*

```
SELECT     *
FROM       FORFILE
WHERE      LOC = 'CALIFORNIA'
```

The asterisk indicates that all the attributes of FORFILE are to be retrieved.

Retrieval 3 (Level 2): Existential Quantifier Equivalent, Nested Block *Find the size of California forests containing cedar trees.*

```
SELECT      SIZE
FROM        FORFILE
WHERE       LOC = 'CALIFORNIA'
            AND
            FOREST IS IN  (SELECT    FOREST
                           FROM      TREE
                           WHERE     SPECIES = 'CEDAR')
```

In this case the use of the nested SELECT block is equivalent to (or thus avoids) the use of the existential quantifier. In the inner block, we collect all FOREST values for forests containing cedar trees. In the outer block, we collect all SIZE and FOREST values for forests in California, but we retrieve only those SIZE values where the FOREST value IS IN the collection of FOREST values from the inner block.

The collection of FOREST values in the inner block constitutes a mathematical set, and IS IN is used instead of the set inclusion symbol ε. This is a more concrete example of what was sketched in Section 15.1 and clearly demonstrates the set theoretic foundation of SQL. The retrieval should be studied carefully and thoroughly understood.

Retrieval 4 (Level 2): Result Formed from Two Relations   *Find the tree numbers for cedar trees, and the size of the forests containing them.*

```
SELECT      SIZE, TREENUMB
FROM        FORFILE, TREE
WHERE       FORFILE.FOREST = TREE.FOREST
            AND
            TREE.SPECIES = 'CEDAR'
```

The DSL ALPHA version of this retrieval is shown under retrieval 4 in Section 14.2.3. The two are similar in this case.

Retrieval 5 (Level 2): Bench-mark Retrieval   *Find the tree numbers and locations of spruce trees on which no electrical measurements have been carried out.*

This is the retrieval we singled out as a bench-mark in Chapter 11 (EOS CODASYL enhancement retrieval 7). The DSL ALPHA version is given in Section 14.2.3 (retrieval 5). Again, we have two ways of expressing this retrieval in SQL. One method involves using the CONTAINS subclause and is equivalent to the use of the universal quantifier. The other method involves the construction that is equivalent to the use of the existential quantifier.

1. Universal quantifier equivalent

```
SELECT      TREENUMB, LOC
FROM        TREE
WHERE
            (SPECIES = 'SPRUCE')
AND         ((SELECT   MEASNUMB
```

```
            FROM       MEASUREMENT
            WHERE      TYPE ⌐ = 'ELECTRICAL')
            CONTAINS
            (SELECT    MEASNUMB
            FROM       MEASUREMENT
            WHERE      TREE.TREENUMB = MEASUREMENT.TREENUMB))
```

2. Existential quantifier equivalent

```
    SELECT    TREENUMB, LOC
    FROM      TREE
    WHERE

              SPECIES = 'SPRUCE'
              AND
              TREENUMB IS NOT IN
              (SELECT    TREENUMB
              FROM       MEASUREMENT
              WHERE      TYPE = 'ELECTRICAL')
```

Of the two expressions, the first requires the most attention. Conceptually, the last SELECT block groups together all the tuples that would otherwise be the members of a TREE_ MEAS owner-coupled set occurrence. None of these "members" must have a TYPE value 'ELECTRICAL' and therefore must form a mathematical subset of, or be contained in, the MEASUREMENT tuples for which the TYPE value is not 'ELECTRICAL'. Thus we may avoid the universal quantifier by using CONTAINS, the SQL equivalent of the set theoretic ⊃. The second version of the retrieval merely employs the SQL equivalent of the negated existential quantifier.

Retrieval 6 (Level 2): Natural Quantifier FOR ONE AND FOR ALL Equivalent   *Find the tree numbers and locations of spruce trees on which only chemical measurements have been carried out; that is, trees on which one and all measurements are chemical.*

```
SELECT    TREENUMB, LOC
FROM      TREE
WHERE     SPECIES = 'SPRUCE'
          AND TREENUMB  IS IN
                        (SELECT    TREENUMB
                        FROM       MEASUREMENT
                        WHERE      TYPE = 'CHEMICAL')
          AND
          ((SELECT MEASNUMB
          FROM       MEASUREMENT
          WHERE      TYPE = 'CHEMICAL')
CONTAINS
          (SELECT    MEASNUMB
          FROM       MEASUREMENT
          WHERE      TREE.TREENUMB = MEASUREMENT.TREENUMB))
```

Instead of CONTAINS we could use the negated existential quantifier equivalent. For a TREE tuple to be retrieved, we specify that there must be one chemical measurement on the tree and that all measurements on the tree are chemical.

Retrieval 7 (Level 2): Single Relationship, Two Quantifier Equivalents — Find the tree numbers and locations of spruce trees on which (a) all measurements were carried out before 19800101; and (b) at least one measurement was electrical.

```
SELECT      TREENUMB, LOC
FROM        TREE
WHERE       SPECIES = 'SPRUCE'
            AND
            ((SELECT    MEASNUMB
            FROM        MEASUREMENT
            WHERE       DATE < 19800101)
CONTAINS
            (SELECT     MEASNUMB
            FROM        MEASUREMENT
            WHERE       TREE.TREENUMB = MEASUREMENT.TREENUMB))
AND
            (TREENUMB IS IN    (SELECT    TREENUMB
                               FROM       MEASUREMENT
                               WHERE      TYPE = 'ELECTRICAL'))
```

On close examination, it should be clear that this expression has precisely the same structure as the previous one and for the same reasons.

Retrieval 8 (Level 2): Use of GROUP BY — Find the tree numbers for trees on which electrical and chemical measurements have been carried out.

We can manage this retrieval by using only the MEASUREMENT relation, but since the relationship between TREE and MEASUREMENT is being employed implicitly, we classify it as a level-2 retrieval.

```
SELECT      TREENUMB
FROM        MEASUREMENT
GROUP BY    TREENUMB HAVING SET (TYPE)
            CONTAINS ('ELECTRICAL', 'CHEMICAL')
```

The semantics of GROUP BY are interesting. In the above example, for each TREENUMB value selected in the SELECT block, all MEASUREMENT tuples with this TREENUMB value are grouped together, as specified by GROUP BY TREENUMB. Thus, in effect, we have grouped together all the members of a TREE_MEAS owner-coupled set occurrence (see Chapter 8), since MEASUREMENT.TREENUMB is a connection key.

From this grouping of MEASUREMENT tuples, the TYPE values are taken as forming the mathematical set SET (TYPE). The set

$$\{'ELECTRICAL', 'CHEMICAL'\}$$

---

must then be a subset of SET (TYPE) for the original TREENUMB value to be acceptable. HAVING should be read as a special form of WHERE.

Retrieval 9 (Level 2): Use of GROUP BY   *Find the names of the forests that have at least the same species as forest* 'XFOR'.

```
SELECT     FOREST
FROM       TREE
GROUP BY   FOREST HAVING SET (SPECIES) CONTAINS
                    (SELECT    SPECIES
                     FROM      TREE
                     WHERE     FOREST = 'XFOR')
```

This expression should be studied carefully. In the inner SELECT block we have a set of the species in the forest 'XFOR'. In the outer SELECT block we take a FOREST value and group together all those TREE tuples with that FOREST value (all the TREE members in a FOR_TREE owner-coupled set occurrence). The SPECIES values from this grouping— that is, SET (SPECIES)—should contain the set from the inner block. The EOS CODASYL enhancement expression is less concise, and involves both SPEC_TREE and FOR_TREE (see Figure 8.2).

Retrieval 10 (Level 3)   *Find the names and sizes of forests that contain all species.*

```
SELECT     FOREST, SIZE
FROM       FORFILE
WHERE      (SELECT    SPECIES
            FROM      TREE
            WHERE     FOREST = FORFILE.FOREST)
            =
           (SELECT    SPECIES
            FROM      SPECFILE)
```

The DSL ALPHA version is given under retrieval 9 in Section 14.2.3.

Retrieval 11 (Level 3): Nested SELECT Blocks   *Find the names of California forests containing only cedar trees, if any, on which only electrical measurements, if any, have been carried out.*

```
SELECT     FOREST
FROM       FORFILE
WHERE      LOC = 'CALIFORNIA'
           AND
           FOREST IS NOT IN
                    (SELECT    FOREST
                     FROM      TREE
                     WHERE     SPECIES ¬ = 'CEDAR'
```

```
                        OR
                        TREENUMB IS IN
                                (SELECT    TREENUMB
                                FROM       MEASUREMENT
                                WHERE      TYPE ¬ = 'ELECTRICAL'))
```

This expression is the equivalent of two nested universal quantifier expressions, although here we have used nested negated existential quantifier equivalents. The alternative expression using nested **CONTAINS** subclauses should be constructed as an exercise. Notice that the above expression retrieves forests with no trees at all.

It is useful here to compare the equivalent CODASYL EOS enhancement expression:

```
FIND NEXT : FORFILE RECORD ((LOCATION = 'CALIFORNIA')&
    FOR ALL TREE MEMBER RECORDS ((SPECIES = 'CEDAR')&
    FOR ALL MEASUREMENT MEMBER RECORDS (TYPE = 'ELECTRICAL')))
```

The reader is invited to consider the consequences of omitting the phrases *if any* from the retrieval request (see retrieval 6).

Retrieval 12 (Level 3): Use of a Label   *Find the names of forests containing more than one species.*

```
SELECT     UNIQUE FOREST
FROM       TREE XTREE
WHERE      FOREST IS IN
                    SELECT    FOREST
                    FROM      TREE
                    WHERE     SPECIES ¬ = XTREE.SPECIES
```

In the outer SELECT block, we consider all the TREE tuples; we take one of them, which we shall call an XTREE tuple. We now consider the FOREST value in the XTREE tuple for extraction. But first we make a list of all FOREST values in TREE for a species different from that in the XTREE tuple. If the FOREST value being considered for extraction is in this auxiliary list, then it is acceptable. SQL is at its most concise, although not at its most readable, in retrievals of this type. The EOS CODASYL enhancement version is not so concise but is possibly more readable. We give the short version without explicit reference to owner-coupled sets.

```
FIND NEXT : FORFILE OWNER RECORD
    ((EXISTS TREE MEMBER RECORD (SPECFILE OWNER OCCURRENCE (1))
& (EXISTS TREE MEMBER RECORD (SPECFILE OWNER OCCURRENCE (2)) )
```

Here we have specified that we wish to retrieve the next FORFILE record with at least one TREE member with a certain SPECFILE owner record and with at least one TREE member with a different SPECFILE owner record. However, in both the SQL and EOS CODASYL versions, labels are required.

Retrieval 13 (Level 2): Recursive Relationship   *Find the date of planting for all those trees for which all immediate descendants, if any, are in the forest* 'XFOR'.

```
SELECT      PLANTED
FROM        TREE XTREE
WHERE
            ((SELECT    TREENUMB
             FROM       TREE
             WHERE      FOREST = 'XFOR')
CONTAINS
             (SELECT    TREENUMB
             FROM       TREE
             WHERE      TREE.PARENT = XTREE.TREENUMB))
```

In this we use a label for TREE and the equivalent of the universal quantifier. The DSL ALPHA version is given under retrieval 10 in Section 14.2.3.

Retrieval 14 (Level 2): Recursive Relationship   *Find the date of planting for those trees that are directly propagated from trees, for which all immediate descendants are in the forest* 'XFOR'.

```
SELECT      PLANTED
FROM        TREE XTREE
WHERE
            ((SELECT    TREENUMB
             FROM       TREE
             WHERE      FOREST = 'XFOR')
CONTAINS
             (SELECT    TREENUMB
             FROM       TREE
             WHERE      TREE.PARENT = XTREE.PARENT))
```

As with the DSL ALPHA case (retrieval 11, Section 14.2.3), this retrieval is superficially similar to the previous one. In this case, we group the TREE tuples in the second nested SELECT block according to whether they have the same PARENT value as the tuple under consideration for extraction.

15.3 ALTERNATIVES TO SQL

SQL is easily the most important relational retrieval sublanguage. It is incorporated in IBM's System R prototype, and we may confidently expect that in the years to come every major relational system will provide for it. It was designed to serve the typical user—that is, persons not expected to have a strong background in mathematics—and successfully avoids the use of the quantifiers so characteristic of DSL ALPHA [Reisner, 1975].

However, at the time of writing it is not possible to state with any certainty to what extent SQL will succeed. The examples used in this chapter were chosen to illustrate both the strengths and weaknesses of the sublanguage. Readers must remember that the sublanguage has yet to be subjected to the test of commercial data-processing environments, and as yet the only demanding environment in which SQL has been extensively used has been the classroom environment. Our observation has been that students have no difficulty with simpler retrievals. However, with more complex retrievals, students with a good mathematical background prefer DSL ALPHA.

We can certainly expect that there will be further advances along the SQUARE-SQL avenue of development, given the history of programming languages. However, we might also conclude that there was justification for increased effort along the alternate natural-quantifier avenue of development mentioned in Section 15.1. Although it properly belongs to the CODASYL approach, the EOS CODASYL enhancement from Chapter 11 is an example of a retrieval language in which the use of quantifiers does not appear unnatural. The quantifiers in the EOS CODASYL enhancement are used in a user-friendly and natural manner simply because they quantify the member records of an owner-coupled set occurrence and not a complete file of records.

The next step is obvious. Would it help to incorporate something akin to the owner-coupled set concept into the relational approach? We believe that it would help a great deal. In fact, it could be argued that the owner-coupled set concept has already been incorporated in the form of the **GROUP BY** facility of SQL. But one thing is certain: any such incorporation should not affect the basic simplicity of the relational conceptual schema. In the following sections, we briefly describe one way in which such an incorporation has been accomplished.

15.3.1 Implicit Owner-Coupled Sets in the Relational Conceptual Schema

Let us look back to the FORESTRY relational conceptual data base (Figure 13.2) and for purposes of illustration take two relations such as FORFILE and TREE, which are connected by a 1:n relationship. In the relational approach, such a relationship is always fully described at the conceptual level, since the required connection keys are always present. (We recall that in the CODASYL approach the child-connection keys may be omitted, in which case the relationship is fully described only by the existence of some pointer system specified at the internal level.) Thus we can refer to the relationship between two relations by specifying the parent and child-connection keys involved; that is, in the case of the FORFILE and TREE relations by specifying the pair

(FORFILE.FOREST, TREE.FOREST)

We note that in general we may not refer to a relationship between two relations by simply specifying the names of the relations involved, since there may be several relationships between them (see Figure 6.5).

There is nothing to prevent us from regarding a 1:n relationship between two relations as being described by an owner-coupled set made up of set occurrences, each with an owner tuple and a collection of member tuples. We can refer to such a set by means of the parent/child (or owner/member) connection-key pair, but we do not have to declare it in the conceptual schema. The owner-coupled set exists implicitly and has been called a *dynamic* set [Bradley, 1978] because it may be made known to the DBCS dynamically when it is to be used in a DML command, as opposed to the *static* declaration of a CODASYL set in a schema. In discussing differences between CODASYL and relational approaches, Date has referred to these owner-coupled sets as *nonessential sets* [Date, 1977]. *Implicit set* is possibly a more appropriate term.

Such implicit or dynamic owner-coupled sets have no effect on storage operations in the relational approach, and a storage operation would still be very simple, involving merely the insertion of a tuple in a relation (see Chapter 16). By incorporating the specification of implicit owner-coupled sets into relational retrieval sublanguages, we are borrowing a proven and powerful concept, but leaving behind all of the complexities that surround its use in CODASYL. (We recall that owner-coupled sets, especially recursive sets, complicate both the CODASYL schema, and insertion and deletion of records.)

The extension of the concept of an owner-coupled set to include implicit sets was the basis of the original extended owner-coupled set (EOS) data model that could be manipulated by a predicate calculus (the EOS predicate calculus), which used quantifiers with owner-coupled sets [Bradley, 1978]. The EOS CODASYL enhancement described in Chapter 11 is a limited adaptation of the EOS calculus. We shall conclude this chapter with three examples of the application of the EOS calculus to the relational FORESTRY data base; one of them involves a functional dependency.

15.3.2 EOS Predicate Calculus Retrievals

The main structure of the EOS calculus is similar to that of DSL ALPHA. Thus if we wish to retrieve the names and locations of forests satisfying certain conditions, we write:

GET W1 (FOREST, LOC) : *EOS-predicate*

where W1 is a named workspace in a relational UWA. W1 receives the result of the retrieval, which is always a relation.

The syntax of the EOS predicate is quite different from that of DSL ALPHA but is very close to that given in Figure 11.1 for the EOS enhancement syntax. However, the distinguishing feature of the EOS predicate in the present context is that the owner-coupled sets employed are implicit or dynamic, and owner-member connection-key pairs are used to refer to them. Since such owner-member connection-key pairs are awkward to write repeatedly, aliases may be used instead and made known to the system in the same manner as are range variables in DSL ALPHA. Thus in a user session we could declare

SET ALIAS FT (FORFILE.FOREST, TREE.FOREST);
                        /*   Set FT is implicit version of CODASYL set FOR_TREE   */
SET ALIAS TM (TREE.TREENUMB, MEASUREMENT.TREENUMB);
                        /*   Set TM is implicit version of CODASYL set TREE_MEAS   */

But two relations and only one implicit set permit simplified syntax (section 11.2.9).

Retrieval A (Level 2): Natural Quantifier   *Find the tree numbers and locations of spruce trees on which chemical and only chemical measurements have been carried out.*

```
GET W1 (TREENUMB, LOC) : TREE TARGET TUPLE ((SPECIES = 'SPRUCE') &
                    OWNER (TM) SET OCCURRENCE
     (FOR ONE AND FOR ALL MEASUREMENT MEMBER TUPLES (TYPE =
                                              CHEMICAL')))
```

This should be compared with SQL retrieval 6.

Retrieval B (Level 3): Adjectival Expression   *Find each company owning an Oregon forest in which at least 20% of the cedar trees have been subjected to chemical and only chemical measurements.*

```
GET W1 (COMPANY) : FORFILE TARGET TUPLE ((LOC = 'OREGON') &
                    OWNER (FT) SET OCCURRENCE
     (FOR AT LEAST 20% OF (SPECIES = 'CEDAR') TREE MEMBER TUPLES
               (OWNER (TM) SET OCCURRENCE
                (FOR ONE AND FOR ALL MEASUREMENT TUPLES
                                            (TYPE = 'CHEMICAL')))))
```

The retrieval above contains two natural quantifiers, as well as an adjectival expression. It could be expressed by SQL, however, provided we extend the sublanguage to permit the construction

(*SELECT-block*) CONTAINS AT LEAST 20% OF (*SELECT-block*)

The resulting expression is

```
SELECT     COMPANY
FROM       FORFILE
WHERE      LOC = 'OREGON'
           AND
           (SELECT     TREENUMB
           FROM        TREE
           WHERE       TREENUMB IS IN
                                        (SELECT     TREENUMB
                                        FROM        MEASUREMENT
                                        WHERE       TYPE = 'CHEMICAL')
                       AND TREENUMB IS NOT IN
                                        (SELECT     TREENUMB
                                        FROM        MEASUREMENT
                                        WHERE       TYPE ¬ = 'CHEMICAL'))
           CONTAINS AT LEAST 20% OF
           (SELECT     TREENUMB
           FROM        TREE
```

```
WHERE      FORFILE.FOREST = TREE.FOREST
           AND
           SPECIES = 'CEDAR')
```

15.3.3 Projection (or Virtual) Owner-Coupled Sets

Readers who have not studied Chapter 7 should skip this section.

As we saw in Chapter 7 in dealing with functional dependencies, there will always be 1:*n* relationships between the attribute values of a relation and the tuples of a relation. As a reminder, suppose we take the relation FORFILE from Figure 13.2 and consider the attribute COMPANY. Since a company can be expected to possess several forests (this will be true in general if the relation is to be in 4NF), there must be a 1:*n* relationship between the derived projection or virtual relation P(COMPANY) and FORFILE, as we saw in Chapter 7.

We thus could have what may be called a *projection* or *virtual* owner-coupled set supporting the 1:*n* relationship between P(COMPANY) and FORFILE. This owner-coupled set is implicit and need not be declared in a conceptual schema. Nevertheless, it may be uniquely specified by the use of its owner-connection key P(COMPANY).COMPANY and member-connection key FORFILE.COMPANY, as shown in Figure 15.1.

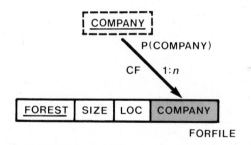

FIGURE 15.1. *The 1:n relationship that exists between the projection of the* FORFILE *attribute* COMPANY *and the relation* FORFILE.

Such an implicit owner-coupled set is useful in formulating (more subtle) retrieval expressions involving 1:*n* relationships occurring within a single relation. As before, we would have to inform the system that we needed to use such an implicit set. We could do this in a user session simply by naming an alias together with the proper connection keys.

SET ALIAS CF (P(COMPANY).COMPANY, FORFILE.COMPANY)

With the new owner-coupled set CF, we might conveniently express the following retrieval, which involves only the relation FORFILE.

Find the locations of forests that belong to companies which own only those forests exceeding 10,000 acres in size.

```
GET W1 (LOC):   FORFILE TARGET TUPLE
                (MEMBER (CF) SET OCCURRENCE
    (FOR ALL FORFILE MEMBER TUPLES (SIZE > 10000))
```

The need to extend the owner-coupled set concept to include virtual owner-coupled sets may be viewed as a drawback to the EOS calculus and results from the fact that the sublanguage requires that it be possible to reference any $1:n$ relationship in a data base, even a functional dependency, as an owner-coupled set. Nevertheless, whenever we have all the $1:n$ relationships involved in a retrieval as named owner-coupled sets—whether projection sets or not—expression of the retrieval is usually easy.

For the sake of completeness, we conclude this section with the SQL equivalent of the above retrieval.

```
SELECT     LOC
FROM       FORFILE, XFORFILE
WHERE
                (SELECT     FOREST
                 FROM       FORFILE
                 WHERE      SIZE > 10000)
           CONTAINS
                (SELECT     FOREST
                 FROM       FORFILE
                 WHERE      COMPANY = XFORFILE.COMPANY)
```

The expression is somewhat subtle. We select a LOC value from a FORFILE tuple, which is also labeled XFORFILE. The next SELECT block contains all forests greater than 10,000 acres in size; in order for the LOC value from the XFORFILE tuple to be retrieved, these forests must contain all the forests with the same company as XFORFILE.COMPANY. It may be argued that SQL has the advantage in retrievals involving the functional dependencies of a relation, since it can handle $1:n$ relationships of any kind without what some would call artificial constructs such as owner-coupled sets, especially virtual owner-coupled sets. Further SQL retrievals involving computations are described in Chapter 16.

15.3.4 Status of Natural Quantifier Alternatives to SQL

The existence of the EOS predicate calculus demonstrates that a user-friendly relational retrieval language employing quantifiers is a possibility. It does not follow that such a language would have to employ implicit owner-coupled sets. But in order for quantifiers to be applied in more natural manner, it is clear that some subgroupings of the tuples in relations would have to be used. Since owner-coupled sets are widely known, their use has obvious advantages. The EOS language is the result of research on the "no man's land" between the relational and CODASYL approaches, and it is therefore not surprising that one adaptation of it may be used in the CODASYL approach (Chapter 11) and another one in the relational approach. It might also be noted that the language can easily be shown to be relationally complete (by a process of demonstrating that it can carry out all the operations of relational algebra described in the following chapter).

EXERCISE

Use SQL to specify each of the retrievals listed for Chapter 11.

REFERENCES

Bradley, J., 1978a, "An Extended Owner-coupled Set Data Model and Predicate Calculus for Data Base Management," *ACM Trans. on Database Sys.*, **3**(4):385–416.

Astrahan, M. M., and others, 1976, "System R: Relational Approach to Data Base Management," *ACM Trans. on Data Base Sys.*, **1**(2):97–137.

Boyce, R. F., and others, 1975, "Specifying Queries as Relational Expressions," *Comm. ACM*, **18**(11):621–28.

Chamberlin, D. D., and R. F. Boyce, 1974, "SEQUEL, a Structured English Query Language," *Proc. ACM SIGMOD Workshop on Data Description, Access and Control*, pp. 249–64.

Date, C. J., 1977, *An Introduction to Data Base Systems*, Addison-Wesley, Reading, Mass.

Kim, W., 1979, "Relational Data Base Systems," *ACM Comput. Surv.*, **11**(3):185–211.

Reisner, P., R. F. Boyce, and D. D. Chamberlin, 1975, "Human Factor Evaluation of Two Data Base Query Languages, SQUARE and SEQUEL," *Proc. AFIPS Nat. Computer Conf.*, vol. 44, IFIPS Press, Montvale, N.J., pp. 447–52.

Relational Algebra and Other Relational Facilities

16

In this final chapter on the relational approach, we look first at a highly original but fundamental relational-retrieval language, *relational algebra*. We also look briefly at how expressions in languages such as DSL ALPHA may be converted into relational algebra procedures and at the subject of *performance optimizers* mentioned in both Chapters 11 and 13. We then examine relational storage and updating operations, which are very simple in the relational approach (assuming the relations to be in 4NF). Finally, we look at some more peripheral relational topics: the *functional* (as opposed to relational) *completeness* of retrieval sublanguages, *integrity constraints* for maintaining the integrity of a relational data base, and *external* data bases derived from the conceptual data base by means of retrieval expressions.

16.1 RELATIONAL ALGEBRA

In marked contrast to both DSL ALPHA and SQL, retrievals in relational algebra are generally effected by the specification of a sequence of operations, in much the same manner as in a conventional computer program. Thus relational algebra is essentially a procedural or navigational retrieval language. However, operations in relational algebra are very high level, and much may be accomplished in a single operation. Furthermore, with simpler retrievals it is possible to nest a sequence of relational-algebraic expressions into a single expression, which gives the language a nonprocedural dimension. Relational algebra was introduced by Codd and was shown to be relationally complete [Codd, 1972]. It is of fundamental importance for research and development in relational data bases.

16.1.1 Relational Algebra Operations

In relational algebra, we employ both the traditional mathematical set operations and certain relational operations.

Set Operations   The sets with which we are dealing are always sets of tuples. Suppose A_TREE and B_TREE are relations consisting of tuples each describing trees. Then we have the following.

1. *Set union operation*
    A_TREE ∪ B_TREE is the relation with tuples describing trees that are in either A_TREE or B_TREE, or in both A_TREE and B_TREE.

2. *Set intersection operation*
    A_TREE ∩ B_TREE is the relation with tuples describing trees that are in both A_TREE and B_TREE.

3. *Set difference operation*
    A_TREE − B_TREE is the relation with tuples describing trees in A_TREE but not in both A_TREE and B_TREE.

4. *Extended Cartesian product operation*
    Suppose a forest can have trees only of a single species. If we take the relations FORFILE and SPECFILE from the FORESTRY data base, then FORFILE ⊗ SPECFILE is the extended Cartesian product. This product is a relation, with each tuple a FORFILE tuple concatenated to a SPECFILE tuple. The concatenation tuples of the product list all possible FORFILE, SPECFILE tuple combinations.

The extended Cartesian product operation applied to sets of tuples is illustrated in Figure 16.1.

Relational Operations   There are four important relational operations: *selection, projection*, *natural join* or *join*, and *division*. We shall illustrate them by means of relations from the FORESTRY data base.

The selection operation   The *selection operation* is the simplest operation. Suppose we

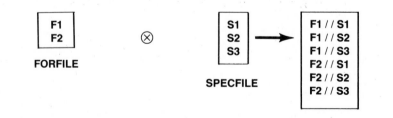

FIGURE 16.1. *Extended Cartesian product applied to the relations* FORFILE *and* SPECFILE.

wish to construct a new relation N_FORFILE, consisting of tuples from FORFILE for which the LOC value is 'CALIFORNIA'. We write the algebraic statement

N_FORFILE = SEL(FORFILE (LOC = 'CALIFORNIA'))

The relation FORFILE is the operand, SEL is the operator, and the relation N_FORFILE is the result. In the parentheses following the operand, we may have any logical expression involving logical relations featuring the operand attributes. Thus X_TREE in

X_TREE = SEL(TREE((SPECIES = 'CEDAR') $\wedge$ (FOREST = 'XFOR')))

is a new relation with tuples from TREE describing cedar trees growing in 'XFOR'.

The projection operation   The selection operation forms a new relation by selecting tuples from the operand relation. The *projection operation* forms a new relation by selecting columns or attributes from an operand relation and eliminating duplicate tuples. We recall that use has already been made of this operation in Chapter 7.

Suppose we need a relation which has tuples specifying forest names with the species growing in them. We code

X_REL = PROJ(TREE(SPECIES,FOREST))

The SPECIES and FOREST columns are taken out of the relation TREE. The result is not a relation, because the SPECIES/FOREST pairs can have duplicates. On elimination of these duplicates, the resulting relation is placed in X_REL. The operation is illustrated in Figure 16.2.

SPECIES	FOREST	TREENUMB
PINE	XFOR	1
BEECH	ZFOR	3
PINE	YFOR	5
SPRUCE	XFOR	8
OAK	YFOR	10
CEDAR	YFOR	13
CEDAR	XFOR	14
SPRUCE	ZFOR	17
SPRUCE	YFOR	20
OAK	YFOR	24
CEDAR	XFOR	26
BEECH	ZFOR	31

TREE

SPECIES	FOREST
PINE	XFOR
BEECH	ZFOR
PINE	YFOR
SPRUCE	XFOR
OAK	YFOR
CEDAR	YFOR
CEDAR	XFOR
SPRUCE	ZFOR
SPRUCE	YFOR

X_REL

FIGURE 16.2. *Illustration of the relational projection operation* PROJ(TREE(SPECIES,FOREST)). *The result is the relation* X_REL.

The natural join operation There are several different *join* operations, but that which is called the *natural join* is the most common and useful. Thus when we refer to a join operation in this chapter it is the natural join which is implied.

A join operation basically joins or concatenates certain tuples from two operand relations. The result is a new relation. The concatenation process is controlled by what are called the *join attributes* or *join fields*. We illustrate by an example (see Figure 16.3). Suppose we need a relation FT in which each tuple describes both a tree and the forest it grows in. We code

FT = FORFILE * TREE (FOREST, FOREST)

Here the operands are the FORFILE and TREE relations, and the join operand is denoted by an asterisk. FOREST in FORFILE and FOREST in TREE are the join attributes.

In order to carry out this join operation, we first select all possible pairs of tuples, for which each pair consists of a FORFILE tuple and a TREE tuple such that the FORFILE.FOREST value is equal to the TREE.FOREST value. The tuples of each pair are then concatenated, and one of the duplicate FOREST columns is removed. (If the duplicate FOREST column is not removed, the operation is known as an *equi-join*.) The relation FT is the result of this natural join and is shown in Figure 16.3.

As mentioned above, there are several different join operations. For example, in a *greater-than join,* tuples of a pair from relations A and B are concatenated if their respective join attributes *a* and *b* satisfy $a > b$. Similarly, there exists a *less-than join,* and so on. For a join operation to be valid, the participating join attributes must both be drawn from the same domain, in which case they are said to be *join compatible*.

FOREST	SIZE	LOC	COMPANY
XFOR	200	MAINE	LOGCO
ZFOR	500	B.C.	BLOMAC
YFOR	150	OREGON	ARBCO

FORFILE

SPECIES	FOREST	TREENUMB	PLANTED
PINE	XFOR	1	—
BEECH	ZFOR	3	—
PINE	YFOR	5	—
SPRUCE	XFOR	8	—

TREE

SPECIES	FOREST	SIZE	LOC	COMPANY	TREENUMB	PLANTED
PINE	XFOR	200	MAINE	LOGCO	1	—
BEECH	ZFOR	500	B.C.	BLOMAC	3	—
PINE	YFOR	150	OREGON	ARBCO	5	—
SPRUCE	XFOR	200	MAINE	LOGCO	8	—

FT

FIGURE 16.3. *Illustration of a natural-join operation of the relations* FORFILE *and* TREE *using the join attributes* FORFILE.FOREST *and* TREE.FOREST.

The division operation The *division operation* is easily the most difficult operation to grasp and may be explained either by a mathematical definition or diagrammatically. We shall take the diagrammatic approach.

Suppose we have the relation X_REL (from the projection operation) which has tuples that specify forests along with the species growing in them, as shown in Figure 16.4*a*. Suppose further that we wish to retrieve a (one-attribute tuple) relation giving all the FOREST values for forests in which the lists of species 'CEDAR', 'SPRUCE', and 'PINE' grow. Let us call this list SPECLIST.

To specify the correct relation F_REL, we consider X_REL as dividend and SPECLIST as a divisor and code

F_REL = X_REL ÷ SPECLIST

To carry out the division operation, we imagine that the tuples of the dividend X_REL are first sorted into groupings. In such a grouping the SPECIES values are the same as those of the divisor SPECLIST and the FOREST values are all the same, as shown in Figure 16.4*b*. Of course not all tuples can form such groupings, but perhaps some can. The quotient F_REL is the set of FOREST values from these groupings.

In general, the dividend relation must be binary; that is, it has only two attributes. The divisor relation must have only one attribute and, in addition, one of the attribute types of the dividend. The quotient has one attribute; the other attribute type is from the dividend.

It is possible to have division operations in which the dividend and divisor are not binary and unary, respectively. As an exercise, the reader might try to construct such an operation [Codd, 1971].

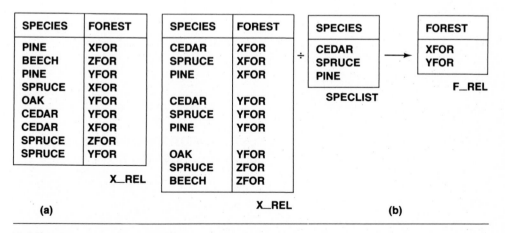

FIGURE 16.4. *Illustration of* X_REL *divided by* SPECLIST; *the quotient is* F_REL.

16.1.2 Algebraic Retrieval Examples

Since we are dealing with an algebra, retrievals may be specified in either of two ways.

    a.   *Procedurally:* Here the retrieval is specified as a sequence of operations. Each operation is specified by means of an expression the value of which is assigned to a named *relational workspace* or *variable*. (For relational workspaces, see Chapter 14.)

    b.   *Nonprocedurally:* The retrieval is specified as a single algebraic expression with subcomponents that are themselves algebraic expressions.

We give both methods in the following examples. We make use of relational workspaces R1, R2, …, as required.

Retrieval 1: Projection and Division   *Find the forests containing all species.*

Procedural

```
R1 = PROJ (TREE(SPECIES,FOREST))
R2 = PROJ (SPECFILE(SPECIES))
R3 = R1 ÷ R2
```

Nonprocedural

```
R3 = PROJ (TREE(SPECIES,FOREST)) ÷ PROJ(SPECFILE(SPECIES))
```

Retrieval 2: Projection, Division, and Join   *Find the names and sizes of forests containing all species.*

Procedural

```
R1 = PROJ (TREE(SPECIES,FOREST))
R2 = PROJ (SPECFILE(SPECIES))
R3 = R1 ÷ R2
R4 = R3 * FORFILE (FOREST, FOREST)
R5 = PROJ (R4(FOREST,SIZE))
```

Nonprocedural

```
R5 = PROJ (((PROJ(TREE(SPECIES,FOREST)) ÷ PROJ(SPECFILE(SPECIES)) )
          * FORFILE(FOREST, FOREST))(FOREST,SIZE))
```

The DSL ALPHA version of this retrieval is given under retrieval 9 in Section 14.2.3; the SQL version is under retrieval 10 in Section 15.2.2.

Retrieval 3: Selection, Join, and Projection   *Find the types of measurements that have been carried out on trees in forests in California.*

Procedural

```
R1 = SEL(FORFILE(LOC = 'CALIFORNIA'))
R2 = R1 * TREE (FOREST,FOREST)
R3 = R2 * MEASUREMENT (TREENUMB,TREENUMB)
R4 = PROJ(R3(TYPE))
```

Nonprocedural

```
R4 = PROJ((((SEL(FOREST(LOC = 'CALIFORNIA'))) * TREE(FOREST,FOREST))
          * MEASUREMENT(TREENUMB,TREENUMB))(TYPE))
```

16.1.3 Application to Functional and Join Dependencies

In Chapter 7 we used diagrammatic techniques to analyze functional and binary-join dependencies. It should now be clear that the projection or virtual files that we employed are nothing other than simple algebraic projections. Relational algebra is thus ideally suited to the analysis of dependencies in relational files and is used in most research projects in this field [Fagin, 1977; Delobel, 1978].

We shall not conduct any further analysis of dependencies here, except to reexamine one aspect of a binary-join dependency in the light of relational algebra. Referring to Figures 7.11 and 7.12, which illustrate the binary-join dependency in the relational file ASSIGNMENT, we can state that the dependency exists because ASSIGNMENT must always be a natural join on the COMPANY fields (attributes) of the two projections P(CON_ENG,COMPANY) and P(COMPANY,LOC). Thus

```
ASSIGNMENT = ENGINEER * OPERATION (COMPANY,COMPANY)
```

must always hold true and is ultimately responsible for the peculiar insertion and deletion characteristics of the file. Similarly, a join dependency of order 3 occurs in a relational file, if it must always be the result of joining three projections together on a common join field (Figure 7.13).

16.1.4 Application to Commercial Data Processing

Our experience with relational algebra leads us strongly to the conclusion that the relational algebra language is unsuited for use in commercial data processing, for two good reasons. First, it is extremely difficult to write algebraic routines for more complex retrievals correctly, and, in the words of one student, it is counterintuitive. Secondly, to read and understand the logic of an algebraic routine written by another person is a very time-consuming affair. Relational algebra can, in fact, be usefully regarded as the "assembler" language of the relational approach. In support of this is the fact that (apart from its theoretical applications) its main practical use appears to be as a target language. Higher relational-retrieval expressions are reduced to algebra routines as a first step in the translation process. We examine this aspect of relational algebra in Section 16.2.

16.2 PERFORMANCE OPTIMIZATION AND THE REDUCTION PROCESS

Reduction is the process of converting a retrieval expression in a language such as DSL ALPHA or SQL to a relational-algebraic procedure, while *performance optimization* is that part of the reduction process that ensures that the resulting procedure is an optimum one in terms of performance; that is, one employing a minimum number of underlying file accesses. This is an important area of research and development at the present time, and most of the subject matter lies beyond the scope of this book. We restrict our coverage to a description of some of the principles involved. A more detailed coverage is to be found in a recent book by Ullman [Ullman, 1980].

16.2.1 Performance Optimization

To see some of the principles involved in performance optimization, we may imagine that the reduction and optimization processes are sequential and separate, that is, we imagine that the reduction process takes place first, giving a certain algebraic procedure, and that this procedure is then subjected to the optimization process, giving rise to an optimized algebraic procedure. We may therefore concern ourselves with some of the principles involved in optimizing a relational-algebraic procedure [Smith, 1975].

We may begin by analyzing the kind of storage file accesses required in the execution of each type of relational algebra operation. We also consider two extreme cases, one where the storage file is very large and can reside only in external (direct access) storage, and the other where the storage file is quite small and can easily be accommodated in main memory.

1. *Select operation*

   The *select operation* can be carried out efficiently and quickly for large storage files, provided there is an inversion for at least one of the fields involved in the selection conditions. The absence of inversions could render the operation prohibitively expensive with 4-digit average search lengths for very large storage files (see Chapter 5). For small storage files, there is no problem.

2. *Join operation*

   The *join operation* can be carried out efficiently with large storage files if there is an inversion for any join field that is not a prime key. However, the operation is efficient only in the sense of low average search lengths for records sought to complete a join, and since very many records will participate in the join, it will inevitably be slow. The operation will be efficient and fast for two small storage files. When one storage file is small and the other large, the operation will be fast if a suitable inversion is available (see Chapter 5).

3. *Project operation*

   The *project operation* can be carried out reasonably quickly with large storage files only when the number of projection fields is low and there is an inversion for each projection field. The technique involved is to intersect pointer fields in one inversion record with the pointer fields in inversion records from a different inversion file, and so on. However, when the number of projection fields is large, sequential processing of the file will be required. With small storage files, there is no problem.

4. *Division operation*
   The *division operation* is a very time-consuming operation with large storage files, and inversions are no help. As usual, it can be carried out efficiently with small storage files.

5. *The mathematical set operations*
   Except in the case of the Cartesian product, it is not likely that we would ever want to carry out *set operations* on large storage files; the operations are all very time consuming. With small storage files, there are no problems.

This analysis is hardly encouraging and indicates that unless steps toward performance optimization are taken, relational algebra procedures can easily perform very badly. For example, consider the following typical retrieval.

Find the sizes and owners of California forests that contain spruce trees.

From a logical point of view, there is nothing wrong with using the procedure

```
R1 = FORFILE * TREE (FOREST,FOREST)    /*  Extremely slow  */
R2 = SEL(R1(FORFILE.LOC = 'CALIFORNIA' & SPECIES = 'SPRUCE'))
                                       /*  Fast if proper inversions are available  */
R3 = PROJ(R2(SIZE,COMPANY)            /*  Fast  */
```

Nevertheless, without optimization, the execution of this procedure will be very slow indeed, assuming FORFILE and TREE to be large. The problem is the join operation right at the beginning. The retrieval could be managed quite differently, as follows.

```
R1 = SEL(FORFILE(LOC = 'CALIFORNIA'))  /*  Fast with proper inversion  */
R2 = SEL(TREE(SPECIES = 'SPRUCE'))     /*  Fast with proper inversion  */
R3 = R1 * R2(FOREST,FOREST)            /*  Fast if R1, R2 are small  */
R4 = PROJ(R3(SIZE,COMPANY))            /*  Fast if R3 is small  */
```

This simple example illustrates most of the principles involved in optimization. Selection operations must be carried out first; the resulting relations are likely to be small, thus permitting fast execution of other algebraic operations. Also, the internal or storage data base must include a sufficient number of inverted files (or equivalents) to permit fast execution of selection operations. Unfortunately, if the relations resulting from selection operations are still very large, performance is likely to be poor.

We shall not attempt to give algorithms for optimization, as the subject is beyond the scope of this book. A great deal of optimization may be carried out as part of the reduction process that we consider in the next section [Palermo, 1974; Wong, 1976; Yao, 1979].

Data-Base Machines as an Aid to Performance   At the time of writing, it is probably safe to state that the implementation of a *high-performance* relational system for large data bases has proved to be difficult, and the problem still awaits a complete solution.[1] We have so far considered only optimization during retrievals, but as we have seen, many inverted storage files or their functional equivalents [Astrahan, 1976] are required for this purpose. Such inversions have their price, as we saw in Chapter 6, and severely reduce performance during updating of the data base.

These problems have led many to conclude that the solution lies in more advanced hardware, which has had a stimulating effect on research and development on new types of external-storage devices. Of particular interest is the concept of a data-base machine connected to the main computer as a *back-end device,* where the connection to a disk unit is through a set of parallel microprocessors with one connected to each disk read/write head [Banerjee, 1978*a*]. This arrangement (which clearly involves much increased computational power) permits a complete cylinder to be read in one access, thus permitting the retrieval of many records based on their data *content* in just one access. Such an external memory is known as a *Partitioned Content Addressable Memory* (PCAM), and experience with a data-base machine employing PCAMs indicates greatly increased performance over conventional systems [Banerjee, 1978*b*]. It does indeed look as if this may be the way forward.

16.2.2 The Reduction Process

As should be clear from a glance at the retrieval diagrams used with DSL ALPHA (and the EOS CODASYL enhancement), the retrieval expressions have a hierarchical, or tree, structure. The same is true for SQL expressions, although this may not be quite so obvious. It should also be clear that a branch of the tree in the DSL ALPHA (or EOS) case will involve either an existentially or a universally (or negated existential equivalent) quantified expression. In the SQL case, we will have either an IS IN or CONTAINS (or IS NOT IN) expression.

Having recognized the tree structure of the expression, the next step in the reduction process is to decompose the expression into a corresponding hierarchy of simple expressions involving at most two relations and one quantifier (or quantifier equivalent, in the case of SQL). We take as our first illustration an example involving DSL ALPHA and existential quantifiers only. Suppose we have the following retrieval.

Find the sizes of Oregon forests containing spruce trees on which chemical measurements have been carried out.

The DSL ALPHA expression is

```
GET W1 (F.SIZE) :
        F.LOC = 'OREGON'
```

---

[1]*It is possible that it will never be solved completely, and that each generation of optimizers will simply be better than the previous generation.*

```
∧   ∃ T TUPLE (F.FOREST = T.FOREST ∧ T.SPECIES = 'SPRUCE'
∧   ∃ M TUPLE (T.TREENUMB = M.TREENUMB ∧ M.TYPE = 'CHEMICAL' ))
```

This expression forms a simple nonbranching hierarchy, and we now decompose it into a similar hierarchy of distinct expressions. We employ the relational workspaces WF, WT, and WM, each of which will be assigned F, W, and T tuples, respectively. For simplicity we take WF TUPLE to mean a tuple from the workspace relation WF. The decomposition is

(4)
```
    GET W1 (WF.SIZE)
```
(3)
```
    GET WF (F):
        F.LOC = 'OREGON' ∧ ∃ WT TUPLE (F.FOREST = WT.FOREST)
```
(2)
```
    GET WT (T):
        T.SPECIES = 'SPRUCE' ∧ ∃ WM TUPLE (T.TREENUMB = WM.TREENUMB)
```
(1)
```
    GET WM (M):
        M.TYPE = 'CHEMICAL'
```

We see that these expressions exactly mirror the original expression. However, execution must take place starting at the bottom of the hierarchy; that is, Expression 1 is executed first, then Expression 2, and so on. The reader should take time to check through the above expressions in execution order to clarify what is happening.

The final step in the reduction involves converting each of the decomposition expressions into an algebra procedure. This is not very difficult because the number of different types of decomposition expressions is quite limited. At the top of a hierarchy, we always have an expression of the same type as Expression 4, and at the bottom we have expressions that look like Expression 1. In the middle, we shall have expressions such as 2 and 3 or expressions involving a single universal (or negated existential) quantifier. We can say that expressions of the same type as Expressions 2 and 3 all have the general structure

```
GET WP (P):
    P-logical-expression θ ∃C TUPLE (P.p = C.c)
```

where P is a parent-file tuple and C is a child-file tuple, p and c being the connection keys. In addition, *P-logical-expression* is a logical expression involving the attributes of P, WP is a workspace relation which will be assigned the result of executing the (command) expression, and θ is logical AND or OR.

This general expression can be reduced to the following *general* algebra routine, which we will call XQUAND, for the case where θ is AND.

```
R1 = SEL (P (P-logical-expression))
R2 = PROJ (C (c))
WP = R1 * R2 (p,c)
```

We are now in a position to complete our reduction of Expressions 1, 2, 3, and 4 in our simple example. Reduction of Expressions 1 and 4 is trivial, and Expressions 2 and 3 are reduced by applying XQUAND. Remembering to begin at the bottom of the expression hierarchy, we have the following as a final algebra routine.

```
WM = SEL (M (TYPE = 'CHEMICAL'))
/*  Now apply XQUAND */
R11 = SEL (T (SPECIES = 'SPRUCE'))
R12 = PROJ (WM (TREENUMB))
WT = R11 * R12 (TREENUMB,TREENUMB)
/*  Now apply XQUAND again   */
R21 = SEL (F(LOC = 'OREGON'))
R22 = PROJ (WT(FOREST))
WF = R21 * R22 (FOREST,FOREST)
/*  Now extract required columns from WF   */
W1 = PROJ (WF (SIZE))
```

This example is, of course, almost trivially simple, but it does illustrate many of the principles. The reader will note that we shall need another algebra routine XQUOR for the case where there is an OR instead of an AND in the general expression involving two files and the existential quantifier. Similarly, we could use algebra routines UQUAND and UQUOR for the general expression involving two files and the universal (or negated existential) quantifier. The logical-AND version of such a general negated existential quantifier expression is

GET WP (P):
> *P-logical-expression* $\wedge \neg$ $\exists C$ TUPLE $(P.p = C.c)$

It reduces to the algebra procedure UQUAND as follows.

```
R1 = SEL (P(P-logical-expression))
R2 = PROJ (C (c))
R3 = R2 * R1 (c,p)
WP = R1 − R3   /*   Set difference operation   */
```

As a final example, we may apply both XQUAND and UQUAND to the reduction of a DSL ALPHA expression in which the hierarchical structure has two branches. Suppose we need the date of planting of cedar trees on which only chemical measurements have been performed (that is, one and all measurements are chemical on a retrieved tree). We have

```
RANGE MEASUREMENT MX
GET W1 (T.PLANTED):
        T.SPECIES = 'CEDAR'
    ∧   ∃M TUPLE (T.TREENUMB = M.TREENUMB) ∧  M.TYPE = 'CHEMICAL')
    ∧¬ ∃MX TUPLE (T.TREENUMB = MX.TREENUMB ∧ MX.TYPE ¬= 'CHEMICAL')
```

Using suffixes L and R to denote left and right, the above expression decomposes into the hierarchy of simpler expressions

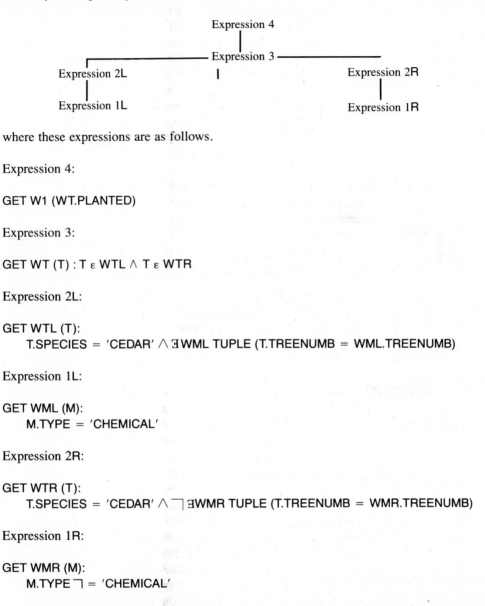

where these expressions are as follows.

Expression 4:

GET W1 (WT.PLANTED)

Expression 3:

GET WT (T) : T ε WTL ∧ T ε WTR

Expression 2L:

GET WTL (T):
    T.SPECIES = 'CEDAR' ∧ ∃WML TUPLE (T.TREENUMB = WML.TREENUMB)

Expression 1L:

GET WML (M):
    M.TYPE = 'CHEMICAL'

Expression 2R:

GET WTR (T):
    T.SPECIES = 'CEDAR' ∧ ¬∃WMR TUPLE (T.TREENUMB = WMR.TREENUMB)

Expression 1R:

GET WMR (M):
    M.TYPE ¬ = 'CHEMICAL'

As in the previous example, execution starts are the bottom of the expression hierarchy and the execution of Expression 3 depends on the results of executing Expressions 2L and 2R. The reader is urged to check through these expressions in execution order.

It should be clear that the algebra procedures XQUAND and UQUAND may be used to reduce Expressions 2L and 2R, respectively. The branching of the hierarchy is managed by Expression 3, which reduces simply to

$$WT = WTL \cap WTR$$

The reader should complete the reduction as an exercise.

16.3 STORAGE AND UPDATING OPERATIONS

There are distinct storage and updating sublanguages for the three relational-retrieval languages presented in this book. However, there is no difference in principle between them, and we shall thus look at such sublanguages only from the point of view of the principles involved. (For SQL under System R, see Appendix 3.)

In contrast to the retrieval sublanguages, the updating and storage sublanguages are extraordinarily simple. In fact, they are all much simpler than their CODASYL counterparts. This simplicity arises not because of the fundamental nature of relations, but rather because tuples (representing real-world entities) are grouped only into relations. Other groupings, such as owner-coupled sets, are not explicitly allowed. Thus when a new tuple has to be stored, it is merely inserted into a relation. In the CODASYL approach, when a new record is to be stored, it is placed in a file and often in many different sets.

Similarly, when a tuple is to be updated, changing an attribute value will not affect the status of a tuple in a relation. Contrast this with CODASYL, where updating of a connection field will require a record to be connected to a different set occurrence. Furthermore, when a tuple is to be deleted, there are no side effects. In CODASYL, as we have seen, deletion of a single record can trigger an avalanche of secondary deletions.

16.3.1 Storage Operation

We have already made use of the STORE command in the loading program in Chapter 14. We repeat it here for the sake of completeness. The syntax is

STORE RELATION (*relation-1*) FROM WORKSPACE (*workspace-relation*);

The tuples to be stored in *relation-1* are in the workspace relation and will be stored in accordance with their primary key values in most implementations. There is no reason to restrict the STORE command to only one tuple.

16.3.2 Update Operation

The essential point about updating is that only the tuples of nonderived relations can be updated without risk of ambiguity. Derived tuples may be updated in System R (see Appendix 3), but only if the underlying storage tuples can be identified.

Tuples to be updated could be placed in a workspace by a special version of a retrieval command which warns the system of intention to update the tuples of the retrieved relation.

HOLD W1 (FORFILE) : COMPANY = 'TREECO'

The predicate is a DSL ALPHA predicate, but we might equally well have a SELECT expression (Date, 1977).

Let us suppose that W1 is a PL/1 structure array and that the company 'TREECO' has changed its name to 'ROOTCO'. We then update the tuples of the structure.

```
BEOR = '1'B; N = 1;
DO WHILE (BEOR);  /*   BEOR: Before End of Relation   */
    IF W1(N).COMPANY = ' ' THEN BEOR = '0'B;
        ELSE DO;
            W1(N).COMPANY = 'ROOTCO';
            N = N + 1;
            END;
END;
```

We now issue an update command.

UPDATE RELATION (FORFILE) FROM WORKSPACE (W1)

We do not intend to discuss the problems of concurrency control in relational systems. However, the special retrieval command HOLD can be interpreted as locking the tuples in W1 against retrieval from FORFILE by competing run-units. The completion of the UP-DATE command execution could then cause these tuples to be unlocked. Another alternative is to have a RELEASE command to unlock them [Reis, 1977]. (In System R, selection and updating are combined in a single command.)

16.3.3 Delete Operation

As with an update operation, only uniquely identified tuples may be deleted. The tuples to be deleted could first be retrieved and placed in a workspace by means of a HOLD command. From this point, they are thus locked against further retrieval. A DELETE command would then remove the tuples in the workspace from the data base. (In System R, selection and deletion are also combined in a single command.)

As an example, we wish to delete all FORFILE tuples for which the COMPANY value is 'ROOTCO'.

HOLD W1 (FORFILE) : COMPANY = 'ROOTCO'
DELETE RELATION (FORFILE) FROM WORKSPACE (W1)

If we have made a mistake, the situation may be saved by

STORE RELATION (FORFILE) FROM WORKSPACE (W1)

since the deleted tuples are still available in the workspace relation W1.

16.4 ADDITIONAL RELATIONAL FACILITIES

Before leaving the subject of relational data bases, there are some important additional facilities that we shall discuss briefly. We shall look at the *computational retrieval power* of relational sublanguages, *integrity constraints,* and *derived subschemas.*

16.4.1 Computational Retrieval Power

We saw that both SQL and relational algebra were relationally complete; that is, the sublanguages could be used to express any retrieval that the fundamental relational calculus (on which DSL ALPHA is based) could express.

However, relational completeness is only one measure of the retrieval power of a sublanguage, and there is a large class of retrievals that cannot be expressed by the relational sublanguages described so far. These retrievals require that computations be carried out on the data in the data base. (Nevertheless, it should be noted that the use of natural quantifiers in the EOS predicate calculus does give this sublanguage some limited computational retrieval power.) In general, we can distinguish two main types of computational retrieval, depending on the use to which the computation is put. These two types are *target computational retrievals* and *predicate computational retrievals.*

1. *Target computational retrievals:* With these retrievals, one or more of the data items retrieved is computed from data in the data base. For example, we might require the maximum and average sizes of forests in each location. Both of these would have to be computed from the values of SIZE and LOC in the relation FORFILE.

2. *Predicate computational retrievals:* Here the set of tuples retrieved depends on the result of computations on data in the data base, but the results of the computations are not themselves retrieved. For example, we might want to retrieve the name and size of forests containing more than 4000 cedar trees. Thus for each FORFILE tuple, we would have to count the number of child TREE tuples with a SPECIES value equal to 'CEDAR'; while the result of such a count is not itself retrieved, it will determine which FORFILE tuples are retrieved.

It is easy to have retrievals that are really combined target and predicate computational retrievals; for example, we might want to retrieve, for forests containing more than 4000 cedar trees, the names and sizes of such forests together with the number of cedar trees.

There appear to be three main strategies for dealing with computational retrievals. The simplest strategy involves using the retrieval sublanguage to retrieve all the data necessary for completion of the request by means of further computational processing. Thus to retrieve the maximum and average sizes of forests in each location, the relation with attributes SIZE and LOC would be first retrieved from FORFILE using SQL or DSL ALPHA. Then a special statistical routine (or a statistical package such as SPSS [Nie, 1975]) would be applied to this relation to produce the final result.[1] This may not appear

---

[1]*SPSS is an acronym for Statistical Package for the Social Sciences.*

to be a very attractive strategy, but if the retrieval involves very complex statistical parameters, it will probably be necessary, at least for the foreseeable future.

The second strategy involves the incorporation of special computational or statistical functions in the retrieval sublanguage. This has been done with SQL and DSL ALPHA [Astrahan, 1976; Date, 1977]. However, only very simple functions have been incorporated, but they allow many computational retrievals to be written in a single expression. The last strategy is to allow for the use of both computational functions and special statistical routines and packages. This last strategy will probably be the most common with complex retrievals.

Before concluding this section, we shall give some examples of both target and predicate computational retrievals using statistical functions with SQL and occasionally with DSL ALPHA and the EOS predicate calculus. The most important functions are COUNT, which counts the number of data elements in a list, SUM, which sums the values of the data items in a list, AVG, which takes the average of the values in a list, and MAX/MIN, which computes the maximum or minimum value in a list. Since in practice we can be certain that computational retrievals will commonly involve cost analysis, let us assume for the purpose of the following retrievals that we have an additional attribute TREECOST in TREE and MEASCOST in MEASUREMENT. TREECOST gives the initial cost of a tree, while MEASCOST gives the cost of carrying out a measurement.

Target Computational Retrievals   We can distinguish two basic types of target computational retrieval, which we shall refer to as *simple* and *partitioned target retrievals*. Simple target retrievals involve one or more complete attributes in any relation. Partitioned target retrievals involve computations on partitions of an attribute. The following examples illustrate these points.

Retrieval 1: COUNT *function, simple target*   **Find the number of electrical measurements carried out on trees in the** FORESTRY **data base.**

```
SELECT      COUNT(MEASNUMB)
FROM        MEASUREMENT
WHERE       TYPE = 'ELECTRICAL'
```

The retrieval is imagined to be carried out in two stages. In the first stage, a list of (necessarily unique) MEASNUMB values is retrieved. Then the function COUNT counts the number of elements in this target set of retrieved values.

Retrieval 2: COUNT *function, simple target*   **Find the total number of species in forests in Oregon.**

```
SELECT      COUNT(UNIQUE SPECIES)
FROM        TREE
WHERE       FOREST IS IN
                (SELECT      FOREST
                 FROM        FORFILE
                 WHERE       LOC = 'OREGON')
```

In the first stage of the retrieval, we retrieve a set of (unique) SPECIES values for forests in Oregon, the number of which is then counted by COUNT. Note that UNIQUE must be specified here.

Retrieval 3: SUM *function, simple target*   **Find the total cost of spruce trees in 1970.**

```
SELECT      SUM(TREECOST)
FROM        TREE
WHERE       SPECIES = 'SPRUCE'
            AND PLANTED < 19710101 AND PLANTED > = 19700101
```

This retrieval differs significantly from the first two. Here, in the first stage of the retrieval, a list of not necessarily unique TREECOST values is retrieved. In the second stage, the values of all the data items in the list, whether duplicates or not, are summed by SUM.

If the retrieval had involved the average, maximum, or minimum cost of spruce trees, the function SUM would be replaced by AVG, MAX, or MIN as required.

Retrieval 4: SUM *function, partitioned target*   **For each tree, find the tree number and the total cost of measurements on that tree.**

```
SELECT      TREENUMB, SUM(MEASCOST)
FROM        MEASUREMENT
GROUP BY    TREENUMB
```

Here it is understood that the SUM function operates on the partition of the relation MEASUREMENT induced by the use of GROUP BY. Had we needed the average, maximum, or minimum cost of measurements, we would have replaced the function SUM by AVG, MAX, or MIN, as required. We now expand the above retrieval to rule out the use of GROUP BY.

Retrieval 5: SUM *function, partitioned target*   **For each cedar tree, find the date of planting and the total cost of electrical measurements.**

To express this retrieval in a straightforward manner, we introduce an auxiliary attribute X, which might be regarded as a (virtual) attribute of the relation TREE. Here X contains summary information about measurements on a given tree.

```
SELECT      PLANTED, X
FROM        TREE
WHERE       SPECIES = 'CEDAR'
AND         X =    (SELECT    SUM(MEASCOST)
                    FROM      MEASUREMENT
                    WHERE     TYPE = 'ELECTRICAL'
                    AND       TREE.TREENUMB = MEASUREMENT.TREENUMB)
```

In this retrieval, for a given TREE tuple, in the inner SELECT block the MEASCOST values for electrical measurements on that given tree are retrieved, summed, and placed in X. For that given tree, the PLANTED and X values are then retrieved. Had we needed average, maximum, or minimum costs, we would have used AVG, MAX, or MIN, respectively, instead of SUM.

This retrieval raises a number of interesting considerations for data-base design. For example, in accounting systems, summary information of the type specified in the above retrieval is very commonly required. Thus it would be convenient to place certain summary attributes in parent relations; these attributes contain summary information about child tuples. In each TREE tuple in the FORESTRY data base, we might have the total number of measurements performed, the total cost of measurements, or the number of the most/least expensive measurement. The advantage would be the saving in computation if this type of information were frequently required. It is also clear that such summary attributes could be included without affecting a relation's 4NF status. However, the disadvantage is that we have introduced a new statistical dependency. Updating the MEASUREMENT relation would require updating of the TREE relation, and if this is either not done or is done incorrectly, then the data base becomes inconsistent. However, a way around this difficulty might be to permit such summary attributes in the external data base only, by means of the derived user views described in Section 16.4.3. In that way, any inconsistency would be short-lived, but the summary attributes would have to be computed each time an external data base was invoked.

Before we turn to predicate computational retrievals, you might be interested in seeing how retrieval 5 would be managed in DSL ALPHA and the EOS predicate calculus. In DSL ALPHA we would write

RANGE MEASUREMENT MX
GET (PLANTED, PSUM (MEASCOST,TREENUMB)) :
    T.SPECIES = 'CEDAR' ∧ T.TREENUMB = M.TREENUMB ∧
    ∃MX TUPLE (MX.TREENUMB = T.TREENUMB ∧ MX.TYPE = 'ELECTRICAL')

Here we simply retrieve the cost of each electrical measurement, together with tree number and date of planting for the tree on which the measurement was carried out. A special version of SUM, the partitioned sum function PSUM, is then applied. It produces a sum of the data items in MEASCOST for each value of TREENUMB. Similarly, we would use PCOUNT, PAVG, PMAX, and PMIN. Such partitioned functions could also be applied in SQL, at least in theory.

With the EOS predicate calculus, as with DSL ALPHA, we could apply the partitioned versions of the computational functions. However, there is a more natural method available here, which stems from the fact that partitions are quite natural in the EOS sublanguage because of the use of owner-coupled sets. With many computational retrievals, we can use the natural quantifier

FOR [COLLECTION OF]

When such a quantifier is applied to the member records of an owner-coupled set, *logical-expression-2* (see Figure 11.1) will describe properties of a collection of member records—

that is, statistical properties—and it is precisely this that we have need for. Retrieval 5 can be expressed as

```
GET (PLANTED, X) : TREE TARGET TUPLE ((SPECIES = 'CEDAR') &
                        OWNER SET (TM) OCCURRENCE
(FOR (TYPE = 'ELECTRICAL') MEASUREMENT MEMBER TUPLES
                                        (X = SUM(MEASCOST) ))
```

Here the function SUM applies only to the quantified MEASUREMENT member tuples; that is, to those MEASUREMENT members which have TYPE value 'ELECTRICAL' and are members of a given owner-coupled set occurrence. As with SQL, we use an auxiliary summary variable X in an obvious manner.

Predicate Computation Retrievals

Retrieval 6: COUNT *function* **Find the sizes of California forests in which the number** *of cedar trees exceeds 4000.*

```
SELECT    SIZE
FROM      FORFILE
WHERE     LOC = 'CALIFORNIA'
AND       4000 <    (SELECT    COUNT(TREENUMB)
                    FROM      TREE
                    WHERE     SPECIES = 'CEDAR'
                    AND       FORFILE.FOREST = TREE.FOREST)
```

Here we take a given FORFILE tuple. In the inner SELECT block, we retrieve the child cedar-tree numbers and count them using the COUNT function. If 4000 is less than the result, then the FORFILE tuple is retrieved provided the LOC value is 'CALIFORNIA'. The retrieval is a predicate retrieval because the retrieved tuples depend on the result of a computation which is not itself retrieved.

It is interesting to note that the EOS version of this retrieval requires no computational functions; the use of a natural quantifier is sufficient.

```
GET (SIZE): FORFILE TARGET TUPLE ((LOC = 'CALIFORNIA') &
                        OWNER SET (FT) OCCURRENCE
EXISTS AT LEAST 4001 TREE MEMBER TUPLES (SPECIES = 'CEDAR'))
```

Alternatively, using the COUNT function and the natural quantifier FOR COLLECTION OF, we could have specified

```
GET (SIZE): FORFILE TARGET TUPLE ((LOC = 'CALIFORNIA') &
                        OWNER SET (FT) OCCURRENCE
FOR (SPECIES = 'CEDAR') TREE MEMBER TUPLES
                            (4000 < COUNT(TREENUMB) ))
```

Retrieval 7: MAX *function*   **Find the most expensive trees.**

```
SELECT     TREENUMB
FROM       TREE
WHERE      TREECOST =    (SELECT    MAX(TREECOST)
                          FROM       TREE)
```

In the inner block, the value of TREECOST which is highest for the whole TREE relation is determined. In the outer block, TREENUMB values from those tuples with this maximum value of TREECOST are selected. The retrieval is clearly a predicate retrieval, because we do not retrieve the maximum value of TREECOST but merely make use of it to select TREE tuples. The next retrieval is similar but involves additional retrieval conditions.

Retrieval 8: MIN *function*   **Find the least expensive cedar trees planted before 1970.**

```
SELECT     TREENUMB
FROM       TREE
WHERE      SPECIES = 'CEDAR' AND PLANTED < 19700101
AND        TREECOST =    (SELECT    MIN(TREECOST)
                          FROM       TREE
                          WHERE      SPECIES = 'CEDAR'
                          AND        PLANTED < 19700101)
```

In the inner block, the minimum value of TREECOST for cedar trees planted before 1970 is determined. Then in the outer block, we select TREE tuples with a TREECOST value equal to this minimum, but since there could exist TREE tuples with this minimum TREE-COST value that are not cedars and were planted before 1970, we are forced to repeat the SPECIES and PLANTED conditions in the outer block. This is not entirely satisfactory, but we have not been able to find a more concise expression. Perhaps the reader can. We end the section with a retrieval that is both a predicate and a target retrieval.

Combined Predicate and Target Computational Retrieval

Retrieval 9: MIN *and* AVG *functions*   What was the cost of the least expensive tree on which the average cost of chemical measurements is less than $500?

```
SELECT     MIN(TREECOST)
FROM       TREE
WHERE      TREENUMB IS IN
               (SELECT    TREENUMB
                FROM       MEASUREMENT, MREF   /*   MREF is a label   */
                WHERE      TYPE = 'CHEMICAL'
                AND        500 >    (SELECT    AVG(MEASCOST)
                                     FROM       MEASUREMENT
```

```
WHERE     TYPE = 'CHEMICAL'
AND
MEASUREMENT.TREENUMB =
MREF.TREENUMB))
```

To understand this expression, the retrieval can be reduced to simple steps. First of all, we should retrieve the tree numbers for trees on which the average cost of chemical measurements is less than $500. This is done in the two inner SELECT blocks by selecting TREENUMB values from MEASUREMENT tuples, where the average cost of chemical measurements for MEASUREMENT tuples with the same TREENUMB value is less than $500. Then, in the outer block, we retrieve all the TREECOST values for TREE tuples with the TREENUMB values selected earlier. Finally, the MIN function takes the minimum value of TREECOST. It is possible to omit TYPE = 'CHEMICAL' on line 6 of the expression without the logic being impaired. Readers can use this fact to test their understanding of the underlying logic.

For comparison purposes, we give the EOS predicate calculus version as well.

```
GET (MIN(TREECOST)):  TREE TARGET TUPLE
                      OWNER SET(TM) OCCURRENCE
(FOR (TYPE = 'CHEMICAL') MEASUREMENT MEMBER TUPLES
                                      (AVG(MEASCOST) < 500))
```

Here again we make use of the natural quantifier FOR COLLECTION OF. We first retrieve the costs of trees where, for the chemical member tuples in the set TM, the average cost of a measurement is less than $500. The function MIN then produces the minimum value of the retrieved TREECOST values.

16.4.2 Integrity Constraints

Integrity constraints will normally be specified in the schema and place a constraint on properties of data in the data base for purposes of ensuring the integrity of the data. We may have *implicit* and *explicit* constraints.

For example, the facts that the TREE relation has tuples, each of which describes a tree, and that the candidate key is TREENUMB require that there not be two trees with the same TREENUMB value. This is an implicit constraint.

An explicit constraint is simply a predicate that must always have the value *true*. For example, suppose that no chemical measurements will be carried out on spruce trees in the forest 'XFOR' in 1980. We could thus place the following in the schema.

```
¬ ∃ T TUPLE ((SPECIES = 'SPRUCE') ∧ (FOREST = 'XFOR')
∧ ∃ M TUPLE (T.TREENUMB = M.MEASNUMB
       ∧ DATE < 19810101 ∧ DATE > 19791231
       ∧ TYPE = 'CHEMICAL' ) )
```

Each time a MEASUREMENT record is either stored or updated, the DBCS will check that this predicate remains true. A storage or update operation that would render the predicate *false* is rejected.

It is clear that integrity constraints employing EOS or equivalent predicates could be usefully employed in the CODASYL approach as well. System R permits explicit integrity constraints [Astrahan, 1976].

16.4.3 Derived Subschemas or User Views

In Chapter 9, we introduced two external schemas, or subschemas, for the FORESTRY data base, namely, the TOP_FORESTRY and BOT_FORESTRY subschemas. The fields of the external records were the same as those of the underlying FORESTRY conceptual records, but we could, if we wished, have had fewer fields.

Such an external schema is thus more or less a subset of the conceptual schema. Similar external schemas are possible in the relational approach, and an example is shown in Figure 16.5. The specification language for such an external schema would be very similar to that used with the conceptual schema in Chapter 13. However, the existence of a high-level, nonprocedural relational-retrieval language permits additional refinements in the specification of external schemas. As we saw, DSL ALPHA or SQL can be used to retrieve a relation derivable from the relations in the data base. Thus these sublanguages could also be used to define derived external relations or "user views" of the data base [Kim, 1979].

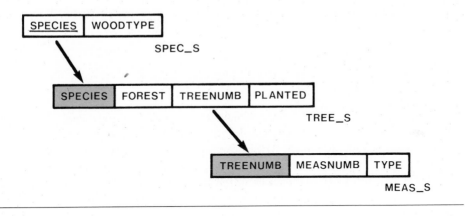

FIGURE 16.5. *Simple external schema.*

A user might, therefore, define an external schema (with the permission of the DBA) of the type shown in Figure 16.6, which is derived from the conceptual schema. Thus the user would have to use a version of a relational-retrieval language in the definition of the external schema. The external data base in Figure 16.6 might be defined by

```
RELATION TREE_TYPE (SPECFILE.SPECIES,
                    SPECFILE.WOODTYPE)
```

```
RANGE FORFILE F, TREE T
RELATION TREEFOR (T.SPECIES,
                  T.TREENUMB,
                  T.PLANTED,
                  T.FOREST,
                  F.SIZE
                  F.COMPANY.) : T.FOREST = F.FOREST
```

The relation TREE_TYPE is a simple "subset" or, more accurately, projection of the conceptual relation SPECFILE. The relation TREEFOR is specified by means of a DSL ALPHA expression and is thus derived from the two relations TREE and FORFILE.

This derived external schema could then be subjected to retrievals by the user in the usual manner, and if the underlying conceptual relation were updated by another user, the system would see to it that this derived external schema were modified to reflect the new underlying conceptual relations. Similarly, should it ever be necessary to change the schema or *base* relations from which the external schema is derived, a new external schema definition would be all that was necessary to provide the user view in Figure 16.6.

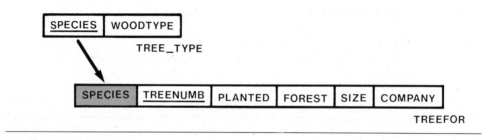

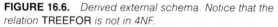

FIGURE 16.6. *Derived external schema. Notice that the relation* TREEFOR *is not in 4NF.*

However, the user of the derived external schema would be limited in his or her ability to update derived relations, although with the TREEFOR relation, theoretically the user could be permitted to store a new TREEFOR tuple and have this storage reflected in the underlying TREE and FORFILE relations. Alternatively, the inserted TREEFOR tuple might be stored in the external data base, but this storage would not be reflected in the underlying conceptual files. System R permits derived external schemas [Astrahan, 1976; Ries, 1977].

It may be noted again that the idea of a derived external schema could be incorporated into the CODASYL approach by making use of retrieval expressions such as those of the EOS predicate calculus. Furthermore, both the primary and secondary hierarchies of the hierarchical approach (see Chapter 17) are user views derived from a fundamental conceptual data base. This fact could facilitate the manipulation of a hierarchical data base, such as an IMS data base (Chapter 17), by means of a relational DBCS.[1]

---

[1]*In 1981, while this book was in press, IBM announced a relational package based on SQL, namely, SQL/DS, to do just that. The package interfaces with DOS/VSE and DL/1.*

EXERCISES

1. Use relational algebra to express the retrievals listed in the exercises for Chapter 11.

2. Use the reduction process outlined in Section 16.2 to generate relational algebra expressions for the DSL ALPHA expressions in Chapter 14 (with the exception of retrieval 9, which requires more advanced techniques).

3. In the following computational retrievals, assume that TREECOST and MEASCOST have been added to TREE and MEASUREMENT, respectively, as described in Section 16.4.1. The retrievals should be expressed in SQL and also, if desired, in the EOS predicate calculus.

   a. Retrieve the cost of the least expensive tree in the forest 'XFOR'.

   b. Retrieve the number of cedar trees listed in the data base.

   c. Retrieve the average cost of electrical measurements on spruce trees.

   d. Retrieve the trees on which the average cost of chemical measurements is less than $100.

   e. What was the total cost of trees in the forest 'XFOR' that were planted before 1970?

   f. Find the names of the companies owning spruce trees on which the maximum cost of an electrical measurement was twice the minimum cost.

   g. Find the names of companies with average forest size exceeding 10,000 acres.

   h. Find the names of companies which own forests with trees costing more than $10,000,000 in all.

REFERENCES

Astrahan, M. M., and others, 1976, "System R: Relational Approach to Data Base Management," *ACM Trans. on Data Base Systems*, **1**(2):97–137.

Banerjee, J., and R. I. Baum, 1978*a*, "Concepts and Capabilities of a Data Base Computer," *ACM Trans. on Data Base Systems*, **3**(4):348–84.

Banerjee, J., and D. K. Hsiao, 1978*b*, "Performance Study of a Data Base Machine in Supporting Relational Data Bases," *Proc. of ACM Conference on Very Large Data Bases*, Berlin, pp. 319–31.

Codd, E. F., 1972, "Relational Completeness of Data Base Sublanguages," in *Data Base Systems, Courant Computer Science Symposia*, vol. 6, Prentice-Hall, Englewood Cliffs, N.J., pp. 65–98.

Date, C. J., 1977, *Introduction to Data Base Systems*, Addison-Wesley, Reading, Mass.

Delobel, C., 1978, "Normalization and Hierarchical Dependencies in the Relational Data Model," *ACM Trans. on Data Base Systems*, **3**(3):201–202.

Fagin, R., 1977, "A New Normal Form for Relational Data Bases," *ACM Trans. on Data Base Systems*, **2**(3):262–79.

Kim, W., 1979, "Relational Data Base Systems," *ACM Comput. Surv.,* **11**(3): 185–211.

Nie, H. N., and others, 1975, *Statistical Package for the Social Sciences,* McGraw-Hill, New York.

Palermo, F. P., 1974, "A Data Base Search Problem," *Information Sys.: COINS IV,* J. T. Tou, (ed.), Plenum Press, New York.

Ries, D. R., and M. Stonebraker, 1977, "Effects of Locking Granularity in a Data Base Management System," *ACM Trans. on Database Systems,* **2**(3):233–46.

Smith, J. M., and P. Y. T. Chang, 1975, "Optimizing the Performance of a Relational Algebra Data Base Interface," *Comm. ACM.,* **18**(10):568–88.

Ullman, J. D., 1980, *Principles of Data Base Systems,* Computer Science Press, Potomac, Maryland.

Wong, E., and K. Youssefi, 1976, "Decomposition: A Strategy for Query Processing," *ACM Trans. on Data Base Systems,* **1**(3):233–41.

Yao, S. B., 1979, "Optimization of Query Evaluation Algorithms," *ACM Trans. on Data Base Systems,* **4**(2):133–55.

The Hierarchical Approach

17

We now turn to the hierarchical approach to data-base management. This approach is fairly widely used, mainly because it is the approach inherent in IMS (Information Management System), a commercial system made available from IBM in the late 1960s [Date, 1977; IBM, 1974, 1977a, 1977b, 1978a, 1978b, 1978c; Kapp, 1978; Walsh, 1980].

Because of the fairly wide use of IMS, some authors have contented themselves with a description of IMS instead of describing the hierarchical approach in general [Date, 1977]. We believe this to be an undesirable strategy from an educational point of view, for two reasons. First, IMS has a special structure of its own and adheres only in broad outline to the ANSI/SPARC three-level structure described in Chapter 6. Secondly, it contains a great deal of implementation detail. The result is that it is difficult for the newcomer to perceive the basic principles of the hierarchical approach, most of which are nevertheless present in IMS.

We shall, therefore, take a compromise approach. We shall study the basic principles of the hierarchical approach in the light of the ANSI/SPARC recommendations and using the extended Bachman diagrams employed throughout this book. Where appropriate, we shall illustrate with a minimum of detail the deployment of these principles in IMS. In this chapter, we concentrate on the hierarchical schemas.

17.1 THE CONCEPTUAL DATA BASE

Contrary to widespread belief, the hierarchical approach is not limited to conceptual data bases that have a hierarchical structure. In theory it may be applied to data bases with network structure, although in practice economics will probably always dictate that implementations be capable of handling limited networks only.

For purposes of comparison, we shall use much the same conceptual data base as we used with the CODASYL and relational approaches, namely the FORESTRY data bases. However, to better illustrate the hierarchical approach, we add an additional file FORESTER to the FORESTRY data base, as shown in the extended Bachman diagram in Figure 17.1.

The conceptual file FORESTER describes the foresters who look after forests. We suppose that a given forest is looked after by one or more foresters and that a given forester looks after only one forest. Thus there is a $1:n$ relationship between FORFILE and FORESTER. The prime key for the FORESTER file is SOCNUMB, the forester's social security number. The FOREST field in FORESTER is the connection field, an occurrence of which contains the name of the forest in which the forester works. This new version of FORESTRY is also in 4NF (Chapter 7).

We recall that in a hierarchy a child record (that is, corresponding to a CODASYL member record) can have at most one parent record (that is, corresponding to a CODASYL owner record). The conceptual FORESTRY data base is therefore not a hierarchy, but a network. For example, a TREE record has three parents in general, a SPECFILE parent, a FORFILE parent, and—most likely—a TREE parent.

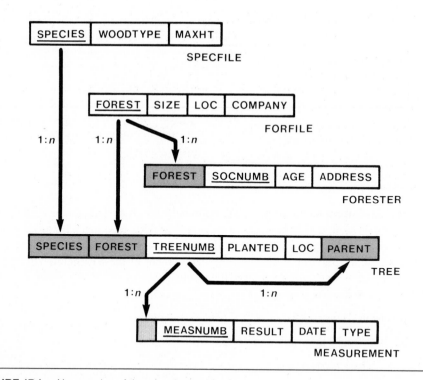

FIGURE 17.1. *New version of the experimental forestry data base* FORESTRY. *An additional conceptual file* FORESTER *has been added and describes foresters. For a given forest, there will be many foresters.*

We shall now examine the principles behind the construction of hierarchical schemas for this conceptual network data base.

17.2 THE HIERARCHICAL SCHEMAS

Strictly speaking, the ANSI/SPARC approach is not quite sufficient with hierarchical data bases. The problem is that we frequently have to deal with what are really two conceptual data bases.

In the general case, we shall have to deal with what is fundamentally a *network conceptual data base,* such as that shown in Figure 17.1.[1] However, in the hierarchical approach, the conceptual data structures must consist of hierarchies, so that we need another conceptual data base, the *hierarchical conceptual data base* which is *derived* from the fundamental network conceptual data base. (Of course, the problem does not arise if the fundamental network data base also happens to be a hierarchy or collection of hierarchies.)

The *hierarchical conceptual schema* reflects this derived hierarchical conceptual data base, and a hierarchical *external schema* is a subset of the hierarchical conceptual schema. The hierarchical *internal schema* specifies an implementation of some (but not all) of the *hierarchies* of the hierarchical conceptual data base.

In a hierarchical conceptual schema, the conceptual records are collected into two basic groupings: *conventional conceptual files* and *hierarchies.* It is important to realize that there can be two classes of hierarchies, which in this chapter we shall call *primary* and *secondary* hierarchies. Primary and secondary hierarchies are fundamental to the hierarchical approach. For the moment, we can say that a primary hierarchy is taken directly from the fundamental network conceptual data base, while a secondary hierarchy is a derived hierarchy that enables the hierarchical conceptual data base to be logically equivalent to the fundamental network conceptual data base.

These concepts may be more clearly illustrated if we refer to the set of diagrams in Figure 17.2. We have the following elements.

1. Fundamental network conceptual data base (Figure 17.2*a*).

    a. Conceptual files A, B, C, D, E, corresponding to the files SPECFILE, FORFILE, TREE, FORESTER, and MEASUREMENT from the FORESTRY data base (Figure 17.1).

    b. A network structure with no individual hierarchies.

2. Hierarchical conceptual data base (Figure 17.2*b*).

    a. Conceptual files A, B, C, D, E.

    b. *Primary hierarchy types* P1 and P2, where each of the conceptual files A, B, C, D,

---

[1]*We use the term* network *in its dictionary sense, not as a name for an approach to data-base management.*

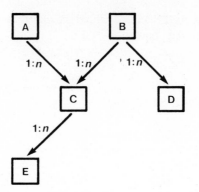

(a) Fundamental network conceptual data base (**FORESTRY**). Files **A, B, C, D,** and **E** correspond to the files in Figure 17.1.

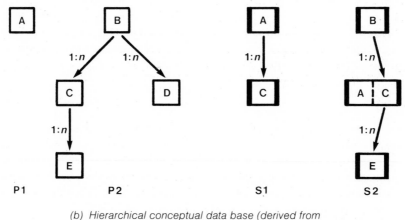

P1   P2   S1   S2

(b) Hierarchical conceptual data base (derived from **FORESTRY**). Main structures are the conceptual primary hierarchies P1 and P2 and the conceptual secondary hierarchies S1 and S2.

FIGURE 17.2. *Overall structure of the schemas in the hierarchical approach.*

and **E** is part of one or more of these hierarchies. Thus all the conceptual files are used at least once in constructing P1 and P2.

c. *Secondary hierarchy types* S1 and S2. The structure of any one of these secondary hierarchies is based on one or more of the primary hierarchies in such a way that the constituent files of a secondary hierarchy are either taken from **A, B, C, D,** or **E** or are composites such as **AB, ABC,** or **AC,** formed by concatenating records from one or more files. We consider the file **AB** here to be the file formed by concatenating (equivalent to a relational natural join on the connection fields) **A** and **B** records.

3. External hierarchical data bases (Figure 17.2*c*).

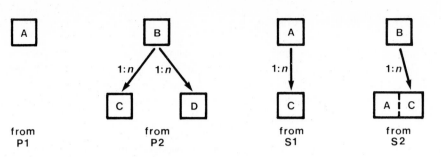

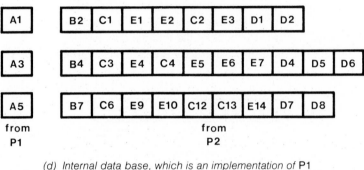

(c) External hierarchical data bases that are subsets or subhierarchies of the primary and secondary hierarchies from (b).

(d) Internal data base, which is an implementation of P1 and P2, containing a pointer system to simulate S1 and S2.

FIGURE 17.2 *(cont'd)*

    a. *External hierarchies,* which are subhierarchies taken from *both* primary and secondary hierarchies in the conceptual schema.

    b. *External files,* which are the files making up the subhierarchies. The records of an external file may have fewer field types than those of the corresponding files in the conceptual hierarchies.

  4. Internal or storage hierarchical data base (Figure 17.2*d*).

    a. *Storage hierarchies,* which are the storage versions of the primary conceptual hierarchies P1 and P2. A storage hierarchy is a *storage* or *physical file,* in which each physical record has an internal hierarchical structure composed of *physical record segments.* Such a physical file may be organized as a sequential, hash, or index-sequential file.

    b. There are no storage versions of the secondary conceptual hierarchies.

    c. Physical record segments, as mentioned in (a), which are storage versions of the conceptual records from the conceptual files A, B, C, D, and E. These physical record segments contain the pointers necessary for the processing of the secondary conceptual hierarchies S1 and S2.

17.2.1 The Conceptual Schema

As we have already seen, in the hierarchical conceptual schema the conceptual records are grouped into conceptual files in much the same way as in the CODASYL approach and also into conceptual hierarchy types (with distinct names). These hierarchy types are classified into primary and secondary hierarchy types. (But note that, as used in this book, *primary* and *secondary* are not IMS terms.)

Primary Hierarchy Types　As an example of primary hierarchy types with the conceptual FORESTRY data base, we could group the conceptual records into the two primary hierarchy types SPEC_HIER and FOR_HIER, as shown using extended Bachman diagrams in Figure 17.3. All of the files in the FORESTRY data base are represented in these two primary hierarchies. If possible, each file is structured into one of the hierarchies, but there is no reason why a file may not be structured into more than one hierarchy. (However, if a file is structured into more than one hierarchy, the file in question may be duplicated in the corresponding storage structures of the internal data base.)

It is important to be clear on what exactly is entailed by a grouping such as a primary

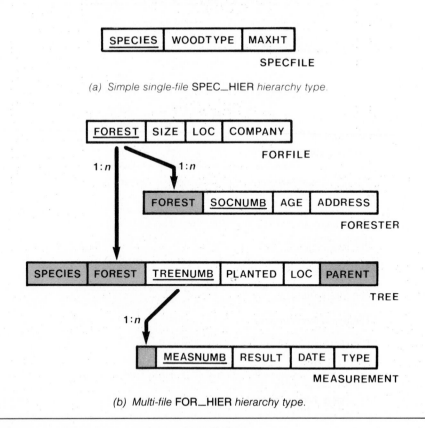

(a) *Simple single-file* SPEC_HIER *hierarchy type.*

(b) *Multi-file* FOR_HIER *hierarchy type.*

FIGURE 17.3.　*Primary hierarchy types in the* FORESTRY *conceptual data base.*

hierarchy type. Let us consider the hierarchy type FOR_HIER more closely. It is made up of hierarchy occurrences or FOR_HIER occurrences. An occurrence will consist of a FORFILE parent record occurrence together with all its child-record occurrences, as well as their child occurrences in the form of a data tree with the FORFILE record as the root record.

A collection of such data trees or hierarchy occurrences forms a hierarchy type, and by way of illustration we have drawn two typical occurrences of FOR_HIER in Figure 17.4. We see that a root FORFILE record is the parent of TREE and FORESTER records, and that each of these TREE child records is the parent of MEASUREMENT child records.

The primary hierarchies are the basic hierarchies of the data base, and it is these hierarchies together with added pointers that are represented in internal storage. In this respect, the primary hierarchies correspond well to the physical hierarchies in internal storage.

We are free to choose the primary hierarchies in any way we please, provided they encompass all the files in the data base. Thus we could have chosen the following instead of the hierarchies in Figure 17.3.

(1) SPECFILE; TREE child of SPECFILE; MEASUREMENT child of TREE.

(2) FORFILE; FORESTER child of FORFILE

However, we usually choose the primary hierarchies in such a way as to facilitate the construction of the secondary hierarchy types which, as already mentioned, are based on the primary types.

Specification of Conceptual Files and Primary Hierarchy Types   The specification of the conceptual files can be considered as quite straightforward. We need to specify the following for a given file.

    a.   File name.

    b.   File fields.

    c.   The primary record key, secondary file keys, and associated record order.

    d.   The connection fields, if any, together with associated restraints.

To specify a (conceptual) primary hierarchy type we need the following.

    a.   The files participating in the hierarchy type.

    b.   The hierarchical order of these files.

    c.   The sequence fields and associated order of the conceptual records within a hierarchical occurrence.

A few words of explanation may be necessary with respect to *hierarchical order* and *sequence fields*. Each file in the hierarchy type may be assigned a hierarchical order number, where the root file has number 1, and the remaining files are assigned 2, 3, 4, ..., as we go down the hierarchy (such as in Figure 17.3) from left to right. This assigns 2 to the TREE file and 3 to the FORESTER. The effect is that when we wish to retrieve

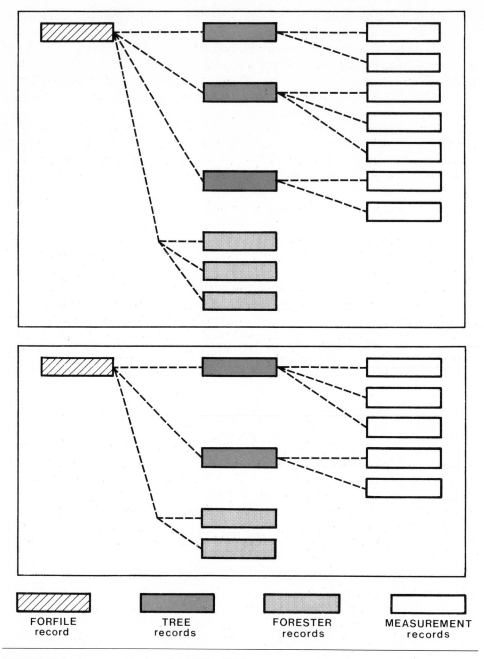

FIGURE 17.4. *Two occurrences of the* FOR_HIER *hierarchy type from Figure 17.3b. A hierarchy occurrence is constructed from conceptual records. Note that the stippled lines are not pointers and are shown to clearly indicate parent and child conceptual records.*

the first child of a given FORFILE record, it will be a TREE record that is retrieved, because TREE has been assigned a lower hierarchical order number than FORESTER.

The sequence field for a file plays a role similar to the set key in CODASYL, in that it determines the order of records for that file within a hierarchical occurrence. Thus if PLANTED (date of planting) is the sequence field for the TREE file, TREE records within a FOR_HIER hierarchy occurrence will be maintained (conceptually) in PLANTED order. They may thus be retrieved from a hierarchy occurrence in PLANTED order.

We shall now give an IMS specification of the FOR_HIER hierarchy type and its constituent files. However, before doing so, we need to say something about the structures and terminology used in IMS.

In IMS there is an entry corresponding to a conceptual schema for each hierarchy, whether primary or secondary. However, there is an entry corresponding to an internal schema for primary hierarchies only. Furthermore, the conceptual schema for a primary hierarchy is integrated with the internal schema for that hierarchy, giving us an *integrated conceptual-internal schema,* which is referred to in IMS as a *Data-Base Description* (DBD). That part of an IMS storage data base specified at the conceptual level by a DBD is referred to in IMS as a *Physical Data Base* (PDB). Thus *for each primary hierarchy,* we must specify a DBD for an underlying PDB.

In the specification of a DBD, we do not specify the files and hierarchy types in distinct entries (as, for example, with files and sets in CODASYL); these specifications are also integrated. We now give just that part of a DBD for the primary hierarchy FOR_HIER that would correspond to the requirements of a conceptual schema. (That is, we are omitting the internal schema part of the DBD.)

01	DBD	NAME = FOR_HIER
02	SEGM	NAME = FORFILE
03	FIELD	NAME = (FOREST, SEQ),
04	FIELD	NAME = SIZE,
05	FIELD	NAME = LOC,
06	FIELD	NAME = COMPANY,
07	SEGM	NAME = TREE, PARENT = FORFILE[1]
08	FIELD	NAME = SPECIES,
09	FIELD	NAME = FOREST,
10	FIELD	NAME = (TREENUMB, SEQ),
11	FIELD	NAME = PLANTED,
12	FIELD	NAME = LOC,
13	FIELD	NAME = PARENT,
14	SEGM	NAME = FORESTER, PARENT = FORFILE[1]
15	FIELD	NAME = FOREST,
16	FIELD	NAME = (SOCNUMB, SEQ),
17	FIELD	NAME = AGE,
18	FIELD	NAME = ADDRESS,

---

[1]PARENT *is an IMS reserve word here, not a field name in the* TREE *file.*

19	SEGM	NAME = MEASUREM, PARENT = TREE[1]
20	FIELD	NAME = (MEASNUMB, SEQ),
21	FIELD	NAME = RESULT,
22	FIELD	NAME = DATE,
23	FIELD	NAME = TYPE

We note the following.

1. The order in which the "segments" appear determines the hierarchical order number assigned. Thus the TREE "segment" is assigned number 2.

2. In IMS it is permitted to distinguish between the order of records from a given file within a hierarchy and the order within the file. In the case of the root records, the order within the file and within the hierarchy will be the same in any case. In the above, we have specified only the hierarchical sequence fields (FOREST, TREENUMB, SOCNUMB, MEASNUMB). Specification of the equivalent of file keys (known in IMS as secondary indexes) has been omitted because it involves a great deal of IMS detail relating to the "internal" part of the internal-conceptual schema.

Finally, we note the need in the hierarchical approach for indicators to serve as position indicators, along the same lines as the currency indicators in CODASYL. We may construct such an indicator using the sequence keys of the constituent records of a hierarchy. For example, let us suppose that we have just retrieved a MEASUREMENT record with MEAS-NUMB value 999, with a parent that has TREENUMB value 666, where the parent of this record has FOREST value XFOR. The position indicator (or *fully concatenated key* in IMS) value would be:

XFOR 666 999

This would be updated as the user program navigates through the FOR_HIER hierarchy.

Secondary Hierarchy Types   *Secondary hierarchy types* are defined in terms of the primary hierarchies and are used to give the user a hierarchical view of the network aspects of the fundamental network conceptual data base such as the FORESTRY data base.

Looking again at the FORESTRY data base in Figure 17.1, it is clear that when we have retrieved a TREE child record for a given FORFILE parent, we shall sometimes need to retrieve the SPECFILE "parent" record for this TREE record. However, we note that SPECFILE is not a parent of TREE in either of the two primary hierarchies FOR_HIER or SPEC_HIER in Figure 17.3.

We therefore refer to SPECFILE as a *secondary parent* of TREE, FORFILE being the *primary parent*. In addition, we may construct a secondary hierarchy based on both FOR HIER and SPEC_HIER and called INTER_ST, as shown in Figure 17.5a. We recall that a secondary hierarchy type is purely conceptual, there being no corresponding internal hierarchy.

We see that INTER_ST has FORFILE records as the roots and is the parent of a file TREESPEC, which has records consisting of TREE records, each concatenated to its

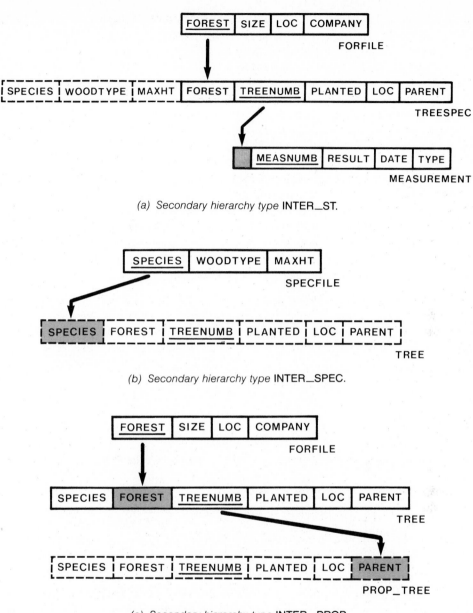

(a) Secondary hierarchy type INTER_ST.

(b) Secondary hierarchy type INTER_SPEC.

(c) Secondary hierarchy type INTER_PROP.

FIGURE 17.5. *Useful secondary or derived hierarchy types based on the primary hierarchy types* SPEC_HIER *and* FOR_HIER *shown in Figure 17.2.*

secondary parent SPECFILE with the ensuing duplicate SPECIES value omitted. Thus INTER_ST enables us to process the child TREE record for a given FORFILE parent record, at the same time being able to obtain the SPECFILE parent records by means of the file TREESPEC. However, if we need to process all the "child" TREE records of a SPECFILE record, we would need to define a new secondary hierarchy such as INTER_ SPEC in Figure 17.5b. In INTER_SPEC, TREE records are secondary children of the SPECFILE records.

On occasion, we need to obtain the records for trees immediately descended from the tree described by a given TREE record. To do this, we can set up a third secondary hierarchy type INTER_PROP. Here we have a new child file PROP_TREE, as shown in Figure 17.5c, which has as secondary parent the TREE file.

Thus if we call nonsecondary parents and children primary parents and children, we may summarize the situation in the three secondary hierarchy types INTER_ST, INTER_ SPEC, and INTER_PROP as follows.

1. INTER_ST.

    a. FORFILE is primary parent of TREESPEC.

    b. SPECFILE is secondary parent of TREESPEC.

    c. TREESPEC is primary child of FORFILE.

    d. TREESPEC is secondary child of SPECFILE.

    e. MEASUREMENT is primary child of TREESPEC.

2. INTER_SPEC.

    a. SPECFILE is secondary parent of TREE.

    b. TREE is secondary child of SPECFILE.

3. INTER_PROP.

    a. TREE is primary child of FORFILE.

    b. TREE is secondary parent of PROP_TREE.

    c. PROP_TREE is secondary child of TREE.

Specification of the Secondary Hierarchy Types   The specification of a secondary hierarchy is a comparatively simple matter; it is necessary only to specify the structure of the hierarchy in terms of its constituent files, together with the source of the records in those files in terms of the primary hierarchies [Date, 1977; IBM, 1978b].

We shall give the IMS specification of the INTER_ST hierarchy for purposes of illustration. IMS uses the terms *physical* and *logical* for *primary* and *secondary;* thus we have IMS physical and logical parents and children. In addition, a secondary hierarchy is regarded as a distinct data base requiring its own conceptual schema and is called a *logical data base* specified in a *logical data-base description*. There is no IMS internal schema corresponding to the conceptual schema (logical data-base description) for a secondary hierarchy. The pointer system necessary to support a secondary hierarchy is specified in the internal part of the internal-conceptual schema for a primary hierarchy (that is, part of a DBD). The reader who is somewhat confused by this might usefully refer to the overview shown in Figure 17.2.

We now give an IMS logical data base description for the INTER_ST secondary hierarchy. (IMS names have at most 8 characters, which we sometimes ignore.)

```
1    DBD        NAME = INTER_ST, ACCESS = LOGICAL
2    DATASET    LOGICAL
3    SEGM       NAME = FORFILE, SOURCE = ((FORFILE,,FOR_HIER))
4    SEGM       NAME = TREESPEC, PARENT = FORFILE,
5               SOURCE = ((SPECFILE,,SPEC_HIER), (TREE, FOR_HIER))
6    SEGM       NAME = MEASUREM, PARENT = TREESPEC,
                SOURCE = ((MEASUREM,,FOR_HIER))
```

This specification is almost self-explanatory. We see that the TREESPEC "segment" is a composite made up of SPECFILE records as described in the SPEC_HIER data-base description, and TREE records as described in the FOR_HIER DBD (lines 7–13).

It would thus appear that by means of secondary hierarchies (or IMS logical data bases) it would be possible to specify a conceptual schema for any network. However, in practice most implementations would place a limit on the kinds of secondary hierarchies allowed. In this respect, IMS has the following important limiting rule.

> A record of a file in a primary hierarchy cannot be both a secondary parent and a secondary child.

Thus we could not specify the secondary hierarchies INTER_SPEC and INTER_PROP in the current version of IMS, since TREE is a secondary child in INTER_SPEC and a secondary parent in INTER_PROP. We could get around this difficulty in IMS simply by eliminating INTER_SPEC and the version of SPEC_HIER shown in Figure 17.3a and specifying a new version of the primary hierarchy SPEC_HIER, in which SPECFILE is the primary parent and TREE the primary child. However, we must pay for this circumvention, for TREE is now specified in both primary hierarchies FOR_HIER and SPEC_HIER. In IMS it is the primary hierarchies that are physically stored (following the addition of suitable pointers), so that the TREE file would be duplicated in storage.

17.2.2 The Internal Schema (Part of a DBD)

In general, the unit of storage is the *storage hierarchy occurrence*, which is the storage version of a primary hierarchy occurrence (such as in Figure 17.4). Each storage hierarchy *occurrence* may thus be regarded as a physical record with an internal hierarchical structure. A collection of storage hierarchy occurrences is a *storage hierarchy* type or *physical file*.

We thus have to deal with storage hierarchy types when we specify the internal schema, where there will be one storage hierarchy type for each primary hierarchy (type). Since each storage hierarchy type is a physical file of hierarchically structured records, there will be two main elements in the internal schema.

1. The *physical file organization,* together with access methods and pointer system to aid processing of the corresponding primary hierarchy type.

2. *Pointer systems* to aid processing of any secondary hierarchy types based on the primary hierarchy type being specified in the internal schema.

We shall look at these elements in turn.

Storage Hierarchy (Physical File) Organization There are many possible ways of organizing the physical files. The techniques used in IMS are probably as good as any, and we shall use them for purposes of illustration [Date, 1977; Kapp, 1978].

First of all, there are three basic ways of cementing together the *physical segments* of the physical records (we recall that a *physical segment* is the storage version of a conceptual record). These three methods use, respectively,

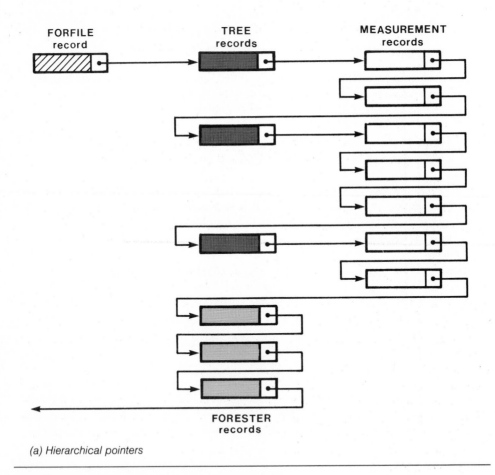

(a) Hierarchical pointers

FIGURE 17.6. *Two basic pointer systems used with the storage or internal schema for the* **FOR_HIER** *hierarchy type from Figure 17.3b. Both systems are available in IMS.*

1. Physical contiguity;

2. Hierarchical pointers;

3. Child/twin pointers.

To understand physical contiguity, consider a FOR_HIER conceptual hierarchy occurrence as shown in Figure 17.4. In the internal version of such an occurrence, the first TREE physical segment would be physically stored right after the root FORFILE segment. The first MEASUREMENT segment would then be stored after the first TREE segment. This procedure would be continued as long as needed.

Hierarchical pointers would connect the segments together, as shown in Figure 17.6a, enabling segments to be retrieved in exactly the same order as in the case of physical contiguity. However, child/twin pointers permit the child segments of a given parent segment to be connected by twin pointers. At the same time a parent is connected to a child by a child pointer, as shown in Figure 17.6b.

These three methods are intimately involved with the file organizations and access

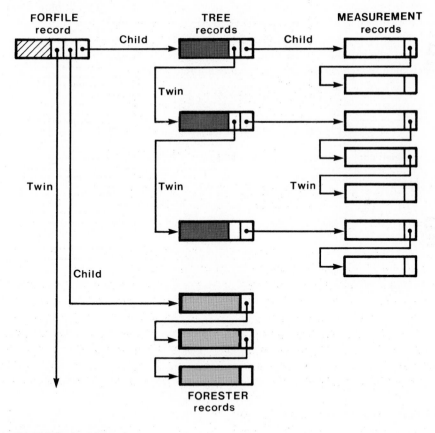

(b) Child/twin pointers.

FIGURE 17.6 *(continued)*

THE HIERARCHICAL SCHEMAS

methods that may be used with a storage hierarchy. The combinations are illustrated in Table 17.1. We may summarize the properties of the four basic file organizations as follows.

HSAM   A HSAM storage hierarchy looks like a CONSECUTIVE file with PL/1 (Chapter 2). The physical file may even reside on magnetic tape. The physical records (storage hierarchy occurrences) are ordered in ascending order by root-segment sequence field. HSAM is an acronym for *Hierarchical Sequential Access Method.*

HISAM   In the simplest case, a storage hierarchy is stored as an index-sequential file, where the index is on the root-segment sequence field. Thus a storage hierarchy occurrence may be accessed either directly or sequentially. Normally, however, two datasets (physical files) are used to store a HISAM storage hierarchy, one for an initial part of a storage hierarchy occurrence and another for the remaining or overflow part of a storage hierarchy occurrence. The overflow dataset is also used to accommodate insertions. It is not quite true to say that access to the subsidiary segments for a given root segment is sequential using the physical contiguity of the segment; physical contiguity may be partially replaced by a HISAM pointer system in the case of overflow or insertion of additional segments. Furthermore, there are two versions of HISAM, one based on ISAM and the other on VSAM (Chapter 4). A full description is beyond the scope of this text; however, Figure 17.7 gives some insight into the kind of detail involved with the ISAM version. HISAM is an acronym for *Hierarchical Index Sequential Access Method.*

POSSIBLE STRUCTURES FOR STORAGE HIERARCHIES IN IMS		
Access Method	**Physical Segment Linkage**	**Type of Access**
HSAM	Physical Contiguity	Sequential access to a root segment and subsidiary segments.
HISAM	Physical Contiguity	Direct (via index) access to a root segment, sequential access to subsidiary segments.
HDAM	Hierarchical Pointers	Direct (hashing) access to a root segment, sequential access to subsidiary segments.
HDAM	Child/Twin Pointers	Direct (hashing) access to a root segment, direct (via pointers) access to subsidiary segments.
HIDAM	Hierarchical Pointers	Direct (via index) access to a root segment, sequential access to subsidiary segments.
HIDAM	Child/Twin Pointers	Direct (via index) access to a root segment, direct (via pointers) access to subsidiary segments.

TABLE 17.1

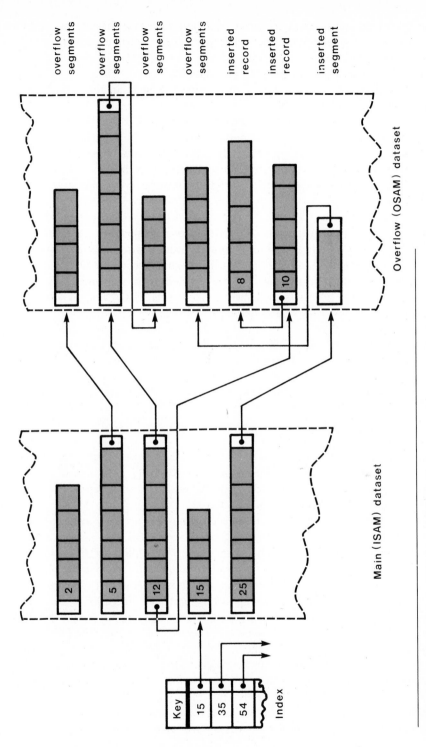

FIGURE 17.7. *Structure of a HISAM storage hierarchy. Each storage hierarchy (physical record) occurrence is made up of segments. On loading, a storage hierarchy is stored in the ISAM dataset, the OSAM (overflow) dataset being used if there are too many segments. The OSAM dataset is also used for inserted segments and inserted storage hierarchy occurrences (labeled inserted record in the diagram). Keys shown are keys to root segments of hierarchy types.*

HDAM   Here the storage hierarchy is organized as a hash file, where hashing is carried out on the root-segment sequence field. Thus there is direct access to the root segments. The subsidiary segments are connected together either by hierarchical or child/twin pointers, as specified in the internal part of the PDB description.

There is a separate overflow area, but it is used only when the main data area is full. Overflow from an address caused by synonyms is handled by the chained progressive overflow technique (Chapter 3). Inserted segments are placed as near as possible to their root segments and connected by either the hierarchical or child/twin pointer system. An address will normally hold several storage hierarchy occurrences plus some segment insertions; that is, the address capacity is greater than one. The principles described in Chapter 3 for minimizing search length apply here. HDAM is an acronym for *Hierarchical Direct-Access Method*.

HIDAM   HIDAM is basically an extension of HISAM. However, this time three datasets may be involved, two for a dense index (in addition to the usual sparse index) and one for the storage hierarchy occurrences. As with HDAM, the subsidiary segments are connected by either hierarchical or child/twin pointers. We thus have direct or sequential access to the root segments and pointer access to the subsidiary segments. HIDAM is an acronym for *Hierarchical Index Sequential Access Method*.

Secondary Pointer System   Since storage hierarchies corresponding to the secondary hierarchies such as INTER_ST, INTER_SPEC, or INTER_PROP from Figure 17.5 would result in excessive duplication of data, it is desirable to have a pointer system embedded in the storage hierarchy occurrences for the primary hierarchies. These secondary pointers enable the DBCS to simulate the secondary hierarchies. We shall now look at some examples of secondary pointers using the secondary hierarchies INTER_ST, INTER_SPEC, and INTER_PROP.

The pointer system, which is embedded in the storage hierarchy corresponding to the primary FOR_HIER in order to simulate the secondary INTER_ST, is shown in Figure 17.8. The storage hierarchy for the primary SPEC_HIER is also involved, and the system can also simulate the secondary hierarchy INTER_SPEC.

The secondary parent pointers permit a TREE record to be connected to its secondary parent in SPECFILE thus simulating the TREESPEC records of INTER_ST. The secondary child and secondary twin pointers permit simulation of the TREE file in INTER_SPEC.

Turning to Figure 17.9, we see that it is necessary to embed only secondary child and secondary twin pointers in the storage hierarchy for the FOR_HIER primary hierarchy to produce a simulation of the INTER_PROP secondary hierarchy. In Figure 17.10 are some occurrences of INTER_PROP that result directly from the pointer system applied to FOR_HIER in Figure 17.9. We note that the relationship between TREE and PROP_TREE is a 1:*n* relationship but is not quite the same as the recursive relationship embodied in the set PROPAGATE in Chapter 8. To see this, let us suppose we wish to retrieve the immediate descendants of tree 5 (which is in forest 'X'). We retrieve the FORFILE record for forest 'X' and then the records for its trees until we find tree 5. We then retrieve the child trees in TREE_PROP, namely, trees 15, 25, and 35. To find the direct descendants of any of these trees, such as tree 25, we shall *have to access the* TREE *file again to retrieve the*

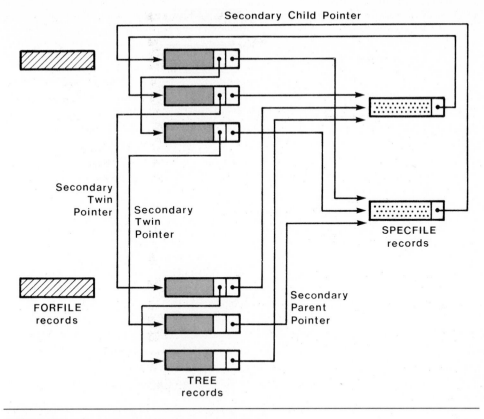

Secondary Child Pointer

Secondary
Twin
Pointer

Secondary
Twin
Pointer

Secondary
Parent
Pointer

FORFILE
records

TREE
records

SPECFILE
records

FIGURE 17.8. *Secondary pointer system used with the storage versions of the* **FOR_HIER** *and* **SPEC_HIER** *hierarchies. The pointer system facilitates processing of the secondary conceptual hierarchies* **INTER_ST** *and* **INTER_ SPEC** *from Figure 17.5. In IMS, such secondary pointers are called* logical pointers. *In this diagram only the* **FORFILE** *and* **TREE** *storage records in two* **FOR_HIER** *storage occurrences are displayed. Conceptual* **FOR_ HIER** *occurrences are displayed in Figure 17.4.*

TREE *record for tree 25.* We can then retrieve the child trees in TREE_PROP of this tree, namely, trees 10, 20, and 30. Thus while the relationship we are dealing with is fundamentally recursive, it appears as a hierarchy to the user and is processed as such.

The secondary pointer systems described here are generally available in IMS and are called *logical pointers.* However, as mentioned earlier, if we were using IMS we would have to redesign our hierarchies to overcome the IMS restriction that a storage segment which is a logical parent cannot also be a logical child; this rule is violated by the segment corresponding to conceptual TREE records. However, we shall ignore this IMS restriction in the interest of a clear presentation of the *principles* involved in the hierarchical approach.

In IMS, as already mentioned, the secondary pointer systems and the access methods described in the previous subsection are specified in the internal part of the DBD for each

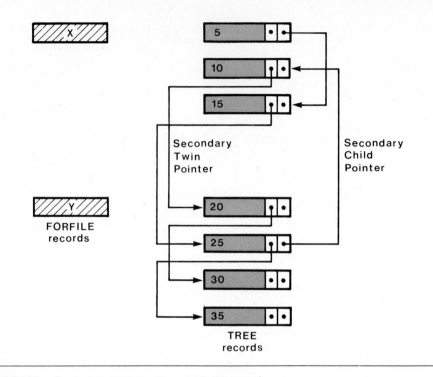

FIGURE 17.9. *Secondary pointer system used with part of the storage version of the* FOR_HIER *hierarchy to facilitate processing of the secondary hierarchy type* INTER_PROP.

primary hierarchy. A detailed description of the methods of specification of these secondary pointers has been given by Date [Date, 1977].

17.2.3 The External Schema

The *external schema* is basically a subset of the conceptual schema. The user sees a collection of external files with records grouped into hierarchical structures [Kapp, 1978; Tsichritzis, 1977].

To be specific, the user sees a collection of subhierarchies consisting of subhierarchy occurrences. A subhierarchy is a part of any hierarchy, *whether primary or secondary,* that is specified in the conceptual schema. In IMS, a subhierarchy must include the root file from the hierarchy from which it is taken, and a user can have only one subhierarchy from any conceptual hierarchy.

If we take the hierarchy FOR_HIER, in IMS we could have the following subhierarchies.

    a.   FOREST; FORESTER child of FOREST.

    b.   FOREST; TREE child of FOREST.

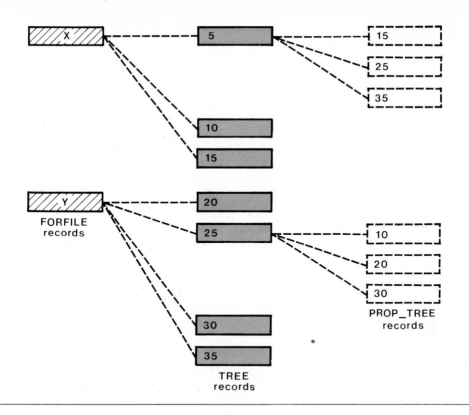

FIGURE 17.10. *Two occurrences of the conceptual hierarchy* INTER_PROP *corresponding to the storage version of the* FOR_HIER *hierarchy from Figure 17.9.*

    c.   FOREST; FORESTER child of FOREST; TREE child of FOREST.

    d.   FOREST; TREE child of FOREST; MEASUREMENT child of TREE.

    e.   FOR_HIER itself.

In IMS, an external schema is called a PCB (*Program Communications Block*) and there is a PCB for each subhierarchy. The following is an example of part of a PCB for the subhierarchy in (d) above.

```
1   PCB           TYPE = DB,DBNAME = FOR_HIER,
2   SENSEG        NAME = FOREST,PROCOPT = G
3   SENSEG        NAME = TREE,PARENT = FOREST,PROCOPT = G
4   SENSEG        NAME = MEASUREM, PARENT = TREE,PROCOPT = G
```

The PROCOPT (process option) entry indicates what kind of processing may be carried out on the conceptual file (IMS "segment") specified. Here G, denoting GET, indicates retrieval, I indicates insertion, and D indicates deletion, and so on.

THE HIERARCHICAL SCHEMAS   **501**

EXERCISES

For each of the data bases in Figures 6.5, 6.10, and 6.16a, use diagrammatic techniques to draw up each of the following.

1. Conceptual level primary and secondary hierarchy types.

2. Required storage hierarchies showing primary and secondary (physical and logical) pointer system.

3. Some external hierarchies.

REFERENCES

Date, C. J., 1977, *An Introduction to Data Base Management Systems,* Addison-Wesley, Reading, Mass.

IBM, 1974, *DL/1 Data Base Techniques for Manufacturing Applications.*

IBM, 1977a, *IMS/VS Storage Utilities,* Order Form SH20–9029.

IBM, 1977b, *IMS/VS General Information,* Order Form GH20–1260–4.

IBM, 1978a, *CICS/VS, General Information,* Order Form GC33–0066–3.

IBM, 1978b, *IMS/VS Application Design Guide,* Order Form SH20–9025.

IBM, 1978c, *IMS/VS Application Programming Reference Manual,* Order Form SH20–9026.

Kapp, D., and J. F. Leben, 1978, *IMS Programming Techniques, A Guide to Using DL/1,* D. Van Nostrand, New York.

Walsh, M., 1980, *Information Management System, Virtual Storage,* Reston Publishing Co., Reston, Va.

Manipulation of Hierarchical Data Bases

18

In this chapter we shall study how loading, updating, and retrieval are carried out with hierarchical data bases, using the FORESTRY data base in particular. For the sake of simple presentation, we shall take retrieval first.

The best-known hierarchical retrieval sublanguage is IBM's DL/1 [IBM, 1977; Kapp, 1978] and this manipulates an IMS data base. However, before we can look at this retrieval language, we must first examine how the user working area and special registers are handled in the hierarchical approach.

18.1 THE UWA AND SPECIAL REGISTERS

The UWA serves much the same function as in the CODASYL approach. On the other hand, while the function of the special registers has a great deal in common with that in the CODASYL approach, there are important differences.

18.1.1 The UWA

In a user program, we must declare structures that are capable of holding external records from the external hierarchies being manipulated by the program. Thus if we have a user program that manipulates external hierarchies which are identical to the conceptual hierarchies FOR_HIER, SPEC_HIER, INTER_ST, INTER_SPEC, and INTER_PROP, then we could declare the following structures using PL/1 in much the same way as we did with CODASYL.

```
DCL 1 FORREC
        2  FOREST...;
        .........;
DCL 1 SPECREC,
        2  SPECIES ..,
        ..........;
DCL 1 TREEREC,
        2  SPECIES ...,
        2  FOREST.....,
        2  TREENUMB...,
        ............;
DCL 1 MEASREC
        2  MEASNUMB ..,
        ...........;
DCL 1 TREESPECREC,   /*   Holds TREESPEC records from INTER_ST   */
        2  SPECIES...,
        ..........;
DCL 1 FORESREC,   /*   Hold FORESTER records from FOR_HIER   */
        2  FOREST ...,
        ..........;
DCL 1 PROPTREEREC   /*   Holds PROP_TREE records from INTER_PROP   */
        LIKE TREEREC;
```

These structures are the same as those we used with CODASYL in Chapter 9, except for
TREESPECREC, FORESREC, and PROPTREEREC. PROPTREEREC must have the
same structure as TREEREC, because we may want to retrieve both a TREE record and
its direct descendant together.

18.1.2 Special Registers

In the hierarchical approach, a user program may be manipulating several external hierarchies, whereas in the CODASYL approach, it is normal for a user program to be
manipulating only one network. Thus it is desirable in the hierarchical approach to have
a collection of special registers *for each external hierarchy being manipulated.*

    This is done in IMS, and we shall look at the more important of the IMS special
registers in a typical collection. Incidentally, a special register collection in IMS is called
a *PCB-mask,* and the registers for all the user-program's external hierarchies are collec-
tively known as the PSB, or *Program Specification Block* [IBM, 1978b; Kapp, 1978].

    It is necessary for the special register collection for an external hierarchy to have a
name, in order that we may refer to it in a retrieval command. A name suggestive of the
hierarchy involved is usual. In IMS, a special register collection is a program structure
variable, part of which is exemplified by the following.

```
DCL 1 SR_FOR_HIER,
        2  HIERARCHY CHAR (8),         /*   Contains the name of the primary or secondary
```

		hierarchy on which the external hierarchy is based. In this case the value will be 'FOR_HIER' */
2 STATUS CHAR (2),	/*	Corresponds to DB_STATUS in CODASYL */
2 FILENAME CHAR (8),	/*	Name of file from which the record has just been retrieved */
2 C_INDICATOR CHAR (15);	/*	Corresponds to CODASYL currency indicators. Contains fully concatenated key for record just retrieved */

The STATUS register is checked after a command has been carried out, especially when the outcome is not predictable. A blank value means that the operation has been successfully carried out, while 'GE' indicates that the record was not found.

C_INDICATOR functions in a manner very similar to the currency indicators in CODASYL. Because DL/1 is essentially navigational, there has to be a method of recording a user-program's position within a hierarchy. Thus if we have just retrieved a MEASUREMENT record from the FOR_HIER hierarchy, C_INDICATOR would contain the FOREST value for the tree on which the measurement was carried out, concatenated to the TREE-NUMB value of the tree involved, and concatenated to the MEASNUMB value for the measurement involved. As a reminder, it is important to remember that there is a collection of special registers such as SR_FOR_HIER for each external hierarchy being used by the program and that the special register collection involved must be referred to in any DL/1 command.

The name chosen for a special register collection and the names of the registers are arbitrary in IMS. Finally, we should mention that each IMS special register collection in IMS has nine registers, of which we have described only four. In the following subsections, we shall assume that we have declared special register collections SR_FOR_HIER, SR_SPEC_HIER, SR_INTER_ST, SR_INTER_SPEC, and SR_INTER_PROP to be used with the external hierarchies identical to the conceptual hierarchies FOR_HIER, SPEC_HIER, INTER_ST, INTER_SPEC, and INTER_PROP, respectively. In all of these special register collections, we use HIERARCHY, STATUS, FILENAME, and C_INDICATOR as register names.

18.2 THE DL/1 RETRIEVAL SUBLANGUAGE

The syntax of DL/1 is basically simple, but it is detailed; for presentation purposes, we shall use a more user-friendly version. There are three basic retrieval commands.

1. GET FIRST or GU command.

2. GET NEXT or GN command.

3. GET NEXT WITHIN PARENT or GNP command.

These apparently simple commands have very involved semantics, however, which we now illustrate by means of retrievals from the FORESTRY data base.

18.2.1 DL/1 Retrieval Examples

The level concept introduced in Chapter 11 is applicable to retrievals with DL/1. Thus, with reference to the FOR_HIER hierarchy, a retrieval involving the FORFILE file is level 1, one involving the FORFILE file and its TREE child file is level 2, and one involving the FORFILE file and its descendant TREE and MEASUREMENT files is level 3. We shall therefore use the level concept to classify the following retrievals.

Retrieval 1: GU Command, Level 1   *Retrieve the first root* (FORFILE) *record in the* FOR_HIER *hierarchy.*

GU (SR_FOR_HIER) FORFILE

As a result of this retrieval, the UWA structure FORREC will have the required FORFILE record and the registers of SR_FOR_HIER will all be updated, so that HIERARCHY has the value 'FOR_HIER', STATUS has a blank value indicating a successful retrieval, FILENAME has the value 'FORFILE', and C_INDICATOR has the FOREST value for the retrieved record. C_INDICATOR thus indicates the current position of the program with respect to FOR_HIER.

Retrieval 2: GN Command, Level 1   *Retrieve the second, third, and fourth root* (FORFILE) *records in* FOR_HIER.

```
GU (SR_FOR_HIER) FORFILE;  /*  Position at first record  */
DO J = 2 TO 4;
    GN (SR_FOR_HIER) FORFILE;
    PUT SKIP LIST (FORREC);
END;
/*  Position at fourth record  */
```

With GU we start at the beginning of a hierarchy—that is, at the root record of the first hierarchical occurrence—establishing a position that is recorded in C_INDICATOR. With GN we move forward to the next hierarchy occurrence sticking to the file specified, the position at the end of a retrieval being recorded in C_INDICATOR.

Retrieval 3: GU Command, Level 1   *Retrieve the first root* (FORFILE) *record (in* FOR_HIER) *for which* LOC *value is* 'CALIFORNIA' *and* COMPANY *value is* 'XCO'.

GU (SR_FOR_HIER) FORFILE ((LOC = 'CALIFORNIA') & (COMPANY = 'XCO'));

Here again we start afresh into FOR_HIER, going forward through the FOR_HIER occurrences until we come to a FORFILE record satisfying the *search argument*. Our resulting position is then recorded in the register C_INDICATOR.

Retrieval 4: GN Command, Level 1   *Retrieve all the root* (FORFILE) *records in* FOR_HIER *for which* LOC *value is* 'CALIFORNIA'.

```
GU (SR_FOR_HIER) FORFILE (LOC = 'CALIFORNIA');
PUT LIST (FORREC);
BEOF = '1'B;   /*  BEOF: Before End of File   */
DO WHILE (BEOF);
    GN (SR_FOR_HIER) FORFILE (LOC = 'CALIFORNIA');
    IF SR_FOR_HIER.STATUS = 'GE'   /*  None found   */
        THEN BEOF = '0'B;
        ELSE PUT SKIP LIST (FORREC);
END;
```

The first position is established by the GU command; subsequent positions are established by each execution of a GN command. Note that search arguments may be used with GN in the same way as with GU.

Retrieval 5: GU Command, Level 2   *Retrieve the first* TREE *record in the* FOR_HIER *hierarchy for which the species is spruce and the forest is in California.*

```
GU (SR_FOR_HIER)  FORFILE (LOC = 'CALIFORNIA')
                  TREE (SPECIES = 'SPRUCE')
```

In the above command, we may say that there are two search arguments, one for FORFILE and one for TREE. In either a GN or GU command, it is *the record specified in the last search argument in the command that is retrieved in DL/1,* unless special provisions are made, as we shall see in retrieval 8.

In executing the above command, the system searches sequentially through the FOR_HIER occurrence within the FORFILE file until the first record with LOC value 'CALIFORNIA' is found. It then goes sequentially through the TREE child records of this FORFILE record until a TREE record with SPECIES value 'SPRUCE' is found. If none is found, the system continues its sequential scan of the FORFILE file. Of course if LOC had been specified as a record key (not the same as sequence field, see Section 17.2.1), that it is possible to specify in the GU command that the FORFILE file be directly accessed [IBM, 1978c].

Retrieval 6: GN Command, Mostly Level 1   *Starting with the* TREE *record retrieved in the previous command, find all the* TREE *records for trees planted before 1980.*

```
GU (SR_FOR_HIER)  FORFILE (LOC = 'CALIFORNIA')
                  TREE (SPECIES = 'SPRUCE');
    /*  Thus we have determined the start position which is recorded in C_INDICATOR   */
BEOF = '1'B;
DO WHILE (BEOF);
    GN (SR_FOR_HIER) TREE (PLANTED < 19800101);
    IF SR_FOR_HIER.STATUS = 'GE' THEN BEOF = '0'B;  /*  None left   */
    ELSE PUT SKIP LIST (TREEREC);
END;
```

With the GN command, we go forward from the start position in TREE determined by the GU command. The GN causes the remaining part of the TREE file to be processed. Following each GN command execution, the sequence key of the parent FORFILE record and child TREE record for the latest position is placed in C_INDICATOR.

Retrieval 7: GU, GN Commands, Level 3   *Retrieve all electrical measurements carried out on spruce trees in forests in California.*

```
GU (SR_FOR_HIER) FORFILE
                    /*   Start position at first FORFILE record   */
BEOF = '1'B;
DO WHILE (BEOF);
    GN (SR_FOR_HIER) FORFILE (LOC = 'CALIFORNIA')
                     TREE (SPECIES = 'SPRUCE')
                     MEASUREMENT (TYPE = 'ELECTRICAL');
    IF SR_FOR_HIER.STATUS = 'GE' THEN BEOF = '0'B;  /*   None left   */
                     ELSE PUT SKIP LIST (MEASREC);
END;
```

At this point it is convenient to demonstrate actual DL/1 syntax as used with PL/1. In practice, the GN command used in the above retrieval could be written as

```
SIX = 6;   /*   SIX is a numeric variable   */
CALL PL1DL1 (SIX,   /*   Call to IMS with 6 + 1 arguments   */
            'GN   ',                       /*   Command   */
            SR_FOR_HIER, MEASREC,   /*   Registers and UWA structure   */
            'FORFILE    (LOC     =   CALIFORNIA   )',
            'TREE       (SPECIES =   SPRUCE       )',
            'MEASUREM  (TYPE     =   ELECTRICAL   )'  );
```

The three search arguments are the final three arguments in the call to IMS. (Blanks have to be inserted so that each part of a search argument has a standard length.)

Retrieval 8: Level 3, Multiple-File Retrieval   *In the previous retrieval, retrieve also the* TREE *parents in addition to the required* MEASUREMENT *records.*

We replace the previous GN command by

```
GN (SR_FOR_HIER) FORFILE (LOC = 'CALIFORNIA')
                 TREE*D (SPECIES = 'SPRUCE')
                 MEASUREMENT (TYPE = 'ELECTRICAL');
```

The *D in the above case indicates that the TREE parent of a retrieval MEASUREMENT record is also to be retrieved. In general, *D indicates retrieval of the complete hierarchical path from where it is specified, down to the bottom-level file specified in the search argument.

Retrieval 9: Complete Hierarchy Retrieval *Retrieve all the records in the hierarchy FOR_HIER in hierarchical sequence.*

```
GU (SR_FOR_HIER) FORFILE;   /*   Position at first record in FOR_HIER   */
PUT LIST (FORREC);
BEOH = '1'B;   /*   BEOH: Before End Of Hierarchy type   */
DO WHILE (BEOH);
     GN (SR_FOR_HIER)   /*   Note the omission of the record search argument indicating
                               next record of any kind in hierarchical sequence is to be
                               retrieved   */
     IF SR_FOR_HIER.STATUS = 'GE'   /*   None left   */   THEN BEOH = '0'B;
     ELSE DO;
          /*   We must determine what record type has been retrieved   */
          IF SR_FOR_HIER.FILENAME = 'MEASUREM'
                    THEN PUT SKIP LIST (MEASREC);
          ELSE IF SR_FOR_HIER.FILENAME = 'TREE'
                    THEN PUT SKIP LIST (TREEREC);
          ELSE IF SR_FOR_HIER.FILENAME = 'FORESTER'
                    THEN PUT SKIP LIST (FORESREC);
                    ELSE PUT SKIP LIST (FORREC);
     END;
END;
```

Commands of this type are unique to the hierarchical approach. The system will examine every record in the FOR_HIER hierarchy in hierarchical sequence, that is, in the sequence determined by the hierarchical pointer system in Figure 17.6a. It is up to the program to determine which type of record is retrieved by the execution of a GN command.

Retrieval 10: GNP Command *Retrieve the records for all electrical measurements carried out on tree 56.*

```
GU (SR_FOR_HIER)          FORFILE
                          TREE (TREENUMB = 56);
          /*   Initial position determined   */
BOOL = '1'B;
DO WHILE (BOOL);
     GNP (SR_FOR_HIER) MEASUREMENT (TYPE = 'ELECTRICAL');
     IF SR_FOR_HIER.STATUS = 'GE'   /*   None left   */   THEN BOOL = '0'B;
     ELSE PUT SKIP LIST (MEASREC);
END;
```

GNP retrieves only records that are subsidiary to the previously retrieved record, in this case the TREE record with TREENUMB value 56. When all the subsidiary MEASURE-MENT records of this TREE record have been examined, the system places 'GE' in the proper STATUS register, signaling that there are no more MEASUREMENT records requiring processing.

Retrieval 11: GNP Command, Level 3 *For each tree in forest* 'XFOR', *retrieve the tree record together with the tree records for its immediate descendants planted before 1980.*

With this retrieval we have to use the hierarchy INTER_PROP.

```
GU (SR_INTER_PROP) FORFILE (FOREST = 'XFOR');
                            /*   Initial position determined   */
BOOL = '1'B;
DO WHILE (BOOL);
    GNP (SR_INTER_PROP)              TREE*D
                                     TREE_PROP (PLANTED < 19800101);
    IF SR_INTER_PROP.STATUS = 'GE'   /*   None left   */   THEN BOOL = '0'B;
    ELSE DO;
        PUT SKIP LIST ('PARENT/CHILD PAIR');
        PUT SKIP LIST (TREEREC, PROPTREEREC);
    END;
END;
```

This program excerpt will give us a lot of redundant output. When the system is positioned at a given TREE record, it examines all the TREE_PROP records subsidiary to this TREE record, so that the same TREE record will be output many times. The reader should devise a program excerpt as an exercise to eliminate this, preferably by modifying the DL/1 commands.

Retrieval 12: GNP Command, Level *n* *Retrieve all the records that are subsidiary to the* FORFILE *record for forest* 'XFOR'.

We return to the FOR_HIER hierarchy.

```
GU (SR_FOR_HIER) FORFILE (FOREST = 'XFOR');
                            /* Initial position determined */
BOOL = '1'B;
DO WHILE (BOOL);
    GNP (SR_FOR_HIER);   /*   Note omission of the record search argument indicating
                               that next record of any kind under FORFILE record is to
                               be retrieved   */
    IF SR_FOR_HIER.STATUS = 'GE'   /*   None left   */   THEN BOOL = '0'B;
    ELSE DO;
        /*   We must find out what record type has been retrieved   */
    IF SR_FOR_HIER.FILENAME = 'MEASUREM'
            THEN PUT SKIP LIST (MEASREC);
    ELSE IF SR_FOR_HIER.FILENAME = 'FORESTER'
            THEN PUT SKIP LIST (FORESREC);
    ELSE PUT SKIP LIST (TREEREC);
    END;
END;
```

This rather unique use of GNP is similar to that for the GN command in retrieval 9, with the difference that here we are restricted to an examination of all the records subsidiary to (or within the parent) FORFILE record for which the FOREST value is 'XFOR'.

Retrieval 13: GN Command, Composite Record *Retrieve the* MEASUREMENT *records for electrical measurements carried out on hardwood trees in California forests.*

We can see that only the INTER_ST hierarchy contains the information required for this retrieval (see Figure 17.5a).

```
GU (SR_INTER_ST) FORFILE;   /*   Initial position at 1st record in hierarchy   */
BOOL = '1'B;
DO WHILE (BOOL);
    GN (SR_INTER_ST)    FORFILE (LOC = 'CALIFORNIA')
                        TREESPEC (WOODTYPE = 'HARDWOOD')
                        MEASUREMENT (TYPE = 'ELECTRICAL');
    IF SR_INTER_ST.STATUS = 'GE'   /*   None left   */   THEN BOOL = '0'B;
    ELSE PUT SKIP LIST (MEASREC);
END;
```

Retrieval 14: Two Hierarchies *Find the records for those species that occur only in Oregon forests.*

This retrieval is somewhat more difficult, given our retrieval tools. As with complex retrievals in the CODASYL approach, we are forced to consider our retrieval strategy carefully, in the interest of maintaining good performance. In such cases, the data-base administrator needs to be consulted to make sure that the underlying storage structures are compatible with the strategy chosen.

In the following program excerpt, we shall make use of the two hierarchies FOR_HIER and INTER_SPEC. First, using INTER_SPEC, we shall examine each species, together with its trees. For each tree, using the hierarchy FOR_HIER, we shall check to see that the parent forest is located in Oregon. This retrieval is really a network retrieval, as it involves the network aspect of the FORESTRY data base. This example illustrates how such retrievals are handled in the hierarchical approach.

```
DCL TEMPORARY CHAR (15);           /*   Holds a FOREST value   */
DCL (BEOF, LOGICAL, OK) BIT (1);   /*   Logical variables   */
N = 1; BEOF = '1'B';
DO WHILE (BEOF);
    IF N = 1 THEN GU (SR_INTER_SPEC) SPECFILE;
                                   /*   Position at first record in SPECFILE   */
    ELSE GN (SR_INTER_SPEC) SPECFILE;
                                   /*   Position at subsequent record in
                                        SPECFILE   */
    IF SR_INTER_SPEC.STATUS = 'GE' /*   None left   */   THEN BEOF = '0'B;
    ELSE DO;
```

```
        M = 0; LOGICAL = '1'B; OK = '1'B;
        DO WHILE (LOGICAL);
            GNP (SR_INTER_SPEC) TREE;    /*   Examination of all trees under
                                                SPECFILE record begins   */
            IF SR_INTER_SPEC.STATUS = 'GE' THEN LOGICAL = '0'B;
            ELSE DO;  /*   Check if it is in an Oregon forest   */
                TEMPORARY = TREEREC.FOREST;
                    /*   Now we look in FOR_HIER hierarchy with this sequence field   */
                M = M + 1;
                GU (SR_FOR_HIER) FORFILE ((FOREST = TEMPORARY)
                                                    & (LOC = 'OREGON'));
                IF SR_FOR_HIER.STATUS = 'GE'   /*   None found, tree not growing
                                                    in Oregon   */
                THEN DO;
                    LOGICAL = '0'B; OK = '0'B;
                END;
            END;
        END;
        IF M > 0 & OK THEN   /*   All trees under SPECFILE record are in Oregon
                                    forests   */
        PUT SKIP LIST (SPECREC);
        N = N + 1;
    END;
END;
```

This example illustrates a fundamental weakness of the hierarchical approach. Retrievals become artificially complex when they involve more than one hierarchy, and there is little that can be done about it.

The above retrieval also demonstrates the need for consultation with the data-base administrator to prevent use of a retrieval strategy that will result in poor performance. For example, with an unsuitable internal schema, the GU command with the FOR_HIER hierarchy in the above retrieval could lead to a sequential search of the entire hierarchy.

Status of DL/1   Because of the fairly widespread use of IMS in commercial installations, DL/1 is quite well known. Unfortunately, because of the complexity of the IMS schema structure and a requirement for very detailed specifications, the occasional academic user cannot easily set up an IMS data base. Such users often have a larger number of smaller data bases, and ease of installation and use is critical. For this reason, DL/1 is not widely used by academic personnel (as distinct from university administrative personnel). This is a pity, for there is a great deal that is positive in DL/1. For example, it is clearly much more nonnavigational than the CODASYL DML. In DL/1, we can express a fairly complex retrieval involving many files, provided the files are all in the same hierarchy. This cannot be done with a CODASYL data base that has a hierarchical structure; instead, a great deal of code involving many nested loops is required.

However, DL/1 is still quite primitive in its retrieval power when compared with some of the relational-retrieval languages or the EOS CODASYL enhancement sublanguage described in Chapter 11.

18.3 LOADING A HIERARCHICAL DATA BASE

Before we can examine the principles behind the initial loading of a hierarchical data base, we need to have a load or insertion command for inserting records into the data base. The IMS INSERT (INSRT) command is a good example of such a command and is worth considering in detail [Date, 1977; IBM, 1978b].

18.3.1 The IMS INSERT Command

Basically we have the same type of problem in inserting a record into either a CODASYL or hierarchical data base. The problem arises because conceptual records in both approaches have two groupings. In the CODASYL approach, it is files and owner-coupled sets; in the hierarchical approach, it is files and hierarchy types.

Thus, as we have seen, with a CODASYL data base a record must be placed in both a file and owner-coupled set occurrences. Similarly, in the hierarchical approach, we must place a record in both a file and a hierarchy occurrence, in a subhierarchy occurrence, and so on.

In the CODASYL approach, we have several methods of selecting the correct set occurrences, depending on what has been specified in the SET SELECTION clause in the schema. In the hierarchical approach, we could also have different methods of selecting the appropriate hierarchy and subhierarchy occurrences, but in IMS there is only one method; it is probably the most useful method.

In IMS, selection of the appropriate hierarchy and subhierarchy occurrences is by means of current indicators for the ancestors of the record to be inserted. As an example, suppose we wish to insert a new MEASUREMENT record into the FOR_HIER hierarchy. We would have

INSRT (SR_FOR_HIER) MEASUREMENT;

The system would look up the current sequence keys of the ancestors of the MEASURE-MENT file, that is, of TREE and FORFILE records. These are in the special register SR_FOR_HIER.C_INDICATOR. The MEASUREMENT record is then inserted into the MEASUREMENT file, into the occurrence of the FOR_HIER hierarchy type indicated by the FORFILE C_INDICATOR sequence key, and into the subhierarchy occurrence headed by the TREE file indicated by the TREE C_INDICATOR sequence key. The MEASURE-MENT record is taken from the UWA structure MEASREC.

Another way of looking at this is to consider that the MEASUREMENT record is inserted at the bottom of the hierarchical or ancestral path currently in C_INDICATOR. Thus, before using the command above, the user would have to ensure that the current indicators in C_INDICATOR were the correct ones. This could be done by issuing an appropriate retrieval command.

For example, suppose we wish to insert a MEASUREMENT record for a measurement carried out on tree 56 in forest 'XFOR'. We could set the position as follows and then insert the record.

```
GU (SR_FOR_HIER) FORFILE (FOREST = 'XFOR')
                 TREE (TREENUMB = 56);
INSRT (SR_FOR_HIER) MEASUREMENT;
```

This is somewhat reminiscent of the use of the CODASYL STORE command. However, the IMS INSERT command also permits a direct specification of the ancestral path, at the bottom of which the record is to be inserted.

Instead of the GU and INSRT commands as used above, we could have used the following single INSRT command:

```
INSRT (SR_FOR_HIER)   FORFILE (FOREST = 'XFOR')
                      TREE (TREENUMB = 56)
                      MEASUREMENT;
```

Here it is the record specified in the last record search argument which is to be inserted; the ancestral path to be used is specified in the other record-search arguments. The CODASYL STORE command has no corresponding facility, although of its utility there can be little doubt. However, as the reader may recall, we have included a proposal along these lines in Section 10.5.3.

In general, when we use INSRT to place a record in the data base, there must be a parent record already stored. This will not be the case, however, when the record being stored is a root. To store a root in IMS, we code, for example,

```
INSRT (SR_FOR_HIER)   FORFILE*D;
```

In addition, we may use the command to store several records of a hierarchical occurrence. Suppose we wish to store a new FORFILE record, together with a descendant TREE record and a descendant MEASUREMENT record. We code

```
INSRT (SR_FOR_HIER)   FORFILE*D
                      TREE
                      MEASUREMENT;
```

Here the root record is stored first, creating a new hierarchy occurrence and causing C_INDICATOR to be updated. The TREE record can then be stored under the FORFILE record, and finally the MEASUREMENT record under the TREE record.

18.3.2 Loading of Primary Hierarchy Types

In loading a hierarchy (type) such as FOR_HIER initially, it is usual to load each complete hierarchy occurrence separately. In loading such an occurrence, the constituent records are presented in hierarchical sequence.

Ideally, the individual hierarchical occurrences making up a hierarchy type could be loaded in any order independent of the underlying internal storage structures. In this respect, IMS loading programs are not data independent, since whether or not the occurrences can be presented in random root-key-sequence order depends on the underlying access method. If it is, for example, HIDAM or HSAM, then the occurrences must be in ascending root-key-sequence order. However, since it is usual to load the occurrences in ascending root-key sequence anyway, this is hardly a drawback.

As an example of hierarchical loading techniques, we shall give a loading program for the FOR_HIER hierarchy type. We shall assume that the records to be loaded are in the CONSECUTIVE files XFORFILE, XTREE, XFORESTER, and XMEASUREMENT. However, XMEASUREMENT records are not the same as MEASUREMENT records; an XMEASUREMENT record has an extra field TREENUMB, which holds the sequence field of its XTREE parent record (see FORESTRY DBD, line 10).

To facilitate loading the constituent records of each FOR_HIER occurrence, the XFORFILE, XTREE, XFORESTER, and XMEASUREMENT records must be available in the correct sequence. Thus the root XFORFILE records must be sorted in ascending FOREST key-sequence order. On the other hand, the remaining subsidiary records must be sorted, not in root-sequence order, but in parent-key order. That is, XTREE records must be sorted in FOREST order, XFORESTER in FOREST order, and XMEASUREMENT records in the TREENUMB order of XTREE records.

The reader should see that obtaining the XMEASUREMENT records in the correct order is not quite so simple. The records cannot just be sorted on a field as with the other files. We leave it to the reader to devise a scheme for sorting.

Loading Program   The loading program that follows is in fact suitable for loading the storage data base for the IMS primary hierarchy FOR_FILE (where in IMS it would be referred to as a PDB). We also use the UWA and special register collection SR_FOR_HIER (IMS terminology: PCB) as defined in Section 18.1.2.

```
DL1PL1 : PROC (POINT) OPTIONS MAIN;
          /*   Program loads FOR_HIER hierarchy from FORESTRY data base shown in Figure
               17.3b   */
                             /*   UWA   */
DCL  1  FORREC,
        ........;
DCL  1  TREEREC,
        .......;
DCL  1  FORESREC,
        ........;
DCL  1  MEASREC,
        .......;
                  /*   Special register collection (PCB-mask)   */
DCL  1  SR_FOR_HIER BASED (POINT),
        ............;
              /*   POINT value passed from IMS to program to invoke special registers   */
DCL  (XFORFILE,
```

```
                XTREE,
                XFOREST,
                XMEAS) FILE RECORD ENV (CONSECUTIVE);
                            /*  Data base loaded from these files  */
     DCL   1   XMEASREC,
               2   TREENUMB FIXED BIN (31),
               2   SUBSTRUCT LIKE MEASREC;
           /*  XMEASREC can hold an XMEAS record, and SUBSTRUCT a MEASUREMENT
               record  */
     DCL   (BOOL,
               LOGICAL) (4) BIT (1);  /*  Logical variables  */
     ON ENDFILE (XFORFILE) LOGICAL (1) = '0'B;
     ON ENDFILE (XTREE) LOGICAL (2) = '0'B;
     ON ENDFILE (XFOREST) LOGICAL (3) = '0'B;
     ON ENDFILE (XMEAS) LOGICAL (4) = '0'B;
     OPEN FILE  (XFORFILE) INPUT,
                (XTREE) INPUT,
                (XFOREST) INPUT,
                (XMEAS) INPUT;
     LOGICAL = '1'B;  /*  All array elements contain '1'B  */
     READ FILE (XFORFILE) INTO (FORREC);
     READ FILE (XTREE) INTO (TREEREC);
     READ FILE (XFOREST) INTO (FORESREC);
     READ FILE (XMEAS) INTO (XMEASREC); MEASREC = SUBSTRUCT;
                            /*  Loading commences  */
         /*  Each execution of following main loop loads a FOR_HIER hierarchy occurrence  */
     DO WHILE (LOGICAL (1));
         INSRT (SR_FOR_HIER) FORFILE*D;  /*  Simplified syntax  */
                        /*  Root loaded for this occurrence of FOR_HIER  */
         IF TREEREC.FOREST = FORREC.FOREST THEN
         BOOL (2) = '1'B;
             /*  Next loop loads all TREE and MEASUREMENT records under FORFILE root
                 record  */
         DO WHILE (BOOL (2) & LOGICAL (2));
             INSRT (SR_FOR_HIER)   TREE;
             IF XMEASREC.TREENUMB = TREEREC.TREENUMB THEN
             BOOL (3) = '1'B;
                 /*  Next loop loads all MEASUREMENT records under previously loaded TREE
                     record  */
             DO WHILE (BOOL (3) & LOGICAL (3));
                 INSRT (SR_FOR_HIER) MEASUREM  /*  ent  */;
                 READ FILE (XMEAS) INTO (XMEASREC); MEASREC = SUBSTRUCT;
                 IF TREEREC.TREENUMB ¬ = XMEASREC.TREENUMB
                                     THEN BOOL (3) = '0'B;
                     /*  That is, all MEASUREMENT records loaded for this TREE
                         record  */
```

```
        END;
            /*  Load next TREE record   */
        READ FILE (XTREE) INTO (TREEREC);
        IF FORREC.FOREST ¬ = TREEREC.FOREST
                            THEN BOOL (2) = '0'B;
    END;
                                /*  All TREE records under this FORFILE root loaded   */
    IF FORESREC.FOREST = FORREC.FOREST THEN
    BOOL (4) = '1'B;
        /*  Next loop loads all FORESTER records under this FORFILE root record   */
    DO WHILE (BOOL (4) & LOGICAL (4));
        INSRT (SR_FOR_HIER) FORESTER;
        READ FILE (XFOREST) INTO (FORESREC);
        IF FORREC.FOREST ¬ = FORESREC.FOREST
                            THEN BOOL (4) = '0'B;
    END;
        /*  All FORESTER records under this FORFILE root record loaded   */
    READ FILE (XFORFILE) INTO (FORREC);
END;
    /*  All FOR_HIER occurrences loaded   */
END;
```

The program above is not at all robust. For example, the loading process could be effectively ruined simply by placing a TREE record (in correct sort order) that has no parent in XFORFILE in the XTREE file. However, the program does illustrate the principles involved. Another method would involve just loading FORFILE records sequentially, and then using direct access to load the remaining records.

18.3.3 Loading of Secondary Hierarchy Types

With IMS, the loading of the secondary hierarchies is a simple matter. We saw in Section 17.2.2 that the storage structures corresponding to the primary hierarchies must contain secondary (IMS: logical) pointers that permit the system to simulate the secondary hierarchies. (These secondary pointers are specified in the internal part of DBD in IMS.)

Thus, having loaded the primary hierarchies, there remains to incorporate the secondary pointers in the underlying structures. This is carried out by executing a special utility program, which is as good a method as any.

18.4 IMS UPDATING COMMANDS AND CONCURRENCY CONTROL

18.4.1 Updating with Primary Hierarchies

In this section, we briefly consider insertion, deletion, and replacement of records with an existing primary hierarchy. We illustrate these operations using IMS commands.

Insertion of Records   This is done by means of the INSRT command, as explained in Section 18.3.1.

Deletion of Records   Before a record can be deleted, it must be retrieved and the system warned of the intention to delete it. Retrieval for deletion purposes is therefore carried out by special versions of the usual GU, GN, and GNP commands. These commands are GHU (GET HOLD FIRST), GHN (GET HOLD NEXT), and GHNP (GET HOLD NEXT WITHIN PARENT); apart from the fact that they *enable* the DELETE (DLET) command, these special retrieval commands otherwise are functionally the same as the standard commands.

As an example of a deletion, let us suppose we wish to delete the record for tree 56 in forest 'XFOR'. We code

```
GHU (SR_FOR_HIER)     FORFILE (FOREST = 'XFOR')
                      TREE (TREENUMB = 56);
DLET (SR_FOR_HIER)
```

The GHU command retrieves the required TREE record and places it in the appropriate UWA structure, at the same time enabling the DLET command. The DLET command then causes the TREE record to be deleted, together with its MEASUREMENT children.

Following deletion, the deleted TREE record is still in the UWA, whence it may be rescued if the deletion was an error. The deleted MEASUREMENT records cannot be recovered.

Replacement of Records   A record may be replaced by a process of deletion followed by insertion. However, we may also use a special command, such as the REPLACE (REPL) command in IMS. As with DLET, REPL can be used only if it has been enabled by the process of retrieving the record to be replaced by means of the GHU, GHN, or GHNP commands.

As an example of its use, let us suppose we wish to replace the record for tree 56 in forest 'XFOR' by the record in the structure NEWTREE. We code

```
GHU (SR_FOR_HIER)     FORFILE (FOREST = 'XFOR')
                      TREE (TREENUMB = 56);
            /*   REPL enabled; retrieved record in structure TREEREC   */
TREEREC = NEWTREE;    /*   UWA TREE record replaced   */
REPL (SR_FOR_HIER);   /*   New TREE record placed in FOR_HIER   */
```

A restriction on the use of this command in IMS prevents the sequence field in the replacement record from being different from that of the replaced record. Thus the record in NEWTREE must also have 56 for the TREENUMB value. This means that use of a process of deletion and insertion is not necessarily technically the same as the use of the replacement command.

18.4.2 Updating Commands with Secondary Hierarchies

The use of updating commands with secondary hierarchies gives rise to great difficulties and illustrates an additional weakness of the hierarchical approach.

To get an idea of the extent of the problem, consider a user of an external hierarchy identical to the secondary hierarchy INTER_ST (see Figure 17.5a). Let us now suppose that the forest 'XFOR' is totally wiped out by a fire, so that this forest and all data connected with it are no longer of interest to the experimental forestry program. In addition, we suppose that the foresters who looked after this forest have decided to switch to a less dangerous occupation. The user would therefore want to delete the record for the forest 'XFOR' with all its subsidiaries. The immediate children of the FOREST record are the composite TREESPEC records. But it is clear that we should not want to delete the SPECFILE component of a child TREESPEC record, since in general a SPECFILE record will describe species of trees in other forests still of interest. In addition, we should like to delete (or have the system delete automatically) those FORESTER records that are children of the FORFILE record being deleted. These children are not children of FORFILE in the INTER_ST hierarchy, but rather in the FOR_HIER hierarchy. If not deleted, they will not have a parent record anyway.

In very simple terms, the problem is how to direct the system not to delete what it otherwise should (the SPECFILE part of a TREESPEC record) and to delete what it otherwise would not (FORESTER children in FOR_HIER). Similar problems arise with the other updating commands when applied to secondary hierarchies.

There are two solutions to the problem.

1. Prohibit updating and allow only retrieval with external hierarchy types that are based on secondary hierarchy types.

2. Require that special updating rules for secondary hierarchy types be specified in the conceptual schema, making the semantics of the updating commands dependent on these rules.

Here we are forced to choose between two evils. The first solution is unsatisfactory as it represents an inconvenient restriction on the freedom of the user. The second solution is also unsatisfactory because it increases the semantic complexity of the updating commands.

In IMS, the second solution is used. The updating rules are specified in the PDBs for the primary hierarchies (on which the secondary hierarchies are based). The associated details are beyond the scope of this text.

18.4.3 Concurrency Control

The concurrency control system with the hierarchical approach would be similar in principle to that used with the CODASYL approach (or the relational approach), in that there is a need for a high-level locking system for conceptual files, and a low-level locking system for individual conceptual records.

We may look briefly at concurrency control in IMS, since it is endowed with locking facilities at both levels [IBM, 1978a, 1978b; Walsh, 1980].

High-Level Locking It must be understood that IMS is equipped with its own tele-processing monitor (or data-communications facility), and as such it is IMS that loads and enables execution of application programs. IMS will enable an application program only if a file which is exclusive to this program is not also exclusive to any concurrently executing run-unit. A file may be specified as being exclusive in the external schema (to be precise, there will be specified PROCOPT = E following the corresponding (sensitive) segment type in the PCB for the hierarchy involved).

We may thus specify an exclusive lock for any file in the hierarchy, and this will ensure that there can only be one run-unit with this lock.

Low-Level Locking Consider two concurrently executing run-units, A and B, with external schemas (PCBs) which have a common file F. If A issues a GET HOLD command for a record f in F, this causes f to be retrieved and the updating commands to be enabled for use by A, as we saw in Section 18.4.1. However, the record f is also assigned a shared lock. This lock will permit B to retrieve f but not to issue a GET HOLD command for f, thus also prohibiting B from updating f.

Since the updating commands are enabled for use by A on f, if A later actually carries out an updating of f, then the record f is assigned a more secure exclusive lock. This exclusive lock is removed from f only when run-unit A has completed execution. Unfortunately, if B is waiting to update f and A runs for a long time, B will be unreasonably delayed. However, in general, a shared lock is removed from a record when its sequence key is no longer in the currency register, which in this chapter has been called C_INDI-CATOR.

It is not difficult to see that this system, like many others, can give rise to deadlock. If A has to update records f and g and B records g and f, then when A has updated f and B has updated g, the two run-units become deadlocked, assuming A must next update g and B must next update f. When this happens, IMS will cancel—for instance—B, rolling back any changes it has already made to the data base. Then A will be allowed to complete its execution, following which B will be restarted.

18.5 STATUS OF THE HIERARCHICAL APPROACH

The hierarchical approach will probably continue to be useful, especially with data bases with a basic structure that is hierarchical in nature. However, with data bases with a fundamental network structure, the disadvantages of the hierarchical approach are all too apparent; with such data bases, CODASYL-like or relational systems are likely to prove superior.

We can probably look forward to conceptually cleaner hierarchical systems based on the ANSI/SPARC proposal. Increased nonnavigational retrieval power for hierarchical retrieval sublanguages can also be expected. In this respect, it is interesting to note that in SYSTEM 2000, another widely used hierarchical system (complete with its own special terminology, of course), the retrieval sublanguage is equipped with more advanced non-navigational facilities [Tsichritzis, 1976].

EXERCISES

1. Use DL/1 to write programs to carry out essentially the same retrievals as those in the Exercises for Chapter 11 (with the exception of Exercise 3).

2. Write a DL/1 program to carry out an explosion of a part from the data base in Figure 6.16*a*.

REFERENCES

Date, C. J., 1977, *An Introduction to Data Base Management Systems,* Addison-Wesley, Reading, Mass.

IBM, 1977, *IMS/VS General Information,* Order Form GH20–1260–4.

IBM, 1978*a, CICS/VS, General Information,* Order Form GC33–0066–3.

IBM, 1978*b, IMS/VS Application Programming Reference Manual,* Order Form SH20–9026.

Kapp, D., and J. F. Leben, 1978, *IMS Programming Techniques, A Guide to Using DL/1,* D. Van Nostrand, New York.

Tsichritzis, D. C., and F. H. Lochovsky, 1976, "Hierarchical Data Base Management: A Survey," *ACM Comput. Surv.,* **8**(1):105–124.

Walsh, M., 1980, *Information Management System, Virtual Storage,* Reston Publishing Co., Reston, Va.

Data-Base Management in Perspective

19

By now the reader should understand what data bases are and how they may be built and managed. It should also be clear that while, in many cases, data bases can replace conventional storage files, the conventional storage file is not likely to disappear from the scene. Conventional storage files are necessary for processing of data prior to loading into a data base, as source files for the loading process itself, as transaction files from which a data base can be updated, as log files in which changes to a data base may be recorded, as unload files to temporarily hold a data base during periods of reorganization, and as backup files for integrity purposes. In addition, conventional storage files will continue to be used where the use of a data base would be uneconomical. For these reasons, every data-base specialist should have a thorough grounding in conventional file techniques.

It appears, then, that the future of conventional file processing is secure. In fact, it may even be safe to predict that far from being displaced by data bases, the use of data bases will most likely occasion an expansion in the amount of conventional file processing because of the intimate relationship between files and data bases as mentioned above.

This leads us to some questions that are frequently asked about data-base management.

    a.   Should an organization which has data processing based on conventional storage files switch to a data-base approach?

    b.   If a switch is advisable, which approach to data-base management should be used?

Unfortunately it is easier to pose these questions than to answer them, and the best thing to do might be to give some quick noncommittal answers and conclude the book as quickly as possible. Candidate noncommittal answers might be "maybe" for question (a) and "take your pick" for question (b). There are no general and satisfactory answers to these questions, and the questions are best posed in relation to some specific case. A specific case will, of course, require its own specific analysis, and the best we can do here is list some general considerations.

19.1 COST-BENEFIT ANALYSIS OF DATA-BASE PROCESSING

Data-base management is expensive, the least expense often being the cost of a DBMS package. Significant expenses are the cost of the data-base systems-analysis and data-base design, the cost of constructing and loading the data base, the cost of data-base administration, the cost of expanded direct-access storage to hold the data base, and the cost of a faster (or even an additional) CPU to compensate for the relatively poor performance of present data-base systems. A further significant cost may be lost productivity in the conversion stage due to increased political activity triggered by the reluctance of some user groups to give up exclusive control over certain data files.

There are costs and politics associated with every major investment project, and an investment in data-base management is no exception. But this is the main point: Conversion to a data-base approach is an investment, and all the traditional tools of investment analysis—cost-benefit analysis for all tangible and intangible costs and benefits and return on investment analysis—should be applied as far as possible. We have seen in this book that there are many benefits associated with the use of a data-base approach. Some of them, such as data independence, will reduce operating costs because of less maintenance of existing programs and fewer production programs to maintain. Other benefits, such as the absence of significant data redundancy in the data base and the use of data-base retrieval sublanguages, permit inexpensive retrieval of data that would be prohibitively expensive with conventional data processing. Such data can help an organization better adapt to a changing environment, thus increasing productivity and the return on the data-base investment. Naturally, it is not always possible to foresee all the costs and benefits, but an attempt should be made.

19.2 SYSTEM SELECTION

At the time of writing, the main choice is between CODASYL owner-coupled set-type systems and hierarchical systems; however, increased competition from relational systems can be expected as time goes on. In addition, there are many hybrid systems, each with its own array of concepts and terminology.

One thing should be clear: Both owner-coupled set-type and relational-type systems are network systems; that is, they are capable of manipulating any conceptual data base in the form of a network. While in theory hierarchical systems could use secondary hierarchies to manage any network, practical considerations limit them to hierarchical structures with only limited network aspects. Thus if the data base has a hierarchical structure, any approach can probably be used. However, if the data base has a strong network structure, the hierarchical approach must be ruled out. This brings us to the now-standard controversy between the relative merits of the owner-coupled set-type approach, particularly the CODASYL approach, and the relational approach.

Many readers, particularly if they favor the relational approach, will have noticed that the CODASYL approach is the first of the three to be introduced in this book, and is given more space. Readers should not infer from this that we favor the CODASYL approach. Both approaches have advantages and disadvantages. However, we prefer using CODASYL as a tool for introducing the subject of data-base management to students, for a very simple reason. Beginning students of data-base management can be presumed to have some knowledge and experience with conventional files. In the CODASYL approach, the user is expected to manipulate data-base files in a manner not all that different from the manipulation of conventional files. Thus with CODASYL, beginning students can more easily get a feel for data bases and their manipulation without too great a conceptual leap from a foundation in conventional file processing. Students are then in a better position to tackle and appreciate the more remote but, at least at present, more powerful relational approach.

Some readers will probably expect us to state our preference with regard to the CODASYL and relational approaches. However, we have no preferred approach at the time of writing. We are strongly in favor of the use of 4NF relational files with all approaches, for the reasons explained in Chapter 7. Furthermore, the concept of the owner-coupled set, which is central to CODASYL, is so natural and useful that we should like to see it employed *implicitly* in relational retrieval *sublanguages,* perhaps along the lines indicated in Chapter 15. Finally, we believe that the benefits of nonnavigational retrieval originating in the relational approach should gradually be incorporated in the CODASYL approach. Chapter 11 gives an example of how this may be done. In the long run, we can hope for agreement on one simple type of 4NF conceptual schema that can be manipulated by a wide variety of sublanguages catering to the wide variety of user needs.

> *"The road goes ever on and on*
> *Out from the door where it began."*
>
> J.R.R. Tolkien, in The Lord of the Rings, 1954

IBM Disk Specifications

APPENDIX 1

	IBM 3330 (1976)	IBM 3380 (1980)
Tracks per cylinder	30	15
Cylinders per drive	555	1,770
Nominal track capacity (S) in bytes	19,254	47,968
Maximum (user-data) track capacity (bytes)	19,069	47,476
Maximum (user-data) cylinder capacity (bytes)	572,070	712,140
Maximum (user-data) drive capacity (bytes)	317,498,850	1,260,487,800
Count-data factor (c) in bytes	185	480
Count-key-data factor (r) in bytes	267	704
Nominal data transmission rate (s) in bytes/sec	1,198,000	3,000,000
Rotation time (R) in msecs	16.7	16.7
Average seek time (P) in msecs	25	16
Independent read/write actuators per drive	1	2

With the IBM 3380 disk there is a modification to the rules for calculating track capacities. The formulae (1) and (2) on page 23 still apply but instead of k we must use 32($\lceil (k + 12)/32 \rceil$), and instead of B we must use 32($\lceil (B + 12)/32 \rceil$) bytes.[1] This is because the key and data subblocks must occupy a multiple of 32 bytes, and a further 12 bytes are reserved for system purposes within both the key and data subblocks.

Thus if we have a 2000-byte transmitted data block (the data subblock B) and a 10-byte key (k), the number of blocks that can be stored on a track is:

$$\lfloor 47,968/(480 + 2,016) \rfloor \quad \text{or 19 blocks, with count-data format}$$

and $\lfloor 47,968/(704 + 32 + 2,016) \rfloor$ or 17 blocks, with count-key data format.

The largest transmitted data block that can be placed on a track is 47,476 bytes long.

---

[1] *See footnote on page 136.*

CODASYL COBOL APPENDIX 2
DML Commands

The following is a list of the CODASYL COBOL versions of the PL/1 commands discussed in Chapters 9 and 10. The section numbering system corresponds to that used in the text. Although the CODASYL specifications refer to *record* names, and so on, to be consistent with the rest of the book, we continue to use *file* names. Syntax for recursive sets is also included, and for the same reason. Syntax for REALMs is omitted by assuming that a REALM can hold just one file. The CODASYL commands in this Appendix incorporate the main CODASYL specification updates to January 1981. (Note that for many commands peripheral semantic descriptions are omitted. Readers interested in the complete semantic descriptions should consult the original specifications.)

9.3.1 READY Command

1. COBOL syntax

$$\underline{READY} \left[[\textit{file-name-1}] \dots \left[\underline{USAGE\_MODE} \text{ IS } \begin{bmatrix} EXCLUSIVE \\ PROTECTED \\ SHARED \end{bmatrix} \begin{Bmatrix} RETRIEVAL \\ UPDATE \end{Bmatrix} \right] \right]$$

2. Command examples

    READY TREE MEASUREMENT
    READY TREE MEASUREMENT USAGE MODE IS RETRIEVAL
    READY

3. Semantics

    a. All files (and owner-coupled sets based on them) that are specified in the command are made available for manipulation. Default value (READY only) is all subschema files and sets.

b. If RETRIEVAL is specified, then only DML commands that cause data to be retrieved from the data base, such as FIND and GET, may be used.

c. If UPDATE is specified, then all other DML commands may be used in addition.

d. If the USAGE MODE clause is omitted, the default is RETRIEVAL.

e. Use of EXCLUSIVE, PROTECTED, and SHARE options is explained in Section 10.4.

4. Remarks
CODASYL REALMs have been omitted by assuming that a REALM can hold only one file.

9.3.2 Record Key FIND Command—First Version (JOD Format 2)

(With all FIND commands, if the word FIND is replaced by FETCH, the record retrieved is in addition placed in the UWA.)

1. COBOL syntax

   FIND ANY *file-name* USING *key-name-1*

2. Command examples

   FIND ANY TREE USING TREENUMB
   FIND ANY SPECFILE USING SPECIES

3. Semantics

   a. The record retrieved becomes the CRU, the current of file, for the file involved and the current of set for all sets in which it participates.

   b. The record does *not* become available in the UWA.

   c. *Key-name-1* is a record or secondary key declared in the subschema; its value is obtainable from the corresponding UWA data item.

   d. If duplicate key values can occur for the key used, then the system retrieves the first record with the specified key value, in the order specified in the subschema for retrieval with that type of key. To retrieve the remaining records with that duplicate key value, the second version of the record key FIND command must be used.

9.3.3 Record Key FIND Command—Second Version

1. COBOL syntax

   FIND DUPLICATE *file-name* USING *key-name-1*

2. Command example

   FIND DUPLICATE TREE USING LOC

3. Semantics

a. Semantic Rules 1, 2, and 3 for the first version also apply to the second version.

b. The key used with the command does not have to be specified as allowing duplicate values to occur.

c. On execution of the command, the DBCS first checks the CRU. If the record type and key value of the CRU match that of the record to be retrieved, then the file is accessed and the *next* record in the file with a duplicate key value is retrieved. *Next* is in the order specified in the subschema for records with duplicate values of that type of key. If the record type or key value do not match that of the CRU, then the file is accessed and the system retrieves the first record with the specified key value, in the order specified in the subschema for retrieval with that type of key.

9.3.4 The GET Command

1. COBOL syntax

   GET *identifier-1* [, *identifier-2*] ...

2. Command examples

   GET TREEREC
   GET TREEREC.PLANTED
   GET TREEREC.PLANTED, TREEREC.FOREST

3. Semantics

   a. The identifier must identify either the record or a field of the record presently the CRU.

   b. The record or data items so identified are assigned to the corresponding UWA structure or variables, respectively.

9.3.5 The CONNECT Command

1. Syntax

   CONNECT [*file-name*] TO $\left\{ \begin{array}{l} \textit{set-name-1}\ [,\ \textit{set-name-2}]\ ... \\ \text{ALL} \end{array} \right\}$.

2. Command examples

   CONNECT TREE TO FOR_TREE
   CONNECT TO FOR_TREE
   CONNECT TREE TO ALL

3. Semantics

   a. The record to be connected is the current record of the file specified, otherwise it is the CRU.

   b. If a set name is specified, it must be a set that has been specified in the subschema.

   c. If ALL is specified, the connection operation will be attempted on all such sets for which the CRU record is a potential member.

---

d.   For each set involved, the record is coupled to the current-of-set occurrence, in accordance with the ordering criteria for the records of the set.

e.   For each set to which the record is coupled, the record becomes the current of set. It also becomes the CRU. Other currency indicators are not updated.

f.   For recursive sets, see the proposal in Section 9.5.2.

9.3.6 The STORE Command

1.   Syntax

STORE *file-name*

2.   Semantics

a.   The command stores in the specified file, the record available in the corresponding UWA structure.

b.   The record is stored consistent with the record and secondary record keys specified in the subschema. These key values should be available in the UWA structure.

c.   The command also couples the UWA record to all **AUTOMATIC** sets for which it can be a member.

d.   The set occurrences of these **AUTOMATIC** sets are selected on the basis of the **SET SELECTION** specifications in the subschema.

e.   UWA data items or variables required by the DBCS in following a **SET SELECTION** specification should be initialized.

f.   Following successful execution of a **STORE** command, the record stored becomes the current of run-unit, current of the file in which it was stored, and current of all sets to which it was coupled.

9.5.3 The RETAINING Clause

1.   COBOL syntax

$$\text{RETAINING} \left[\left\{ \begin{array}{c} \underline{\text{RECORD}} \\ \textit{set-name-1} \ \{\textit{set-name-2}\} \ \dots \end{array} \right\} \right] \underline{\text{CURRENCY}}$$

2.   Semantics

If **RETAINING CURRENCY** is specified, just the CRU is updated, otherwise rules (b) and (c) of the PL/1 version apply.

10.1.2 Sequential FIND Command (JOD Format 1)

1.   COBOL syntax

$$\underline{\text{FIND}} \left\{ \begin{array}{c} \underline{\text{FIRST}} \\ \underline{\text{NEXT}} \end{array} \right\} \textit{file-name} \left[\left\{ \underline{\text{USING}} \ \textit{identifier-1} \right\} [, \textit{identifier-2}] \ \dots \right]$$

2. Command examples

FIND FIRST TREE
FIND NEXT TREE USING PLANTED, LOC

3. Semantics

a. When FIRST is specified, the first record in the specified file is retrieved in record-key order. If USING is also specified, the first record in record-key order which satisfies the target conditions is retrieved.

b. Target conditions are specified by the identifier values in the USING clause. A record satisfies the target conditions when for each USING clause identifier the corresponding record field has a matching value.

c. When NEXT is specified, the next record in record-key sequence following the current of file is retrieved. If USING is also specified, it is the next record following the current of file and satisfying the target conditions that is retrieved.

d. The record retrieved becomes the CRU, the current of file and also the current of set for all sets in which it participates.

10.1.3 Data-Base Key-Order FIND Command (JOD Format 4)

1. COBOL syntax

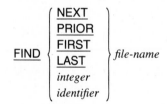

2. Command examples

FIND LAST TREE
FIND N TREE
FIND FIRST TREE

3. Semantics

a. The record is retrieved from the file specified and becomes the CRU, the current of file, and the current of set for all sets in which it participates.

b. The records in the file may be considered to be available in ascending or descending data-base key order.

c. Specification of FIRST or LAST, respectively, retrieves the first or last of the records from the file specified.

d. If n is the value of *integer* or if n is the value of the program variable specified by *identifier,* then the nth record is retrieved. With negative n, we process backwards through the file.

CODASYL COBOL DML COMMAND

e. If the current of file record was the *n*th, specification of NEXT or PRIOR in the command causes the $(n + 1)$th or $(n - 1)$th record to be retrieved, respectively.

4. Remarks
    CODASYL REALMs are omitted by assuming that a REALM can hold only one file.

10.1.4 Record-Key FIND Command (JOD Format 2)

This is the workhorse FIND command introduced in Section 9.3.2. We mention it here for the sake of completeness.

10.1.5 Controlled Set-Scan FIND Command (JOD Format 4)

1. COBOL syntax

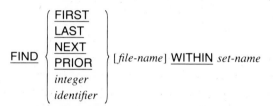

$$\text{FIND} \left\{ \begin{array}{l} \underline{\text{FIRST}} \\ \underline{\text{LAST}} \\ \underline{\text{NEXT}} \\ \underline{\text{PRIOR}} \\ integer \\ identifier \end{array} \right\} [\textit{file-name}] \ \underline{\text{WITHIN}} \ set\text{-}name$$

2. Command examples

    FIND FIRST TREE WITHIN FOR_TREE
    FIND LAST WITHIN TREE_MEAS

3. Semantics

    a. The record is retrieved from the file specified and becomes CRU, current of file, and the current of set for all sets in which it participates.

    b. The records of a set occurrence for the set specified are retrieved in the order specified for member records in the subschema set specification.

    c. The set occurrence selected is the current of set for the set specified.

    d. FIRST retrieves the first member record and LAST retrieves the last member record.

    e. If *n* is the value of *integer* or if *n* is the value of the program variable specified by *identifier*, then the *n*th record in the set occurrence is retrieved. If *n* is negative, the order of retrieval is from last to first.

    f. If the current-of-set record is the *n*th, specification of NEXT or PRIOR retrieves the $(n + 1)$th or $(n - 1)$th member of the set occurrence, respectively.

Recursive Sets and the Controlled Set-Scan FIND Command   We have the problem that there is one current record of set (CRS) for a recursive set, but two current occurrences of set. The two current occurrences are the one for which the CRS is the owner (which we refer to as CS_OWN) and the one for which the CRS is a member (which we refer to as CS_MEM).

The solution is to be able to specify in the command precisely to which of the two possible set occurrences we refer, and this may be accomplished by inserting CS_OWN or CS_MEM in the FIND command.

1. COBOL syntax

$$\text{FIND} \left\{ \begin{array}{l} \underline{\text{FIRST}} \\ \underline{\text{LAST}} \\ \vdots \end{array} \right\} \textit{file-name} \underline{\text{WITHIN}} \left[\begin{array}{l} \text{CS\_OWN} \\ \text{CS\_MEM} \end{array} \right] \textit{set-name}$$

2. Command examples

   FIND FIRST WITHIN CS_OWN PROPAGATE
   FIND N TREE WITHIN CS_MEM PROPAGATE

3. Semantics
   The semantics are the same as the PL/1 version.

10.1.6 Set-Scan Target FIND Command (JOD Format 7)

To handle recursive sets, we propose that CS_OWN and CS_MEM be used as indicated below.

1. COBOL syntax

   $$\underline{\text{FIND}} \textit{ file-name } \underline{\text{WITHIN}} \textit{ set-name} \left[\begin{array}{l} \underline{\text{CURRENT}} \\ \text{CS\_OWN} \\ \text{CS\_MEM} \end{array} \right]$$

   $$\left[\underline{\text{USING}} \textit{ identifier-1 } [, \textit{ identifier-2}] \dots \right]$$

2. Command examples

   a. Nonrecursive set

      FIND TREE WITHIN FOR_TREE CURRENT USING PLANTED, LOC
      FIND MEASUREMENT WITHIN TREE_MEAS CURRENT USING TYPE

   b. Recursive set

      FIND TREE WITHIN PROPAGATE CS_OWN USING PLANTED

3. Semantics (nonrecursive set)

   a. The set occurrence is selected by means of the current record of set for the set specified.

   b. The record retrieved becomes the CRU, the current of file for the file specified, and the current of set for all sets in which it participates.

   c. The member records of the selected set occurrences are scanned in the order specified for member records in the subschema set specification until the first member record satisfying the using specifications is found. In all cases, the scan starts with the first member record of the set occurrence.

---

4. Semantics (recursive set)

    a. Rules b and c for nonrecursive sets still hold.

    b. If CS_OWN is specified, the set occurrence selected has the CRS as its owner. If CS_MEM is specified, the set occurrence selected has the CRS as a member. If neither is specified, CS_MEM is assumed by default.

10.1.7 Set-Scan Duplicate Target FIND Command (JOD Format 3)

To handle recursive sets, we propose that CS_OWN and CS_MEM be used as indicated below.

1. COBOL syntax

$$\text{\underline{FIND DUPLICATE WITHIN}} \quad \left[\begin{array}{c} \text{\underline{CS\_OWN}} \\ \text{\underline{CS\_MEM}} \end{array} \right] \quad \textit{set-name}$$

$$\text{\underline{USING}} \quad \textit{identifier-1} \, [, \, \textit{identifier-2}] \, \ldots$$

2. Command examples

```
FIND DUPLICATE WITHIN TREE_MEAS USING TYPE
FIND DUPLICATE WITHIN CS_OWN PROPAGATE USING PLANTED
```

3. Semantics

    a. The search is carried out in the order specified for member records in the subschema set specification for the set specified.

    b. The search starts at the member record following the record which is the current of set. However, if the current of set is the owner, the search starts at the first member record.

    c. As with the previous command, the USING subclause defines the target record.

    d. The set occurrence selected by means of the current of set; if the set is recursive, the CS_OWN/CS_MEM specification pinpoints which set occurrence is to be used. The default value is CS_MEM.

    e. The record retrieved becomes the CRU, and so on.

10.1.8 Owner FIND Command (JOD Format 6)

For recursive sets, we propose that CS_OWN and CS_MEM be used.

1. COBOL syntax

$$\text{\underline{FIND} \underline{OWNER} \underline{WITHIN}} \quad \left[\begin{array}{c} \text{\underline{CS\_OWN}} \\ \text{\underline{CS\_MEM}} \end{array} \right] \quad \textit{set-name}$$

2. Command examples

```
FIND OWNER WITHIN TREE_MEAS
FIND OWNER WITHIN CS_MEM PROPAGATE
```

3. Semantics

    a. The set occurrence is selected by means of the current of set for the set specified.

    b. For recursive sets, the proper set occurrence is specified using **CS_OWN** or **CS_ MEM**, with the usual meaning. The default value is **CS_MEM**.

    c. The owner record of the set specified becomes the CRU, and so on.

10.1.10 The KEEP Command

The keep command permits a data-base key value corresponding to a currency indicator to be assigned to a keep-list.

1. COBOL syntax

    <u>KEEP</u> [*data-base-key-identifier*] <u>USING</u> *keep-list-name*

2. Command examples

    KEEP USING TREEKEEP
    KEEP TREE USING TREEKEEP   /*   We assume that TREEKEEP has been declared in the external schema as a keep-list. */

3. Semantics

    a. The data-base key is placed at the end of the list of keys in the specified keep-list.

    b. If *data-base-key-identifier* is omitted, then the data-base key assigned is that of the CRU currency indicator.

    c. When *data-base-key-identifier* denotes a file or set, then the data-base key from the corresponding currency indicator is assigned to the keep-list.

10.1.11 The Currency FIND Command (JOD Format 5)

1. COBOL syntax

    <u>FIND</u> *data-base-key-identifier*

2. Command examples

    FIND TREE   /* File name */
    FIND PROPAGATE   /* Set name */
    FIND TREEKEEP   /* Keep-list name */

3. Semantics

    a. The record retrieved becomes the CRU, the current of file and the current of set for all sets in which it participates.

    b. When a file name or a set name is denoted by *data-base-key-identifier*, the record referenced by the data-base key of the corresponding currency indicator is retrieved.

    c. When a keep-list is denoted by *data-base-key-identifier*, the record referenced by the first data-base key in the keep-list is retrieved.

10.2.2 The MODIFY Command

1. COBOL syntax

   MODIFY [*identifier 1*] ...

2. Command examples

   MODIFY TREE
   MODIFY FOREST, PLANTED

3. Semantics

   a. The record being updated is the current record of either the file directly specified or the file whose fields are directly specified, otherwise it is the CRU.

   b. The fields specified by the identifiers are updated using the corresponding UWA values. When no fields are specified, all the fields of the target record are updated using the UWA field values.

   c. If an updated field is either a set-sort key or a secondary or order key, the record is repositioned in either its set occurrence or its file, respectively.

   d. If an updated field is a member-connection field in a value-based set, then the record's set-occurrence membership is updated consistent with the new connection-field value and set-ordering criteria. However, whenever the set involved has retention class FIXED, then a request to update the connection field will be rejected.

   e. The execution of a MODIFY makes the record modified the CRU, and

   (1) if the current-of-set indicator points to the record being modified, it will be set to null whenever a record's position in or membership of a set occurrence of that set is updated; and

   (2) if the current-of-file indicator points to the record being modified, it will be set to null whenever a record's position in the file is changed because an order key is updated.

10.2.3 The RECONNECT Command

1. COBOL syntax

   RECONNECT [*file-name*] WITHIN *set-name-1* [,*set-name-2*] ...

2. Command examples

   RECONNECT WITHIN TREE_MEAS
   RECONNECT MEASUREMENT WITHIN TREE_MEAS

3. Semantics
   They are the same as the PL/1 version, except that the record affected is the current of the file specified, otherwise it is the CRU.

10.2.4 The DISCONNECT Command

1. COBOL syntax

$$\underline{\text{DISCONNECT}} \ [\textit{file-name}] \ \underline{\text{FROM}} \quad \left\{ \begin{array}{l} \textit{set-name-1} \ [, \ \textit{set-name-2}] \ \dots \\ \underline{\text{ALL}} \end{array} \right\}$$

2. Command examples

   DISCONNECT TREE FROM FOR_TREE
   DISCONNECT FROM ALL

3. Semantics

   a. The record to be uncoupled is the current of the file specified, otherwise it is the CRU.

   b. The sets from which the record is to be uncoupled are specified using the set-name identifiers. If ALL is specified, the record is to be uncoupled from all sets for which it is a member record.

   c. For a set so specified, the set occurrence required is identified by the CRU. For recursive sets, the CRU points to two set occurrences, and we propose that the one used be that for which the CRU is a member record.

   d. A record can be uncoupled only from a set which has the OPTIONAL retention class.

   e. Following the execution of the command, the record uncoupled becomes the CRU, and for each set from which the record has been uncoupled, the current-of-set indicator is set to null if it identified the record uncoupled.

10.2.5 The ERASE Command

1. COBOL syntax

   ERASE [ALL] [\textit{file-name}]

2. Semantics
   They are the same as the PL/1 version, except that the record affected (the object record) is the current of the file specified, otherwise it is the CRU.

System R
Prototype
Specifics

APPENDIX 3

As stated in Chapter 13, IBM's System R prototype is an important example of a comprehensive relational data base system. Many of the principles on which its design is based have been described in PART 2 of the text, additional details being presented here for the sake of completeness. Readers should bear in mind that System R is currently a prototype and not a product, and that the material presented here may well be significantly affected by the evolution of the system from prototype to product status. System R currently runs under OS/MVS (see Chapter 1) and VM/CMS (a related operating system); it was first constructed under VM/CMS.

A3.1 SYSTEM ARCHITECTURE

To illustrate the architecture of the system we will make use of a simple data base consisting of the relations FORFILE and TREE from the FORESTRY data base in Figure 13.2. This conceptual data base is illustrated in Figure A3.1a; the attributes are the same as those in Figure 13.2, except that obvious abbreviations are used. We are also free to make use of more conventional terminology, since strict relational terms (Chapter 13) appear to be little used with System R. Thus we may use the terms *(relational) file* or *table* for *relation,* and *field* or *column* for *attribute.*

A3.1.1 A System R Data Base

A System R data base conforms reasonably well to the ANSI/SPARC 3-level architecture, and consists of storage, conceptual and various external data bases as illustrated in Figure A3.2 for the data base from Figure A3.1a. The conceptual relational files are referred to

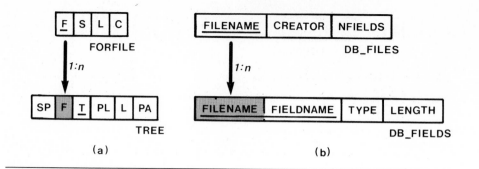

Figure A3.1 *Extended Bachman diagram showing (a) part of the FORESTRY data base from Figure 8.2, and (b) part of the System R data dictionary. The equivalent of the ANSI/SPARC conceptual and external schema descriptions are stored in the data dictionary, which is available to users for retrieval of information about the data base.*

as *base tables,* and at the internal level there is exactly one storage file for each base table at the conceptual level. At the internal level there may also be a set of indexes on any field or composite field from a base table. For non key fields, these indexes are the same as inversions (see Chapter 5). In addition, storage files may be connected by *links,* which in effect are parent-to-child and child-to-next-child pointers (as is possible in CODASYL internal data bases, see Figure 12.3a). We note here that the concept of a key is not used explicitly in System R.

An external file may be a base table, or it may be a projection of a base table (see Chapter 16), or it may be derived from more than one base table (Section 16.4.3). If an external file is not a base table, then it is known as a *view.* Thus in Figure 2, V1 is a view equivalent to a projection of FORFILE, V2 is a view equivalent to a retrieval on FORFILE and TREE, but FORFILE is strictly speaking not a view since it is a base table. As we will see, all views are defined by means of SQL expressions.

In System R the definitions of the equivalent of the ANSI/SPARC conceptual and external schemas are stored in the *data dictionary* (Section 6.4.4). The data dictionary is part of the data base. It consists of a collection of related base tables, two of which are shown in Figure A3.1b. As with the other base tables, there is a storage file for each data dictionary base table. In addition, a user may employ SQL to extract data from views defined on the dictionary base tables. (The names used with that part of the data dictionary shown in Figure A3.1b are not those used with System R.) The relational file DB_FILES has a record for each conceptual file in the data base, the name of a file being the key. Other fields in a DB_FILES record contain information about the creator of the file described and the number of fields it contains. The relational file DB_FIELDS has a record for every field in every file in the data base, the name of a field and the file containing it serving as a key. Other fields in a DB_FIELDS record are the data type of the field described and its length in bytes. There is clearly a 1:n relationship between records in DB_FILES and DB_FIELDS.

We note that since the System R data dictionary is available to users for manipulation by means of SQL commands, System R may be said to include a data dictionary facility

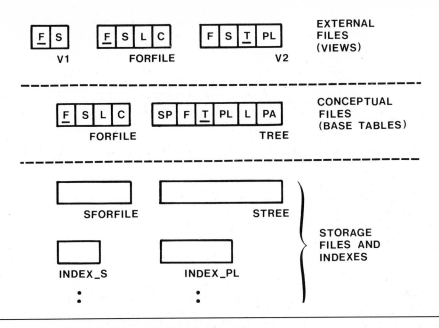

EXTERNAL
FILES
(VIEWS)

CONCEPTUAL
FILES
(BASE TABLES)

STORAGE
FILES AND
INDEXES

Figure A3.2 *The data base from Figure A3.1a shown here as a 3-level System R data base. The external files are chosen arbitrarily. A similar 3 levels for the data dictionary from Figure A3.1b is not shown. The data dictionary is considered to be part of a System R data base.*

as described in section 6.4.4. However, since the equivalent of ANSI/SPARC schemas are stored in the data dictionary, updates to the dictionary would require authorization from the data base administrator.

A3.1.2 Overview of the System R Data Base Management System

The essential software components of System R are the Relational Data (Base) System (the RD System) and the Research Software System (the RS System). The RD System is roughly equivalent to the DBCS of Chapter 6, and can carry out commands passed to it by either an applications program or terminal control system (Figure A3.3). One terminal control system for interactive use of System R is the User Friendly System (the UF System). The set of commands acceptable to the RD System together with the objects of these commands is referred to as the RD Interface. (In like manner we could have referred to the CODASYL DML commands and their objects in Chapters 9 and 10 as the CODA-SYL Interface.)

The RD System passes commands in turn to the RS System (although not quite directly as we shall see). The RS System is responsible for accessing the data base, and may thus be regarded as a data base access method. However individual storage files are accessed by means of the standard operating system file access methods. The very high level commands acceptable to the RS System and the objects of these commands are referred to as the RS Interface. The RS Interface thus functions as a target language for

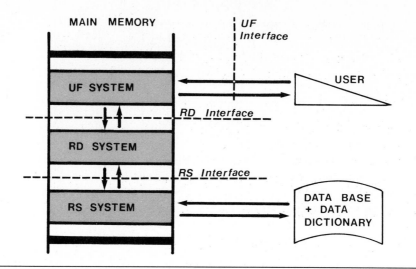

MAIN MEMORY

UF Interface

UF SYSTEM

USER

RD Interface

RD SYSTEM

RS Interface

RS SYSTEM

DATA BASE + DATA DICTIONARY

Figure A3.3. *Overview of the major components of System R in an interactive environment. Additional details are shown in Figure A3.4. A user may issue both SQL DDL commands to define the equivalent of the ANSI/SPARC schemas, and SQL DML commands to manipulate the data base. The UF System is the terminal control system, the RD System is roughly equivalent to a Data Base Control System, and the RS System is a data base access method.*

reduction of SQL commands. Finally the interface that the UF System presents to a terminal user, the UF Interface, is the SQL DDL and DML (together with some additional commands for display management).

A3.1.3 Defining a System R Data Base

In System R the Data Definition Language (DDL) for defining schema equivalents, and the Data Manipulation Language (DML) for manipulating a data base, are both considered to be part of System R SQL. However since SQL is an acronym for Structured *Query* Language, this can give rise to confusion and we find it convenient to distinguish between the SQL DDL and SQL DML. We now illustrate some important SQL DDL commands.

We will assume that a data base will most frequently be defined in the interactive mode, so that in what follows the reader might bear Figure A3.3 in mind. To define a conceptual schema for the data base in Figure 1a, we use CREATE TABLE commands:

```
CREATE TABLE     FORFILE     (F        (CHAR(15), NONULL),
                              S        (INTEGER),
                              L        (CHAR(10)),
                              C        (CHAR(20))   )
```

```
CREATE TABLE    TREE    (SP        (CHAR(20), NONULL),
                         F         (CHAR(15), NONULL),
                         T         (INTEGER, NONULL),
                         PL        (INTEGER),
                         L         (INTEGER),
                         PA        (INTEGER)   )
```

As a result of these commands suitable entries will be made in the data dictionary, and space allocated for the storage versions of FORFILE and TREE. Note that we have not specified keys. However we have stated that the key fields FORFILE.F and TREE.T may not have null values. Keys are not a feature of System R, and even the uniqueness of a key field can only be specified using an indirect method involving index specifications for storage files (described next). Furthermore domain specifications are not a feature of System R, and a user may equate any pair of fields with compatible data types, so that the system will accept nonsensical requests.

Indexes may be defined at the internal level by means of CREATE INDEX commands:

```
CREATE UNIQUE INDEX INDEX_T ON TREE (T)
CREATE INDEX INDEX_PL ON TREE (PL)
```

In the first command we use the UNIQUE option to define an index on the key field T in the base table TREE. The index is to be called INDEX_T and UNIQUE ensures that there is only one TREE record with a given value of T. If UNIQUE were omitted for all indexes on TREE fields (or composite fields) then duplicate conceptual records would be a possibility, so that TREE would not be a relation. Thus a System R data base is not necessarily relational in the strict sense of the term. In the second command above we create an index called INDEX_PL on the field PL in the TREE file. Since duplicate PL values may occur in TREE, INDEX_PL is in fact an inversion of TREE on the field PL. Execution of a CREATE INDEX command causes the definition of the index to be stored in a RS System *directory*, not the data dictionary.

A view may be defined my means of a DEFINE VIEW command:

```
DEFINE VIEW V2 (F, S, T, PL)
    AS   SELECT F, S, T, PL FROM FORFILE, TREE
         WHERE FORFILE.F = TREE.F
```

This causes the definition of the view V2 (see Figure A3.2) to be stored in the data dictionary. Note that the retrieval expressed by the SELECT expression is not actually carried out at this point; the expression is merely used by the RD System in manipulations of the data base based on the view V2. Any SQL SELECT expression may be used following AS to define a view. This means that it is also possible to use one view to define another.

A3.1.4. Alterations to a Data Base Definition

At any time following the definition of a System R data base, it is possible to employ the SQL DDL commands described in the previous section to define new base tables, new indexes, and additional views. However we may also use the DROP command at any time to eliminate base tables, indexes, or views. Thus:

```
DROP TABLE FORFILE
DROP INDEX INDEX-PL
DROP VIEW V1
```

The first command not only causes the removal of the FORFILE definitions from the data dictionary, it also causes the deletion of the storage file for FORFILE and associated indexes. Similarly the second command causes deletion of RS System directory entries concerning INDEX_PL together with the deletion of the actual index. The last command causes deletion of dictionary entries for the view V1.

A further possibility is the addition of one or more new column definitions to the dictionary entries for a base table, for example the definition of the additional field X for the base table FORFILE. We use an EXPAND TABLE command as follows:

```
EXPAND TABLE FORFILE
            ADD FIELD X (INTEGER)
```

Note that the word FIELD rather than COLUMN or ATTRIBUTE is used in this command. This command does not cause data to be placed in the new column X in the data base. This must be done using SQL DML commands.

The fact that a user (with proper authorization) may alter the definition of a System R data base at any time is a novel feature. SQL DDL commands to alter a definition may be issued not only at any point during a terminal session but also at any point within an application program manipulating the data base by means of SQL DML statements. Thus a quite flexible equivalent of the Performance Control Language mentioned in Section 12.3.3 has been incorporated into System R in a user-friendly manner.

A3.2. MANIPULATION OF A SYSTEM R DATA BASE

It is convenient to distinguish between interactive manipulation of a System R data base, and manipulation by means of an application program. We take interactive manipulation first.

A3.2.1 Interactive manipulation of a System R Data Base

In a typical terminal session a user passes SQL DML commands to the UF System. Each SQL command is executed as it is received and the results returned to the user via the UF System. To understand how such an SQL command is executed consider Figure A3.4.

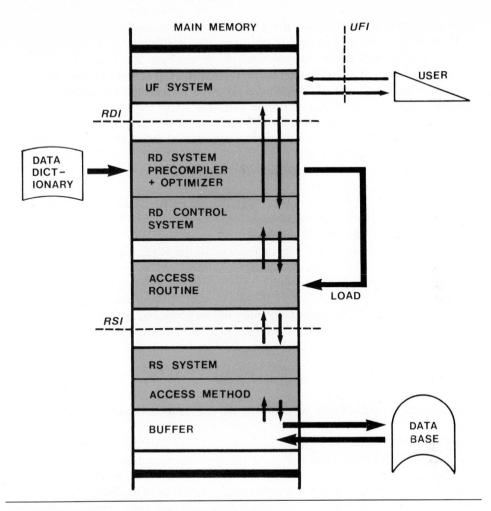

Figure A3.4 *Interactive manipulation of a System R data base via SQL commands. The RD System from Figure A3.3 has two main components, namely a precompiler and the actual data base control system. An SQL command received at the RD Interface (RDI) is converted to an access routine by the precompiler and loaded and executed by the RD control system. The access routine contains calls to the RS System.*

The most important point is that the RD System has in fact two major components, namely a precompiler, and a run-time control system that is reasonably close to the DBCS from Chapter 6. Following receipt of an SQL command, the UF System passes the equivalent of the command to the RD System. The RD System precompiler translates the command into a procedure that manipulates the data base by means of calls to the RS System. This procedure (or *access routine*) has been optimized by the precompiler's optimizer (see Section 16.2). The procedure is then loaded, and executed under the control of the RD control system. The RS System carries out the fairly high level commands passed to it from the access routine, making use of a standard operating system access method to access individual storage files and indexes.

The System R SQL retrieval language is the same as that described in Chapter 15, and Section 16.4.1 but with some additional peripheral capabilities. An UPDATE command consists of a retrieval part and an update part. The retrieval part identifies a record or records to be updated by means of an SQL predicate, while the update part specifies the updating to be carried out. (In Section 16.3, separate commands are used for the two parts.) Thus to increase by 1,000 acres this size of California forests containing spruce trees we could issue the SQL command.

```
UPDATE FORFILE
SET S = S + 1000   /*   End of update part   */
WHERE L = 'CALIFORNIA' AND F IS IN
      (SELECT F FROM TREE
      WHERE
      SP = 'SPRUCE')   /*   End of SQL predicate   */
```

Similarily a DELETE command consists of two parts, one to identify records to be deleted, and one to carry out a deletion. Thus to delete all elm trees we could code:

```
DELETE TREE   /*   Delete part   */
WHERE SP = 'ELM'   /*   SQL predicate   */
```

To store a new record in forfile we could use the insertion command:

```
INSERT INTO FORFILE:
<'ZFOR', 500, 'OREGON' 'XCO'>
```

Note that the update, delete, and insert commands are normally applied to the *base tables*, and may be applied to *views* only when underlying base table records are unambiguously identified.

A3.2.2 Manipulation from an Applications Program

An application program may contain many SQL DML commands. If these commands were converted to access routines by the precompiler at run time, then the application program would run very slowly. It is more sensible, especially if application program is to be run repeatedly in a production environment, to convert the SQL commands to access routines at compile time. Thus the SQL commands are translated only once, no matter how often a program runs. This is the method used in System R, and is outlined in Figures A3.5 and A3.6.

Consider Figure A3.5 first. PL/1 source program is first processed by the RD System precompiler. The precompiler makes use of the data dictionary to produce an access routine for each SQL command in the program, together with a new version of the PL/1 source program. This new version contains a call to the RD System (called XRDI) for each

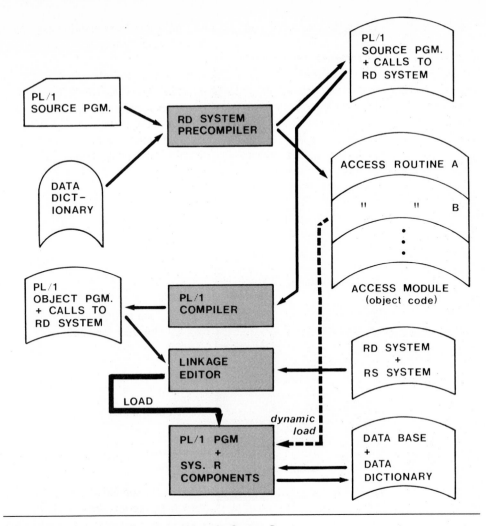

Figure A3.5 *Preparation for manipulation of a System R data base by means of a PL/1 program. For each System R command in the source program, the precompiler inserts a call to the RD System and constructs an access routine. The access module containing these access routines is later loaded for execution at run time (see Figure A3.6).*

SQL command. The new PL/1 source program is then compiled by the PL/1 compiler, and the resulting object program then linked to the RD and RS systems for loading and execution.

What happens at execution time is illustrated in Figure A3.6. Suppose that the precompiler had produced an access routine **A** for a given SQL command (the collection of access routines for the SQL commands in the program is called an *access module* and is not initially loaded for execution). At the point in the application program where the given SQL command is to be executed, the PL/1 program calls the RD System (by means of a

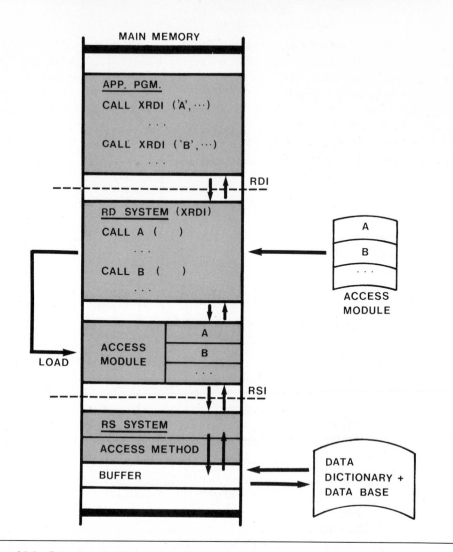

Figure A3.6 *Execution of a PL/1 program that manipulates a System R data base. The program contains calls to the RD System which reads in and dynamically loads the access module prepared by the precompiler at compile time. The access routines of the access module call the RS System under RD System control.*

call to the routine XRDI) informing it about the need to use the access routine A. The RD System then loads the Access Module, enabling the access routine A to be executed under RD System control. The access routine then issues calls to the RS system as described in the previous section

We conclude with a description of how SQL commands may be embedded in a PL/1 program, similar techniques being used with COBOL. Within a PL/1 program, the first data base command must be $BEGIN TRANSACTION, and the last data base command must be $END TRANSACTION. If the program terminates without an $END TRANSAC-TION command, all changes to the data base since the $BEGIN TRANSACTION command are cancelled. Furthermore, System R commands must be prefixed by a '$' to permit their identification by the precompiler.

Field names defined in the data dictionary for base tables and views cannot be referenced in a PL/1 program. Instead variables equivalent to the variables of a User Working Area (see Chapters 6, 9, and 18) must be used. Suppose X is such a UWA variable. Its *declaration* must be prefixed by a '$', it may be referenced in a PL/1 program as X, but it must be referenced in a $SQL expression as $X. This is illustrated in the program that follows. Finally there is a status variable called SYR_CODE which is part of a structure variable SYR. A status code is returned to SYR_CODE following execution of a $SQL command. It is not necessary to give the full declaration for SYR, since the statement $SYR causes the precompiler to incorporate the necessary expansion. We now give an example involving updating, deletion and insertion with the base table FORFILE. Note that *User Working Area* is not a System R term.

```
SQ1: PROC OPTIONS (MAIN);
           /*   User Working Area   */
$DCL FOREST CHAR (15);
$DCL SIZE FIXED BIN (31);
$DCL LOC CHAR (10);
$DCL C CHAR (20);   /*   C is not an error; note all UWA types match types in data dictionary
                          (Section A3.1)   */
           /*   End of UWA   */
$SYR;   /*   Expanded by precompiler to include SYR_CODE declaration   */
$BEGIN TRANSACTION;

GET LIST (SIZE, LOC);   /*   Assume values 1000, 'OREGON' read in   */
$UPDATE FORFILE
SET S = S + $SIZE
WHERE L = $LOC AND C = 'XCO';   /*   Size of Xco forests in Oregon increased   */
IF SYR_CODE ¬= 'OK' THEN CALL ERROR_ PROC;   /*   Prints error message   */

GET LIST (C);   /*   Assume value 'ZCO' read in   */
DELETE FORFILE WHERE C = $C;   /*   All Zco forest records deleted   */
IF SYR_CODE ¬= 'OK' THEN CALL ERROR_PROC;

GET LIST (FOREST, SIZE, LOC);   /*   Part of the new record read into UWA   */
INSERT IN FORFILE (F, S, L):
    ⟨$FOREST, $SIZE, $LOC⟩;   /*   Record with null C value stored   */

$END TRANSACTION;
END;
```

We note that an example of a $SQL retrieval is not included in the above program. It could only be inserted as a conventional SQL expression (with '$' modifications) provided that

---

only one record was certain to be retrieved. An example using the UWA from the program above might be:

```
$SELECT F, L, C
INTO $FOREST, $LOC, $C
FROM FORFILE WHERE L = 'GREENLAND';
PUT SKIP LIST (FOREST, LOC, C);
```

Here we are assuming that Greenland has only one forest. Note that the retrieved fields are placed in the UWA variables following INTO.

However normally a $SQL command will retrieve many records, which may only be dealt with by an artifice (or object) referred to as a *cursor*. For the user it would be most convenient if a $SQL retrieval command simply placed the retrieved records in a UWA structural array. Another reasonably convenient device would have been to allow for a $SELECT NEXT command to place the next record satisfying the retrieval conditions in the UWA variables (in a manner similar to the EOS CODASYL Enhancement in Chapter 11). Instead a $SQL command can be imagined to place the records in a buffer, which can be accessed record at a time, but only by means of a cursor which must be *declared*, *opened* and *closed*. The following program to print out some retrieved records illustrates the mechanism. The facility is clearly in need of improvement.

```
SQ2: PROC OPTIONS (MAIN);
        /*   UWA   */
$DCL FOREST CHAR (15);
$DCL SIZE FIXED BIN (31);   /*   End of UWA   */
DCL BEORR BIT (1) INIT ('1'B);   /*   Before End of Retrieved Relation   */
$SYR;   /*   Expanded by precompiler to include SYR_CODE declaration   */
        /*   We now declare a cursor arbitrarily named CURS   */
$LET CURS BE (SELECT F, S
                INTO $FOREST, $SIZE
                FROM FORFILE WHERE L = 'OREGON');
    /*   The above is a declaration, not a command. CURS can point to one of the records
    specified in the SELECT (without a '$') expression   */

$BEGIN TRANSACTION;   /*   Ready for processing   */
$OPEN CURS;   /*   Cursor activated   */
$FETCH CURS;   /*   First time used, CURS identifies first record specified in the SELECT
                    expression. This record is now available in the UWA variables specified
                    in the SELECT expression   */
DO WHILE (BEORR);   /*   We print all the records specified by the SELECT expression   */
    PUT SKIP LIST (FOREST, SIZE);
    $FETCH CURS;   /*   Next record specified in SELECT expression placed in the UWA
                        variables   */
    IF SYR_CODE ¬= 'OK' THEN   /*   Numeric codes used in practice   */
    IF SYR_CODE = 'END OF RELATION'
```

```
        THEN BEORR = 'O'B';
        ELSE CALL ERROR_PROC;   /*   which prints message and
                                     stops the processing   */
END;
$CLOSE CURS;  /*   Cursor deactivated   */
        /*   Had we used a UWA variable $LOC to hold the value 'OREGON' in the SELECT
        expression, then we could now assign 'COLORADO' to LOC, and activate ($OPEN)
        the cursor again. This time a different set of records would be identified by the
        cursor.   */
$END TRANSACTION;
END;
```

It is also possible to use the cursor to identify records to be updated or deleted, and the record involved may be referred to in an UPDATE or DELETE expression as the CURRENT OF CURS, CURS being the name of the cursor involved.

FURTHER READING

Astrahan, M. M., and others, 1976. "System R: Relational Approach to Database Management", ACM Trans. on Database Systems, 1 (2):97–137.

Astrahan, M. M., and others, 1980. "A History and Evaluation of System R", IBM Research Report RJ2843.

Astrahan, M. M., and others, 1980. "Performance of the System R Access Path Selection Mechanism", Proc. IFIP Congress 1980, North-Holland, New York, 487–91.

Chamberlin, D. D., and others, 1981. "Support for Repetitive Transactions and AD HOC Queries in System R", ACM Trans. on Database Systems, 6 (1):70–94.

Date, C. J. An Introduction to Data Base Systems, 3rd edition. Addison/Wesley, Reading, Mass. 1981.

King, W. F., 1980. "Relational data base systems: where we stand today", IFIP Congress 1980, North-Holland, New York, 369–81.

GLOSSARY

DATA DICTIONARY (OR GLOSSARY) OF DATA BASE FIELDS

1. RESOURCE Data Base (Figure 6.5)

AGENCY	In GOV_ AGENCY, the name of a government agency; in CONCESSION, the name of the agency granting the drilling concession.
CHIEF	In GOV_ AGENCY, the head of the agency; in PETROFIRM, the head of the oil company.
COMPANY	In PETROFIRM, the name of an oil company; in DRILL_HOLE, the name of the oil company owning the well.
CONCESS	In DRILL_HOLE, the number of the concession containing the well.
CONCESSNO	In CONCESSION, the number of a drilling concession, in PROPERTY, the number of the concession containing the property.
COST	In CONCESSION, the price paid for the drilling concession; in DRILL_HOLE, the cost of drilling the well.
COUNTRY	In GOV_AGENCY, the country or state supporting the agency.
DRILL_FIRM	In DRILLER, the name of a drilling firm; in DRILL_HOLE, the name of the drilling firm that drilled the well.
FORMER	In CONCESSION, the name of the oil company that owned the concession immediately prior to the present owner.
HOLE	In DRILL_HOLE, the number of a hole or well.
LOC	In CONCESSION, the country, state or region (for example, the North Sea) containing the concession. in DRILL_HOLE, the position of the well *relative* to the property limits.
OWNER	In PROPERTY, the legal owner of the property (in unsettled regions or at sea: a government).
PNUMBER	In PROPERTY, the number of a property (in unsettled regions or at sea: the number of the parent concession).
PRESENT	In CONCESSION, the name of an oil company presently owning a concession.
PROP	In DRILL_HOLE, the number of the property containing the well.
REGIST	In DRILLER, the country or state of registration of the drilling company.
SIZE	In CONCESSION, the size or area of the concession.

2. FORESTRY Data Base (Figures 8.2, 13.2, and 17.1)

ADDRESS	In FORESTER, the address of the forester.
AGE	In FORESTER, the age of the forester.
COMPANY	In FORFILE, the company that owns the forest.
DATE	In MEASUREMENT, the date on which the measurement was performed.
FOREST	In FORFILE, the name of a forest; in FORESTER, the forest looked after by the forester; in TREE, the forest containing the tree.
LOC	In FORFILE, the country or state containing the forest; in TREE, the *relative* position of a tree within a forest.
MAXHT	In SPECFILE, the maximum height of the species of tree.
MEASNUMB	In MEASUREMENT, the number of a measurement.
PARENT	In TREE, the number of the parent of the tree.
PLANTED	In TREE, the date of planting of the tree.
RESULT	In MEASUREMENT, the result of the measurement.
SIZE	In FORFILE, the size or area of the forest
SOCNUMB	In FORESTER, the social security number of a forester
SPECIES	In SPECFILE, the name of a species of tree; in TREE, the species of the tree.
TREENUMB	In TREE, the number of a tree; in MEASUREMENT, the number of the tree measured.
TYPE	In MEASUREMENT, the type of the measurement.
WOODTYPE	In SPECFILE, the type of wood yielded by the species.

INDEX

access method, 9, 17, 79
  user-written, 17
accounting, 473
address capacity (size), 72
adjectival expression (EOS), 450, 388–90
algebra (relational), 455–68
aggregates (CODASYL), 266, 368–369
alternate indexes (VSAM), 154
ANSI/SPARC, 222–235, 257–261
approaches (to DBMS), 231–235
AREA (CODASYL), 261
ASCENDING/DESCENDING, *see* order
association, *see* relationship
Astrahan, M. M., 415, 425, 426, 239, 453, 471, 480,
  A3
attribute (relations), 417
auditor, 226
Augenstein, M. J., 130, 139
Auslander, M. A., 17
AUTOMATIC storage class, 273
  recursive sets, 281
average search length,
  computation of, 101, 102
  for retrieval, 76–85, 102
  for updating, 44
AVG function (SQL), 471

Bachman, C., 206, 208, 237, 338, 364, 369
Bachman diagram, *see* diagram
balanced merge,
  2-way, 167–174
  k-way, 174–180
balanced tree, 130–33
Banerjee, J., 464, 479
base table (System R), 540
based variables, 49
basic quantifiers, *see* quantifiers
batch processing,
  data bases, 229
  files, 45
Baum, R. I., 479
Bayer, R. 133, 149
BCNF, 243
BEGIN TRANSACTION (System R), 540
bench-mark retrieval,
  EOS CODASYL, 380
  DSL ALPHA, 433
  SQL, 442–43
bill-of-materials, 215, 220–22
binary-join dependency, 239, 242, 248–52, 461
binary search,
  in 1-level index, 129
  in index block, 136
binomial theorem, 111
BJD, *see* binary-join dependency
Blasgen, M. W., 415, 416, 426
block,

data block, 5, 19–22, 22–25, 125
  in hash files, 97
  index block, 125
  storage block, 23
BLKSIZE, 37, 38, 118
block factor, 9, 38
block gap, *see* interblock gap
block interval (indexes), 115, 118, 125
block, size, 20–22, 25, 45, 38
block splitting (indexes), 117, 125
Boyce-Codd normal form, *see* BCNF
Boyce, R. F., 439, 453
BOTLOAD program, 307
Bradley, J., 239, 255, 269, 284, 449, 453, 494
Bratbergsengen, K., 66, 81, 113
B-tree, 133–134
buffer, 5, 9, 47–57
built-in functions, *see* retrievals, computational

candidate key, 418
cards, 35
Cartesian product, 251, 419, 456
  expanded, 253, 254, 419
  partitioned, 251, 253, 254
cascade merge, 189, 190
categories (of entities), 53, 424
central processing unit (CPU), 4
CF (current of file), 292
chain,
  CODASYL DSDL, 402–403
  IMS, 494, 495, 499, 500
  multiple linked lists, 161
  overflow (hash files), 80, 84–95, 120–23
chained progressive overflow, 80–84
Chamberlin, D. D., 415, 426, 416, 439, 453, 550
Chang, P., 284
Chang, P. Y. T., 480
channel, 4, 6
  address word, 10
  program, 5, 9, 79, 121, 122, 133, 136
CHECK (CODASYL), 282
child,
  connection field, 206
  file, 210
  record, 212, 487
child/twin pointers, 495
Chomsky, N., 372, 395
chronological order (owner-coupled sets), 277–279
Cincom Corp., 260, 284
Clemons, E. K., *364, 369*
CLOSE,
  files, 35, 88
  System R, 550
  TITLE option, 170, 171, 174
clustered placement (DSDL), 401
COBOL, 31, 118
  CODASYL, *see* CODASYL

System R, *(continued)*
  precompiler, 547
  RD system, 541
  RS system, 541
  UF system, 545
  SQL, 540
System R data base
  definition, 539
  manipulation, 544
system set (CODASYL), 321–22

Tainiter, R., 77, 113
Tanenbaum, A. M., 149
Tanenbaum, A. S., 7, 29
tape, 18–22
tape format, 19
TARGET (EOS calculus), 450
target record, 372
Taylor, F. E., 292, 314
teleprocessing monitor, 291–93
Teory, T. J., 226, 237
TEST program, 92
testing hash distributions, 91
third normal form, 243, 244, 253
TITLE option (PL/1), 170–71
TOPLOAD program, 303
TOTAL, 260, 284, 367
track (disk), 22
  capacity, 23, 26
  index, *see* ISAM
  utilization, 25, 75, 79, 94, 95
Traiger, I. N., 426
tree (data),
  balanced, 130–33
  B-tree, 133–34
  IMS hierarchy, 232, 483
Tremblay, J. P., 115, 118, 149
Tsichritzis, D. C., 202, 204, 231, 237, 260, 421, 426,
    520, 521
tuple concept, 234, 218
twin pointers (IMS), 495

UF interface, A3
Ullman, J. D., 239, 255, 462, 480
union operation, 456
universal quantifier, *see* quantifier
update commands (data base),
  CODASYL, 300–03, 310–11, 334–38
  IMS, 513–14, 517–20
  relational, 468–69
  System R, 545
update commands (files),
  CONSECUTIVE, 34
  ISAM/VSAM, 140–41
  REGIONAL(1), 90
updating data bases,
  CODASYL, 296, 333–39, 356–64
  IMS, 517–20
  relational, 468–69
  System R, A3
updating files, *see* file updating

update problems
  1NF files, 246
  2NF files, 247
  3NF files, 252, 254
user-friendly interface, *see* UF interface
user working/work area,
  CODASYL, 274, 294–296
  IMS, 503
  relational, 427
  System R, 543
utilization of storage,
  disk, 25, 75, 79, 94, 95, 108
  tape, 19, 20
UWA, *see* userworking area

validation of data, 282–83, 303–04
value-based set (CODASYL), 269–71
variable-length blocks, 54, 155
variable-length/format records
  sequential files, 52–58
  inverted files, 154–55
views, (user), 414, 477–88, 543
virtual address, 15
virtual file,
  MULTICS, 17
  projection (relational), 241
virtual operating system, 8, 12–17, 166
virtual owner-coupled set, *see* owner-coupled set
VM/370, 416, A3
VSAM, 118
  alternate indexes, 154
  commands, 138–41
  creation of, 142
  free space, 126
  index, 123–128
  insertions, 125–128

Waghorn, W., 364, 370
Wagner, R. E., 125, 149
Walsh, M., 481, 502, 519, 521
Weinberg, G. M., 31, 60
Whinston, A. B., 371, 395
Whitney, K. K. M., 415, 426
Wibe, K., 113
Wiederhold, G., 138, 149, 151, 194, 231, 237
Wong, E., 463, 480
workspace (relational), 427, 428
WRITE, 12
  CONSECUTIVE locate mode, 52
  CONSECUTIVE move mode, 33
  ISAM/VSAM, 139–41
  REGIONAL(1), 88–90
  REGIONAL(2), 78–79

Yao, S. B., 463, 480
Yeh, R. T., 261, 284
Youssefi, K., 480
Yuen, P. S. J., 113
Yurkanan, C. V., 395

Zloof, M. M., 416, 426